Data Simplification

Data Simplification
Taming Information With Open Source Tools

Jules J. Berman

AMSTERDAM • BOSTON • HEIDELBERG • LONDON
NEW YORK • OXFORD • PARIS • SAN DIEGO
SAN FRANCISCO • SINGAPORE • SYDNEY • TOKYO
Morgan Kaufmann is an imprint of Elsevier

Morgan Kaufmann is an imprint of Elsevier
50 Hampshire Street, 5th Floor, Cambridge, MA 02139, USA

British Library Cataloguing in Publication Data
A catalogue record for this book is available from the British Library

Library of Congress Cataloging-in-Publication Data
A catalog record for this book is available from the Library of Congress

ISBN: 978-0-12-803781-2

For information on all MK publications
visit our website at https://www.elsevier.com/

Working together
to grow libraries in
developing countries

www.elsevier.com • www.bookaid.org

Publisher: Todd Green
Acquisition Editor: Todd Green
Editorial Project Manager: Amy Invernizzi
Production Project Manager: Punithavathy Govindaradjane
Designer: Mark Rogers

Typeset by SPi Global, India

For my best friend, Bailey.

Contents

Foreword

It is common knowledge that every computer scientist, programmer, statistician, informatician, and knowledge domain expert must know how to analyze data. It is less commonly known that very few of these data professionals are given the skills required to prepare their data in a form that supports credible analysis. As Berman points out, data analysis has no value unless it can be verified, validated, reanalyzed, and repurposed, as needed. *Data Simplification: Taming Information with Open Source Tools* is a practical guide to the messiness of complex and heterogeneous data used in discovery science (ie, our optimistic resolve to understand what our data is trying to tell us). Berman successfully makes the case for data simplification as a discipline within data science.

In this important work, Berman deals with the practical aspects of complex data sets and creates a workflow for tackling problems in so-called big data research. No book to date has effectively dealt with the sources of data complexity in such a comprehensive, yet practical fashion. Speaking from my own area of involvement, biomedical researchers wrestling with genome/imaging/computational phenotype analyses will find Berman's approach to data simplification particularly constructive.

The book opens with a convincing demonstration that complex data requires simplification in order to answer high impact questions. Berman shows that the process of data simplification is not, itself, simple. He provides a set of principles, methods and tools to unlock the secrets of "big data." More importantly, he provides a roadmap to the use of free, open source tools in the data simplification process; skills that need to be emphasized to the data science community irrespective of scientific discipline. It is fair to acknowledge that our customary reliance on costly and "comprehensive" software/development solutions will sometimes increase the likelihood that a data project will fail.

As there is a "gold rush" encouraging the workforce training of data scientists, this gritty "Rules of the Road" monograph should serve as a constant companion for modern data scientists. Berman convincingly portrays the value of programmers and analysts who have facility with Perl, Python, or Ruby and who understand the critical role of metadata, indexing, and data visualization. These professionals will be high on my shopping list of talent to add to our biomedical informatics team in Pittsburgh.

Data science is currently the focus of an intense, worldwide effort extending to all biomedical institutions. It seems that we have reached a point where progress in the biomedical sciences is paused, waiting for us to draw useful meaning from the dizzying amount of new data being collected by high throughput technologies, electronic health records, mobile medical sensors, and the exabytes generated from imaging modalities in research and clinical practice. Here at the University of Pittsburgh, we are deeply involved in the efforts of the U.S. National Institutes of Health to tame complex biomedical data, through our membership in the NIH Big Data to Knowledge (BD2K) Consortium (https://datascience.nih.gov/bd2k). Our continuing fascination with "more" data and "big" data have been compounded by the amplification and hype of an array of software tools and solutions that claim to "solve" big data problems. Although, much of data science innovation focuses on hardware, cloud computing, and novel algorithms to solve BD2K problems, the critical issues remain at the level of the utility of the data (eg, simplification) addressed in this important book by Berman.

Data Simplification provides easy, free solutions to the unintended consequences of data complexity. This book should be the first (and probably most important) guide to success in the data sciences. I will be providing copies to my trainees, programmers, analysts, and faculty, as required reading.

Michael J. Becich, MD, PhD
Associate Vice-Chancellor for Informatics in the Health Sciences
Chairman and Distinguished University Professor, Department of Biomedical Informatics
Director, Center for Commercial Application (CCA) of Healthcare Data
University of Pittsburgh School of Medicine

Preface

Complex data is difficult to understand and analyze. Large data projects, using complex sets of data, are likely to fail; furthermore, the more money spent on a data project, the greater the likelihood of failure.[1–9] What is true for data projects is also true in the experimental sciences; large and complex projects are often unrepeatable.[10–28] Basically, complexity is something that humans have never mastered. As a species, we work much better when things are made simple.

Intelligent data scientists soon learn that it is nearly impossible to conduct competent and reproducible analyses of highly complex data. Inevitably, something always goes wrong. This book was written to provide a set of general principles and methods for data simplification. Here are the points that establish the conceptual framework of *Data Simplification: Taming Information with Open Source Tools*:

(1) The first step in data analysis is data simplification. Most modern data scientists can expect that the majority of their time will be spent collecting, organizing, annotating, and simplifying their data, preparatory to analysis. A relatively small fraction of their time will be spent directly analyzing the data. When data has been simplified, successful analysis can proceed using standard computational methods, on standard computers.

(2) Results obtained from unsimplified projects are nearly always irreproducible. Hence, the results of analyses on complex data cannot be validated. Conclusions that cannot be validated have no scientific value.

(3) Data simplification is not simple. There is something self-defeating about the term, "data simplification." The term seems to imply a dumbing down process wherein naturally complex concepts are presented in a manner that is palatable to marginally competent scientists. Nothing can be further from the truth. Creating overly complex data has always been the default option for lazy-minded or cavalier scientists who lacked the will or the talent to produce a simple, well-organized, and well-annotated collection of data. The act of data simplification will always be one of the most challenging tasks facing data scientists, often requiring talents drawn from multiple disciplines. The sad truth is that there are very few data professionals who are competent to perform data simplification; and fewer still educators who can adequately teach the subject.

(4) No single software application will solve your data simplification needs.[29] Applications that claim to do everything for the user are, in most instances, applications that require the user to do everything for the application. The most useful software solutions often come in the form of open source utilities, designed to perform one method very well and very fast. In this book, dozens of freely available utilities are demonstrated.

(5) Data simplification tools are data discovery tools, in the hands of creative individuals. The act of data simplification always gives the scientist a better understanding of the meaning of the data. Data that has been organized and annotated competently provides us with new questions, new hypotheses, and new approaches to problem solving. Data that is complex only provides headaches.

(6) Data simplification is a prerequisite for data preservation. Data that has not been simplified has no useful shelf life. After a data project has ended, nobody will be able to understand what was done. This means no future projects will build upon the original data, or find new purposes for the data. Moreover, conclusions drawn from the original data will never be verified or validated. This means that when you do not simplify your data, your colleagues will not accept your conclusions. Those who understand the principles and practice of data simplification will produce credible data that can be validated and repurposed (see Glossary items, Validation, Data repurposing, Data Quality Act).

(7) Data simplification saves money. Data simplification often involves developing general solutions that apply to classes of data. By eliminating the cost of using made-to-order proprietary software, data scientists can increase their productivity and reduce their expenses.

(8) Learning the methods and tools of data simplification is a great career move. Data simplification is the next big thing in the data sciences. The most thoughtful employers understand that it's not always about keeping it simple. More often, it's about making it simple (see Glossary item, KISS).

(9) Data scientists should have familiarity with more than one programming language. Although one high-level language has much the same functionality as another, each language may have particular advantages in different situations. For example, a programmer may prefer Perl when her tasks involve text parsing and string pattern matches. Another programmer might prefer Python if she requires a variety of numeric or analytic functions and a smooth interface to a graphing tool. Programmers who work with classes of data objects, or who need to model new classifications, might prefer the elegant syntax and rich class libraries available in Ruby (see Glossary item, Syntax). Books that draw on a single programming language run the risk of limiting the problem-solving options of their readers. Although there are many high-quality programming languages, I have chosen Perl, Python, and Ruby as the demonstration languages for this book. Each of these popular languages is free, open source, and can be installed easily and quickly on virtually any operating system. By offering solutions in several different programming languages, this book may serve as a sort of Rosetta stone for data scientists who must work with data structures produced in different programming environments.

ORGANIZATION OF THIS BOOK

Chapter 1, The Simple Life, explores the thesis that complexity is the rate-limiting factor in human development. The greatest advances in human civilization and the most dramatic evolutionary improvements in all living organisms have followed the acquisition of methods that reduce or eliminate complexity.

Chapter 2, Structuring Text, reminds us that most of the data on the Web today is unstructured text, produced by individuals, trying their best to communicate with one another. Data simplification often begins with textual data. This chapter provides readers with tools and strategies for imposing some basic structure on free-text.

Chapter 3, Indexing Text, describes the often undervalued benefits of indexes. An index, aided by proper annotation of data, permits us to understand data in ways that were not anticipated when the original content was collected. With the use of computers, multiple indexes designed for different purposes, can be created for a single document or data set. As data accrues, indexes can be updated. When data sets are combined, their respective indexes can be merged. A good way of thinking about indexes is that the document contains all of the complexity; the index contains all of the simplicity. Data scientists who understand how to create and use indexes will be in the best position to search, retrieve, and analyze textual data. Methods are provided for automatically creating customized indexes designed for specific analytic pursuits and for binding index terms to standard nomenclatures.

Chapter 4, Understanding Your Data, describes how data can be quickly assessed, prior to formal quantitative analysis, to develop some insight into what the data means. A few simple visualization tricks and simple statistical descriptors can greatly enhance a data scientist's understanding of complex and large data sets. Various types of data objects, such as text files, images, and time-series data, can be profiled with a summary signature that captures the key features that contribute to the behavior and content of the data object. Such profiles can be used to find relationships among different data objects, or to determine when data objects are not closely related to one another.

Chapter 5, Identifying and Deidentifying Data, tackles one of the most under-appreciated and least understood issues in data science. Measurements, annotations, properties, and classes of information have no informational meaning unless they are attached to an identifier that distinguishes one data object from all other data objects, and that links together all of the information that has been or will be associated with the identified data object. The method of identification and the selection of objects and classes to be identified relates fundamentally to the organizational model of complex data. If the simplifying step of data identification is ignored or implemented improperly, data cannot be shared, and conclusions drawn from the data cannot be believed. All well-designed information systems are, at their heart, identification systems: ways of naming data objects so that they can be retrieved. Only well-identified data can be usefully deidentified. This chapter discusses methods for identifying data and deidentifying data.

Chapter 6, Giving Meaning to Data, explores the meaning of meaning, as it applies to computer science. We shall learn that data, by itself, has no meaning. It is the job of the data scientist to assign meaning to data, and this is done with data objects, triples, and classifications (see Glossary items, Data object, Triple, Classification, Ontology). Unfortunately, coursework in the information sciences often omits discussion of the critical issue of "data meaning"; advancing from data collection to data analysis without stopping to design data objects whose relationships to other data objects are defined and discoverable. In this chapter, readers will learn how to prepare and classify meaningful data.

Chapter 7, Object-Oriented Data, shows how we can understand data, using a few elegant computational principles. Modern programming languages, particularly object-oriented programming languages, use introspective data (ie, the data with which data objects describe themselves) to modify the execution of a program at run-time; an elegant process known as reflection. Using introspection and reflection, programs can integrate data objects with related data objects. The implementations of introspection, reflection and integration, are among the most important achievements in the field of computer science.

Chapter 8, Problem Simplification, demonstrates that it is just as important to simplify problems as it is to simplify data. This final chapter provides simple but powerful methods for analyzing data, without resorting to advanced mathematical techniques. The use of random number generators to simulate the behavior of systems, and the application of Monte Carlo, resampling, and permutative methods to a wide variety of common problems in data analysis, will be discussed. The importance of data reanalysis, following preliminary analysis, is emphasized.

CHAPTER ORGANIZATION

Every chapter has a section in which free utilities are listed, and their functions, in the service of data simplification, are described. The utilities listed in this book confer superpowers on the user; nothing less. Like a magical incantation, or a bite from a radioactive spider, software utilities endow sedentary data scientists with the power to create elaborate graphs with the click of a mouse, perform millions of mathematical calculations in the blink of an eye, and magically unlock the deepest secrets held in a tangled web of chaotic data. Happily, every data scientist can enjoy a nearly limitless collection of no-cost, opens source programming languages, utilities, specifications, and undifferentiated software that can help them perform all of the tasks involved in data simplification. Bearing in mind that today's exciting innovation is tomorrow's abandonware, I've confined my recommendations to tools whose popularity has survived the test of time (see Glossary items, Utility, Open source, Free software, Free software license, FOSS, Specification, Undifferentiated software, GNU software license, Abandonware).

Every chapter has its own glossary. Traditionally, glossaries are intended to define technical terms encountered in the text. Definitions, though helpful, seldom explain the purpose served by a term or concept. In this book, the glossaries are designed to add depth and perspective to concepts that were touched upon in the chapters. Readers will find that the glossaries can be enjoyed as stand-alone documents, worthy of reading from beginning to ending.

Every chapter has its own Reference section. Serious readers will want to obtain and study the primary sources. With very few exceptions, the articles cited in the reference sections are available for public download from the Web. A cursory review of the citations should indicate that the articles are chosen from many different scientific disciplines, reinforcing the premise that science, at its most creative, is always multidisciplinary.

HOW TO READ THIS BOOK

Readers will almost certainly be overwhelmed by the multitude of algorithms and code snippets included in this book. Please keep in mind that there is plenty of time to master methodology. It might be best to absorb the fundamental concepts discussed in each chapter. For your first reading, it is sufficient to understand how various methods may fit into a general approach to simplifying data. When you need to use the tools or the scripts from the book, please do not try to retype snippets of code; you'll only introduce errors. Use the free downloadable file, containing all of the code from the book, at the publisher's web site (http://booksite.elsevier.com/9780128037812/) (see Glossary item, Script).

NOTA BENE

Readers will notice that many of the examples of classifications are drawn from the classification of living organisms. The reasons for this is that the classification of living organisms is the largest, most mature, and the best classification in existence. It was developed with the most intense efforts of thousands of scientists, over hundreds of years. Almost every imaginable design flaw and conceptual error that can be produced by the human mind has been committed and corrected in the development of this classification. Hence, this classification offers a seemingly endless number of examples of what to avoid and what to seek when designing, or implementing, a classification. Anyone who has any serious interest in data organization, regardless of his or her chosen scientific discipline, must endure some exposure to the history and the current status of the classification of living organisms.

The book contains many scripts, and snippets of scripts, written in Perl, Python, or Ruby. The book also contains command line calls to numerous open source utilities. These code samples should be operable on Windows and Linux systems and on any operating system that supports scripts written in Perl, Python, or Ruby. Although all of the code was thoroughly checked to ensure that it functioned properly, readers may encounter occasional malfunctions and nonfunctions due to inconsistencies and incompatibilities between versions of operating systems and/or versions of programming languages; or due to unavailability of utilities and language-specific modules; or due to the author's inadvertent coding errors; or due to typographic mistakes; or due to idiosyncrasies among individual computers. As an example of the last item, readers should know that whenever a command line in this book begins with the DOS prompt: "c:\ftp>", this represents a drive location on the author's computer. Readers must substitute the prompt that applies to their own computer in all these instances.

This book is a work of literature; nothing more. Neither the author nor the publisher is responsible for code that does not work to the reader's satisfaction. The provided code is not intended to serve as functional applications. It is best to think of the code in this book as instructional text intended to demonstrate various options and approaches that might be applied to data-related projects. To reduce the number of errors introduced when code is transcribed by hand, all of the coding examples from the book can be downloaded from the publisher's web site for *Data Simplification: Taming Information with Open Source Tools*.

GLOSSARY

Abandonware Software that is abandoned (eg, no longer updated, supported, distributed, or sold) after its economic value is depleted. In academic circles, the term is often applied to software that is developed under a research grant. When the grant expires, so does the software. Most of the software in existence today is abandonware

Autocoding When nomenclature coding is done automatically, by a computer program, the process is known as "autocoding" or "autoencoding." See Coding. See Nomenclature. See Autoencoding.

Autoencoding Synonym for autocoding. See Autocoding.

Blended Class Also known as class noise, subsumes the more familiar, but less precise term, "Labeling error." Blended class refers to inaccuracies (eg, misleading results) introduced in the analysis of data due to errors in class assignments (ie, assigning a data object to class A when the object should have been assigned to class B). If you are testing the effectiveness of an antibiotic on a class of people with bacterial pneumonia, the accuracy of your results will be forfeit when your study population includes subjects with viral pneumonia, or smoking-related lung damage. Errors induced by blending classes are often overlooked by data analysts who incorrectly assume that the experiment was designed to ensure that each data group is composed of a uniform and representative population. A common source of class blending occurs when the classification upon which the experiment is designed is itself blended. For example, imagine that you are a cancer researcher and you want to perform a study of patients with malignant fibrous histiocytomas (MFH), comparing the clinical course of these patients with the clinical course of patients who have other types of tumors. Let's imagine that the class of tumors known as MFH does not actually exist; that it is a grab-bag term erroneously assigned to a variety of other tumors that happened to look similar to one another. This being the case, it would be impossible to produce any valid results based on a study of patients diagnosed as MFH. The results would be a biased and irreproducible cacophony of data collected across different, and undetermined, classes of tumors. Believe it or not, this specific example, of the blended MFH class of tumors, is selected from the real-life annals of tumor biology.[30, 31] The literature is rife with research of dubious quality, based on poorly designed classifications and blended classes. A detailed discussion of this topic is found in Section 6.5, Properties that Cross Multiple Classes. One caveat. Efforts to eliminate class blending can be counterproductive if undertaken with excess zeal. For example, in an effort to reduce class blending, a researcher may choose groups of subjects who are uniform with respect to every known observable property. For example, suppose you want to actually compare apples with oranges. To avoid class blending, you might want to make very sure that your apples do not included any kumquats, or persimmons. You should be certain that your oranges do not include any limes or grapefruits. Imagine that you go even further, choosing only apples and oranges of one variety (eg, Macintosh apples and navel oranges), size (eg 10 cm), and origin (eg, California). How will your comparisons apply to the varieties of apples and oranges that you have excluded from your study? You may actually reach conclusions that are invalid and irreproducible for more generalized populations within each class. In this case, you have succeeded in eliminated class blending, at the expense of losing representative populations of the classes. See Simpson's paradox.

Child Class The direct or first generation subclass of a class. Sometimes referred to as the daughter class or, less precisely, as the subclass. See Parent class. See Classification.

Class A class is a group of objects that share a set of properties that define the class and that distinguish the members of the class from members of other classes. The word "class," lowercase, is used as a general term. The word "Class," uppercase, followed by an uppercase noun (eg Class Animalia), represents a specific class within a formal classification. See Classification.

Classification A system in which every object in a knowledge domain is assigned to a class within a hierarchy of classes. The properties of superclasses are inherited by the subclasses. Every class has one immediate superclass (ie, parent class), although a parent class may have more than one immediate subclass (ie, child class). Objects do not change their class assignment in a classification, unless there was a mistake in the assignment. For example, a rabbit is always a rabbit, and does not change into a tiger. Classifications can be thought of as the simplest and most restrictive type of ontology, and serve to reduce the complexity of a knowledge domain.[32] Classifications can be easily modeled in an object-oriented programming language and are nonchaotic (ie, calculations performed on the members and classes of a classification should yield the same output, each time the calculation is performed). A classification should be distinguished from an ontology. In an ontology, a class may have more than one parent class and an object may be a member of more than one class. A classification can be considered a special type of ontology wherein each class is limited to a single parent class and each object has membership in one and only one class. See Nomenclature. See Thesaurus. See Vocabulary. See Classification. See Dictionary. See Terminology. See Ontology. See Parent class. See Child class. See Superclass. See Unclassifiable objects.

Coding The term "coding" has three very different meanings; depending on which branch of science influences your thinking. For programmers, coding means writing the code that constitutes a computer programmer. For cryptographers, coding is synonymous with encrypting (ie, using a cipher to encode a message). For medics, coding is calling an emergency team to handle a patient in extremis. For informaticians and library scientists, coding involves assigning an alphanumeric identifier, representing a concept listed in a nomenclature, to a term. For example, a surgical pathology report may include the diagnosis, "Adenocarcinoma of prostate." A nomenclature may assign a code C4863000 that uniquely identifies the concept "Adenocarcinoma." Coding the report may involve annotating every occurrence of the word "Adenocarcinoma" with the "C4863000" identifier. For a detailed explanation of coding, and its importance for searching and retrieving data, see the full discussion in Section 3.4, "Autoencoding and Indexing with Nomenclatures." See Autocoding. See Nomenclature.

Command Line Instructions to the operating system, that can be directly entered as a line of text from the a system prompt (eg, the so-called C prompt, "c:\>", in Windows and DOS operating systems; the so-called shell prompt, "$", in Linux-like systems).

Command Line Utility Programs lacking graphic user interfaces that are executed via command line instructions. The instructions for a utility are typically couched as a series of arguments, on the command line, following the name of the executable file that contains the utility. See Utility.

Data Quality Act In the U.S., the data upon which public policy is based must have quality and must be available for review by the public. Simply put, public policy must be based on verifiable data. The Data Quality Act of 2002, requires the Office of Management and Budget to develop government-wide standards for data quality.[33]

Data Object A data object is whatever is being described by the data. For example, if the data is "6 feet tall," then the data object is the person or thing to which "6 feet tall" applies. Minimally, a data object is a metadata/data pair, assigned to a unique identifier (ie, a triple). In practice, the most common data objects are simple data records, corresponding to a row in a spreadsheet or a line in a flat-file. Data objects in object-oriented programming languages typically encapsulate several items of data, including an object name, an object unique identifier, multiple data/metadata pairs, and the name of the object's class. See Triple. See Identifier. See Metadata.

Data Repurposing Involves using old data in new ways, that were not foreseen by the people who originally collected the data. Data repurposing comes in the following categories: (1) Using the preexisting data to ask and answer questions that were not contemplated by the people who designed and collected the data; (2) Combining preexisting data with additional data, of the same kind, to produce aggregate data that suits a new set of questions that could not have been answered with any one of the component data sources; (3) Reanalyzing data to validate assertions, theories, or conclusions drawn from the original studies; (4) Reanalyzing the original data set using alternate or improved methods to attain outcomes of greater precision or reliability than the outcomes produced in the original analysis; (5) Integrating heterogeneous data sets (ie, data sets with seemingly unrelated types of information), for the purpose an answering questions or developing concepts that span diverse scientific disciplines; (6) Finding subsets in a population once thought to be homogeneous; (7) Seeking new relationships among data objects; (8) Creating on-the-fly, novel data sets through data file linkages; (9) Creating new concepts or ways of thinking about old concepts, based on a reexamination of data; (10) Fine-tuning existing data models; and (11) Starting over and remodeling systems.[34] See Heterogeneous data.

Dictionary A terminology or word list accompanied by a definition for each item. See Nomenclature. See Vocabulary. See Terminology.

Exe File A file with the filename suffix ".exe". In common parlance, filenames with the ".exe" suffix are executable code. See Executable file.

Executable File A file that contains compiled computer code that can be read directly from the computer's CPU, without interpretation by a programming language. A language such as C will compile C code into executables. Scripting languages, such as Perl, Python, and Ruby interpret plain-text scripts and send instructions to a runtime engine, for execution. Because executable files eliminate the interpretation step, they typically run faster than plain-text scripts. See Exe file.

FOSS Free and open source software. Equivalent to FLOSS (Free Libre Open Source Software), an abbreviation that trades redundancy for international appeal. See Free Software Movement versus Open Source Initiative.

Free Software Movement Versus Open Source Initiative Beyond trivial semantics, the difference between free software and open source software relates to the essential feature necessary for "open source" software (ie, access to the source code) and to the different distribution licenses of free software and open source software. Sticklers insist that free software always comes with permission to modify and redistribute software in a prescribed manner as discussed in the software license; a permission not always granted in open source software. In practice, there is very little difference between free software and open source software. Richard Stallman has written an essay that summarizes the two different approaches to creating free software and open source software.[35]

Free Software The concept of free software, as popularized by the Free Software Foundation, refers to software that can be used freely, without restriction. The term "free" does not necessarily relate to the actual cost of the software.

Free Software License Virtually all free software is distributed under a license that assigns copyright to the software creator and protects the creator from damages that might result from using the software. Software sponsored by the Free Software Foundation, and much of the software described as either free software or open source software is distributed under one of the GNU software licenses. See GNU software license.

GNU Software License The GNU organization publishes several licenses, used for software produced by GNU and by anyone who would like to distribute their software under the terms of the GNU license. GNU licenses are referred to as copyleft licenses, because they primarily serve the software users, rather than the software creators. One of the GNU licenses, the General Public License, covers most software applications. The GNU Lesser General Public License, formerly known as the GNU Library General Public License is intended for use with software libraries or unified collections of files comprising a complex application, language, or other body of work.[36]

HTML HyperText Markup Language is an ASCII-based set of formatting instructions for web pages. HTML formatting instructions, known as tags, are embedded in the document, and double-bracketed, indicating the start point and end points for instruction. Here is an example of an HTML tag instructing the web browser to display the word "Hello" in italics: <i>Hello</i>. All web browsers conforming to the HTML specification must contain software routines that recognize and implement the HTML instructions embedded within in web documents. In addition to formatting instructions, HTML also includes linkage instructions, in which the web browsers must retrieve and display a listed web page, or a web resource, such as an image. The protocol whereby web browsers, following HTML instructions, retrieve web pages from other internet sites, is known as HTTP (HyperText Transfer Protocol).

Halting a Script The most common problem encountered by programmers is nonexecution (ie, your script will not run). But another problem, which can be much worse, occurs when your program never wants to stop. This can occur when a block or loop has no exit condition. For most scripting languages, when you notice that a script seems to be running too long, and you want to exit, just press the ctrl-break keys. The script should eventually stop and return your system prompt.

Heterogeneous Data Two sets of data are considered heterogeneous when they are dissimilar to one another, with regard to content, purpose, format, organization, or annotations. One of the purposes of data science is to discover relationships among heterogeneous data sources. For example, epidemiologic data sets may be of service to molecular biologists who have gene sequence data on diverse human populations. The epidemiologic data is likely to contain different types of data values, annotated and formatted in a manner different from the data and annotations in a gene sequence database. The two types of related data, epidemiologic and genetic, have dissimilar content; hence they are heterogeneous to one another.

Identification The process of providing a data object with an identifier, or the process of distinguishing one data object from all other data objects on the basis of its associated identifier. See Identifier.

Identifier A string that is associated with a particular thing (eg person, document, transaction, data object), and not associated with any other thing.[37] Object identification usually involves permanently assigning a seemingly random sequence of numeric digits (0–9) and alphabet characters (a-z and A-Z) to a data object. A data object can be a specific piece of data (eg, a data record), or an abstraction, such as a class of objects or a number or a string or a variable. See Identification.

Instance An instance is a specific example of an object that is not itself a class or group of objects. For example, Tony the Tiger is an instance of the tiger species. Tony the Tiger is a unique animal and is not itself a group of animals or a class of animals. The terms instance, instance object, and object are sometimes used interchangeably, but the special value of the "instance" concept, in a system wherein everything is an object, is that it distinguishes members of classes (ie, the instances) from the classes to which they belong.

Introspection A method by which data objects can be interrogated to yield information about themselves (eg, properties, values, and class membership). Through introspection, the relationships among the data objects can be examined. Introspective methods are built into object-oriented languages. The data provided by introspection can be applied, at run-time, to modify a script's operation; a technique known as reflection.

Specifically, any properties, methods, and encapsulated data of a data object can be used in the script to modify the script's run-time behavior. See Reflection.

KISS Acronym for Keep It Simple Stupid. The motto applies to almost any area of life; nothing should be made more complex than necessary. As it happens, much of what we encounter, as data scientists, comes to us in a complex form (ie, nothing to keep simple). A more realistic acronym is MISS (Make It Simple Stupid).

Meaning In informatics, meaning is achieved when described data is bound to a unique identifier of a data object. "Claude Funston's height is five feet eleven inches," comes pretty close to being a meaningful statement. The statement contains data (five feet eleven inches), and the data is described (height). The described data belongs to a unique object (Claude Funston). Ideally, the name "Claude Funston" should be provided with a unique identifier, to distinguish one instance of Claude Funston from all the other persons who are named Claude Funston. The statement would also benefit from a formal system that ensures that the metadata makes sense (eg, What exactly is height, and does Claude Funston fall into a class of objects for which height is a property?) and that the data is appropriate (eg, Is 5 feet 11 inches an allowable measure of a person's height?). A statement with meaning does not need to be a true statement (eg, The height of Claude Funston was not 5 feet 11 inches when Claude Funston was an infant). See Semantics. See Triple. See RDF.

Metadata The data that describes data. For example, a data element (also known as data point) may consist of the number, "6." The metadata for the data may be the words "Height, in feet." A data element is useless without its metadata, and metadata is useless unless it adequately describes a data element. In XML, the metadata/data annotation comes in the form < metadata tag>data<end of metadata tag > and might be look something like:

```
<weight_in_pounds>150</weight_in_pounds>
```

In spreadsheets, the data elements are the cells of the spreadsheet. The column headers are the metadata that describe the data values in the column's cells, and the row headers are the record numbers that uniquely identify each record (ie, each row of cells). See XML.

Microarray Also known as gene chip, gene expression array, DNA microarray, or DNA chips. These consist of thousands of small samples of chosen DNA sequences arrayed onto a block of support material (usually, a glass slide). When the array is incubated with a mixture of DNA sequences prepared from cell samples, hybridization will occur between molecules on the array and single stranded complementary (ie, identically sequenced) molecules present in the cell sample. The greater the concentration of complementary molecules in the cell sample, the greater the number of fluorescently tagged hybridized molecules in the array. A specialized instrument prepares an image of the array, and quantifies the fluorescence in each array spot. Spots with high fluorescence indicate relatively large quantities of DNA in the cell sample that match the specific sequence of DNA in the array spot. The data comprising all the fluorescent intensity measurements for every spot in the array produces a gene profile characteristic of the cell sample.

Multiclass Classification A misnomer imported from the field of machine translation, and indicating the assignment of an instance to more than one class. Classifications, as defined in this book, impose one-class classification (ie, an instance can be assigned to one and only one class). It is tempting to think that a ball should be included in class "toy" and in class "spheroids," but mutliclass assignments create unnecessary classes of inscrutable provenance, and taxonomies of enormous size, consisting largely of replicate items. See Multiclass inheritance. See Taxonomy.

Multiclass Inheritance In ontologies, multiclass inheritance occurs when a child class has more than one parent class. For example, a member of Class House may have two different parent classes: Class Shelter, and Class Property. Multiclass inheritance is generally permitted in ontologies but is forbidden in one type of restrictive ontology, known as a classification. See Classification. See Parent class. See Multiclass classification.

Namespace A namespace is the realm in which a metadata tag applies. The purpose of a namespace is to distinguish metadata tags that have the same name, but a different meaning. For example, within a single XML file, the metadata tag "date" may be used to signify a calendar date, or the fruit, or the social engagement. To avoid confusion, metadata terms are assigned a prefix that is associated with a Web document that defines the term (ie, establishes the tag's namespace). In practical terms, a tag that can have different descriptive meanings in different contexts is provided with a prefix that links to a web document wherein the meaning of the tag, as it applies in the XML document is specified.

Nomenclature A nomenclatures is a listing of terms that cover all of the concepts in a knowledge domain. A nomenclature is different from a dictionary for three reasons: (1) the nomenclature terms are not annotated with definitions, (2) nomenclature terms may be multi-word, and (3) the terms in the nomenclature are limited to the scope of the selected knowledge domain. In addition, most nomenclatures group synonyms under a group code. For example, a food nomenclature might collect submarine, hoagie, po' boy, grinder, hero, and torpedo under an alphanumeric code such as "F63958". Nomenclatures simplify textual documents by uniting synonymous terms under a common code. Documents that have been coded with the same nomenclature can be integrated with other documents that have been similarly coded, and queries conducted over such documents will yield the same results, regardless of which term is entered (ie, a search for either hoagie, or po' boy will retrieve the same information, if both terms have been annotated with the synonym code, "F63948"). Optimally, the canonical concepts listed in the nomenclature are organized into a hierarchical classification.[38,39] See Coding. See Autocoding.

Nonatomicity Nonatomicity is the assignment of a collection of objects to a single, composite object, that cannot be further simplified or sensibly deconstructed. For example, the human body is composed of trillions of individual cells, each of which lives for some length of time, and then dies. Many of the cells in the body are capable of dividing to produce more cells. In many cases, the cells of the body that are capable of dividing can be cultured and grown in plastic containers, much like bacteria can be cultured and grown in Petri dishes. If the human body is composed of individual cells, why do we habitually think of each human as a single living entity? Why don't we think of humans as bags of individual cells? Perhaps the reason stems from the coordinated responses of cells. When someone steps on the cells of your toe, the cells in your brain sense pain, the cells in your mouth and vocal cords say ouch, and an army of inflammatory cells rush to the scene of the crime. The cells in your toe are not capable of registering an actionable complaint, without a great deal of assistance. Another reason that organisms, composed of trillions of living cells, are generally considered to have nonatomicity, probably relates to the "species" concept in biology. Every cell in an organism descended from the same zygote, and every zygote in every member of the same species descended from the same ancestral organism. Hence, there seems to be little benefit to assigning unique entity status to the individual cells that compose organisms, when the class structure for organisms is based on descent through zygotes. See Species.

Notation 3 Also called n3. A syntax for expressing assertions as triples (unique subject + metadata + data). Notation 3 expresses the same information as the more formal RDF syntax, but n3 is easier for humans to read.[40] RDF and n3 are interconvertible, and either one can be parsed and equivalently tokenized (ie, broken into elements that can be reorganized in a different format, such as a database record). See RDF. See Triple.

Ontology An ontology is a collection of classes and their relationships to one another. Ontologies are usually rule-based systems (ie, membership in a class is determined by one or more class rules). Two important features distinguish ontologies from classifications. Ontologies permit classes to have more than one parent class. For example, the class of automobiles may be a direct subclass of "motorized devices" and a direct subclass of "mechanized transporters." In addition, an instance of a class can be an instance of any number of additional classes. For example, a Lamborghini may be a member of class "automobiles" and of class "luxury items." This means that the lineage of an instance in an ontology can be highly complex, with a single instance occurring in multiple classes, and with many connections between classes. Because recursive relations are permitted, it is possible to build an ontology wherein a class is both an ancestor class and a descendant class of itself. A classification is a highly restrained ontology wherein instances can belong to only one class, and each class may have only one parent class. Because classifications have an enforced linear hierarchy, they can be easily modeled, and the lineage of any instance can be traced unambiguously. See Classification. See Multiclass classification. See Multiclass inheritance.

Open Access A document is open access if its complete contents are available to the public. Open access applies to documents in the same manner as open source applies to software.

Open Source Software is open source if the source code is available to anyone who has access to the software. See Open source movement. See Open access.

Open Source Movement Open source software is software for which the source code is available. The Open Source Software movement is an offspring of the Free Software movement. Although a good deal of free software is no-cost software, the intended meaning of the term "free" is that the software can be used without restrictions. The Open Source Initiative posts an open source definition RopaR and a list of approved licenses that can be attached to open source products.

Parent Class The immediate ancestor, or the next-higher class (ie, the direct superclass) of a class. For example, in the classification of living organisms, Class Vertebrata is the parent class of Class Gnathostomata. Class Gnathostomata is the parent class of Class Teleostomi. In a classification, which imposes single class inheritance, each child class has exactly one parent class; whereas one parent class may have several different child classes. Furthermore, some classes, in particular the bottom class in the lineage, have no child classes (ie, a class need not always be a superclass of other classes). A class can be defined by its properties, its membership (ie, the instances that belong to the class), and by the name of its parent class. When we list all of the classes in a classification, in any order, we can always reconstruct the complete class lineage, in their correct lineage and branchings, if we know the name of each class's parent class. See Instance. See Child class. See Superclass.

RDF Resource Description Framework (RDF) is a syntax in XML notation that formally expresses assertions as triples. The RDF triple consists of a uniquely identified subject plus a metadata descriptor for the data plus a data element. Triples are necessary and sufficient to create statements that convey meaning. Triples can be aggregated with other triples from the same data set or from other data sets, so long as each triple pertains to a unique subject that is identified equivalently through the data sets. Enormous data sets of RDF triples can be merged or functionally integrated with other massive or complex data resources. For a detailed discussion see Open Source Tools for Chapter 6, "Syntax for Triples." See Notation 3. See Semantics. See Triple. See XML.

RDF Schema Resource Description Framework Schema (RDFS). A document containing a list of classes, their definitions, and the names of the parent class(es) for each class. In an RDF Schema, the list of classes is typically followed by a list of properties that apply to one or more classes in the Schema. To be useful, RDF Schemas are posted on the Internet, as a Web page, with a unique Web address. Anyone can incorporate the classes and properties of a public RDF Schema into their own RDF documents (public or private) by linking named classes and properties, in their RDF document, to the web address of the RDF Schema where the classes and properties are defined. See Namespace. See RDFS.

RDFS Same as RDF Schema.

Reflection A programming technique wherein a computer program will modify itself, at run-time, based on information it acquires through introspection. For example, a computer program may iterate over a collection of data objects, examining the self-descriptive information for each object in the collection (ie, object introspection). If the information indicates that the data object belongs to a particular class of objects, then the program may call a method appropriate for the class. The program executes in a manner determined by descriptive information obtained during run-time; metaphorically reflecting upon the purpose of its computational task. See Introspection.

Reproducibility Reproducibility is achieved when repeat studies produce the same results, over and over. Reproducibility is closely related to validation, which is achieved when you draw the same conclusions, from the data, over and over again. Implicit in the concept of "reproducibility" is that the original research must somehow convey the means by which the study can be reproduced. This usually requires the careful recording of methods, algorithms, and materials. In some cases, reproducibility requires access to the data produced in the original studies. If there is no feasible way for scientists to undertake a reconstruction of the original study, or if the results obtained in the original study cannot be obtained in subsequent attempts, then the study is irreproducible. If the work is reproduced, but the results and the conclusions cannot be repeated, then the study is considered invalid. See Validation. See Verification.

Script A script is a program that is written in plain-text, in a syntax appropriate for a particular programming language, that needs to be parsed through that language's interpreter before it can be compiled and executed. Scripts tend to run a bit slower than executable files, but they have the advantage that they can be understood by anyone who is familiar with the script's programming language. Scripts can be identified by the so-called shebang line at the top of the script. See Shebang. See Executable file. See Halting a script.

Semantics The study of meaning (Greek root, semantikos, signficant meaning). In the context of data science, semantics is the technique of creating meaningful assertions about data objects. A meaningful assertion, as used here, is a triple consisting of an identified data object, a data value, and a descriptor for the data value. In practical terms, semantics involves making assertions about data objects (ie, making triples), combining assertions about data objects (ie, merging triples), and assigning data objects to classes; hence relating triples to other triples. As a word of warning, few informaticians would define semantics in these terms, but most definitions for semantics are functionally equivalent to the definition offered here. Most language is unstructured and meaningless. Consider the assertion: Sam is tired. This is an adequately structured sentence with a subject verb and object. But what is the meaning of the sentence? There are a lot of people named Sam. Which Sam is being referred to in this sentence? What does it mean to say that Sam is tired? Is "tiredness" a constitutive property of Sam, or does it only apply to specific moments? If so, for what moment in time is the assertion, "Sam is tired" actually true? To a computer, meaning comes from assertions that have a specific, identified subject associated with some sensible piece of fully described data (metadata coupled with the data it describes). See Triple. See RDF.

Shebang Standard scripts written in Ruby, Perl, or Python all begin with a shebang, a colloquialism referring to the concatenation of the pound character, "#" (known by the musically-inclined as a SHarp character), followed by an exclamation sign, "!" (connoting a surprise or a bang). A typical shebang line (ie, top line) for Perl, Ruby, Python, and Bash scripts is:

```
#!/usr/local/bin/perl
#!/usr/local/bin/ruby
#!/usr/local/bin/python
#!/usr/local/bin/sh
```

In each case, the shebang is followed by the directory path to the script, and this is traditionally followed by optional programming arguments specific to each language. The shebang line, though essential in some Unix-like systems, is unnecessary in the Windows operating system. In this book, I use the shebang line to indicate, at a glance, the language in which a script is composed.

Simpson's Paradox Occurs when a correlation that holds in two different data sets is reversed if the data sets are combined. For example, baseball player A may have a higher batting average than player B for each of two seasons, but when the data for the two seasons are combined, player B may have the higher 2-season average. Simpson's paradox is just one example of unexpected changes in outcome when variables are unknowingly hidden or blended.[41]

Species Species is the bottom-most class of any classification or ontology. Because the species class contains the individual objects of the classification, it is the only class which is not abstract. The special significance of the species class is best exemplified in the classification of living organisms. Every species of organism contains individuals that share a common ancestral relationship to one another. When we look at a group of squirrels, we know that each squirrel in the group has its own unique personality, its own unique genes (ie, genotype), and its own unique set of physical features (ie, phenotype). Moreover, although the DNA sequences of individual squirrels are unique, we assume that there is a commonality to the genome of squirrels that distinguishes it from the genome of every other species. If we use the modern definition of species as an evolving gene pool, we see that the species can be thought of as a biological life form, with substance (a population of propagating genes), and a function (evolving to produce new species).[42–44] Put simply, species speciate; individuals do not. As a corollary, species evolve; individuals simply propagate. Hence, the species class is a separable biological unit with form and function. We, as individuals, are focused on the lives of individual things, and we must be reminded of the role of species in biological and nonbiological classifications. The concept of species is discussed in greater detail in Section 6.4. See Blended class. See Nonatomicity.

Specification A specification is a formal method for describing objects (physical objects such as nuts and bolts or symbolic objects, such as numbers, or concepts expressed as text). In general, specifications do not require the inclusion of specific items of information (ie they do not impose restrictions on the content that is included in or excluded from documents), and specifications do not impose any order of appearance of the data contained in the document (ie, you can mix up and rearrange specified objects, if you like). Specifications are not generally certified by a standards organization. They are generally produced by special interest organizations, and the legitimacy of a specification depends on its popularity. Examples of specifications are RDF (Resource Description Framework) produced by the W3C (World Wide Web Consortium), and TCP/IP (Transfer Control Protocol/Internet Protocol), maintained by the Internet Engineering Task Force. The most widely implemented specifications are simple and easily implemented. See Specification versus standard.

Specification Versus Standard Data standards, in general, tell you what must be included in a conforming document, and, in most cases, dictates the format of the final document. In many instances, standards bar inclusion of any data that is not included in the standard (eg, you should not include astronomical data in an clinical x-ray report). Specifications simply provide a formal way for describing the data that you choose to include in your document. XML and RDF, a semantic dialect of XML, are examples of specifications. They both tell you how data should be represented, but neither tell you what data to include, or how your document or data set should appear. Files that comply with a standard are rigidly organized and can be easily parsed and manipulated by software specifically designed to adhere to the standard. Files that comply with a specification are typically self-describing documents that contain within themselves all the information necessary for a human or a computer to derive meaning from the file contents. In theory, files that comply with a specification can be parsed and manipulated by generalized software designed to parse the markup language of the specification (eg, XML, RDF) and to organize the data into data structures defined within the file. The relative strengths and weaknesses of standards and specifications are discussed in Section 2.6, "Specifications Good, Standards Bad." See XML. See RDF.

Superclass Any of the ancestral classes of a subclass. For example, in the classification of living organisms, the class of vertebrates is a superclass of the class of mammals. The immediate superclass of a class is its parent class. In common parlance, when we speak of the superclass of a class, we are usually referring to its parent class. See Parent class.

Syntax Syntax is the standard form or structure of a statement. What we know as English grammar is equivalent to the syntax for the English language. Charles Mead distinctly summarized the difference between syntax and semantics: "Syntax is structure; semantics is meaning."[45] See Semantics.

Taxonomic Order In biological taxonomy, the hierarchical lineage of organisms are divided into a descending list of named orders: Kingdom, Phylum (Division), Class, Order, Family, and Genus, Species. As we have learned more and more about the classes of organisms, modern taxonomists have added additional ranks to the classification (eg, supraphylum, subphylum, suborder, infraclass, etc.). Was this really necessary? All of this taxonomic complexity could be averted by dropping named ranks and simply referring to every class as "Class." Modern specifications for class hierarchies (eg, RDF Schema) encapsulate each class with the name of its superclass. When every object yields its class and superclass, it is possible to trace any object's class lineage. For example, in the classification of living organisms, if you know the name of the parent for each class, you can write a simple script that generates the complete ancestral lineage for every class and species within the classification.[46] See Class. See Taxonomy. See RDF Schema. See Species.

Taxonomy A taxonomy is the collection of named instances (class members) in a classification or an ontology. When you see a schematic showing class relationships, with individual classes represented by geometric shapes and the relationships represented by arrows or connecting lines between the classes, then you are essentially looking at the structure of a classification, minus the taxonomy. You can think of building a taxonomy as the act of pouring all of the names of all of the instances into their proper classes. A taxonomy is similar to a nomenclature; the difference is that in a taxonomy, every named instance must have an assigned class. See Taxonomic order.

Terminology The collection of words and terms used in some particular discipline, field, or knowledge domain. Nearly synonymous with vocabulary and with nomenclature. Vocabularies, unlike terminologies, are not to be confined to the terms used in a particular field. Nomenclatures, unlike terminologies, usually aggregate equivalent terms under a canonical synonym.

Thesaurus A vocabulary that groups together synonymous terms. A thesaurus is very similar to a nomenclature. There are two minor differences. Nomenclatures included multi-word terms; whereas a thesaurus is typically composed of one-word terms. In addition, nomenclatures are typically restricted to a well-defined topic or knowledge domain (eg, names of stars, infectious diseases, etc.). See Nomenclature. See Vocabulary. See Classification. See Dictionary. See Terminology. See Ontology.

Triple In computer semantics, a triple is an identified data object associated with a data element and the description of the data element. In the computer science literature, the syntax for the triple is commonly described as: subject, predicate, object, wherein the subject is an identifier, the predicate is the description of the object, and the object is the data. The definition of triple, using grammatical terms, can be off-putting to the data scientist, who may think in terms of spreadsheet entries: a key that identifies the line record, a column header containing the metadata description of the data, and a cell that contains the data. In this book, the three components of a triple are described as: (1) the identifier for the data object, (2) the metadata that describes the data, and (3) the data itself. In theory, all data sets, databases, and spreadsheets can be constructed or deconstructed as collections of triples. See Introspection. See Data object. See Semantics. See RDF. See Meaning.

Unclassifiable Objects Classifications create a class for every object and taxonomies assign each and every object to its correct class. This means that a classification is not permitted to contain unclassified objects; a condition that puts fussy taxonomists in an untenable position. Suppose you have an object, and you simply do not know enough about the object to confidently assign it to a class. Or, suppose you have an object that seems to fit more than one class, and you can't decide which class is the correct class. What do you do? Historically, scientists have resorted to creating a "miscellaneous" class into which otherwise unclassifiable objects are given a temporary home, until more suitable accommodations can be provided. I have spoken with numerous data managers, and everyone seems to be of a mind that "miscellaneous" classes, created as a stopgap measure, serve a useful purpose. Not so. Historically, the promiscuous application of "miscellaneous" classes have proven to be a huge impediment to the advancement of science. In the case of the classification of living organisms, the class of protozoans stands as a case in point. Ernst Haeckel, a leading biological taxonomist in his time, created the Kingdom Protista (ie, protozoans), in 1866, to accommodate a wide variety of simple organisms with superficial commonalities. Haeckel himself understood that the protists were a blended class that included unrelated organisms, but he believed that further study would resolve the confusion. In a sense, he was right, but the process took much longer than he had anticipated; occupying generations of taxonomists over the following 150 years. Today, Kingdom Protista no longer exists. Its members have been reassigned to other classes. Nonetheless, textbooks of microbiology still describe the protozoans, just as though this name continued to occupy a legitimate place among terrestrial organisms. In the meantime, therapeutic opportunities for eradicating so-called protozoal infections, using class-targeted agents, have no doubt been missed.[47] You might think that the creation of a class of living organisms, with no established scientific relation to the real world, was a rare and ancient event in the annals of biology, having little or no chance of being repeated. Not so. A special pseudoclass of fungi, deuteromyctetes (spelled with a lowercase "d," signifying its questionable validity as a true biologic class) has been created to hold fungi of indeterminate speciation. At present, there are several thousand such fungi, sitting in a taxonomic limbo, waiting to be placed into a definitive taxonomic class.[47, 48] See Blended class.

Undifferentiated Software Intellectual property disputes have driven developers to divide software into two categories: undifferentiated software and differentiated software. Undifferentiated software comprises the fundamental algorithms that everyone uses whenever they develop a new software application. It is in nobody's interest to assign patents to basic algorithms and their implementations. Nobody wants to devote their careers to prosecuting or defending tenuous legal claims over the ownership of the fundamental building blocks of computer science. Differentiated software comprises customized applications that are sufficiently new and different from any preceding product that patent protection would be reasonable.

Utility In the context of software, a utility is an application that is dedicated to performing one specific task very well and very fast. In most instances, utilities are short programs, often running from the command line, and thus lacking any graphic user interface. Many utilities are available at no cost, with open source code. In general, simple utilities are preferable to multipurpose software applications.[29] **Remember, an application that claims to do everything for the user is, most often, an application that requires the user to do everything for the application.** See Command line. See Command line utility.

Validation Validation is the process that checks whether the conclusions drawn from data analysis are correct.[49] Validation usually starts with repeating the same analysis of the same data, using the methods that were originally recommended. Obviously, if a different set of conclusions is drawn from the same data and methods, the original conclusions cannot be validated. Validation may involve applying a different set of analytic methods to the same data, to determine if the conclusions are consistent. It is always reassuring to know that conclusions are repeatable, with different analytic methods. In prior eras, experiments were validated by repeating the entire experiment, thus producing a new set of observations for analysis. Many of today's scientific experiments are far too complex and costly to repeat. In such cases, validation requires access to the complete collection of the original data, and to the detailed protocols under which the data was generated. One of the most useful methods of data validation involves testing new hypotheses, based on the assumed validity of the original conclusions. For example, if you were to accept Darwin's analysis of barnacle data, leading to his theory of evolution, then you would expect to find a chronologic history of fossils in ascending layers of shale. This was the case; thus, paleontologists studying the Burgess shale reserves provided some validation to Darwin's conclusions. Validation should not be mistaken for proof. Nonetheless, the repeatability of conclusions, over time, with the same or different sets of data, and the demonstration of consistency with related observations, is about all that we can hope for in this imperfect world. See Verification. See Reproducibility.

Verification The process by which data is checked to determine whether the data was obtained properly (ie, according to approved protocols), and that the data accurately measured what it was intended to measure, on the correct specimens, and that all steps in data processing were done using well-documented protocols. Verification often requires a level of expertise that is at least as high as the expertise of the individuals who produced the data.[49] Data verification requires a full understanding of the many steps involved in data collection and can be a time-consuming task. In one celebrated case, in which two statisticians reviewed a microarray study performed at Duke University, the time devoted to their verification effort was reported to be 2000 hours.[50] To put this statement in perspective, the official work-year, according to the U.S. Office of Personnel Management, is 2087 hours. Verification is different from validation. Verification is performed on data; validation is done on the results of data analysis. See Validation. See Microarray. See Introspection.

Vocabulary A comprehensive collection of the words and their associated meanings. In some quarters, "vocabulary" and "nomenclature" are used interchangeably, but they are different from one another. Nomenclatures typically focus on terms confined to one knowledge domain. Nomenclatures typically do not contain definitions for the contained terms. Nomenclatures typically group terms by synonymy. Lastly, nomenclatures include multi-word terms. Vocabularies are collections of single words, culled from multiple knowledge domains, with their definitions, and assembled in alphabetic order. See Nomenclature. See Thesaurus. See Taxonomy. See Dictionary. See Terminology.

XML Acronym for eXtensible Markup Language, a syntax for marking data values with descriptors (ie, metadata). The descriptors are commonly known as tags. In XML, every data value is enclosed by a start-tag, containing the descriptor and indicating that a value will follow, and an end-tag, containing the same descriptor and indicating that a value preceded the tag. For example: <name>Conrad Nervig</name>. The enclosing angle brackets, "<>", and the end-tag marker, "/", are hallmarks of HTML and XML markup. This simple but powerful relationship between metadata and data allows us to employ metadata/data pairs as though each were a miniature database. The semantic value of XML becomes apparent when we bind a metadata/data pair to a unique object, forming a so-called triple. See Triple. See Meaning. See Semantics. See HTML.

REFERENCES

1. Kappelman LA, McKeeman R, Lixuan Zhang L. Early warning signs of IT project failure: the dominant dozen. *Information Systems Management* 2006;**23**:31–6.
2. Arquilla J. The Pentagon's biggest boondoggles. *The New York Times (Opinion Pages)* March 12, 2011.
3. Lohr S. Lessons from Britain's Health Information Technology Fiasco. *The New York Times* September 27, 2011.
4. Department of Health Media Centre. *Dismantling the NHS National Programme for IT. Press Release* September 22, 2011. Available from: http://mediacentre.dh.gov.uk/2011/09/22/dismantling-the-nhs-national-programme-for-it/ [accessed 12.06.2012].
5. Whittaker Z. UK's delayed national health IT programme officially scrapped. *ZDNet* September 22, 2011.
6. Lohr S. Google to end health records service after it fails to attract users. *The New York Times* Jun 24, 2011.
7. Schwartz E. Shopping for health software, some doctors get buyer's remorse. *The Huffington Post Investigative Fund* January 29, 2010.
8. Heeks R, Mundy D, Salazar A. *Why health care information systems succeed or fail.* Manchester: Institute for Development Policy and Management, University of Manchester; June 1999. Available from: http://www.sed.manchester.ac.uk/idpm/research/publications/wp/igovernment/igov_wp09.htm. [accessed 12.07.2012].
9. Beizer B. *Software testing techniques.* 2nd ed. Hoboken, NJ: Van Nostrand Reinhold; 1990.
10. Unreliable Research. Trouble at the lab. *The Economist* October 19, 2013.
11. Kolata G. Cancer fight: unclear tests for new drug. *The New York Times* April 19, 2010.
12. Ioannidis JP. Why most published research findings are false. *PLoS Med* 2005;**2**:e124.
13. Baker M. Reproducibility crisis: blame it on the antibodies. *Nature* 2015;**521**:274–6.
14. Naik G. Scientists' elusive goal: reproducing study results. *Wall Street Journal* December 2, 2011.
15. Innovation or Stagnation. *Challenge and opportunity on the critical path to new medical products.* Silver Spring, MD: U.S. Department of Health and Human Services, Food and Drug Administration; 2004.
16. Hurley D. Why are so few blockbuster drugs invented today? *The New York Times* November 13, 2014.
17. Angell M. The truth about the drug companies. *The New York Review of Books* July 15, 2004; vol. 51.
18. Crossing the Quality Chasm. *A new health system for the 21st century.* Washington, DC: Quality of Health Care in America Committee, Institute of Medicine; 2001.
19. Wurtman RJ, Bettiker RL. The slowing of treatment discovery, 1965–1995. *Nat Med* 1996;**2**:5–6.
20. Ioannidis JP. Microarrays and molecular research: noise discovery? *Lancet* 2005;**365**:454–5.
21. Weigelt B, Reis-Filho JS. Molecular profiling currently offers no more than tumour morphology and basic immunohistochemistry. *Breast Cancer Res* 2010;**12**:S5.
22. The Royal Society. *Personalised medicines: hopes and realities.* London: The Royal Society; 2005. Available from: https://royalsociety.org/~/media/Royal_Society_Content/policy/publications/2005/9631.pdf [accessed 01.01.2015].
23. Vlasic B. Toyota's slow awakening to a deadly problem. *The New York Times* February 1, 2010.

24. Lanier J. The complexity ceiling. In: Brockman J, editor. *The next fifty years: science in the first half of the twenty-first century*. New York: Vintage; 2002. p. 216–29.
25. Ecker JR, Bickmore WA, Barroso I, Pritchard JK, Gilad Y, Segal E. Genomics: ENCODE explained. *Nature* 2012;**489**:52–5.
26. Rosen JM, Jordan CT. The increasing complexity of the cancer stem cell paradigm. *Science* 2009;**324**:1670–3.
27. Labos C. It ain't necessarily so: why much of the medical literature is wrong. *Medscape News and Perspectives* September 09, 2014.
28. Gilbert E, Strohminger N. *We found only one-third of published psychology research is reliable — now what? The Conversation* August 27, 2015; Available at: http://theconversation.com/we-found-only-one-third-of-published-psychology-research-is-reliable-now-what-46596 [accessed 27.08.2015].
29. Brooks FP. No silver bullet: essence and accidents of software engineering. *Computer* 1987;**20**:10–9.
30. Al-Agha OM, Igbokwe AA. Malignant fibrous histiocytoma: between the past and the present. *Arch Pathol Lab Med* 2008;**132**:1030–5.
31. Nakayama R, Nemoto T, Takahashi H, Ohta T, Kawai A, Seki K, et al. Gene expression analysis of soft tissue sarcomas: characterization and reclassification of malignant fibrous histiocytoma. *Mod Pathol* 2007;**20**:749–59.
32. Patil N, Berno AJ, Hinds DA, Barrett WA, Doshi JM, Hacker CR, et al. Blocks of limited haplotype diversity revealed by high-resolution scanning of human chromosome 21. *Science* 2001;**294**:1719–23.
33. Data Quality Act. 67 Fed. Reg. 8,452, February 22, 2002, addition to FY 2001 Consolidated Appropriations Act (Pub. L. No. 106-554. codified at 44 U.S.C. 3516).
34. Berman JJ. *Repurposing legacy data: innovative case studies*. United States: Elsevier; 2015.
35. Stallman R. *Why "Free Software" is better than "Open Source"*. Boston: Free Software Foundation; 2015. Available from: http://www.gnu.org/philosophy/free-software-for-freedom.html [accessed 14.11.2015].
36. What is copyleft? Available from: http://www.gnu.org/copyleft/ [accessed 31.08.2015].
37. Paskin N. Identifier interoperability: a report on two recent ISO activities. *D-Lib Mag* 2006;**12**:1–23.
38. Berman JJ. *Tumor classification: molecular analysis meets Aristotle. BMC Cancer* 2004;**4**:10. Available from:http://www.biomedcentral.com/1471-2407/4/10 [accessed 01.01.2015].
39. Berman JJ. *Tumor taxonomy for the developmental lineage classification of neoplasms. BMC Cancer* 2004;**4**:88. http://www.biomedcentral.com/1471-2407/4/88 [accessed 01.01. 2015].
40. Berman JJ, Moore GW. *Implementing an RDF schema for pathology images*. Pittsburgh, PA: Pathology Informatics; 2007. Available from:http://www.julesberman.info/spec2img.htm [accessed 01.01.2015].
41. Tu Y, Gunnell D, Gilthorpe MS. Simpson's Paradox, Lord's Paradox, and suppression effects are the same phenomenon — the reversal paradox. *Emerg Themes Epidemiol* 2008;**5**:2.
42. DeQueiroz K. Ernst Mayr and the modern concept of species. *Proc Natl Acad Sci U S A* 2005;**102**(Suppl. 1):6600–7.
43. DeQueiroz K. Species concepts and species delimitation. *Syst Biol* 2007;**56**:879–86.
44. Mayden RL. Consilience and a hierarchy of species concepts: advances toward closure on the species puzzle. *J Nematol* 1999;**31**(2):95–116.
45. Mead CN. Data interchange standards in healthcare IT — computable semantic interoperability: now possible but still difficult, do we really need a better mousetrap? *J Healthc Inf Manag* 2006;**20**:71–8.
46. Berman JJ. *Methods in medical informatics: fundamentals of healthcare programming in Perl, Python, and Ruby*. Boca Raton: Chapman and Hall; 2010.
47. Berman JJ. *Taxonomic guide to infectious diseases: understanding the biologic classes of pathogenic organisms*. Waltham: Academic Press; 2012.
48. Guarro J, Gene J, Stchigel AM. Developments in fungal taxonomy. *Clin Microbiol Rev* 1999;**12**:454–500.
49. Committee on Mathematical Foundations of Verification, Validation, and Uncertainty Quantification, Board on Mathematical Sciences and their Applications, Division on Engineering and Physical Sciences, National

Research Council, Validation, and Uncertainty Quantification; Board on Mathematical Sciences and their Applications, Division on Engineering and Physical Sciences, National Research Council. *Assessing the reliability of complex models: mathematical and statistical foundations of verification, validation, and uncertainty quantification*. Washington, DC: National Academy Press; 2012 Available from: http://www.nap.edu/catalog.php?record_id=13395 [accessed 01.01.2015].

50. The Economist. Misconduct in science: an array of errors. *The Economist* September 10, 2011.

Author Biography

Jules Berman holds two bachelor of science degrees from MIT (Mathematics, and Earth and Planetary Sciences), a PhD from Temple University, and an MD, from the University of Miami. He was a graduate researcher in the Fels Cancer Research Institute, at Temple University, and at the American Health Foundation in Valhalla, New York. His post-doctoral studies were completed at the U.S. National Institutes of Health, and his residency was completed at the George Washington University Medical Center in Washington, D.C. Dr. Berman served as Chief of Anatomic Pathology, Surgical Pathology, and Cytopathology at the Veterans Administration Medical Center in Baltimore, Maryland, where he held joint appointments at the University of Maryland Medical Center and at the Johns Hopkins Medical Institutions. In 1998, he transferred to the U.S. National Institutes of Health, as a Medical Officer, and as the Program Director for Pathology Informatics in the Cancer Diagnosis Program at the

National Cancer Institute. Dr. Berman is a past president of the Association for Pathology Informatics, and the 2011 recipient of the association's Lifetime Achievement Award. He is a listed author on over 200 scientific publications and has written more than a dozen books in his three areas of expertise: informatics, computer programming, and cancer biology. Dr. Berman is currently a freelance writer.

THE SIMPLE LIFE

1

1.1 SIMPLIFICATION DRIVES SCIENTIFIC PROGRESS

> Make everything as simple as possible, but not simpler.
> -Albert Einstein (see Glossary item, Occam's razor)

Advances in civilization have been marked by increasing complexity. To a great extent, modern complexity followed from the invention of books, which allowed us to build upon knowledge deposited by long-deceased individuals.

Because it is easy to admire complexity, it can be difficult to appreciate its opposite: simplification. Few of us want to revert to a simple, prehistoric lifestyle, devoid of the benefits of engines, electricity, automobiles, airplanes, mass production of food and manufactured items, and medical technology. Nonetheless, a thoughtful review of human history indicates that some of our greatest scientific advances involved simplifying complex activities (see Glossary item, Science). Here are just a few examples:

1. **Nouns and names**. By assigning specific names to individuals (eg, Turok Son of Stone, Hagar the Horrible), ancient humans created a type of shorthand for complex objects, thus releasing themselves from the task of providing repeated, detailed descriptions of the persons to whom we refer.
2. **Classifications**. Terms that apply to classes of things simplified our ability to communicate abstract concepts. The earliest classes may have been the names of species (eg, antelope) or families (eg, birds). In either case, class abstractions alleviated the need for naming every bird in a flock (see Glossary items, Abstraction, Species, Systematics, Taxonomy, and Classification).
3. **Numerals**. Early humans must have known that counting on fingers and toes can be confusing. Numbers simplified counting, and greatly extended the maximum conceivable value of a tally. Without an expandable set of integers, communicating "how much" and "how many" must have been an exasperating experience.
4. **Glyphs, runes, stone tablets, and papyrus**. Written language, and the media for preserving thoughts, relieved humans from committing everything to memory. The practice of writing things down simplified the task of recordkeeping and allowed ancient humans to create records that outlived the record-keepers (see Glossary item, Persistence).
5. **Libraries**. Organized texts (ie, books) and organized collections of texts (ie, libraries) simplified the accrual of knowledge across generations. Before there were books and libraries, early

1

religions relied on the oral transmission of traditions and laws, an unreliable practice that invited impish tampering. The popularization of books marked the demise of oral traditions and the birth of written laws that could be copied, examined, discussed, and sometimes discarded.

6. **Mathematics**. Symbolic logic permitted ancient man to understand the real world through abstractions. For example, the number 2, a mathematical abstraction with no physical meaning, can apply to any type of object (eg, 2 chickens, 2 rocks, or 2 universes). Mathematics freed us from the tedious complexities of the physical realm, and introduced humans to a new world, ruled by a few simple axioms.

The list of ancient simplifications can go on and on. In modern times, simplifications have sparked new scientific paradigms and rejuvenated moribund disciplines. In the information sciences, HTML, a new and very simple method for formatting text and linking web documents and other data objects across the Internet, has revolutionized communications and data sharing. Likewise, XML has revolutionized our ability to annotate, understand, and merge data objects. The rudiments of HTML and XML can be taught in a few minutes (see Glossary items, HTML, XML, Data object).

In the computer sciences, language compilers have greatly reduced the complexity of programming. Object-oriented programming languages have simplified programming even further. Modern programmers can be much more productive than their counterparts who worked just a few decades ago. Likewise, Monte Carlo and resampling methods have greatly simplified statistics, enabling general scientists to model complex systems with ease (see Sections 8.2 and 8.3 of Chapter 8). More recently, MapReduce has simplified calculations by dividing large and complex problems into simple problems, for distribution to multiple computers (see Glossary item, MapReduce).

The methods for sequencing DNA are much simpler today than they were a few decades ago, and projects that required the combined efforts of multiple laboratories over several years, can now be accomplished in a matter of days or hours, within a single laboratory.

Physical laws and formulas simplify the way we understand the relationships among objects (eg, matter, energy, electricity, magnetism, and particles). Without access to simple laws and formulas, we could not have created complex products of technology (ie, computers, smartphones, and jet planes).

1.2 THE HUMAN MIND IS A SIMPLIFYING MACHINE

Science is in reality a classification and analysis of the contents of the mind.
-Karl Pearson in The Grammar of Science, 1900[1]

The unrestricted experience of reality is complex and chaotic. If we were to simply record all the things and events that we see when we take a walk on a city street or a country road, we would be overwhelmed by the magnitude and complexity of the collected data: images of trees, leaves, bark, clouds, buildings, bricks, stones, dirt, faces, insects, heat, cold, wind, barometric pressure, color, shades, sounds, loudness, harmonics, sizes and positions of things, relationships in space between the positions of different objects, movements, interactions, changes in shape, emotional responses, to name just a few.[2]

We fool ourselves into thinking that we can gaze at the world and see what is to be seen. In fact, what really happens is that light received by retinal receptors is processed by many neurons, in many pathways, and our brain creates a representation of the data that we like to call consciousness. The ease with which we can be fooled by optical illusions serves to show that we only "see" what our brains tell us to see; not what is really there. Vision is somewhat like sitting in a darkened theater and watching a Hollywood extravaganza, complete with special effects and stage props. Dreams are an example of pseudo-visual productions directed by our subconscious brains, possibly as an antidote to nocturnal boredom.

Life, as we experience it, is just too weird to go unchecked. We maintain our sanity by classifying complex data into simple categories of things that have defined properties and roles. In this manner, we can ignore the details and concentrate on patterns. When we walk down the street, we see buildings. We know that the buildings are composed of individual bricks, panes of glass, and girders of steel; but we do not take the time to inventory all the pieces of the puzzle. We humans classify data instinctively, and much of our perception of the world derives from the classes of objects that we have invented for ourselves.

What we perceive is dependent upon the choices we make, as we classify our world. If we classify animals as living creatures, just like ourselves, with many of the same emotional and cognitive features as we have, then we might be more likely to treat animals much the same way as we treat our fellow humans. If we classify animals as a type of food, then our relationships with animals might be something different. If we classify 3-week-old human embryos as young humans, then our views on abortion might be quite different from someone who classifies 3-week-old human embryos as small clusters of cells without organs or a nervous system.

Classification is heavy stuff. We simplify our world through classification, but, in so doing, we create our personal realities. For this reason, the process of classification should be done correctly. If I had to choose an area of science that was neglected during my early education, it would be ontology, the science of classification. Every data scientist should understand that there is a logic to creating a classification and that a poor data classification can ruin the most earnest efforts to analyze complex data. Chapter 6 is devoted to the concepts of meaning and classification, as it applies to the data sciences (see Glossary items, Classification, Ontology).

1.3 SIMPLIFICATION IN NATURE

The dream of every cell, to become two cells!

-Francois Jacob

Is our universe complex? Maybe so, but it is very clear that forces have been at work to simplify our reality. Despite the enormity of our universe, there seem to be just a few types of cosmological bodies (eg, stars, planets, black holes, gases, debris, and dark matter). These bodies assemble into galaxies, and our galaxies display a relatively narrow range of shapes and sizes. We see that simple and stable systems can emerge from chaos and complexity (see Glossary item, System). Because stable systems, by definition, persist longer than unstable systems, the stable systems will eventually outnumber the unstable, chaotic systems. As time progresses, simplicity trumps complexity.

What is true on the grand scale seems to apply to the small scale of things. Despite the enormous number of protons, neutrons, and electrons available to form complex elements, we find that there are just 98 naturally occurring elements. Under extreme laboratory conditions, we can produce about 20 additional elements that exist briefly before decaying. Spectrographic surveys of space indicate that the universe accommodates no elements other than those natural elements encountered in our own solar system.

Why is the periodic table of elements such a simple and short piece of work? Why can we not make heavier and heavier atoms, without restraint? As it happens, the nature of the physical realm is highly restrictive. It is estimated that electrons in the ground state (ie, lowest energy state) move at about 1% of the speed of light. The number of electrons orbiting the nucleus of an element equals the number of protons in the nucleus; hence, heavy elements contain many more electrons than the light elements. As the number of electrons increases, so do the orbits occupied by the electrons. Each additional orbit in the heavy elements has a higher energy level than the preceding orbit, and this means that the velocity of the electrons in the higher orbits exceeds the velocity of the electrons in the lower orbits. Eventually, as the electrons in an atom occupy orbits of higher and higher energies, the outermost electrons must move at a speed that exceeds the speed of light. Electrons cannot exceed the speed of light; hence, there is a strict limit to the number of allowed electron orbits; hence, there is a strict limit to the number of elements; hence, the periodic table is simple and short.

Is the realm of living organisms more complex than the physical realm? There are estimated to be somewhere between 10 million and 100 million species of living organisms on planet Earth. At first blush, the profusion of species would suggest incomprehensible complexity. Nonetheless, all of the species of living organisms can be listed under a simple classification composed of some dozens of classes. A high school student, perusing the classification of living organisms, can acquire a fair knowledge of the evolutionary development of life on earth. A skeptic might remark that the classes of living organisms are artefactual and arbitrary. What does it mean to say that there are a 100 classes of living organisms, when a we might have assigned species to 1000 classes or 1,000,000 classes if we had chosen so? As it happens, the true classes of organisms are discoveries, not inventions. A species is a biological unit, much like a single organism is a biological unit (Glossary item, Species). A strong argument can be made that the number of classes of organisms is fixed. It is the job of biologists to correctly assign organisms to their proper species, and to provide a hierarchy of classes that exactly accommodate the lineage produced by the evolution of life on this planet (see Glossary items, Classification system versus identification system, Cladistics, Clade, Monophyletic class, and Taxonomic order). Essentially, the classification of living organisms is an exercise in discovering the simplicity in nature. Because the classification of living organisms is the oldest and most closely examined classification known to science, data analysts are well-advised to learn from past failures and triumphs resulting from this grand, communal endeavor. In Sections 6.2 through 6.4 of Chapter 6, we will return to the process whereby simple classifications are built to model complex systems.

Aside from the simple manner in which all organisms can be classified, it seems obvious enough that life is complex. Furthermore, the complexity found in a highly evolved organism, such as a human, is obviously much greater than the complexity of the first organisms arising on earth. Hence, it seems safe to conclude that among living organisms, complexity has continually increased throughout the history of the evolution of life on our planet. Well, yes and no. The complexity of living organisms has increased over time, but simplification has occurred in tandem with complexification. For example, all living organisms contain DNA, and the DNA in organisms obeys a simple coding system. A biologist who works with human DNA one year may switch over to a study of fruit flies or corn the next year, without bothering to acquire new equipment. The protein, DNA, and RNA motifs in our cells are simple variations of a relatively small number of motifs and subunits developed long ago and shared by most living organisms.[3] A biologist who studies fruit flies and humans will learn that the same genes that control the embryonic development in humans also control the embryonic development of fruit flies and mice.[4] In some cases, a human gene can substitute for an insect gene, with little or no difference in outcome. Basically, what we see as the limitless complexity of nature is accounted for by variations on a few simple themes.

When we look at all the different types of animals in the world, we focus on diversity. We forget that there are just a few dozen body plans available to animals, and all of these plans were developed about half a billion years ago, in the Cambrian period.[5] Since then, nothing much has happened. It is as though we have spent a half billion years recovering from a wave of complexification. Today, we look at a horse and its rider, and we think that we are looking at two totally unrelated animals. Not so. Humans and horses have the same body plan, the same skeleton, and the same bones.[6] The differences lie in bone size and shape, attachment facets, and a few involutionary adjustments (eg, loss of a tail). A visiting Martian, with no appreciation of the subtleties, might fail to distinguish any one mammal from another.

Evolution simplifies organisms by conserving great evolutionary achievements among descendant classes. For example, the evolutionary development of photosynthetic oxygenation occurred once only; all organisms capable of photosynthetic oxygenation presumably use the same basic equipment inherited from one lucky cyanobacterium (see Glossary item, Chloroplast evolution). Likewise, about one billion years ago, the first eukaryotes appeared as one-celled organisms containing a nucleus and at least one mitochondrion. Nature never needed to reinvent the mitochondrion. The mitochondria that exist today, throughout the kingdom of eukaryotes, apparently descended from one early ancestor. So it goes for ribosome-associated proteins that translate ribonucleic acids into protein, and hox genes that orchestrate embryonic development.[4] The genomes of living cells, containing upwards of billions of nucleotides, seem hopelessly complex, but nature reduces the complexity and size of genomes when conditions favor a simpler and shorter set of genes (see Glossary item, Obligate intracellular organism).[7,8] Henner Brinkmann and Herve Philippe summarized the situation nicely: "In multiple cases evolution has proceeded via secondary simplification of a complex ancestor, instead of the constant march towards rising complexity generally assumed."[9]

1.4 THE COMPLEXITY BARRIER

Nobody goes there anymore. It's too crowded.

-Yogi Berra

It seems that many scientific findings, particularly those findings based on analyses of large and complex data sets, are yielding irreproducible results. We find that we cannot depend on the data that we depend on. If you don't believe me, consider these shocking headlines:

1. "Unreliable research: Trouble at the lab."[10] *The Economist*, in 2013 ran an article examining flawed biomedical research. The magazine article referred to an NIH official who indicated that "researchers would find it hard to reproduce at least three-quarters of all published biomedical findings, the public part of the process seems to have failed." The article described a study conducted at the pharmaceutical company Amgen, wherein 53 landmark studies were repeated. The Amgen scientists were successful at reproducing the results of only 6 of the 53 studies. Another group, at Bayer HealthCare, repeated 63 studies. The Bayer group succeeded in reproducing the results of only one-fourth of the original studies.

2. "A decade of reversal: an analysis of 146 contradicted medical practices."[11] The authors reviewed 363 journal articles, reexamining established standards of medical care. Among these articles were 146 manuscripts (40.2%) claiming that an existing standard of care had no clinical value.

3. "Cancer fight: unclear tests for new drug."[12] This *New York Times* article examined whether a common test performed on breast cancer tissue (Her2) was repeatable. It was shown that for patients who tested positive for Her2, a repeat test indicated that 20% of the original positive assays were actually negative (ie, falsely positive on the initial test).[12]

4. "Reproducibility crisis: blame it on the antibodies."[13] Biomarker developers are finding that they cannot rely on different batches of a reagent to react in a consistent manner, from test to test. Hence, laboratory analytic methods, developed using a controlled set of reagents, may not have any diagnostic value when applied by other laboratories, using different sets of the same analytes.[13]

5. "Why most published research findings are false."[14] Modern scientists often search for small effect sizes, using a wide range of available analytic techniques, and a flexible interpretation of outcome results. The manuscript's author found that research conclusions are more likely to be false than true.[14,15]

6. "We found only one-third of published psychology research is reliable — now what?"[16] The manuscript authors suggest that the results of a first study should be considered preliminary and tentative. Conclusions have no value until they are independently validated.

Anyone who attempts to stay current in the sciences soon learns that much of the published literature is irreproducible[17]; and that almost anything published today might be retracted tomorrow. This appalling truth applies to some of the most respected and trusted laboratories in the world.[18-25] Those of us who have been involved in assessing the rate of progress in disease research are painfully aware of the numerous reports indicating a general slowdown in medical progress.[26-33]

For the optimists, it is tempting to assume that the problems that we may be experiencing today are par for the course, and temporary. It is the nature of science to stall for a while and lurch forward in sudden fits. Errors and retractions will always be with us as long as humans are involved in the scientific process.

For the pessimists, such as myself, there seems to be something going on that is really new and different; a game changer. This game changer is the "complexity barrier," a term credited to Boris Beizer, who used it to describe the impossibility of managing increasingly complex software products.[34] The complexity barrier, known also as the complexity ceiling, applies to virtually every modern area of science and engineering.[35,36]

Some of the mistakes that lead to erroneous conclusions in data-intensive research are well-known, and include the following:

1. Errors in sample selection, labeling, and measurement.[37-39] For example, modern biomedical data is high-volume (eg, gigabytes and larger), heterogeneous (ie, derived from diverse sources), private (ie, measured on human subjects), and multidimensional (eg, containing thousands of different measurements for each data record). The complexities of handling such data correctly are daunting[40] (see Glossary items, Curse of dimensionality, Dimensionality).

2. Misinterpretation of the data[41,14,42,31,43-45]

3. Data hiding and data obfuscation[46,47]

4. Unverified and unvalidated data[48-51,43,52]

5. Outright fraud[47,25,53]

When errors occur in complex data analyses, they are notoriously difficult to discover.[48]

Aside from human error, intrinsic properties of complex systems may thwart our best attempts at analysis. For example, when complex systems are perturbed from their normal, steady-state activities, the rules that govern the system's behavior become unpredictable.[54] Much of the well-managed complexity of the world is found in machines built with precision parts having known functionality. For example, when an engineer designs a radio, she knows that she can assign names to the components, and these components can be relied upon to behave in a manner that is characteristic of its type. A capacitor will behave like a capacitor, and a resistor will behave like a resistor. The engineer need not worry that the capacitor will behave like a semiconductor or an integrated circuit. The engineer knows that the function of a machine's component will never change; but the biologist operates in a world wherein components change their functions, from organism to organism, cell to cell, and moment to moment. As an example, cancer researchers discovered an important protein that plays a role in the development of cancer. This protein, p53, was considered to be the primary cellular driver for human malignancy. When p53 mutated, cellular regulation was disrupted, and cells proceeded down a slippery path leading to cancer. In the past few decades, as more information was obtained, cancer researchers have learned that p53 is just one of many proteins that play some role in carcinogenesis, and that the role played by p53 changes depending on the species, tissue type, cellular microenvironment, genetic background of the cell, and many other factors. Under one set of circumstances, p53 may modify DNA repair; under another set of circumstances, p53 may cause cells to arrest the growth cycle.[55,56] It is difficult to predict the biological effect of a protein that changes its primary function based on prevailing cellular conditions.

At the heart of all data analysis is the assumption that systems have a behavior that can be described with a formula or a law, or that can lead to results that are repeatable and to conclusions that can be validated. We are now learning that our assumptions may have been wrong, and that our best efforts at data analysis may be irreproducible.

Complexity seems to be the root cause of many failures in software systems; and the costs of such failures run very high. It is common for large, academic medical centers to purchase information systems that cost in excess of $500 million. Despite the enormous investment, failures are not uncommon.[57–59] About three-quarters of hospital information systems are failures.[60] Furthermore, successfully implemented electronic health record systems do not always improve patient outcomes.[61] Based on a study of the kinds of failures that account for patient safety errors in hospitals, it has been suggested that hospital information systems will not greatly reduce safety-related incidents.[62] Clinical decision support systems, built into electronic health record systems, have not had much impact on physicians' practices.[63] These systems tend to be too complex for the hospital staff to master and are not well-utilized.[64]

It is believed that the majority of information technology projects fail, and that failure is positively correlated with the size and cost of the projects.[65] We know that public projects costing hundreds of billions of dollars have failed quietly, without raising much attention.[66,67] Projects that are characterized by large size, high complexity, and novel technology aggravate any deficiencies in management, personnel, or process practices.[65,68,35,36,69]

In 2004, the National Cancer Institute launched an ambitious project, known as the Cancer Biomedical Informatics Grid, abbreviated as (CaBig(tm)), aimed at developing standards for annotating and sharing biomedical data, and tools for data analysis (see Glossary items, Standard, Grid, and Data sharing).[64] For a time, the project received generous support from academia and industry. In 2006, the Cancer Biomedical Informatics Grid was selected as a laureate in ComputerWorld's honors program.[70] ComputerWorld described the project as "Effectively forming a World Wide Web of cancer research," with "promises to speed progress in all aspects of cancer research and care." The great promises of the project came with a hefty price tag. By 2010, the National Cancer Institute had sunk at least 350 million dollars into the effort.[71] Though the project was ambitious, there were rumblings in the cancer informatics community that very little had been achieved. In view of past and projected costs, an ad hoc committee was assigned to review the program. In a report issued to the public in 2011, the committee found that the project had major deficiencies and suggested a year-long funding moratorium.[71] Soon thereafter, the project leader left the National Cancer Institute, and the Cancer Bioinformatics Grid was unceremoniously terminated.[72]

After CaBig(tm) was terminated, Barry Smith, a big thinker in the rather small field of ontology, wrote an editorial entitled "CaBIG(tm) Has Another Fundamental Problem: It Relies on "Incoherent" Messaging Standard" (see Glossary item, Ontology).[73] In his editorial, Smith suggested that HL7, a data model specification used by CaBig(tm) could not possibly work, and that it had proven itself a failure for those people who actually tried to implement the specification and use it for its intended purposes.[73]

At about the same time that CaBig was being terminated, a major project in the United Kingdom was also scuttled. The United Kingdom's National Health Service had embarked on a major overhaul of its information systems, with the goal of system-wide interoperability and data integration (see Glossary items, Interoperability, Integration). After investing $17 billion dollars, the project was ditched when members of Parliament called the effort "unworkable."[74–76] This failed program had been called "the world's biggest civil information technology program."[74] Back in 2001, a report published by the NHS Information Authority cited fundamental flaws in HL7.[77] The project was also hampered by intrinsic difficulties in establishing a workable identifier system (to be discussed further in Sections 5.1 and 5.2 of Chapter 5). **There are generally multiple problems that, together, account for the failure of a complex system**.[78–80]

Science and society may have reached a complexity barrier beyond which nothing can be analyzed and understood with any confidence. In light of the irreproducibility of complex data analyses, it seems prudent to make the following two recommendations:

1. Simplify your complex data, before you attempt analysis.
2. Assume that the first analysis of primary data is tentative and often wrong. **The most important purpose of data analysis is to lay the groundwork for data reanalysis** (see Glossary items, Primary data, Secondary data, Conclusions).

1.5 GETTING READY

What is needed is not only people with a good background in a particular field, but also people capable of making a connection between item 1 and item 2, which might not ordinarily seem connected.

-Isaac Asimov[81]

Like many individuals, I am no cook. Nonetheless, I can prepare a few dishes when the need arises: scrambled eggs, oatmeal, and spaghetti. In a pinch, I'll open a can of tuna, or baked beans. My wife insists that such activities do not qualify as cooking, but I maintain that the fundamental skills, such as heating, boiling, mixing, and measuring, are all there. It's cooking if I can eat it.

If you are planning to have a data-centric career, then you must learn to cook up your own scripts. Otherwise, you will be limited by the built-in functionalities provided by software applications. To make a substantive contribution to your field, you must have the ability to organize and analyze diverse types of data, using algorithms collected from a variety of different scientific disciplines. Creativity often involves finding relationships that were missed by your peers, but you will never find those relationships if you lock yourself in a specialized software application. Programming languages free scientists to follow their creative instincts.

Some of our most common and indispensable computational tasks are ridiculously easy to achieve, in any programming environment. We do not ask a master chef to fill a glass of water at the sink. Why would we seek the services of a professional programmer when we need to alphabetically sort a list, or find records in a data set that match a query string, or annotate a collection of files with a name and date (see Glossary items, Query, String)? The bulk of the work involved in data analysis projects will require skills in data organization, data curation, data annotation, data merging, data transforming, and a host of computationally simple techniques that you should learn to do for yourself.[64,40] (see Glossary items, Curator, Transform)

There are hundreds of fine programming languages available; each with its own strengths and weaknesses. If you intend to confine your programming efforts to simple tasks, such as basic arithmetic operations, simple descriptive statistics, and search and replace methods, then you may wish to avoid the languages preferred by professional programmers(eg, C and Java). Furthermore, advanced GUI (Graphic User Interface) languages such as Visual Basic, require a level of programmatic overhead that you will not need. Specialty languages, such as R, for statistics, may come in handy, but they are not essential for every data scientist.[82] Some tasks should be left to specialists. Perl, Python, and Ruby are powerful, no-cost programming languages, with versions available for most popular operating systems. Instructional online tutorials, as well as a rich literature of print books, provide nonprogrammers with the skills they need to write the programs that they will use as data scientists.[40,83–85]

If you hope to simplify your data, it is advisable to begin your projects by eyeballing your data files. For this, you will need a simple text editor and some data visualization tools. The easiest way to review a large data file is to open it and browse; much the same way that you might browse the contents of books in a library. Most word processing software applications are not suited to opening and browsing large files, exceeding about 50 megabytes in length. Text editors, unlike word processors, are designed to perform simple tasks on large, plain-text files (ie, unformatted text, also known as ASCII text) on the order of a gigabyte in length (see Glossary items, ASCII, American Standard Code for Information Interchange). There are many freely available text editors that can quickly open and search large files. Two popular text editors are Emacs and vi. Downloadable versions are available for Linux, Windows, and Macintosh systems. Text editors are useful for composing computer programs, which are always written in plain-text (see Glossary item, Plain-text). Data scientists will find it useful to acquire facility with a fast and simple text editor (see Glossary items, Data science, Data scientist).

For data visualization, Gnuplot or Matplotlib should suffice. Gnuplot is an easy-to-use general data visualization and analysis tool that is available at no cost.[86] If you prefer to program in Python, then Matplotlib is a good choice. Similar to Gnuplot in functionality, Matplotlib is designed to work smoothly within Python scripts, on output data provided by Python's numpy and scipy modules (see Glossary items, Numpy, Scipy). Gnuplot and Matplotlib support a remarkable range of data analysis options (see Open Source Tools for Chapter 4).[87]

As a preliminary step, it is important to know whether your data is comprehensive (ie, containing all of the data relevant to an intended purpose), representative (ie, containing a useful number of data objects of every type of data included in the data set), reasonably organized (eg, with identifiers for individual records and with a consistent set of features associated with each data record), and adequately annotated (eg, timestamped appropriately, and accompanied with descriptions of the data elements) (see Glossary items, Timestamp, Time, Trusted timestamp, Universal and timeless).

The outlook for data scientists who choose to be creative with their data has never been better. You can stop obsessing over your choice of operating system and programming language; modern scripting languages provide cross-platform compatibility. You can forget about buying expensive software applications; nearly everything you need is available at no cost. Feel free to think in terms of simple utilities (eg, command-line programs or specialized modules) that will implement specific algorithms, as required (see Glossary item, Algorithm). Write your own short scripts designed to perform one particular computational task quickly, using a minimal amount of code, and without the overhead of a graphic user interface. A few hours of effort will start you on your way towards data independence.

By far, the most important asset of any data analyst is her brain. A set of personal attributes that include critical thinking, an inquisitive mind, and the patience to devote hundreds of hours to reviewing data is certain to come in handy. Expertise in analytic algorithms is a valuable, yet sometimes overrated, skill (see Glossary items, New analytic method, Method). Most data analysis projects require the ability to understand the data, and this can often be accomplished with simple data visualization tools. The application of rigorous mathematical and statistical algorithms typically comes at the end of the project, after the key relationships among data objects have been discovered (see Glossary items, Object, Data object). It is important to remember that if your old data is verified, organized, annotated, and preserved, the analytic process can be repeated and improved. In most cases, the first choice of analytic method is not the best choice. No single analytic method is critical when the data analyst has the opportunity to repeat his work, applying many different methods, all the while attaining a better understanding of the data.[87]

OPEN SOURCE TOOLS

Today, most software exists, not to solve a problem, but to interface with other software.

-IO Angell

PERL

Perl comes bundled with Linux distributions. Versions of the Perl interpreter are available for most operating systems.

For Windows users, the Strawberry Perl distribution comes bundled with a CPAN installer, a C compiler (gcc+), and a wealth of bundled modules (see Glossary item, CPAN). Strawberry Perl is a compilation of open source software components, available as 32-bit or 64-bit binary versions (see Glossary items, Binary data, Exe file). Strawberry Perl is available at: strawberryperl.com

Further information is available at: https://www.perl.org/get.html

General instruction for Perl programming is available in my book, "Perl Programming for Medicine and Biology."[83]

PYTHON

Like Perl, Python comes bundled on Linux distributions. Python installations for various operating systems are available at: https://www.python.org/downloads/

A Python download site for Windows is: https://www.python.org/downloads/windows/

Students and professionals in healthcare and related sciences may enjoy my book, "Methods in Medical Informatics: Fundamentals of Healthcare Programming in Perl, Python, and Ruby."[84]

RUBY

Ruby was built to have many of the syntactic features of Perl but with the native object orientation of Smalltalk.

Ruby installations for various operating systems can be downloaded from: https://www.ruby-lang.org/en/downloads/

A Windows installer for Ruby is found at: http://rubyinstaller.org/

An excellent Ruby book is "Programming Ruby: The Pragmatic Programmer's Guide," by Dave Thomas.[88] Students and professionals in healthcare and related sciences may enjoy my book, "Ruby Programming for Medicine and Biology."[85]

TEXT EDITORS

When I encounter a large data file, in plain ASCII format, the first thing I do is open the file and take a look at its content (see Glossary items, ASCII, Plain-text). Unless the file is small (ie, under about 50 megabytes), most commercial word processors fail at this task. You will want to use an editor designed to work with large ASCII files (see Glossary item, Text editor). Two of the more popular, freely available editors are Emacs and vi (also available under the name vim). Downloadable versions are available for Linux, Windows, and Macintosh systems. On most computers, these editors will open files of several hundred megabytes, at least.[64]

vim download site: http://www.vim.org/download.php

Emacs download site: https://www.gnu.org/software/emacs/

For those with 64-bit Windows, an emacs version is available at: http://sourceforge.net/projects/emacsbinw64/?source=typ_redirect

One of the advantages of Emacs is its implicit, prettified display of source code. Perl, Python, and Ruby scripts are all displayed with colored fonts distinguishing commands, comments, quoted text, and conditionals.

OPENOFFICE

OpenOffice is a free word processing application that also displays and edits powerpoint-type files and excel-type files. It can also produce mathematical symbols, equations and notations, providing much of the functionality of LaTeX (see Glossary item, LaTeX). OpenOffice is available at: https://www.openoffice.org/download/

LIBREOFFICE

A spin-off project from OpenOffice, intended to offer equivalent functionality plus greater extensibility. LibreOffice is available at: https://www.libreoffice.org/

COMMAND LINE UTILITIES

The "command line" is a one-line instruction, sent to the operating system, and entered at the operating system prompt. The command line is an important feature of most operating systems.[89] The term "command line utility" refers to a utility that can be launched via a command line instruction. By convention, command line utilities permit the user to include arguments (ie, required or optional parameters that modify the behavior of the utility, added to the command line in no particular order).

To enter command line arguments, you must have a command prompt (also called the "shell prompt" or just "the shell" in unix-like operating systems). In the Windows operating system, the "Command Prompt" application provides the functionality of the old "DOS" screen. The "Command Prompt" application sits inconspicuously among the minor Windows system programs. Once you find Command Prompt among the list of available programs in your system, it would be wise to move its icon to a place of honor on your desktop, for easy access. Entering the word "help" at the command prompt produces a long list of the available DOS commands (Fig. 1.1).

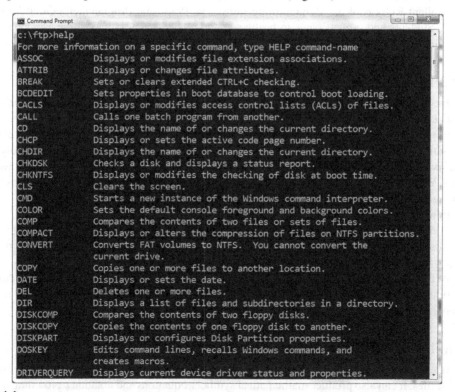

FIGURE 1.1

At the DOS prompt, which happens to be set to the c:\ftp subdirectory in this example, the "help" line displays several screens of commands, any of which can be asserted from the command line.

The most common use of the Command prompt is to execute DOS commands (eg, dir, cd, type, copy, ren, rd), familiar to anyone who has used DOS-based computers, prior to the advent of Windows (Fig. 1.2).

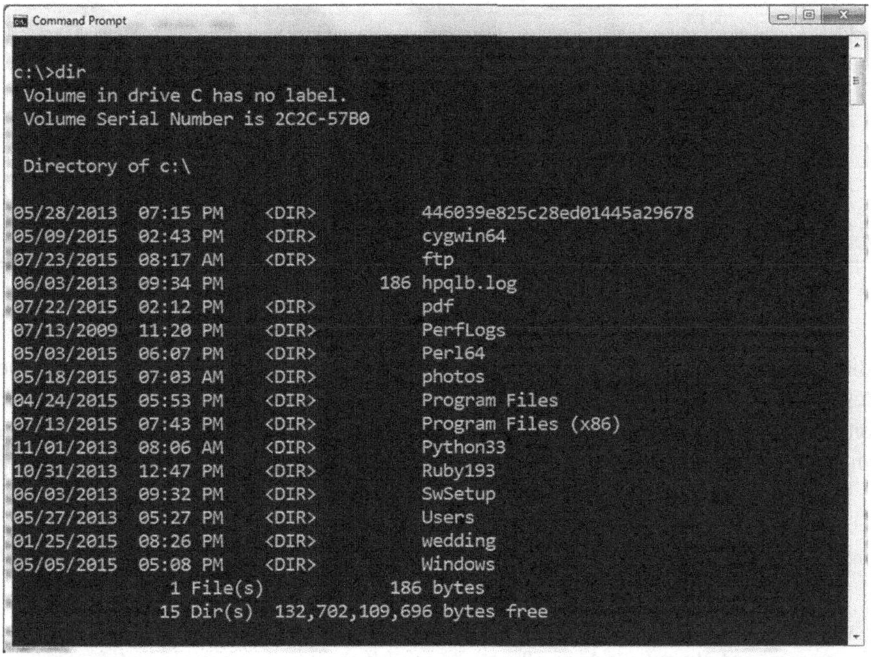

```
Command Prompt

c:\>dir
 Volume in drive C has no label.
 Volume Serial Number is 2C2C-57B0

 Directory of c:\

05/28/2013  07:15 PM    <DIR>          446039e825c28ed01445a29678
05/09/2015  02:43 PM    <DIR>          cygwin64
07/23/2015  08:17 AM    <DIR>          ftp
06/03/2013  09:34 PM               186 hpqlb.log
07/22/2015  02:12 PM    <DIR>          pdf
07/13/2009  11:20 PM    <DIR>          PerfLogs
05/03/2015  06:07 PM    <DIR>          Perl64
05/18/2015  07:03 AM    <DIR>          photos
04/24/2015  05:53 PM    <DIR>          Program Files
07/13/2015  07:43 PM    <DIR>          Program Files (x86)
11/01/2013  08:06 AM    <DIR>          Python33
10/31/2013  12:47 PM    <DIR>          Ruby193
06/03/2013  09:32 PM    <DIR>          SwSetup
05/27/2013  05:27 PM    <DIR>          Users
01/25/2015  08:26 PM    <DIR>          wedding
05/05/2015  05:08 PM    <DIR>          Windows
               1 File(s)            186 bytes
              15 Dir(s)  132,702,109,696 bytes free
```

FIGURE 1.2

The DOS prompt window, displaying the DOS prompt (ie, c:\>), and a DOS command (ie, dir), and the screen dump exhibiting the results of the dir command, listing the current directory contents of the author's home computer.

The command line gains power when it invokes applications and utilities. Here is an example of a command line instruction that calls an ImageMagic utility (Fig. 1.3).

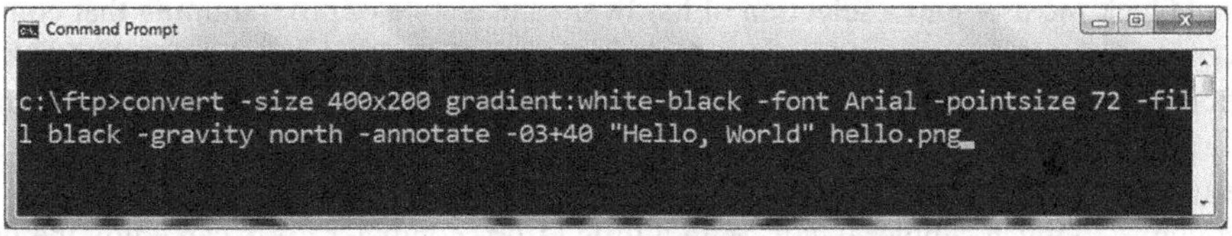

```
Command Prompt

c:\ftp>convert -size 400x200 gradient:white-black -font Arial -pointsize 72 -fil
l black -gravity north -annotate -03+40 "Hello, World" hello.png
```

FIGURE 1.3

A single command line, albeit a lengthy one, that calls ImageMagick's "convert" utility to create a gray gradient background to the words "Hello, World."

The first word following the system prompt is "convert," the name of an ImageMagick utility (see Glossary item, ImageMagick). The full name of the utility is convert.exe, but the operating system is programmed to know that "convert" represents an executable file within the current directory, or in the list of files in its PATH (ie, the operating system's go-to list of executable files) (see Glossary items, Exe file, Executable file). The convert utility expects a list of parameters and the name of an output file.

The resulting image is shown (Fig. 1.4):

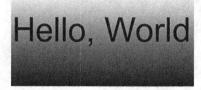

FIGURE 1.4

The output file, hello.png, produced from the command line, displayed in Fig. 1.3.

How did I know the proper command line syntax for ImageMagick's convert utility? The ImageMagick download, widely available from multiple locations on the Internet, comes with detailed documentation. This documentation indicates that ImageMagick contains "convert," among many other utilities, and provides instructions for implementing these utilities via the command line. The following command line requests instructions, via the "-help" argument, for using the montage utility.

```
c:\>montage -help
```

There are many thousands of publicly available command line utilities. Like anything on the Internet, utilities may not always work as advertised, and it may be impossible to know when a utility has been corrupted with malicious code. It is best to download only trusted utilities, from trusted websites. In this book, I try to confine my suggested utilities to tested and popular resources (see Glossary item, Data resource).

CYGWIN, LINUX EMULATION FOR WINDOWS

Three decades ago, every computer user was faced with deciding which operating system to use (eg, Unix, DOS, Macintosh, Amiga) and which programming language to learn (eg, C, Basic, Fortran). The choice would lock the user into a selection of hardware and a style of programming that could not be easily reversed. Over the next two decades, the importance of the decision did not diminish, but the proliferation of programming languages made the decision much more difficult. The computer magazine literature from the 90s was crammed with titles devoted to one particular operating system or one particular programming language.

Everything is so much simpler today. With a little effort, computer users can enjoy the particular benefits offered by most operating systems and most programming languages, from their home computer. For myself, I use Windows as my default operating system, because it comes preinstalled on most computers sold in the United States. One of the very first things I do after booting a new computer is to install Cygwin, a linux-like interface for Windows.

Cygwin, and supporting documentation, can be downloaded from: http://www.cygwin.com/

Cygwin opens in a window that produces a shell prompt (equivalent to the Windows C prompt) from which Unix programs can be launched. For myself, I use Cygwin primarily as a source of Linux utilities, of which there are hundreds. In addition, Cygwin comes bundled with some extremely useful applications, such as Perl, Python, and Gnuplot. Cygwin distributions containing Ruby are also available (Fig. 1.5).

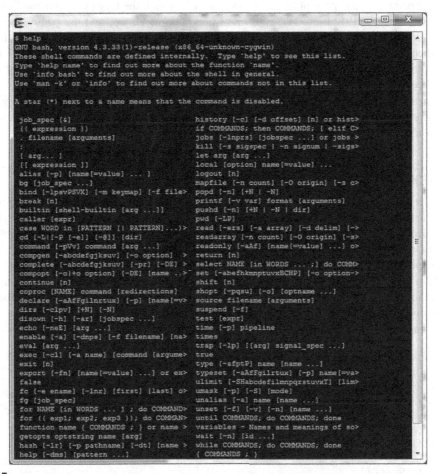

FIGURE 1.5

The Cygwin screen, emulating a Linux system, under the Windows operating system.

Windows users are not restricted to launching Linux applications from the Cygwin shell prompt. A command line from the Windows C prompt will launch Cygwin utilities. Likewise, a system call from a Perl, Python, or Ruby script can make interactive calls to Cygwin applications (see Glossary item, System call).

Here are a few examples:

```
c:\cygwin64\bin>wc c:\ftp\simplify.txt
output:
10718 123383 849223 c:\ftp\simplify.txt
```

Here, we begin at the C prompt for the subdirectory in which the Cygwin command line utilities are stored (ie, c:\cygwin64\bin>). We enter the Linux command, wc, and the path/filename for a plain-text file. The Linux "wc" command is a word counter. The "wc" command is followed by the path/filename of the interrogated file. The three numbers returned, "10718 123383 849223" are the number of lines in the file, the number of words in the file, and the number of bytes in the file, respectively.

Data scientists eventually learn that there are some tasks that are best left to Linux. Having Cygwin installed on your Windows system will make life easier for you, and for your collaborators, who may prefer to work in Linux.

DOS BATCH SCRIPTS

When you have a succession of DOS commands that you use routinely, it is often convenient to collect them all in a plain-text file that will run your commands in tandem. Such files are called batch files and can be created in any text editor by simply listing the commands, line-by-line, and appending the suffix ".bat" to the named file that holds the commands.

The simplest batch files are often the most useful. As an example, you may have a collection of working files that you would like to back up, at the end of each work day, onto an external thumb drive. Assuming the thumb drive is assigned the f: directory, just list your copy commands, mount your thumb drive, and invoke the name of the batch file at the command prompt.

Here is an example of a batch file, fback.bat, that copies 10 of my work-in-progress files to a thumb drive.

```
copy diener.txt f:
copy simplify.txt f:
copy re-ana.txt f:
copy phenocop.txt f:
copy mystery.txt f:
copy disaster.txt f:
copy factnote.txt f:
copy perlbig.txt f:
copy create.txt f:
copy exploreo.txt f:
```

To invoke the batch file, just enter its name from the subdirectory in which it resides. For example:

```
c:\ftp>fback.bat
```

Batch files will initiate any action that would otherwise be launched from the command line. This includes calling utilities. For example, the magick.bat batch file, vida infra, launches ImageMagick's "convert" application and applies contrast twice, yielding a modified file named results.png. The current directory is changed to the location wherein the Cygwin executables reside. From this location, Cygwin's version of ImageMagick's imdisplay (image display) application is launched, to display the "results.png" image file, at which time, the directory is changed back to its start location. Notice that the magick.bat batch file invokes a Linux application, contained in the Cygwin application, directly from a DOS line; a neat trick. Of course, this batch file requires ImageMagick and Cygwin to be installed on your computer.

```
convert c:\ftp\eqn.jpg -contrast -contrast c:\ftp\results.png
cd c:\cygwin64\home\E-Rock\
imdisplay c:\ftp\results.png
cd c:\ftp
```

In the prior example, the name of the image file used in the batch file was preassigned (ie, so-called hard-coded into the script). For most practical applications, you won't know which files to modify until you are ready to launch the batch file. Batch files have a simple syntax for substituting variable names, into a batch command, at the moment when the batch file is launched. Strings separated by spaces appearing after the name of the batch file are assigned to numbered variables that are passed to the batch file.

Here is the command line that launches the showpic.bat batch file:

```
c:\cygwin64\home\E-Rock>showpic.bat eqn.jpg
```

Following the name of the batch file, there is a parameter, "c:\ftp\eqn.jpg" which will be passed implicitly to the batch file, as the numbered variable, "%1." We can see how the passed parameter is used, when we inspect the code for the showpic.bat batch file.

```
imdisplay %1
```

The batch file loads the provided path/filename into the variable, %1, and displays the eqn.jpg image.

Batch files can include conditional statements and loop iterators. The following batch file, a.bat, contains a conditional statement and a go-to command. If the user supplies a parameter (a path/filename in this case) when the batch file is invoked, an application (which happens to be "a.exe" here; you would need to substitute your own exe file) is launched, using the provided filename. If no filename is provided, the application is launched using "c:\ftp\perlbig.txt" as the default parameter. Here is the a.bat batch file:

```
cd C:\ftp\back\aurora
if not "%1" == "" goto start
```

```
a.exe c:\ftp\perlbig.txt
goto end
:start
a.exe c:\ftp\%1
:end
cd c:\ftp
exit
```

Experienced programmers simplify their lives by composing short batch files that automate routine processes.

LINUX BASH SCRIPTS

The bash script, also known as the shell script, is the Unix equivalent of the DOS batch script; a batch of shell commands collected into a short plain-text file, and executed by invoking the name of the file, from the command prompt. The name, bash, is a concatenation of the first two characters of "Batch"+"Shell." There are thousands of open source and available bash files that users will find helpful.

One of the peculiarities of Linux bash files is that prior to launch, downloaded bash files will, in most cases, need to have their file permissions reset. At the Linux shell prompt, the "chmod + x" command, shown here, changes the mode of the file (mybashfile in this instance) to permit user access.

```
$ chmod +x mybashfile
```

Here is an example demonstrating the typical syntax for launching a bash file from the Cygwin shell:

```
$ mybashfile infile.gif out.gif -s 5 -d 5 -c 5 -g 1 -p 2 -b white
```

Typically, the name of the bash file, in this case "mybashfile", is followed by the name of an existing file on which the bash file will operate ("infile.gif" here), followed by the name of an output file ("out.gif" here), followed by a list of options and parameters that modify the behavior of the bash file. The options are preceded by a dash (-s, -d, -c, -g, -p, -b) and each option is immediately followed by a space, and then an input parameter, also called the input argument. How do we know what options to use and what arguments to supply? By convention, bash files include a help screen that can be invoked with the name of the bashfile followed by "-h" or "-help"

```
$ mybashfile -h
```

As a curious subpopulation of humanity, Linux devotees are eager to spend any amount of time, no matter how large, writing applications intended to save any amount of time, no matter how small. Consequently, when it comes to parsimonious approaches to data simplification, nothing beats Linux utilities. Linux programmers have prepared, through the decades, an amazing library of bash scripts, capable of performing a wide range of useful tasks.[90,91] A great source of hundreds of brilliant and useful image utilities, available as bash files, is found at Fred Weinhaus' site: http://www. fmwconcepts.com/imagemagick/plot3D/index.php

INTERACTIVE LINE INTERPRETERS

Interpreted languages, such as Python, Ruby, and Perl permit scripts to be run line-by-line; whereas executable files (eg, C programs) are compiled and executed in toto, as though the entire program consisted of a single, long line of code. Because scripts are interpreted line-by-line, they can be developed via line interpreters, permitting programmers to test each line of code, as the script is being written.

Python, Ruby, and Perl provide line interpreters for programmers who take pride in crafting perfect lines of code. In the following examples, a line of code prints the sum of 5+5.

The line interpreter for Python is invoked by typing "python" at the system prompt:

```
c:\>python
Python 3.3.2 (v3.3.2:d047928ae3f6, May 16 2013, 00:06:53) [MSC v.1600 64 bit (AMD64)] on
win32
Type "help", "copyright", "credits", or "license" for more information.
>>> print(5 + 5)
10
>>>
```

The line interpreter for Ruby is invoked by typing "irb" at the system prompt:

```
c:\>irb
irb(main):001:0> puts (5+5)
10
=> nil
```

The Ruby line interpreter keeps track of the line number of the code.

Perl will interpret a line of code by invoking "perl" followed by an argument composed of the evaluate instruction (e) and the command.

```
c:\>perl -e "print 5+5";
10
```

Perl users may choose to interpret code lines using the Perl debugger. The debugger is activated with one of Perl's famously obscure, syntactically abbreviated operating system command lines, from the system prompt:

```
c:\ftp>perl -d -e 1
```

The command line activates a line-by-line interface to the Perl interpreter as shown:

```
c:\ftp>perl -d -e 1

Loading DB routines from perl5db.pl version 1.33
Editor support available.

Enter h or 'h h' for help, or 'perldoc perldebug' for more help.

main::(-e:1): 1

  DB<1> print(gmtime());
3937203411501220

  DB<2> print(1+6);

7

  DB<3> print(4/0);
Illegal division by zero at (eval 11)[C:/Perl64/lib/perl5db.pl:640] line 2.
```

Like the Ruby "irb" line interpreter, the Perl debugger keeps track of the line number.

PACKAGE INSTALLERS

Perl, Python, and Ruby have a seemingly endless number of open source packages that extend the functionality of the standard distribution of each language. All three languages provide package managers that will download any package you desire, from an archive site on the web, and install the language-specific package on your computer. Once installed, the packages can be called into service in scripts.

Currently, there are over 64,000 Python packages available at the Python Package Index repository at: https://pypi.python.org/pypi

The installer for Python is Pip. Pip comes preinstalled in Python 2.7.9 and later (Python version 2 series) and Python 3.4 and later (Python 3 series). A usage example for pip is::

```
$ pip install rdflib          (on Linux shell)
c:\>pip install rdflib        (on Windows)
```

Currently, the Comprehensive Perl Archive Network (CPAN) has nearly 154,000 Perl modules, with over 12,000 contributors. You can search the multitude of Perl modules to your heart's content, at: https://metacpan.org/

The CPAN modules are available for installation through the CPAN installer, included in the newer distributions of Perl. For Windows users, a CPAN installer in included in the Strawberry Perl installation (vida supra).

At the C prompt, enter "cpan"

```
c:\>cpan
```

Perl then produces a "cpan" prompt from which you can enter an "install" command, followed by the name of the CPAN module you would like to install (the Chart::Gnuplot module in this example).

```
cpan> install Chart::Gnuplot
```

Public installation modules for Ruby are known as Gems. There are currently nearly 7000 Gems available from: https://rubygems.org/

The Gem installer comes standard with Ruby. A usage example, for installing the sqlite3 gem, is:

```
c:\>gem install sqlite3-ruby -v=1.2.3
```

SYSTEM CALLS

A system call is a command line, inserted into a software program, that interrupts the script while the operating system executes the command line. Immediately afterword, the script resumes at the next line of code. Any utility that runs from the command line can be embedded in any scripting language that supports system calls, and this includes all of the languages discussed in this book.

Here are the properties of system calls that make them useful to programmers:

1. System calls can be inserted into iterative loops (eg, while loops, for loops) so that they can be repeated any number of times, on collections of files, or data elements (see Glossary item, Iterator).
2. Variables that are generated at run-time (ie, during the execution of the script) can be included as arguments added to the system call.
3. The results of the system call can be returned to the script, and used as variables.
4. System calls can utilize any operating system command and any program that would normally be invoked through a command line, including external scripts written in other programming languages. Hence, a system call can initiate an external script written in an alternate programming language, composed at run-time within the original script, using variables generated in the original script, and capturing the output from the external script for use in the original script (see Glossary item, Metaprogramming)!

System calls enhance the power of any programming language by providing access to a countless number of external methods and by participating in iterated actions using variables created at run-time.

How does the system call help with the task of data simplification? Data simplification is very often focused on uniformity and reproducibility. If you have 100,000 images, data simplification might involve calling ImageMagick to resize every image to the same height and width (see Glossary item, ImageMagick). If you need to convert spreadsheet data to a set of triples, than you might need to provide a UUID string to every triple in the database all at once (see Glossary items, UUID, Universally Unique IDentifier, Triple). If you are working on a Ruby project and you need to assert one of Python's numpy methods on every data file in a large collection of data files, then you might want to create a short Python file that can be accessed, via a system call, from your Ruby script (see Glossary item, Numpy).

Once you get the hang of including system calls in your scripts, you will probably use them in most of your data simplification tasks. It's important to know how system calls can be used to great advantage, in Perl, Python, and Ruby. A few examples follow.

The following short Perl script makes a system call, consisting of the DOS "dir" command:

```
#!/usr/bin/perl
system("dir");
exit;
```

The "dir" command, launched as a system call, displays the files in the current directory. Here is the equivalent script, in Python:

```
#!/usr/local/bin/python
import os
os.system("dir")
exit
```

Notice that system calls in Python require the importation of the os (operating system) module into the script.

Here is an example of a Ruby system call, to ImageMagick's "Identify" utility. The system call instructs the "Identify" utility to provide a verbose description of the image file3320_out.jpg, and to pipe the output into the text file, myimage.txt.

```
#!/usr/bin/ruby
system("Identify -verbose c:/ftp/3320_out.jpg >myimage.txt")
exit
```

Here is an example of a Perl system call, to ImageMagick's "convert" utility, that incorporates a Perl variable ($file, in this case) that is passed to the system call. If you run this script on your own computer, please note that the system( ) command must appear as a single line of code. The system line was broken here, into two lines, to accommodate the printed page.

```
#!/usr/local/bin/perl
$file = "try2.gif";
system("convert -size 350x40 xc:lightgray -font Arial -pointsize 32 -fill black
 -gravity north -annotate +0+0 \"Hello, World\" $file");
exit;
```

The following Python script opens the current directory and parses through every filename, looking for jpeg image files. When a jpeg file is encountered, the script makes a system call to imagemagick, instructing imagemagick's "convert" utility to copy the jpeg file to the thumb drive (designated as the f: drive), in the form of a grayscale image. If you try this script at home, be advised that it requires a mounted thumb drive, in the "f:" drive.

```
#!/usr/local/bin/python
import os, re, string
filelist = os.listdir(".")
for file in filelist:
    if ".jpg" in file:
        img_in = file
        img_out = "f:/" + file
        command = "convert " + img_in + " -set colorspace Gray -separate -average " + img_out
        os.system(command)
exit
```

Let's look at a Ruby script that calls a Perl script, a Python script, and another Ruby script, from within one Ruby script.

Here are the Perl, Python, and Ruby scripts that will be called from within a Ruby script:

```
hi.py
#!/usr/local/bin/python
print("Hi, I'm a Python script")
exit

hi.pl
#!/usr/local/bin/perl
print "Hi, I'm a Perl script\n";
exit;

hi.rb
#!/usr/local/bin/ruby
puts "Hi, I'm a Ruby script"
exit
```

Here is the Ruby script, call_everyone.rb, that calls external scripts, written in Python, Perl, and Ruby:

```
#!/usr/local/bin/ruby
system("python hi.py")
system("perl hi.pl")
system("ruby hi.rb")
exit
```

Here is the output of the Ruby script, call_everyone.rb:

```
c:\ftp>call_everyone.rb
Hi, I'm a Python script
Hi, I'm a Perl script
Hi, I'm a Ruby script
```

If you have some facility with a variety of language-specific methods and utilities, you can deploy them all from within your favorite scripting language.

GLOSSARY

ANSI The American National Standards Institute (ANSI) accredits standards developing organizations to create American National Standards (ANS). A so-called ANSI standard is produced when an ANSI-accredited standards development organization follows ANSI procedures and receives confirmation, from ANSI, that all the procedures were followed. ANSI coordinates efforts to gain international standards certification from the ISO (International Standards Organization) or the IEC (International Electrotechnical Commission). ANSI works with hundreds of ANSI-accredited standards developers.

ASCII ASCII is the American Standard Code for Information Interchange, ISO 14962-1997. The ASCII standard is a way of assigning specific 8-bit strings (a string of 0s and 1s of length 8) to the alphanumeric characters and punctuation. Uppercase letters are assigned a different string of 0s and 1s than their matching lowercase letters.

There are 256 ways of combining 0s and 1s in strings of length 8. This means that that there are 256 different ASCII characters, and every ASCII character can be assigned a number-equivalent, in the range of 0 to 255. The familiar keyboard keys produce ASCII characters that happen to occupy ASCII values under 128. Hence, alphanumerics and common punctuation are represented as 8-bits, with the first bit, "0," serving as padding. Hence, keyboard characters are commonly referred to as 7-bit ASCII. These are the classic printable ASCII characters:

```
!"#$%&'()*+,-./0123456789:;<=> ?@ABCDEFGHIJKLMNOPQRSTUVWXYZ
[\]^_'abcdefghijklmnopqrstuvwxyz{|}~
```

Files composed exclusively of common keyboard characters are commonly referred to as plain-text files or as 7-bit ASCII files. See Text editor. See Plain-text. See ISO.

Abstraction In the context of object-oriented programming, abstraction is a technique whereby a method is simplified to a generalized form that is applicable to a wide range of objects, but for which the specific characteristics of the object receiving the method may be used to return a result that is suited to the object. Abstraction, along with polymorphism, encapsulation, and inheritance, are essential features of object-oriented programming languages. See Polymorphism. See Inheritance. See Encapsulation.

Algorithm An algorithm is a logical sequence of steps that lead to a desired computational result. Algorithms serve the same function in the computer world as production processes serve in the manufacturing world. Fundamental algorithms can be linked to one another, to create new algorithms. Algorithms are the most important intellectual capital in computer science. In the past half-century, many brilliant algorithms have been developed.[92],[93]

American Standard Code for Information Interchange See ASCII.

Autocoding When nomenclature coding is done automatically, by a computer program, the process is known as "autocoding" or "autoencoding." See Coding. See Nomenclature. See Autoencoding.

Autoencoding Synonym for autocoding. See Autocoding.

Binary data Computer scientists say that there are 10 types of people. Those who think in terms of binary numbers, and those who do not. Pause for laughter and continue. All digital information is coded as binary data. Strings of 0s and 1s are the fundamental units of electronic information. Nonetheless, some data is more binary than other data. In text files, 8-bit sequences are equivalent to decimals in the range of 0 to 256, and these decimal numbers are mapped as characters, as determined by the ASCII standard. In several raster image formats (ie, formats consisting of rows and columns of pixel data), 24-bit pixel values are chopped into red, green, and blue values of 8-bits each. Files containing various types of data (eg, sound, movies, telemetry, formatted text documents) all have some kind of low-level software that takes strings of 0s and 1s and converts them into data that has some particular meaning for a particular use. So-called plain-text files, including html files and xml files are distinguished from binary data files and referred to as plain-text or ASCII files. Most computer languages have an option wherein files can be opened as "binary," meaning that the 0s and 1s are available to the programmer, without the intervening translation into characters or stylized data. See ASCII.

Blended class Also known as class noise, subsumes the more familiar, but less precise term, "Labeling error." Blended class refers to inaccuracies (eg, misleading results) introduced in the analysis of data due to errors in class assignments (ie, assigning a data object to class A when the object should have been assigned to class B). If you are testing the effectiveness of an antibiotic on a class of people with bacterial pneumonia, the accuracy of your results will be forfeit when your study population includes subjects with viral pneumonia, or smoking-related lung damage. Errors induced by blending classes are often overlooked by data analysts who incorrectly assume that the experiment was designed to ensure that each data group is composed of a uniform population. A common source of class blending occurs when the classification upon which the experiment is designed is itself blended. For example, imagine that you are a cancer researcher and you want to perform a study of patients with malignant fibrous histiocytomas (MFH), comparing the clinical course of these patients with the clinical course of patients who have other types of tumors. Let's imagine that the class of tumors known as MFH does not actually exist; that it is a grab-bag term erroneously assigned to a variety of other tumors that happened to look similar to one another. This being the case, it would be impossible to produce any valid results based on a study of patients diagnosed as having MFH. The results would be a biased and irreproducible cacophony of data collected across different, and undetermined, classes of tumors. Believe it or not, this specific example, of the blended MFH class of tumors, is selected from the real-life annals of tumor biology.[94,95] The literature is rife with research of dubious quality, based on poorly designed classifications and blended classes. A detailed discussion of this topic is found in Section 6.5 of Chapter 6, Properties that Cross Multiple Classes. One caveat. Efforts to eliminate class blending can be counterproductive if undertaken with excess zeal. For example, in an effort to reduce class blending, a researcher may choose groups of subjects who are uniform with respect to every known observable property. For example, suppose you want to actually compare apples with oranges. To avoid class blending, you might want to make very sure that your apples do not include any kumquats, or persimmons. You should be certain that your oranges do not include any limes or grapefruits. Imagine that you go even further, choosing only apples and oranges of one variety (eg, Macintosh apples and navel oranges), size (eg, 10 cm), and origin (eg, California). How will your comparisons apply to the varieties of apples and oranges that you have excluded from your study? You may actually reach conclusions that are invalid and irreproducible for more generalized populations within each class. In this case, you have succeeded in eliminating class blending, while losing representative populations of the classes. See Simpson's paradox.

CPAN The Comprehensive Perl Archive Network, known as CPAN, has nearly 154,000 Perl packages, with over 12,000 contributors. These packages greatly extend the functionality of Perl, and include virtually every type of Perl method imaginable (eg, math, statistics, communications, plotting, and numerical analyses). Any CPAN Perl package can be easily downloaded and automatically installed on your computer's Perl directory when you use the CPAN installer. For instructions, see Open Source Tools. You can search the multitude of Perl modules to your heart's content at: https://metacpan.org/.

Check digit A checksum that produces a single digit as output is referred to as a check digit. Some of the common identification codes in use today, such as ISBN numbers for books, come with a built-in check digit. Of course, when using a single digit as a check value, you can expect that some transmitted errors will escape the check, but the check digit is useful in systems wherein occasional mistakes are tolerated; or wherein the purpose of the check digit is to find a specific type of error (eg, an error produced by a substitution in a single character or digit), and wherein the check digit itself is rarely transmitted in error. See Checksum.

Checksum An outdated term that is sometimes used synonymously with one-way hash or message digest. Checksums are performed on a string, block, or file yielding a short alphanumeric string intended to be specific for the input data. Ideally, If a single bit were to change, anywhere within the input file, then the checksum for the input file would change drastically. Checksums, as the name implies, involve summing values (typically weighted character values), to produce a sequence that can be calculated on a file before and after transmission. Most of the errors that were commonly introduced by poor transmission could be detected with checksums. Today, the old checksum algorithms have been largely replaced with one-way hash algorithms. A checksum that produces a single digit as output is referred to as a check digit. See Check digit. See Message digest. See HMAC.

Child class The direct or first generation subclass of a class. Sometimes referred to as the daughter class or, less precisely, as the subclass. See Parent class. See Classification.

Chloroplast evolution Chloroplasts are the organelles (little membrane-wrapped replicating structures within cells) that produce glucose and oxygen, via a process that can be loosely described as: carbon dioxide + water + light energy $\rightarrow$ carbohydrate + oxygen. Chloroplasts are found in plants. Aside from photosynthesis occurring in plants, we can also observe photosynthesis in cyanobacteria. Photosynthesis produced by cyanobacteria is thought to be account for the conversion of our atmosphere from an anoxic environment to an oxygen-rich environment. Did photosynthesis, a complex chemical pathway, evolve twice in terrestrial history;

once in cyanobacteria and once again in primitive plants? Present thinking on the subject holds that the evolution of photosynthesis occurred only once, in the distant past, and all photosynthesis ever since, in cyanobacteria and in plants, arose from this one event. It is presumed that plants acquired photosynthesis when they engulfed photosynthesizing cyanobacteria that evolved into self-replicating chloroplasts. This startling conclusion is based on a simple observation that chloroplasts, unlike other plant organelles, are wrapped by two membrane layers. One layer is believed to have been contributed by the captured cyanobacteria, and one layer presumably contributed by the ancient plant cell as it wrapped the cyanobacteria in its own cell membrane. Whether a complex pathway, such as photosynthesis, can re-evolve in other organisms, is a matter of conjecture.[96]

Clade A class, plus all of its descendant classes. A clade should be distinguished from a lineage, the latter being a class and its ascendant classes. Because a class can have more than one child class, a pictogram of a clade will often look like a branching tree. In a classification, where each class is restricted to having one parent class, ascending lineages (from the Latin linea, "a line"), are represented as a nonbranching line of ancestors, leading to the root (ie, top class) of the classification. Of course, in an ontology, where there are no restrictions on the number of parents a class may have, pictograms of clades and lineages will tend to be florid.

Cladistics The technique of producing a hierarchy of clades, wherein each clade is a monophyletic class. See Monophyletic class.

Class A class is a group of objects that share a set of properties that define the class and that distinguish the members of the class from members of other classes. The word "class," lowercase, is used as a general term. The word "Class," uppercase, followed by an uppercase noun (eg, Class Animalia), represents a specific class within a formal classification. See Classification.

Classification A system in which every object in a knowledge domain is assigned to a class within a hierarchy of classes. The properties of classes are inherited by their subclasses. Every class has one immediate superclass (ie, parent class), although a parent class may have more than one immediate subclass (ie, child class). Objects do not change their class assignment in a classification, unless there was a mistake in the assignment. For example, a rabbit is always a rabbit, and does not change into a tiger. Classifications can be thought of as the simplest and most restrictive type of ontology, and serve to reduce the complexity of a knowledge domain.[3] Classifications can be easily modeled in an object-oriented programming language and are nonchaotic (ie, calculations performed on the members and classes of a classification should yield the same output, each time the calculation is performed). A classification should be distinguished from an ontology. In an ontology, a class may have more than one parent class and an object may be a member of more than one class. A classification can be considered a special type of ontology wherein each class is limited to a single parent class and each object has membership in one, and only one, class. See Nomenclature. See Thesaurus. See Vocabulary. See Classification. See Dictionary. See Terminology. See Ontology. See Parent class. See Child class. See Superclass. See Unclassifiable objects.

Classification system versus identification system It is important to distinguish a classification system from an identification system. An identification system matches an individual organism with its assigned object name (or species name, in the case of the classification of living organisms). Identification is based on finding several features that, taken together, can help determine the name of an organism. For example, if you have a list of characteristic features: large, hairy, strong, African, jungle-dwelling, knuckle-walking; you might correctly identify the organism as a gorilla. These identifiers are different from the phylogenetic features that were used to classify gorillas within the hierarchy of organisms (Animalia: Chordata: Mammalia: Primates: Hominidae: Homininae: Gorillini: Gorilla). Specifically, you can identify an animal as a gorilla without knowing that a gorilla is a type of mammal. You can classify a gorilla as a member of Class Gorillini without knowing that a gorilla happens to be large. **One of the most common mistakes in science is to confuse an identification system with a classification system. The former simply provides a handy way to associate an object with a name; the latter is a system of relationships among objects.**

Coding The term "coding" has three very different meanings, depending on which branch of science influences your thinking. For programmers, coding means writing the code that constitutes a computer program. For cryptographers, coding is synonymous with encrypting (ie, using a cipher to encode a message). For medics, coding is calling an emergency team to handle a patient in extremis. For informaticians and library scientists, coding involves assigning an alphanumeric identifier, representing a concept listed in a nomenclature, to a term. For example, a surgical pathology report may include the diagnosis, "Adenocarcinoma of prostate." A nomenclature may assign a code C4863000 that uniquely identifies the concept "Adenocarcinoma." Coding the report may involve annotating every occurrence of the work "Adenocarcinoma" with the "C4863000" identifier. For a detailed explanation of nomenclature coding, and its importance for searching and retrieving data, see the full discussion in Section 3.4 of Chapter 3, Autoencoding and Indexing with Nomenclatures. See Autocoding. See Nomenclature.

Conclusions Conclusions are the interpretations made by studying the results of an experiment or a set of observations. The term "results" should never be used interchangeably with the term "conclusions." **Remember, results are verified. Conclusions are validated.**[97] See Verification. See Validation. See Results.

Curator The word "curator" derives from the Latin, "curatus," taken care of the same root for "curative," indicating that curators "take care of" things. A data curator collects, annotates, indexes, updates, archives, searches, retrieves, and distributes data. Curator is another of those somewhat arcane terms (eg, indexer, data archivist, and lexicographer) that are being rejuvenated in the new millennium. It seems that if we want to enjoy the benefits of a data-centric world, we will need the assistance of curators, trained in data organization.

Curse of dimensionality As the number of attributes for a data object increases, the multidimensional space becomes sparsely populated, and the distances between any two objects, even the two closest neighbors, becomes absurdly large. When you have thousands of dimensions (eg, data values in a data record, cells in the rows of a spreadsheet), the space that holds the objects is so large that distances between data objects become difficult or impossible to compute, and most computational algorithms become useless.

Data object A data object is whatever is being described by the data. For example, if the data is "6-feet tall," then the data object is the person or thing to which "6-feet tall" applies. Minimally, a data object is a metadata/data pair, assigned to a unique identifier (ie, a triple). In practice, the most common data objects are simple data records, corresponding to a row in a spreadsheet or a line in a flat-file. Data objects in object-oriented programming languages typically encapsulate several items of data, including an object name, an object unique identifier, multiple data/metadata pairs, and the name of the object's class. See Triple. See Identifier. See Metadata.

Data resource A collection of data made available for data retrieval. The data can be distributed over servers located anywhere on earth or in space. The resource can be static (ie, having a fixed set of data), or in flux. Plesionyms for data resource are: data warehouse, data repository, data archive, data store.

Data science A vague term encompassing all aspects of data collection, organization, archiving, distribution, and analysis. The term has been used to subsume the closely related fields of informatics, statistics, data analysis, programming, and computer science.

Data scientist Anyone who practices data science and who has some expertise in a field subsumed by data science (ie, informatics, statistics, data analysis, programming, and computer science).

Data sharing Providing one's own data to another person or entity. This process may involve free or purchased data, and it may be done willingly, or under coercion, as in compliance with regulations, laws, or court orders.

Database A software application designed specifically to create and retrieve large numbers of data records (eg, millions or billions). The data records of a database are persistent, meaning that the application can be turned off, then on, and all the collected data will be available to the user (see Open Source Tools for Chapter 7).

Dictionary A terminology or word list accompanied by a definition for each item. See Nomenclature. See Vocabulary. See Terminology.

Dimensionality The dimensionality of a data object consists of the number of attributes that describe the object. Depending on the design and content of the data structure that contains the data object (ie, database, array, list of records, object instance, etc.), the attributes will be called by different names, such as field, variable, parameter, feature, or property. Data objects with high dimensionality create computational challenges, and data analysts typically reduce the dimensionality of data objects wherever possible.

Dublin Core metadata The Dublin Core metadata is a set of tags that describe the content of an electronic file. These tags were developed by a group of librarians who met in Dublin, Ohio. Syntactical usage of the Dublin Core elements is described in Open Source Tools for Chapter 2.

Encapsulation The concept, from object-oriented programming, that a data object contains its associated data. Encapsulation is tightly linked to the concept of introspection, the process of accessing the data encapsulated within a data object. Encapsulation, Inheritance, and Polymorphism are available features of all object-oriented languages. See Inheritance. See Polymorphism.

Exe file A file with the filename suffix ".exe." In common parlance, filenames with the ".exe" suffix are executable code. See Executable file.

Executable file A file that contains compiled computer code that can be read directly from the computer's CPU, without interpretation by a programming language. A language such as C will compile C code into executables. Scripting languages, such as Perl, Python, and Ruby interpret plain-text scripts and send instructions to a run-time engine, for execution. Because executable files eliminate the interpretation step, they typically run faster than plain-text scripts. See Exe file.

Gaussian copula function A formerly praised and currently vilified formula, developed for Wall Street, that calculates the risk of default correlation (ie, the likelihood of two investment vehicles defaulting together). The formula uses the current market value of the vehicles, without factoring in historical data. The formula is easy to implement, and was a favored model for calculating risk in the securitization market. In about 2008, the Gaussian copula function stopped working; soon thereafter came the 2008 global market collapse. In some circles, the Gaussian copula function is blamed for the disaster.[98]

Generalization Generalization is the process of extending relationships from individual objects to classes of objects. For example, when Isaac Newton observed the physical laws that applied to apples falling to the ground, he found a way to relate the acceleration of an object to its mass and to the force of gravity. His apple-centric observations applied to all objects and could be used to predict the orbit of the moon around the earth, or the orbit of the earth around the sun. Newton generalized from the specific to the universal. Similarly, Darwin's observations on barnacles could be generalized to yield the theory of evolution, thus explaining the development of all terrestrial organisms. Science would be of little value if observed relationships among objects could not be generalized to classes of objects. See Science.

Grid A collection of computers and computer resources that are coordinated to provide a desired functionality. The Grid is the intellectual predecessor of cloud computing. Cloud computing is less physically and administratively restricted than Grid computing.

HMAC Hashed Message Authentication Code. When a one-way hash is employed in an authentication protocol, it is often referred to as an HMAC. See Message digest. See Checksum.

HTML HyperText Markup Language is an ASCII-based set of formatting instructions for web pages. HTML formatting instructions, known as tags, are embedded in the document, and double-bracketed, indicating the start point and end points for instruction. Here is an example of an HTML tag instructing the web browser to display the word "Hello" in italics: <i>Hello</i>. All web browsers conforming to the HTML specification must contain software routines that recognize and implement the HTML instructions embedded within web documents. In addition to formatting instructions, HTML also includes linkage instructions, in which the web browsers must retrieve and display a listed web page, or a web resource, such as an image. The protocol whereby web browsers, following HTML instructions, retrieve web pages from other Internet sites, is known as HTTP (HyperText Transfer Protocol).

ISO International Standards Organization. The ISO is a nongovernmental organization that develops international standards (eg, ISO-11179 for metadata and ISO-8601 for date and time). See ANSI.

Identification The process of providing a data object with an identifier, or the process of distinguishing one data object from all other data objects on the basis of its associated identifier. See Identifier.

Identifier A string that is associated with a particular thing (eg person, document, transaction, and data object), and not associated with any other thing.[99] Object identification usually involves permanently assigning a seemingly random sequence of numeric digits (0–9) and alphabet characters (a–z and A–Z) to a data object. A data object can be a specific piece of data (eg, a data record), or an abstraction, such as a class of objects or a number, a string, or a variable. See Identification.

ImageMagick An open source utility that supports a huge selection of robust and sophisticated image editing methods. There is a detailed discussion of ImageMagick in Open Source Tools for Chapter 4.

Inheritance In object-oriented languages, data objects (ie, classes and object instances of a class) inherit the methods (eg, functions and subroutines) created for the ancestral classes in their lineage. See Abstraction. See Polymorphism. See Encapsulation.

Instance An instance is a specific example of an object that is not itself a class or group of objects. For example, Tony the Tiger is an instance of the tiger species. Tony the Tiger is a unique animal and is not itself a group of animals or a class of animals. The terms instance, instance object, and object are sometimes used interchangeably, but the special value of the "instance" concept, in a system wherein everything is an object, is that it distinguishes members of classes (ie, the instances) from the classes to which they belong.

Integration Integration, in the computer sciences, involves relating diverse data extracted from different data sources. Data merging is a type of data integration, wherein various sources of data are combined in a manner that preserves meaning and value. The terms "integration" and "interoperability" are sometimes confused with one another. An easy way of thinking about these terms is that **integration applies to data, while interoperability applies to software**.

Interoperability It is desirable and often necessary to create software that operates with other software, regardless of differences in operating systems and programming language. There are a wide variety of methods by which this can be achieved. The topic of software interoperability has become complex, but it remains a fundamental issue to all attempts to share analytic methodologies. The terms "integration" and "interoperability" should not be confused with one another. An easy way of thinking about these terms is that integration applies to data, while interoperability applies to software.[40]

Introspection A method by which data objects can be interrogated to yield information about themselves (eg, properties, values, and class membership). Through introspection, the relationships among the data objects can be examined. Introspective methods are built into object-oriented languages. The data provided by introspection can be applied, at run-time, to modify a script's operation; a technique known as reflection. Specifically, any properties, methods, and encapsulated data of a data object can be used in the script to modify the script's run-time behavior. See Reflection.

Iterator Iterators are simple programming shortcuts that call functions that operate on consecutive members of a data structure, such as a list, or a block of code. Typically, complex iterators can be expressed in a single line of code. Perl, Python, and Ruby all have iterator methods.

LaTeX LaTeX is a document preparation system that operates in conjunction with TeX, a typesetting system. Because LaTeX is designed to accommodate scientific and mathematical notations (eg, exponents, integrals, and summations), LaTeX is used widely by publishers of scientific text. LaTeX is discussed in the Open Source Tools section of Chapter 4.

MapReduce A method by which computationally intensive problems can be processed on multiple computers, in parallel. The method can be divided into a mapping step and a reducing step. In the mapping step, a master computer divides a problem into smaller problems that are distributed to other computers. In the reducing step, the master computer collects the output from the other computers. MapReduce is intended for large and complex data resources, holding petabytes of data.

Marshaling Marshaling, like serializing, is a method for achieving data persistence (ie, saving variables and other data structures produced in a program, after the program has stopped running). Marshaling methods preserve data objects, with their encapsulated data and data structures. See Persistence. See Serializing.

Meaning In informatics, meaning is achieved when described data is bound to a unique identifier of a data object. The assertion that "Claude Funston's height is five feet eleven inches," comes pretty close to being a meaningful statement. The statement contains data (five feet eleven inches), and the data is described (height). The described data belongs to a unique object (Claude Funston). Ideally, the name "Claude Funston" should be provided with a unique identifier, to distinguish one instance of Claude Funston from all the other persons who are named Claude Funston. The statement would also benefit from a formal system that ensures that the metadata makes sense (eg, What exactly is height, and does Claude Funston fall into a class of objects for which height is a property?) and that the data is appropriate (eg, Is 5 feet 11 inches an allowable measure of a person's height?). A statement with meaning does not need to be a true statement (eg, The height of Claude Funston was not 5 feet 11 inches when Claude Funston was an infant). See Semantics. See Triple. See RDF.

Message digest Within the context of this book, "message digest," "digest," "HMAC," and "one-way hash" are equivalent terms. See HMAC.

Metadata The data that describes data. For example, a data element (also known as data point) may consist of the number, "6." The metadata for the data may be the words "Height, in feet." A data element is useless without its metadata, and metadata is useless unless it adequately describes a data element. In XML, the metadata/data annotation comes in the form <metadata tag> data <end of metadata tag> and might look something like:

```
<weight_in_pounds>150</weight_in_pounds>
```

In spreadsheets, the data elements are the cells of the spreadsheet. The column headers are the metadata that describe the data values in the columns' cells, and the row headers are the record numbers that uniquely identify each record (ie, each row of cells). See XML.

Metaprogramming A metaprogram is a program that creates or modifies other programs. Metaprogramming is a powerful feature found in languages that are modifiable at runtime. Perl, Python, and Ruby are all metaprogramming languages. There are several techniques that facilitate metaprogramming features, including introspection and reflection. See Reflection. See Introspection.

Method Roughly equivalent to functions, subroutines, or code blocks. In object-oriented languages, a method is a subroutine available to an object (class or instance). In Ruby and Python, instance methods are declared with a "def" declaration followed by the name of the method, in lowercase. Here is an example, in Ruby, for the "hello" method, written for the Salutations class.

```
class Salutations
    def hello
      puts "hello there"
    end
end
```

Microarray Also known as gene chip, gene expression array, DNA microarray, or DNA chips. These consist of thousands of small samples of chosen DNA sequences arrayed onto a block of support material (such as a glass slide). When the array is incubated with a mixture of DNA sequences prepared from cell samples, hybridization will occur between molecules on the array and single-stranded complementary (ie, identically sequenced) molecules present in the cell sample. The greater the concentration of complementary molecules in the cell sample, the greater the number of fluorescently tagged hybridized molecules in the array. A specialized instrument prepares an image of the array, and quantifies the fluorescence in each array spot. Spots with high fluorescence indicate relatively large quantities of DNA in the cell sample that match the specific sequence of DNA in the array spot. The data comprising all the fluorescent intensity measurements for every spot in the array produces a gene profile characteristic of the cell sample.

Monophyletic class A class of organisms that includes a parent organism and all its descendants, while excluding any organisms that did not descend from the parent. If a subclass of a parent class omits any of the descendants of the parent class, then the parent class is said to be paraphyletic. If a subclass of a parent class includes organisms that did not descend from the parent, then the parent class is polyphyletic. A class can be paraphyletic and polyphyletic, if it excludes organisms that were descendants of the parent and if it includes organisms that did not descend from the parent. The goal of cladistics is to create a hierarchical classification that consists exclusively of monophyletic classes (ie, no paraphyly, no polyphyly). See Cladistics. See Clade.

Multiclass classification A misnomer imported from the field of machine translation, and indicating the assignment of an instance to more than one class. Classifications, as defined in this book, impose one-class classification (ie, an instance can be assigned to one and only one class). It is tempting to think that a ball should be included in class "toy" and in class "spheroids," but multiclass assignments create unnecessary classes of inscrutable provenance, and taxonomies of enormous size, consisting largely of replicate items. See Multiclass inheritance. See Taxonomy.

Multiclass inheritance In ontologies, multiclass inheritance occurs when a child class has more than one parent class. For example, a member of Class House may have two different parent classes: Class Shelter, and Class Property. Multiclass inheritance is generally permitted in ontologies but is forbidden in one type of restrictive ontology, known as a classification. See Classification. See Parent class. See Multiclass classification.

Namespace A namespace is the realm in which a metadata tag applies. The purpose of a namespace is to distinguish metadata tags that have the same name, but a different meaning. For example, within a single XML file, the metadata tag "date" may be used to signify a calendar date, or the fruit, or the social engagement. To avoid confusion, metadata terms are assigned a prefix that is associated with a Web document that defines the term (ie, establishes the tag's namespace). In practical terms, a tag that can have different descriptive meanings in different contexts is provided with a prefix that links to a web document wherein the meaning of the tag, as it applies in the XML document is specified.

New analytic method The chief feature that distinguishes a new analytic method from an old analytic method is that we have not yet learned the limitations and faults associated with the new method. Although it is true that all great analytic methods were, at one time, new methods, it is also true that all terrible analytic methods were, at one time, new methods. Historically, there have been many more failed methods than successful methods. Hence, most new analytic methods are bad methods. See Gaussian copula function.

Nomenclature A nomenclature is a listing of terms that cover all of the concepts in a knowledge domain. A nomenclature is different from a dictionary for three reasons: (1) the nomenclature terms are not annotated with definitions, (2) nomenclature terms may be multi-word, and (3) the terms in the nomenclature are limited to the scope of the selected knowledge domain. In addition, most nomenclatures group synonyms under a group code. For example, a food nomenclature might collect submarine, hoagie, po' boy, grinder, hero, and torpedo under an alphanumeric code such as "F63958." Nomenclatures simplify textual documents by uniting synonymous terms under a common code. Documents that have been coded with the same nomenclature can be integrated with other documents that have been similarly coded, and queries conducted over such documents will yield the same results, regardless of which term is entered (ie, a search for either hoagie, or po' boy will retrieve the same information, if both terms have been annotated with the synonym code, "F63948"). Optimally, the canonical concepts listed in the nomenclature are organized into a hierarchical classification.[100,101] See Coding. See Autocoding.

Nonatomicity Nonatomicity is the assignment of a collection of objects to a single, composite object, that cannot be further simplified or sensibly deconstructed. For example, the human body is composed of trillions of individual cells, each of which lives for some length of time, and then dies. Many of the cells in the body are capable of dividing to produce more cells. In many cases, the cells of the body that are capable of dividing can be cultured and grown in plastic containers, much like bacteria can be cultured and grown in Petri dishes. If the human body is composed of individual cells, why do we habitually think of each human as a single living entity? Why don't we think of humans as bags of individual cells? Perhaps the reason stems from the coordinated responses of cells. When someone steps on the cells of your toe, the cells in your brain sense pain, the cells in your mouth and vocal cords say "ouch," and an army of inflammatory cells rush to the scene of the crime. The cells in your toe are not capable of registering an actionable complaint, without a great deal of assistance. The reason that organisms, composed of trillions of living cells, are generally considered to have nonatomicity, probably relates to the "species" concept in biology. Every cell in an organism descended from the same zygote, and every zygote in every member of the same species descended from the same ancestral organism. Hence, there seems to be little benefit to assigning unique entity status to the individual cells that compose organisms, when the class structure for organisms is based on descent through zygotes. See Species.

Notation 3 Also called n3. A syntax for expressing assertions as triples (unique subject+metadata+data). Notation 3 expresses the same information as the more formal RDF syntax, but n3 is easier for humans to read.[102] RDF and N3 are interconvertible, and either one can be parsed and equivalently tokenized (ie, broken into elements that can be reorganized in a different format, such as a database record). See RDF. See Triple.

Numpy Also known as Numerical Python, numpy is an open source extension of Python that supports matrix operations and a variety of other mathematical functions. Examples of Python scripts containing numpy methods are found in Chapter 4.

Object See Data object.

Obligate intracellular organism An obligate intracellular organism can only reproduce within a host cell. Obligate intracellular organisms live off the bounty of the host cell. Thus, it would be redundant for such organisms to maintain all of the complex metabolic processes that a free-living organism must synthesize and maintain. Consequently, obligate intracellular organisms adapt simplified cellular anatomy, often dispensing with much of the genome, much of the cytoplasm, and most of the organelles that were present in their ancestral classes, prior to their switch to intracellular (ie, parasitic) living.

Occam's razor Also known as lex parsimoniae (law of parsimony). Asserts that the least complex solution is, more often than not, the correct solution. See Parsimony. See Solomonoff's theory of inductive inference.

Ontology An ontology is a collection of classes and their relationships to one another. Ontologies are usually rule-based systems (ie, membership in a class is determined by one or more class rules). Two important features distinguish ontologies from classifications. Ontologies permit classes to have more than one parent class. For example, the class of automobiles may be a direct subclass of "motorized devices" and a direct subclass of "mechanized transporters." In addition, an instance of a class can be an instance of any number of additional classes. For example, a Lamborghini may be a member of class "automobiles" and of class "luxury items." This means that the lineage of an instance in an ontology can be highly complex, with a single instance occurring in multiple classes, and with many connections between classes. Because recursive relations are permitted, it is possible to build an ontology wherein a class is both an ancestor class and a descendant class of itself. A classification is a highly restrained ontology wherein instances can belong to only one class, and each class may have only one parent class. Because classifications have an enforced linear hierarchy, they can be easily modeled, and the lineage of any instance can be traced unambiguously. See Classification. See Multiclass classification. See Multiclass inheritance.

Parent class The immediate ancestor, or the next-higher class (ie, the direct superclass) of a class. For example, in the classification of living organisms, Class Vertebrata is the parent class of Class Gnathostomata. Class Gnathostomata is the parent class of Class Teleostomi. In a classification, which imposes single class inheritance, each child class has exactly one parent class; whereas one parent class may have several different child classes. Furthermore, some classes, in particular the bottom class in the lineage, have no child classes (ie, a class need not always be a superclass of other classes). A class can be defined by its properties, its membership (ie, the instances that belong to the class), and by the name of its parent class. When we list all of the classes in a classification, in any order, we can always reconstruct the complete class lineage, in their correct lineage and branchings, if we know the name of each class's parent class. See Instance. See Child class. See Superclass.

Parsimony Use of the smallest possible collection of resources in solving a problem or achieving a goal. See Occam's razor. See Solomonoff's theory of inductive inference.

Persistence   Persistence is the ability of data to remain available in memory or storage after the program in which the data was created has stopped executing. Databases are designed to achieve persistence. When the database application is turned off, the data remains available to the database application when it is restarted at some later time. See Database. See Marshaling. See Serializing.

Plain-text   Plain-text refers to character strings or files that are composed of the characters accessible to a typewriter keyboard. These files typically have a ".txt" suffix to their names. Plain-text files are sometimes referred to as 7-bit ASCII files because all of the familiar keyboard characters have ASCII values under 128 (ie, can be designated in binary with, just seven 0s and 1s. In practice, plain-text files exclude 7-bit ASCII symbols that do not code for familiar keyboard characters. To further confuse the issue, plain-text files may contain ASCII characters above 7 bits (ie, characters from 128 to 255) that represent characters that are printable on computer monitors, such as accented letters. See ASCII.

Polymorphism   Polymorphism is one of the constitutive properties of an object-oriented language (along with inheritance, encapsulation, and abstraction). Methods sent to object receivers have a response determined by the class of the receiving object. Hence, different objects, from different classes, receiving a call to a method of the same name, will respond differently. For example, suppose you have a method named "divide" and you send the method (ie, issue a command to execute the method) to an object of Class Bacteria and an object of Class Numerics. The Bacteria, receiving the divide method, will try to execute by looking for the "divide" method somewhere in its class lineage. Being a bacteria, the "divide" method may involve making a copy of the bacteria (ie, reproducing) and incrementing the number of bacteria in the population. The numeric object, receiving the "divide" method, will look for the "divide" method in its class lineage and will probably find some method that provides instructions for arithmetic division. Hence, the behavior of the class object, to a received method, will be appropriate for the class of the object. See Inheritance. See Encapsulation. See Abstraction.

Primary data   The original set of data collected to serve a particular purpose or to answer a particular set of questions, and intended for use by the same individuals who collected the data. See Secondary data.

Query   One of the first sticking points in any discussion of heterogeneous database queries is the definition of "query." Informaticians use the term "query" to mean a request for records that match a specific set of data element features (eg, name, age, etc.) Ontologists think of a query as a question that matches the competence of the ontology (ie, a question for which the ontology can infer an answer). Often, a query is a parameter or set of parameters that is matched against properties or rules that apply to objects in the ontology. For example, "weight" is a property of physical objects, and this property may fall into the domain of several named classes in an ontology. The query may ask for the names of the classes of objects that have the "weight" property and the numbers of object instances in each class. A query might select several of these classes (eg, including dogs and cats, but excluding microwave ovens), along with the data object instances whose weights fall within a specified range (eg, 20 to 30 pounds).

RDF   Resource Description Framework (RDF) is a syntax in XML notation that formally expresses assertions as triples. The RDF triple consists of a uniquely identified subject plus a metadata descriptor for the data plus a data element. Triples are necessary and sufficient to create statements that convey meaning. Triples can be aggregated with other triples from the same data set or from other data sets, so long as each triple pertains to a unique subject that is identified equivalently through the data sets. Enormous data sets of RDF triples can be merged or functionally integrated with other massive or complex data resources. For a detailed discussion, see Open Source Tools for Chapter 6, "Syntax for triples." See Notation 3. See Semantics. See Triple. See XML.

RDF Schema   Resource Description Framework Schema (RDFS). A document containing a list of classes, their definitions, and the names of the parent class(es) for each class. In an RDF Schema, the list of classes is typically followed by a list of properties that apply to one or more classes in the Schema. To be useful, RDF Schemas are posted on the Internet, as a Web page, with a unique Web address. Anyone can incorporate the classes and properties of a public RDF Schema into their own RDF documents (public or private) by linking named classes and properties, in their RDF document, to the web address of the RDF Schema where the classes and properties are defined. See Namespace. See RDFS.

RDFS Same as RDF Schema.

Reflection A programming technique wherein a computer program will modify itself, at run-time, based on information it acquires through introspection. For example, a computer program may iterate over a collection of data objects, examining the self-descriptive information for each object in the collection (ie, object introspection). If the information indicates that the data object belongs to a particular class of objects, then the program may call a method appropriate for the class. The program executes in a manner determined by descriptive information obtained during run-time; metaphorically reflecting upon the purpose of its computational task. See Introspection.

Reproducibility Reproducibility is achieved when repeat studies produce the same results, over and over. Reproducibility is closely related to validation, which is achieved when you draw the same conclusions, from the data, over and over again. Implicit in the concept of "reproducibility" is that the original research must somehow convey the means by which the study can be reproduced. This usually requires the careful recording of methods, algorithms, and materials. In some cases, reproducibility requires access to the data produced in the original studies. If there is no feasible way for scientists to undertake a reconstruction of the original study, or if the results obtained in the original study cannot be obtained in subsequent attempts, then the study is irreproducible. If the work is reproduced, but the results and the conclusions cannot be repeated, then the study is considered invalid. See Validation. See Verification.

Results The term "results" is often mistaken for the term "conclusions." Interchanging the two concepts is a source of confusion among data scientists. In the strictest sense, "results" consist of the full set of experimental data collected by measurements. In practice, "results" are provided as a small subset of data distilled from the raw, original data. In a typical journal article, selected data subsets are packaged as a chart or graph that emphasizes some point of interest. Hence, the term "results" may refer, erroneously, to subsets of the original data, or to visual graphics intended to summarize the original data. Conclusions are the inferences drawn from the results. Results are verified; conclusions are validated. The data that is generated from the original data should not be confused with "secondary" data. See Secondary data. See Conclusions. See Verification. See Validation.

Science Of course, there are many different definitions of science, and inquisitive students should be encouraged to find a conceptualization of science that suits their own intellectual development. For me, science is all about finding general relationships among objects. In the so-called physical sciences, the most important relationships are expressed as mathematical equations (eg, the relationship between force, mass and acceleration; the relationship between voltage, current and resistance). In the so-called natural sciences, relationships are often expressed through classifications (eg, the classification of living organisms). Scientific advancement is the discovery of new relationships or the discovery of a generalization that applies to objects hitherto confined within disparate scientific realms (eg, evolutionary theory arising from observations of organisms and geologic strata). Engineering would be the area of science wherein scientific relationships are exploited to build new technology. See Generalization.

Scipy Scipy, like numpy, is an open source extension to Python.[103] It includes many very useful mathematical routines commonly used by scientists, including: integration,interpolation, Fourier transforms, signal processing, linear algebra, and statistics. Examples and discussion are provided in Open Source Tools for Chapter 4.

Secondary data Data collected by someone else. Much of the data analyses performed today are done on secondary data.[104] Most verification and validation studies depend upon access to high-quality secondary data. Because secondary data is prepared by someone else, who cannot anticipate how you will use the data, it is important to provide secondary data that is simple and introspective. See Introspection. See Primary data.

Semantics The study of meaning (Greek root, semantikos, signficant meaning). In the context of data science, semantics is the technique of creating meaningful assertions about data objects. A meaningful assertion, as used here, is a triple consisting of an identified data object, a data value, and a descriptor for the data value. In practical terms, semantics involves making assertions about data objects (ie, making triples), combining assertions about data objects (ie, merging triples), and assigning data objects to classes; hence relating triples to other triples. As a word of warning, few informaticians would define semantics in these terms, but most definitions for semantics are functionally equivalent to the definition offered here. Most language is unstructured and meaningless. Consider the assertion: Sam is tired. This is an adequately structured sentence with a subject verb and object. But what is the meaning of the sentence? There are a lot of people named Sam. Which Sam is being referred to in this sentence? What does it mean to say that Sam is tired? Is "tiredness" a constitutive property of Sam, or does it only apply to specific moments? If so, for what moment in time is the assertion, "Sam is tired" actually true? To a computer, meaning comes from assertions that have a specific, identified subject associated with some sensible piece of fully described data (metadata coupled with the data it describes). As you may suspect, virtually all data contained in databases does not fully qualify as "meaningful." See Triple. See RDF.

Serializing Serializing is a plesionym (ie, near-synonym) for marshaling and is a method for taking data produced within a script or program, and preserving it in an external file, that can be saved when the program stops, and quickly reconstituted as needed, in the same program or in different programs. The difference, in terms of common usage, between serialization and marshaling is that serialization usually involves capturing parameters (ie, particular pieces of information), while marshaling preserves all of the specifics of a data object, including its structure, content, and code). As you might imagine, the meaning of terms might change depending on the programming language and the intent of the serializing and marshaling methods. See Persistence. See Marshaling.

Simpson's paradox Occurs when a correlation that holds in two different data sets is reversed if the data sets are combined. For example, baseball player A may have a higher batting average than player B for each of two seasons, but when the data for the two seasons are combined, player B may have the higher 2-season average. Simpson's paradox is just one example of unexpected changes in outcome when variables are unknowingly hidden or blended.[105]

Solomonoff's theory of inductive inference Solomonoff's theory of inductive inference is Occam's razor, as applied to mathematics and computer science. The shortest, most computable functions that describe or predict data are the correct functions, assuming that all competing functions describe the existing data equally well. See Occam's razor. See Parsimony.

Species Species is the bottom-most class of any classification or ontology. Because the species class contains the individual objects of the classification, it is the only class which is not abstract. The special significance of the species class is best exemplified in the classification of living organisms. Every species of organism contains individuals that share a common ancestral relationship to one another. When we look at a group of squirrels, we know that each squirrel in the group has its own unique personality, its own unique genes (ie, genotype), and its own unique set of physical features (ie, phenotype). Moreover, although the DNA sequences of individual squirrels are unique, we assume that there is a commonality to the genome of squirrels that distinguishes it from the genome of every other species. If we use the modern definition of species as an evolving gene pool, we see that the species can be thought of as a biological life form, with substance (a population of propagating genes), and a function (evolving to produce new species).[106–108] Put simply, species speciate; individuals do not. As a corollary, species evolve; individuals simply propagate. Hence, the species class is a separable biological unit with form and function. We, as individuals, are focused on the lives of individual things, and we must be reminded of the role of species in biological and nonbiological classifications. The concept of species is discussed in greater detail in Section 6.4 of Chapter 6. See Blended class. See Nonatomicity.

Specification A specification is a formal method for describing objects (physical objects such as nuts and bolts or symbolic objects, such as numbers, or concepts expressed as text). In general, specifications do not require the inclusion of specific items of information (ie, they do not impose restrictions on the content that is included in or excluded from documents), and specifications do not impose any order of appearance of the data contained in the document (ie, you can mix up and rearrange specified objects, if you like). Specifications are not generally certified by a standards organization. They are typically produced by special interest organizations, and the legitimacy of a specification depends on its popularity. Examples of specifications are RDF (Resource Description Framework) produced by the W3C (World Wide Web Consortium), and TCP/IP (Transfer Control Protocol/Internet Protocol), maintained by the Internet Engineering Task Force. The most widely implemented specifications are simple and easily implemented. See Specification versus standard.

Specification versus standard Data standards, in general, tell you what must be included in a conforming document, and, in most cases, dictates the format of the final document. In many instances, standards bar inclusion of any data that is not included in the standard (eg, you should not include astronomical data in a clinical x-ray report). Specifications simply provide a formal way for describing the data that you choose to include in your document. XML and RDF, a semantic dialect of XML, are examples of specifications. They both tell you how data should be represented, but neither tell you what data to include, or how your document or data set should appear. Files that comply with a standard are rigidly organized and can be easily parsed and manipulated by software specifically designed to adhere to the standard. Files that comply with a specification are typically self-describing documents that contain within themselves all the information necessary for a human or a computer to derive meaning from the file contents. In theory, files that comply with a specification can be parsed and manipulated by generalized software designed to parse the markup language of the specification (eg, XML, RDF) and to organize the data into data structures defined within the file. The relative strengths and weaknesses of standards and specifications are discussed in Section 2.6 of Chapter 2, "Specifications Good, Standards Bad." See XML. See RDF.

Standard A standard is a set of rules for doing a particular task or expressing a particular kind of information. The purpose of standards is to ensure that all objects that meet the standard have certain physical or informational features in common, thus facilitating interchange, reproducibility, interoperability, and reducing costs of operation. In the case of standards for data and information, standards typically dictate what data is to be included, how that data should be expressed and arranged, and what data is to be excluded. Standards are developed by any of hundreds of standards developing agencies, but there are only a few international agencies that bestow approval of standards. See ISO. See Specification. See Specification versus standard.

String A string is a sequence of characters (ie, letters, numbers, punctuation). For example, this book is a long string. The complete sequence of the human genome (3 billion characters, with each character an A,T,G, or C) is an even longer string. Every subsequence of a string is also a string. A great many clever algorithms for searching, retrieving, comparing, compressing, and otherwise analyzing strings, have been published.[109]

Superclass Any of the ancestral classes of a subclass. For example, in the classification of living organisms, the class of vertebrates is a superclass of the class of mammals. The immediate superclass of a class is its parent class. In common parlance, when we speak of the superclass of a class, we are usually referring to its parent class. See Parent class.

System A set of objects whose interactions produce all of the observable properties, behaviors and events that we choose to observe. Basically, then, a system is whatever we decide to look at (eg, the brain, the cosmos, a cell, a habitat). The assumption is that the objects that we are not looking at (ie, the objects excluded from the system), have little or no effect on the objects within the system. Of course, this assumption will not always be true, but we do our best.

System call Refers to a command, within a running script, that calls the operating system into action, momentarily bypassing the programming interpreter for the script. A system call can do essentially anything the operating system can do via a command line.

Systematics The term "systematics" is, by tradition, reserved for the field of biology that deals with taxonomy (ie, the listing of the distinct types of organisms) and with classification (ie, the classes of organisms and their relationships to one another). There is no reason why biologists should lay exclusive claim to the field of systematics. As used herein, systematics equals taxonomics plus classification, and this term applies just as strongly to stamp collecting, marketing, operations research, and object-oriented programming as it does to the field of biology.

Taxonomic order In biological taxonomy, the hierarchical lineage of organisms are divided into a descending list of named orders: Kingdom, Phylum (Division), Class, Order, Family, Genus, and Species. As we have learned more and more about the classes of organisms, modern taxonomists have added additional ranks to the classification (eg, supraphylum, subphylum, suborder, infraclass, etc.). Was this really necessary? All of this taxonomic complexity could be averted by dropping named ranks and simply referring to every class as "Class." Modern specifications for class hierarchies (eg, RDF Schema) encapsulate each class with the name of its superclass. When every object yields its class and superclass, it is possible to trace any object's class lineage. For example, in the classification of living organisms, if you know the name of the parent for each class, you can write a simple script that generates the complete ancestral lineage for every class and species within the classification.[84] See Class. See Taxonomy. See RDF Schema. See Species.

Taxonomy A taxonomy is the collection of named instances (class members) in a classification or an ontology. When you see a schematic showing class relationships, with individual classes represented by geometric shapes and the relationships represented by arrows or connecting lines between the classes, then you are essentially looking at the structure of a classification, minus the taxonomy. You can think of building a taxonomy as the act of pouring all of the names of all of the instances into their proper classes. A taxonomy is similar to a nomenclature; the difference is that in a taxonomy, every named instance must have an assigned class. See Taxonomic order.

Terminology The collection of words and terms used in some particular discipline, field, or knowledge domain. Nearly synonymous with vocabulary and with nomenclature. Vocabularies, unlike terminologies, are not confined to the terms used in a particular field. Nomenclatures, unlike terminologies, usually aggregate equivalent terms under a canonical synonym.

Text editor A text editor (also called ASCII editor) is a software program designed to display simple, unformatted text files. Text editors differ from word processing software applications that produce files with formatting information embedded within the file. Text editors, unlike word processors, can open large files (in excess of 100 megabytes), very quickly. They also allow you to move around the file with ease. Examples of free and open source text editors are Emacs and vi. See ASCII.

Thesaurus A vocabulary that groups together synonymous terms. A thesaurus is very similar to a nomenclature. There are two minor differences. Nomenclatures included multi-word terms; whereas a thesaurus is typically composed of one-word terms. In addition, nomenclatures are typically restricted to a well-defined topic or knowledge domain (eg, names of stars, infectious diseases, etc.). See Nomenclature. See Vocabulary. See Classification. See Dictionary. See Terminology. See Ontology.

Time A large portion of data analysis is concerned, in one way or another, with the times that events occur or the times that observations are made, or the times that signals are sampled. Here are three examples demonstrating why this is so: (1) most scientific and predictive assertions relate how variables change with respect to one another, over time; and (2) a single data object may have many different data values, over time, and only timing data will tell us how to distinguish one observation from another; (3) computer transactions are tracked in logs, and logs are composed of time-annotated descriptions of the transactions. Data objects often lose their significance if they are not associated with an accurate time measurement. Because accurate time data is easily captured by modern computers, there is no reason why data elements should not be annotated with the time at which they are made. See Timestamp. See Trusted timestamp.

Timestamp Many data objects are temporal events and all temporal events must be given a timestamp indicating the time that the event occurred, using a standard measurement for time. The timestamp must be accurate, persistent, and immutable. The Unix epoch time (equivalent to the Posix epoch time) is available for most operating systems and consists of the number of seconds that have elapsed since January 1, 1970, midnight, Greenwich mean time. The Unix epoch time can easily be converted into any other standard representation of time. The duration of any event can be easily calculated by subtracting the beginning time from the ending time. Because the timing of events can be maliciously altered, scrupulous data managers may choose to employ a trusted timestamp protocol by which a timestamp can be verified. See Trusted timestamp

Transform A transform is a mathematical operation that takes a function or a time series (eg, values obtained at intervals of time) and transforms it into something else. An inverse transform takes the transform function and produces the original function. Transforms are useful when there are operations that can be more easily performed on the transformed function than on the original function.

Triple In computer semantics, a triple is an identified data object associated with a data element and the description of the data element. In the computer science literature, the syntax for the triple is commonly described as: subject, predicate, object, wherein the subject is an identifier, the predicate is the description of the object, and the object is the data. The definition of triple, using grammatical terms, can be off-putting to the data scientist, who may think in terms of spreadsheet entries: a key that identifies the line record, a column header containing the metadata description of the data, and a cell that contains the data. In this book, the three components of a triple are described as: (1) the identifier for the data object, (2) the metadata that describes the data, and (3) the data itself. In theory, all data sets, databases, and spreadsheets can be constructed or deconstructed as collections of triples. See Introspection. See Data object. See Semantics. See RDF. See Meaning.

Trusted timestamp It is sometimes necessary to establish, beyond doubt, that a timestamp is accurate and has not been modified. Through the centuries, a great many protocols have been devised to prove that a timestamp is trustworthy. One of the simplest methods, employed in the late twentieth century, involved creating a digest of a document (eg, a concatenated sequence consisting of the first letter of each line in the document) and sending the sequence to a newspaper for publication in the "Classifieds" section. After publication of the newspaper, anyone in possession of the original document could extract the same sequence from the document, thus proving that the document had existed on the date that the sequence appeared in the newspaper's classified advertisements. Near the end of the twentieth century, one-way hash values became the sequences of choice for trusted timestamp protocols. Today, newspapers are seldom employed to establish trust in timestamps. More commonly, a message digest of a confidential document is sent to a timestamp authority that adds a date to the digest and returns a message, encrypted with the timestamp authority's private key, containing the original one-way hash plus the trusted date. The received message can be decrypted with the timestamp authority's public key, to reveal the date/time and the message digest that is unique for the original document. It seems like the modern trusted timestamp protocol is a lot of work, but those who use these services can quickly and automatically process huge batches of documents. See Message digest.

UUID UUID (Universally Unique IDentifier) is a protocol for assigning unique identifiers to data objects, without using a central registry. UUIDs were originally used in the Apollo Network Computing System.[110] Most modern programming languages have modules for generating UUIDs. See Identifier.

Unclassifiable objects Classifications create a class for every object and taxonomies assign each and every object to its correct class. This means that a classification is not permitted to contain unclassified objects; a condition that puts fussy taxonomists in an untenable position. Suppose you have an object, and you simply do not know enough about the object to confidently assign it to a class. Or, suppose you have an object that seems to fit more than one class, and you can't decide which class is the correct class. What do you do? Historically, scientists have resorted to creating a "miscellaneous" class into which otherwise unclassifiable objects are given a temporary home, until more suitable accommodations can be provided. I have spoken with numerous data managers, and everyone seems to be of a mind that "miscellaneous" classes, created as a stopgap measure, serve a useful purpose. Not so. Historically, the promiscuous application of "miscellaneous" classes have proven to be a huge impediment to the advancement of science. In the case of the classification of living organisms, the class of protozoans stands as a case in point. Ernst Haeckel, a leading biological taxonomist in his time, created the Kingdom Protista (ie, protozoans), in 1866, to accommodate a wide variety of simple organisms with superficial commonalities. Haeckel himself understood that the protists were a blended class that included unrelated organisms, but he believed that further study would resolve the confusion. In a sense, he was right, but the process took much longer than he had anticipated; occupying generations of taxonomists over the following 150 years. Today, Kingdom Protista no longer exists. Its members have been reassigned to classes among the animals, plants, and fungi. Nonetheless, textbooks of microbiology still describe the protozoans, just as though this name continued to occupy a legitimate place among terrestrial organisms. In the meantime, therapeutic opportunities for eradicating so-called protozoal infections, using class-targeted agents, have no doubt been missed.[111] You might think that the creation of a class of living organisms, with no established scientific relation to the real world, was a rare and ancient event in the annals of biology, having little or no chance of being repeated. Not so. A special pseudo-class of fungi, deuteromyctetes (spelled with a lowercase "d," signifying its questionable validity as a true biologic class) has been created to hold fungi of indeterminate speciation. At present, there are several thousand such fungi, sitting in a taxonomic limbo, waiting to be placed into a definitive taxonomic class.[112,111] See Blended class.

Universal and timeless Wherein a set of data or methods can be understood and utilized by anyone, from any discipline, at any time. It's a tall order, but a worthy goal. Much of the data collected over the centuries of recorded history is of little value because it was never adequately described when it was specified (eg, unknown time of recording, unknown source, unfamiliar measurements, unwritten protocols). Efforts to resuscitate large collections of painstakingly collected data are often abandoned simply because there is no way of verifying, or even understanding, the original data.[87] Data scientists who want their data to serve for posterity should use simple specifications, and should include general document annotations such as the Dublin Core. The importance of creating permanent data is discussed in Section 8.5 of Chapter 8, Data Permanence and Data Immutability. See Dublin Core metadata.

Universally Unique IDentifier See UUID.

Validation Validation is the process that checks whether the conclusions drawn from data analysis are correct.[97] Validation usually starts with repeating the same analysis of the same data, using the methods that were originally recommended. Obviously, if a different set of conclusions is drawn from the same data and methods, the original conclusions cannot be validated. Validation may involve applying a different set of analytic methods to the same data, to determine if the conclusions are consistent. It is always reassuring to know that conclusions are repeatable, with different analytic methods. In prior eras, experiments were validated by repeating the entire experiment, thus producing a new set of observations for analysis. Many of today's scientific experiments are far too complex and costly to repeat. In such cases, validation requires access to the complete collection of the original data, and to the detailed protocols under which the data was generated. One of the most useful methods of data validation involves testing new hypotheses, based on the assumed validity of the original conclusions. For example, if you were to accept Darwin's analysis of barnacle data leading to his theory of evolution, then you would expect to find a chronologic history of fossils in ascending layers of shale. This was the case; thus, paleontologists studying the Burgess shale provided some validation to Darwin's conclusions. Validation should not be mistaken for proof. Nonetheless, the repeatability of conclusions, over time, with the same or different sets of data, and the demonstration of consistency with related observations, is about all that we can hope for in this imperfect world. See Verification. See Reproducibility.

Verification The process by which data is checked to determine whether the data was obtained properly (ie, according to approved protocols), and that the data accurately measured what it was intended to measure. Verification often requires a level of expertise that is at least as high as the expertise of the individuals who produced the data.[97] Data verification requires a full understanding of the many steps involved in data collection and can be a time-consuming task. In one celebrated case, in which two statisticians reviewed a micro-array study performed at Duke University, the number of hours devoted to their verification effort was reported to be 2000 hours[48] To put this statement in perspective, the official work-year, according to the U.S. Office of Personnel Management, is 2087 hours Verification is different from validation. Verification is performed on data; validation is done on the results of data analysis. See Validation. See Microarray. See Introspection.

Vocabulary A comprehensive collection of words and their associated meanings. In some quarters, "vocabulary" and "nomenclature" are used interchangeably, but they are different from one another. Nomenclatures typically focus on terms confined to one knowledge domain. Nomenclatures typically do not contain definitions for the contained terms. Nomenclatures typically group terms by synonymy. Lastly, nomenclatures include multi-word terms. Vocabularies are collections of single words, culled from multiple knowledge domains, with their definitions, and assembled in alphabetic order. See Nomenclature. See Thesaurus. See Taxonomy. See Dictionary. See Terminology.

XML Acronym for eXtensible Markup Language, a syntax for marking data values with descriptors (ie, metadata). The descriptors are commonly known as tags. In XML, every data value is enclosed by a start-tag, containing the descriptor and indicating that a value will follow, and an end-tag, containing the same descriptor and indicating that a value preceded the tag. For example: <name>Conrad Nervig </name>. The enclosing angle brackets, "<>", and the end-tag marker, "/", are hallmarks of HTML and XML markup. This simple but powerful relationship between metadata and data allows us to employ metadata/data pairs as though each were a miniature database. The semantic value of XML becomes apparent when we bind a metadata/data pair to a unique object, forming a so-called triple. See Triple. See Meaning. See Semantics. See HTML.

REFERENCES

1. Pearson K. *The grammar of science.* London: Adam and Black; 1900.
2. Berman JJ. *Neoplasms: principles of development and diversity.* Sudbury: Jones & Bartlett; 2009.
3. Patil N, Berno AJ, Hinds DA, Barrett WA, Doshi JM, Hacker CR, et al. Blocks of limited haplotype diversity revealed by high-resolution scanning of human chromosome 21. *Science* 2001;**294**:1719–23.
4. Ramos OM, Barker D, Ferrier DEK. Ghost loci imply hox and parahox existence in the last common ancestor of animals. *Curr Biol* 2012;**22**:1951–6.
5. Bromham L. What can DNA tell us about the Cambrian explosion? *Integr Comb Biol* 2003;**43**:148–56.
6. Dawkins R. *The greatest show on Earth: the evidence for evolution paperback.* New York: Free Press; 2009.
7. Feltman R. The mysterious genes of carnivorous bladderwort reveal themselves. The Washington Post, February 23, 2015.
8. Ball P. Smallest genome clocks in at 182 genes. *Nature* 2006;.
9. Brinkmann H, Philippe H. The diversity of eukaryotes and the root of the eukaryotic tree. *Adv Exp Med Biol* 2007;**607**:20–37.
10. Unreliable research: trouble at the lab. The Economist, October 19, 2013.
11. Prasad V, Vandross A, Toomey C, Cheung M, Rho J, Quinn S, et al. A decade of reversal: an analysis of 146 contradicted medical practices. *Mayo Clin Proc* 2013;**88**:790–8.
12. Kolata G. Cancer fight: unclear tests for new drug. The New York Times, April 19, 2010.
13. Baker M. Reproducibility crisis: blame it on the antibodies. *Nature* 2015;**521**:274–6.
14. Ioannidis JP. Why most published research findings are false. *PLoS Med* 2005;**2**.
15. Labos C. It ain't necessarily so: why much of the medical Literature is wrong. Medscape News and Perspectives, September 09, 2014.
16. Gilbert E, Strohminger N. We found only one-third of published psychology research is reliable — now what? The Conversation, August 27, 2015. Available at: http://theconversation.com/we-found-only-one-third-of-published-psychology-research-is-reliable-now-what-46596 [accessed 27.08.15].
17. Naik G. Scientists' elusive goal: reproducing study results. Wall Street J, December 2, 2011.
18. Zimmer C. A sharp rise in retractions prompts calls for reform. The New York Times, April 16, 2012.
19. Altman LK. Falsified data found in gene studies. The New York Times, October 30, 1996.
20. Weaver D, Albanese C, Costantini F, Baltimore D. Retraction: altered repertoire of endogenous immunoglobulin gene expression in transgenic mice containing a rearranged mu heavy chain gene. *Cell* 1991;**65**:536.
21. Chang K. Nobel winner in physiology retracts two papers. The New York Times, September 23, 2010.
22. Fourth paper retracted at Potti's request. The Chronicle, March 3, 2011.
23. Whoriskey P. Doubts about Johns Hopkins research have gone unanswered, scientist says. The Washington Post, March 11, 2013.
24. Lin YY, Kiihl S, Suhail Y, Liu SY, Chou YH, Kuang Z, et al. Retraction: functional dissection of lysine deacetylases reveals that HDAC1 and p300 regulate AMPK. *Nature* 2013;**482**:251–5.

25. Shafer SL. Letter: To our readers. Anesthesia and Analgesia, February 20, 2009.
26. Innovation or stagnation: challenge and opportunity on the critical path to new medical products. U.S. Department of Health and Human Services, Food and Drug Administration; 2004.
27. Hurley D. Why are so few blockbuster drugs invented today? The New York Times, November 13, 2014.
28. Angell M. The truth about the drug companies. The New York Review of Books, vol. 51, July 15, 2004.
29. Crossing the quality chasm: a new health system for the 21st century. Quality of Health Care in America Committee, editors. Institute of Medicine, Washington, DC; 2001.
30. Wurtman RJ, Bettiker RL. The slowing of treatment discovery, 1965–1995. *Nat Med* 1996;**2**:5–6.
31. Ioannidis JP. Microarrays and molecular research: noise discovery? *Lancet* 2005;**365**:454–5.
32. Weigelt B, Reis-Filho JS. Molecular profiling currently offers no more than tumour morphology and basic immunohistochemistry. *Breast Cancer Res* 2010;**12**:S5.
33. Personalised medicines: hopes and realities. The Royal Society, London; 2005. Available from: https://royalsociety.org/~/media/Royal_Society_Content/policy/publications/2005/9631.pdf [accessed 01.01.15].
34. Beizer B. Software Testing Techniques. Van Nostrand Reinhold; Hoboken, NJ 2 edition, 1990.
35. Vlasic B. Toyota's slow awakening to a deadly problem. The New York Times, February 1, 2010.
36. Lanier J. The complexity ceiling. In: Brockman J, editor. *The next fifty years: science in the first half of the twenty-first century*. New York: Vintage; 2002. p. 216–29.
37. Bandelt H, Salas A. Contamination and sample mix-up can best explain some patterns of mtDNA instabilities in buccal cells and oral squamous cell carcinoma. *BMC Cancer* 2009;**9**:113.
38. Knight J. Agony for researchers as mix-up forces retraction of ecstasy study. *Nature* 2003;**425**:109.
39. Gerlinger M, Rowan AJ, Horswell S, Larkin J, Endesfelder D, Gronroos E, et al. Intratumor heterogeneity and branched evolution revealed by multiregion sequencing. *N Engl J Med* 2012;**366**:883–92.
40. Berman JJ. *Biomedical Informatics*. Sudbury, MA: Jones and Bartlett; 2007.
41. Ioannidis JP. Is molecular profiling ready for use in clinical decision making? *Oncologist* 2007;**12**:301–11.
42. Ioannidis JP. Some main problems eroding the credibility and relevance of randomized trials. *Bull NYU Hosp Jt Dis* 2008;**66**:135–9.
43. Ioannidis JP, Panagiotou OA. Comparison of effect sizes associated with biomarkers reported in highly cited individual articles and in subsequent meta-analyses. *JAMA* 2011;**305**:2200–10.
44. Ioannidis JP. Excess significance bias in the literature on brain volume abnormalities. *Arch Gen Psychiatry* 2011;**68**:773–80.
45. Pocock SJ, Collier TJ, Dandreo KJ, deStavola BL, Goldman MB, Kalish LA, et al. Issues in the reporting of epidemiological studies: a survey of recent practice. *BMJ* 2004;**329**:883.
46. Harris G. Diabetes drug maker hid test data, files indicate. The New York Times, July 12, 2010.
47. Berman JJ. Machiavelli's Laboratory. Amazon Digital Services, Inc.; 2010.
48. Misconduct in science: an array of errors. The Economist. September 10, 2011.
49. Begley S. In cancer science, many 'discoveries' don't hold up. Reuters, March 28, 2012.
50. Abu-Asab MS, Chaouchi M, Alesci S, Galli S, Laassri M, Cheema AK, et al. Biomarkers in the age of omics: time for a systems biology approach. *OMICS* 2011;**15**:105–12.
51. Moyer VA. Screening for prostate cancer: U.S. Preventive Services Task Force recommendation statement. *Ann Intern Med* 2012;**157**(2):120–34.
52. How science goes wrong. The Economist, October 19, 2013.
53. Martin B. Scientific fraud and the power structure of science. *Prometheus* 1992;**10**:83–98.
54. Rosen JM, Jordan CT. The increasing complexity of the cancer stem cell paradigm. *Science* 2009;**324**:1670–3.
55. Madar S, Goldstein I, Rotter V. Did experimental biology die? Lessons from 30 years of p53 research. *Cancer Res* 2009;**69**:6378–80.
56. Zilfou JT, Lowe SW. Tumor Suppressive Functions of p53. *Cold Spring Harb Perspect Biol* 2009;**00**: a001883.

57. Lohr S. Google to end health records service after it fails to attract users. The New York Times, June 24, 2011.
58. Schwartz E. Shopping for health software, some doctors get buyer's remorse. The Huffington Post Investigative Fund, January 29, 2010.
59. Heeks R, Mundy D, Salazar A. Why health care information systems succeed or fail. Institute for Development Policy and Management, University of Manchester, June 1999. Available from: http://www.sed.manchester.ac.uk/idpm/research/publications/wp/igovernment/igov_wp09.htm [accessed 12.07.12].
60. Littlejohns P, Wyatt JC, Garvican L. Evaluating computerised health information systems: hard lessons still to be learnt. *Br Med J* 2003;**326**:860–3.
61. Linder JA, Ma J, Bates DW, Middleton B, Stafford RS. Electronic health record use and the quality of ambulatory care in the United States. *Arch Intern Med* 2007;**167**:1400–5.
62. Patient Safety in American Hospitals. HealthGrades, July 2004. Available from: http://www.healthgrades.com/media/english/pdf/hg_patient_safety_study_final.pdf [accessed 09.09.12].
63. Gill JM, Mainous AG, Koopman RJ, Player MS, Everett CJ, Chen YX, et al. Impact of EHR-based clinical decision support on adherence to guidelines for patients on NSAIDs: a randomized controlled trial. *Ann Fam Med* 2011;**9**:22–30.
64. Berman JJ. *Principles of big data: preparing, sharing, and analyzing complex information.* Burlington, MA: Morgan Kaufmann; 2013.
65. Kappelman LA, McKeeman R, Lixuan Zhang L. Early warning signs of IT project failure: the dominant dozen. *Inf Syst Manag* 2006;**23**:31–6.
66. Arquilla J. The Pentagon's biggest boondoggles. The New York Times (Opinion Pages), March 12, 2011.
67. Van Pelt M. IT governance in federal project management. George Mason University, Fairfax, Virginia, December 8, 2009.
68. Brooks FP. No silver bullet: essence and accidents of software engineering. *Computer* 1987;**20**:10–9.
69. Basili VR, Perricone BT. Software errors and complexity: an empirical investigation. *Commun ACM* 1984;**27**:556–63.
70. The ComputerWorld honors program case study. Available from: http://www.cwhonors.org/case_studies/NationalCancerInstitute.pdf [accessed 31.08.12].
71. An assessment of the impact of the NCI cancer Biomedical Informatics Grid (caBIG). Report of the Board of Scientific Advisors Ad Hoc Working Group, National Cancer Institute, March, 2011.
72. Komatsoulis GA. Program announcement to the CaBIG community. National Cancer Institute. https://cabig.nci.nih.gov/program_announcement [accessed 31.08.12].
73. Smith B. caBIG has another fundamental problem: it relies on "incoherent" messaging standard. *Cancer Lett* 2011;**37**(16).
74. Lohr S. Lessons from Britain's health information technology fiasco. The New York Times, September 27, 2011.
75. Dismantling the NHS national programme for IT. Department of Health Media Centre Press Release, September 22, 2011. Available from: http://mediacentre.dh.gov.uk/2011/09/22/dismantling-the-nhs-national-programme-for-it/ [accessed 12.06.12].
76. Whittaker Z. UK's delayed national health IT programme officially scrapped. ZDNet, September 22, 2011.
77. Robinson D, Paul Frosdick P, Briscoe E. HL7 Version 3: an impact assessment. NHS Information Authority, March 23, 2001.
78. Leveson NG. *A new approach to system safety engineering.* Self-published ebook; 2002.
79. Leveson N. Medical devices: the Therac-25. In: Leveson N, editor. *Appendix A in 'Safeware: system safety and computers'.* Reading: Addison-Wesley; 1995.
80. Leveson NG. Engineering a safer world. System safety for the 21st century. Self-published book, 2009. Available from: http://sunnyday.mit.edu/book2.pdf [accessed 12.10.09].

81. Asimov I. Isaac Asimov Mulls "How do people get new ideas?" MIT Technology Review, October 20, 2014.
82. Lewis PD. *R for medicine and biology*. Sudbury: Jones and Bartlett Publishers; 2009.
83. Berman JJ. *Perl programming for medicine and biology*. Sudbury, MA: Jones and Bartlett; 2007.
84. Berman JJ. *Methods in medical informatics: fundamentals of healthcare programming in Perl, Python, and Ruby*. Boca Raton: Chapman and Hall; 2010.
85. Berman JJ. *Ruby programming for medicine and biology*. Sudbury, MA: Jones and Bartlett; 2008.
86. Janert PK. *Gnuplot in action: understanding data with graphs*. Manning; 2009.
87. Berman JJ. *Repurposing legacy data: innovative case studies*. Elsevier/Morgan Kaufmann imprint; 2015.
88. Thomas D. *Programming Ruby 1.9 & 2.0: the pragmatic programmers' guide*. 4th ed. Frisco, TX: Pragmatic Bookshelf; 2013.
89. Stephenson N. *In the beginning…was the command line*. New York: William Morrow Paperbacks; 1999.
90. Robbins A, Beebe NHF. *Classic shell scripting hidden commands that unlock the power of unix*. O'Reilly Media; 2005.
91. Newham C. *Learning the bash shell: unix shell programming*. O'Reilly Media; 2005.
92. Cipra BA. The best of the 20th century: editors name top 10 algorithms. *SIAM News* 2000;**33**(4).
93. Wu X, Kumar V, Quinlan JR, Ghosh J, Yang Q, Motoda H, et al. Top 10 algorithms in data mining. *Knowl Inf Syst* 2008;**14**:1–37.
94. Al-Agha OM, Igbokwe AA. Malignant fibrous histiocytoma: between the past and the present. *Arch Pathol Lab Med* 2008;**132**:1030–5.
95. Nakayama R, Nemoto T, Takahashi H, Ohta T, Kawai A, Seki K, et al. Gene expression analysis of soft tissue sarcomas: characterization and reclassification of malignant fibrous histiocytoma. *Mod Pathol* 2007;**20**:749–59.
96. Nowack EC, Melkonian M, Glockner G. Chromatophore genome sequence of paulinella sheds light on acquisition of photosynthesis by eukaryotes. *Curr Biol* 2008;**18**:410–8.
97. Committee on mathematical foundations of verification, validation, and uncertainty quantification; Board on mathematical sciences and their applications, Division on engineering and physical sciences, National research council. Assessing the reliability of complex models: mathematical and statistical foundations of verification, validation, and uncertainty quantification. National Academy Press; 2012. Available from: http://www.nap.edu/catalog.php?record_id=13395 [accessed 01.01.15].
98. Salmon F. Recipe for disaster: the formula that killed wall street. Wired Magazine 17:03, February 23, 2009.
99. Paskin N. Identifier interoperability: a report on two recent ISO activities. *D-Lib Mag* 2006;**12**:1–23.
100. Berman JJ. Tumor classification: molecular analysis meets Aristotle. BMC Cancer 4:10, 2004. Available from: http://www.biomedcentral.com/1471-2407/4/10 [accessed 01.01.15].
101. Berman JJ. *Tumor taxonomy for the developmental lineage classification of neoplasms. BMC Cancer* 2004;**4**:88. http://www.biomedcentral.com/1471-2407/4/88 [accessed 01.01.15].
102. Berman JJ, Moore GW. Implementing an RDF Schema for pathology images 2007. Available from: http://www.julesberman.info/spec2img.htm [accessed 01.01.15].
103. SciPy reference guide, Release 0.7. Written by the SciPy community, December 07, 2008.
104. Smith AK, Ayanian JZ, Covinsky KE, Landon BE, McCarthy EP, Wee CC, et al. Conducting high-value secondary dataset analysis: an introductory guide and resources. *J Gen Intern Med* 2011;**26**:920–9.
105. Tu Y, Gunnell D, Gilthorpe MS. Simpson's paradox, lord's paradox, and suppression effects are the same phenomenon — the reversal paradox. *Emerg Themes Epidemiol* 2008;**5**:2.
106. DeQueiroz K. Ernst Mayr and the modern concept of species. *Proc Natl Acad Sci U S A* 2005;**102** (Suppl. 1):6600–7.
107. DeQueiroz K. Species concepts and species delimitation. *Syst Biol* 2007;**56**:879–86.
108. Mayden RL. Consilience and a hierarchy of species concepts: advances toward closure on the species puzzle. *J Nematol* 1999;**31**(2):95–116.

109. Gusfield D. *Algorithms on strings, trees and sequences.* Cambridge University Press; 1997.
110. Leach P, Mealling M, Salz R. A universally unique identifier (UUID) URN namespace. Network Working Group, Request for Comment 4122, Standards Track. Available from: http://www.ietf.org/rfc/rfc4122.txt [accessed 01.01.15].
111. Berman JJ. *Taxonomic guide to infectious diseases: understanding the biologic classes of pathogenic organisms.* Waltham: Academic Press; 2012.
112. Guarro J, Gene J, Stchigel AM. Developments in fungal taxonomy. *Clin Microbiol Rev* 1999;**12**:454–500.

STRUCTURING TEXT

2.1 THE MEANINGLESSNESS OF FREE TEXT

> I've had a perfectly wonderful evening. But this wasn't it.
>
> -Groucho Marx

English is such a ridiculous language that an objective observer might guess that it was designed for the purpose of impeding communication. As someone who has dabbled in machine translation, here are just a few points that I find particularly irritating:

1. **Homonyms**. One word can have dozens of meanings, depending on context. Unfortunately, you cannot really depend on context, particularly when writing machine translation software (see Glossary item, Machine translation). Here are a few egregious examples:

   Both the martini and the bar patron, were drunk.
   The bandage was wound around a wound.
   He farmed to produce produce.
   Present the present in the present time.
   Don't object to the data object.
   Teach a sow to sow seed.
   Wind the sail before the wind comes.

   Homonymic misunderstandings are the root cause of all puns, the lowest and most despised form of humor.

2. **Janus sentences**. A single word can have opposite meanings, or opposite words may have equivalent meanings, depending on its idiomatic context. For example, if you were asked "Have you been here?" and you have not, you might answer, "No, I haven't." If I were to negate the same question, and ask, "Haven't you been here?," you would likewise answer "No, I haven't." Same answer, opposite question.

   If you were told that the light is out in your room, then you would know that the light was not working. If you were told that the stars are out tonight, then you would know that the stars are shining, as expected.

   Antonyms become synonyms, as if by whim. If I were to cash in my chips, I would collect the money owed me. If I cashed out my chips, the meaning does not change. In or out, it's all the same. Contrariwise, overlook and oversee should, logically, be synonyms; but they are antonyms.

3. **Word meanings change with case**. As examples, Nice and nice, Polish and polish, Herb and herb, August and august. Likewise, all abbreviations whose letters form a legitimate word will mean one thing when appearing in uppercase (eg, AIDS, the disease; US, the country; OR, the state) and another thing when appearing in lowercase (eg, "aids," to help; "us," the first person plural; and "or," the option).

4. **Noncompositionality of words**. The meaning of individual words cannot be reliably deduced by analyzing root parts. For example, there is neither pine or apple in pineapple, no egg in eggplant, and hamburgers are made from beef, not ham. You can assume that a lover will love, but you cannot assume that a finger will "fing." Vegetarians will eat vegetables, but humanitarians will not eat humans.[1]

5. **Unrestricted extensibility**. Sentences are extensible, but comprehension is not. For example, the following four sentences are examples of proper English.

   The cat died.
   The cat the dog chased died.
   The cat the dog the rat bit chased died.
   The cat the dog the rat the elephant admired bit chased died.

   If we think about these sentences long enough, we might conclude that the following assertions applied:

   The elephant admired the rat.
   The rat bit the dog.
   The dog chased the cat.
   The cat died.

6. **Reifications**. The most unforgivable flaw in English is the common usage of reification; the process whereby the subject of a sentence is inferred, without actually being named (see Glossary item, Reification). Reification is accomplished with pronouns and other subject references.[1]

Here is an example:
"It never rains here."

The word "it" seems to be the subject of the sentence; but what is "it" really? "It" seems to be the thing that never rains at a particular location specified as "here" (wherever "here" is). What would be the noun word for which "it" is the pronoun?

The sentence "It never rains here" is meaningless because there is no way of determining the subject of the sentence (ie, the object to which the sentence applies).

Let's look at another example of reification; this one taken from a newspaper article.[1]

"After her husband disappeared on a 1944 recon mission over Southern France, Antoine de Saint-Exupery's widow sat down and wrote this memoir of their dramatic marriage."

There are two reified persons in the sentence: "her husband," and "Antoine de Saint-Exupery's widow." In the first phrase, "her husband" is a relationship (ie, "husband") established for a pronoun (ie, "her") referenced to the person in the second phrase. The person in the second phrase is reified by a relationship to Saint-Exupery (ie, "widow"), who just happens to be the reification of the person in the first phrase (ie, "Saint-Exupery is her husband").

A final example is:
"Do you know who I am?"

There are no identifiable individuals; everyone is reified and reduced to an unspecified pronoun ("you," "I"). Though there are just a few words in the sentence, half of them are superfluous. The words "Do," "who," and "am" are merely fluff, with no informational purpose. In an object-oriented world, the question would be transformed into an assertion, "You know me," and the assertion would be sent an object method, "true?".[1] We are jumping ahead. Objects, assertions, and methods will be discussed in later chapters.

We write self-referential reifying sentences every time we use a pronoun. Strictly speaking, such sentences are meaningless and cannot be sensibly evaluated by software programs (see Glossary item, Meaning). The subjects of the sentence are not properly identified, the references to the subjects are ambiguous.

A Hungarian friend once told me that "English is a language that, if you sit down and learn it all by yourself, you will end up speaking a language that nobody else on earth speaks." By this, he meant that English makes no sense. The meaning of English language comes from common usage, not through semantic logic.

If English is meaningless, then how can we produce software that accurately translates English to other languages? As you might guess, idiomatic and complex sentences are difficult to translate. Machine translation of free-text is greatly facilitated when text is written as simple, short, declarative sentences. Over the years, there have been several attempts at simplifying English, most notably "Controlled English," and "Basic English."

Controlled English is a disciplined approach to sentence construction that avoids some of the intrinsic flaws in written language. Pogson, in 1988, formalized the rules for Controlled English. Pogson's key points are as follows[2,3]:

1. Each word in the text may convey only one meaning and context. If "iris" is an anatomic part of the eye, then it cannot be used as a flower. If "report" is used as a noun, then it should not be used as a verb elsewhere in the text.
2. For each meaning, only one term may be used (eg, if you use the term "chair," then you should not use the term "seat" to describe the same piece of furniture, elsewhere in the text).

C.K. Ogden, in 1930, introduced Basic English, wherein words are constrained to a list of about 850 words that have clear definitions and that convey more than 90% of the concepts commonly described in narrative text.[4] Basic English was championed by some very influential people, including Winston Churchill. Numerous books have been "translated" into Basic English, including the Bible.[3]

Most recently, a type of simplified English has been developed for Wikipedia readers who do not speak English as their first language.[5] Simplified versions of many Wikipedia pages have been composed, thus extending the reach of this remarkable Web resource.

Although Controlled English, Basic English, and Simplified English all serve to reduce the complexity of language, they could go much further to improve the computation of sentence parsing. Here are a few additional suggestions for creating sentences that can be understood by humans and by computers[3]:

1. Sentences should be short and declarative, with an obvious subject, predicate, and object. The shorter the sentence, the lower the likelihood of misinterpretation.
2. Negations should include the word "not" and double negations should never be used. Most importantly, negations should not be expressed as positive assertions. "John is absent" is a positive

statement that has the same meaning as "John is not present." The former requires the computer to understand the meaning of "absence," whereas the latter only requires the computer to recognize a common negation operator ("not").

3. Abbreviations and acronyms should be avoided, wherever feasible. If an abbreviation must be used, then it should appear in all uppercase letters, without periods. Abbreviations can be pluralized by adding a lowercase "s."

4. Natural language parsers must know where one sentence ends and the next begins. The "period" alone cannot serve as a reliable sentence delimiter. Wanton periods appear in honorifics, abbreviations, quantitative values, and Web addresses (eg, Mr., Ph.D., U.S., $5.15, gov.com). Using the period as the sentence terminator would result in the abrupt separation and loss of terms that would otherwise be connected. Consider using a period, exclamation point or a question mark followed by a double-space. If a sentence naturally ends at a carriage return, two spaces should be added after the period, as buffer. The consistent use of two spaces after a period runs counter to the preference of the printing industry, where single space sentence delimiters currently prevail. Regardless, the consistent inclusion of double spaces between sentences greatly simplifies computer parsing, and should be used when circumstances permit (see Glossary item, Monospaced font).

5. Reifications should be abandoned, whenever feasible. Use "Rain seldom occurs at this location," rather than "It doesn't rain here much."

We labor under the delusion that the sentences we write have specific, unambiguous meaning. This is simply not true. Most sentences are ambiguous. In Chapter 6, we will discuss how to create meaningful sentences.

2.2 SORTING TEXT, THE IMPOSSIBLE DREAM

> Consistency is the last refuge of the unimaginative.
>
> **-Oscar Wilde**

The world loves an alphabetically sorted list. A quick glance at any alphabetized list of words or terms from a text document always reveals a great deal about the content. If you've scanned the first 100 words on an alphabetized list, and you're still looking at words that begin with "ab," then you can infer that the document is long and that its vocabulary is rich.

For programmers, the greatest value of alphabetized lists comes with fast search and retrieval algorithms. As it happens, it is computationally trivial to find any word in an alphabetically sorted list. Surprisingly, increasing the length of the list does not appreciably increase the length of time required to locate the item; hence, searches on alphabetized lists are virtually instantaneous. If you were a computer, here is how you would search an alphabetized list:

1. Go to the center of the list and take a look at the word at that location.

2. Ask whether the word you are searching has an alphabetic rank less than the word you've just plucked from the center of the list. If so, then you know that your search-word is located somewhere

in the first half of the list. Otherwise, your search-word must belong in the second half of the list. Hence, you've reduced the length of the list you must search by one-half.

3. Repeat steps 1 and 2, halving the length of the search-list with each iteration, until you come to the word in the list that matches your search-word.

Imagine that your list of alphabetized words contained a thousand billion words (ie, about 2 exp 30 words). If the words were held in an alphabetized list, then you would be able to find your word in just 30 repetitions of steps 1 and 2. This is so because every repetition of the algorithm reduces the search by a factor of 2.

Alphabetized lists of words enhance our ability to quickly merge lists to produce an aggregate alphabetized list. The merge is performed by item-by-item alphabetic comparisons, until one of the two lists is exhausted. If the same two lists were merged, without presorting each list, then producing an alphabetized list would require a new sort on a list whose length was the sum of the two lists being merged.

Sorting has such great importance to computer scientists that every introductory programming text contains a section or chapter devoted to sorting routines. Most modern programming languages come with a built-in sort command that will arrange lists of items into alphanumeric order.

On the face of it, alphanumeric sorting is one of the simplest and most useful computational functions provided by modern computers. It is a shame that there exists no satisfactory set of rules that define the product of the sort. In point of fact, there is no guarantee that any two operating systems, provided with the same list of words or numbers, will produce identical sorted lists. Furthermore, it is logically impossible to create a set of sorting rules that will produce a sensible and helpful sorted list, under all possible sets of circumstances. Put simply, sorting is a process that cannot be done correctly.

Just for a taste of how idiosyncratic sorting can be, here are examples of how a few filenames in a directory would be sorted in Linux, DOS, and by a text editor with a sorting feature.

Unix directory sort:

```
1. X_HIST.PL
2. xlxs_spreadsheet.pdf
3. XMLVOCAB.PL
4. XOXOHWRD.ZBK
5. xy.TXT
6. XY_RAND.PL
7. xyrite.TXT
```

DOS directory sort:

```
1. xlxs_spreadsheet.pdf
2. XMLVOCAB.PL
3. XOXOHWRD.ZBK
4. xy.TXT
5. xyrite.TXT
6. XY_RAND.PL
7. X_HIST.PL
```

Wordprocessor directory sort:

```
XMLVOCAB.PL
XOXOHWRD.ZBK
XY_RAND.PL
X_HIST.PL
xlxs_spreadsheet.pdf
xy.TXT
xyrite.TXT
```

No two sorts, for the same list of filenames, were equivalent. How so?

Whenever we sort words or phrases (ie, sequences of words), we must make decisions about the positional hierarchy of characters, the relevancy of characters, and the equivalences among characters and sequences of characters. Whichever decisions we make may conflict with decisions that others have made. Furthermore, the decisions that we make will prove to be wrong decisions, under unexpected conditions.

Before moving forward, we should ask ourselves, "Why does the hierarchical positioning of characters matter?" We must understand that algorithms that search and retrieve words and phrases from sorted lists will fail if the list is sorted in a manner that is different from the search algorithm's method for determining the precedence of which of two words/phrases are higher in the list. For example, in step 2 of the search algorithm described previously, we compare our search term with the term found at the middle of the alphabetized list. If our search term alphabetically precedes the term located at the middle of the list, we will devote the next iteration of the search to items in the first half of the list. If the list had been sorted in a manner that put the search term in the second half of the list (ie, if the sorted list used a different method for establishing alphabetic precedence), then the search term will not be found and retrieved, using our search algorithm.

The first order of business in any sorting routine is to determine whether the sort will be done word-for-word or letter-by-letter. In a word-for-word sort, New Brunswick comes before Newark, NJ. This is because "New" precedes "Newark." The word-for-word sort is sometimes referred to as the nothing-before-something search. In this case, the "nothing" following "New" precedes the "ark" in "Newark." If we had done a letter-by-letter search, Newark, NJ precedes New Brunswick, because the letter that follows "New" in "Newark" is an "a" that precedes the letter that follows "New" in "New Brunswick" (ie, "B").

The next order of business in sorting routines is to determine how to deal with uppercase and lowercase letters. Should the uppercase letters precede the lowercase letters? How about punctuation? Should we delete punctuation marks prior to the sort, or should we replace punctuation marks with a space, or should we leave them untouched? Should we treat punctuation marks that occur inside a word (eg, "isn't") differently from punctuation marks that occur outside words (eg, "The end.")? What should we do with punctuation marks that occur inside and outside of a word (eg, "U.S.A.")? Should "*P* value" reside next to *P*-value" or should Page be sandwiched in between?

How do we alphabetize names that contain an umlauted character? Do you pretend the umlaut isn't there, and put it in alphabetic order with the plain characters? The same problem applies to every special character (eg, "üéâäàèïÇÉúê").

How do we alphabetize single characters created by combining two characters (eg, "æ"). Should we render Cæsar, unto "Caesar"?

How do we handle surnames preceded by modifiers? Do you alphabetize de Broglie under "D" or under "d" or under "B"? If you choose B, then what do you do with the concatenated form of the name, "deBroglie"?

You are probably thinking that now is the time to consult some official guidelines. The National Information Standard Organization has published an informative tract, titled, "Guidelines for Alphabetical Arrangement of Letters and Sorting of Numerals and Other Symbols."[6] These guidelines describe several sorting methods: word-for-word, letter-by-letter, ASCIIbetical, and modified ASCIIbetical. The Guidelines refer us to various sets of alphabetization rules: American Library Association, British Standards Institution, Chicago Manual of Style, and Library of Congress. None of these guidelines are compatible with one another and all are subject to revisions.

For the computer savvy, the choice is obvious: use ASCIIbetical sorting. ASCIIbetical sorting is based on assigning every character to its ASCII value, and sorting character by character (including punctuation, spaces and nonprintable characters). This type of sorting is by far the easiest way to arrange any sequence alphanumerically, and can be accomplished in a manner that produces an identically sorted output in any operating system or in any programming environment (Fig. 2.1).

ASCII sorts have their limitations, listing terms in a way that you might not prefer. For example, consider the following Perl script, sortlet.pl that sorts a set of words and phrases by ASCII values:

```perl
#!/usr/local/bin/perl
@word_array = ("MacIntire", "Macadam", "wilson", "tilson", "Wilson",
"I cannot go", "I can not go", "I can also go", "I candle maker",
"O'Brien", "OBrien", "O'Brien's", "O'Briens", "OBrien's", "Oar", "O'Brienesque");
@word_array = sort (@word_array);
print join("\n", @word_array);
exit;
```

Here is the output of the sortlet.pl script:

```
C:\ftp\pl>perl sortlet.pl
I can also go
I can not go
I candle maker
I cannot go
MacIntire
Macadam
O'Brien
O'Brien's
O'Brienesque
O'Briens
OBrien
OBrien's
Oar
Wilson
tilson
wilson
```

Dec	Hex	Chr	Dec	Hex	Chr	Dec	Hex	Chr	Dec	Hex	Chr
000	0x00	^@	032	0x20		064	0x40	@	096	0x60	`
001	0x01	^A	033	0x21	!	065	0x41	A	097	0x61	a
002	0x02	^B	034	0x22	"	066	0x42	B	098	0x62	b
003	0x03	^C	035	0x23	#	067	0x43	C	099	0x63	c
004	0x04	^D	036	0x24	$	068	0x44	D	100	0x64	d
005	0x05	^E	037	0x25	%	069	0x45	E	101	0x65	e
006	0x06	^F	038	0x26	&	070	0x46	F	102	0x66	f
007	0x07	^G	039	0x27	'	071	0x47	G	103	0x67	g
008	0x08	^H	040	0x28	(	072	0x48	H	104	0x68	h
009	0x09	^I	041	0x29	)	073	0x49	I	105	0x69	i
010	0x0a	^J	042	0x2a	*	074	0x4a	J	106	0x6a	j
011	0x0b	^K	043	0x2b	+	075	0x4b	K	107	0x6b	k
012	0x0c	^L	044	0x2c	,	076	0x4c	L	108	0x6c	l
013	0x0d	^M	045	0x2d	-	077	0x4d	M	109	0x6d	m
014	0x0e	^N	046	0x2e	.	078	0x4e	N	110	0x6e	n
015	0x0f	^O	047	0x2f	/	079	0x4f	O	111	0x6f	o
016	0x10	^P	048	0x30	0	080	0x50	P	112	0x70	p
017	0x11	^Q	049	0x31	1	081	0x51	Q	113	0x71	q
018	0x12	^R	050	0x32	2	082	0x52	R	114	0x72	r
019	0x13	^S	051	0x33	3	083	0x53	S	115	0x73	s
020	0x14	^T	052	0x34	4	084	0x54	T	116	0x74	t
021	0x15	^U	053	0x35	5	085	0x55	U	117	0x75	u
022	0x16	^V	054	0x36	6	086	0x56	V	118	0x76	v
023	0x17	^W	055	0x37	7	087	0x57	W	119	0x77	w
024	0x18	^X	056	0x38	8	088	0x58	X	120	0x78	x
025	0x19	^Y	057	0x39	9	089	0x59	Y	121	0x79	y
026	0x1a	^Z	058	0x3a	:	090	0x5a	Z	122	0x7a	z
027	0x1b	^[	059	0x3b	;	091	0x5b	[	123	0x7b	{
028	0x1c	^\	060	0x3c	<	092	0x5c	\	124	0x7c	|
029	0x1d	^]	061	0x3d	=	093	0x5d	]	125	0x7d	}
030	0x1e	^^	062	0x3e	>	094	0x5e	^	126	0x7e	~
031	0x1f	^_	063	0x3f	?	095	0x5f	_	127	0x7f	
128	0x80	?	160	0xa0		192	0xc0	A	224	0xe0	à
129	0x81	?	161	0xa1	¡	193	0xc1	A	225	0xe1	á
130	0x82	‚	162	0xa2	¢	194	0xc2	A	226	0xe2	â
131	0x83	ƒ	163	0xa3	£	195	0xc3	A	227	0xe3	a
132	0x84	„	164	0xa4	¤	196	0xc4	Ä	228	0xe4	ä
133	0x85	…	165	0xa5	¥	197	0xc5	Å	229	0xe5	å
134	0x86	†	166	0xa6	¦	198	0xc6	Æ	230	0xe6	æ
135	0x87	‡	167	0xa7	§	199	0xc7	Ç	231	0xe7	ç
136	0x88	^	168	0xa8	¨	200	0xc8	E	232	0xe8	è
137	0x89	‰	169	0xa9	©	201	0xc9	É	233	0xe9	é
138	0x8a	Š	170	0xaa	ª	202	0xca	E	234	0xea	ê
139	0x8b	‹	171	0xab	«	203	0xcb	E	235	0xeb	ë
140	0x8c	Œ	172	0xac	¬	204	0xcc	I	236	0xec	ì
141	0x8d	?	173	0xad		205	0xcd	I	237	0xed	í
142	0x8e	Ž	174	0xae	®	206	0xce	I	238	0xee	î
143	0x8f	?	175	0xaf	¯	207	0xcf	I	239	0xef	ï
144	0x90	?	176	0xb0	°	208	0xd0	Ð	240	0xf0	d
145	0x91	'	177	0xb1	±	209	0xd1	Ñ	241	0xf1	ñ
146	0x92	'	178	0xb2	²	210	0xd2	O	242	0xf2	ò
147	0x93	"	179	0xb3	³	211	0xd3	O	243	0xf3	ó
148	0x94	"	180	0xb4	´	212	0xd4	O	244	0xf4	ô
149	0x95	•	181	0xb5	µ	213	0xd5	O	245	0xf5	o
150	0x96	–	182	0xb6	¶	214	0xd6	Ö	246	0xf6	ö
151	0x97	—	183	0xb7	·	215	0xd7	×	247	0xf7	÷
152	0x98	~	184	0xb8	¸	216	0xd8	O	248	0xf8	o
153	0x99	™	185	0xb9	¹	217	0xd9	U	249	0xf9	ù
154	0x9a	š	186	0xba	º	218	0xda	U	250	0xfa	ú
155	0x9b	›	187	0xbb	»	219	0xdb	U	251	0xfb	û
156	0x9c	œ	188	0xbc	¼	220	0xdc	Ü	252	0xfc	ü
157	0x9d	?	189	0xbd	½	221	0xdd	Ý	253	0xfd	ý
158	0x9e	ž	190	0xbe	¾	222	0xde		254	0xfe	
159	0x9f	Ÿ	191	0xbf	¿	223	0xdf	ß	255	0xff	ÿ

FIGURE 2.1

The ASCII chart. Notice that the familiar typewriter (keyboard) characters fall within the first 126 ASCII values. Notice also that the lowercase letters have higher ASCII values than the uppercase letters and that the punctuation marks are scattered in three areas: under the uppercase letters and between the uppercase letters and lower case letters, as well as over the lowercase letters.

Notice that Macadam follows MacIntire, tilson is sandwiched between Wilson and wilson, and Oar follows O'Brien.

It gets much worse. Consider the following six characters, and their ASCII values:

```
Ä (ASCII 142)
ä (ASCII 132)
A (ASCII 65)
a (ASCII 97)
á (ASCII 160)
å (ASCII 134)
```

The numeric ASCII values for the variant forms of "A" are scattered, ranging from 65 to 160. This means that an ASCII sort based on ASCII values of characters will place words containing different versions of "A" in widely scattered locations in the sorted output list. The scattering of specially accented letters would apply to virtually every specially accented character.

Here's an absolutely impossible sorting job for you to sink your teeth into. HTML is a pure-ASCII format that recognizes most of the printable ASCII characters, rendering them much like they would be rendered in any text editor. Several of the printable ASCII characters are ignored by browsers, most notably the acute angle brackets, "< and >." The reason for this is that the acute angle brackets are used as formatting symbols for tags. If they were rendered as characters, every embedded tag would be visible in the browser. Whenever you need to render an angle bracket in an HTML page, you must use special encodings, specifically "<" for the left bracket (ie, the bracket that looks like a less-than symbol), and ">" for the right bracket (ie, the bracket that looks like a greater-than symbol). By substituting a four-character encoding for a single ASCII character, it becomes impossible to produce a sensible character-by-character sort on HTML character strings.

The situation is made even more impossible (if such a thing exists) by the use of alternative sequences of characters that are meant to represent single ASCII characters. For example, consider the following HTML document, and its browser rendering.

```
<html><head></head>
<h2>
<br>&#224; &agrave;
<br>&#225; &aacute;
<br>&#226; &acirc;
<br>&#227; &atilde;
<br>&#228; &auml;
<br>&#229; &aring;
<br>&#230; &aelig;
<br>&#231; &ccedil;
<br>&#232; &egrave;
<br>&#233; &eacute;
<br>&#234; &ecirc;
<br>&#235; &euml;
```

```
<br>&#236; &igrave;
<br>&#237; &iacute;
<br>&#238; &icirc;
<br>&#239; &iuml;
</h2>
</html>
```

There is simply no way to order a word sensibly when the characters in the word can be represented by any one of several encodings (Fig. 2.2).

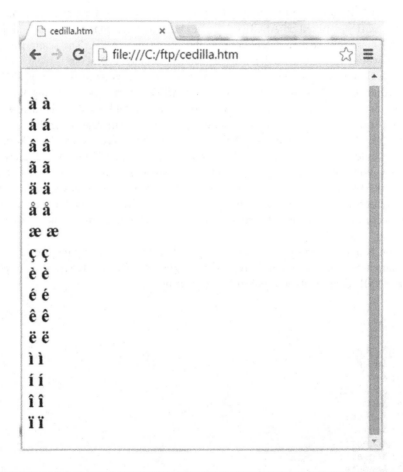

FIGURE 2.2

A Web browser rendition of each of the characters represented in the preceding HTML document. Notice that each pair of encodings, listed line-by-line in the HTML document, is represented by a character that is not included in the standard keyboard.

Textual data would be simple to sort if every character in a data file consisted exclusively of so-called printable ASCII. Here are the printable ASCII characters:

```
!"#$%&'()*+,-./0123456789:;<=>
?@ABCDEFGHIJKLMNOPQRSTUVWXYZ
[\]^_'abcdefghijklmnopqrstuvwxyz{|}~
```

The so-called printable ASCII characters are the subset of printable characters that appear on the standard computer keyboard. Technically, the list of printable characters includes at least a dozen special characters (eg, accented letters, diacriticals, common symbols). As used here and elsewhere, the printable characters are the keyboard characters listed above.

If the printable ASCII characters are what you truly desire, any corpus of text can be converted into printable ASCII with one line of Perl code, that I refer to as my Procrustean translator. Procrustes was a mythical Greek giant who was a thief and a murderer. He would capture travelers and tie them to an iron bed. If they were longer than the bed, he would hack off their limbs until they fit.

The Perl script, unprintable.pl, that replaces unprintable ASCII characters with a space and leaves everything else unchanged:

```perl
#!/usr/local/bin/perl
$var = "µ½¼ßüéâäàèïÇÉúêæ That's all folks!";
$var =~ tr/\012\015\040-\176/ /c;
print $var;
exit;
```

Output of the Perl script, unprintable.pl:

```
c:\ftp>unprintable.pl
               That's all folks!
```

The so-called unprintable letters inside the input variable, "µ½¼ßüéâäàèïÇÉúêæ" were replaced by spaces, and the printable characters, "That's all folks!" were left intact. The Procrustean translator lacks subtlety, but it gets the job done.

Here is a nearly equivalent Python script, printable.py:

```python
#!/usr/local/bin/python
# -*- coding: iso-8859-15 -*-
import string
in_string = "prinüéêçâäàtable"
out_string = filter(lambda x: x in string.printable, in_string)
print out_string
exit
```

Notice that printable.py contains a specialized line that informs the Python interpreter that the script is coded in the iso-8859-15 character set, a variant of ASCII that replaces some of the nonalphabetic ASCII characters with Europeanized nonkeyboard alphabetic characters.

Here is the output of printable.py

```
c:\ftp>printable.py
printable
```

A less brutal script would attempt to map common nonkeyboard characters to their closes printable versions. For example, ü would be replaced by u, é by e, â by a, Ç by c. Some nonprintable characters can be replaced by words (eg, μ by microns, ½ by one-half, ß by beta). Any such program would need to be updated from time to time, to cope with evolving character standards, such as UTF (see Glossary item, UTF).

Here is a short Perl script, non_keyboard.pl, that strips nonkeyboard characters, with the exception of about two dozen commonly occurring nonkeyboard characters that can be mapped to recognizably near-equivalent printable characters or printable words.

```perl
#!/usr/local/bin/perl
$var = "μ½¼ßüéâäàèïÇÉúêæ";
$var =~ s/×/ x /g;
$var =~ s/-/\-/g;
$var =~ s/—/\-/g;
$var =~ s/"/\"/g;
$var =~ s/"/\"/g;
$var =~ s/'/\'/g;
$var =~ s/'/\'/g;
$var =~ s/μ/ microns /g;
$var =~ s/½/ one-half /g;
$var =~ s/¼/ one-quarter /g;
$var =~ s/ß/ beta /g;
$var =~ s/æ/ae/g;
$var =~ tr/üéâäàèïÇÉúê/ueaaaeiCEue/;
$var =~ tr/\012\015\040-\176/ /c;
print "The input, \"μ½¼ßüéâäàèïÇÉúêæ\" has been modified to \"$var\"";
exit;
```

Here is the output of the non_keyboard.pl script.

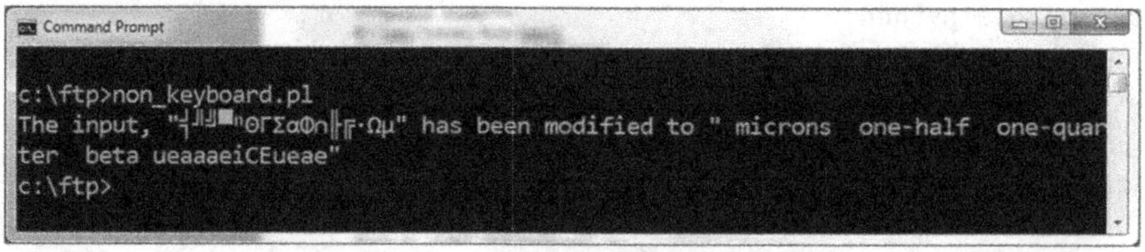

FIGURE 2.3

The output of the Perl script non_keyboard.pl. The nonprintable input string has been translated to the printable output string, "microns one-half one-quarter beta ueaaaeiCEueae."

Notice that the input string appearing in the non_keyboard.pl Perl script is "µ½¼ßüéâäàèïÇÉúêæ," while the rendition of the same input screen, on the monitor, is a collection of straight-angled rods and several Greek letters. This happens because the monitor translates ASCII values to a different set of display characters than does the text editor used to produce the non_keyboard.pl Perl script. This is one more example of the unwanted and perplexing consequences that occur when employing nonprintable characters within textual data sets (Fig. 2.3).

Of course, this short script can be modified to translate any quantity of text files containing nonkeyboard characters into text files composed exclusively of keyboard characters. If you need to sort text ASCIIbetically, then you should seriously consider running your files through a script that enforces pure printable-ASCII content.

2.3 SENTENCE PARSING

We'd all have been better off to have read half as many books. Twice.

-Dick Cavett

Sentences are the units of language that contain complete thoughts and meaningful assertions. Hence, you might expect that programming languages would be designed to parse through text files sentence-by-sentence. This is not the case. Programming languages parse through text documents line-by-line (see Glossary item, Line). For the data scientist who is trying to make sense of plain-text data, information extracted from lines of text can be deceiving. For example, consider these two lines

```
By all means, pull the emergency cord
if you want us all to die!
```

Here, we have one sentence, with a newline break after the word "cord." If we had constructed a program that parsed and interpreted text line-by-line, we might have concluded that pulling the emergency cord is a good thing. If we had constructed a program that parsed and interpreted text sentence-by-sentence, we might have averted catastrophe.

The process of structuring text begins with extracting sentences. Here is a short Perl script, sentence.pl, that operates on the first paragraph of verse from Lewis Carroll's poem, Jabberwocky.

```
#!/usr/local/bin/perl
$all_text =
"And, has thou slain the Jabberwock? Come
to my arms, my beamish boy! O frabjous
day! Callooh! Callay! He chortled in his
joy. Lewis Carroll, excerpted from
Jabberwocky";
```

```
$all_text =~ s/\n/ /g;
$all_text =~ s/([^A-Z]+[\.\!\?][ \n]{1,3})([A-Z])/$1\n$2/g;
print $all_text;
exit;
```

Here is the output of the sentence.pl script. Notice that the lines of the original text have been assembled as individual sentences.

```
c:\ftp\pl>sentence.pl
And, has thou slain the Jabberwock?
Come to my arms, my beamish boy!
O frabjous day!
Callooh!
Callay!
He chortled in his joy.
Lewis Carroll, excerpted from Jabberwocky
```

The script loads the text into a single string variable and removes the newline characters (ie, the line breaks), replacing them with a space. Next, the script inserts a line break character at patterns that are likely to occur at the ends of sentences. Specifically, the pattern match searches for a sequence of lowercase letters, followed by a sentence delimiting character (ie, a period, a question mark or an exclamation mark), followed by one to three spaces, followed by an uppercase letter. We will use sentence parsing routines in scripts that appear in later chapters. For now, here is the equivalent script, sentence.py, in Python:

```
#!/usr/local/bin/python
import re
all_text =\
"And, has thou slain the Jabberwock? Come \
to my arms, my beamish boy! O frabjous \
day! Callooh! Callay! He chortled in his \
joy. Lewis Carroll, excerpted from \
Jabberwocky";
sentence_list = re.split(r'[\.\!\?] +(?=[A-Z])', all_text)
print '\n'.join(sentence_list)
exit
```

Here is the equivalent script, sentence.rb, in Ruby:

```
#!/usr/local/bin/ruby
all_text =\
"And, has thou slain the Jabberwock? Come \
to my arms, my beamish boy! O frabjous \
day! Callooh! Callay! He chortled in his \
```

```
joy. Lewis Carroll, excerpted from \
Jabberwocky";
all_text.split(/[\.\!\?]+(?=[A-Z])/).each {|phrase| puts phrase}
exit
```

After a textual document is parsed into sentences, the next step often involves feeding the sentences to a natural language processor (see Glossary items, Natural language processing, Machine learning, Dark data). Each sentence is parsed into assigned grammatical tokens (eg, A = adjective, D = determiner, N = noun, P = preposition, V = main verb). A determiner is a word such as "a" or "the," that specifies the noun.[7]

Consider the sentence, "The quick brown fox jumped over lazy dogs." This sentence can be grammatically tokenized as:

the::D
quick::A
brown::A
fox::N
jumped::V
over::P
the::D
lazy::A
dog::N

We can express the sentence as a sequence of its tokens listed in the order of occurrence in the sentence: DAANVPDAN. This does not seem like much of a breakthrough, but imagine having a large collection of such token sequences representing every sentence from a large text corpus. With such a data set, we could begin to understand the rules of sentence structure. Commonly recurring sequences, like DAANVPDAN, might be assumed to be proper sentences. Sequences that occur uniquely in a large text corpus are probably poorly constructed sentences. Before long, we might find ourselves constructing logic rules that reduce the complexity of sentences by dropping subsequences which, when removed, yield a sequence that occurs more commonly than the original sequence. For example, our table of sequences might indicate that we can convert DAANVPDAN into NVPAN (ie, "Fox jumped over lazy dog"), without sacrificing too much of the meaning from the original sentence and preserving a grammatical sequence that occurs commonly in the text corpus.

This short example serves as an overly simplistic introduction to natural language processing. We can begin to imagine that the grammatical rules of a language can be represented by sequences of tokens that can be translated into words or phrases from a second language, and reordered according to grammatical rules appropriate to the target language. Many natural language processing projects involve transforming text into a new form, with desirable properties (eg, other languages, an index, a collection of names, a new text with words and phrases replaced with canonical forms extracted from a nomenclature).[7]

2.4 ABBREVIATIONS

A synonym is a word you use when you can't spell the other one.

-Baltasar Gracian

People confuse shortening with simplifying; a terrible mistake. In point of fact, next to reifying pronouns, abbreviations are the most vexing cause of complex and meaningless language. Before we tackle the complexities of abbreviations, let's define our terms. An abbreviation is a shortened form of a word or term. An acronym is a an abbreviation composed of letters extracted from the words composing a multi-word term. There are two major types of abbreviations: universal/permanent and local/ephemeral. The universal/permanent abbreviations are recognized everywhere and have been used for decades (eg, USA, DNA, UK). Some of the universal/permanent abbreviations ascend to the status of words whose long-forms have been abandoned. For example, we use laser as a word. Few who use the term know that "laser" is an acronym for "light amplification by stimulated emission of radiation." Likewise, we use "AIDS" as a word, forgetting that it is an acronym for "acquired immune deficiency syndrome." The acronym is inaccurate, as AIDS is not a primary immunodeficiency disease; it is a viral disease for which immunodeficiency is a secondary complication. Local/ephemeral abbreviations are created for terms that are repeated within a particular document or a particular class of documents. Synonyms and plesionyms (ie, near-synonyms) allow authors to represent a single concept using alternate terms (see Glossary item, Plesionymy).[8]

Abbreviations make textual data complex, for three principle reasons:

1. No rules exist with which abbreviations can be logically expanded to their full-length form.
2. A single abbreviation may mean different things to different individuals, or to the same individual at different times.
3. A single term may have multiple different abbreviations. (In medicine, angioimmunoblastic lymphadenopathy can be abbreviated as ABL, AIL, or AIML.) These are the so-called polysemous abbreviations (see Glossary item, Polysemy). In the medical literature, a single abbreviations may have dozens of different expansions.[8]

Some of the worst abbreviations fall into one of the following categories:

Abbreviations that are neither acronyms nor shortened forms of expansions. For example, the short form of "diagnosis" is "dx," although no "x" is contained therein. The same applies to the "x" in "tx," the abbreviation for "therapy," but not the "X" in "TX" that stands for Texas. For that matter, the short form of "times" is an "x," relating to the notation for the multiplication operator. Roman numerals I, V, X, L, and M are abbreviations for words assigned to numbers, but they are not characters included in the expanded words (eg, there is no "I" in "one"). EKG is the abbreviation for electrocardiogram, a word totally bereft of any "K." The "K" comes from the German orthography. There is no letter "q" in subcutaneous, but the abbreviation for the word is sometimes "subq;" never "subc." What form of alchemy converts ethanol to its common abbreviation, "EtOH?"

Mixed-form abbreviations. In medical lingo "DSV" represents the dermatome of the fifth (V) sacral nerve. Here a preposition, an article, and a noun (of, the, nerve) have all been unceremoniously excluded from the abbreviation; the order or the acronym components have been transposed (dermatome sacral fifth); an ordinal has been changed to a cardinal (fifth changed to five), and the cardinal has been shortened to its roman numeral equivalent (V).

Prepositions and articles arbitrarily retained in an acronym. When creating an abbreviation, should we retain or abandon prepositions? Many acronyms exclude prepositions and articles. USA is the acronym for United States of America; the "of" is ignored. DOB (Date Of Birth) remembers the "of."

Single expansions with multiple abbreviations. Just as abbreviations can map to many different expansions, the reverse can occur. For instance, high-grade squamous intraepithelial lesion can be abbreviated as HGSIL or HSIL. Xanthogranulomatous pyelonephritis can be abbreviated as xgp or xgpn.

Recursive abbreviations. The following example exemplifies the horror of recursive abbreviations. The term SMETE is the abbreviation for the phrase "science, math, engineering, and technology education." NSDL is a real-life abbreviation, for "National SMETE digital Library community." To fully expand the term (ie, to provide meaning to the abbreviation), you must recursively expand the embedded abbreviation, to produce "National science, math, engineering, and technology education digital Library community."

Stupid or purposefully nonsensical abbreviations. The term GNU (Gnu is not UNIX) is a recursive acronym. Fully expanded, this acronym is of infinite length. Although the N and the U expand to words ("Not Unix"), the letter G is simply inscrutable. Another example of an inexplicable abbreviation is PT-LPD (post-transplantation lymphoproliferative disorders). The only logical location for a hyphen would be smack between the letters p and t. Is the hyphen situated between the T and the L for the sole purpose of irritating us?

Abbreviations that change from place to place. Americans sometimes forget that most English-speaking countries use British English. For example an esophagus in New York is an oesophagus in London. Hence TOF makes no sense as an abbreviation of tracheo-esophageal fistula here in the U.S., but this abbreviation makes perfect sense to physicians in England, where a patients may have a tracheo-oesophageal fistula. The term GERD (representing the phrase gastroesophageal reflux disease) makes perfect sense to Americans, but it must be confusing in Britain, where the esophagus is not an organ.

Abbreviations masquerading as words. Our greatest vitriol is reserved for abbreviations that look just like common words. Some of the worst offenders come from the medical lexicon: axillary node dissection (AND), acute lymphocytic leukemia (ALL), Bornholm eye disease (BED), and expired air resuscitation (EAR). Such acronyms aggravate the computational task confidently translating common words. Acronyms commonly appear as uppercase strings, but a review of a text corpus of medical notes has shown that words could not be consistently distinguished from homonymous word-acronyms.[9]

Fatal abbreviations. Fatal abbreviations are those which can kill individuals if they are interpreted incorrectly. They all seem to originate in the world of medicine:

MVR, which can be expanded to any of: mitral valve regurgitation, mitral valve repair, or mitral valve replacement;

LLL, which can be expanded to any of: left lower lid, left lower lip, or left lower lung;

DOA, dead on arrival, date of arrival, date of admission, drug of abuse.

Is a fear of abbreviations rational, or does this fear emanate from an overactive imagination? In 2004, the Joint Commission on Accreditation of Healthcare Organizations, a stalwart institution not known to be squeamish, issued an announcement that, henceforth, a list of specified abbreviations should be excluded from medical records Rboodr.

Examples of Forbidden abbreviations are:

IU (International Unit), mistaken as IV (intravenous) or 10 (ten).

Q.D., Q.O.D. (Latin abbreviation for once daily and every other day), mistaken for each other.

Trailing zero (X.0 mg) or a lack of a leading zero (.X mg), in which cases the decimal point may be missed. Never write a zero by itself after a decimal point (X mg), and always use a zero before a decimal point (0.X mg).

MS, MSO4, MgSO4, all of which can be confused with one another and with morphine sulfate or magnesium sulfate. Write "morphine sulfate" or "magnesium sulfate."

Abbreviations on the hospital watch list were:

mg (for microgram), mistaken for mg (milligrams), resulting in a 1000-fold dosing overdose.

h.s., which can mean either half-strength or the Latin abbreviation for bedtime or may be mistaken for q.h.s., taken every hour. All can result in a dosing error.

T.I.W. (for three times a week), mistaken for three times a day or twice weekly, resulting in an overdose.

The list of abbreviations that can kill, in the medical setting, is quite lengthy. Fatal abbreviations probably devolved through imprecise, inconsistent, or idiosyncratic uses of an abbreviation, by the busy hospital staff who enter notes and orders into patient charts. For any knowledge domain, the potentially fatal abbreviations is the most important to catch.

Nobody has ever found an accurate way of disambiguating and translating abbreviations.[8] There are, however a few simple suggestions, based on years of exasperating experience, that might save you time and energy.

1. Disallow the use of abbreviations, whenever possible. Abbreviations never enhance the value of information. The time saved by using an abbreviation is far exceeded by the time spent attempting to deduce its correct meaning.

2. When writing software applications that find and expand abbreviations, the output should list every known expansion of the abbreviation. For example, the abbreviation, "ppp," appearing in a medical report, should have all these expansions inserted into the text, as annotations: pancreatic polypeptide, palatopharyngoplasty, palmoplantar pustulosis, pancreatic polypeptide, pentose phosphate pathway, platelet poor plasma, primary proliferative polycythaemia, or primary proliferative polycythemia. Leave it up to the knowledge domain experts to disambiguate the results.

2.5 ANNOTATION AND THE SIMPLE SCIENCE OF METADATA

All parts should go together without forcing. You must remember that the parts you are reassembling were disassembled by you. Therefore, if you can't get them together again, there must be a reason. By all means, do not use a hammer.

-IBM Manual, 1925

Free text is most useful when it is marked with tags that describe the text. Tags can also provide marked text with functionality (eg, linkage to a Web page, linkage to some other section of text, linkage to an image, activation of a script). By marking text with tags, it is possible to transform a document into an ersatz database, that can be integrated with other documents, and queried. This section describes the fundamentals of markup, particularly HTML and XML.

HTML (HyperText Markup Language) is a collection of format descriptors for text and data. All Web browsers are designed to interpret embedded HTML metadata tags and to display the enclosed data (see Glossary item, Metadata). Tags tell browsers how they should display the tagged object (the object described with metadata).

For example:

```
<font size=72>This book, <i>Data Simplification</i>, is <b>way cool.</b></font>
```

The <font size=72> tag provides the Web browser with the size of the text that needs to be displayed. The </font> tag marks the end of the text to which the font size instruction applies. Similarly, within the enclosed text, a <i> tag indicates the start of italicized text, and a <b> tag indicates the start of bolded text (Fig. 2.4).

This book, *Data Simplification*, is **way cool.**

FIGURE 2.4

A sentence, with HTML mark-up, as it is displayed in a Web browser.

Before there was HTML, there were file formats that contained embedded tags indicating how the text should be displayed by the word processing application. In the 1980s, XyWrite files were popular among professional writers, because they contained embedded formatting instructions that were accepted by the publishing industry. The commercial XyWrite word processing application was fast and could handle large files. What XyWrite and its competitors could not do, and what HTML provided, was markup instructions for linking parts of one document with parts of another document, and for retrieving specified objects (eg, other Web pages, image files, external programs) from some selected location on the Internet. Internet locations are known as URLs (Uniform Resource Locators). When your browser encounters a link tag, it sends a request to have the object at the URL delivered to the browser. The request and response are negotiated using HTTP (HyperText Transfer Protocol). Your browser formats the Web page, and assembles the linked external data objects specified by the HTML tags found in the Web page document (see Glossary item, Data object).

The strength of HTML is its remarkable simplicity. A few dozen HTML tags are all that are needed to create glorious Web pages, with active links to any location in the Web universe.

HTML is referred to as a specification, because it specifies formatting information for the browser (see Glossary items, Specification, Specification versus standard). It is the browser that produces a visual output that conforms to the specified instructions embedded in textual metadata.

While HTML tells Web browsers how to format Web pages (ie, what Web pages should look like when they are displayed in a browser), HTML tells us nothing about the data being displayed. XML (eXtensible Markup Language) is a markup protocol that binds data elements to metadata, the descriptors of the data (see Glossary item, Protocol).[10,11] Surprisingly, this simple relationship between data and the data that describes data is the most powerful innovation in data organization since the invention of the book. Seldom does a technology emerge with all the techniques required for its success, but this seems to be the case for XML.

In XML, data descriptors (known as XML tags) enclose the data they describe with angle-brackets, much as HTML encloses text with formatting instructions.

<date>June 16, 1904</date>

The tag, <date> and its end-tag, </date> enclose a data element, which in this case is the unabbreviated month, beginning with an uppercase letter and followed by lowercase letters, followed by a space, followed by a two-digit numeric for the date of the month, followed by a comma and space, followed by the 4-digit year. The XML tag could have been defined in a separate document detailing the data format of the data element described by the XML tag. ISO-11179 is a standard that explains how to specify the properties of tags (see Glossary item, ISO-11179).

If we had chosen to, we could have broken the <date> tag into its constituent parts.

```
<date>
<month>June</month>
<day>16</day>
<year>1904</year>
</date>
```

Six properties of XML explain its extraordinary utility.[10,11] These are:

1. *Enforced and defined structure (XML rules and schema)*: An XML file is well-formed if it conforms to the basic rules for XML file construction recommended by the W3C (Worldwide Web Consortium). This means that it must be a plain-text file, with a header indicating that it is an XML file, and must enclose data elements with metadata tags that declare the start and end of the data element. The tags must conform to certain rules (eg, alphanumeric strings without intervening spaces) and must also obey the rules for nesting data elements.[10,12] A metadata/data pair may be contained within another metadata/data pair (so-called nesting), but a metadata/data pair cannot straggle over another metadata/data pair. Most browsers will parse XML files, rejecting files that are not well-formed. The ability to ensure that every XML file conforms to basic rules of metadata tagging and nesting makes it possible to extract XML files as sensible data structures.

2. *Reserved namespaces*: Namespaces preserve the intended meaning of tags whose meanings might otherwise change Web page to Web page (see Glossary item, Namespace). When you encounter the XML tag <date>, would you know whether the tag referred to a calendar date, or the fruit known as date, or the social encounter known as date? A namespace is the realm in which a metadata tag applies. The purpose of a namespace is to distinguish metadata tags that have the same name, but a different meaning. For example, within a single XML file, the metadata tag "date" may be used to signify a calendar date, or the fruit, or the social engagement. To avoid confusion, metadata terms are assigned a prefix that is associated with a Web document that defines the term (ie, establishes the tag's namespace). For example, an XML page might contain three "date" tags, each prefixed with a code that identifies the namespace that defines the intended meaning for the date tag.

```
<calendar:date>June 16, 1904</calendar:date>
<agriculture:date>Thoory</agriculture:date>
<social:date>Pyramus and Thisbe<social:date>
```

At the top of the XML document you would expect to find links to the three URL locations (ie, Web addresses) where the namespaces appearing in the XML snippet (ie, "calendar:," "agriculture:," and "social:") can be found. If you followed the links to these three namespaces, you would find the definition of "date" used within each respective namespace. See URL.

3. *Linking data via the internet*: XML comes with specifications for linking XML documents with other XML documents, or with any external file that has a specific identifier or Web location (see Glossary items, URN, URL). This means that there is a logical and standard method for linking any XML document or any part of any XML document, including individual data elements, to any other uniquely identified resource (eg, Web page).

4. *Logic and meaning*: Although the technical methodologies associated with XML can be daunting, the most difficult issues always relate to the meaning of things. A variety of formal approaches have been proposed to reach the level of meaning within the context of XML. The simplest of these is the Resource Description Framework (see Glossary item, RDF). The importance of the RDF model is that it binds data and metadata to a unique object with a Web location. Consistent use of the RDF model assures that data anywhere on the Web can always be connected through unique objects using RDF descriptions. The association of described data with a unique object confers meaning and greatly advances our ability to integrate data over the internet. RDF will be discussed in much greater detail in Open Source Tools for Chapter 6.

5. *Self-awareness*: Because XML can be used to describe anything, it can certainly be used to describe a query related to an XML page. Furthermore, it can be used to describe protocols for transferring data, performing Web services, or describing the programmer interface to databases. It can describe the rules for interoperability for any data process, including peer-to-peer data sharing. When an XML file is capable of displaying autonomous behavior, composing queries, merging replies and transforming its own content, it is usually referred to as a software agent.

6. *Formal metadata*: The International Standards Organization has created a standard way of defining metadata tags, (the ISO-11179 specification (see Glossary items, ISO, ANSI, American National Standards Institute).

2.6 SPECIFICATIONS GOOD, STANDARDS BAD

> The nice thing about standards is that you have so many to choose from.
>
> **-Andrew S. Tanenbaum**

Data standards are the false gods of informatics. They promise miracles, but they can't deliver. The biggest drawback of standards is that they change all the time. If you take the time to read some of the computer literature from the 1970s or 1980s, you will come across the names of standards that have long since fallen into well-deserved obscurity. You may find that the computer literature from the 1970s is nearly impossible to read with any level of comprehension, due to the large number of now-obsolete standards-related acronyms scattered through every page. Today's eternal standard is tomorrow's indecipherable gibberish.[7]

The Open Systems Interconnection (OSI) was an internet protocol created in 1977 with approval from the International Organization for Standardization. It has been supplanted by TCP/IP, the protocol that everyone uses today. A handful of programming languages has been recognized as standards by the

American National Standards Institute. These include Basic, C, Ada, and Mumps. Basic and C are still popular languages. Ada, recommended by the Federal Government, back in 1995 for all high performance software applications, is virtually forgotten.[13] Mumps is still in use, particularly in hospital information systems, but it changed its name to M, lost its allure to a new generation of programmers, and now comes in various implementations that may not strictly conform to the original standard.

In many cases, as a standard matures, it often becomes hopelessly complex. As the complexity becomes unmanageable, those who profess to use the standard may develop their own idiosyncratic implementations. Organizations that produce standards seldom provide a mechanism to ensure that the standard is implemented correctly. Standards have long been plagued by noncompliance or (more frequently) under-compliance. Over time, so-called standard-compliant systems tend to become incompatible with one another. The net result is that legacy data, purported to conform to a standard format, is no longer understandable (see Glossary items, Legacy data, Dark data).

Malcolm Duncan has posted an insightful and funny essay entitled "The Chocolate Teapot (version 2.3)."[14] In this essay, he shows how new versions of standards may unintentionally alter the meanings of classes of terms contained in earlier versions, making it impossible to compare or sensibly aggregate and interpret terms and concepts contained in any of the versions.[7]

Suppose you have a cooking-ware terminology with a "teapot" item. Version 1 of the nomenclature may list only one teapot material, porcelain, and only two permissible teapot colors, blue or white. Version 2 of the terminology might accommodate two teapot subtypes: blue teapot and white teapot (ie, in version 2, blue and white are subtypes of teapot, not colors of teapot). If a teapot were neither blue nor white, it would be coded under the parent term, "teapot." Suppose version 3 accommodates some new additions to the teapot pantheon: chocolate teapot, ornamental teapot, china teapot, and industrial teapot. Now the teapot world is shaken by a tempest of monumental proportions. The white and the blue teapots had been implicitly considered to be made of porcelain, like all china teapots. How does one deal with a white teapot that is not porcelain or a porcelain teapot that is a china teapot? If we had previously assumed that a teapot was an item in which tea is made, how do we adjust, conceptually, to the new term "ornamental teapot?" If the teapot is ornamental, then it has no tea-making functionality, and if it cannot be used to make tea, how can it be a teapot? Must we change our concept of the teapot to include anything that looks like a teapot? If so, how can we deal with the new term "industrial teapot," which is likely to be a big stainless steel vat that has more in common, structurally, with a microbrewery fermenter than with an ornamental teapot? What is the meaning of a chocolate teapot? Is it something made of chocolate, is it chocolate-colored, or does it brew chocolate-flavored tea? Suddenly we have lost the ability to map terms in version 3 to terms in versions 1 and 2 (see Glossary item, Nomenclature mapping). We no longer understand the classes of objects (ie, teapots) in the various versions of our cookware nomenclature. We cannot unambiguously attach nomenclature terms to objects in our data collection (eg, blue china teapot). We no longer have a precise definition of a teapot or of the subtypes of teapot.

Regarding versioning, it is a very good rule of thumb that when you encounter a standard whose name includes a version number (eg, International Classification of Diseases-10 or Diagnostic and Statistical Manual of Mental Disorders-5), you can be certain that the standard is unstable, and must be continually revised. Some continuously revised standards cling tenaciously to life, when they really deserve to die. In some cases, a poor standard is kept alive indefinitely by influential leaders in their fields, or by entities who have an economic stake in perpetuating the standard.

Raymond Kammer, then Director of the U.S. National Institute of Standards and Technology, understood the downside of standards. In a year 2000 government report, he wrote that "the consequences of standards can be negative. For example, companies and nations can use standards to disadvantage competitors. Embodied in national regulations, standards can be crafted to impede export access, sometimes necessitating excessive testing and even redesigns of products. A 1999 survey by the National Association of Manufacturers reported that about half of U.S. small manufacturers find international standards or product certification requirements to be barriers to trade. And according to the Transatlantic Business Dialogue, differing requirements add more than 10% to the cost of car design and development."[15]

As it happens, data standards are seldom, if ever, implemented properly. In some cases, the standards are simply too complex to comprehend. Try as they might, every implementation of a complex standard is somewhat idiosyncratic. Consequently, no two implementations of a complex data standard are equivalent to one another. In many cases, corporations and government agencies will purposefully veer from the standard to accommodate some local exigency. In some cases, a corporation may find it prudent to include nonstandard embellishments to a standard to create products or functionalities that cannot be easily reproduced by their competitors. In such cases, customers accustomed to a particular manufacturer's rendition of a standard may find it impossible to switch providers (see Glossary item, Lock in).

The process of developing new standards is costly. Interested parties must send representatives to many meetings. In the case of international standards, meetings occur in locations throughout the planet. Someone must pay for the expertise required to develop the standard, improve drafts, and vet the final version. Standards development agencies become involved in the process, and the final product must be approved by one of the agencies that confer final approval. After a standard is approved, it must be accepted by its intended community of users. Educating a community in the use of a standard is another expense. In some cases, an approved standard never gains traction. Because standards cost a great deal of money to develop, it is only natural that corporate sponsors play a major role in the development and deployment of new standards. Software vendors are clever and have learned to benefit from the standards-making process. In some cases, members of a standards committee may knowingly insert a fragment of their own patented property into the standard. After the standard is released and implemented, in many different vendor systems, the patent holder rises to assert the hidden patent. In this case, all those who implemented the standard may find themselves required to pay a royalty for the use of intellectual property sequestered within the standard (see Glossary items, Patent farming, Intellectual property).[1]

Savvy standards committees take measures to reduce patent farming. Such measures may take the form of agreements, signed by all members of the standards committee, to refrain from asserting patent claims on the standard. There are several ways to circumvent and undermine these agreements. If a corporation holds patents on components of a standard, the corporation can sell their patents to a third party. The third party would be a so-called patent holding company that buys patents in selected technologies with the intention of eventually asserting patents over an array of related activities.[16] If the patent holder asserts the patent, the corporation might profit from patent farming, through their sale of the patent, without actually breaking the agreement (see Glossary item, Patent farming).

Corporations can profit from standards indirectly, by obtaining patents on the uses of the standard; not on the patent itself. For example, an open standard may have been created that can be obtained at no cost, and that is popular among its intended users, and that contains no hidden intellectual property (see Glossary items, Open standard, Intellectual property). An interested corporation or individual may discover a novel use for the standard. The corporation or individual can patent the use of the standard, without needing to patent the standard itself. The patent holder will have the legal right to assert the patent over anyone who uses the standard for the purpose claimed by the patent. This patent protection will apply even when the standard is free and open.[1]

Despite the problems inherent in standards, government committees cling to standards as the best way to share data. The perception is that in the absence of standards, the necessary activities of data sharing, data verification, data analysis, and any meaningful validation of the conclusions will be impossible to achieve.[17] This long-held perception may not be true. Data standards, intended to simplify our ability to understand and share data, may have increased the complexity of data science. As each new standard is born, our ability to understand our data seems to diminish. Luckily, many of the problems produced by the proliferation of data standards can be avoided by switching to a data annotation technique broadly known as "specification." Although the terms "specification" and "standard" are used interchangeably, by the incognoscenti, the two terms are quite different from one another. A specification is a formal way of describing data. A standard is a set of requirements, created by a standards development organization, that comprise a predetermined content and format for a set of data (see Glossary items, Specification, Specification versus standard).

A specification is an accepted method for describing objects (physical objects such as nuts and bolts; or symbolic objects, such as numbers; or concepts expressed as text). In general, specifications do not require explicit items of information (ie, they do not impose restrictions on the content that is included in or excluded from documents), and specifications do not impose any order of appearance of the data contained in the document (ie, you can mix up and rearrange the data records in a specification if you like). Specifications are not generally certified by a standards organization. Examples of specifications are RDF (Resource Description Framework) produced by the W3C (World Wide Web Consortium), and TCP/IP (Transfer Control Protocol/Internet Protocol), maintained by the Internet Engineering Task Force. The most widely implemented specifications are simple; thus, easily adaptable.

Specifications, unlike standards, do not tell you what data must be included in a document. A specification simply provides a uniform way of representing the information you choose to include. Some of the most useful and popular specifications are XML, RDF, Notation 3, and Turtle (see Glossary items, XML, RDF, Notation 3, Turtle). In general, specifications do not require explicit items of information (ie, they do not impose restrictions on the content that is included in or excluded from documents), and specifications do not impose any order of appearance of the data contained in the document (ie, you can mix up and rearrange the data records in a specification if you like). Specifications are not typically certified by a standards organization, but they are developed by special interest groups. Their legitimacy depends on their popularity.

Files that comply with a specification can be parsed and manipulated by generalized software designed to parse the markup language of the specification (eg, XML, RDF) and to organize the data into data structures defined within the file.

Specifications serve most of the purposes of a standard, plus providing many important functions that standards typically lack (eg, full data description, data exchange across diverse types of data sets, data merging, and semantic logic) (see Glossary item, Semantics). Data specifications spare us most of the heavy baggage that comes with a standard, which includes: limited flexibility to include changing diverse data objects, locked-in data descriptors, licensing and other intellectual property issues, competition among standards that compete within the same data domain, and bureaucratic overhead (see Glossary item, Intellectual property).[7]

Most importantly, specifications make standards fungible. A good specification can be ported into a data standard, and a reasonably good data standard can be ported into a specification. For example, there are dozens of image formats (eg, jpeg, png, gif, tiff). Although these formats have not gone through a standards development process, they are used by billions of individuals and have achieved the status as de facto standards. For most of us, the selection of any particular image format is inconsequential. Data scientists have access to robust image software that will convert images from one format to another.

The most common mistake committed by data scientists is to convert legacy data (ie, old data incompatible with the data held in a newer information system) directly into a contemporary standard, and using analytic software that is designed to operate exclusively upon the chosen standard (see Glossary item, Legacy data). Doing so only serves to perpetuate your legacy-related frustrations. You can be certain that your data standard and your software application will be unsuitable for the next generation of data scientists. It makes much more sense to port legacy data into a general specification, from which data can be ported to any current or future data standard.

OPEN SOURCE TOOLS

> Some people, when confronted with a problem, think 'I know, I'll use regular expressions.' Now they have two problems.
>
> **-Jamie Zawinski**

ASCII

ASCII is the American Standard Code for Information Interchange, ISO-14962-1997. The ASCII standard is a way of assigning specific 8-bit strings (a string of 0s and 1s of length 8) to the alphanumeric characters and punctuation. Uppercase letters are assigned a different string of 0s and 1s than their corresponding lowercase letters. There are 256 ways of combining 0s and 1s in strings of length 8, and this means there are 256 different ASCII characters.

The familiar keyboard keys produce ASCII characters that happen to occupy ASCII values under 128. Hence, alphanumerics and common punctuation are represented as 8-bits, with the first bit, "0" serving as padding; and keyboard characters are commonly referred to as 7-bit ASCII. Files composed of common keyboard characters, are commonly referred to as plain-text files or as 7-bit ASCII files. Applications that display and edit unformatted, 7-bit ASCII files, are referred to as text editors. For some uses, the 256 ASCII character limit is too constraining. There are many languages in the world, with their own alphabets or with their own versions of ASCII Romanized alphabet. Consequently, a new character code (UNICODE) has been designed as an expansion of ASCII. To maintain facile software conversion from ASCII to Unicode, ASCII is embedded in the Unicode standard (see Glossary items, Text editor, Plain-text).

REGULAR EXPRESSIONS

Every graduate student working through any of the fields of science anticipates a future life involved with the deep analysis of data. This dream can come true, to some extent, but the majority of every scientist's time is devoted to the dirty job of structuring data into a useful format. I feel justified in referring to this activity as "dirty," because most of the terms that describe this activity convey the notion that data needs to be cleansed or rehabilitated prior to use (see Glossary items, Data cleaning, Data flattening, Data fusion, Data merging, Data mining, Data munging, Data reduction, Data scraping, Data scrubbing, Data wrangling). The common denominator for data restructuring is pattern matching; finding a pattern in the data that requires substitution or transformation, or relocation. Hence, every serious data scientist must master Regular expressions, the universal syntax for expressing string patterns.

Regular expressions, commonly referred to as Regex, refers to the standard pattern-matching syntax used in most modern programming languages, including Perl, Python, and Ruby. Some word processing applications, such as OpenOffice, also support Regex string searches.

Here are the basic pattern notations used in Regex:

```
g      Match globally, (find all occurrences).
i      Do case-insensitive pattern matching.
m      Treat string as multiple lines.
o      Compile pattern only once.
s      Treat string as single line.
x      Use extended regular expressions.
^      Match the beginning of the line.
.      Match any character (except newline).
$      Match the end of the line (or before newline at the end).
|      Alternation.
()     Grouping.
[]     Character class.
*      Match 0 or more times.
+      Match 1 or more times.
?      Match 1 or 0 times.
{n}    Match exactly n times.
{n,}   Match at least n times.
{n,m}  Match at least n but not more than m times.
\n     newline(LF, NL).
\W     Match a non-word character.
\s     Match a whitespace character.
\S     Match a non-whitespace character.
\d     Match a digit character.
\D     Match a non-digit character.
```

Perl, Ruby, and Python each have the equivalent of a substitution operator that looks for a specific pattern match, within a string, and, finding a match, substitutes another string at the location of the matching pattern.

In Perl, the substitution operator syntax looks like this:

```
$string =~ s/<pattern that you match>/<replacement pattern>/options;
```

Here is a Perl snippet demonstrating Regex substitution:

```
$string =~ s/[\n]+/ /g;
$string =~ s/([^A-Z]+\.[ ]{1,2})([A-Z])/$1\n$2/g;
```

This short snippet uses Perl's substitution operator on a string, to do the following:

1. The first command of the snippet substitutes a space character for every occurrence in the string of one or more carriage returns. By removing all of the carriage returns in the string, the line can produce an output string that occupies a single line.
2. The second command looks through the string for a succession of characters that are not uppercase letters of the alphabet. If such a substring is followed by a period, followed by one or two spaces, followed by a an uppercase letter of the alphabet, it will make a substitution.
3. The substitution will consist of the found pattern described in the first parenthesized group in the search pattern (ie, the string of characters that are not uppercase letters of the alphabet, followed by a period, followed by one or two spaces) and it will insert this found string, followed by a carriage return, followed by the uppercase letter that followed in the string.
4. The second command will continue searching the string for additional pattern matches, making appropriate substitutions for every matching pattern, until it exhausts the original. The string to be searched can comfortably hold the length of an entire book. String length is only limited by the RAM memory of your computer.

What did this complex and seemingly pointless task accomplish? Roughly, the two-line snippet is a sentence parser that transforms a plain-text string into a series of lines, each line composed of a sentence. If you do not immediately see how this is accomplished, here is a hint. Nearly every sentence ends with a non-uppercase character, followed by a period, followed by one or two spaces, followed by the first letter of the next sentence, an uppercase character.

For the uninitiated, Regex can be daunting. The florid inscrutability of Regex expressions, found in virtually every Perl script, contributed greatly to the somewhat cynical assessment, attributed to Keith Bostic, that Perl looks the same before and after encryption (see Glossary item, Encryption). Nonetheless, Regex is an absolute necessity for any data scientist who needs to extract or transform data (ie, every data scientist). Regular expression patterns are identical from language to language. However, the syntax of commands that operate with regular expressions (eg, string substitutions, extractions, and other actions that occur at the location of a pattern match) will vary somewhat among the different programming languages that support Regex.

As another example of the power of Regex, here is a short Perl script that parses through a plain-text book, extracting any text that matches a pattern commonly encountered by given name followed by a family name.

```
#!/usr/local/bin/perl
undef($/);
open (TEXT, "english_lit.txt");
open (OUT, ">english_lit_names.txt");
$line = <TEXT>;
close TEXT;
while ($line =~ /\b[A-Z][a-z]+[ \n]{1}[A-Z][a-z]+\b/g)
   {
   $name = $&;
   $name =~ s/\n/ /;
   next if ($name =~ /^The/);
   next if ($name =~ /^In/);
```

```
    next if ($name =~ /^Of/);
    next if ($name =~ /^In/);
    next if ($name =~ /^In/);
    next if ($name !~ /[A-Z][a-z]+/);
    $namelist{$name} = "";
    }
while ($line =~ /\b[A-Z][a-z]+[\,\n]+[A-Z][\,\.\n]*[A-Z]?[\,\.\n]*[A-Z]?[\,\.\n]*\b/g)
    {
    $name = $&;
    next if ($name =~ /^The/);
    next if ($name =~ /^In/);
    $name =~ s/[\,\.\n]//g;
    next if ($name =~ /{3,}/);
    $name =~ s/ +$//;
    next if ($name !~ /[A-Z][a-z]+/);
    $namelist{$name} = "";
    }
print OUT join("\n", sort(keys(%namelist)));
close OUT;
system 'notepad english_lit_names.txt';
exit;
```

This short script will parse a full-length book almost instantly, producing a long list of alphabetized two-word terms, most of which are legitimate names:

Short sample of output

```
Abbess Hilda
About Project
Abraham Cowley
Abraham Cowper
Abt Vogler
Academy Classics
Adam Bede
Adam Smith
Adelaide Procter
Adelaide Witham
Ado About
After Alfred
Again Beowulf
Albion Series
Aldine Edition
Aldine Poets
Aldine Series
Alexander Pope
Alexander Selkirk
Alfred Lord
Alfred Tennyson
Algernon Charles
Alice Brown
```

```
All Delight
Alloway Kirk
Although Bacon
American Book
American Indians
American Revolution
American Taxation
Amerigo Vespucci
Among Browning
Among Coleridge
Among My
Among Ruskin
Amos Barton
```

You can see that the script is not perfect. The output includes two-word strings that are not names (eg, Ado About, Among My), and it undoubtedly excludes legitimate names (eg, ee cummings, Madonna). Still, it's a start. In Section 3.3 of Chapter 3, we will see how we can add a few lines of code and transform this script into an indexing application.

FORMAT COMMANDS

Format commands are short routines built into many programming languages, that display variables as neat columns of padded or justified words and numbers. Format commands have equivalent functionality in most higher level programming languages (eg, Python, Ruby, Perl, C, Java). The generic name of the format command is usually "printf." The syntax for the printf command involves assigning a field specifier for fields or columns, followed by the list of the variables that will fit the specified fields. Each field specifier consists of a percent sign, followed by an integer that specifies the size of the column, followed by a dot, followed by an integer specifying the maximum size of the element to be placed in the field, followed by a letter indicating the type of element (eg, string, decimal integer, etc.). The following the list of specifiers constitute the most common instructions in printf statements.[18]

Here is a list of printf field specifiers.

```
%% a percent sign
%c a character with the given number
%s a string
%d a signed integer, in decimal
%u an unsigned integer, in decimal
%o an unsigned integer, in octal
%x an unsigned integer, in hexadecimal
%e a floating-point number, in scientific notation
%f a floating-point number, in fixed decimal notation
%g a floating-point number, in %e or %f notation
```

Here is an example of a Perl one-liner, launched from Perl's debugger environment (see Open Source Tools for Chapter 1, Interactive Line Interpreters for Perl, Python, and Ruby).

```
DB<1> printf("%-10.10s %0.1u %7.6u %4.3u\n", "hello", 3, 28, 15, );
```

The one-liner Perl command saves 10 spaces for a string, printing the string from left to right, beginning with the first space. Following the reserved 10 spaces is an unsigned, single character, then a saved length of 7 spaces, allowing for a 6 character unsigned integer, then a saved length of 4 spaces, allowing 3 spaces for an unsigned integer, then a carriage-return character.

Here is the output, from the Perl debugger:

```
hello   3 000028 015
```

Strictly speaking, Python has no printf function. It uses the % operator instead, but it serves the same purpose and uses an equivalent syntax.

Here is a Python one-liner launched from the Python interpreter:

```
>>> "%-20.20s %8.06d" % ("hello", 35)
```

The Python code creates 20 spaces, then prints a string of characters, beginning at the first space. Following that, 8 spaces are saved for an integer, and prints out 6 characters, padding zeros if the supplied integer is smaller than 6 characters in length. Here is the output:

```
'hello                000035'
```

Here is an example of the printf command, used in the Ruby script, printf_ruby.rb:

```
#!/usr/local/bin/ruby
freq = Hash.new(0)
my_string = "Peter Piper picked a peck of pickled peppers.
            A peck of pickled peppers Peter Piper picked.
            If Peter Piper picked a peck of pickled peppers,
            Where is the peck of pickled peppers that Peter
            Piper picked?"
my_string.downcase.scan(/\w+/){|word| freq[word] = freq[word]+1}
freq.sort_by {|k, v| v}.reverse.each {|k,v| printf "%-10.10s %0.2u\n", k, v}
exit
```

Here is the output of the printf_ruby.rb script.

```
c:\ftp>printf_ruby.rb
peter      04
piper      04
picked     04
peck       04
of         04
peppers    04
pickled    04
```

```
a            03
if           01
where        01
is           01
the          01
that         01
```

In this example, the printf command tells the interpreter of the programming language to expect a character string followed by an integer; and that the character string should start at the left-most space, padded out to fill 10 spaces, to be followed immediately by a 2 digit integer, indicating the number of occurrences of the word, and a newline space. The comma-separated parameters that follow (ie, k, freq(k)) supply the interpreter with the string and the number that will be used in the execution of the printf command.

CONVERTING NONPRINTABLE FILES TO PLAIN-TEXT

Removing all the nonprintable characters from a file is a blunt and irreversible tactic. Sometimes, it suffices to transform a file into printable characters, from which you can reconstitute the original file, if needed. The Base64 algorithm reads binary files 6 bits at a time (instead of the 8-bit read for ASCII streams). Whereas an 8-bit chunk corresponds to a base 256 number (ie, 2 to the 8 exponent), a 6-bit chunk corresponds to a base 64 number (ie, 2 to the 6 exponent). The 6-bit chunks are assigned to a range of printable ASCII characters. Binary files that are transformed to Base64 can be reverse-transformed back to the original file.

Here is a short Ruby script, base64_ruby.rb, that takes a sentence, encodes it to Base64, and reverses the process to produce the original text.

```
#!/usr/local/bin/ruby
require 'base64'
data = "Time flies like an arrow. Fruit flies like a banana."
base64_transformed_data = Base64.encode64(data)
puts base64_transformed_data
base64_reverse = Base64.decode64(base64_transformed_data)
puts base64_reverse
exit
```

Output:

```
c:\ftp>base64_ruby.rb
VGltZSBmbGllcyBsaWtlIGFuIGFycm93LiAgRnJ1aXQgZmxpZXMgbGlrZSBh
IGJhbmFuYS4=
Time flies like an arrow. Fruit flies like a banana.
```

Here is a Perl script, base64_perl, that will take any file, ASCII or binary, and produce a printable Base64 translation. In the example below, the script encodes the Gettysburg address into Base64 text.

```
#!/usr/local/bin/perl
use MIME::Base64;
open (TEXT,"gettysbu.txt");
binmode TEXT;
$/ = undef;
$string = <TEXT>;
close TEXT;
$encoded = encode_base64($string);
print $encoded;
$decoded = decode_base64($encoded);
print "\n\n$decoded";
exit;
```

Here are the first few lines of output from the base64_perl script:

```
c:\ftp>base64_perl.pl
Rm91ciBzY29yZSBhbmQgc2V2ZW4geWVhcnMgYWdvIG91ciBmYXRoZXJzIGJyb3VnaHQgZm9ydGgg
b24gdGhpcwOKY29udGluZW50IGEgbmV3IG5hdGlvbiwgY29uY2VpdmVkIGluIGxpYmVydHkgYW5k
```

Here is the equivalent script, in Python[19]:

```
#!/usr/local/bin/python
import base64
sample_file = open ("gettysbu.txt", "rb")
string = sample_file.read()
sample_file.close()
print base64.encodestring(string)
print base64.decodestring(base64.encodestring(string))
exit
```

Adobe Acrobat Portable Document Format (ie, the ubiquitous PDF files), are unsuitable for text processing algorithms; they contain obscure formatting instructions, in a nonprintable ASCII format. Version 11 of Adobe Reader has a built-in pdf-to-text conversion tool, but the Adobe tool does not provide the power and flexibility of a utility that can be called from a script. A script that contains a system call to a utility can convert input files from multiple storage locations, and seamlessly integrate the returned output into subsequent script commands (see Glossary item, System call).

For rugged data simplification efforts, you may want to use the Xpdf utility. Xpdf is open source software that includes a PDF text extractor (pdftotext.exe) and a number of related utilities that operate on PDF files. Xpdf runs under multiple operating systems. The suite of Xpdf executables can be downloaded at: http://www.foolabs.com/xpdf/download.html

Once downloaded, the pdftotext utility can be called from the subdirectory in which it resides.
c:\ftp\xpdf>pdftotext zerolet.pdf

Here is a short Perl script that produces a text file for each of the .pdf files in a subdirectory. The script is intended to be launched from the same directory in which the pdftotext.exe file resides.

```
#!/usr/local/bin/perl
opendir(XPDF_SUBDIR, ".") || die ("Unable to open directory");
```

```
@from_files = readdir(XPDF_SUBDIR);
closedir(XPDF_SUBDIR);
foreach $filename (@from_files)
  {
  if ($filename =~ /\.pdf/)
    {
    system("pdftotext.exe $filename");
    }
  }
exit;
```

Here is the equivalent Python script:

```
#!/usr/local/bin/python
import os, re, string
filelist = os.listdir(".")
for file in filelist:
  if ".pdf" in file:
    command = "pdftotext.exe " + file
    os.system(command);
exit
```

Here is the equivalent Ruby script:

```
#!/usr/local/bin/ruby
filelist = Dir.glob("*.pdf")
filelist.each do
  |filename|
  system("pdftotext.exe #{filename}")
  end
exit
```

DUBLIN CORE

The specification for general file descriptors is the Dublin Core.[20] This set of about 15 common data elements, developed by a committee of librarians, specify the header information in electronic files and documents. The Dublin Core elements include such information as the date that the file was created, the name of the entity that created the file, and a general comment on the contents of the file. The Dublin Core elements aid in indexing and retrieving electronic files and should be included in every electronic document. The Dublin Core metadata specification is found at: http://dublincore. org/documents/dces/

Some of the most useful Dublin Core elements are[1]:

Contributor   the entity that contributes to the document
Coverage   the general area of information covered in the document
Creator   entity primarily responsible for creating the document
Date   a time associated with an event relevant to the document
Description   description of the document

Format	file format
Identifier	a character string that uniquely and unambiguously identifies the document
Language	the language of the document
Publisher	the entity that makes the resource available
Relation	a pointer to another, related document, typically the identifier of the related document
Rights	the property rights that apply to the document
Source	an identifier linking to another document from which the current document was derived
Subject	the topic of the document
Title	title of the document
Type	genre of the document

An XML syntax for expressing the Dublin Core elements is available.[21,22]

GLOSSARY

ANSI The American National Standards Institute (ANSI) accredits standards developing organizations to create American National Standards (ANS). A so-called ANSI standard is produced when an ANSI-accredited standards development organization follows ANSI procedures and receives confirmation from ANSI that all the procedures were followed. ANSI coordinates efforts to gain international standards certification from the ISO (International Standards Organization) or the IEC (International Electrotechnical Commission). ANSI works with hundreds of ANSI-accredited standards developers.

ASCII ASCII is the American Standard Code for Information Interchange, ISO-14962-1997. The ASCII standard is a way of assigning specific 8-bit strings (a string of 0s and 1s of length 8) to the alphanumeric characters and punctuation. Uppercase letters are assigned a different string of 0s and 1s than their matching lowercase letters. There are 256 ways of combining 0s and 1s in strings of length 8. This means that that there are 256 different ASCII characters, and every ASCII character can be assigned a number-equivalent, in the range of 0 to 255. The familiar keyboard keys produce ASCII characters that happen to occupy ASCII values under 128. Hence, alphanumerics and common punctuation are represented as 8-bits, with the first bit, "0," serving as padding. Hence, keyboard characters are commonly referred to as 7-bit ASCII. These are the classic ASCII characters:

```
!"#$%&'()*+,-./0123456789:;<=> ?@ABCDEFGHIJKLMNOPQRSTUVWXYZ
[\]^_'abcdefghijklmnopqrstuvwxyz{|}~
```

Files composed exclusively of common keyboard characters are commonly referred to as plain-text files or as 7-bit ASCII files. See Text editor. See Plain-text. See ISO.

American National Standards Institute See ANSI.

Autovivification In programming, autovivification is a feature of some programming languages wherein a variable or data structure seemingly brings itself into life, without definition or declaration, at the moment when its name first appears in a program. The programming language automatically registers the variable and endows it with a set of properties consistent with its type, as determined by the context, within the program. Perl supports autovivification. Python and Ruby, under most circumstances, do not. In the case of Ruby, new class objects (ie, instances of the class) are formally declared and created, by sending the "new" method to the class assigned to the newly declared object. See Reification.

Dark data Unstructured and ignored legacy data, presumed to account for most of the data in the "infoverse." The term gets its name from "dark matter" which is the invisible stuff that accounts for most of the gravitational attraction in the physical universe.

Data cleaning More correctly, data cleansing, and is synonymous with data fixing or data correcting. Data cleaning is the process by which errors, spurious anomalies, and missing values are somehow handled. The options for data cleaning are: correcting the error, deleting the error, leaving the error unchanged, or imputing a value.[23] Data cleaning should not be confused with data scrubbing. See Data scrubbing.

Data flattening In the field of informatics, data flattening is a popular but ultimately counterproductive method of data organization and data reduction. Data flattening involves removing data annotations that are deemed unnecessary for the intended purposes of the data (eg, timestamps, field designators, identifiers for individual data objects referenced within a document). Data flattening makes it difficult or impossible to verify data or to discover relationships among data objects. A detailed discussion of the topic is found in Section 4.5, "Reducing Data." See Verification. See Data repurposing. See Pseudosimplification.

Data fusion Data fusion is very closely related to data integration. The subtle difference between the two concepts lies in the end result. Data fusion creates a new and accurate set of data representing the combined data sources. Data integration is an on-the-fly usage of data pulled from different domains and, as such, does not yield a residual fused set of data.

Data merging A nonspecific term that includes data fusion, data integration, and any methods that facilitate the accrual of data derived from multiple sources. See Data fusion.

Data mining Alternate form, datamining. The term "data mining" is closely related to "data repurposing" and both endeavors employ many of the same techniques. Accordingly, the same data scientists engaged in data mining efforts are likely to be involved in data repurposing efforts. In data mining, the data, and the expected purpose of the data, are typically provided to the data miner, often in a form suited for analysis. In data repurposing projects, the data scientists are expected to find unintended purposes for the data, and the job typically involves transforming the data into a form suitable for its new purpose.

Data munging Refers to a multitude of tasks involved in preparing data for some intended purpose (eg, data cleaning, data scrubbing, data transformation). Synonymous with data wrangling.

Data object A data object is whatever is being described by the data. For example, if the data is "6 feet tall," then the data object is the person or thing to which "6 feet tall" applies. Minimally, a data object is a metadata/data pair, assigned to a unique identifier (ie, a triple). In practice, the most common data objects are simple data records, corresponding to a row in a spreadsheet or a line in a flat-file. Data objects in object-oriented programming languages typically encapsulate several items of data, including an object name, an object unique identifier, multiple data/metadata pairs, and the name of the object's class. See Triple. See Identifier. See Metadata.

Data reduction When a very large data set is analyzed, it may be impractical or counterproductive to work with every element of the collected data. In such cases, the data analyst may choose to eliminate some of the data, or develop methods whereby the data is approximated. Some data scientists reserve the term "data reduction" for methods that reduce the dimensionality of multivariate data sets.

Data repurposing Involves using old data in new ways, that were not foreseen by the people who originally collected the data. Data repurposing comes in the following categories: (1) Using the preexisting data to ask and answer questions that were not contemplated by the people who designed and collected the data; (2) Combining preexisting data with additional data, of the same kind, to produce aggregate data that suits a new set of questions that could not have been answered with any one of the component data sources; (3) Reanalyzing data to validate assertions, theories, or conclusions drawn from the original studies; (4) Reanalyzing the original data set using alternate or improved methods to attain outcomes of greater precision or reliability than the outcomes produced in the original analysis; (5) Integrating heterogeneous data sets (ie, data sets with seemingly unrelated types of information), for the purpose of answering questions or developing concepts that span diverse scientific disciplines; (6) Finding subsets in a population once thought to be homogeneous; (7) Seeking new relationships among data objects; (8) Creating, on-the-fly, novel data sets through data file linkages; (9) Creating new concepts or ways of thinking about old concepts, based on a re-examination of data; (10) Fine-tuning existing data models; and (11) Starting over and remodeling systems.[7] See Heterogeneous data.

Data scraping Pulling together desired sections of a data set or text, using software.

Data scrubbing A term that is very similar to data deidentification and is sometimes used improperly as a synonym for data deidentification. Data scrubbing refers to the removal, from data records, of information that is considered unwanted. This may include identifiers, private information, or any incriminating or otherwise objectionable language contained in data records, as well as any information deemed irrelevant to the purpose served by the record. See Deidentification.

Data wrangling Jargon referring to a multitude of tasks involved in preparing data for eventual analysis. Synonymous with data munging.[24]

Deidentification The process of removing all of the links in a data record that can connect the information in the record to an individual. This usually includes the record identifier, demographic information (eg, place of birth), personal information (eg, birthdate), biometrics (eg, fingerprints), and so on. The process of deidentification will vary based on the type of records examined. Deidentifying protocols exist wherein deidentified records can be reidentified, when necessary. See Reidentification. See Data scrubbing.

Encryption A common definition of encryption involves an algorithm that takes some text or data and transforms it, bit-by-bit, into an output that cannot be interpreted (ie, from which the contents of the source file cannot be determined). Encryption comes with the implied understanding that there exists some reverse transformation that can be applied to the encrypted data, to reconstitute the original source. As used herein, the definition of encryption is expanded to include any protocols by which files can be shared, in such a way that only the intended recipients can make sense of the received documents. This would include protocols that divide files into pieces that can only be reassembled into the original file using a password. Encryption would also include protocols that alter parts of a file while retaining the original text in other parts of the file. As described in Chapter 5, there are instances when some data in a file should be shared, while only specific parts need to be encrypted. The protocols that accomplish these kinds of file transformations need not always employ classic encryption algorithms. See Winnowing and chaffing.

HTML Hyper Text Markup Language is an ASCII-based set of formatting instructions for Web pages. HTML formatting instructions, known as tags, are embedded in the document, and double-bracketed, indicating the start point and end points for instruction. Here is an example of an HTML tag instructing the Web browser to display the word "Hello" in italics: <i>Hello</i>. All Web browsers conforming to the HTML specification must contain software routines that recognize and implement the HTML instructions embedded within in Web documents. In addition to formatting instructions, HTML also includes linkage instructions, in which the Web browsers must retrieve and display a listed Web page, or a Web resource, such as an image. The protocol whereby Web browsers, following HTML instructions, retrieve Web pages from other internet sites, is known as HTTP (HyperText Transfer Protocol).

Heterogeneous data Two sets of data are considered heterogeneous when they are dissimilar to one another, with regard to content, purpose, format, organization, or annotations. One of the purposes of data science is to discover relationships among heterogeneous data sources. For example, epidemiologic data sets may be of service to molecular biologists who have gene sequence data on diverse human populations. The epidemiologic data is likely to contain different types of data values, annotated and formatted in a manner different from the data and annotations in a gene sequence database. The two types of related data, epidemiologic and genetic, have dissimilar content; hence they are heterogeneous to one another.

ISO International Standards Organization. The ISO is a nongovernmental organization that develops international standards (eg, ISO-11179 for metadata and ISO-8601 for date and time). See ANSI.

ISO-11179 The ISO standard for defining metadata, such as XML tags. The standard requires that the definitions for metadata used in XML (the so-called tags) be accessible and should include the following information for each tag: Name (the label assigned to the tag), Identifier (the unique identifier assigned to the tag), Version (the version of the tag), Registration Authority (the entity authorized to register the tag), Language (the language in which the tag is specified), Definition (a statement that clearly represents the concept and essential nature of the tag), Obligation (indicating whether the tag is required), Datatype (indicating the type of data that can be represented in the value enclosed by the tag), Maximum Occurrence (indicating any limit to the number of times that the tag appears in a document), and Comment (a remark describing how the tag might be used).[25] See ISO.

Identification The process of providing a data object with an identifier, or the process of distinguishing one data object from all other data objects on the basis of its associated identifier. See Identifier.

Identifier A string that is associated with a particular thing (eg person, document, transaction, data object), and not associated with any other thing.[26] Object identification usually involves permanently assigning a seemingly random sequence of numeric digits (0-9) and alphabet characters (a-z and A-Z) to a data object. A data object can be a specific piece of data (eg, a data record), or an abstraction, such as a class of objects or a number or a string or a variable. See Identification.

Intellectual property Data, software, algorithms, and applications that are created by an entity capable of ownership (eg, humans, corporations, universities). The owner entity holds rights over the manner in which the intellectual property can be used and distributed. Protections for intellectual property may come in the form of copyrights, patents, and laws that apply to theft. Copyright applies to published information. Patents apply to novel processes and inventions. Certain types of intellectual property can only be protected by being secretive. For example, magic tricks cannot be copyrighted or patented; this is why magicians guard their intellectual property against theft. Intellectual property can be sold outright, or used under a legal agreement (eg, license, contract, transfer agreement, royalty, usage fee, and so on). Intellectual property can also be shared freely, while retaining ownership (eg, open source license, GNU license, FOSS license, Creative Commons license).

Introspection A method by which data objects can be interrogated to yield information about themselves (eg, properties, values, and class membership). Through introspection, the relationships among the data objects can be examined. Introspective methods are built into object-oriented languages. The data provided by introspection can be applied, at run-time, to modify a script's operation; a technique known as reflection. Specifically, any properties, methods, and encapsulated data of a data object can be used in the script to modify the script's run-time behavior. See Reflection.

Legacy data Data collected by an information system that has been replaced by a newer system, and which cannot be immediately integrated into the newer system's database. For example, hospitals regularly replace their hospital information systems with new systems that promise greater efficiencies, expanded services, or improved interoperability with other information systems. In many cases, the new system cannot readily integrate the data collected from the older system. The previously collected data becomes a legacy to the new system. In many cases, legacy data is simply "stored" for some arbitrary period of time, in case someone actually needs to retrieve any of the legacy data. After a decade or so, the hospital finds itself without any staff members who are capable of locating the storage site of the legacy data, or moving the data into a modern operating system, or interpreting the stored data, or retrieving appropriate data records, or producing a usable query output.

Line A line in a nonbinary file is a sequence of characters that terminate with an end-of-line character. The end-of-line character may differ among operating systems. For example, the DOS end-of-line character is ASCII 13 (ie, the carriage return character) followed by ASCII 10 (ie, the line feed character), simulating the new line movement in manual typewriters. The Linux end-of-line character is ASCII 10 (ie, the line feed character only). When programming in Perl, Python, or Ruby, the newline character is represented by "\n" regardless of which operating system or file system is used. For most purposes, use of "\n" seamlessly compensates for discrepancies among operating systems with regard to their preferences for end-of-line characters. Binary files, such as image files or telemetry files, have no designated end-of-line characters. When a file is opened as a binary file, any end-of-line characters that happen to be included in the file are simply ignored as such, by the operating system.

Lock in Also appearing as lock-in and, more specifically, as vendor lock-in. Describes the situation when a data manager is dependent on a single manufacturer, supplier, software application, standard, or operational protocol and cannot use alternate sources without violating a license, incurring substantial costs, or suffering great inconvenience. One of the most important precepts of data simplification is to avoid vendor lock-in, whenever possible. Aside from vendor lock-in, data scientists should understand that user communities participate complicitly in efforts to lock-in inferior software, and standards. After a user has committed time, money, resources to a particular methodology, or has built professional ties with a community that supports the methodology, he or she will fight tooth and nail to preserve the status quo. It can be very difficult for new methods to replace entrenched methods, and this could be described as user lock-in.

Machine learning Refers to computer systems and software applications that learn or improve as new data is acquired. Examples would include language translation software that improves in accuracy as additional language data is added to the system, and predictive software that improves as more examples are obtained. Machine learning can be applied to search engines, optical character recognition software, speech recognition software, vision software, and neural networks. Machine learning systems are likely to use training data sets and test data sets.

Machine translation Ultimately, the job of machine translation is to translate text from one language into another language. The process of machine translation begins with extracting sentences from text, parsing the words of the sentence into grammatical parts, and arranging the grammatical parts into an order that imposes logical sense on the sentence. Once this is done, each of the parts can be translated by a dictionary that finds equivalent terms in a foreign language, then reassembled as a foreign language sentence by applying grammatical positioning rules appropriate for the target language. Because these steps apply the natural rules for sentence constructions in a foreign language, the process is often referred to as natural language machine translation. It is important to note that nowhere in the process of machine translation is it necessary to find meaning in the source text, or to produce meaning in the output. Machine translation algorithms preserve ambiguities, without attempting to impose a meaningful result.

Meaning In informatics, meaning is achieved when described data is bound to a unique identifier of a data object. "Claude Funston's height is 5 feet 11 inches," comes pretty close to being a meaningful statement. The statement contains data (5 feet 11 inches), and the data is described (height). The described data belongs to a unique object (Claude Funston). Ideally, the name "Claude Funston" should be provided with a unique identifier, to distinguish one instance of Claude Funston from all the other persons who are named Claude Funston. The statement would also benefit from a formal system that ensures that the metadata makes sense (eg, What exactly is height, and does Claude Funston fall into a class of objects for which height is a property?) and that the data is appropriate (eg, Is 5 feet 11 inches an allowable measure of a person's height?). A statement with meaning does not need to be a true statement (eg, The height of Claude Funston was not 5 feet 11 inches when Claude Funston was an infant). See Semantics. See Triple. See RDF.

Metadata The data that describes data. For example, a data element (also known as data point) may consist of the number, "6." The metadata for the data may be the words "Height, in feet." A data element is useless without its metadata, and metadata is useless unless it adequately describes a data element. In XML, the metadata/data annotation comes in the form <metadata tag>data<end of metadata tag> and might be look something like:

```
<weight_in_pounds>150</weight_in_pounds>
```

In spreadsheets, the data elements are the cells of the spreadsheet. The column headers are the metadata that describe the data values in the column's cells, and the row headers are the record numbers that uniquely identify each record (ie, each row of cells). See XML.

Microarray Also known as gene chip, gene expression array, DNA microarray, or DNA chips. These consist of thousands of small samples of chosen DNA sequences arrayed onto a block of support material (usually, a glass slide). When the array is incubated with a mixture of DNA sequences prepared from cell samples, hybridization will occur between molecules on the array and single stranded complementary (ie, identically sequenced) molecules present in the cell sample. The greater the concentration of complementary molecules in the cell sample, the greater the number of fluorescently tagged hybridized molecules in the array. A specialized instrument prepares an image of the array, and quantifies the fluorescence in each array spot. Spots with high fluorescence indicate relatively large quantities of DNA in the cell sample that match the specific sequence of DNA in the array spot. The data comprising all the fluorescent intensity measurements for every spot in the array produces a gene profile characteristic of the cell sample.

Monospaced font Alternate terms are fixed-pitch, fixed-width, or nonproportional font. Most modern fonts have adjustable spacing, to make the best use of the distance between successive letters and to produce a pleasing look to the printed words. For example, "Te" printed in proportional font might push the "e" under the roof of the top bar of the "T." You will never see the "e" snuggled under the bar of the "T" in a monospaced font. Hence, when using proportional font, the spacings inserted into text will have variable presentations, when displayed on the monitor or when printed on paper. Programmers should use monospaced fonts when composing software; think of the indentations in Python and Ruby and the use of spaces as padding in quoted text and formatting commands. Examples of monospaced fonts include: Courier, Courier New, Lucida Console, Monaco, and Consolas.

Namespace A namespace is the realm in which a metadata tag applies. The purpose of a namespace is to distinguish metadata tags that have the same name, but a different meaning. For example, within a single XML file, the metadata tag "date" may be used to signify a calendar date, or the fruit, or the social engagement. To avoid confusion, metadata terms are assigned a prefix that is associated with a Web document that defines the term (ie, establishes the tag's namespace). In practical terms, a tag that can have different descriptive meanings in different contexts is provided with a prefix that links to a Web document wherein the meaning of the tag, as it applies in the XML document, is specified. An example of namespace syntax is provided in Section 2.5.

Natural language processing A field broadly concerned with how computers interpret human language (ie, machine translation). At its simplest level, this may involve parsing through text, and organizing the grammatical units of individual sentences (ie, tokenization). The grammatical units can be trimmed, reorganized, matched against concept equivalents in a nomenclature or a foreign language dictionary, and reassembled as a simplified, grammatically uniform, output or as a translation into another language.

Nomenclature mapping Specialized nomenclatures employ specific names for concepts that are included in other nomenclatures, under other names. For example, medical specialists often preserve their favored names for concepts that cross into different fields of medicine. The term that pathologists use for a certain benign fibrous tumor of the skin is "fibrous histiocytoma," a term spurned by dermatologists, who prefer to use "dermatofibroma" to describe the same tumor. As another horrifying example, the names for the physiologic responses caused by a reversible cerebral vasoconstricitive event include: thunderclap headache, Call-Fleming syndrome, benign angiopathy of the central nervous system, postpartum angiopathy, migrainous vasospasm, and migraine angiitis. The choice of term will vary depending on the medical specialty of the physician (eg, neurologist, rheumatologist, obstetrician). To mitigate the discord among specialty nomenclatures, lexicographers may undertake a harmonization project, in which nomenclatures with overlapping concepts are mapped to one another.

Notation 3 Also called n3. A syntax for expressing assertions as triples (unique subject + metadata + data). Notation 3 expresses the same information as the more formal RDF syntax, but n3 is easier for humans to read.[27] RDF and n3 are interconvertible, and either one can be parsed and equivalently tokenized (ie, broken into elements that can be reorganized in a different format, such as a database record). See RDF. See Triple.

Open standard It is disappointing to admit that many of the standards that apply to data and software are neither free nor open. Standards developing organizations occasionally require the members of their communities to purchase a license as a condition for obtaining, viewing, or using the standard. Such licenses may include encumbrances that impose strict limits on the way that the standard is used, distributed, modified, shared, or transmitted. Restrictions on the distribution of the standard may extend to any and all materials annotated with elements of the standard, and may apply to future versions of the standard. The concept of an open standard, as the name suggests, provides certain liberties, but many standards, even open standards, are encumbered with restrictions that users must abide.

Patent farming The practice of hiding intellectual property within a standard, or method, or device is known as patent farming or patent ambushing.[28] After a standard is adopted into general use, the patent farmer announces the presence of his or her hidden patented material and presses for royalties. The patent farmer plants seeds in the standard and harvests his crop when the standard has grown to maturity; a rustic metaphor for some highly sophisticated and cynical behavior.

Plain-text Plain-text refers to character strings or files that are composed of the characters accessible to a typewriter keyboard. These files typically have a ".txt" suffix to their names. Plain-text files are sometimes referred to as 7-bit ASCII files because all of the familiar keyboard characters have ASCII vales under 128 (ie, can be designated in binary with, just seven 0s and 1s. In practice, plain-text files exclude 7-bit ASCII symbols that do not code for familiar keyboard characters. To further confuse the issue, plain-text files may contain ASCII characters above 7 bits (ie, characters from 128 to 255) that represent characters that are printable on computer monitors, such as accented letters. See ASCII.

Plesionymy Plesionyms are nearly synonymous words, or pairs of words that are sometimes synonymous; other times not. For example, the noun forms of "smell" and "odor" are synonymous. As a verb, "smell" does the job, but "odor" comes up short. You can smell a fish, but you cannot odor a fish. Smell and odor are plesionyms to one another. Plesionymy is another challenge for machine translators.

Polysemy In polysemy, a single word, character string or phrase has more than one meaning. Polysemy can be thought of as the opposite of synonymy, wherein different words mean the same thing. Polysemy is a particularly vexing problem in the realm of medical abbreviations. A single acronym may have literally dozens of possible expansions.[8] For example, ms is the abbreviation for manuscript, mass spectrometry, mental status, millisecond, mitral stenosis, morphine sulfate, multiple sclerosis, or the female honorific.

Protocol A set of instructions, policies, or fully-described procedures for accomplishing a service, operation, or task. Data is generated and collected according to protocols. There are protocols for conducting experiments, and there are protocols for measuring the results. There are protocols for choosing the human subjects included in a clinical trial, and there are protocols for interacting with the human subjects during the course of the trial. All network communications are conducted via protocols; the Internet operates under a protocol (TCP-IP, Transmission Control Protocol-Internet Protocol). One of the jobs of the modern data scientist is to create and curate protocols.

Pseudosimplification Refers to any method intended to simplify data that reduces the quality of the data, interferes with introspection, modifies the data without leaving a clear trail connecting the original data to the modified data, eliminates timestamp data, transforms the data in a manner that defies reverse transformation, or that unintentionally increases the complexity of data. See Data flattening.

RDF Resource Description Framework (RDF) is a syntax in XML notation that formally expresses assertions as triples. The RDF triple consists of a uniquely identified subject plus a metadata descriptor for the data plus a data element. Triples are necessary and sufficient to create statements that convey meaning. Triples can be aggregated with other triples from the same data set or from other data sets, so long as each triple pertains to a unique subject that is identified equivalently through the data sets. Enormous data sets of RDF triples can be merged or functionally integrated with other massive or complex data resources. For a detailed discussion see Open Source Tools for Chapter 6, Syntax for Triples. See Notation 3. See Semantics. See Triple. See XML.

Reflection A programming technique wherein a computer program will modify itself, at run-time, based on information it acquires through introspection. For example, a computer program may iterate over a collection of data objects, examining the self-descriptive information for each object in the collection (ie, object introspection). If the information indicates that the data object belongs to a particular class of objects, then the program may call a method appropriate for the class. The program executes in a manner determined by descriptive information obtained during run-time; metaphorically reflecting upon the purpose of its computational task. See Introspection.

Reidentification A term casually applied to any instance whereby information can be linked to a specific person, after the links between the information and the person associated with the information have been removed. Used this way, the term reidentification connotes an insufficient deidentification process. In the health care industry, the term "reidentification" means something else entirely. In the U.S., regulations define "reidentification" under the "Standards for Privacy of Individually Identifiable Health Information.[29]" Therein, reidentification is a legally sanctioned process whereby deidentified records can be linked back to their human subjects, under circumstances deemed legitimate and compelling, by a privacy board. Reidentification is typically accomplished via the use of a confidential list of links between human subject names and deidentified records, held by a trusted party. In the healthcare realm, when a human subject is identified through fraud, trickery, or through the deliberate use of computational methods to break the confidentiality of insufficiently deidentified records (ie, hacking), the term "reidentification" would not apply.[1]

Reification A programming term that has some similarity to "autovivification." In either case, an abstract piece of a program brings itself to life, at the moment when it is assigned a name. Whereas autovivification generally applies to variables and data structures, reification generally applies to blocks of code, methods, and data objects. When a named block of code becomes reified, it can be invoked anywhere within the program, by its name. See Autovivification.

Reproducibility Reproducibility is achieved when repeat studies produce the same results, over and over. Reproducibility is closely related to validation, which is achieved when you draw the same conclusions, from the data, over and over again. Implicit in the concept of "reproducibility" is that the original research must somehow convey the means by which the study can be reproduced. This usually requires the careful recording of methods, algorithms, and materials. In some cases, reproducibility requires access to the data produced in the original studies. If there is no feasible way for scientists to undertake a reconstruction of the original study, or if the results obtained in the original study cannot be obtained in subsequent attempts, then the study is irreproducible. If the work is reproduced, but the results and the conclusions cannot be repeated, then the study is considered invalid. See Validation. See Verification.

Semantics The study of meaning (Greek root, semantikos, significant meaning). In the context of data science, semantics is the technique of creating meaningful assertions about data objects. A meaningful assertion, as used here, is a triple consisting of an identified data object, a data value, and a descriptor for the data value. In practical terms, semantics involves making assertions about data objects (ie, making triples), combining assertions about data objects (ie, merging triples), and assigning data objects to classes; hence relating triples to other triples. As a word of warning, few informaticians would define semantics in these terms, but most definitions for semantics are functionally equivalent to the definition offered here. Most language is unstructured and meaningless. Consider the assertion: Sam is tired. This is an adequately structured sentence with a subject verb and object. But what is the meaning of the sentence? There are a lot of people named Sam. Which Sam is being referred to in this sentence? What does it mean to say that Sam is tired? Is "tiredness" a constitutive property of Sam, or does it only apply to specific moments? If so, for what moment in time is the assertion, "Sam is tired" actually true? To a computer, meaning comes from assertions that have a specific, identified subject associated with some sensible piece of fully described data (metadata coupled with the data it describes). See Triple. See RDF.

Specification A specification is a formal method for describing objects (physical objects such as nuts and bolts or symbolic objects, such as numbers, or concepts expressed as text). In general, specifications do not require the inclusion of specific items of information (ie, they do not impose restrictions on the content that is included in or excluded from documents), and specifications do not impose any order of appearance of the data contained in the document (ie, you can mix up and rearrange specified objects, if you like). Specifications are not generally certified by a standards organization. They are generally produced by special interest organizations, and the legitimacy of a specification depends on its popularity. Examples of specifications are RDF (Resource Description Framework) produced by the W3C (World Wide Web Consortium), and TCP/IP (Transfer Control Protocol/Internet Protocol), maintained by the Internet Engineering Task Force. The most widely implemented specifications are simple and easily implemented. See Specification versus standard.

Specification versus standard Data standards, in general, tell you what must be included in a conforming document, and, in most cases, dictate the format of the final document. In many instances, standards bar inclusion of any data that is not included in the standard (eg, you should not include astronomical data in an clinical X-ray report). Specifications simply provide a formal way for describing the data that you choose to include in your document. XML and RDF, a semantic dialect of XML, are examples of specifications. They both tell you how data should be represented, but neither tell you what data to include, or how your document or data set should appear. Files that comply with a standard are rigidly organized and can be easily parsed and manipulated by software specifically designed to adhere to the standard. Files that comply with a specification are typically self-describing documents that contain within themselves all the information necessary for a human or a computer to derive meaning from the file contents. In theory, files that comply with a specification can be parsed and manipulated by generalized software designed to parse the markup language of the specification (eg, XML, RDF) and to organize the data into data structures defined within the file. The relative strengths and weaknesses of standards and specifications are discussed in Section 2.6, "Specifications Good, Standards Bad." See XML. See RDF.

System call Refers to a command, within a running script, that calls the operating system into action, momentarily bypassing the programming interpreter for the script. A system call can do essentially anything the operating system can do via a command line.

Text editor A text editor (also called ASCII editor) is a software program designed to display simple, unformatted text files. Text editors differ from word processing software applications that produce files with formatting information embedded within the file. Text editors, unlike word processors, can open large files (in excess of 100 Megabytes), very quickly. They also allow you to move around the file with ease. Examples of free and open source text editors are Emacs and vi. See ASCII.

Triple In computer semantics, a triple is an identified data object associated with a data element and the description of the data element. In the computer science literature, the syntax for the triple is commonly described as: subject, predicate, object, wherein the subject is an identifier, the predicate is the description of the object, and the object is the data. The definition of triple, using grammatical terms, can be off-putting to the data scientist, who may think in terms of spreadsheet entries: a key that identifies the line record, a column header containing the metadata description of the data, and a cell that contains the data. In this book, the three components of a triple are described as: (1) the identifier for the data object, (2) the metadata that describes the data, and (3) the data itself. In theory, all data sets, databases, and spreadsheets can be constructed or deconstructed as collections of triples. See Introspection. See Data object. See Semantics. See RDF. See Meaning.

Turtle Another syntax for expressing triples. From RDF came a simplified syntax for triples, known as Notation 3 or n3,[30] From n3 came Turtle, thought to fit more closely to RDF. From Turtle came an even more simplified form, known as N-Triples. See RDF. See Notation 3.

URL Unique Resource Locator. The Web is a collection of resources, each having a unique address, the URL. When you click on a link that specifies a URL, your browser fetches the page located at the unique location specified in the URL name. If the Web were designed otherwise (ie, if several different Web pages had the same Web address, or if one Web address were located at several different locations), then the Web could not function with any reliability.

URN Unique Resource Name. Whereas the URL identifies objects based on the object's unique location in the Web, the URN is a system of object identifiers that are location-independent. In the URN system, data objects are provided with identifiers, and the identifiers are registered with, and subsumed by, the URN. For example:

```
urn:isbn-13:9780128028827
```

Refers to the unique book, "Repurposing Legacy Data: Innovative Case Studies," by Jules Berman

```
urn:uuid:e29d0078-f7f6-11e4-8ef1-e808e19e18e5
```

Refers to a data object tied to the UUID identifier e29d0078-f7f6-11e4-8ef1-e808e19e18e5 In theory, if every data object were assigned a registered URN, and if the system were implemented as intended, the entire universe of information could be tracked and searched. See URL. See UUID.

UTF Any one of several Unicode Transformation Formats that accommodate a larger set of character representations than ASCII. The larger character sets included in the UTF standards include diverse alphabets (ie, characters other than the 26 Latinized letters used in English). See ASCII.

UUID (Universally Unique IDentifier) is a protocol for assigning unique identifiers to data objects, without using a central registry. UUIDs were originally used in the Apollo Network Computing System.[31] Most modern programming languages have modules for generating UUIDs. See Identifier.

Validation Validation is the process that checks whether the conclusions drawn from data analysis are correct.[32] Validation usually starts with repeating the same analysis of the same data, using the methods that were originally recommended. Obviously, if a different set of conclusions is drawn from the same data and methods, the original conclusions cannot be validated. Validation may involve applying a different set of analytic methods to the same data, to determine if the conclusions are consistent. It is always reassuring to know that conclusions are repeatable, with different analytic methods. In prior eras, experiments were validated by repeating the entire experiment, thus producing a new set of observations for analysis. Many of today's scientific experiments are far too complex and costly to repeat. In such cases, validation requires access to the complete collection of the original data, and to the detailed protocols under which the data was generated. One of the most useful methods of data validation involves testing new hypotheses, based on the assumed validity of the original conclusions. For example, if you were to accept Darwin's analysis of barnacle data, leading to his theory of evolution, then you would expect to find a chronologic history of fossils in ascending layers of shale. This was the case; thus, paleontologists studying the Burgess shale reserves provided some validation to Darwin's conclusions. Validation should not be mistaken for proof. Nonetheless, the repeatability of conclusions, over time, with the same or different sets of data, and the demonstration of consistency with related observations, is about all that we can hope for in this imperfect world. See Verification. See Reproducibility.

Verification The process by which data is checked to determine whether the data was obtained properly (ie, according to approved protocols), and that the data accurately measured what it was intended to measure, on the correct specimens, and that all steps in data processing were done using well-documented protocols. Verification often requires a level of expertise that is at least as high as the expertise of the individuals who produced the data.[32] Data verification requires a full understanding of the many steps involved in data collection and can be a time-consuming task. In one celebrated case, in which two statisticians reviewed a microarray study performed at Duke University, the time devoted to their verification effort was reported to be 2000 hours.[33] To put this statement in perspective, the official work-year, according to the U.S. Office of Personnel Management, is 2087 hours. Verification is different from validation. Verification is performed on data; validation is done on the results of data analysis. See Validation. See Microarray. See Introspection.

Winnowing and chaffing Better known to contrarians as chaffing and winnowing. A protocol invented by Ronald Rivest for securing messages against eavesdroppers, without technically employing encryption.[34] As used in this book, the winnowing and chaffing protocol would be considered a type of encryption. A detailed discussion of winnowing and chaffing is found in Open Source tools for Chapter 8. See Encryption.

XML Acronym for eXtensible Markup Language, a syntax for marking data values with descriptors (ie, metadata). The descriptors are commonly known as tags. In XML, every data value is enclosed by a start-tag, containing the descriptor and indicating that a value will follow, and an end-tag, containing the same descriptor and indicating that a value preceded the tag. For example: <name>Conrad Nervig </name >. The enclosing angle brackets, "<>," and the end-tag marker, "/," are hallmarks of HTML and XML markup. This simple but powerful relationship between metadata and data allows us to employ metadata/data pairs as though each were a miniature database. The semantic value of XML becomes apparent when we bind a metadata/data pair to a unique object, forming a so-called triple. See Triple. See Meaning. See Semantics. See HTML.

REFERENCES

1. Berman JJ. *Principles of big data: preparing, sharing, and analyzing complex information.* Burlington, MA: Morgan Kaufmann; 2013.
2. Pogson G. Controlled English: enlightenment through constraint. *Lang Technol* 1988;**6**:22–5.
3. Berman JJ. *Biomedical informatics.* Sudbury, MA: Jones and Bartlett; 2007.

4. Ogden CK. *Basic English: a general introduction with rules and grammar*. London: Paul Treber; 1930.
5. Coster W, Kauchak D. Simple English Wikipedia: a new text simplification task. In: Proceedings of the 49th annual meeting of the association for computational linguistics: human language technologies; 2011. Available at: http://www.aclweb.org/anthology/P11-2117 [accessed 07.09.15].
6. Weller S, Cajigas I, Morrell J, Obie C, Steel G, Gould SJ, et al. Alternative splicing suggests extended function of PEX26 in peroxisome biogenesis. *Am J Hum Genet* 2005;**76**(6):987–1007.
7. Berman JJ. *Repurposing legacy data: innovative case studies*. Burlington, MA: Elsevier, Morgan Kaufmann imprint; 2015.
8. Berman JJ. Pathology abbreviated: a long review of short terms. *Arch Pathol Lab Med* 2004;**128**:347–52.
9. Nadkarni P, Chen R, Brandt C. UMLS concept indexing for production databases. *JAMIA* 2001;**8**:80–91.
10. Berman JJ, Bhatia K. Biomedical data integration: using XML to link clinical and research datasets. *Expert Rev Mol Diagn* 2005;**5**:329–36.
11. Berman JJ. Pathology data integration with eXtensible Markup Language. *Hum Pathol* 2005;**36**:139–45.
12. Ahmed K, Ayers D, Birbeck M, Cousins J, Dodds D, Lubell J, et al. *Professional XML meta data*. Birmingham, UK: Wrox; 2001.
13. FIPS PUB 119-1. Supersedes FIPS PUB 119. 1985 November 8. Federal Information Processing Standards Publication 119-1 1995 March 13. Announcing the Standard for ADA. Available from: http://www.itl.nist.gov/fipspubs/fip119-1.htm, [accessed 26.08.12].
14. Duncan M. *Terminology version control discussion paper: the chocolate teapot*. Medical Object Oriented Software Ltd.; 2009. Available from: http://www.mrtablet.demon.co.uk/chocolate_teapot_lite.htm [accessed 30.08.12].
15. Kammer RG. The role of standards in today's society and in the future. Statement of Raymond G. Kammer, Director, National Institute of Standards and Technology, Technology Administration, Department of Commerce, Before the House Committee on Science Subcommittee on Technology, September 13, 2000.
16. Cahr D, Kalina I. Of pacs and trolls: how the patent wars may be coming to a hospital near you. *ABA Health Law* 2006;**19**:15–20.
17. National Committee on Vital and Health Statistics. Report to the Secretary of the U.S. Department of Health and Human Services on Uniform Data Standards for Patient Medical Record Information. July 6, 2000. Available from: http://www.ncvhs.hhs.gov/hipaa000706.pdf.
18. Berman JJ. *Ruby programming for medicine and biology*. Sudbury, MA: Jones and Bartlett; 2008.
19. Berman JJ. *Methods in medical informatics: fundamentals of healthcare programming in Perl, Python, and Ruby*. Boca Raton: Chapman and Hall; 2010.
20. Kunze J. Encoding Dublin Core metadata in HTML. Dublin Core Metadata Initiative. Network working group request for comments 2731. The Internet Society. Available at: http://www.ietf.org/rfc/rfc2731.txt; 1999 [accessed 01.08.15].
21. Dublin Core Metadata Initiative. Available from: http://dublincore.org; 2015 [accessed 14.11.15].
22. Dublin Core Metadata Element Set, Version 1.1: Reference description. Available from: http://dublincore.org/documents/1999/07/02/dces/ [accessed 14.11.15].
23. Van den Broeck J, Cunningham SA, Eeckels R, Herbst K. Data cleaning: detecting, diagnosing, and editing data abnormalities. *PLoS Med* 2005;**2**:e267.
24. Lohr S. For big-data scientists, "janitor work" is key hurdle to insights. *The New York Times*; 2014.
25. ISO/IEC 11179, Information technology—metadata registries. ISO/IEC JTC1 SC32 WG2 Development/Maintenance. Available from: http://metadata-standards.org/11179/ [accessed 02.11.14].
26. Paskin N. Identifier interoperability: a report on two recent ISO activities. *D-Lib Mag* 2006;**12**:1–23.
27. Berman JJ, Moore GW. *Implementing an RDF Schema for pathology images*; 2007. Available from: http://www.julesberman.info/spec2img.htm [accessed 01.01.15l.

28. Gates S. *Qualcomm v. Broadcom—The federal circuit weighs in on "patent ambushes"*; 2008. Available from: http://www.mofo.com/qualcomm-v-broadcom—the-federal-circuit-weighs-in-on-patent-ambushes-12-05-2008[accessed 22.01.13].

29. Department of Health and Human Services. 45 CFR (Code of Federal Regulations), Parts 160 through 164. Standards for privacy of individually identifiable health information (final rule). *Fed Regist* 2000;**65** (250):82461–510.

30. Primer: Getting into RDF & Semantic Web using N3. Available from: http://www.w3.org/2000/10/swap/Primer.html [accessed 17.09.15].

31. Leach P, Mealling M, Salz R. A universally unique identifier (UUID) URN namespace. Network Working Group, Request for Comment 4122, Standards Track. Available from: http://www.ietf.org/rfc/rfc4122.txt [accessed 01.01.15].

32. Committee on Mathematical Foundations of Verification, Validation, and Uncertainty Quantification, Board on Mathematical Sciences and Their Applications, Division on Engineering and Physical Sciences, National Research Council. *Assessing the reliability of complex models: mathematical and statistical foundations of verification, validation, and uncertainty quantification.* National Academy Press; 2012 Available from: http://www.nap.edu/catalog.php?record_id=13395 [on 01.01.15.

33. Misconduct in science: an array of errors. The Economist. September 10, 2011.

34. Rivest RL. MIT Lab for computer science. March 18, 1998 (rev. April 24, 1998).

INDEXING TEXT

3.1 HOW DATA SCIENTISTS USE INDEXES

If I had known what it would be like to have it all, I might have been willing to settle for less.

-Lily Tomlin

Have computers brought death to the once-familiar index? So I've been told. A friend of mine once suggested that the ubiquitous "search" box has made the index obsolete. If you're reading almost any kind of text on your computer screen, pushing the "Ctrl-F" keys will produce a "search" box that prompts for a word or term, and highlights all the occurrences in the text. Why would anyone go to the trouble of visiting an index, if they can find any term, on the spot, and instantly?

The index may be disparaged today, but there was a time when indexes were considered to be an essential component of every serious text[1] (See Glossary item, Indexes). In Wheeler's 1920 book, "Indexing: Principles, Rules and Examples," the author wrote, "The importance of book indexes is so widely recognized and the want of them so frequently deplored that no argument in their favor seems necessary."[2] Wheeler was right to believe that indexes are important, but he was wrong to suggest that no argument in their favor is necessary.

Instructional books are not lists of facts, and novels are not the print versions of movies. Every book, regardless of its topic, is a representation of the mind of the author. Every sentence tells us something about how the author interprets reality, and anyone who takes the time to read a single-author book is influenced by the author's conjured worldview. A single-author book is the closest thing we have to a Vulcan mind meld. The index organizes the author's message by reimagining the text. Great indexes provide a way of seeing the world created by the book, often in a manner that was unintended by the book's author. Ultimately, an index gives us an opportunity to grow beyond the text, discovering relationships among concepts that were missed by the author. By all rights, indexers should be given published credit for their creative products, much like authors are given credit for their works.[3]

Here are a few of the specific strengths of an index that cannot be duplicated by "find" operations on terms entered into a query box.[4]

1. An index can be read, as a stand-alone document, to acquire a quick view of the book's contents.[5]
2. When you do a "find" search in a query box, your search may come up empty if there is nothing in the text that matches your query. This can be very frustrating if you know that the text covers the topic entered into the query box. Indexes avoid the problem of fruitless searches. By browsing the index, you can find the term you need, without foreknowledge of its exact

wording within the text. When you find a term in the index, you may also find closely related terms, subindexed under your search term, or alphabetically indexed above or below your search term.

3. Searches on computerized indexes are nearly instantaneous, because the index is precompiled. Even when the text is massive (eg, gigabytes, terabytes), information retrieval via an index will be nearly instantaneous.

4. Indexes can be tied to a classification or other specialized nomenclature. Doing so permits the analyst to know the relationships among different topics within the index, and within the text[6] (See Glossary items, Nomenclature, Terminology, Vocabulary, Classification, Indexes vs. classifications).

5. Many indexes are cross-indexed, providing a set of relationships among different terms, that a clever data analyst might find useful.

6. Indexes can be merged. If the location entries for index terms are annotated with some identifier for the source text, then searches on a merged index will yield locators that point to specific locations from all of the sources.

7. Indexes can be embedded directly in the text.[7] Whereas conventional indexes contain locators to the text, embedded indexes are built into the locations where the index term is found in the text, with each location listing other locations where the term can be found. These onsite lists of terms can be hidden from the viewer with formatting instructions (eg, pop-up link tags in the case of HTML). Programmers can reconstitute conventional indexes from location-embedded tags, as required.

8. Indexes can be created to satisfy a particular goal; and the process of creating a made-to-order index can be repeated again and again. For example, if you have a massive or complex data resource devoted to ornithology, and you have an interest in the geographic location of species, you might want to create an index specifically keyed to localities, or you might want to add a locality subentry for every indexed bird name in your original index. Such indexes can be constructed as add-ons, when needed.

9. Indexes can be updated. If terminology or classifications change, there is nothing stopping you from re-building the index with an updated specification, without modifying your source data.

10. Indexes are created after the database has been created. In some cases, the data manager does not envision the full potential of a data resource until after it is built. The index can be designed to encourage novel uses for the data resource.

11. Indexes can occasionally substitute for the original text. A telephone book is an example of an index that serves its purpose without being attached to a related data source (eg, caller logs, switching diagrams).

You'll notice that the majority of the listed properties of indexes were impossible to achieve before the advent of computers. Today, a clever data scientist can prepare innovative and powerful indexes, if she has the following three ingredients:

1. The ability to write simple indexing scripts. Examples of short but powerful scripts for building indexes are provided in this chapter.

2. Nomenclatures with which to collect and organize terms from the text. The search for a specific index term can be greatly enhanced by expanding the search to include all terms that are synonymous with the search term. Nomenclatures organize equivalent terms under a canonical concept.

3. Access to data resources whose indexes can be sensibly merged. In the past several decades, data scientists have gained access to large, public, electronic data resources; perfect for indexing.

Data scientists should think of indexes as a type of data object. As such, an index is programmable, meaning that a savvy programmer can add all manner of functionality to indexes. For example, consider the index created for the Google search engine. The Google index uses a computational method known as PageRank. The rank of a page is determined by two scores: the relevancy of the page to the query phrase; and the importance of the page. The relevancy of the page is determined by factors such as how closely the page matches the query phrase, and whether the content of the page is focused on the subject of the query. The importance of the page is determined by how many Web pages link to and from the page, and the importance of the Web pages involved in the linkages. It is easy to see that the methods for scoring relevance and importance are subject to algorithmic variances, particularly with respect to the choice of measures (ie, the way in which a page's focus on a particular topic is quantified), and the weights applied to each measurement. The reasons that PageRank query responses are returned rapidly is that the score of a page's importance is precomputed, and stored in an index, with the page's Web addresses. Word matches from the query phrase to Web pages are quickly assembled using an index consisting of words, the pages containing the words, and the locations of the words in the pages.[8] The success of Page Rank, as employed by Google, is legendary (See Glossary item, Page Rank).[9]

An international standard (ISO 999) describes the fundamental principles of indexing (See Glossary item, ISO). Aside from following a few rules for arranging headings and subheadings, the field of computerized indexing is one of the most open and active fields in the data sciences. Indexes should be accepted as a useful device for understanding and simplifying data.

3.2 CONCORDANCES AND INDEXED LISTS

> From a programmer's point of view, the user is a peripheral that types when you issue a read request.
>
> -P. Williams

The easiest type of index to build is the concordance; a list of all the different words contained in a text, with the locations in the text where each word appears (See Glossary item, Concordance). The next easiest index to build is the extracted term index, wherein all of the terms extracted from the text are built into a list, along with the locations of each term. This section will describe computational methods for building both types of basic indexes.

Here, in a short Perl script, concord_gettysbu.pl, are instructions for building the concordance for the Gettysburg address:

```perl
#!/usr/local/bin/perl
open (TEXT, "gettysbu.txt");
open(OUT, ">concordance.txt");
$/ = "";
$line = <TEXT>;
foreach $word (split(/[\s\n]/,$line))
   {
   $word_location = $word_location + 1;
```

```
    $locations{$word} = $locations{$word} . "\,$word_location";
    }
foreach $word (sort keys %locations)
    {
    $locations{$word} =~ s/^[ \,]+//o;
    print OUT "$word $locations{$word}\n";
    }
exit;
```

The script parses the words of the text, and collects the locations where each word occurs (as the distance, in words, from the start of the file), and produces an ASCIIbetical listing of the words, with their respective locations. The concordance is deposited in the file "concordance.txt." We will be using this file in two more scripts that follow in this section. The first few lines of output are shown:

```
But 102
Four 1
God 240
It 91,160,186
Now 31
The 118,139
We 55,65
a 14,36,59,70,76,104,243
above 131
add 136
advanced. 185
ago 6
all 26
altogether 93
```

A concordance script, in Python:

```
#!/usr/local/bin/python
import re
import string
sentence_list = []
word_list = []
word_dict = {}
format_list = []
count = 0
in_text = open('gettysbu.txt', "r")
in_text_string = in_text.read()
in_text_string = in_text_string.replace("\n"," ")
in_text_string = in_text_string.replace(" +"," ")
sentence_list = re.split(r'[\.\!\?] +(?=[A-Z])',in_text_string)
for sentence in sentence_list:
    count = count + 1
    sentence = string.lower(sentence)
    word_list = sentence.split()
```

```
    for word in word_list:
        if word_dict.has_key(word):
            word_dict[word] = word_dict[word] + ',' + str(count)
        else:
            word_dict[word] = str(count)
keylist = word_dict.keys()
keylist.sort()
for key in keylist:
  print key, word_dict[key]
exit
```

A concordance script, in Ruby[10]:

```
#!/usr/local/bin/ruby
f = File.open("gettysbu.txt")
wordplace = Hash.new(""); wordarray = Array.new
f.each do
  |line|
  line.downcase!
  line.gsub!(/[^a-z]/," ")
  wordarray = line.split.uniq
  next if wordarray == []
  wordarray.each{|word| wordplace[word] = "#{wordplace[word]} #{f.lineno}"}
  wordarray = []
end
wordplace.keys.sort.each{|key| puts "#{key} #{wordplace[key]}"}
exit
```

At this point, building a concordance may appear to be an easy, but somewhat pointless exercise. Does the concordance provide any functionality beyond that provided by the ubiquitous "search" box? There are five very useful properties of concordances that you might not have anticipated.

1. You can always reconstruct the original text from the concordance. Hence, after you've built your concordance, you can discard the original text.
2. You can merge concordances without forfeiting your ability to reconstruct the original texts, just as long as you tag locations with some character sequence that identifies the text of origin.
3. You can use a concordance to search for the locations where multi-word terms appear.
4. You can use the concordance to retrieve the sentences and paragraphs in which a search word or a search term appears, in the absence of the original text. The concordance alone can reconstruct and retrieve the appropriate segments of text, on-the-fly, thus bypassing the need to search the original text.
5. A concordance provides a profile of the book, and can be used to compute a similarity score among different books.

Perhaps most amazing is that all five of these useful properties of concordances can be achieved with minor modifications to one of the trivial scripts, vida supra, that build the concordance.

There's insufficient room to explore and demonstrate all five properties of concordances, but let's examine a script, concord_reverse.pl, that reconstructs the original text, from a concordance.

```perl
#!/usr/local/bin/perl
open (TEXT, "concordance.TXT")||die;
$line = " ";
while ($line ne "")
   {
   $line = <TEXT>;
   $line =~ s/\n/\./o;
   $line =~ / /;
   $location_word = $`;
   @location_array = split(/\./,$');
   foreach $location (@location_array)
      {
      $concordance_hash{$location} = $location_word;
      }
   }
$n = 1;
while (exists($concordance_hash{$n}))
   {
   print $concordance_hash{$n} . " ";
   $n = $n + 1;
   }
exit;
```

Here are the first few lines of output:

> Four score and seven years ago our fathers brought forth on this continent a new
> nation, conceived in liberty and dedicated to the proposition that all men are
> created equal. Now we are engaged in a great civil war, testing whether that
> nation or any nation so conceived and so dedicated can long endure. We are met on
> a great battlefield of that war. We have come to dedicate a portion of that field

Had we wanted to write a script that produces a merged concordance for multiple books, we could have simply written a loop that repeated the concordance-building process for each text. Within the loop, we would have tagged each word location with a short notation indicating the particular source book. For example, locations from the Gettysburg address could have been prepended with "G:" and locations from the Bible might have been prepended with a "B:"

Here is a Perl script, proximity_reconstruction.pl, that prints out the a sequence of words flanking the word "who" in every location of the Gettysburg address where the word "who" appears, working exclusively from a concordance.

```perl
#!/usr/local/bin/perl
open (TEXT, "concordance.TXT")||die;
$line = " ";
while ($line ne "")
  {
  $line = <TEXT>;
```

```
$line =~ s/\n/\,/o;
$line =~ / /;
$location_word = $`;
@location_array = split(/\,/,$');
$word_hash{$location_word} = [@location_array];
foreach $location (@location_array)
   {
   $concordance_hash{$location} = $location_word;
   }
}
@word_locations_array = @{$word_hash{"who"}};
foreach $center_place (@word_locations_array)
   {
   $n = 1;
   print "Match.. ";
   while ($n < 11)
      {
      $location = $n + $center_place -5;
      print $concordance_hash{$location} . " ";
      $n = $n + 1;
      }
   print "\n";
   }
exit;
```

Here is the output of the proximity_reconstruction.pl script, which searches for words in the proximity of "who" appearing in the Gettysburg address.

```
c:\ftp>proximity_reconstruction.pl
Match.. final resting-place for those who here gave their lives that
Match.. men, living and dead who struggled here have consecrated it
Match.. unfinished work which they who fought here have thus far
```

Notice that the chosen search word, "who" sits in the center of each line.

Using the provided script as a template, you should be able to write your own scripts, in Perl, Python, or Ruby, that can instantly locate any chosen single word or multi-word terms, producing every sentence, or paragraph in which any search term is contained. Because concordances are precompiled, with the locations of every word, your search and retrieval scripts will run much faster than scripts that rely on Regex matches conducted over the original text (See Glossary item, Regex). Speed enhancements will be most noticeable for large text files.

Aside from reconstructing the full text from the concordance, a concordance provides a fairly good idea of the following information:

1. The topic of the text, based on the words appearing in the concordance. For example, a text having "begat" and "anointed" and "thy" is most likely to be the Old Testament.
2. The complexity of the language. A complex or scholarly text will have a larger vocabulary than a romance novel.

3. A precise idea of the length of the text, achieved by adding all of the occurrences of each of the words in the concordance.
4. The co-locations among words (ie, which words often precede or follow one another).
5. The care with which the text was prepared, achieved by counting the misspelled words.

3.3 TERM EXTRACTION AND SIMPLE INDEXES

> I was working on the proof of one of my poems all the morning, and took out a comma. In the afternoon I put it back again.
>
> -Oscar Wilde

Terms are phrases, most often noun phrases, and are sometimes individual words that have a precise meaning within a knowledge domain. Indexing software extracts and organizes the terms included in a text, providing all the text locations where each of the collected terms occurs.

Indexing can be a difficult process, requiring creativity. A good indexer will always attempt to answer the following four questions, before beginning a new project.

1. How do I find the relevant terms in the text? It is easy to collect the words in a text, but the concept of a term is highly subjective.
2. Which terms should be excluded? Perhaps the index should be parsimonious, including only the most important terms. After it is decided which terms are important and which terms are not, how shall we handle important terms that appear hundreds of times throughout the text? Is it realistic to think that anyone would use an index wherein a single term may appear at hundreds of locations in the text? Which locations, if any, of commonly occurring terms can be omitted from the index?
3. How should I organize the terms in the index? Which terms need to be cross-indexed, or subindexed under other terms?
4. For whom am I creating the index, and for what purposes? An index for an ebook will be used quite differently than an index for a printed book. An index for a terabyte corpus of text will be used differently than an index for an ebook.

Putting aside epistemology for the moment, let us examine the mechanics of extracting terms of a particular type or pattern, and annotating their locations. In Open Source Tools for Chapter 2, we demonstrated how regular expressions could be used to extract a list of proper names (ie, given name plus family name), from a public domain book, downloaded from Project Gutenberg (See Glossary item, Project Gutenberg). We will use the same book here, under filename "english_lit.txt." The short Perl script, namesget2.pl, extracts proper names and adds their byte locations (ie, the number of bytes counting from the start of the text).

```
#!/usr/local/bin/perl
undef($/);
open (TEXT, "english_lit.txt");
$line = <TEXT>;
while ($line =~ /\b[A-Z][a-z]+[ \n]{1}[A-Z][a-z]+\b/g)
  {
  $name = $&;
  $name_place = length($`);
```

```
  $name =~ s/\n/ /;
  next if ($name !~ /[A-Z][a-z]+/);
  $namelist{$name} = "$namelist{$name}\, $name_place";
  }
@namelist = sort(keys(%namelist));
foreach $name (@namelist)
  {
  print "$name $namelist{$name}\n";
  }
exit;
```

The first two dozen lines of output, from the Perl script namesget2.pl, are shown:

```
Abbess Hilda , 75574, 75713
About Project , 1302966
Abraham Cowley , 409655
Abraham Cowper , 1220412
Abt Vogler , 997769, 1003750, 1008995
Academy Classics , 1212052
Adam Bede , 1073581
Adam Smith , 628914, 785572, 932577
Adelaide Procter , 1026546
Adelaide Witham , 1186897
Ado About , 315615
After Alfred , 91274
Again Beowulf , 41291, 42464
Albion Series , 96018
Aldine Edition , 942820
Aldine Poets , 211090
Aldine Series , 495306
Alexander Pope , 12315, 751310
Alexander Selkirk , 674969, 730407
Alfred Lord , 1189113
Alfred Tennyson , 13458, 1189448
Algernon Charles , 1024420, 1196870
Alice Brown , 1199231
```

The Perl script for extracting proper names from a text file, looks for a specific pattern, indicating the likely location of a proper name.

```
while ($line =~ /\b[A-Z][a-z]+[ \n]{1}[A-Z][a-z]+\b/g)
```

In this case, the script extracts pairs of words in which each word begins with an uppercase letter. A byproduct of the pattern match is the string preceding the match (designated as the special Perl variable, "$`"). The length of the string contained in the "$`" variable is the byte location of the pattern match (ie, the byte location of the term that we hope will be a proper name).

Note that we prefer, in this case, to use the byte location of names, rather than page location. The concept of the page number is fading fast into obsolescence, as modern e-readers allow users to customize the appearance of text on their screens (eg, font size, font type, page width, image size). In the case of the e-reader, the page number has no absolute value. The story is not much different for printed books. With print-on-demand services, one book may be published with variable pagination, depending on the print settings selected. Basically, page numbers are a concept that adds complexity, without adding much useful information. Nonetheless, if indexes with page numbers are desired, it is simple enough to create a look-up table wherein ranges of character locations are mapped to page numbers. With such a table, an index annotated with character locations (ie, byte locations) could be transformed into an index annotated with page numbers, with just a few lines of code.

In most cases, good indexes cannot be built by looking for specific patterns, such as we might find for proper names. The indexer must be very clever. There are several available methods for finding and extracting index terms from a corpus of text,[11] but no method is as simple, fast, and scalable as the "stop word" method[12] (See Glossary items, Term extraction algorithm, Scalable). The "stop word" method operates under the empiric observation that all text is composed of words and phrases that represent specific concepts, that are connected by high frequency words of minimal information content.[4]

Consider the first sentence from James Joyce's "Ulysses": "Stately, plump Buck Mulligan came from the stairhead, bearing a bowl of lather on which a mirror and a razor lay crossed."

The terms in the sentence are the noun-phrases, the literary equivalents of data objects: Buck Mulligan, stairhead, bowl of lather, mirror, razor. The remainder of the sentences are words that describe data objects (ie, metadata relating the reader to the data object or relating data objects to one another). The way that noun phrases relate to one another are somewhat limited. If we simply deleted all of the relational words from a sentence, we would be left with a list of noun phrases, and the noun phrases, with their locations, could populate our index.

Here are a few examples:

"The diagnosis is chronic viral hepatitis."
"An epidural hemorrhage can occur after a lucid interval."

Let's eliminate sequences of relational words and replace them with a delimiter sequence, in this case "***."

"*** diagnosis *** chronic viral hepatitis."
"*** epidural hemorrhage *** lucid interval."

The indexable terms are the word sequences that remain when the delimiter sequences are removed:

diagnosis
chronic viral hepatitix
epidural hemorrhage
lucid interval

Let's write a simple Perl script that extracts common relational terms from a text, extracting the remaining word sequences. All we need is a list of commonly occurring relational terms, and a public domain text file. For our sample text, we will use the same text file, english_lit.txt, that we used earlier in this section, and in Open Source Tools for Chapter 2. Our list of common words is sometimes called a stop word list or a barrier word list, because it contains the words that demarcate the beginnings and endings of indexable terms (See Glossary item, Stop words). The Perl script, name_index.pl, includes our stop word list as an array variable.

```perl
#!/usr/local/bin/perl
@stoparray = qw(a about above according across actual actually added after afterwards
again against ahead all almost alone along already also although always am among amongst
amount an and another any anyhow anyone anything anyway anywhere approximately are
arising around as at award away back be became because become becomes becoming been before
beforehand behind being below beside besides best better between beyond birthday both
bottom but by call can cannot can't certain come comes coming completely computer con-
cerning consider considered considering consisting could couldn't cry describe despite
detail did discussion do does doesn't doing done down due during each eight either eleven
else elsewhere empty enough especially even ever every everyone everything everywhere
except few fifteen fifty fill find fire first five followed following for former formerly
forty forward found four from front full further get give given giving go had hardly has
hasn't have haven't having he hence her here hereafter hereby herein hereupon hers her-
self him himself his honor how however hundred i if in indeed inside instead interest into
is isn't it items its itself just keep largely last later latter least less let lets like
likely little look looks made mainly make makes making many may maybe me meantime mean-
while meet meets might million mine miss more moreover most mostly move mr mrs much must my
myself name namely near nearly neither never nevertheless next nine ninety no nobody none
nonetheless nor not nothing now nowhere obtain obtained of off often on once one only onto
or other others otherwise our ours ourselves out outside over overall own part per perhaps
please possible possibly previously put quite rather really recent recently regarding
reprinted resulted resulting same see seem seemed seeming seems seen serious seven
seventy several she should shouldn't show showed shown shows side significant signifi-
cantly since sincere six sixty so so-called some somehow someone something sometime
sometimes somewhere still stop studies study such suggest system take taken takes taking
ten than that the their theirs them themselves then there thereafter thereby therefore
therein thereupon these they thick thin third thirty this those though thousand three
through throughout thru thus to together too top toward towards trillion twelve twenty
two under undergoing unless unlike unlikely until up upon upward us use used using various
versus very via was way ways we well were weren't what whatever whats when whence whenever
where whereafter whereas whereby wherein whereupon wherever whether which while whither
who whoever whole whom whomever whos whose why will with within without would wouldn't yes
yet you your yours yourself yourselves );
open (TEXT, "english_lit.txt");
open (OUT, ">phrase_list.txt");
undef($/);
$whole_book = <TEXT>;
$whole_book =~ s/[\n\t]/ /g;
foreach $stopword (@stoparray)
    {
    $whole_book =~ s/\-/ /g;
    $whole_book =~ s/ *\b$stopword\b */ vvvvv /ig;
    }
@sentence_array = split(/[a-z]+\. +[A-Z]/, $whole_book);
```

```
foreach $sentence (@sentence_array)
  {
  $sentence = lc($sentence);
  push(@phrasearray, split(/ *vvvvv */, $sentence));
  }
@phrasearray = grep($_ ne $prev && (($prev) = $_), sort(@phrasearray));
print OUT join("\n", @phrasearray);
exit;
```

The output file contains over 40,000 terms, extracted from the a plain-text book of English literature, 1.3 megabytes in length. Here's a short sampling from the output file, phrase_list.txt:

```
shelley's "adonais,"
shelley's _adonais_.
shelley's characters
shelley's crude revolutionary doctrines.
shelley's father,
shelley's greater mood.
shelley's influence
shelley's italian life.
shelley's longer poems. _adonais_
shelley's miscellaneous works,
shelley's poem
shelley's poem _adonais_,
shelley's poetry.
shelley's poetry?
shelley's revolt
shelley's revolutionary enthusiasm,
shelley's works.
.
.
.
short descriptive passages
short descriptive poems
short english abstracts.
short essays
short halves, separated
short hymns
short miscellaneous poems
short period
short poem reflecting
short poems
short poems expressing
short poems suggested
short poems, edited
short space
short span
short stanzas,
short stories
short story teller
short story,
short sword
```

This simple algorithm, or something much like it, is a fast and efficient method to build a collection of index terms. The working part of the script, that finds and extracts index terms, uses under a dozen lines of code. Notice that the algorithm breaks the text into sentences, before substituting a delimiter (ie, "vvvvv") for the stop word sequences. This is done to avoid the extraction of sequences that overlap sentences.

Here is a Python script, extractor.py, that will extract term phrases from any file that is composed of lists of sentences (ie, a text file with one sentence per line of file).[12] The stop words are expected to reside in the file, stop.txt, wherein the stop words are listed one word per line of file).

```python
#!/usr/local/bin/python
import re, string
item_list = []
stopfile = open("stop.txt",'r')
stop_list = stopfile.readlines()
stopfile.close()
in_text = open('list_of_sentences.txt', "r")
count = 0
for line in in_text:
  count = count + 1
  for stopword in stop_list:
    stopword = re.sub(r'\n', '', stopword)
    line = re.sub(r' *\b' + stopword + r'\b *', '\n', line)
  item_list.extend(line.split("\n"))
item_list = sorted(set(item_list))
out_text = open('phrases.txt', "w")
for item in item_list:
  print>>out_text, item
exit
```

Here is an equivalent Ruby script, extractor.rb.[12]

```ruby
#!/usr/local/bin/ruby
phrase_array = []
stoparray = IO.read("stop.txt").split(/\n/)
sentence_array = IO.read("list_of_sentences.txt").split(/\n/)
out_text = File.open("phrases.txt", "w")
sentence_array.each do
  |sentence|
  stoparray.each do
    |stopword|
    sentence.gsub!(/ *\b#{stopword}\b */, "\n") if sentence.include? stopword
  end
  phrase_array = phrase_array + sentence.split(/\n/)
end
out_text.puts phrase_array.sort.uniq
exit
```

The output is an alphabetic file of the phrases that might appear in a book's index.

3.4 AUTOENCODING AND INDEXING WITH NOMENCLATURES

The beginning of wisdom is to call things by their right names.

- Chinese proverb

Nomenclatures are listings of terms that cover all of the concepts in a knowledge domain (See Glossary items, Nomenclature, Thesaurus, Vocabulary, Dictionary). A nomenclature is different from a dictionary for three reasons: (1) the nomenclature terms are not annotated with definitions, (2) nomenclature terms may be multi-word, and (3) the terms in the nomenclature are limited to the scope of the selected knowledge domain. In addition, most nomenclatures group synonyms under a group code. For example, a food nomenclature might collect submarine, hoagie, po' boy, grinder, hero, and torpedo under an alphanumeric code such as "F63958." The canonical concepts listed in a nomenclature are typically organized into a hierarchical classification.[13,14]

Nomenclatures simplify textual documents by uniting synonymous terms under a common code. Extending the example of the submarine sandwich, you can imagine that if a text document were to attach the code "F63958" to every textual occurrence of any of the synonyms of submarine sandwich, then it would be a simple matter to write a script that retrieved every paragraph in which "submarine sandwich" occurred, as well as every paragraph in which any and all of its synonymous terms occurred.

When you use the "find" or "search" dialog boxes available to word processors and e-readers, the search routine locates every occurrence of your search term in the text that you are reading. If you are lucky, the "find" box will support either a Regex or a "wildcard" search, retrieving every location matching a particular pattern. Under no circumstances will a "find" box support a search that retrieves all of the occurrences of every word or term that is synonymous with your query. That is the job of an index.

You may be thinking that a clever person, fully aware of what she is looking for, will know the synonyms for a search term and will simply repeat her "find" box query with each alternate term, or, if the "find" box permits, will execute an OR command, listing all the synonyms that apply, in a singly query. In practice, this never happens. Individuals are seldom equipped with the determination, patience, and expertise to formulate on-the-spot, comprehensive queries. A well-crafted nomenclature will contain synonymous terms that are unlikely to be anticipated by any individual. As an example, consider the Developmental Lineage Classification and Taxonomy of Neoplasms; this taxonomy contains 120 synonyms listed for "liver cancer."[13-17] Here are just a few of 120 synonymous or plesionymous terms collected under the nomenclature code, "C3099000":

```
adenoca of the liver
adenocarcinoma arising in liver
adenocarcinoma involving liver
liver with cancer
liver carcinoma
carcinoma arising in liver cells
hcc - hepatocellular carcinoma
primary liver carcinoma
hepatic carcinoma
hepatoma
hepatocarcinoma
liver cell carcinoma
```

Nomenclatures play an important role in data simplification by providing the synonymy required for comprehensive indexing and retrieval of nomenclature concepts. The process of attaching a nomenclature code to a fragment of text is called "coding," an act not to be confused with the programmer's use of "coding" to mean developing a software program. In the medical field, coding has become something of an industry. Healthcare providers hire armies of "coders" to attach disease codes and billing codes to the medical reports and transactions prepared for electronic medical records. Mistakes in coding can have dire consequences. In 2009, the Department of Veterans Affairs sent out hundreds of letters to veterans with the devastating news that they had contracted Amyotrophic Lateral Sclerosis, also known as Lou Gehrig's disease, a fatal degenerative neurologic condition. About 600 of the recipients did not, in fact, have the disease. The VA retracted these letters, attributing the confusion to a coding error.[18] Coding text is difficult. Human coders are inconsistent, idiosyncratic, and prone to error. Coding accuracy for humans seems to fall in the range of 85% to 90%.[19]

Try as they might, human coders cannot keep up with the terabytes of data produced each week by modern information systems. Consequently, there is a great need for fast and accurate software capable of automatic coding, alternatively called autocoding or autoencoding (See Glossary items, Coding, Autoencoding). Autocoding algorithms involve parsing text, word by word, looking for exact matches between runs of words and entries in a nomenclature.[20,21] When a match occurs, the words in the text that matched the nomenclature term are assigned the nomenclature code that corresponds to the matched term.

Here is one possible algorithmic strategy for autocoding the sentence: "Margins positive malignant melanoma." For this example, you would be using a nomenclature that lists all of the tumors that occur in humans. Let us assume that the terms "malignant melanoma" and "melanoma" are included in the nomenclature. They are both assigned the same code, for example "Q5673013," because the people who wrote the nomenclature considered both terms to be biologically equivalent.[4]

Let's pretend that we are computers, tasked with autocoding the diagnostic sentence, "Margins positive malignant melanoma":

1. Begin parsing the sentence, one word at a time. The first word is "Margins." You check against the nomenclature, and find that "margins" is not a term listed in the nomenclature. Save the word "margins." We'll use it in step 2.
2. You go to the second word, "positive" and find no matches in the nomenclature. You retrieve the former word "margins" and check to see if there is a 2-word term, "margins positive" listed in the nomenclature. There is not. Save "margins" and "positive" and continue.
3. You go to the next word, "malignant." There is no match in the nomenclature. You check to determine whether the 2-word term "positive malignant" and the 3-word term "margins positive malignant" are in the nomenclature. They are not.
4. You go to the next word, "melanoma." You check and find that melanoma is in the nomenclature. You check against the two-word term "malignant melanoma," the three-word term "positive malignant melanoma," and the four-word term "margins positive malignant melanoma." There is a match for "malignant melanoma" but it yields the same code as the code for "melanoma."
5. The autocoder appends the code, "Q5673013" to the sentence, and proceeds to the next sentence, where it repeats the algorithm.

The algorithm seems like a lot of work, requiring many comparisons, but it is actually quite efficient. A complete nomenclature, with each nomenclature term paired with its code, can be held in a single variable, in rapid access memory (See Glossary item, Variable). Look-ups to determine whether a word or phrase is included in the nomenclature, are fast. As it happens, there are methods that will speed things along much faster than our sample algorithm. My own previously published method can process text at a rate more than a 1000-fold faster than natural language methods.[20]

Implementations of a very fast autocoder are available in my previously published manuscripts and books.[20–22,10,12] Complete implementations are too large to include here, but the block containing the basic parsing and matching algorithm can be expressed in a few lines of code.

The Ruby code snippet for extracting terms in a sentence that match a nomenclature item, and producing its nomenclature code (ie, autocoding the terms in a text), is shown:

```ruby
absfile.each do
   |sentence|
   sentence.chomp!
   outfile.puts "\nAbstract title..." + sentence.capitalize + "."
   sentence_array = sentence.split
   length = sentence_array.size
   length.times do
      (1..sentence_array.size).each do
         |place_length|
         phrase = sentence_array.slice(0,place_length).join(" ")
         if literalhash.has_key?(phrase)
            outfile.puts "Term..." + phrase.capitalize + " " + literalhash[phrase]
         end
      end
   sentence_array.shift
   end
end
```

Here is the equivalent Python code:

```python
for line in absfile:
   sentence = line
   sentence = sentence.rstrip()
   sentence_array = sentence.split(" ")
   length = len(sentence_array)
   for i in range(length):
     for place_length in range(len(sentence_array)):
         last_element = place_length + 1
         phrase = ' '.join(sentence_array[0:last_element])
         if literalhash.has_key(phrase):
            print>>outfile,"Term..." + phrase + " " + literalhash[phrase]
      sentence_array.pop(0)
   exit
```

Here's the equivalent Perl code:

```perl
$line = " ";
while($line ne "")
   {
   $line = <ABSFILE>;
   $sentence = $line;
   $sentence =~ s/\n//o;
   @sentence_array = split(/ /,$sentence);
   $cycles = scalar(@sentence_array);
   for($n=0;$n<$cycles;$n++)
      {
      for($i=0;$i<scalar(@sentence_array);$i++)
         {
         @part_array = @sentence_array[0..$i];
         $phrase = join(" ", @part_array);
         if (exists($literalhash{$phrase}))
            {
            print OUTFILE "Term...".ucfirst($phrase)." ".$literalhash{$phrase}."\n";
            }
         }
      shift(@sentence_array);
      }
   }
exit;
```

In all three implementations, the first order of business (not shown) involves building the associative array, or dictionary object, for the nomenclature (See Glossary items, Associative array, Hash). This data structure is assigned the variable "literalhash," or "$literalhash" in Perl (See Glossary item, Metasyntactic variable). The "literalhash" object consists of key/value pairs, wherein every unique nomenclature term is a key matched with its nomenclature code value. Once the dictionary object is prepared, a simple word-by-word parsing routine, vida supra, matches nomenclature phrases encountered in a body of text with its nomenclature code.

Autocoding projects never end. Once you think you've finished annotating every term with its correct nomenclature code, thus ensuring that synonymous and plesionymous terms can be found and retrieved together, you learn that the whole job must be repeated.[20–23] Why is autocoding a Sisyphean task? Several reasons:

(1) *Nomenclatures keep changing*: Newer versions of nomenclatures may have a new set of codes that are incompatible with the old set of codes. It happens all the time. In the medical field newer versions of the International Classification of Diseases are not fully compatible with older versions, necessitating double coding (eg, applying new and old versions of the International Classification of Diseases codes to the U.S. mortality tables). Nomenclature revisions are a common consequence of terminology expansions. As a nomenclature increases in size and scope, preexisting relationships among concepts may not always accommodate newer concepts introduced into later versions of the same nomenclature.[24] For example, an automotive

nomenclature from the 1980s would list the DeLorean as a manufactured car, but a current nomenclature might list it as a discontinued model, or a classic, or an antique. Needless to say, nomenclatures are overhauled when two or more nomenclatures merge.

(2) *Data resources often need to switch nomenclatures*: When old information systems are replaced with new systems, vendors of the newer system may impose a different nomenclature on their data. The codes preserved in the legacy system become unusable, unless they can be directly mapped to codes in the new system (See Glossary item, Nomenclature mapping). Because concepts and terms among nomenclatures will differ, even when both nomenclatures cover the same knowledge domain, mapping projects are seldom successful. In most cases, the legacy data is either ignored, or it is recoded with the new nomenclature.

(3) *Data resources may need to be multi-coded*: Using several different nomenclatures, at once, to satisfy the different needs of different data users.

Is there a way to simply avoid coding, and recoding, without sacrificing the advantages of nomenclature-based data retrieval? Yes, there is a way.[25] Textual data can be interrogated, retrieving all the data that is relevant to a search term or its synonymous terms, using any nomenclature, and without bothering to preannotate the data source with nomenclature codes. Here is how it is done:

1. Pick a nomenclature, any nomenclature, that covers the knowledge domain of the text that you will be searching. If you like, you can choose more than one nomenclature. It makes no difference. For the sake of this exercise, the text will be a collection of magazines that focus on cooking. We'll choose a nomenclature that covers types of food items.
2. Prepare a concordance from the text that you'll be searching (as previously described in Section 3.2).
3. Select a demonstration search term. We'll pick "submarine sandwich."
4. Retrieve all synonyms for "submarine sandwich." The nomenclature groups equivalent terms together, so finding the synonyms and plesionyms for "submarine sandwich" is instantaneous. The synonym list found in the nomenclature is: "submarine sandwich, hoagie, po' boy, grinder, hero, and torpedo."
5. Loop through the list of synonyms, and use the concordance to give you every location where the first word of the nomenclature item (eg, "submarine" in "submarine sandwich") appears in the text. If the item consists of more than one word, as in the case of "submarine sandwich," use the concordance to exclude locations where the word "submarine" is not immediately followed by the word "sandwich." For example, if "submarine" is found at word location 2741, then we would need to find the word "sandwich" at location 2742. Failing that, location 2741 would be deleted from the list of locations where the term "submarine sandwich" is found. Repeat this process for every synonym of "submarine sandwich."
6. At the end of the process, you will have retrieved the location of every term in your text corpus that matches any of the nomenclature's synonyms for "submarine sandwich."

You may be thinking that there are a lot of steps to this process and that the time to collect a nomenclature search must surely exceed the length of time for a simple look-up using your favorite application's search utility. Actually, this is not the case. On-the-fly nomenclature searches are extremely fast because every step involves locating ordered items in pre-compiled lists (ie, the pre-compiled nomenclature list and the pre-compiled concordance). The algorithms for searches on ordered lists are much faster than searches conducted by parsing through every character of a long text, while hunting for a word pattern match. Using any nomenclature of your choice, you can find all matches to all synonymous terms from a body of text of any size, with near-instantaneous speed. Public domain Perl code for the "on-the-fly autocoding" script, along with a full description of the algorithm, is available in an open access publication (See Glossary item, Public domain)[25].

3.5 COMPUTATIONAL OPERATIONS ON INDEXES

> She was incapable of saying please, incapable of saying thank you and incapable of saying sorry, all the while creating a surge in the demand for these expressions.
>
> **-Edward St. Aubyn, in his book, "At Last"**

In Section 3.1, How Data Scientists Use Indexes. The claim was made that indexes are programmable objects, and can be used for purposes that were unimaginable prior to the advent of computers (See Glossary item, Burrows-Wheeler transform). In this section, we will see that an index of terms can be used in an encryption protocol. Encryption protocols are often specified as a sequence of mutually accepted actions between two entities (See Glossary item, Encryption). For our example, let us pretend that the two entities are Alice and Bob, and they need to negotiate a confidential exchange of information.[26] A generalized confidentiality problem can be presented as a negotiation protocol between Alice and Bob.[26]

Bob has a file containing the medical records of millions of patients. Alice has secret software that can annotate Bob's file, enhancing its value many-fold. Alice won't give Bob her secret algorithm, but is willing to demonstrate the algorithm if Bob gives her his database. Bob won't give Alice the database, but he can give her little snippets of the database containing insufficient information to match patients with records.

Bob prepares an algorithm that transforms his file into two pieces. Piece 1 is a file that contains all of the phrases (ie, extracted terms) from the original file with each phrase attached to its one-way hash value (See Glossary item, One-way hash). We will be learning more about one-way hashes in Chapter 5. For now, all you need to know is that a one-way hash value is a fixed-length pseudorandom sequence of characters computed on, in this case, fragments of text. The one-way hash has two very important properties: (1) a given phrase will always yield the same one-way hash value when operated on by the one-way hash algorithm and (2) there is no feasible way to determine the phrase by inspecting or manipulating the hash value. This second property holds true even if the hashing algorithm is known. Bob will give Alice Piece 1.

Piece 2 is a file wherein each phrase from the original file is replaced by its one-way hash value. High frequency words (ie, stop words) are left in place in Piece 2. Piece 2 and Piece 1 are used to reconstruct the original text or an annotated version of the original text, using Alice's modifications to Piece 1. The reconstruction algorithm simply steps through all the character strings found in Piece 2. When it encounters a hash-value, the algorithm looks at the list of hash-values in Piece 1 and substitutes the phrase associated with the hash-value back into the Piece 2 file. This continues until the end of Piece 2 is reached, at which time the Piece 2 file has been restored as the original file (plus any annotations that Alice may have added to the terms in Piece 1). This completes the confidential negotiation.

The following is an example of a single line of Bob's text that has been converted into two pieces according to the described algorithm.

Here is Bob's original text, which Bob does not want Alice to see.

```
"they suggested that the manifestations were as severe in the mother as in the sons and
that this suggested autosomal dominant inheritance."
```

Here is Bob's Piece 1, prepared by extracting the phrases from the original text, and producing the one-way hash values for each of the extracted phrases.

```
684327ec3b2f020aa3099edb177d3794 => suggested autosomal dominant inheritance
3c188dace2e7977fd6333e4d8010e181 => mother
8c81b4aaf9c2009666d532da3b19d5f8 => manifestations
db277da2e82a4cb7e9b37c8b0c7f66f0 => suggested
e183376eb9cc9a301952c05b5e4e84e3 => sons
22cf107be97ab08b33a62db68b4a390d => severe
```

Here is Bob's piece 2, created by substituting phrases in the original text with their one-way hash values, leaving the stop words in place. Bob keeps the original text, and piece 2, and does not send either to Alice (who must work exclusively from piece 1).

```
they db277da2e82a4cb7e9b37c8b0c7f66f0 that the 8c81b4aaf9c2009666d532da3b19d5f8 were
as 22cf107be97ab08b33a62db68b4a390d in the 3c188dace2e7977fd6333e4d8010e181 as in the
e183376eb9cc9a301952c05b5e4e84e3 and that this 684327ec3b2f020aa3099edb177d3794.
```

Properties of Piece 1 and Piece 2

Piece 1 (the listing of phrases and their one-way hashes)
1. Contains no information on the frequency of occurrence of the phrases found in the original text (because recurring phrases map to the same hash code and appear as a single entry in Piece 1).
2. Contains no information on the order or locations of the phrases found in the original text.
3. Contains all the concepts found in the original text. Stop words are a popular method of parsing text into concepts.
4. Bob can destroy Piece 1 and recreate it at any time, from the original text.
5. Alice can use the phrases in Piece 1 to transform, annotate, or search the concepts found in the original file.
6. Alice can transfer Piece 1 to a third party without violating Bob's confidentiality.
7. Alice can keep Piece 1 and add it to her database of Piece 1 files collected from all of her clients.
8. Piece 1 is not necessarily unique. Different original files may yield the same Piece 1 (if they're composed of the same phrases). Therefore Piece 1 cannot be used to authenticate the original file used to produce Piece 1 (See Glossary item, Authentication).

Properties of Piece 2
1. Contains no information that can be used to connect any private information to any particular data record.

2. Contains nothing but hash values of phrases and stop words, in their correct order of occurrence in the original text.

3. Anyone obtaining Piece 1 and Piece 2 can reconstruct the original text.

4. The original text can be reconstructed from Piece 2, and any file into which Piece 1 has been merged. There is no necessity to preserve Piece 1 in its original form.

5. Bob can lose or destroy Piece 2, and recreate it later from the original file, using the same algorithm.

If Alice had Piece 1 and Piece 2 she could simply use Piece 1 to find the text phrases that match the hash-values in Piece 2. Substituting the phrases back into Piece 2 will recreate Bob's original line of text. Bob must ensure that Alice never obtains Piece 2.

Alice uses her software (which is her secret) to annotate phrases from Piece 1. Presumably, Alice's software does something that enhances the value of the phrases. Such enhancements might involve annotating each phrase with a nomenclature code, a link to a database, an image file, or a location where related information is stored. Alice substitutes the transformed text (or simply appends the transformed text) for each phrase back into Piece 1, co-locating it with the original one-way hash number associated with the phrase.

Let's pretend that Alice has an autocoder that provides a standard nomenclature code to medical phrases that occur in text. Alice's software transforms the original phrases from Piece 1, preserving the original hash values, and appending a nomenclature code to every phrase that matches a nomenclature term. Here is the file, basically a modification of Piece 1, produced by Alice's software.

```
684327ec3b2f020aa3099edb177d3794 => suggested (autosomal dominant
inheritance=C0443147)
3c188dace2e7977fd6333e4d8010e181 => (mother=C0026591)
8c81b4aaf9c2009666d532da3b19d5f8 => manifestations
db277da2e82a4cb7e9b37c8b0c7f66f0 => suggested
e183376eb9cc9a301952c05b5e4e84e3 => (son=C0037683)
22cf107be97ab08b33a62db68b4a390d => (severe=C0205082)
```

Alice returns the modified piece 1 (ie, the coded phrase list) to Bob. Bob now takes the transformed Piece 1 and substitutes the transformed phrases for each occurrence of the hash values occurring in Piece 2 (which he has saved for this very purpose).

The reconstructed sentence is now:

```
they suggested that the manifestations were as (severe=C0205082) in the (mother=C0026591)
as in the (son=C0037683) and that this suggested (autosomal dominant heritance=C0443147)
```

The original sentence has been annotated with nomenclature codes. This was all accomplished without sharing confidential information that might have been contained in the text. Bob never had access to Alice's software. Alice never had the opportunity to see Bob's original text.

The negotiation between Bob and Alice need not be based on the exchange of text. The same negotiation would apply to any set of data elements that can be transformed or annotated. The protocol has practical value in instances when the sender and receiver each have something to hide: the contents of the original data in the case of the sender; and the secret software, in the case of the receiver.

Data scientists who are reluctant to share their data, based on confidentiality or privacy issues, should know that there are a variety of protocols that permit data to be safely shared, without breaching the secrecy of information contained in the data files. The protocol discussed here, developed by the author, is just one of many widely available negotiation protocols.[27] Encryption protocols will be discussed in greater detail in Chapter 5 (See Glossary items, Deidentification, Reidentification, Scrubbing, Data scrubbing, Deidentification versus anonymization)

OPEN SOURCE TOOLS

Perl: The only language that looks the same before and after RSA encryption.

-Keith Bostic

WORD LISTS

Word lists, for just about any written language for which there is an electronic literature, are easy to create. Here is a short Python script, words.py, that prompts the user to enter a line of text. The script drops the line to lowercase, removes the carriage return at the end of the line, parses the result into an alphabetized list, removes duplicate terms from the list, and prints out the list, with one term assigned to each line of output. This words.py script can be easily modified to create word lists from plain-text files (See Glossary item, Metasyntactic variable).

```
#!/usr/local/bin/python
import sys, re, string
print "Enter a line of text to be parsed into a word list"
line = sys.stdin.readline()
line = string.lower(line)
line = string.rstrip(line)
linearray = sorted(set(re.split(r' +', line)))
for i in range(0, len(linearray)):
    print(linearray[i])
exit
```

Here is some a sample of output, when the input is the first line of Joyce's Finnegan's Wake:

```
c:\ftp>words.py
Enter a line of text to be parsed into a word list
a way a lone a last a loved a long the riverrun, past Eve and Adam's, from swerv
e of shore to bend of bay, brings us by a commodius vicus
a
adam's,
and
bay,
```

```
bend
brings
by
commodius
eve
from
last
lone
long
loved
of
past
riverrun,
shore
swerve
the
to
us
vicus
way
```

Here is a nearly equivalent Perl script, words.pl, that creates a wordlist from a file. In this case, the chosen file happens to be "gettbysu.txt," containing the full-text of the Gettysburg address. We could have included the name of any plain-text file.

```perl
#!/usr/local/bin/perl
open(TEXT, "gettysbu.txt");
undef($/);
$var = lc(<TEXT>);
$var =~ s/\n/ /g;
$var =~ s/\'s//g;
$var =~ tr/a-zA-Z\'\- //cd;
@words = sort(split(/ +/, $var));
@words = grep($_ ne $prev && (($prev) = $_), @words);
print (join("\n",@words));
exit;
```

The words.pl script was designed for speed. You'll notice that it slurps the entire contents of a file into a string variable. If we were dealing with a very large file that exceeded the functional RAM memory limits of our computer, we could modify the script to parse through the file line-by-line.

Aside from word lists you create for yourself, there are a wide variety of specialized knowledge domain nomenclatures that are available to the public.[28,29,14,30–32] Linux distributions often bundle a wordlist, under filename "words," that is useful for parsing and natural language processing applications. A copy of the Linux wordlist is available at:

http://www.cs.duke.edu/~ola/ap/linuxwords

Curated lists of terms, either generalized, or restricted to a specific knowledge domain, are indispensable for developing a variety of applications (eg, spell-checkers, natural language processors, machine translation, coding by term, indexing). Personally, I have spent an inexcusable amount of time creating my own lists, when no equivalent public domain resources were available.

DOUBLET LISTS

Doublet lists (lists of two-word terms that occur in common usage or in a body of text) are a highly underutilized resource. The special value of doublets is that single word terms tend to have multiple meanings, while doublets tend to have specific meaning.

Here are a few examples:***

The word "rose" can mean the past tense of rise, or the flower. The doublet "rose garden" refers specifically to a place where the rose flower grows.

The word "lead" can mean a verb form of the infinitive, "to lead," or it can refer to the metal. The term "lead paint" has a different meaning than "lead violinist." Furthermore, every multiword term of length greater than two can be constructed with overlapping doublets, with each doublet having a specific meaning.

For example, "Lincoln Continental convertible" = "Lincoln Continental" + "Continental convertible." The three words, "Lincoln, "Continental," and "convertible" all have different meanings, under different circumstances. But the two doublets, "Lincoln Continental" and "Continental Convertible" would be unusual to encounter on their own, and have unique meanings.

Perusal of any nomenclature will reveal that most of the terms included in nomenclatures consist of two or more words. This is because single word terms often lack specificity. For example, in a nomenclature of recipes, you might expect to find, "Eggplant Parmesan" but you may be disappointed if you look for "Eggplant" or "Parmesan." In a taxonomy of neoplasms, available at: http://www.julesberman. info/figs/neocl_f.htm, containing over 120,000 terms, only a few hundred of those terms are single word terms.[33]

Lists of doublets, collected from a corpus of text, or from a nomenclature, have a variety of uses in data simplification projects.[33,20,25] We will show examples in Section 5.4.

For now, you should know that compiling doublet lists, from any corpus of text, is extremely easy.

Here is a Perl script, doublet_maker.pl, that creates a list of alphabetized doublets occurring in any text file of your choice (filename.txt in this example):

```perl
#!/usr/local/bin/perl
open(TEXT,"filename.txt")||die"cannot";
open(OUT,">doublets.txt")||die"cannot";
undef($/);
$var = <TEXT>;
$var =~ s/\n/ /g;
$var =~ s/\'s//g;
$var =~ tr/a-zA-Z\'\- //cd;
@words = split(/ +/, $var);
foreach $thing (@words)
   {
   $doublet = "$oldthing $thing";
```

```
    if ($doublet =~ /^[a-z]+[a-z]+$/)
      {
      $doublethash{$doublet}="";
      }
    $oldthing = $thing;
    }
close TEXT;
@wordarray = sort(keys(%doublethash));
print OUT join("\n",@wordarray);
close OUT;
exit;
```

Here is an equivalent Python script, doublet_maker.py:

```
#!/usr/local/bin/python
import anydbm, string, re
in_file = open('filename.txt', "r")
out_file = open('doubs.txt',"w")
doubhash = {}
for line in in_file:
  line = line.lower()
  line = re.sub('[.,<>?/;:"[]\{}|=+-_ ()*&^%$#@!`~1234567890]', ' ', line)
  hoparray = line.split()
  hoparray.append(" ")
  for i in range(len(hoparray)-1):
    doublet = hoparray[i] + " " + hoparray[i + 1]
    if doubhash.has_key(doublet):
        continue
    doubhash_match = re.search(r'[a-z]+ [a-z]+', doublet)
    if doubhash_match:
        doubhash[doublet] = ""
for keys,values in sorted(doubhash.items()):
    out_file.write(keys + '\n')
exit
```

Here is an equivalent Ruby script, doublet_maker.rb that creates a doublet list from file filename. txt:

```
#!/usr/local/bin/ruby
intext = File.open("filename.txt", "r")
outtext = File.open("doubs.txt", "w")
doubhash = Hash.new(0)
line_array = Array.new(0)
while record = intext.gets
  oldword = ""
  line_array = record.chomp.strip.split(/\s+/)
  line_array.each do
    |word|
    doublet = [oldword, word].join(" ")
```

```
    oldword = word
    next unless (doublet =~ /^[a-z]+\s[a-z]+$/)
    doubhash[doublet] = ""
    end
end
doubhash.each {|k,v| outtext.puts k }
exit
```

I have deposited a public domain doublet list, available for download at: http://www.julesberman.info/doublets.htm

The first few lines of the list are shown:

```
a bachelor
a background
a bacteremia
a bacteria
a bacterial
a bacterium
a bad
a balance
a balanced
a banana
```

NGRAM LISTS

Ngrams are subsequences of text, of length n words. A complete collection of ngrams consists of all of the possible ordered subsequences of words in a text. Because sentences are the basic units of statements and ideas, when we speak of ngrams, we are confining ourselves to ngrams of sentences. Let's examine all the ngrams for the sentence, "Ngrams are ordered word sequences."

```
Ngrams (1-gram)
are (1-gram)
ordered (1-gram)
word (1-gram)
sequences (1-gram)
Ngrams are (2-gram)
are ordered (2-gram)
ordered word (2-gram)
word sequences (2-gram)
Ngrams are ordered (3-gram)
are ordered word (3-gram)
ordered word sequences (3-gram)
Ngrams are ordered word (4-gram)
are ordered word sequences (4-gram)
Ngrams are ordered word sequences (5-gram)
```

Google has collected ngrams from scanned literature dating back to 1500. The public can enter their own ngrams into Google's ngram viewer, and receive a graph of the published occurrences of the phrase, through time.[9]

For example, we can use Google's Ngram viewer to visualize the frequency of occurrence of the single word, "photon" (Fig. 3.1).

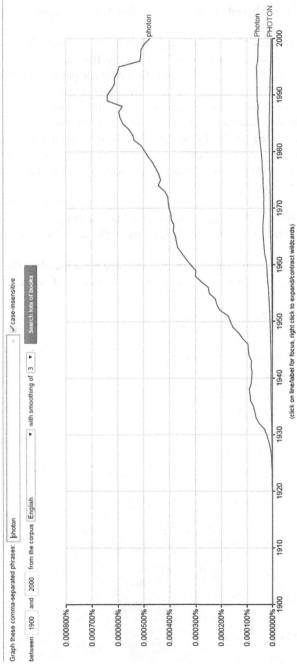

FIGURE 3.1

Google Ngram for the word "photon," from a corpus of literature covering years 1900 to 2000. Notice that the first appearances of the term "photon" closely corresponds to its discovery, in the second decade of the 20th century.

Source: Google Ngram viewer, with permission from Google.

The result fits into an historical narrative. The name "photon" comes from the Greek word for light. The word seems to have been used first in 1916, and is credited to Leonard T. Troland. When we chart the appearance of "photon" in published literature, we see that it does not appear until about 1920, when it rapidly entered common usage.

We can use the Ngram viewer to find trends (eg, peaks, valleys, and periodicities) in data. Consider the Google Ngram Viewer results for the two-word ngram, "yellow fever."

We see that the term "yellow fever" (a mosquito-transmitted hepatitis) appeared in the literature beginning about 1800, with several subsequent peaks. The dates of the peaks correspond roughly to outbreaks of yellow fever in Philadelphia (epidemic of 1793), New Orleans (epidemic of 1853), with U.S. construction efforts in the Panama Canal (1904–14), and with well-documented WWII Pacific outbreaks (about 1942). Following the 1942 epidemic, an effective vaccine was available, and the incidence of yellow fever, as well as the literature occurrences of the "yellow fever" n-gram, dropped precipitously. In this case, a simple review of ngram frequencies provides an accurate chart of historic yellow fever outbreaks (Fig. 3.2).[4,9]

Google's own ngram viewer supports simple lookups of term frequencies. For more advanced analyses (eg, finding co-occurrences of all ngrams against all other ngrams), data scientists can download the ngram data files, available at no cost from Google, and write their own programs, suited to their repurposing goals.

Here is a short Perl script that will take a sentence and produce a list of all the contained ngrams. This short script can easily be adapted to parse large collections of sentences, and to remove punctuation.

The Perl script, ngram_list.pl:

```perl
#!/usr/local/bin/perl
$text = "ngrams are ordered word sequences";
@text_list = split(" ", $text);
while(scalar(@text_list) !=0)
  {
  push(@parts_list, join(" ", @text_list));
  shift(@text_list);
  }
foreach $part (@parts_list)
  {
  $previous = "";
  @word_list = split(" ", $part);
  while(scalar(@word_list) !=0)
    {
    $ngram_list{join(" ", @word_list)} = "";
    $first_word = shift(@word_list);
    $ngram_list{$first_word} = "";
    $previous = $previous . " " . $first_word;
    $previous =~ s/^ //o;
    $ngram_list{$previous} = "";
    }
  }
print(join("\n", sort(keys(%ngram_list))));
exit;
```

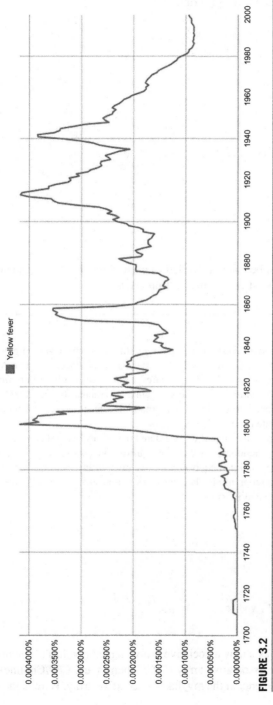

FIGURE 3.2

Google Ngram for the phrase "yellow fever," counting occurrences of the term in a large corpus, from the years 1700 to 2000. Peaks roughly correspond to yellow fever epidemics.

Source: Google Ngram viewer, with permission from Google.

Here is the output of the ngram_list.pl script:

```
c:\ftp>ngram_list.pl
are
are ordered
are ordered word
are ordered word sequences
ngrams
ngrams are
ngrams are ordered
ngrams are ordered word
ngrams are ordered word sequences
ordered
ordered word
ordered word sequences
sequences
word
word sequences
```

The ngram_list.pl script can be easily modified to parse through all the sentences of any text, regardless of length, building the list of ngrams as it proceeds.

GLOSSARY

ANSI The American National Standards Institute (ANSI) accredits standards developing organizations to create American National Standards (ANS). A so-called ANSI standard is produced when an ANSI-accredited standards development organization follows ANSI procedures and receives confirmation, from ANSI, that all the procedures were followed. ANSI coordinates efforts to gain international standards certification from the ISO (International Standards Organization) or the IEC (International Electrotechnical Commission). ANSI works with hundreds of ANSI-accredited standards developers.

Associative array A data structure consisting of an unordered list of key/value data pairs. Also known as hash, hash table, map, symbol table, dictionary, or dictionary array. The proliferation of synonyms suggests that associative arrays, or their computational equivalents, have great utility. Associative arrays are used in Perl, Python, Ruby and most modern programming languages. Here is an example in which an associative array (ie, a member of Class Hash) is created in Ruby.

```
#!/usr/local/bin/ruby
my_hash = Hash.new
my_hash["C05"] = "Albumin"
my_hash["C39"] = "Choline"
my_hash.each {
 |key,value|
 STDOUT.print(key, " --- ", value, "\n")}
exit
```

The first line of the script creates a new associative array, named my_hash. The next two lines create two key/value elements for the associative array (C05/Albumin and C39/Choline). The next line instructs ruby to print out the elements in the my_hash associative array. Here is the output of the short ruby script. *

```
Output:
C05 --- Albumin
C39 --- Choline
```

Authentication A process for determining if the data object that is received (eg, document, file, image) is the data object that was intended to be received. The simplest authentication protocol involves one-way hash operations on the data that needs to be authenticated. Suppose you happen to know that a certain file, named z.txt will be arriving via email and that this file has an MD5 hash of "uF7pBPGgxKtabA/2zYlscQ==." You receive the z.txt, and you perform an MD5 one-way hash operation on the file, as shown here:

```
#!/usr/bin/python
import base64
import md5
md5_object = md5.new()
sample_file = open ("z.txt", "rb")
string = sample_file.read()
sample_file.close()
md5_object.update(string)
md5_string = md5_object.digest()
print(base64.encodestring(md5_string))
exit
```

Let's assume that the output of the MD5 hash operation, performed on the z.txt file, is "uF7pBPGgxKtabA/2zYlscQ==." This would tell us that the received z.txt file is authentic (ie, it is the file that you were intended to receive); because no other file has the same MD5 hash. Additional implementations of one-way hashes are described in Open Source Tools for Chapter 5. The authentication process, in this example, does not tell you who sent the file, the time that the file was created, or anything about the validity of the contents of the file. These would require a protocol that included signature, timestamp, and data validation, in addition to authentication. In common usage, authentication protocols often include entity authentication (ie, some method by which the entity sending the file is verified). Consequently, authentication protocols are often confused with signature verification protocols. An ancient historical example serves to distinguish the concepts of authentication protocols and signature protocols. Since earliest recorded history, fingerprints were used as a method of authentication. When a scholar or artisan produced a product, he would press his thumb into the clay tablet, or the pot, or the wax seal closing a document. Anyone doubting the authenticity of the pot could ask the artisan for a thumbprint. If the new thumbprint matched the thumbprint on the tablet, pot, or document, then all knew that the person creating the new thumbprint and the person who had put his thumbprint into the object were the same individual. Of course, this was not proof that the object was the creation of the person with the matching thumbprint. For all anyone knew, there may have been a hundred different pottery artisans, with one person pressing his thumb into every pot produced. You might argue that the thumbprint served as the signature of the artisan. In practical terms, no. The thumbprint, by itself, does not tell you whose print was used. Thumbprints could not be read, at least not in the same way as a written signature. The ancients needed to compare the pot's thumbprint against the thumbprint of the living person who made the print. When the person died, civilization was left with a bunch of pots with the same thumbprint, but without any certain way of knowing whose thumb produced them. In essence, because there was no ancient database that permanently associated thumbprints with individuals, the process of establishing the identity of the pot-maker became very difficult once the artisan died. A good signature protocol permanently binds an authentication code to a unique entity (eg, a person). Today, we can find a fingerprint at the scene of a crime; we can find a matching signature in a database; and we can link the fingerprint to one individual. Hence, in modern times, fingerprints are true "digital" signatures, no pun intended.

Modern uses of fingerprints include keying (eg, opening locked devices based on an authenticated fingerprint), tracking (eg, establishing the path and whereabouts of an individual by following a trail of fingerprints or other identifiers), and body part identification (ie, identifying the remains of individuals recovered from mass graves or from the sites of catastrophic events based on fingerprint matches). Over the past decade, flaws in the vaunted process of fingerprint identification have been documented, and the improvement of the science of identification is an active area of investigation.[34] See HMAC. See Digital signature.

Autocoding When nomenclature coding is done automatically, by a computer program, the process is known as "autocoding" or "autoencoding." See Coding. See Nomenclature. See Autoencoding.

Autoencoding Synonym for autocoding. See Autocoding.

Autovivification In programming, autovivification is a feature of some programming languages wherein a variable or data structure seemingly brings itself into life, without definition or declaration, at the moment when its name first appears in a program. The programming language automatically registers the variable and endows it with a set of properties consistent with its type, as determined by the context, within the program. Perl supports autovivification. Python and Ruby, under most circumstances, do not. In the case of Ruby, new class objects (ie, instances of the class) are formally declared and created, by sending the "new" method to the class assigned to the newly declared object. See Reification.

Blended class Also known as class noise, subsumes the more familiar, but less precise term, "Labeling error." Blended class refers to inaccuracies (eg, misleading results) introduced in the analysis of data due to errors in class assignments (ie, assigning a data object to class A when the object should have been assigned to class B). If you are testing the effectiveness of an antibiotic on a class of people with bacterial pneumonia, the accuracy of your results will be forfeit when your study population includes subjects with viral pneumonia, or smoking-related lung damage. Errors induced by blending classes are often overlooked by data analysts who incorrectly assume that the experiment was designed to ensure that each data group is composed of a uniform and representative population. A common source of class blending occurs when the classification upon which the experiment is designed is itself blended. For example, imagine that you are a cancer researcher and you want to perform a study of patients with malignant fibrous histiocytomas (MFH), comparing the clinical course of these patients with the clinical course of patients who have other types of tumors. Let's imagine that the class of tumors known as MFH does not actually exist; that it is a grab-bag term erroneously assigned to a variety of other tumors that happened to look similar to one another. This being the case, it would be impossible to produce any valid results based on a study of patients diagnosed as MFH. The results would be a biased and irreproducible cacophony of data collected across different, and undetermined, classes of tumors. Believe it or not, this specific example, of the blended MFH class of tumors, is selected from the real-life annals of tumor biology.[35,36] The literature is rife with research of dubious quality, based on poorly designed classifications and blended classes. A detailed discussion of this topic is found in Section 6.5, "Properties that Cross Multiple Classes." One caveat. Efforts to eliminate class blending can be counterproductive if undertaken with excess zeal. For example, in an effort to reduce class blending, a researcher may choose groups of subjects who are uniform with respect to every known observable property. For example, suppose you want to actually compare apples with oranges. To avoid class blending, you might want to make very sure that your apples do not include any kumquats, or persimmons. You should be certain that your oranges do not include any limes or grapefruits. Imagine that you go even further, choosing only apples and oranges of one variety (eg, Macintosh apples and navel oranges), size (eg 10 cm), and origin (eg, California). How will your comparisons apply to the varieties of apples and oranges that you have excluded from your study? You may actually reach conclusions that are invalid and irreproducible for more generalized populations within each class. In this case, you have succeeded in eliminating class blending, at the expense of losing representative populations of the classes. See Simpson's paradox.

Burrows-Wheeler transform Abbreviated as BWT, the Burrows-Wheeler transform produces a compressed version of an original file, along with a concordance to the contents of the file. Using a reverse BWT, you can reconstruct the original file, or you can find any portion of a file preceding or succeeding any location in the file. The BWT transformation is an amazing example of simplification, applied to informatics. A detailed discussion of the BWT is found in Open Source Tools for Chapter 8. See Concordance.

Check digit A checksum that produces a single digit as output is referred to as a check digit. Some of the common identification codes in use today, such as ISBN numbers for books, come with a built-in check digit. Of course, when using a single digit as a check value, you can expect that some transmitted errors will escape the check, but the check digit is useful in systems wherein occasional mistakes are tolerated; or wherein the purpose of the check digit is to find a specific type of error (eg, an error produced by a substitution in a single character or digit), and wherein the check digit itself is rarely transmitted in error. See Checksum.

Checksum An outdated term that is sometimes used synonymously with one-way hash or message digest. Checksums are performed on a string, block, or file yielding a short alphanumeric string intended to be specific for the input data. Ideally, If a single bit were to change, anywhere within the input file, then the checksum for the input file would change drastically. Checksums, as the name implies, involve summing values (typically weighted character values) to produce a sequence that can be calculated on a file before and after transmission. Most of the errors that were commonly introduced by poor transmission could be detected with checksums. Today, the old checksum algorithms have been largely replaced with one-way hash algorithms. A checksum that produces a single digit as output is referred to as a check digit. See Check digit. See One-way hash. See Message digest. See HMAC.

Child class The direct or first generation subclass of a class. Sometimes referred to as the daughter class or, less precisely, as the subclass. See Parent class. See Classification.

Class A class is a group of objects that share a set of properties that define the class and that distinguish the members of the class from members of other classes. The word "class," lowercase, is used as a general term. The word "Class," uppercase, followed by an uppercase noun (eg Class Animalia), represents a specific class within a formal classification. See Classification.

Classification A system in which every object in a knowledge domain is assigned to a class within a hierarchy of classes. The properties of superclasses are inherited by the subclasses. Every class has one immediate superclass (ie, parent class), although a parent class may have more than one immediate subclass (ie, child class). Objects do not change their class assignment in a classification, unless there was a mistake in the assignment. For example, a rabbit is always a rabbit, and does not change into a tiger. Classifications can be thought of as the simplest and most restrictive type of ontology, and serve to reduce the complexity of a knowledge domain.[37] Classifications can be easily modeled in an object-oriented programming language and are nonchaotic (ie, calculations performed on the members and classes of a classification should yield the same output, each time the calculation is performed). A classification should be distinguished from an ontology. In an ontology, a class may have more than one parent class and an object may be a member of more than one class. A classification can be considered a special type of ontology wherein each class is limited to a single parent class and each object has membership in one, and only one, class. See Nomenclature. See Thesaurus. See Vocabulary. See Classification. See Dictionary. See Terminology. See Ontology. See Parent class. See Child class. See Superclass. See Unclassifiable objects.

Coding The term "coding" has three very different meanings; depending on which branch of science influences your thinking. For programmers, coding means writing the code that constitutes a computer program. For cryptographers, coding is synonymous with encrypting (ie, using a cipher to encode a message). For medics, coding is calling an emergency team to handle a patient in extremis. For informaticians and library scientists, coding involves assigning an alphanumeric identifier, representing a concept listed in a nomenclature, to a term. For example, a surgical pathology report may include the diagnosis, "Adenocarcinoma of prostate." A nomenclature may assign a code C4863000 that uniquely identifies the concept "Adenocarcinoma." Coding the report may involve annotating every occurrence of the work "Adenocarcinoma" with the "C4863000" identifier. For a detailed explanation of coding, and its importance for searching and retrieving data, see the full discussion in Section 3.4. See Autocoding. See Nomenclature.

Concordance A concordance is an index consisting of every word in the text, along with every location wherein each word can be found. It is computationally trivial to reconstruct the original text from the concordance. Before the advent of computers, concordances fell into the provenance of religious scholars, who painstakingly recorded the locations of the all words appearing in the Bible, ancient scrolls, and any texts whose words were considered to be divinely inspired. Today, a concordance for a Bible-length book can be constructed in about a second. Furthermore, the original text can be reconstructed from the concordance, in about the same time.

Data scrubbing A term that is very similar to data deidentification and is sometimes used improperly as a synonym for data deidentification. Data scrubbing refers to the removal, from data records, of information that is considered unwanted. This may include identifiers, private information, or any incriminating or otherwise objectionable language contained in data records, as well as any information deemed irrelevant to the purpose served by the record. See Deidentification.

Deidentification The process of removing all of the links in a data record that can connect the information in the record to an individual. This usually includes the record identifier, demographic information (eg, place of birth), personal information (eg, birthdate), biometrics (eg, fingerprints), and so on. The process of deidentification will vary based on the type of records examined. Deidentifying protocols exist wherein deidentificatied records can be reidentified, when necessary. See Reidentification. See Data scrubbing.

Deidentification versus anonymization Anonymization is a process whereby all the links between an individual and the individual's data record are irreversibly removed. The difference between anonymization and deidentification is that anonymization is irreversible. Because anonymization is irreversible, the opportunities for verifying the quality of data are limited. For example, if someone suspects that samples have been switched in a data set, thus putting the results of the study into doubt, an anonymized set of data would afford no opportunity to resolve the problem by reidentifying the original samples. See Reidentification.

Dictionary A terminology or word list accompanied by a definition for each item. See Nomenclature. See Vocabulary. See Terminology.

Digital signature As it is used in the field of data privacy, a digital signature is an alphanumeric sequence that could only have been produced by a private key owned by one particular person. Operationally, a message digest (eg, a one-way hash value) is produced from the document that is to be signed. The person "signing" the document encrypts the message digest using her private key, and submits the document and the encrypted message digest to the person who intends to verify that the document has been signed. This person decrypts the encrypted message digest with her public key (ie, the public key complement to the private key) to produce the original one-way hash value. Next, a one-way hash is performed on the received document. If the resulting one-way hash is the same as the decrypted one-way hash, then several statements hold true: the document received is the same document as the document that had been "signed." The signer of the document had access to the private key that complemented the public key that was used to decrypt the encrypted one-way hash. The assumption here is that the signer was the only individual with access to the private key. Digital signature protocols, in general, have a private method for encrypting a hash, and a public method for verifying the signature. Such protocols operate under the assumption that only one person can encrypt the hash for the message, and that the name of that person is known; hence, the protocol establishes a verified signature. It should be emphasized that a digital signature is quite different from a written signature; the latter usually indicates that the signer wrote the document or somehow attests to the veracity of the document. The digital signature merely indicates that the document was received from a particular person, contingent on the assumption that the private key was available only to that person. To understand how a digital signature protocol may be maliciously deployed, imagine the following scenario: I contact you and tell you that I am Elvis Presley and would like you to have a copy of my public key plus a file that I have encrypted using my private key. You receive the file and the public key; and you use the public key to decrypt the file. You conclude that the file was indeed sent by Elvis Presley. You read the decrypted file and learn that Elvis advises you to invest all your money in a company that manufactures concrete guitars; which, of course, you do.

Elvis knows guitars. The problem here is that the signature was valid, but the valid signature was not authentic. See Authentication.

Encryption A common definition of encryption involves an algorithm that takes some text or data and transforms it, bit-by-bit, into an output that cannot be interpreted (ie, from which the contents of the source file cannot be determined). Encryption comes with the implied understanding that there exists some reverse transform that can be applied to the encrypted data, to reconstitute the original source. As used herein, the definition of encryption is expanded to include any protocols by which files can be shared, in such a way that only the intended recipients can make sense of the received documents. This would include protocols that divide files into pieces that can only be reassembled into the original file using a password. Encryption would also include protocols that alter parts of a file while retaining the original text in other parts of the file. As described in Chapter 5, there are instances when some data in a file should be shared, while only specific parts need to be encrypted. The protocols that accomplish these kinds of file transformations need not always employ classic encryption algorithms. See Winnowing and chaffing.

HMAC Hashed Message Authentication Code. When a one-way hash is employed in an authentication protocol, it is often referred to as an HMAC. See One-way hash. See Message digest. See Checksum.

Hash A hash, also known as associative array and as dictionary, is a data structure comprising an unordered list of key/value pairs. The term "hash" must be distinguished from the unrelated term, "One-way hash." See One-way hash.

ISO International Standards Organization. The ISO is a nongovernmental organization that develops international standards (eg, ISO-11179 for metadata and ISO-8601 for date and time). See ANSI.

Index An index is a an ordered collection of words, phrases, concepts, or subsets of classes of information (eg, geographic names, names of persons, dates of events), linked to the locations where they occur in the text. The terms in an index are selected and ordered based on the indexer's conceptualization of the text, and of the utility of the text to the intended readers. Furthermore, the index is seldom, if ever, created by the author(s) of the text. Hence, the index is a reconceptualization of the original text, in tabular form, comprising a new, creative, work.[5] See Indexes.

Indexes Every writer must search deeply into his or her soul to find the correct plural form of "index." Is it "indexes" or is it "indices?" Latinists insist that "indices" is the proper and exclusive plural form. Grammarians agree, reserving "indexes" for the third person singular verb form; "The student indexes his thesis." Nonetheless, popular usage of the plural of "index," referring to the section at the end of a book, is almost always "indexes," the form used herein. See Index.

Indexes versus classifications Indexes and classifications both help us to expand and simplify our perception of a subject or a knowledge domain. The key difference between the two concepts is that indexes are methods of searching and retrieving data objects; whereas classifications are methods of describing the relationships among data objects.

Instance An instance is a specific example of an object that is not itself a class or group of objects. For example, Tony the Tiger is an instance of the tiger species. Tony the Tiger is a unique animal and is not itself a group of animals or a class of animals. The terms instance, instance object, and object are sometimes used interchangeably, but the special value of the "instance" concept, in a system wherein everything is an object, is that it distinguishes members of classes (ie, the instances) from the classes to which they belong.

Message digest Within the context of this book, "message digest," "digest," "HMAC," and "one-way hash" are equivalent terms. See One-way hash. See HMAC.

Metasyntactic variable A Variable name that imports no specific meaning, such as x, n, foo, foobar. Dummy variables are often used in iterating loops. For example:

```
for($i=0;$i<1000;$i++)
```

Good form dictates against the liberal use of metasyntactic variables. In most cases, programmers should create variable names that describe the purpose of the variable (eg, time_of_day, column_sum, current_line_from_file).

Multiclass classification A misnomer imported from the field of machine translation, and indicating the assignment of an instance to more than one class. Classifications, as defined in this book, impose one-class classification (ie, an instance can be assigned to one and only one class). It is tempting to think that a ball should be included in class "toy" and in class "spheroids," but multiclass assignments create unnecessary classes of inscrutable provenance, and taxonomies of enormous size, consisting largely of replicate items. See Multiclass inheritance. See Taxonomy.

Multiclass inheritance In ontologies, multiclass inheritance occurs when a child class has more than one parent class. For example, a member of Class House may have two different parent classes: Class Shelter, and Class Property. Multiclass inheritance is generally permitted in ontologies but is forbidden in one type of restrictive ontology, known as a classification. See Classification. See Parent class. See Multiclass classification.

Namespace A namespace is the realm in which a metadata tag applies. The purpose of a namespace is to distinguish metadata tags that have the same name, but a different meaning. For example, within a single XML file, the metadata tag "date" may be used to signify a calendar date, or the fruit, or the social engagement. To avoid confusion, metadata terms are assigned a prefix that is associated with a Web document that defines the term (ie, establishes the tag's namespace). In practical terms, a tag that can have different descriptive meanings in different contexts is provided with a prefix that links to a web document wherein the meaning of the tag, as it applies in the XML document, is specified.

Nomenclature A nomenclatures is a listing of terms that cover all of the concepts in a knowledge domain. A nomenclature is different from a dictionary for three reasons: (1) the nomenclature terms are not annotated with definitions, (2) nomenclature terms may be multi-word, and (3) the terms in the nomenclature are limited to the scope of the selected knowledge domain. In addition, most nomenclatures group synonyms under a group code. For example, a food nomenclature might collect submarine, hoagie, po' boy, grinder, hero, and torpedo under an alphanumeric code such as "F63958." Nomenclatures simplify textual documents by uniting synonymous terms under a common code. Documents that have been coded with the same nomenclature can be integrated with other documents that have been similarly coded, and queries conducted over such documents will yield the same results, regardless of which term is entered (ie, a search for either hoagie, or po' boy will retrieve the same information, if both terms have been annotated with the synonym code, "F63948"). Optimally, the canonical concepts listed in the nomenclature are organized into a hierarchical classification.[13,14] See Coding. See Autocoding.

Nomenclature mapping Specialized nomenclatures employ specific names for concepts that are included in other nomenclatures, under other names. For example, the term that pathologists use for a certain benign fibrous tumor of the skin is "fibrous histiocytoma," a term spurned by dermatologists, who prefer to use "dermatofibroma" to describe the same tumor. As another horrifying example, the names for the physiologic responses caused by a reversible cerebral vasoconstricitve event include: thunderclap headache, Call-Fleming syndrome, benign angiopathy of the central nervous system, postpartum angiopathy, migrainous vasospasm, and migraine angiitis. The choice of term will vary depending on the medical specialty of the physician (eg, neurologist, rheumatologist, obstetrician). To mitigate the discord among specialty nomenclatures, lexicographers may undertake a harmonization project, in which nomenclatures with overlapping concepts are mapped to one another.

Nonatomicity Nonatomicity is the assignment of a collection of objects to a single, composite object, that cannot be further simplified or sensibly deconstructed. For example, the human body is composed of trillions of individual cells, each of which lives for some length of time, and then dies. Many of the cells in the body are capable of dividing to produce more cells. In many cases, the cells of the body that are capable of dividing can be cultured and grown in plastic containers, much like bacteria can be cultured and grown in Petri dishes.

If the human body is composed of individual cells, why do we habitually think of each human as a single living entity? Why don't we think of humans as bags of individual cells? Perhaps the reason stems from the coordinated responses of cells. When someone steps on the cells of your toe, the cells in your brain sense pain, the cells in your mouth and vocal cords say ouch, and an army of inflammatory cells rush to the scene of the crime. The cells in your toe are not capable of registering an actionable complaint, without a great deal of assistance. Another reason that organisms, composed of trillions of living cells, are generally considered to have nonatomicity, probably relates to the "species" concept in biology. Every cell in an organisms descended from the same zygote, and every zygote in every member of the same species descended from the same ancestral organism. Hence, there seems to be little benefit to assigning unique entity status to the individual cells that compose organisms, when the class structure for organisms is based on descent through zygotes. See Species.

One-way hash A one-way hash is an algorithm that transforms one string into another string (a fixed-length sequence of seemingly random characters) in such a way that the original string cannot be calculated by operations on the one-way hash value (ie, the calculation is one-way only). One-way hash values can be calculated for any string, including a person's name, a document, or an image. For any given input string, the resultant one-way hash will always be the same. If a single byte of the input string is modified, the resulting one-way hash will be changed, and will have a totally different sequence than the one-way hash sequence calculated for the unmodified string. Most modern programming languages have several methods for generating one-way hash values. Here is a short Ruby script that generates a one-way hash value for a file:

```
#!/usr/local/bin/ruby
require 'digest/md5'
file_contents = File.new("simplify.txt").binmode
hash_string = Digest::MD5.base64digest(file_contents.read)
puts hash_string
exit
```

Here is the one-way hash value for the file, simplify.txt, using the md5 algorithm:

```
OCfZez7L1A6WFcT+oxMh+g==
```

If we copy our example file to another file, with an alternate filename, the md5 algorithm will generate the same hash value. Likewise, if we generate a one-way hash value, using the md5 algorithm implemented in some other language, such as Python or Perl, the outputs will be identical. One-way hash values can be designed to produce long fixed-length output strings (eg, 256 bits in length). When the output of a one-way hash algorithm is very long, the chance of a hash string collision (ie, the occurrence of two different input strings generating the same one-way hash output value) is negligible. Clever variations on one-way hash algorithms have been repurposed as identifier systems.[38–41] Examples of one-way hash implementations in Perl and Python are found in Open Source Tools for Chapter 5, "Encryption." See HMAC. See Message digest. See Checksum.

Ontology An ontology is a collection of classes and their relationships to one another. Ontologies are usually rule-based systems (ie, membership in a class is determined by one or more class rules). Two important features distinguish ontologies from classifications. Ontologies permit classes to have more than one parent class and more than one child class. For example, the class of automobiles may be a direct subclass of "motorized devices" and a direct subclass of "mechanized transporters." In addition, an instance of a class can be an instance of any number of additional classes. For example, a Lamborghini may be a member of class "automobiles" and of class "luxury items." This means that the lineage of an instance in an ontology can be highly complex, with a single instance occurring in multiple classes, and with many connections between classes. Because recursive relations are permitted, it is possible to build an ontology wherein a class is both an ancestor class and a descendant class of itself. A classification is a highly restrained ontology wherein instances can belong to only one class, and each class may have only one direct parent class. Because classifications have an enforced linear hierarchy, they can be easily modeled, and the lineage of any instance can be traced unambiguously. See Classification. See Multiclass classification. See Multiclass inheritance.

Page Rank Page Rank, alternately PageRank, is a computational method popularized by Google that searches through an index of every Web page, to produce an ordered set of Web pages whose content can be matched against a query phrase. The rank of a page is determined by two scores: the relevancy of the page to the query phrase; and the importance of the page. The relevancy of the page is determined by factors such as how closely the page matches the query phrase, and whether the content of the page is focused on the subject of the query. The importance of the page is determined by how many Web pages link to and from the page, and the importance of the Web pages involved in the linkages. It is easy to see that the methods for scoring relevance and importance are subject to many algorithmic variations, particularly with respect to the choice of measures (ie, the way in which a page's focus on a particular topic is quantified), and the weights applied to each measurement. The reasons that Page Rank query are fast is that the score of a page's importance is pre-computed, and stored with the page's Web addresses. Word matches from the query phrase to Web pages are quickly assembled using a pre-computed index of words, the pages containing the words, and the locations of the words in the pages.[8] The success of Page Rank, as employed by Google, is legend. Page ranking is an example of Object ranking, a computation method employed in ranking data objects. Object ranking involves providing objects with a quantitative score that provides some clue to the relevance or the popularity of an object.

Parent class The immediate ancestor, or the next-higher class (ie, the direct superclass) of a class. For example, in the classification of living organisms, Class Vertebrata is the parent class of Class Gnathostomata. Class Gnathostomata is the parent class of Class Teleostomi. In a classification, which imposes single class inheritance, each child class has exactly one parent class; whereas one parent class may have several different child classes. Furthermore, some classes, in particular, the bottom class in the lineage, have no child classes (ie, a class need not always be a superclass of other classes). A class can be defined by its properties, its membership (ie, the instances that belong to the class), and by the name of its parent class. When we list all of the classes in a classification, in any order, we can always reconstruct the complete class lineage, in in their correct lineage and branchings, if we know the name of each class's parent class. See Instance. See Child class. See Superclass.

Project Gutenberg An organization that has converted nearly 50,000 books into freely available ebooks. Most of the Project Gutenberg ebooks were prepared from works published prior to 1923, for which copyright protections have expired. Such books fall into the public domain. More information is available at: www.gutenberg.org. See Public domain.

Public domain Data that is not owned by an entity. Public domain materials include documents whose copyright terms have expired, materials produced by the federal government, materials that contain no creative content (ie, materials that cannot be copyrighted), or materials donated to the public domain by the entity that holds copyright. Public domain data can be accessed, copied, and redistributed without violating piracy laws. It is important to note that plagiarism laws and rules of ethics apply to public domain data. You must properly attribute authorship to public domain documents. If you purposely fail to attribute authorship or if you purposefully and falsely attribute authorship to the wrong person (eg, yourself), then this is unethical, and an act of plagiarism.

RDF Schema Resource Description Framework Schema (RDFS). A document containing a list of classes, their definitions, and the names of the parent class(es) for each class. In an RDF Schema, the list of classes is typically followed by a list of properties that apply to one or more classes in the Schema. To be useful, RDF Schemas are posted on the Internet, as a Web page, with a unique Web address. Anyone can incorporate the classes and properties of a public RDF Schema into their own RDF documents (public or private) by linking named classes and properties, in their RDF document, to the web address of the RDF Schema where the classes and properties are defined. See Namespace. See RDFS.

RDFS Same as RDF Schema.

Regex Shortened form of "Regular Expression." See Regular expression.

Regular expression Short form, Regex. A regular expression is a widely used syntax for specifying character patterns. Most programming languages and many word processing applications use regular expressions for describing character patterns that can be matched against character strings. A detailed description of regular expressions is found in Open Source Tools for Chapter 2.

Reidentification A term casually applied to any instance whereby information can be linked to a specific person, after the links between the information and the person associated with the information have been removed. Used this way, the term reidentification connotes an insufficient deidentification process. In the health care industry, the term "reidentification" means something else entirely. In the U.S., regulations define "reidentification" under the "Standards for Privacy of Individually Identifiable Health Information."[42] Therein, reidentification is a legally sanctioned process whereby deidentified records can be linked back to their human subjects, under circumstances deemed legitimate and compelling, by a privacy board. Reidentification is typically accomplished via the use of a confidential list of links between human subject names and deidentified records, held by a trusted party. In the healthcare realm, when a human subject is identified through fraud, trickery, or through the deliberate use of computational methods to break the confidentiality of insufficiently deidentified records (ie, hacking), the term "reidentification" would not apply.[4]

Reification A programming term that has some similarity to "autovivification." In either case, an abstract piece of a program brings itself into life, at the moment when it is assigned a name. Whereas autovivification generally applies to variables and data structures, reification generally applies to blocks of code, methods, and data objects. When a named block of code becomes reified, it can be invoked anywhere within the program, by its name. See Autovivification.

Scalable Software is scalable if it operates smoothly, whether the data is small or large. Software programs that operate by slurping all data into a RAM variable (ie, a data holder in RAM memory) are not scalable, because such programs will eventually encounter a quantity of data that is too large to store in RAM. As a rule of thumb, programs that process text at speeds less than a megabyte per second are not scalable, as they cannot cope, in a reasonable time frame, with quantities of data in the gigabyte and higher range.

Scrubbing Data scrubbing is a lot like any other kind of scrubbing. The purpose is to get rid of the dirt and to leave behind a clean product. As an example, when medical records are scrubbed, the most important component to remove is usually patient names and identifiers (eg, social security numbers), any other information present in the text that may help determine the identity of the patient (eg, address, date of birth, eye color, tattoo descriptions), and any information that is not relevant to the intended purpose of the record (eg, complaints directed to the hospital staff, television channel preferences, income). There are two general approaches to scrubbing algorithms: (1) developing numerous routines that find and delete data that needs to be scrubbed and (2) developing routines that find the information needed in a research study, and deleting all other data from the records. Data scrubbing is discussed in depth in Section 5.4.

Simpson's paradox Occurs when a correlation that holds in two different data sets is reversed if the data sets are combined. For example, baseball player A may have a higher batting average than player B for each of two seasons, but when the data for the two seasons are combined, player B may have the higher 2-season average. Simpson's paradox is just one example of unexpected changes in outcome when variables are unknowingly hidden or blended.[43]

Species Species is the bottom-most class of any classification or ontology. Because the species class contains the individual objects of the classification, it is the only class which is not abstract. The special significance of the species class is best exemplified in the classification of living organisms. Every species of organism contains individuals that share a common ancestral relationship to one another. When we look at a group of squirrels, we know that each squirrel in the group has its own unique personality, its own unique genes (ie, genotype), and its own unique set of physical features (ie, phenotype). Moreover, although the DNA sequences of individual squirrels are unique, we assume that there is a commonality to the genome of squirrels that distinguishes it from the genome of every other species. If we use the modern definition of species as an evolving gene pool, we see that the species can be thought of as a biological life form, with substance (a population of propagating genes), and a function (evolving to produce new species).[44–46] Put simply, species speciate; individuals do not. As a corollary, species evolve; individuals simply propagate. Hence, the species class is a separable biological unit with form and function. We, as individuals, are focused on the lives of individual things, and we must be reminded of the role of species in biological and nonbiological classifications. The concept of species is discussed in greater detail in Section 6.4. See Blended class. See Nonatomicity.

Stop words High frequency words such as "the, and, an, but, if," that tend to delineate phrases or terms in text. Also called "barrier words." An example of the use of stop words in text processing is provided in Section 3.2.

Superclass Any of the ancestral classes of a subclass. For example, in the classification of living organisms, the class of vertebrates is a superclass of the class of mammals. The immediate superclass of a class is its parent class. In common parlance, when we speak of the superclass of a class, we are usually referring to its parent class. See Parent class.

Taxonomic order In biological taxonomy, the hierarchical lineage of organisms are divided into a descending list of named orders: Kingdom, Phylum (Division), Class, Order, Family, and Genus, Species. As we have learned more and more about the classes of organisms, modern taxonomists have added additional ranks to the classification (eg, supraphylum, subphylum, suborder, infraclass, etc.). Was this really necessary? All of this taxonomic complexity could be averted by dropping named ranks and simply referring to every class as "Class." Modern specifications for class hierarchies (eg, RDF Schema) encapsulate each class with the name of its superclass. When every object yields its class and superclass, it is possible to trace any object's class lineage. For example, in the classification of living organisms, if you know the name of the parent for each class, you can write a simple script that generates the complete ancestral lineage for every class and species within the classification.[12] See Class. See Taxonomy. See RDF Schema. See Species.

Taxonomy A taxonomy is the collection of named instances (class members) in a classification or an ontology. When you see a schematic showing class relationships, with individual classes represented by geometric shapes and the relationships represented by arrows or connecting lines between the classes, then you are essentially looking at the structure of a classification, minus the taxonomy. You can think of building a taxonomy as the act of pouring all of the names of all of the instances into their proper classes. A taxonomy is similar to a nomenclature; the difference is that in a taxonomy, every named instance must have an assigned class. See Taxonomic order.

Term extraction algorithm Terms are phrases, most often noun phrases, and sometimes individual words, that have a precise meaning within a knowledge domain. For example, "software validation." "RDF triple" and "World Wide Telescope" are examples of terms that might appear in the index or the glossary of this book. The most useful terms might appear up to a dozen times in the text, but when they occur on every page, their value as a searchable item is diminished; there are just too many instances of the term to be of practical value. Hence, terms are sometimes described as noun phrases that have low-frequency and high information content. Various algorithms are available to extract candidate terms from textual documents. The computer-generated list of candidate terms can be examined by a curator who determines whether they should be included in the index created for the document from which they were extracted. The curator may also compare the extracted candidate terms against a standard nomenclature, to determine whether the candidate terms should be added to the nomenclature.[4] Examples of term extraction algorithms are provided in Section 3.2.

Terminology The collection of words and terms used in some particular discipline, field, or knowledge domain. Nearly synonymous with vocabulary and with nomenclature. Vocabularies, unlike terminologies, are not be confined to the terms used in a particular field. Nomenclatures, unlike terminologies, usually aggregate equivalent terms under a canonical synonym.

Thesaurus A vocabulary that groups together synonymous terms. A thesaurus is very similar to a nomenclature. There are two minor differences. Nomenclatures included multi-word terms; whereas a thesaurus is typically composed of one-word terms. In addition, nomenclatures are typically restricted to a well-defined topic or knowledge domain (eg, names of stars, infectious diseases, etc.). See Nomenclature. See Vocabulary. See Classification. See Dictionary. See Terminology. See Ontology.

Unclassifiable objects Classifications create a class for every object and taxonomies assign each and every object to its correct class. This means that a classification is not permitted to contain unclassified objects; a condition that puts fussy taxonomists in an untenable position. Suppose you have an object, and you simply do not know enough about the object to confidently assign it to a class. Or, suppose you have an object that seems to fit more than one class, and you can't decide which class is the correct class. What do you do? Historically, scientists have resorted to creating a "miscellaneous" class into which otherwise unclassifiable objects are given a temporary home, until more suitable accommodations can be provided. I have spoken with numerous data managers, and everyone seems to be of a mind that "miscellaneous" classes, created as a stopgap measure, serve a useful purpose. Not so. Historically, the promiscuous application of "miscellaneous" classes have proven to be a huge impediment to the advancement of science. In the case of the classification of living organisms, the class of protozoans stands as a case in point. Ernst Haeckel, a leading biological taxonomist in his time, created the Kingdom Protista (ie, protozoans), in 1866, to accommodate a wide variety of simple organisms with superficial commonalities. Haeckel himself understood that the protists were a blended class that included unrelated organisms, but he believed that further study would resolve the confusion. In a sense, he was right, but the process took much longer than he had anticipated; occupying generations of taxonomists over the following 150 years. Today, Kingdom Protista no longer exists. Its members have been reassigned to other classes. Nonetheless, textbooks of microbiology still describe the protozoans, just as though this name continued to occupy a legitimate place among terrestrial organisms. In the meantime, therapeutic opportunities for eradicating so-called protozoal infections, using class-targeted agents, have no doubt been missed.[47] You might think that the creation of a class of living organisms, with no established scientific relation to the real world, was a rare and ancient event in the annals of biology, having little or no chance of being repeated. Not so. A special pseudoclass of fungi, deuteromycetes (spelled with a lowercase "d," signifying its questionable validity as a true biologic class) has been created to hold fungi of indeterminate speciation. At present, there are several thousand such fungi, sitting in a taxonomic limbo, waiting to be placed into a definitive taxonomic class.[48,47] See Blended class.

Variable In algebra, a variable is a quantity, in an equation, that can change; as opposed to a constant quantity, that cannot change. In computer science, a variable can be perceived as a container that can be assigned a value. If you assign the integer 7 to a container named "x," then "x" equals 7, until you re-assign some other value to the container (ie, variables are mutable). In some computer languages, when you issue a command assigning a value to a new (undeclared) variable, the variable automatically comes into existence to accept the assignment. The process whereby an object comes into existence, because its existence was implied by an action (such as value assignment), is called reification. See Reification. See Autovivification.

Vocabulary A comprehensive collection of words and their associated meanings. In some quarters, "vocabulary" and "nomenclature" are used interchangeably, but they are different from one another. Nomenclatures typically focus on terms confined to one knowledge domain. Nomenclatures typically do not contain definitions for the contained terms. Nomenclatures typically group terms by synonymy. Lastly, nomenclatures include multi-word terms. Vocabularies are collections of single words, culled from multiple knowledge domains, with their definitions, and assembled in alphabetic order. See Nomenclature. See Thesaurus. See Taxonomy. See Dictionary. See Terminology.

Winnowing and chaffing Better known to contrarians as chaffing and winnowing. A protocol invented by Ronald Rivest for securing messages against eavesdroppers, without technically employing encryption.[49] As used in this book, the winnowing and chaffing protocol would be considered a type of encryption. A detailed discussion of winnowing and chaffing is found in Open Source tools for Chapter 8. See Encryption.

REFERENCES

1. Wheatley HB. *How to make an index*. London: Elliott Stock; 1902.
2. Wheeler MT. *Indexing: principles, rules and examples*. 3rd ed. Albany, NY: New York State Library; 1920.
3. Wallis E, Lavell C. Naming the indexer: where credit is due. *Indexer* 1995;**19**:266–8.

4. Berman JJ. *Principles of big data: preparing, sharing, and analyzing complex information.* Burlington, MA: Morgan Kaufmann; 2013.
5. Mallon T. The best part of every book comes last. *The New York Times* 1991.
6. Shah NH, Jonquet C, Chiang AP, Butte AJ, Chen R, Musen MA. Ontology-driven indexing of public datasets for translational bioinformatics. *BMC Bioinform* 2009;**10**(Suppl. 2):S1.
7. Lamb J. Embedded indexing. *IEEE Trans Ind Electron* 2005;**24**:206–9.
8. Brin S, Page L. The anatomy of a large-scale hypertextual Web search engine. *Comput Netw ISDN Syst* 1998;**33**:107–17.
9. Berman JJ. *Repurposing legacy data: innovative case studies.* Burlington, MA: Elsevier, Morgan Kaufmann Imprint; 2015.
10. Berman JJ. *Ruby programming for medicine and biology.* Sudbury, MA: Jones and Bartlett; 2008.
11. Krauthammer M, Nenadic G. Term identification in the biomedical literature. *J Biomed Inform* 2004;**37**:512–26.
12. Berman JJ. *Methods in medical informatics: fundamentals of healthcare programming in perl, python, and ruby.* Boca Raton, FL: Chapman and Hall; 2010.
13. Berman JJ. Tumor classification: molecular analysis meets Aristotle. *BMC Cancer* 2004;**4**:10. Available from: http://www.biomedcentral.com/1471-2407/4/10 [accessed on 01.01.15].
14. Berman JJ. Tumor taxonomy for the developmental lineage classification of neoplasms. *BMC Cancer* 2004;**4**:88. http://www.biomedcentral.com/1471-2407/4/88 [accessed on 01.01.15].
15. Berman JJ. Modern classification of neoplasms: reconciling differences between morphologic and molecular approaches. *BMC Cancer* 2005;**5**:100. Available from: http://www.biomedcentral.com/1471-2407/5/100 [accessed on 01.01.15].
16. Berman JJ. *Neoplasms: principles of development and diversity.* Sudbury, MA: Jones & Bartlett; 2009.
17. Berman JJ. *Precancer: the beginning and the end of cancer.* Sudbury, MA: Jones and Bartlett; 2010.
18. Hayes A. VA to apologize for mistaken Lou Gehrig's disease notices. *CNN* 2009. Available from: http://www.cnn.com/2009/POLITICS/08/26/veterans.letters.disease [accessed on 04.09.12].
19. Hall PA, Lemoine NR. Comparison of manual data coding errors in 2 hospitals. *J Clin Pathol* 1986;**39**:622–6.
20. Berman JJ. Doublet method for very fast autocoding. *BMC Med Inform Decis Mak* 2004;**4**:16.
21. Moore GW, Berman JJ. Performance analysis of manual and automated systematized nomenclature of medicine (Snomed) coding. *Am J Clin Pathol* 1994;**101**:253–6.
22. Berman JJ. Resources for comparing the speed and performance of medical autocoders. *BMC Med Inform Decis Mak* 2004;**4**:8.
23. Berman JJ, Moore GW. SNOMED-encoded surgical pathology databases: a tool for epidemiologic investigation. *Mod Pathol* 1996;**9**:944–50.
24. Campbell JR, Carpenter P, Sneiderman C, Cohn S, Chute CG, Warren J. Phase II evaluation of clinical coding schemes completeness, taxonomy, mapping, definitions, and clarity. *J Am Med Inform Assoc* 1997;**4**:238–50.
25. Berman JJ. Nomenclature-based data retrieval without prior annotation: facilitating biomedical data integration with fast doublet matching. *In Silico Biol* 2005;**5**:0029. Available from: http://www.bioinfo.de/isb/2005/05/0029/ [accessed on 06.09.15].
26. Berman JJ. Threshold protocol for the exchange of confidential medical data. *BMC Med Res Methodol* 2002;**2**:12. Available from: http://www.biomedcentral.com/1471-2288/2/12 [accessed on 27.08.15].
27. Schneier B. *Applied cryptography: protocols, algorithms and source code in C.* New York, NY: Wiley; 1994.
28. Medical Subject Headings. U.S. National Library of Medicine. Available from: https://www.nlm.nih.gov/mesh/filelist.html [accessed on 29.07.15].
29. Berman JJ. A tool for sharing annotated research data: the "category 0" UMLS (unified medical language system) vocabularies. *BMC Med Inform Decis Mak* 2003;**3**:6.
30. Hayes CF, O'Connor JC. *English-Esperanto dictionary.* London: Review of Reviews Office; 1906. Available from: http://www.gutenberg.org/ebooks/16967 [accessed on 29.07.15].

31. Sioutos N, de Coronado S, Haber MW, Hartel FW, Shaiu WL, Wright LW. NCI thesaurus: a semantic model integrating cancer-related clinical and molecular information. *J Biomed Inform* 2007;**40**:30–43.

32. NCI Thesaurus. Bethesda, MD: National Cancer Institute, U.S. National Institutes of Health. Available from: ftp://ftp1.nci.nih.gov/pub/cacore/EVS/NCI_Thesaurus/ [accessed on 29.07.15].

33. Berman JJ. Automatic extraction of candidate nomenclature terms using the doublet method. *BMC Med Inform Decis Mak* 2005;**5**:35.

34. A Review of the FBI's Handling of the Brandon Mayfield Case. U.S. Department of Justice, Office of the Inspector General, Oversight and Review Division; 2006.

35. Al-Agha OM, Igbokwe AA. Malignant fibrous histiocytoma: between the past and the present. *Arch Pathol Lab Med* 2008;**132**:1030–5.

36. Nakayama R, Nemoto T, Takahashi H, Ohta T, Kawai A, Seki K, et al. Gene expression analysis of soft tissue sarcomas: characterization and reclassification of malignant fibrous histiocytoma. *Mod Pathol* 2007;**20**:749–59.

37. Patil N, Berno AJ, Hinds DA, Barrett WA, Doshi JM, Hacker CR, et al. Blocks of limited haplotype diversity revealed by high-resolution scanning of human chromosome 21. *Science* 2001;**294**:1719–23.

38. Faldum A, Pommerening K. An optimal code for patient identifiers. *Comput Methods Prog Biomed* 2005;**79**:81–8.

39. Rivest R. Request for Comments: 1321, The MD5 Message-Digest Algorithm. Network Working Group. https://www.ietf.org/rfc/rfc1321.txt [accessed on 01.01.15].

40. Bouzelat H, Quantin C, Dusserre L. Extraction and anonymity protocol of medical file. *Proc AMIA Annu Fall Symp* 1996;**1996**:323–7.

41. Quantin CH, Bouzelat FA, Allaert AM, Benhamiche J, Faivre J, Dusserre L. Automatic record hash coding and linkage for epidemiological followup data confidentiality. *Methods Inf Med* 1998;**37**:271–7.

42. Department of Health and Human Services. 45 CFR (Code of Federal Regulations), parts 160 through 164. Standards for privacy of individually identifiable health information (final rule). *Fed Regist* 2000;**65**(250):82461–510.

43. Tu Y, Gunnell D, Gilthorpe MS. Simpson's paradox, Lord's paradox, and suppression effects are the same phenomenon — the reversal paradox. *Emerg Themes Epidemiol* 2008;**5**:2.

44. DeQueiroz K. Ernst Mayr and the modern concept of species. *Proc Natl Acad Sci U S A* 2005;**102** (Suppl. 1):6600–7.

45. DeQueiroz K. Species concepts and species delimitation. *Syst Biol* 2007;**56**:879–86.

46. Mayden RL. Consilience and a hierarchy of species concepts: advances toward closure on the species puzzle. *J Nematol* 1999;**31**(2):95–116.

47. Berman JJ. *Taxonomic guide to infectious diseases: understanding the biologic classes of pathogenic organisms*. Waltham, MA: Academic Press; 2012.

48. Guarro J, Gene J, Stchigel AM. Developments in fungal taxonomy. *Clin Microbiol Rev* 1999;**12**:454–500.

49. Rivest RL. MIT Lab for Computer Science; 1998 (rev. April 24, 1998).

UNDERSTANDING YOUR DATA

4

Now take a sharp knife and slice the tip off the cone through a plane parallel to the table. The fresh-cut surface (or "section") traces out a circle. Now cut through the cone at an angle, and the section becomes an ellipse. Or try a vertical cut, slicing a side off the cone down to the table. This section is an open curve known as a hyperbola. The mathematics of the most important curves of nature can all be described as sections of a simple cone.
-Tom Siefgried, in "The Bit and the Pendulum" (Fig. 4.1)[1]

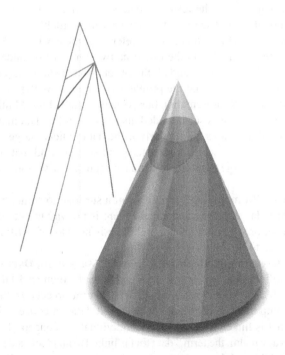

FIGURE 4.1

The beauty of a circle, ellipse, parabola, and hyperbola, displayed as cross sections of a simple cone (See Glossary item, Beauty).

Source: Wikipedia, submitted into the public domain by its author, SergV.

4.1 RANGES AND OUTLIERS

> Another important early step is potentially time-consuming, but of great importance: sitting down with a large set of potential inputs and examining them by hand...Four hours spent with a pile of articles and a highlighter may forestall many unpleasant surprises.
>
> -K. Bretonnel Cohen and Lawrence Hunter in an article entitled, "Getting Started in Text Mining"[2]

It is common for data scientists to omit the first and most important step in data analysis: surveying the content of their data. Data scientists, eager to answer some particular question, may choose to forgo the preliminaries, crunching headlong into the data, with reckless abandon. This is almost always a mistake.[3,4] Taking a few hours to look at the data will often yield new insights, will occasionally uncover systemic deficiencies in the data. When reviewing a new trove of secondary data, it is always wise to scan the data, with the following five questions in mind[5]:

1. **Are the data sets complete, and do they represent the subject domain?** Having a large set of data does not guarantee that your data is complete and representative. Danah Boyd, a social media researcher, gives the example of a scientist who is analyzing the complete set of tweets made available by Twitter.[6] If Twitter removes tweets containing expletives, or tweets composed of nonword character strings, or tweets containing highly charged words, or tweets containing certain types of private information, then the resulting data set, no matter how large it may be, is not representative of the population of senders. If the tweets are available as a set of messages, without any identifier for senders, then the compulsive tweeters (eg, those who send hundreds or thousands of tweets) will be overrepresented, and the one-time tweeters will be underrepresented. If each tweet were associated with an account, and all the tweets from a single account were collected as a unique record, then there would still be the problem created by tweeters who maintain multiple accounts (See Glossary items, Representation bias, Negative study bias, Multiple comparisons bias). If the data at hand cannot support your intended analysis, then the data may yet be sufficient to answer an alternate set of questions, particularly if the data indicate large effects and achieve statistical significance. When all seems lost, data scientists may find that small data sets can be merged with other small or large data sets to produce representative and complete aggregate data collections.

2. **Is the data annotated with metadata?** It may seem a surprise to some, but most of the data collected in the world today is poorly annotated. There is no way to determine how the data elements were obtained, or what they mean, and there is no way of verifying the quality of the data. Such data has little to no value.

3. **Do the data objects have unique identifiers? (See Glossary item, Data object).** If data objects are not uniquely identified, then it becomes impossible to distinguish 10 data values that apply to one object versus 10 data values that apply to 10 different objects. In the case of data on human subjects, it is important to distinguish "identified data," a concept that is central to data science, from "data that is linked to an identified individual," a concept that has legal and ethical importance. In the privacy realm, the term, "data that is linked to an identified individual," is shortened to "identified data," and this indulgence has caused no end of confusion. All good data must be identified. Private data can be deidentified, in the regulatory sense, by removing any links between the data and the person to whom the data applies (See Glossary items, Deidentification,

Deidentification versus anonymization, Reidentification). The data itself should never be deidentified (ie, a unique alphanumeric identifier for every data object must exist). Removing links that connect the data object to an individual is all that is necessary for so-called privacy deidentification.

4. **Is the data set annotated with basic Dublin Core information?** Specifically, does the data set come with the kinds of basic information that indicates who created the data, who owns the data, when the data set was created, and who may use the data? Data scientists cannot assume that they have the right to use any data set that they happened to acquire.

5. **Is the data legal?** If so, is the data encumbered? Has the data been obtained ethically? Data scientists cannot assume that they have no legal liability, financial obligations, or ethical responsibilities when they use secondary data (See Glossary item, Secondary data).

Data quality is serious business. The U.S. government passed the Data Quality Act in 2001, as part of the FY 2001 Consolidated Appropriations Act (Pub. L. No. 106-554). The Act requires Federal Agencies to base their policy decisions on high-quality data and to permit the public to challenge and correct inaccurate data.[7,8] The drawback to this legislation is that science is a messy process, and data may not always attain a high quality. Data that fails to meet standards of quality may be rejected by government committees or may be used to abrogate policies that were based on the data.[9,10] Reviewing your data, before you commit yourself to a data analysis project, is an excellent idea.

After you have had a chance to look at the data, it is prudent to determine the highest and the lowest observed values in your data collection (ie, the range of the data). These two numbers are often the most important numbers in any set of data; even more important than determining the average or the standard deviation. Where the data begins and ends tells the data scientists a great deal about the intrinsic meaning of the data. Moreover, your data must fit within the range of the device that produced the data measurements. Most devices have a range for which they can detect data fairly accurately, the so-called dynamic range (See Glossary item, Accuracy versus precision). Below that range, they might register the measurement as zero, or some fixed minimum value, or as some random value (ie, noise). Above the range, the instrument might register a fixed maximum value, or some number larger than the measurable maxima (ie, more noise). Ideally, all of the data elements in your collection will fall well within the dynamic range of the measurement instrument. In any case, it is vital to know the range of the measured data and the dynamic range of the measurement instrument. Data values higher than or lower than the dynamic range do not contain useful information.

It really is not unusual for otherwise intelligent data scientists to develop sophisticated data models for totally spurious measurements that lie outside the dynamic range of their instruments (See Glossary item, Data modeling). Here is an example. You are looking at human subject data that includes weights. You find that the maximum weight in the data set is 300 pounds, exactly. There are many individuals in the data set who have a weight of 300 pounds, but no individuals with a weight exceeding 300 pounds. You also find that the number of individuals weighing 300 pounds is much greater than the number of individuals weighting 290 pounds. What does this tell you? Obviously, the people included in the data set have been weighed on a scale that tops off at 300 pounds. Most of the people whose weight was recorded as 300 will have a false weight measurement. Had we not looked for the maximum value in the data set, we would have assumed, incorrectly, that the weights were valid.[11]

It might be useful to get some idea of how weights are distributed in the population exceeding 300 pounds (ie, the population outside the dynamic range of the scale). One way of estimating the error is to look at the number of people weighing 295 pounds, 290 pounds, 285 pounds, etc. By observing the trend, and knowing the total number of individuals who weigh at least 300 pounds, you can estimate the number of people falling into the weight categories exceeding 300 pounds.

Here is another example where knowing the maximum for a data set measurement is useful. You are looking at a collection of data on meteorites. The measurements include weights. You notice that the largest meteorite in the large collection weighs 66 tons (equivalent to about 60,000 kilograms), and has a diameter of about 3 meters. Small meteorites are more numerous than large meteorites, but almost every weight category is accounted for by one or more meteorites, up to 66 tons. After that, nothing. You check the published data on meteorites and find that none of your colleagues have reported finding meteorites weighing in excess of about 66 tons. Why do meteorites have a maximum size of about 66 tons (See Glossary items, Meta-analysis, Missing values)?

A little checking tells you that meteors in space can come in just about any size, from a speck of dust to a moon-sized rock. Collisions with earth have involved meteorites much larger than 3 meters. You check the astronomical records and you find that the meteor that may have caused the extinction of large dinosaurs about 65 million years ago, was estimated at 6–10 kilometers (at least 2000 times the diameter of the largest meteorite found on earth).

There is a very simple reason why the largest meteorite found on earth weighs about 66 tons, while the largest meteorites to impact the earth are known to be thousands of time heavier. When meteorites exceed 66 tons, the impact energy can exceed the energy produced by an atom bomb blast. Meteorites larger than 66 tons leave an impact crater, but the meteor itself disintegrates on impact.[11]

As it turns out, much is known about meteorite impacts. The kinetic energy of the impact is determined by the mass of the meteor and the square of the velocity. The minimum velocity of a meteor at impact is about 11 km per second (equivalent to the minimum escape velocity for sending an object from earth into space). The fastest impacts occur at about 70 km per second. From this data, the energy released by meteors, on impact with the earth, can be easily calculated.

By observing the maximum weight of meteors found on earth we learn a great deal about meteoric impacts. When we look at the distribution of weights, we can see that small meteorites are more numerous than larger meteorites. If we develop a simple formula that relates the size of a meteorite with its frequency of occurrence, we can predict the likelihood of the arrival of a meteorite on earth, for every weight of meteorite, including those weighing more than 66 tons, over any interval of time.

Here is another profound example of the value of knowing the maximum value in a data distribution. If you look at the distance from the earth to various cosmic objects (eg, stars, black holes, nebulae) you will quickly find that there is an empiric limit to the distance of objects from earth. Of the many thousands of cataloged stars and galaxies, none of them has a distance that is greater than 13 billion light years. Why? If astronomers could see a star that is 15 billion light years from earth, then the light that is received here on earth must have traveled 15 billion light years to reach us. The time required for light to travel 15 billion light years is 15 billion years; by definition. The universe was born in a big bang about 14 billion years ago. This would imply that the light from the star located 15 billion miles from earth must have begun its journey about a billion years before the universe came into existence. Impossible!

By looking at the distribution of distances of observed stars, and noting that the distances never exceed about 13 billion years, we can infer that the universe must be at least 13 billion years old. You can also infer that the universe does not have an infinite age and size; otherwise, we would see stars at a greater distance than 13 billion light years. If you assume that stars popped into the universe not long after its creation, then you can infer that the universe has an age of about 13 or 14 billion years. All of these deductions, confirmed independently by theoreticians and cosmologists, were made without statistical analysis, by noting the maximum number in a distribution of numbers.[11]

When all of your observations fall within a narrow data range, you may expect to find a process, or a set of processes, that regulate the system as a whole. For example, consider the blood chemistry tests that have been performed routinely by doctors, for nearly a century. By the third decade of the twentieth century, physicians had at their disposal most of the common blood tests known to modern medicine (eg, electrolytes, blood cells, lipids, glucose, nitrogenous compounds). Although blood tests were available in the 1920s, physicians lacked the benefit of analyses on huge sets of individuals. Lacking computers and databases, it took considerable time for clinical scientists to aggregate their data and compile a set of results. What the data revealed was profoundly important. Blood tests performed on normal populations produced results that fell into a very narrow range. This was particularly true for electrolytes (eg, sodium and calcium) and to a somewhat lesser extent for blood cells (eg, white blood cells, red blood cells). Furthermore, for any individual, multiple recordings at different times of the day and on different days, tended to produce consistent results (eg, sodium concentration in the morning was equivalent to sodium concentration in the evening). These finding were totally unexpected, at the time.[5]

Analysis of the data also showed that significant deviations from the normal concentrations of any one of these blood chemicals is always an indicator of disease. Backed by data, but lacking any deep understanding of the physiologic role of blood components, physicians learned to associate abnormal blood test results with specific diseases. The observation of a narrow normal range, in a variety of blood tests, and the association of deviations from the normal range with specific disease processes, was the most important breakthrough in medicine in the first two decades of the twentieth century. The discovery of the "normal range" revolutionized the field of physiology. Thereafter, physiologists concentrated their efforts toward understanding how the body regulates its blood constituents. Their early studies led to nearly everything we now know about homeostatic control mechanisms.

Data scientists may become overly fastidious with their data, rejecting opportunities to pursue important lines of inquiry when the data is not to their liking. For example, outliers and missing data values are the bane of statisticians (See Glossary item, Outlier). Nonetheless, data scientists should appreciate that anomalous data values are sometimes clues to generalizable observations. Assuming that an outlier is a valid observation (ie, not spurious and not the product of a preanalytic error), it is worth remembering that outliers must obey the same physical laws that apply to every other observation. The circumstances that cause one data object to behave like a maverick will often explain the behavior of objects that travel with the herd.

As an example of the importance of rare outliers, consider the discovery of statins, drugs that dramatically reduce serum lipid levels and prevent coronary artery diseases. The Framingham Heart Study is often given credit for establishing the connection between high cholesterol levels and heart disease, back in 1961. Although the Framingham Heart Study provided important statistical evidence, based on a careful study of a large number of individuals, it is historical fact that physicians were well aware of the association between cholesterol and heart attacks decades prior to 1961. An association between high cholesterol levels and arteriosclerosis was recognized by 1921.[12] The genetic link between cholesterol and heart attacks was demonstrated in 1938, when it was shown that patients with familial hypercholesterolemia had a high risk of developing heart disease.[13] Twenty-five years later, case reports of families with familial hypercholesterolemia revealed two distinct forms of the disease (See Glossary item, Case report). A homozygous form affected infants at birth, producing blood cholesterol outliers of about 800 mg/dl, many times higher than those observed within in the normal populations. Children with the homozygous form of familial hypercholesterolemia suffered heart attacks as early as 5 years of age. A heterozygous form of the disease, occurring in the same families, produced somewhat higher levels of cholesterol, 300–400 mg/dl, still several times higher than levels observed in the normal population, and produced heart attacks at the age of 35–60 years.[13] Observations that heart attacks occurred in inherited hypercholesterolemic syndromes inspired a search of cholesterol-lowering drugs. In the 1970s, Akiron Endo found that several species of fungi extrude defensive compounds that inhibit the synthesis of cholesterol in fungal pathogens. Endo eventually found Mevastatin, the first effective inhibitor of human HMG-CoA reductase, the rate-limiting enzyme in the cholesterol biosynthetic pathway.[14] Other statins followed. Wise data scientists understand that outliers are not exceptions to the general rules. Outliers are the exceptions upon which the general rules are made.

4.2 SIMPLE STATISTICAL DESCRIPTORS

> He uses statistics as a drunken man uses lamp-posts… for support rather than illumination.
>
> **-Andrew Lang (1844–1912)**

It is wise to begin every data analysis project with an estimate. Simple estimates are, in most cases, more useful and more reliable than advanced analytic methods. The reason being that estimates, unlike analytic methods, require a keen understanding of the data. No matter how inappropriate the situation, analytic methods produce an output for any data input. Hence, if you have two wildly incompatible solutions to a problem, one produced by an estimate and another produced by an advanced analytic technique, then you should probably keep the estimate and discard the complex analysis. On the other hand, if the estimate and the analytic technique are close to one another, the likelihood that both approaches are correct is high.

Here are a few examples of simple estimates and observations that have proven very useful.

The sun is about 93 million miles from the earth. At this enormous distance, the light hitting earth arrives as nearly parallel rays, and the shadow produced by the earth is nearly cylindrical. This means that the shadow of the earth is approximately the same size as the earth itself. If the earth's circular shadow during a lunar eclipse has a diameter about 2.5 times the diameter of the moon itself, then the moon must have a diameter approximately 1/2.5 times that of the earth. The diameter of the earth is about 8000 miles, so the diameter of the moon must be about 8000/2.5 or about 3000 miles.[11]

The true diameter of the moon is smaller, about 2160 miles. Our estimate is inaccurate because the earth's shadow is actually conical, not cylindrical. If we wanted to use a bit more trigonometry, we'd arrive at a closer approximation. Still, we arrived at a fair approximation of the moon's size from one, simple division based on a casual observation made during a lunar eclipse. Credit for the first scientist to use this estimation goes to the Greek astronomer Aristarchus of Samos (310 BCE–230 BCE). In this particular case, a direct measurement of the moon's distance was impossible. Aristarchus' only option was the rough estimate. His predicament was not unique. Sometimes estimation is the only recourse for data analysts.

A modern-day example wherein measurements failed to help the data analyst is the calculation of deaths caused by heat waves. If individuals are dying from heat-related illness, then municipalities must budget supportive services, such as municipal cooling stations, the free delivery of ice, increased staffing for emergency personnel, and so on. If the number of heat-related deaths is high, the governor may justifiably call a state of emergency.

Medical examiners perform autopsies to determine causes of death. During a heat wave, the number of deceased individuals with a heat-related cause of death seldom rises as much as anyone would expect.[15] The reason for this is that stresses produced by heat cause death by exacerbating preexisting nonheat-related conditions. The cause of death can seldom be pinned on heat. The paucity of autopsy-proven heat deaths can be relieved, somewhat, by permitting pathologists to declare a heat-related death when the environmental conditions at the site of death are consistent with hyperthermia (eg, a high body temperature of the deceased measured shortly after death). Adjusting the criteria for declaring heat-related deaths is a poor remedy. In many cases, the body is not discovered anytime near the time of death, invalidating the use of body temperature. More importantly, different municipalities may develop their own criteria for heat-related deaths (eg, different temperature threshold measures, different ways of factoring night-time temperatures and humidity measurements). Basically, there is no accurate, reliable, or standard way to measure the incidence of heat-related deaths.[11,15]

How might a data estimator handle this problem? It's simple. You take the total number of deaths that occurred during the heat wave. Then you go back over your records of deaths occurring in the same period, in the same geographic region, over a series of years in which a heat wave did not occur. You average that number, giving you the expected number of deaths in a normal (ie, without a heat wave) period. You subtract that number from the number of deaths that occurred during the heat wave, and that gives you an estimate of the number of people who died from heat-related mortality. This strategy, applied to the 1995 Chicago heat wave, led to the estimate that heat-related deaths accounted for a rise in the number of deaths, from 485 to 739.[16]

The average behavior of a collection of objects can be applied toward calculations that would exceed computational feasibility if applied to individual objects. Here is an example. Years ago, I worked on a project that involved simulating cell colony growth, using a Monte Carlo method (See Glossary item, Monte Carlo simulation).[17] Each simulation began with a single cell that divided, producing two cells, unless the cell happened to die prior to cell division. Each simulation applied a certain chance of cell death, somewhere around 0.5, for each cell, at each cell division. When you simulate colony growth, beginning with a single cell, the chance that the first cell will die on the first cell division would be about 0.5; hence there is about a 50% chance that the colony will die out on the first cell division. A Monte Carlo simulation randomly assigned death or life at each cell division, for each cell in the colony (See Glossary item, Monte Carlo simulation). When the colony manages to reach a large size (eg, ten million cells), the simulation markedly slows, as the Monte Carlo algorithm must parse through ten million cells, calculating whether each cell will live or die, and assigning two offspring cells for each simulated division, and removing cells that were assigned a simulated "death." When the computer simulation slowed to a crawl, I found that the whole population displayed an "average" behavior. There was no longer any need to perform a Monte Carlo simulation on every cell in the population. I could simply multiply the total number of cells by the cell death probability (for the entire population), and this would tell me the total number of cells that survived the cycle. For a large colony of cells, with a death probability of 0.5 for each cell, half the cells will die at each cell cycle, and the other half will live and divide, produce two progeny cells; hence the population of the colony will remain stable. When dealing with large numbers, it becomes possible to dispense with the Monte Carlo simulation, and to estimate each generational outcome with a pencil and paper.

Substituting the average behavior for a population of objects, rather than calculating the behavior of every single object, is called mean field approximation (See Glossary item, Mean field approximation). Mean field approximation has been used with great success to understand the behavior of gases, epidemics, crystals, viruses, and all manner of large population problems.

Data distributions are sometimes multimodal, with several peaks and troughs. Multimodality always says something about the data under study. It tells us that the population is somehow nonhomogeneous. Hodgkin lymphoma is an example of a cancer with a bimodal age distribution. There is a peak in occurrences at a young age, and another peak of occurrences at a more advanced age. This two-peak phenomenon can be found whenever Hodgkin lymphoma is studied in large populations[11,18] (Fig. 4.2).

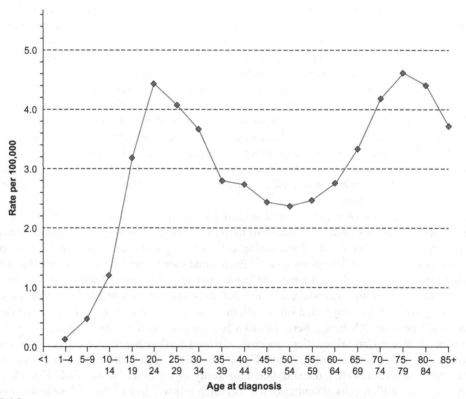

FIGURE 4.2

The number of occurrences of Hodgkin lymphoma in persons of different ages. The distribution is bimodal, with one peak of occurrences at about 35 years of age, and a second peak at about 75 years of age.

Source: The National Cancer Institute's Surveillance Epidemiology End Results, available from: http://seer.cancer.gov/.[19]

In the case of Hodgkin lymphoma, lymphomas occurring in the young may share diagnostic features with the lymphomas occurring in the older population, but the occurrence of lymphomas in two separable populations may indicate that some important distinction may have been overlooked: a different environmental cause, or different genetic alterations of lymphomas in the two age sets, or two different types of lymphomas that were mistakenly classified under one name, or there may be something wrong with the data, such as misdiagnoses, mix-ups during data collection, or blended classes (See Glossary item, Blended class). In general, the larger the data set, the easier it is to find incongruities (such as multimodality). Explaining the causes for data incongruities is always a scientific challenge.

The importance of inspecting data for multimodality applies to black holes. Most black holes have mass equivalents under 33 solar masses. Another set of black holes are supermassive, with mass equivalents of 10 or 20 billion solar masses. When there are objects of the same type, whose masses differ by a factor of a billion, scientists infer that there is something fundamentally different in the origin or development of these two variant forms of the same object. Black hole formation is an active area of interest, but current theory suggests that lower-mass black holes arise from preexisting heavy stars. The supermassive black holes presumably grow from large quantities of matter available at the center of galaxies. The observation of bimodality inspired astronomers to search for black holes whose masses are intermediate between black holes with near-solar masses and the supermassive black holes. Intermediate black holes have been found, and, not surprisingly, they come with a set of fascinating properties that distinguish them from other types of black holes. Fundamental advances in our understanding of the universe may sometimes follow from simple observations of multimodal data distributions.[11]

When we look at data, searching for graphs with multiple peaks, the fundamental question we are asking is: "Does this population contain several different populations?" If so, we must pursue a host of new questions, beginning with: "What makes this subpopulation different from the combined population represented in our graph?" It was possible, in the case of occurrences of Hodgkin lymphoma to distinguish two distinct population peaks, by simple inspection. In most cases, life is not so simple. We can expect to find subsets of data that are somewhat different from the general population, but not so different that we can be certain that the differences are negligible. Simply put, we will not know whether the data represents a sampling from one homogeneous population or a sampling of a separate class of data objects contained within a mixed population. In Section 8.3, we will look at a very simple computational method that we can use when trying to distinguishing subclasses of data objects.

Statisticians have invented two numbers that tell us most of what we need to know about data sets in the small data realm: the mean and the standard deviation. The mean, also known as the average, tells us the center of the bell-shaped curve, and the standard deviation tells us something about the width of the bell. The average is one of the simplest statistics to compute: simply divide the sum total of data by the number of data objects. Though the average is simple to compute, its computation may not always be fast. Finding the exact average requires that the entire data set be parsed; a significant time-waste when the data set is particularly large, or when averages need to be recomputed frequently. When the data can be randomly accessed, it may save considerable time to select a subset of the data (eg, 100 items), compute the average for the subset, and assume that the average of the subset will approximate the average for the full set of data.[11]

For categorical data, often based on observations, not experiments, computing the mean and the standard deviation is often a waste of time. Such data is seldom distributed as a normal curve

(See Glossary items, Observational data, Categorical data). The mean and standard deviation have limited value outside of normal distributions.

4.3 RETRIEVING IMAGE INFORMATION

> The question is not what you look at, but what you see.
> **-Henry David Thoreau in Journal, 5 August 1851**

Data simplification, as it applies to images, typically involves performing some addition, modification, or annotation to many images, all at once. These activities are generally described under the term batch processing. Batch processing usually begins by collecting hundreds or thousands of image files, from subdirectories on your own computer, or from network servers. Once the files are available, a batch processing script may perform routines such as those listed here:

1. Converting every image to one particular image format
2. Changing the image filenames to conform to a particular naming convention (eg, prepending a department's name to each image filename)
3. Converting every image to a black and white version
4. Collecting a particular type of information about each image (eg, height and width, histogram data, image profile, one-way hash value, extracting a piece of each image or a region of interest)
5. Annotating the header of each image (eg, inserting the Dublin Core elements into the text header)
6. Transforming each image (eg, encrypting the image file)

In the case of image files, if you use an image processor to remove blemishes from an image, or to adjust the contrast to your liking, then you are adding to the complexity of the image. It is often impractical to document minor changes made to an image using image processing software. Data simplification for images is achieved when all of the images have an identical, well-documented, and purposeful adjustment made in a uniform manner and at the same time.

ImageMagick, described in Open Source Tools in this chapter, is a free and open source utility that can perform a huge assortment of imaging processes from command line instructions. After ImageMagick is installed, the suite of utilities (eg, "convert," "identify," "montage," "imdisplay," "mogrify") can be called directly from the system prompt.

As an example, the following short Python script calls ImageMagick's image display utility to display an image file. Notice that this script uses "imdisplay," bundled with Cygwin (See Open Source Tools for Chapter 1, Cygwin, Linux emulation for Windows).

```
#!/usr/local/bin/python
import os
os.system("cd c:/cygwin64/")
os.system("imdisplay c:/some_image_file.jpg")
exit
```

The real power of calling ImageMagick utilities from scripts is achieved when large numbers of image files are handled together.

Here is a short Perl script, batch_grey.pl, that copies and converts each of the image files residing in the current directory to a new grayscale file, with the string "_bw" appended to the original filename:

```
#!/usr/bin/perl
opendir(FILES, ".") || die ("Unable to open directory");
@in_files = readdir(FILES);
closedir(FILES);
foreach $filename (@in_files)
    {
    if ($filename =~ /([a-z0-9\_]+)(\.[gifbmpjpgn]{3}) *$/i)
      {
      $out_file = $1 . "_bw" . $2;
      system("convert ${filename} -set colorspace Gray -separate -average ${out_file}");
      }
    }
exit;
```

Here is an equivalent Python script, batch_grey.py:

```
#!/usr/local/bin/python
import os, re, string
filelist = os.listdir(".")
for file in filelist:
  if ".jpg" in file or ".bmp" in file or ".gif" in file or ".png" in file:
    outfile = "bw_" + file
    command = "convert " + file + " -set colorspace Gray -separate -average " + outfile
    os.system(command)
exit
```

Here is an equivalent Ruby script, batch_grey.rb:

```
#!/usr/local/bin/ruby
filelist = Dir.glob("*.*")
filelist.each do
  |file|
  if file =~ /([a-z0-9\_]+)(\.[gifbmpjpgn]{3}) *$/i
    out_file = $1 + "_bw" + $2
    system("convert " + file + " -set colorspace Gray -separate -average " + out_file)
  end
end
exit
```

Several image algorithms require sets of images, all of the same size. The Ruby script, batch_resized.rb, calls the ImageMagick "convert" utility to copy each image file in the current directory as a resized file, with the string "_resized" appended to the filename.

```
#!/usr/local/bin/ruby
filelist = Dir.glob("*.*")
filelist.each do
  |file|
  if file =~ /([a-z0-9\_]+)(\.[gifbmpjpgn]{3}) *$/i
    out_file = $1 + "_resized" + $2
    system("convert " + file + " -resize 325x500! " + out_file)
  end
end
exit
```

Every image contains a wealth of self-descriptive textual information that is packed into a so-called "header"; a block of bytes reserved for plain-text data, preceding the first pixels of the binary image file. For data scientists, the information in the image headers can be just as useful as the visual image. ImageMagick provides a very simple way of capturing the textual data in the image header, as shown:

```
c:\ftp>identify -verbose 071.jpg > 071_header.txt
```

The command line calls ImageMagick's "identify" utility to extract a verbose description of the image "071.jpg" from its header, and to insert the header text into the file named "071_header.txt" (Fig. 4.3).

Using ImageMagick, users can insert any text of their own choosing into the "comment" section of the header, using the following command:

```
c:\ftp>convert eqn.jpg -set comment "hello world yet again" eqn.jpg
```

Now, when we apply the "identify-verbose" command on the "eqn.jpg" image file, we see that the header has, under "Properties:" the comment, "hello world yet again" (Fig. 4.4).

If we wish, we can command ImageMagick to show us just the comments section of the image header. This is accomplished with the "-format" option and the special characters "%c" specifying the comment field, as shown:

```
c:\ftp>identify -verbose -format "%c" eqn.jpg
hello world yet again
```

Rather than inserting a text string in your header comment, we may wish to insert an entire file. Here is a simple ImageMagick command that inserts a 46 kilobyte file into the comment section of an image header:

```
c:\ftp>convert eqn.jpg -set comment @temp.txt eqn.jpg
```

In this example, at the DOS prompt, the file temp.txt is inserted as a header comment. The "@" character, in ImageMagick, signifies that a filename follows. The size of the file permitted in an image header may vary with image formats. For JPEG files, ImageMagick will insert text files into the comment section, up to a maximum size of about 47 kilobytes; more than ample for annotative information.

```
Image: 071.jpg
  Format: JPEG (Joint Photographic Experts Group JFIF format)
  Mime type: image/jpeg
  Class: DirectClass
  Geometry: 500x600+0+0
  Resolution: 72x72
  Print size: 6.94444x8.33333
  Units: PixelsPerInch
  Type: TrueColor
  Endianess: Undefined
  Colorspace: sRGB
  Depth: 8-bit
  Channel depth:
    red: 8-bit
    green: 8-bit
    blue: 8-bit
  Channel statistics:
    Pixels: 300000
    Red:
      min: 0 (0)
      max: 255 (1)
      mean: 49.0092 (0.192193)
      standard deviation: 61.5447 (0.241352)
      kurtosis: 0.17845
      skewness: 1.28082
      entropy: 0.626998
    Green:
      min: 0 (0)
      max: 255 (1)
      mean: 58.0278 (0.227556)
      standard deviation: 74.1386 (0.29074)
      kurtosis: 0.220811
      skewness: 1.33528
      entropy: 0.631847
    Blue:
      min: 0 (0)
      max: 255 (1)
      mean: 36.0148 (0.141235)
      standard deviation: 42.5795 (0.166978)
      kurtosis: 2.66097
      skewness: 1.7666
      entropy: 0.657041
  Image statistics:
    Overall:
      min: 0 (0)
      max: 255 (1)
      mean: 47.6839 (0.186936)
      standard deviation: 60.8202 (0.238511)
      kurtosis: 1.49029
      skewness: 1.63091
      entropy: 0.638609
  Rendering intent: Perceptual
  Gamma: 0.454545
  Chromaticity:
    red primary: (0.64,0.33)
    green primary: (0.3,0.6)
    blue primary: (0.15,0.06)
    white point: (0.3127,0.329)
  Background color: white
  Border color: srgb(223,223,223)
  Matte color: grey74
  Transparent color: black
  Interlace: None
  Intensity: Undefined
  Compose: Over
  Page geometry: 500x600+0+0
  Dispose: Undefined
  Iterations: 0
  Compression: JPEG
  Quality: 85
  Orientation: Undefined
  Properties:
    date:create: 2015-05-18T07:40:10-04:00
    date:modify: 2013-09-18T18:30:46-04:00
    jpeg:colorspace: 2
    jpeg:sampling-factor: 2x2,1x1,1x1
    signature: 7a1cefa11d8db117c0ab68875e70dec44f4aaf99963ab89f1f079c6864bcc31579
  Artifacts:
    filename: 071.jpg
    verbose: true
  Tainted: False
  Filesize: 31.1KB
  Number pixels: 300K
  Pixels per second: 10.71MB
  User time: 0.010u
  Elapsed time: 0:01.027
  Version: ImageMagick 6.9.0-3 Q16 x64 2014-12-30 http://www.imagemagick.org
```

FIGURE 4.3

The prodigious output of ImageMagick's "identify-verbose" command on the jpeg image 071.jpg.

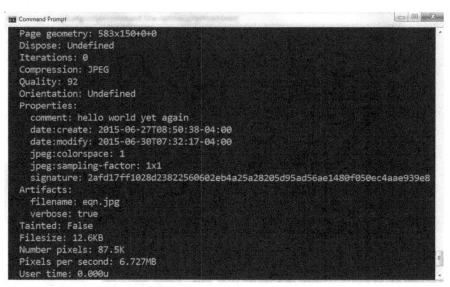

FIGURE 4.4

The output of ImageMagick's "-set comment" command on the image file, eqn.jpg. Notice the comment field, near the center of the image, indicates that text "hello world yet again" has been added to the image header.

The power of calling ImageMagick utilities from scripts comes from applying a set of operations on large numbers of files, all at once. Applying these methods, files can be annotated uniformly (eg, with the same sets of metadata) and analyzed uniformly; thus simplifying projects that involve image processing.

4.4 DATA PROFILING

> Our similarities are different.
>
> **-Yogi Berra**

Data profiling involves creating a distillation of the most salient features of a data object, that can be used for comparison with other objects. When a unique, identifying profile can be expressed as a character string, or a number, it is called a data signature. The algorithms for creating data profiles are countless. Various profiling algorithms have been suggested for text,[20] fingerprints, cancers genes,[21] images, and web pages (See Glossary items, CODIS, Signature, Digital signature). Some of the attractions of profiling are:

1. A profile is always smaller than the object being profiled, making it easier to compare different data objects.
2. Profiles can be precomputed and encapsulated within the data object or archived with the data object's identifier. By precomputing and storing profiles, a data object can be quickly compared against many profiles (See Glossary item, Page Rank).

3. The process of developing successful profiles always teaches you something about the class of data objects you are studying. When a profile works well, its underlying assumptions about the important attributes of the data object are most likely correct.
4. Profiles can be used for data retrieval. Similar items are intended to have similar profiles. If all of the profiles for a data set are precomputed, a simple and fast algorithm can retrieve all items with near-profiles (ie, profiles that have a short distance from one another).

One of the easiest profiles to implement is the phash profile for images.[22] The phash signature contains information about the edges in an image, and is represented as a fixed length string.

ImageMagick's compare utility will calculate phash profiles for images and measure the profile distance between the two images. The syntax for the comparison is:

```
compare -metric phash image1 image2 diffimage
```

Here is an example of a phash comparison for two photos of rocks:

```
c:\photos\rocks>compare -metric phash Adamite_wiki.jpg autunite.jpg diffimage

297.975
```

A distance of 297.975 is not great, indicating that the photos are somewhat similar.
Here is an example of a phash comparison of two images that closely resemble one another:

```
c:\photos\rocks>compare -metric phash Crassostrea_gigas_oyster_2.jpg
Crassostrea_gigas_oyster.jpg diffimage

99.2882
```

A distance of 99.2882 is small, indicating close similarity.
Let's compare an image file with itself.

```
c:\photos\rocks>compare -metric phash autunite.jpg autunite.jpg diffimage
0
```

As we might expect, the distance between an image file and itself is zero.
If you want to produce your own phash profiles for images, you can download Fred Weinhaus' phashconvert bash script that operates in Linux systems or under Cygwin in Windows systems.
The download site is: http://www.fmwconcepts.com/imagemagick/phashconvert/index.php
Fred Weinhaus has produced hundreds of bash scripts that use ImageMagick commands. These scripts are open source and free for noncommercial uses.
After downloading phashconvert, remember to reset the usage permissions at the Linux systems prompt:

```
$ chmod +x phashconvert
```

Here are a few samples of the phashconvert bash utility operating on two different image files:

```
$ phashconvert orca.jpg
0024006301930270033105330305065606951100044708700624110000020-
0530177005603270026029300180738017704180082060400400025002201850183033703300298
0297077007530422042706150611

$ phashconvert tar1.jpg
0034-0190148012303710039035800150751012804680115072900430026-
0370131001403090138029801180631028204020169060802510024002801280136030503270294
0316062206660395042106000644
```

An excellent way of profiling text is to produce a Zipf distribution. George Kingsley Zipf (1902–1950) was an American linguist who demonstrated that, for most languages, a small number of words account for the majority of occurrences of all the words found in prose. Specifically, he found that the frequency of any word is inversely proportional to its placement in a list of words, ordered by their decreasing frequencies in text. The first word in the frequency list will occur about twice as often as the second word in the list, three times as often as the third word in the list, and so on. Many naturally observable collections of data follow a Zipf distribution (eg, most wealth is controlled by a relatively small number of individuals, most crimes are committed by a small portion of the population, a few countries account for the bulk of the world's energy consumption, a few classes of animals account for the majority of terrestrial animal species).[23,24] Zipf distributions cannot be sensibly described by the standard statistical measures that apply to normal distributions (eg, averages and standard deviations).[23,24] Zipf distributions, which technically only apply to word distributions in languages, are instances of a generalized rule, known as Pareto's principle.

The Ruby script, zipf.rb, produces a Zipf distribution with a few lines of code.

```
#!/usr/local/bin/ruby
freq = Hash.new(0)
my_string = "Peter Piper picked a peck of pickled peppers.
            A peck of pickled peppers Peter Piper picked.
            If Peter Piper picked a peck of pickled peppers,
            Where is the peck of pickled peppers that Peter
            Piper picked?"
my_string.downcase.scan(/\w+/){|word| freq[word] = freq[word]+1}
freq.sort_by {|k, v| v}.reverse.each {|k,v| printf "%-10.10s %0.2u\n", k, v}
exit
```

Here is the output of the zipf.rb script.

```
output:
peter    04
piper    04
picked   04
peck     04
of       04
```

```
peppers 04
pickled 04
a       03
if      01
where   01
is      01
the     01
that    01
```

Basically, the Zipf distribution is a frequency distribution of the occurrences of words found in a text, arranged in descending order of frequency.

Here is an equivalent script, in Perl:

```
#!/usr/local/bin/perl
$my_string = <<"EOF";
Peter Piper picked a peck of pickled peppers.
A peck of pickled peppers Peter Piper picked.
If Peter Piper picked a peck of pickled peppers,
Where is the peck of pickled peppers that Peter
Piper picked?
EOF
$my_string =~ s/\n\.\?/ /g;
$my_string = lc($my_string);
while ($my_string =~ /\b([a-z]+)\b/g)
  {
  $freq{$1}++;
  }
while ((my $key, my $value) = each(%freq))
  {
    $value = "000000" . $value;
    $value = substr($value,-6,6);
    push (@termarray, "$value $key");
  }
print join("\n", (reverse (sort (@termarray))));
exit;
```

Here is an equivalent script, in Python:

```
#!/usr/local/bin/python
import re
import string
word_list = []
freq_list = []
format_list = []
freq = {}
my_string = "Peter Piper picked a peck of pickled peppers. A peck of pickled peppers Peter \
Piper picked. If Peter Piper picked a peck of pickled peppers, Where is the peck of pickled \
peppers that Peter Piper picked?".lower()
word_list = re.findall(r'(\b[a-z]{1,}\b)', my_string)
```

```
for item in word_list:
  count = freq.get(item,0)
  freq[item] = count + 1
for key, value in freq.iteritems():
  value = "000000" + str(value)
  value = value[-6:]
  format_list += [value + " " + key]
format_list = reversed(sorted(format_list))
print("\n".join(format_list))
exit
```

After you have produced a Zipf distribution list, you can visualize the distribution, using a graphing application. Here is a short Gnuplot script, gettysburg.gp, that produces a histogram (ie, bin frequency plot) from the Zipf distribution of Lincoln's Gettysburg address.

In the example described here, we put the raw output of the Zipf distribution of the Gettysburg address in the file gettysburg.dat, and we put the Gnuplot script in the file gettysburg.gp. Both files will be stored in the c:\ directory.

```
set xtics border in scale 1,0.5 nomirror rotate by -90 offset character 0,0,0;
set term png size 1300,800;
set output 'c:\out.png';
unset key;
set xrange [0:80];
set style fill solid;
plot 'c:\gettysb.dat' using 2:xticlabels(1) with histogram;
```

Notice that the output of the graph will be ported into a .png file (out.png) in the c:\ directory.

We run the script by changing the directory to the location wherein gnuplot.exe resides, which happens to be, on my computer, "c:\Program Files (x86)\gnuplot\bin"

Once in the directory that holds gnuplot.exe, we invoke the name of the executable file, followed by the path and filename of the gnuplot script, gettysburg.gp (Fig. 4.5):

```
c:\Program Files (x86)\gnuplot\bin>gnuplot.exe c:\gettysburg.gp
```

A typical book contains somewhere between 5000 and 10,000 unique words, depending somewhat on the subject matter, and on the verbal facility of the author. In most cases, the first thirty words in the Zipf distribution account for more than 25% of all word occurrences. By profiling word frequencies, we learn something about the subject matter of the text.[11] It is easy to imagine how we might compare different texts with a distance measure for the normalized frequencies of the commonly occurring words in the two texts (See Glossary item, Euclidean distance).

We note that some of the most frequently occurring words correspond to "stop words," discussed in detail in Section 3.3. The scripts provided here could be easily modified to excluded "stop words" from the Zipf distribution, thus producing a list composed of so-called high-information words. The high-information words with the top occurrence frequencies tell us the most about the book, because these words represent the concepts that the book stresses.[11]

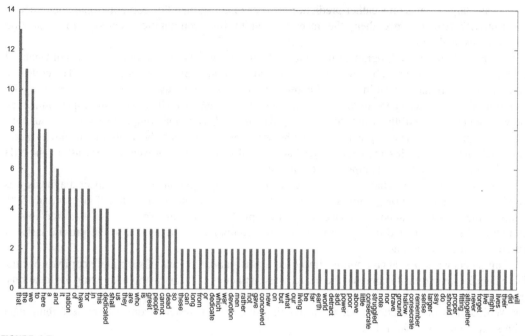

FIGURE 4.5

Gnuplot output of the Gnuplot script, gettysburg.gp.

4.5 REDUCING DATA

When debugging, novices insert corrective code; experts remove defective code.

-Richard Pattis

When thinking of dimensionality, it may be best to think in terms of the attributes of a data record. A medical record may hold hundreds or thousands of data attributes (eg, height, weight, respirations, temperature, blood pressure, hundreds of blood tests, all measured at various dates and times, and each separate measurement representing another attribute). These attributes are often referred to as dimensional data elements, because each attribute can reside in its own dimension in a multidimensional space.

When dealing with issues related to finding and retrieving records that hold many attributes (ie, records of high dimensionality), there is very little downside to multidimensionality. If you're searching for the value of attribute number 5000 in record number 10 million, a good database should have no trouble handling your query. Problems do not arise until you begin to ask questions about the relationships among the different attributes. For example, how does the value of attribute 4632 of record 8,933,425 modify the behavior of attribute 294 or record 12,396,772?

Fifty years ago, finding relationships in large, multidimensional data sets was simply impossible. Computers lacked the computational power to perform the types of combinatorial gymnastics that the job required. In 1961, a meteorologist, Edward Lorenz, found that small changes in initial conditions could have large effects on weather predictions. Lorenz later termed this computational phenomenon the Butterfly Effect. Since then, the race was on to find computation methods for analyzing multidimensional data.

In 2003, when I was a Program Director and Medical Officer at the National Institutes of Health, I attended a briefing convened by a top-level science administrator. She explained that the data collected on human cancers had grown in size and complexity over the previous decade. In response, the NIH would need to acquire supercomputers to deal with all the data (See Glossary item, Supercomputer). New combinatorial algorithms and software would be needed. The supercomputers would use our clinical and experimental data to predict how the behavior of tumors could be altered by different therapeutic regimens. Using this approach, which had worked successfully for weather forecasters, the NIH would harness the power of computers, to cure cancer.

More than twelve years have passed since the day that supercomputer-based cancer diagnosis was envisioned; without tangible progress. It is fair to remark that the microscope, a tool invented in 1590, remains the primary diagnostic device used in hospital laboratories. Today, you will find lots of computers in hospitals and medical offices, but the computers are relegated to the prosaic tasks of record-keeping and billing.[11]

Computers work best at computing simplified mathematical models of seemingly complex events. For example, we can easily compute the trajectories of planets and stars without knowing the locations, masses, and trajectories of every object in the universe. We only need to understand a few laws of physics. With almost no exceptions, our understanding of complex systems comes from describing data with simple mathematical rules.

Mathematicians abhor complex and multidimensional data and consider all such data cursed (See Glossary item, Curse of dimensionality). The curse, as you might expect, is based on mathematical principles. Let's imagine two data objects, each with 10,000 matched attributes. The second object is much like the first object, but each of its attributes is just 5 units larger than the paired attribute in the first object. The number 5 doesn't seem to be a very big difference, but when we calculate the Euclidean distance between object 1 and object 2, we take the square root of the sum of the squares of the differences for 10,000 attributes (See Glossary item, Euclidean distance). In Ruby:

```
irb(main):001:0> Math.sqrt((5**2) * 10000) => 500.0
```

What intuitively would be a distance of 5 between the two objects, is actually a distance of 500.

Because the distance between data objects is large, the multidimensional space that holds the data objects must be sparse (ie, the odds of two different data objects being very close to one another are nearly zero). When the number of dimensions is so large that distances between objects become difficult or impossible to compute, most computational algorithms become useless.

Accordingly, there is much emphasis today on reducing the dimensionality of complex data. The simplest form of dimensionality reduction involves measuring the correlation among attributes (See Pearson's correlation in Open Source Tools for Chapter 8). When two attributes correlate perfectly with one another, one of the attributes can be eliminated. For example, suppose I measure the height of buildings in feet, and include those measurements as an attribute in a data set. Suppose further that I do not understand the relationship between feet and centimeters, leading me to add another attribute in which the height of buildings are measured in centimeters. The feet-height measurements will correlate perfectly with the centimeter-height measurements. One of the two attributes can be safely eliminated.

Likewise, if I can find an attribute that has zero correlation with any other attribute, then I might assume that the attribute consists of noise (ie, random or nearly random data). Noisy data adds nothing but complexity to our calculations and can lead to overfitting (See Glossary item, Overfitting).

Several useful and clever algorithms have been developed that specifically address the curse of dimensionality. Prominent among these is Principle Component analysis. Principle component analysis involves taking a list of parameters and reducing it to a smaller list, with each component of the smaller list constructed from combinations of variables in the larger list. Correspondence analysis is similar to principal component analysis, but is applied to categorical data, rather than continuous data (See Glossary item, Principal component analysis)

Although it is useful, sometimes imperative, to reduce the dimensionality of data, it is important not to confuse dimensional reduction with data flattening. Data flattening is a term that is used differently by data analysts, database experts, and informaticians. Though the precise meaning changes from subfield to subfield, the term always seems to connote a simplification of the data, and the elimination of unnecessary structural restraints. In the field of informatics, data flattening is a popular, but ultimately counterproductive method of data organization and data reduction. Data flattening involves removing data annotations that are not needed for the interpretation of data (eg, timestamps, data field designators, identifiers for individual data objects contained in a document). Imagine, for the sake of illustration, a drastic option that was seriously considered by a large medical institution. This institution, which shall remain nameless, had established an excellent electronic medical record (EMR) system. The EMR assigns a unique and permanent identifier string to each patient, and attaches the identifier string to every hospital transaction involving the patient (eg, biopsy reports, pharmacy reports, nursing notes, laboratory reports). All of the data relevant to a patient, produced anywhere within the hospital system is linked by the patient's unique identifier. The patient's EMR can be assembled, instantly, whenever needed, via a database query. Over time, the patient records in well-designed information systems accrue a huge number of annotations (See Glossary items, Annotation, Timestamp, Universally Unique Identifier, Metadata). The database manager is saddled with the responsibility of maintaining the associations among all of the annotations. For example, an individual with a particular test, conducted at a particular time, on a particular day, will have annotations that link the test to a test procedure protocol, an instrument identifier, a test code, a laboratory name, a test sample, a sample accession time, and so on. If data objects could be stripped of most of their annotations, then the overall data management burden on the hospital information system would be reduced. This can be achieved by composing simplified records and deleting the internal annotations. For example, all of the data relevant to a patient's laboratory test could be reduced to the patient's name, the date, the name of the test, and the test result. All of the other annotations can be deleted. This process is called data flattening. Should a medical center, or any entity that collects data, flatten their data? The positive result would be a streamlining of the system, with a huge reduction in annotation overhead. The negative result would be the loss of the information that connects well-defined data objects (eg, test result with test protocol, test instrument with test result, name of laboratory technician with test sample, name of clinician with name of patient). Because the fundamental activity of the data scientist is to find relationships among data objects, data flattening reduces the scope and value of data analyses. Without annotations and metadata, the data from different information systems cannot be sensibly merged. Furthermore, if there is a desire or a need to reanalyze flattened data, then the data scientist will not be able to verify the data and validate the conclusions drawn from the data (See Glossary items, Verification, Validation, Results, Pseudosimplification).[5]

OPEN SOURCE TOOLS

A mathematician is a person who says that, when three people are supposed to be in a room but five came out, two have to go in so the room gets empty

-Origin unknown

GNUPLOT

Gnuplot is an open source graphing and statistical utility that can plot data extracted from data files or generated by mathematical functions, in two dimensions or three dimensions. An excellent reference book on the subject is "Gnuplot in Action: Understanding Data with Graphs," by Philipp Janert.[25]

The easiest way to access Gnuplot is to use the version that comes bundled in Cygwin (Fig. 4.6).

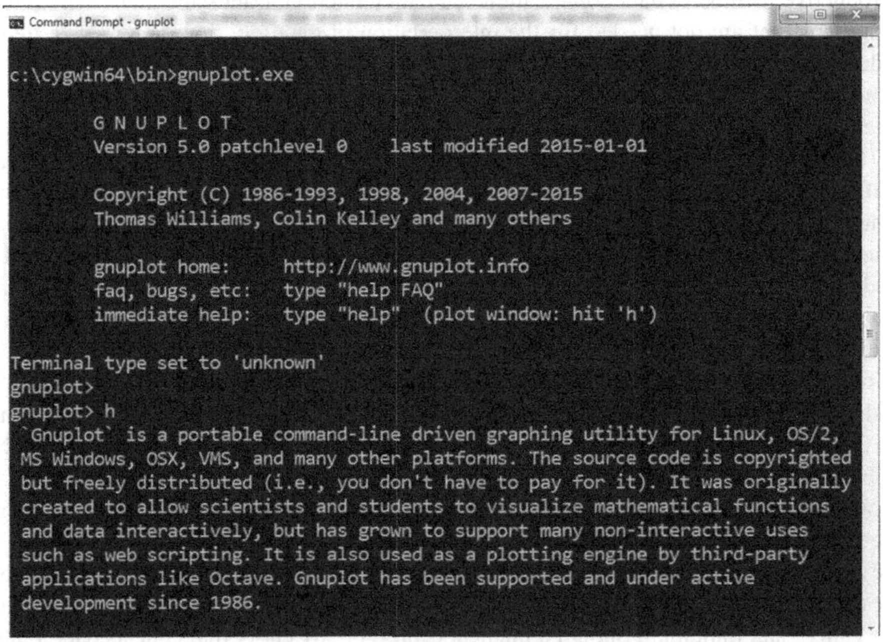

FIGURE 4.6

When Cygwin is installed in your Windows system, Gnuplot can be invoked directly from the command-line prompt at the subdirectory in which CygWin is installed (eg, "c:\cygwin64\bin>", on my computer).

Or, you can download a Windows version of Gnuplot from: http://sourceforge.net/projects/gnuplot/files/latest/download?source=files

Gnuplot can be operated any of several convenient ways: as a DOS command line, as a Linux command line (eg, via Cygwin), as an interactive series of command lines through the Gnuplot console, as a Gnuplot script, or via system calls from scripts (eg, from Perl, Python, or Ruby) (Fig. 4.7).

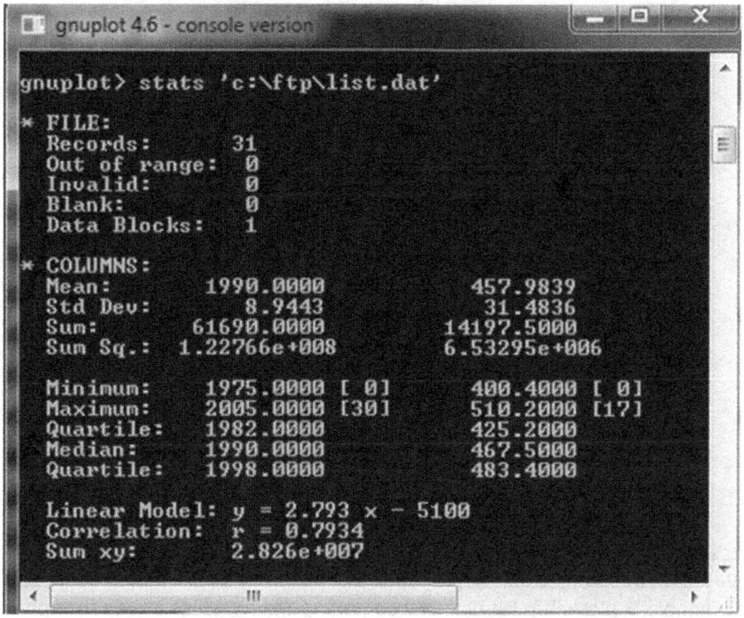

FIGURE 4.7

Shown here is the Gnuplot console, under Windows, which produces a gnuplot> prompt from which you can enter command lines. In this example, the "stats" command, followed by the path/filename of a data file, tabulates helpful statistics for the data.

Basically, all Gnuplot graph commands have the same format, consisting of the word "plot" (for two-dimensional graphs), or "splot," for three-dimensional graphs, followed by the name of the data file to be plotted. If the data file consists of two columns of data, Gnuplot assumes that the first column holds the x-coordinate values and the second column holds the y-value coordinates. Everything else about Gnuplot is just bells and whistles that you can pick up by studying example scripts available on multiple web sites (Fig. 4.8).

Three-dimensional plots are easy to create in Gnuplot. Here is an example wherein the Gnuplot command line calls for a three-dimensional plot, using the "splot" command. When the data file contains three data columns, Gnuplot automatically assigns each column to the x, y, and z coordinates (Fig. 4.9).

Programmers who write many scripts, in different programming languages, are likely to prefer to prepare their Gnuplot instructions as external scripts, using a simple text editor. You may find it easier to develop, modify, and store external scripts than to deal with the oddities of Gnuplot's interactive console. If so, prepare your Gnuplot scripts as external files, with the suffix .gp, and simply call your scripts directly from the subdirectory in which Gnuplot resides, or from the Gnuplot console, using the "load" command.

For example, the following gnuplot command line loads and interprets the Gnuplot script, peter.gp, which contains a set of gnuplot command lines.

```
gnuplot> load 'c:\ftp\peter.gp'
```

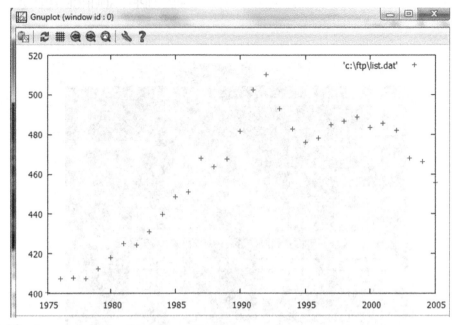

FIGURE 4.8

A basic Gnuplot graph, produced by entering the word "plot" followed by a the path/name of a data file, from the gnuplot prompt: gnuplot> plot 'c:\ftp\list.dat'. The command line produces a simple graph, listing data points and *x-y* coordinate ranges extracted from the data file, and pasting the name of the data file (list.dat) into the upper right quadrant.

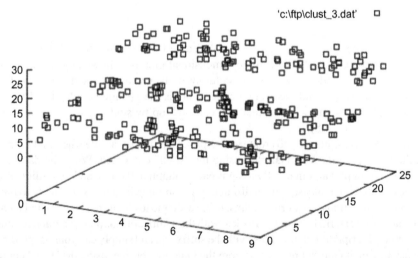

FIGURE 4.9

A three dimension plot, using a prepared, three-column, data file. The Gnuplot command line is: "gnuplot>splot 'c:\ftp\clust_3.dat' with points lt −1 pt 4". The plot is created by the "splot" instruction followed by the data file's path/filename. The remainder of the command line, "with points lt −1 pt 4", modify the appearance of the displayed data points.

MATPLOTLIB

MatPlotlib is a Python module that plots data. If you have MatPlotLib, you can choose your favorite type of graph (eg, bar plot, line plot, filled line plot, scatter plot, boxplot, histogram, pie chart, stream plot, color maps) from a list of hundreds, available from the matplotlib gallery, at: http://matplotlib.org/gallery.html

When you've chosen a sample graph that seems suitable for your data and your purposes, just insert the source code into your own Python scripts, substituting your own data values and variables, wherever appropriate.

Here, the MatPlotLib module is used, in a Python script, to plot a sine wave (Fig. 4.10):

```
#!/usr/local/bin/python
import numpy
import matplotlib.pyplot as plt
cent_array = numpy.linspace(1,50,2000)
sine_array = map(lambda x: numpy.sin(x), cent_array)
plt.plot(cent_array, sine_array)
plt.show()
exit
```

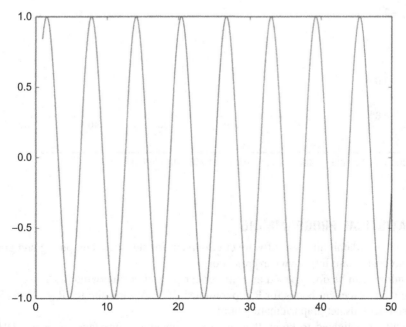

FIGURE 4.10

A sinusoidal distribution produced with MatPlotLib.

Here the sum of cosine and sine waves are plotted (Fig. 4.11):

```
#!/usr/local/bin/python
import numpy
import matplotlib.pyplot as plt
cent_array = numpy.linspace(1,50,2000)
mixed_sine_cosine_array = \
map(lambda x: (0.1*numpy.sin(0.7*x)) + (0.7*numpy.cos(0.1*x)), cent_array)
plt.plot(cent_array, mixed_sine_cosine_array)
plt.show()
exit
```

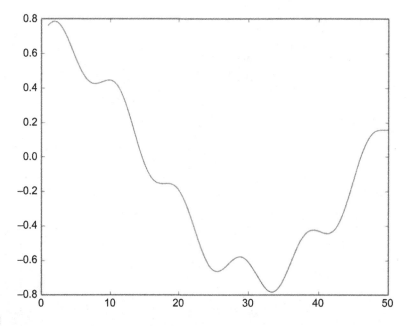

FIGURE 4.11

A sinusoidal and cosinusoidal distribution are summed with MatPlotLib.

R, FOR STATISTICAL PROGRAMMING

R, like Gnuplot and Matplotlib, is a software environment for statistical computing and graphics. It is available at no cost, from: http://www.r-project.org/

R for Windows can be downloaded at: http://cran.r-project.org/bin/windows/base/

There are many excellent books for R programmers.[26–28] A good site for R graphing is found at: http://www.statmethods.net/graphs/creating.html

R users will be delighted to know that there are convenient interfaces to R available for Perl (Statistics::R), Ruby (RinRuby) and Python (Rpy).

One caveat: R offers so many advanced statistical options that scientists are often tempted to use R routines that they do not fully understand. In most cases, the unglamorous descriptive statistical tools described in this chapter (eg, average, standard deviation), and the nonparametric resampling approach to be described in Chapter 8, are simple, transparent, and sufficient for quotidian activities. For myself, a data scientist without statistician credentials, I prefer to use Gunplot, Matplotlib and the standard functions in Perl, Python, and Ruby, leaving R to the card-carrying statisticians.

NUMPY

Numpy (Numerical Python) is an open source extension to Python that supports matrix operations, as well as a rich assortment of mathematical functions.

Numpy can be easily downloaded from sourceforge.net: http://sourceforge.net/projects/numpy/

Here is a short Python script, numpy_dot.py, that creates a 3×3 matrix, inverts the matrix, and calculates the dot produce of the matrix and its inverted counterpart.

```
#!/usr/bin/python
import numpy
from numpy.linalg import inv
a = numpy.array([[1,4,6], [9,15,55], [62,-5, 4]])
print(a)
print(inv(a))
c = numpy.dot(a, inv(a))
print(numpy.round_(c))
exit
```

The numpy_dot.py script employs numpy, numpy's linear algebra module, numpy's matrix inversion method, and the numpy dot product method. We will describe the dot product, in detail, in Open Source Tools for Chapter 8. Here is the output of the script, displaying the original matrix, its inversion, and the dot product, which happens to be the unity matrix:.

```
c:\ftp\py>numpy_dot.py
[[ 1  4  6]
 [ 9 15 55]
 [62 -5  4]]
[[ 4.19746899e-02 -5.76368876e-03  1.62886856e-02]
 [ 4.22754041e-01 -4.61095101e-02 -1.25297582e-04]
 [-1.22165142e-01  3.17002882e-02 -2.63124922e-03]]
[[1. 0. 0.]
 [0. 1. 0.]
 [0. 0. 1.]]
```

There is an abundance of documentation for numpy, available at: http://docs.scipy.org/doc/

It is easy to see why numerically inclined programmers might opt for Python, over other languages, just to enjoy easy access to the numpy methods.

SCIPY

Scipy is an open source collection of mathematics-related Python modules.[29] Scipy modules include: integration, interpolation, Fourier transforms, signal processing, linear algebra, statistics (See Glossary items, Signal, Fourier transform, Fourier series). In addition, Scipy comes bundled with MatPlotLib.

Scipy can be downloaded from: http://www.scipy.org/scipylib/download.html

Like numpy, scipy is a treasure trove of useful, easily implemented, algorithms.

You can spare yourself the trouble of downloading individual installations of numpy and scipy by downloading Anaconda, a free distribution that bundles hundreds of python packages, along with a recent version of Python. Anaconda is available at: https://store.continuum.io/cshop/anaconda/

IMAGEMAGICK

ImageMagick is an open source utility that supports a huge selection of robust and sophisticated image editing methods. Its source code download site is: http://www.imagemagick.org/download/

Users may find it convenient to download the executable binaries, for their specific operating system, from: http://www.imagemagick.org/script/binary-releases.php

Hundreds of ImageMagick methods are described in detail, and useful examples are provided, at: http://www.imagemagick.org/Usage/

There are several things you should know about ImageMagick:

1. Unlike the commercial image processing applications, ImageMagick has no graphic user interface. ImageMagick is intended to serve as a command line utility.
2. ImageMagick is powerful. There are hundreds of available methods for creating and modifying images.
3. ImageMagick can be called from Python, Perl, or Ruby via system calls or via language-specific ImageMagick interface modules (ie, PerlMagick, PythonMagick, or RMagick)

Here are a few examples of ImageMagick command lines that can be launched from the system prompt:

Converts an image in SVG format to JPEG format.

```
convert mtor_pathway.svg mtor_pathway.jpg
```

Creates a thumbnail image from image.jpg and converts it to gif format.

```
convert -size 600x800 image.jpg -thumbnail 120x160 image_thumb.gif
```

Applies contrast twice to an image, and produce a new file for the results.

```
convert original.jpg -contrast -contrast result.png
```

Puts the contents of file words.txt into the comment section of tar1.jpg and keeps the same filename for the output file.

```
convert -comment @words.txt tar1.jpg tar1.jpg
```

Displays a verbose description of an image, including the header contents.

```
identify -verbose tar1.jpg
```

The real power of ImageMagick comes when it is inserted into scripts, allowing the programmer to perform batch operations of image collections.

Here is a Python script, image_resize.py, that creates a resized copy of every jpeg file in the current directory.

```
#!/usr/local/bin/python
import sys, os, re
filelist = os.listdir(".")
pattern = re.compile(".jpg$")
for filename in filelist:
  if pattern.search(filename):
    out_filename = pattern.sub('_small.jpg', filename)
    print(out_filename)
    cmdstring = "convert " + filename + " -resize 400x267! " + out_filename
    os.system(cmdstring)
  else:
    continue
exit
```

Here is a Perl script, factth.pl, that reduces the size of every image in a subdirectory that exclusively contains image files. In this case, the all-image subdirectory is "c:\ftp\factth".

```
#!/usr/local/bin/perl
$newdir = "c\:\\ftp\\factth";
opendir (MYDIR, $newdir) || die ("Can't open directory");
chdir ($newdir);
while ($file = readdir (MYDIR))
  {
  next if (-d $file);
  next if ($file eq "." || $file eq "..");
  system("convert $file -resize 30% $file");
  }
closedir (MYFILE);
exit;
```

DISPLAYING EQUATIONS IN LATEX

LaTeX is a document preparation system that operates in conjunction with TeX, a typesetting system. Because LaTeX is designed to accommodate scientific and mathematical notations (eg, exponents, integrals, summations), LaTeX is used widely by publishers of scientific text. LaTeX is the subject of numerous books referenced at: http://LaTeX-project.org/guides/books.html

Within LaTeX is a notation system for expressing any mathematical formula in simple ASCII format. Formula expressed in ASCII can be converted, by the LaTeX application, into elegant symbolic form. The mathematical formulas displayed in this book were prepared in ascii notation, converted by LaTeX algorithms into image files, and printed.

Just as there are mini-languages for pattern matching (ie, Regex) and string formatting (ie, format commands), there is a mini-language for expressing mathematical formulas in ASCII. Data scientists should familiarize themselves with LaTeX formula notation.

Here are a few examples:

Normalized compression distance in LaTeX notation: NCD_Z(x,y) = \frac{Z(xy) - min\left\{Z(x), Z(y)\right\}}{max\left\{Z(x),Z(y)\right\}}

The normalized compression distance is displayed elsewhere in this chapter, in Fig. 4.13.

Pearson's formula in LaTeX notation: \frac{\sum (x_i - \overline{x})(y_i - \overline{y})}{\sqrt {\sum{(x_i - \overline{x})^2}}{\sqrt{\sum{(y_i - \overline{y})^2}}}

Pearson's formula is displayed elsewhere in this chapter, in Fig. 4.15.

Euler's identity in LaTeX notation: e^(^i^\pi^) + 1=0

Pearson's formula is displayed elsewhere, in Fig. 6.1.

The Sample size formula in LaTeX notation: n = (Z_{\alpha/2} \sigma / E)^2

It is not necessary to install LaTeX and TeX, just to display formulas. Python's MatPlotLib module will do it for you. The following short python script takes the sample size formula, in ascii notation, and coverts it to LaTeX symbols (Fig. 4.12).

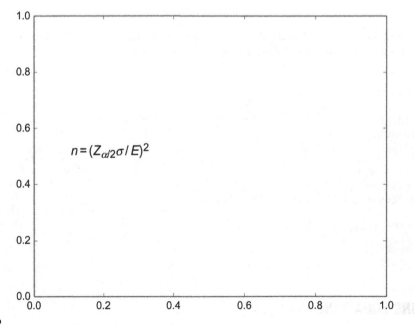

FIGURE 4.12

The sample size formula converted to a stylized image, using a two-line MatPlotLib script (See Glossary items, Power, Sample size).

```
#!/usr/local/bin/python
import matplotlib.pyplot as plt
plt.text(0.1, 0.5, r'$n = (Z_{\alpha/2} \sigma / E)^2$', fontsize=40)
plt.show()
exit
```

NORMALIZED COMPRESSION DISTANCE

Most compression algorithms work by finding repeated sequences in data streams, and replacing such patterns with shorter strings, that can be transformed back to the original patterns, when the file is decompressed. For example, a file may have long runs of 1s, and these long runs can be replaced by a few characters and a tagging system that can reconstitute runs of 1s. Though the different compression algorithms vary greatly, they all look for repeating features (eg, waves, runs, fractals, regions). Files filled with randomly chosen characters are incompressible, because long random sequences do not repeat. Files composed of nonrandom characters will be compressible (ie, repeated patterns will emerge). Furthermore, files that are similar to one another, when concatenated, will undergo greater compression than the concatenation of two files that are dissimilar to one another. The reason being that two similar files will share repeated regions, thus facilitating compression. Files that are dissimilar to one another, will not share many repeating regions, thus impairing compression of the concatenated files.[30] This simple fact is the basis of the normalized compression distance.

The normalized compression distance, shown below, is a very simple measurement of similarity between two files (Fig. 4.13).

$$NCD_Z(x, y) = \frac{Z(xy) - min\{Z(x), Z(y)\}}{max\{Z(x), Z(y)\}}$$

FIGURE 4.13

The normalized compression distance, between two strings, x and y, is the compression size of the concatenation of x and y minus the compression size of x or y, whichever is smaller, divided by the compression size of x or y, whichever is largest.

Two highly similar strings will have a normalized compression distance of close to 0. Two dissimilar strings will have a normalized compression distance close to 1 (ie, the largest possible normalized distance from one another).[31] Aside from its ease of implementation, the normalized compression distance is particularly useful because it makes no assumptions about the relative size of files (ie, two files of different sizes can be concatenated), and it is a nonparametric test, making no assumptions about the distribution of data contained in the strings or files (See Glossary item, Nonparametric statistics).

Let's look at an example, using the Gettysburg address, a plain-text file of length 1463 bytes. When I take the Gettysburg address and compress it, with gzip, the file size shrinks to 738 bytes. When I concatenate the Gettysburg address with itself, thus doubling its size, the size of the compressed file is only 761 bytes (ie, hardly larger than the compressed size of the Gettysburg address by itself). The computed normalized compression distance of the Gettysburg address, with itself, is

(761 − 738)/738 = 0.031, a number very close to zero, indicating that there is very little compression distance between the Gettysburg address and itself.

For the sake of completion, let us compute the normalized compression distance between two files, each composed of randomly chosen characters.

Here is how to make a file consisting of random characters, using Python:

```
#!/usr/local/bin/python
from random import randint
outfile = open ("random_1.raw", "wb")
for n in range(160000):
  c = chr(randint(0,255))
  outfile.write(c)
exit
```

It just so happens that we chose to create files of size 160,000 bytes, a size that is divisible by 8 (the number of bits in an ASCII character), and which happens to be the square of 400 (ie, 160,000 = 400 × 400). These fortunate circumstances permit us the luxury of representing our file as an image of 400 rows and 400 columns, with each pixel being a random character of 8 bits length (ie, varying from 0 to 255), equivalent to the shades of gray available to individual pixels. ImageMagick can convert a raw data file, of the type just described, into an image file that we can view.

```
c:\ftp>convert -size 400x400 -depth 8 gray:random_1.raw random_1.bmp
```

Here is the resultant image (Fig. 4.14):

FIGURE 4.14

An image composed entirely of pixels randomly chosen from 256 shades of gray.

You may find it an interesting observation that any two images composed of random pixels will look identical to one another, to the human eye. Our brains have no way of distinguishing the differences among individual pixels. Yet, such files are maximally dissimilar, and are separated by the largest possible normalized compression distances.

We can run the same Python script to produce a second random file. We'll call the first random file random_1.raw, and the second random file, random_1.raw. Now we are ready to write a Python script, compression_dist.py, that calculates the normalized compression distance between two files. In this case, the two files will be the two random files we have just created.

```python
#!/usr/local/bin/python
import gzip
import os

first_in = open('random_1.raw', 'rb')
first_out = gzip.open('random_1.gz', 'wb')
first_out.writelines(first_in)
first_out.close()
first_in.close()
random_1_size = os.path.getsize('random_1.gz')

second_in = open('random_2.raw', 'rb')
second_out = gzip.open('random_2.gz', 'wb')
second_out.writelines(second_in)
second_out.close()
second_in.close()
random_2_size = os.path.getsize('random_2.gz')

os.system("c:/cygwin64/bin/cat c:/ftp/random_1.raw \
c:/ftp/random_2.raw > c:/ftp/random_cat.raw")

cat_in = open('random_cat.raw', 'rb')
cat_out = gzip.open('random_cat.gz', 'wb')
cat_out.writelines(cat_in)
cat_out.close()
cat_in.close()
random_cat_size = os.path.getsize('random_cat.gz')

dist = float(random_cat_size - random_1_size)/float(random_2_size)
print(dist)
exit
```

Here is the output:

```
c:\ftp>norm_comp.py
0.999843825159
```

The normalized compression distance between our two random files is 0.999843825159, indicating that two files composed of random characters have, as we surmised, a normalized compression distance of about 1.

PEARSON'S CORRELATION

Similarity scores are based on comparing one data object with another, attribute by attribute, usually summing the squares of the differences in magnitude for each attribute, and using the calculation to compute a final outcome, known as the correlation score. One of the most popular correlation methods is Pearson's correlation, which produces a score that can vary from -1 to $+1$. Two objects with a high score (near $+1$) are highly similar.[18] Two uncorrelated objects would have a Pearson score near zero. Two objects that correlated inversely (ie, one falling when the other rises) would have a Pearson score near -1 (See Glossary items, Correlation distance, Normalized compression distance).

The Pearson correlation for two objects, with paired attributes, sums the product of their differences from their object means, and divides the sum by the product of the squared differences from the object means (Fig. 4.15).

$$\frac{\sum (x_i - \overline{x})(y_i - \overline{y})}{\sqrt{\sum (x_i - \overline{x})^2}\sqrt{\sum (y_i - \overline{y})^2}}$$

FIGURE 4.15

Formula for Pearson's correlation. \frac{\sum (x_i - \overline{x})(y_i - \overline{y})}{\sqrt{\sum{(x_i - \overline{x})^ 2}}{\sqrt{\sum{(y_i - \overline{y}) ˜2}}}.

You will notice that the Pearson's correlation is parametric, in the sense that it relies heavily on the "mean" parameter for the two objects. This means that Pearson's correlation might have higher validity for a normal distribution, with a centered mean, than for a distribution that is not normally distributed, such as a Zipf distribution (See Glossary items, Nonparametric statistics, Zipf distribution).

Python's Scipy module offers a Pearson function. In addition to computing Pearson's correlation, the Scipy function produces a two-tailed p-value, which provides some indication of the likelihood that two totally uncorrelated objects might produce a Pearson's correlation value as extreme as the calculated value (See Glossary item, p-value).

Let's look at a short Python script, pearson.py, that calculates the Pearson correlation on two lists.

```
#!/usr/bin/python
from scipy.stats.stats import pearsonr
a = [1,2,3,4]
b = [2,4,6,8]
print pearsonr(a,b)
exit
```

Here's the output of pearson.py

```
c:\ftp\py>sci_pearson.py
(1.0, 0.0)
```

The first output number is the Pearson correlation value. The second output number is the two-tailed *p*-value. We see that the two list objects are perfectly correlated, with a Pearson's correlation of 1. This is what we would expect, as the attributes of list b are exactly twice the value of their paired attributes in list a. In addition, the double-tailed *p*-value is zero, indicating that it unlikely that two uncorrelated lists would yield the calculated correlation value.

Let's look at the Pearson correlation for another set of paired list attributes.

```
#!/usr/bin/python
from scipy.stats.stats import pearsonr
a = [1,4,6,9,15,55,62,-5]
b = [-2,-8,-9,-12,-80,14,15,2]
print pearsonr(a,b)
exit
```

Here's the output:

```
c:\ftp\py>sci_pearson.py
(0.32893766587262174, 0.42628658412101167)
```

In this case, the Pearson correlation is intermediate between 0 and 1, indicating some correlation. How does the Pearson correlation help us to simplify and reduce data? If two lists of data have a Pearson correlation of 1 or of −1, this implies that one set of the data is redundant. We can assume the two lists have the same information content. For further explanation, see Section 4.5. Reducing Data in this chapter.

If we were comparing two sets of data and found a Pearson correlation of zero, then we might assume that the two sets of data were uncorrelated, and that it would be futile to try to model (ie, find a mathematical relationship for) the data (See Glossary item, Overfitting).

THE RIDICULOUSLY SIMPLE DOT PRODUCT

There are many different correlation measurements, and all of them are based on assumptions about how well-correlated sets of data ought to behave. A data analyst who works with gene sequences might impose a different set of requirements, for well-correlated data, than a data analyst who is investigating fluctuations in the stock market. Hence, there are many correlation values that are available to data scientists, and these include: Pearson, Cosine, Spearman, Jaccard, Gini, Maximal Information Coefficient, and Complex Linear Pathway score. The simplest of all the correlation scores is the dot product. In a recent paper comparing the performance of 12 correlation formulas, the simple dot product led the pack.[32] (Fig. 4.16).

$$\sum_i x_i y_i$$

FIGURE 4.16

The lowly dot product. For two vectors, the dot product is the sum of the products of the corresponding values. To normalize the dot product, we would divide the dot product by the product of the lengths of the two vectors.

The Python script, dot_big.py, examines the various dot products that can be calculated for three vectors,

```
a = [1,4,6,9,15,55,62,-5]
b = [-2,-8,-9,-12,-80,14,15,2]
c = [2,8,12,18,30,110,124,-10]
```

Notice that vector c has twice the value of each paired attribute in vector a.

```
#!/usr/bin/python
from __future__ import division
import numpy
from numpy import linalg
a = [1,4,6,9,15,55,62,-5]
b = [-2,-8,-9,-12,-80,14,15,2]
c = [2,8,12,18,30,110,124,-10]
a_length = linalg.norm(a)
b_length = linalg.norm(b)
c_length = linalg.norm(c)
print "Vector a is ", (a)
print "Vector b is ", (b)
print "Vector c is ", (c)
print "Length of a is ", (a_length)
print "Length of b is ", (b_length)
print "Length of c is ", (c_length)
print "Dot of a and b is ", (numpy.dot(a,b))
print "Dot of b and a is ", (numpy.dot(b,a))
print "Dot of a and a is ", (numpy.dot(a,a))
print "Dot of b and b is ", (numpy.dot(b,b))
print "Dot of a and c is ", (numpy.dot(a,c))
print "Dot of c and b is ", (numpy.dot(c,b))
print "Normalized dot of a and b is ", (numpy.dot(a,b) / (a_length * b_length))
print "Normalized dot a and a is ", (numpy.dot(a,a) / (a_length * a_length))
print "Normalized dot of b and b is ", (numpy.dot(b,b) / (b_length * b_length))
print "Normalized dot of a and c is ", (numpy.dot(a,c) / (a_length * c_length))
print "Normalized dot of b and c is ", (numpy.dot(b,c) / (b_length * c_length))
exit
```

output:

```
c:\ftp>dot_big.py
Vector a is [1, 4, 6, 9, 15, 55, 62, -5]
Vector b is [-2, -8, -9, -12, -80, 14, 15, 2]
Vector c is [2, 8, 12, 18, 30, 110, 124, -10]
```

```
Length of a is 85.1645466142
Length of b is 84.36824047
Length of c is 170.329093228
Dot of a and b is 294
Dot of b and a is 294
Dot of a and a is 7253
Dot of b and b is 7118
Dot of a and c is 14506
Dot of c and b is 588
Normalized dot of a and b is 0.0409175385118
Normalized dot a and a is 1.0
Normalized dot of b and b is 1.0
Normalized dot of a and c is 1.0
Normalized dot of b and c is 0.0409175385118
```

Inspecting the output, we see that the normalized dot product of a vector with itself is 1. The normalized dot product of a and c is also 1, because c is perfectly correlated with a, being twice its value, attribute by attribute. Hence we observe that the normalized dot product of a and b is equal to the normalized dot product of a and c (0.0409175385118).

GLOSSARY

Accuracy versus precision Accuracy measures how close your data comes to being correct. Precision provides a measurement of reproducibility (ie, whether repeated measurements of the same quantity produce the same result). Data can be accurate but imprecise. If you have a 10-pound object, and you report its weight as 7.2376 pounds, on every occasion when the object is weighed, then your precision is remarkable, but your accuracy is dismal. See Precision.

Annotation Annotation involves associating data with additional data to provide description, disambiguation (eg, adding identifiers to distinguish the data from other data), links to related data, or timestamps to mark when the data was created. One of the most important functions of annotation is to provide data elements with metadata, facilitating our ability to find relationships among different data objects. Annotation is vital for effective search and retrieval of large and complex sets of data.

Authentication A process for determining if the data object that is received (eg, document, file, image) is the data object that was intended to be received. The simplest authentication protocol involves one-way hash operations on the data that needs to be authenticated. Suppose you happen to know that a certain file, named z.txt will be arriving via email and that this file has an MD5 hash of "uF7pBPGgxKtabA/2zYlscQ==". You receive the z.txt, and you perform an MD5 one-way hash operation on the file, as shown here:

```
#!/usr/bin/python
import base64
import md5
md5_object = md5.new()
sample_file = open ("z.txt", "rb")
string = sample_file.read()
sample_file.close()
md5_object.update(string)
md5_string = md5_object.digest()
print(base64.encodestring(md5_string))
exit
```

Let's assume that the output of the MD5 hash operation, performed on the z.txt file, is "uF7pBPGgxKtabA/2zYlscQ==". This would tell us that the received z.txt file is authentic (ie, it is the file that you were intended to receive); because no other file has the same MD5 hash. Additional implementations of one-way hashes are described in Open Source Tools for Chapter 5. The authentication process, in this example, does not tell you who sent the file, the time that the file was created, or anything about the validity of the contents of the file. These would require a protocol that included signature, timestamp, and data validation, in addition to authentication. In common usage, authentication protocols often include entity authentication (ie, some method by which the entity sending the file is verified). Consequently, authentication protocols are often confused with signature verification protocols. An ancient historical example serves to distinguish the concepts of authentication protocols and signature protocols. Since earliest of recorded history, fingerprints were used as a method of authentication. When a scholar or artisan produced a product, he would press his thumb into the clay tablet, or the pot, or the wax seal closing a document. Anyone doubting the authenticity of the pot could ask the artisan for a thumbprint. If the new thumbprint matched the thumbprint on the tablet, pot, or document, then all knew that the person creating the new thumbprint and the person who had put his thumbprint into the object were the same individual. Of course, this was not proof that the object was the creation of the person with the matching thumbprint. For all anyone knew, there may have been a hundred different pottery artisans, with one person pressing his thumb into every pot produced. You might argue that the thumbprint served as the signature of the artisan. In practical terms, no. The thumbprint, by itself, does not tell you whose print was used. Thumbprints could not be read, at least not in the same way as a written signature. The ancients needed to compare the pot's thumbprint against the thumbprint of the living person who made the print. When the person died, civilization was left with a bunch of pots with the same thumbprint, but without any certain way of knowing whose thumb produced them. In essence, because there was no ancient database that permanently associated thumbprints with individuals, the process of establishing the identity of the pot-maker became very difficult once the artisan died. A good signature protocol permanently binds an authentication code to a unique entity (eg, a person). Today, we can find a fingerprint at the scene of a crime; we can find a matching signature in a database; and we can link the fingerprint to one individual. Hence, in modern times, fingerprints are true "digital" signatures, no pun intended. Modern uses of fingerprints include keying (eg, opening locked devices based on an authenticated fingerprint), tracking (eg, establishing the path and whereabouts of an individual by following a trail of fingerprints or other identifiers), and body part identification (ie, identifying the remains of individuals recovered from mass graves or from the sites of catastrophic events based on fingerprint matches). Over the past decade, flaws in the vaunted process of fingerprint identification have been documented, and the improvement of the science of identification is an active area of investigation.[33] See HMAC. See Digital signature.

Beauty To mathematicians, beauty and simplicity are virtually synonymous, both conveying the idea that someone has managed to produce something of great meaning or value from a minimum of material. Euler's identity, relating e, i, pi, 0, and 1 in a simple equation, is held as an example of beauty in mathematics. When writing this book, I was tempted to give it the title, "The Beauty of Data," but I feared that a reductionist flourish, equating data simplification with beauty, was just too obscure.

Blended class Also known as class noise, subsumes the more familiar, but less precise term, "Labeling error." Blended class refers to inaccuracies (eg, misleading results) introduced in the analysis of data due to errors in class assignments (ie, assigning a data object to class A when the object should have been assigned to class B). If you are testing the effectiveness of an antibiotic on a class of people with bacterial pneumonia, the accuracy of your results will be forfeit when your study population includes subjects with viral pneumonia, or smoking-related lung damage. Errors induced by blending classes are often overlooked by data analysts who incorrectly assume that the experiment was designed to ensure that each data group is composed of a uniform and representative population. A common source of class blending occurs when the classification upon which the experiment is designed is itself blended. For example, imagine that you are a cancer researcher and you want to perform a study of patients with malignant fibrous histiocytomas (MFH), comparing the clinical course of these patients with the clinical course of patients who have other types of tumors. Let's imagine that the class of tumors known as MFH does not actually exist; that it is a grab-bag term erroneously assigned to a variety of other tumors that happened to look similar to one another. This being the case, it would be impossible to produce any valid results based on a study of patients diagnosed as MFH. The results would be a biased and irreproducible cacophony of data collected across different, and undetermined, classes tumors. Believe it or not, this specific example, of the blended MFH class of tumors, is selected from the real-life annals of tumor biology.[34,35] The literature is rife with research of dubious quality, based on poorly designed classifications and blended classes. A detailed discussion of this topic is found in Section 6.5, Properties that Cross Multiple Classes. One caveat. Efforts to eliminate class blending can be counterproductive if undertaken with excess zeal. For example, in an effort to reduce class blending, a researcher may choose groups of subjects who are uniform with respect to every known observable property. For example, suppose you want to actually compare apples with oranges. To avoid class blending, you might want to make very sure that your apples do not included any kumquats, or persimmons. You should be certain that your oranges do not include any limes or grapefruits. Imagine that you go even further, choosing only apples and oranges of one variety (eg, Macintosh apples and navel oranges), size (eg, 10 cm), and origin (eg, California). How will your comparisons apply to the varieties of apples and oranges that you have excluded from your study? You may actually reach conclusions that are invalid and irreproducible for more generalized populations within each class. In this case, you have succeeded in eliminating class blending, at the expense of losing representative populations of the classes. See Simpson's paradox.

CODIS Abbreviation for Combined DNA Index System. CODIS is a collection of the unique nucleotide sequences of the equivalent 13 segments of DNA, for every individual included in the database.[36] The CODIS database is used by law enforcement personnel and contains identifying DNA sequences for individuals who have been processed within the criminal justice system. DNA obtained at a crime scene can be matched against DNA samples contained in the database. Hence, the identity of individuals whose DNA is found at a crime scene can often be established. In the absence of a match, it is sometimes possible to establish the genetic relationship (ie, paternal or maternal relatives) between crime scene samples and individuals included in the database.

Case report The case report, also known as the case study, is a detailed description of a single event or situation, often devoted to an outlier, or a unique occurrence of an observation. The concept of the case study is important in the field of data simplification because it highlights the utility of seeking general truths based on observations of rare events. Case reports are common in the biomedical literature, often beginning with a comment regarding the extreme rarity of the featured disease. You can expect to see phrases such as "fewer than a dozen have been reported in the literature" or "the authors have encountered no other cases of this lesion," or such and such a finding makes this lesion particularly uncommon and difficult to diagnose; and so on. The point that the authors are trying to convey is that the case report is worthy of publication specifically because the observation is rare. Too often, case reports serve merely as a cautionary exercise, intended to ward against misdiagnosis. The "beware this lesion" approach to case reporting misses the most important aspect of this type of publication; namely that science, and most aspects of human understanding, involve generalizing from the specific. When Isaac Newton saw an apple falling, he was not thinking that he could write a case report about how he once saw an apple drop, thus warning others not to stand under apple trees lest a rare apple might thump them upon the head. Newton generalized from the apple to all objects, addressing universal properties of gravity, and discovering the laws by which gravity interacts with matter. The case report gives us an opportunity to clarify the general way things work, by isolating one specific and rarely observed factor.[37,38] **Data scientists must understand that rare cases are not exceptions to the general laws of reality; they are the exceptions upon which the general laws of reality are based**. See Outlier.

Categorical data Categorical data is non-numeric data in which objects are assigned categories, with categories having no numeric order. Yes or no, male or female, heads or tails, snake-eyes or boxcars, are types of unordered categorical data. Traditional courses in mathematics and statistics stress the analysis of numeric data, but data scientists soon learn that much of their work involves the collection and analysis of non-numeric data (eg, resampling statistics, as discussed in Section 8.3 of Chapter 8). See Resampling statistics.

Check digit A checksum that produces a single digit as output is referred to as a check digit. Some of the common identification codes in use today, such as ISBN numbers for books, come with a built-in check digit. Of course, when using a single digit as a check value, you can expect that some transmitted errors will escape the check, but the check digit is useful in systems wherein occasional mistakes are tolerated; or wherein the purpose of the check digit is to find a specific type of error (eg, an error produced by a substitution in a single character or digit), and wherein the check digit itself is rarely transmitted in error. See Checksum.

Checksum An outdated term that is sometimes used synonymously with one-way hash or message digest. Checksums are performed on a string, block or file yielding a short alphanumeric string intended to be specific for the input data. Ideally, If a single bit were to change anywhere within the input file, then the checksum for the input file would change drastically. Checksums, as the name implies, involve summing values (typically weighted character values), to produce a sequence that can be calculated on a file before and after transmission. Most of the errors that were commonly introduced by poor transmission could be detected with checksums. Today, the old checksum algorithms have been largely replaced with one-way hash algorithms. A checksum that produces a single digit as output is referred to as a check digit. See Check digit. See Message digest. See HMAC.

Conclusions Conclusions are the interpretations made by studying the results of an experiment or a set of observations. The term "results" should never be used interchangeably with the term "conclusions." **Remember, results are verified. Conclusions are validated**. See Verification. See Validation. See Results.

Correlation distance The correlation distance provides a measure of similarity between two variables. Two similar variables will rise and fall together, and it is this coordinated variation in value that is measured by correlation distance scores.[39,40] See Pearson's correlation.

Curse of dimensionality As the number of attributes for a data object increases, the multidimensional space becomes sparsely populated, and the distances between any two objects, even the two closest neighbors, becomes absurdly large. When you have thousands of dimensions (eg, data values in a data record, cells in the rows of a spreadsheet), the space that holds the objects is so large that distances between data objects become difficult or impossible to compute, and best computational algorithms become useless.

DSP See Digital Signal Processing.

Data cleaning More correctly, data cleansing, and synonymous with data fixing or data correcting. Data cleaning is the process by which errors, spurious anomalies, and missing values are somehow handled. The options for data cleaning are: correcting the error, deleting the error, leaving the error unchanged, or imputing a different value.[41] Data cleaning should not be confused with data scrubbing. See Data scrubbing.

Data flattening In the field of informatics, data flattening is a popular but ultimately counterproductive method of data organization and data reduction. Data flattening involves removing data annotations that are deemed unnecessary for the intended purposes of the data (eg, timestamps, field designators, identifiers for individual data objects referenced within a document). Data flattening makes it difficult or impossible to verify data or to discover relationships among data objects. A detailed discussion of the topic is found in Section 4.5, Reducing Data. See Verification. See Data repurposing. See Pseudosimplification.

Data modeling Refers to the intellectual process of finding a mathematical expression (often, an equation) or a symbolic expression that describes or summarizes a system or a collection of data. In many cases, mathematical models describe how different variables will change with one another. Data models always simplify the systems they describe, and many of the greatest milestones in the physical sciences have arisen from a bit of data modeling supplemented by scientific genius (eg, Newton's laws of mechanics and optics, Kepler's laws of planetary orbits). In many cases, the modeler simply plots the data and looks for familiar shapes and patterns that suggest a particular type of data distribution (eg, logarithmic, linear, normal, periodic, Power law, etc.). The modeler has numerous means of testing whether the data closely fits the model.

Data object A data object is whatever is being described by the data. For example, if the data is "6 feet tall," then the data object is the person or thing to which "6 feet tall" applies. Minimally, a data object is a metadata/data pair, assigned to a unique identifier (ie, a triple). In practice, the most common data objects are simple data records, corresponding to a row in a spreadsheet or a line in a flat-file. Data objects in object-oriented programming languages typically encapsulate several items of data, including an object name, an object unique identifier, multiple data/metadata pairs, and the name of the object's class. See Triple. See Identifier. See Metadata.

Data repurposing Involves using old data in new ways, that were not foreseen by the people who originally collected the data. Data repurposing comes in the following categories: (1) Using preexisting data to ask and answer questions that were not contemplated by the people who designed and collected the data; (2) Combining preexisting data with additional data, of the same kind, to produce aggregate data that suits a new set of questions that could not have been answered with any one of the component data sources; (3) Reanalyzing data to validate assertions, theories, or conclusions drawn from the original studies; (4) Reanalyzing the original data set using alternate or improved methods to attain outcomes of greater precision or reliability than the outcomes produced in the original analysis; (5) Integrating heterogeneous data sets (ie, data sets with seemingly unrelated types of information), for the purpose an answering questions or developing concepts that span diverse scientific disciplines; (6) Finding subsets in a population once thought to be homogeneous; (7) Seeking new relationships among data objects; (8) Creating, on-the-fly, novel data sets through data file linkages; (9) Creating new concepts or ways of thinking about old concepts, based on a re-examination of data; (10) Fine-tuning existing data models; and (11) Starting over and remodeling systems.[5] See Heterogeneous data.

Data scrubbing A term that is very similar to data deidentification and is sometimes used improperly as a synonym for data deidentification. Data scrubbing refers to the removal, from data records, of information that is considered unwanted. This may include identifiers, private information, or any incriminating or otherwise objectionable language contained in data records, as well as any information deemed irrelevant to the purpose served by the record. See Deidentification.

Deidentification The process of removing all of the links in a data record that can connect the information in the record to an individual. This usually includes the record identifier, demographic information (eg, place of birth), personal information (eg, birthdate), biometrics (eg, fingerprints), and so on. The process of deidentification will vary based on the type of records examined. Deidentifying protocols exist wherein deidentified records can be reidentified, when necessary. See Reidentification. See Data scrubbing.

Deidentification versus anonymization Anonymization is a process whereby all the links between an individual and the individual's data record are irreversibly removed. The difference between anonymization and deidentification is that anonymization is irreversible. Because anonymization is irreversible, the opportunities for verifying the quality of data are limited. For example, if someone suspects that samples have been switched in a data set, thus putting the results of the study into doubt, an anonymized set of data would afford no opportunity to resolve the problem by reidentifying the original samples. See Reidentification.

Digital Signal Processing Digital Signal Processing (DSP) is the field that deals with creating, transforming, sending, receiving, and analyzing digital signals. Digital signal processing began as a specialized subdiscipline of signal processing. For most of the twentieth century, many technologic advances came from converting nonelectrical signals (temperature, pressure, sound, and other physical signals) into electric signals that could be carried via electromagnetic waves, and later transformed back into physical actions. Because electromagnetic waves sit at the center of so many transform processes, even in instances when the input and outputs are nonelectrical in nature, the field of electrical engineering and signal processing have paramount importance in every field of engineering. In the past several decades, signals have moved from the analog domain (ie, waves) into the digital realm (ie, digital signals expressed as streams of 0s and 1s). Over the years, as techniques have developed by which any kind of signal can be transformed into a digital signal, the subdiscipline of digital signal processing has subsumed virtually all of the algorithms once consigned to its parent discipline. In fact, as more and more processes have been digitized (eg, telemetry, images, audio, sensor data, communications theory), the field of digital signal processing has come to play a central role in data science. See Digital signal.

Digital signal A signal is a description of how one parameter varies with some other parameter. The most familiar signals involve some parameter varying over time (eg, sound is air pressure varying over time). When the amplitude of a parameter is sampled at intervals, producing successive pairs of values, the signal is said to be digitized. See Digital Signal Processing.

Digital signature As it is used in the field of data privacy, a digital signature is an alphanumeric sequence that could only have been produced by a private key owned by one particular person. Operationally, a message digest (eg, a one-way hash value) is produced from the document that is to be signed. The person "signing" the document encrypts the message digest using her private key, and submits the document and the encrypted message digest to the person who intends to verify that the document has been signed. This person decrypts the encrypted message digest with her public key (ie, the public key complement to the private key) to produce the original one-way hash value. Next, a one-way hash is performed on the received document. If the resulting one-way hash is the same as the decrypted one-way hash, then several statements hold true: the document received is the same document as the document that had been "signed." The signer of the document had access to the private key that complemented the public key that was used to decrypt the encrypted one-way hash. The assumption here is that the signer was the only individual with access to the private key. Digital signature protocols, in general, have a private method for encrypting a hash, and a public method for verifying the signature. Such protocols operate under the assumption that only one person can encrypt the hash for the message, and that the name of that person is known; hence, the protocol establishes a verified signature. It should be emphasized that a digital signature is quite different from a written signature; the latter usually indicates that the signer wrote the document or somehow attests to the veracity of the document. The digital signature merely indicates that the document was received from a particular person, contingent on the assumption that the private key was available only to that person. To understand how a digital signature protocol may be maliciously deployed, imagine the following scenario: I contact you and tell you that I am Elvis Presley and would like you to have a copy of my public key plus a file that I have encrypted using my private key. You receive the file and the public key; and you use the public key to decrypt the file. You conclude that the file was indeed sent by Elvis Presley. You read the decrypted file and learn that Elvis advises you to invest all your money in a company that manufactures concrete guitars; which, of course, you do. Elvis knows guitars. The problem here is that the signature was valid, but the valid signature was not authentic. See Authentication.

Euclidean distance Two points, $(x1, y1)$, $(x2, y2)$ in Cartesian coordinates are separated by a hypotenuse distance, that being the square root of the sum of the squares of the differences between the respective x-axis and y-axis coordinates. In n-dimensional space, the Euclidean distance between two points is the square root of the sum of the squares of the differences in coordinates for each of the n-dimensional coordinates. Data objects are often characterized by multiple feature values, and these feature values can be listed as though they were coordinate values for an n-dimensional object. The smaller the Euclidean distance between two objects, the higher the similarity to each other. Several of the most popular correlation and clustering algorithms involve pairwise comparisons of the Euclidean distances between data objects in a data collection. Data scientists are not limited to scaled feature measurements, such as length. For example, another type of distance measurement, the Mahalanobis distance, measures correlation differences among variables. Hence, the Mahalanobis distance is not influenced by the relative scale of the different feature attributes of objects. The Mahalanobis distance is commonly applied within clustering and classifier algorithms.[11]

Fourier series Periodic functions (ie, functions with repeating trends in the data, or waveforms) can be represented as the sum of oscillating functions (ie, functions involving sines, cosines, or complex exponentials). The summation function is the Fourier series.

Fourier transform A transform is a mathematical operation that takes a function or a time series (eg, values obtained at intervals of time) and transforms it into something else. An inverse transform takes the transform function and produces the original function. Transforms are useful when there are operations that can be more easily performed on the transformed function than on the original function. Possibly the most useful transform is the Fourier transform, which can be computed with great speed on modern computers, using a modified form known as the fast Fourier Transform. Periodic functions and waveforms (periodic time series) can be transformed using this method. Operations on the transformed function can sometimes eliminate periodic artifacts or frequencies that occur below a selected threshold (eg, noise). The transform can be used to find similarities between two signals. When the operations on the transform function are complete, the inverse of the transform can be calculated and substituted for the original set of data. See Fourier series.

HMAC Hashed Message Authentication Code. When a one-way hash is employed in an authentication protocol, it is often referred to as an HMAC. See Message digest. See Checksum.

HTML HyperText Markup Language is an ASCII-based set of formatting instructions for web pages. HTML formatting instructions, known as tags, are embedded in the document, and double-bracketed, indicating the start point and end points for instruction. Here is an example of an HTML tag instructing the web browser to display the word "Hello" in italics: $<i>$Hello$</i>$. All web browsers conforming to the HTML specification must contain software routines that recognize and implement the HTML instructions embedded within web documents. In addition to formatting instructions, HTML also includes linkage instructions, in which the web browsers must retrieve and display a listed web page, or a web resource, such as an image. The protocol whereby web browsers, following HTML instructions, retrieve web pages from other internet sites, is known as HTTP (HyperText Transfer Protocol).

Heterogeneous data Two sets of data are considered heterogeneous when they are dissimilar to one another, with regard to content, purpose, format, organization, or annotations. One of the purposes of data science is to discover relationships among heterogeneous data sources. For example, epidemiologic data sets may be of service to molecular biologists who have gene sequence data on diverse human populations. The epidemiologic data is likely to contain different types of data values, annotated and formatted in a manner different from the data and annotations in a gene sequence database. The two types of related data, epidemiologic and genetic, have dissimilar content; hence they are heterogeneous to one another.

Identification The process of providing a data object with an identifier, or the process of distinguishing one data object from all other data objects on the basis of its associated identifier. See Identifier.

Identifier A string that is associated with a particular thing (eg, person, document, transaction, data object), and not associated with any other thing.[42] Object identification usually involves permanently assigning a seemingly random sequence of numeric digits (0–9) and alphabet characters (a–z and A–Z) to a data object. A data object can be a specific piece of data (eg, a data record), or an abstraction, such as a class of objects or a number or a string or a variable. See Identification.

Introspection A method by which data objects can be interrogated to yield information about themselves (eg, properties, values, and class membership). Through introspection, the relationships among the data objects can be examined. Introspective methods are built into object-oriented languages. The data provided by introspection can be applied, at run-time, to modify a script's operation; a technique known as reflection. Specifically, any properties, methods, and encapsulated data of a data object can be used in the script to modify the script's run-time behavior. See Reflection.

Mean field approximation A method whereby the average behavior for a population of objects substitutes for the behavior of individual objects in the population. This method greatly simplifies calculations. It is based on the observation that large collections of objects can be characterized by their average behavior. Mean field approximation has been used with great success to understand the behavior of gases, epidemics, crystals, viruses, and all manner of large population phenomena.

Meaning In informatics, meaning is achieved when described data is bound to a unique identifier of a data object. "Claude Funston's height is five feet eleven inches," comes pretty close to being a meaningful statement. The statement contains data (five feet eleven inches), and the data is described (height). The described data belongs to a unique object (Claude Funston). Ideally, the name "Claude Funston" should be provided with a unique identifier, to distinguish one instance of Claude Funston from all the other persons who are named Claude Funston. The statement would also benefit from a formal system that ensures that the metadata makes sense (eg, What exactly is height, and does Claude Funston fall into a class of objects for which height is a property?) and that the data is appropriate (eg, Is 5 feet 11 inches an allowable measure of a person's height?). A statement with meaning does not need to be a true statement (eg, The height of Claude Funston was not 5 feet 11 inches when Claude Funston was an infant). See Semantics. See Triple. See RDF.

Message digest Within the context of this book, "message digest," "digest," "HMAC," and "one-way hash" are equivalent terms. See HMAC.

Meta-analysis Meta-analysis involves combining data from multiple similar and comparable studies to produce a summary result. The hope is that by combining individual studies, the meta-analysis will carry greater credibility and accuracy than any single study. Three of the most recurring flaws in meta-analysis studies are selection bias (eg, negative studies are often omitted from the literature), inadequate knowledge of the included sets of data (eg, incomplete methods sections in the original articles), and nonrepresentative data (eg, when the published data is nonrepresentative samples of the original data sets).

Metadata The data that describes data. For example, a data element (also known as data point) may consist of the number, "6." The metadata for the data may be the words "Height, in feet." A data element is useless without its metadata, and metadata is useless unless it adequately describes a data element. In XML, the metadata/data annotation comes in the form < metadata tag>data<end of metadata tag > and might be look something like:

```
<weight_in_pounds>150</weight_in_pounds>
```

In spreadsheets, the data elements are the cells of the spreadsheet. The column headers are the metadata that describe the data values in the column's cells, and the row headers are the record numbers that uniquely identify each record (ie, each row of cells). See XML.

Microarray Also known as gene chip, gene expression array, DNA microarray, or DNA chips. These consist of thousands of small samples of chosen DNA sequences arrayed onto a block of support material (such as a glass slide). When the array is incubated with a mixture of DNA sequences prepared from cell samples, hybridization will occur between molecules on the array and single stranded complementary (ie, identically sequenced) molecules present in the cell sample. The greater the concentration of complementary molecules in the cell sample, the greater the number of fluorescently tagged hybridized molecules in the array. A specialized instrument prepares an image of the array, and quantifies the fluorescence in each array spot. Spots with high fluorescence indicate relatively large quantities of DNA in the cell sample that match the specific sequence of DNA in the array spot. The data comprising all the fluorescent intensity measurements for every spot in the array produces a gene profile characteristic of the cell sample.

Missing values Most complex data sets have missing data values. Somewhere along the line, data elements were not entered, or records were lost, or some systemic error produced empty data fields. Various mathematical approaches to missing data have been developed; commonly involving assigning values on a statistical basis (ie, assignment by imputation). Imputation methods are based on the assumption that missing data arises at random. When missing data arises nonrandomly, there is no satisfactory statistical fix. The data curator must track down the source of the errors, and somehow rectify the situation. In either case, the issue of missing data introduces a potential bias, and it is crucial to fully document the method by which missing data is handled. See Data cleaning.

Monte Carlo simulation Monte Carlo simulations were introduced in 1946 by John von Neumann, Stan Ulam, and Nick Metropolis.[43] For this technique, the computer generates random numbers and uses the resultant values to simulate repeated trials of a probabilistic event. Monte Carlo simulations can easily simulate various processes (eg, Markov models and Poisson processes) and can be used to solve a wide range of problems, discussed in detail in Section 8.2. The Achilles heel of the Monte Carlo simulation, when applied to enormous sets of data, is that so-called random number generators may introduce periodic (nonrandom) repeats over large stretches of data.[44] What you thought was a fine Monte Carlo simulation, based on small data test cases, may produce misleading results for large data sets. The wise data analyst will avail himself of the best possible random number generator, and will test his outputs for randomness (See Open Source Tools for Chapter 5, Pseudorandom number generators). Various tests of randomness are available.[45,46]

Multiple comparisons bias When you compare a control group against a treated group using multiple hypotheses based on the effects of many different measured parameters, you will eventually encounter statistical significance, based on chance alone.

Negative study bias When a project produces negative results (fails to confirm a hypothesis), there may be little enthusiasm to publish the work.[47] When statisticians analyze the results from many different published manuscripts (ie, perform a meta-analysis), their work is biased by the pervasive absence of negative studies.[48] In the field of medicine, negative study bias creates the false sense that a particular treatment yields a positive result.

New data It is natural to think of certain objects as being "new," meaning, with no prior existence; and other objects being "old," having persisted from an earlier time, and into the present. In truth, there are very few "new" objects in our universe. Most objects arise in a continuum, through a transformation or a modification of an old object. When we study Brownian motion, wherein the a particle's direction of motion, at time "t", is chosen randomly, we are aware that the location of the particle, at time "t" is predetermined by all of its prior locations, at times "$t-1$", "$t-2$", down to "$t=0$". The new "$t+1$" data is influenced by every occurrence of old data. For another example, the air temperature 1 minute from now is largely determined by weather events that are occurring now, but the weather occurring now is largely determined by all of the weather events that have occurred in the history of our planet. When we speak of "new" data, alternately known as prospectively acquired data or as prospective data, we must think in terms that relate the new data to the "old" data that preceded it. The dependence of new data on old data can be approached computationally. The autocorrelation function is a method for producing a type of measurement indicating the dependence of data elements on prior data elements. Long-range dependence occurs when a value is dependent on many prior values. Long-range dependence is determined when the serial correlation (ie, the autocorrelation over multiple data elements) is high when the number of sequential elements is large.[49]

Nonparametric statistics Statistical methods that are not based on assumptions about the distribution of the sample population (eg, not based on the assumption that the sample population fits a Gaussian distribution). Median, mode, and range are examples of common nonparametric statistics. See p-value.

Normalized compression distance String compression algorithms (eg, zip, gzip, bunzip) should yield better compression from a concatenation of two similar strings than from a concatenation of two highly dissimilar strings. The reason being that the same string patterns that are employed to compress a string (ie, repeated runs of a particular pattern) are likely to be found in another, similar string. If two strings are completely dissimilar, then the compression algorithm would fail to find repeated patterns that enhance compressibility. The normalized compression distance is a similarity measure based on the enhanced compressibility of concatenated strings of high similarity.[31] A full discussion, with examples, is found in Open Source Tools for this chapter.

Notation 3 Also called n3. A syntax for expressing assertions as triples (unique subject+metadata+data). Notation 3 expresses the same information as the more formal RDF syntax, but n3 is easier for humans to read.[50] RDF and n3 are interconvertible, and either one can be parsed and equivalently tokenized (ie, broken into elements that can be reorganized in a different format, such as a database record). See RDF. See Triple.

Observational data Data obtained by measuring preexisting things or things that occurred without the help of the scientist. Observational data needs to be distinguished from experimental data. In general, experimental data can be described with a Gaussian curve, because the experimenter is trying to measure what happens when a controlled process is performed on every member of a uniform population. Such experiments typically produce Gaussian (ie, bell-shaped or normal) curves for the control population and the test population. The statistical analysis of experiments reduces to the chore of deciding whether the resulting Gaussian curves are different from one another. In observational studies, data is collected on categories of things, and the resulting data sets often follow a Zipf distribution, wherein a few types of data objects account for the majority of observations.

For this reason, many of the assumptions that apply to experimental data (ie, the utility of parametric statistical descriptors including average, standard deviation, and p-values), will not necessarily apply to observational data sets. See New data. See Zipf distribution. See Nonparametric statistics. See p-value.

Outlier Outliers are extreme data values (ie, values that lie beyond anything you would expect to see). The occurrence of outliers hinders the task of developing models, equations, or curves that closely fit all the available data. In some cases, outliers are simply mistakes that can be ignored by the data analyst. In other cases, the outlier may be the most important data in the data set. There is no simple method to know the import of an outlier; it usually falls to the judgment of the data analyst.

Overfitting Overfitting occurs when a formula describes a set of data very closely, but does not lead to any sensible explanation for the behavior of the data, and does not predict the behavior of comparable data sets. In the case of overfitting, the formula is said to describe the noise of the system, rather than the characteristic behavior of the system. Overfitting occurs frequently with models that perform iterative approximations on training data, coming closer and closer to the training data set with each iteration. Neural networks are an example of a data modeling strategy that is prone to overfitting.[11]

p-value The p-value is the probability of getting a set of results that are as extreme or more extreme than the set of results you observed, assuming that the null hypothesis is true (that there is no statistical difference between the results). The p-value has come under great criticism over the decades, with a growing consensus that the p-value is subject to misinterpretation or used in situations wherein it does not apply.[51] Repeated samplings of data from large data sets will produce small p-values that cannot be directly applied to determining statistical significance. It is best to think of the p-value as just another piece of information that tells you something about how sets of observations compare with one another; and not as a test of statistical significance.

Page Rank Page Rank, alternately PageRank, is a computational method popularized by Google that searches through an index of every web page, to produce an ordered set of web pages whose content can be matched against a query phrase. The rank of a page is determined by two scores: the relevancy of the page to the query phrase; and the importance of the page. The relevancy of the page is determined by factors such as how closely the page matches the query phrase, and whether the content of the page is focused on the subject of the query. The importance of the page is determined by how many Web pages link to and from the page, and the importance of the Web pages involved in the linkages. It is easy to see that the methods for scoring relevance and importance are subject to many algorithmic variations, particularly with respect to the choice of measures (ie, the way in which a page's focus on a particular topic is quantified), and the weights applied to each measurement. The reasons that Page Rank queries are fast is that the score of a page's importance is precomputed, and stored with the page's Web addresses. Word matches from the query phrase to Web pages are quickly assembled using a precomputed index of words, the pages containing the words, and the locations of the words in the pages.[52] The success of Page Rank, as employed by Google, is legend. Page ranking is an example of Object ranking, a computation method employed in ranking data objects (see Data object). Object ranking involves providing objects with a quantitative score that provides some clue to the relevance or the popularity of an object.

Pareto's principle A generalized rule recognizing that, for many distributions, about 80% of occurrences are accounted for by under 20% of the possible causes or sources. For example, a few causes are responsible for more than 80% of deaths (ie, heart disease, cancer, stroke). A few types of cancer are responsible for the bulk of occurrences of cancer (ie, skin cancer, lung cancer, and colorectal cancer). Pareto's principle is also known as the 80-20 rule, the law of the vital few, and the principle of factor sparsity. The Zipf distribution is a special case of Pareto's principle.[23,24] See Zipf distribution. See Power law.

Pearson's correlation Similarity scores are based on comparing one data object with another, attribute by attribute, usually summing the squares of the differences in magnitude for each attribute, and using the calculation to compute a final outcome, known as the correlation score. One of the most popular correlation methods is Pearson's correlation, which produces a score that can vary from -1 to $+1$. Two objects with a high score (near $+1$) are highly similar.[18] See Correlation distance.

Power In statistics, power describes the likelihood that a test will detect an effect, if the effect actually exists. In many cases, power reflects sample size. The larger the sample size, the more likely that an experiment will detect a true effect; thus correctly rejecting the null hypothesis. See Sample size.

Power law A mathematical formula wherein a particular value of some quantity varies as an inverse power of some other quantity.[23,24] The power law applies to many natural phenomena and describes the Zipf distribution or Pareto's principle. The power law is unrelated to the power of a statistical test. See Zipf distribution. See Pareto's principle.

Precision Precision is the degree of exactitude of a measurement and is verified by its reproducibility (ie, whether repeated measurements of the same quantity produce the same result). Accuracy measures how close your data comes to being correct. Data can be accurate, but imprecise; or precise, but inaccurate. If you have a 10-pound object, and you report its weight as 7.2376 pounds, every time you weigh the object, then your precision is remarkable, but your accuracy is dismal. What are the practical limits of precision measurements? Let us stretch our imaginations, for a moment, and pretend that we have just found an artifact left by an alien race that excelled in the science of measurement. As a sort of time capsule for the universe, their top scientists decided to collect the history of their civilization, encoded in binary. Their story looked something like "001011011101000..." extended to about 5 million places. Rather than print the sequence out on a piece of paper or a computer disk, these aliens simply converted the sequence to a decimal length (ie, .001011011101000...") and marked the length on a bar composed of a substance that would never change its size. To decode the bar, and recover the history of the alien race, one would simply need to have a highly precise measuring instrument, that would yield the original binary sequence. Computational linguists could translate the sequence to text, and the recorded history of the alien race would be revealed! Of course, the whole concept is built on an impossible premise. Nothing can be measured accurately to 5 million places. We live in a universe with practical limits (ie, the sizes of atomic particles, the speed of light, the Heisenberg uncertainty principle, the maximum mass of a star, the second law of thermodynamics, the unpredictability of highly complex systems, division by zero). There are many things that we simply cannot do, no matter how hard we try. The most precise measurement achieved by modern science has been in the realm of atomic clocks, where accuracy of 18 decimal places has been claimed.[53] Nonetheless, many scientific disasters are caused by our ignorance of our own limitations, and our persistent gullibility, leading us to believe that precision claimed is precision obtained. For a discussion of how imprecision can be used to our advantage, see Open Source Tools for Chapter 5, Steganography. See Accuracy versus precision.

Primary data The original set of data collected to serve a particular purpose or to answer a particular set of questions, and intended for use by the same individuals who collected the data. See Secondary data.

Principal component analysis A computationally intensive method for reducing the dimensionality of data sets.[4] This method takes a list of parameters and reduces it to a smaller list of variables, with each component of the smaller list constructed from combinations of variables in the longer list. Principal component analysis provides an indication of which variables in both the original and the new list are least correlated with the other variables.

Pseudosimplification Refers to any method intended to simplify data that reduces the quality of the data, interferes with introspection, modifies the data without leaving a clear trail connecting the original data to the modified data, eliminates timestamp data, transforms the data in a manner that defies reverse transformation, or that unintentionally increases the complexity of data. See Data flattening.

RDF Resource Description Framework (RDF) is a syntax in XML notation that formally expresses assertions as triples. The RDF triple consists of a uniquely identified subject plus a metadata descriptor for the data plus a data element. Triples are necessary and sufficient to create statements that convey meaning. Triples can be aggregated with other triples from the same data set or from other data sets, so long as each triple pertains to a unique subject that is identified equivalently through the data sets. Enormous data sets of RDF triples can be merged or functionally integrated with other massive or complex data resources. For a detailed discussion see Open Source Tools for Chapter 6, "Syntax for Triples." See Notation 3. See Semantics. See Triple. See XML.

Reflection A programming technique wherein a computer program will modify itself, at run-time, based on information it acquires through introspection. For example, a computer program may iterate over a collection of data objects, examining the self-descriptive information for each object in the collection (ie, object introspection). If the information indicates that the data object belongs to a particular class of objects, then the program may call a method appropriate for the class. The program executes in a manner determined by descriptive information obtained during run-time; metaphorically reflecting upon the purpose of its computational task. See Introspection.

Reidentification A term casually applied to any instance whereby information can be linked to a specific person, after the links between the information and the person associated with the information have been removed. Used this way, the term reidentification connotes an insufficient deidentification process. In the healthcare industry, the term "reidentification" means something else entirely. In the U.S., regulations define "reidentification" under the "Standards for Privacy of Individually Identifiable Health Information."[54] Therein, reidentification is a legally sanctioned process whereby deidentified records can be linked back to their human subjects, under circumstances deemed legitimate and compelling, by a privacy board. Reidentification is typically accomplished via the use of a confidential list of links between human subject names and deidentified records, held by a trusted party. In the healthcare realm, when a human subject is identified through fraud, trickery, or through the deliberate use of computational methods to break the confidentiality of insufficiently deidentified records (ie, hacking), the term "reidentification" would not apply.[11]

Representation bias Occurs when the population sampled does not represent the population intended for study (ie, the population for which the conclusions of the study will apply). For example, the population for which the normal range of prostate specific antigen (PSA) was based, was selected from a county in the state of Minnesota. The male population under study consisted almost exclusively of white men (ie, virtually no African-Americans, Asians, Hispanics, etc.). It may have been assumed that PSA levels would not vary with race. It was eventually determined that the normal PSA ranges varied greatly by race.[55] The Minnesota data had a large sample size, but did not represent racial subpopulations. Hence, conclusions drawn were not necessarily valid for individuals belonging to subpopulations that were not included in the data.

Reproducibility Reproducibility is achieved when repeat studies produce the same results, over and over. Reproducibility is closely related to validation, which is achieved when you draw the same conclusions, from the data, over and over again. Implicit in the concept of "reproducibility" is that the original research must somehow convey the means by which the study can be reproduced. This usually requires the careful recording of methods, algorithms, and materials. In some cases, reproducibility requires access to the data produced in the original studies. If there is no feasible way for scientists to undertake a reconstruction of the original study, or if the results obtained in the original study cannot be obtained in subsequent attempts, then the study is irreproducible. If the work is reproduced, but the results and the conclusions cannot be repeated, then the study is considered invalid. See Validation. See Verification.

Resampling statistics A technique whereby a sampling of observations is artifactually expanded by randomly selecting observations and adding them back to the same data set; or by creating new sets of data by randomly selecting, without removing, data elements from the original data. For further discussion, see Section 8.3, Resampling and Permutating.

Results The term "results" is often mistaken for the term "conclusions." Interchanging the two concepts is a source of confusion among data scientists. In the strictest sense, "results" consist of the full set of experimental data collected by measurements. In practice, "results" are provided as a small subset of data distilled from the raw, original data. In a typical journal article, selected data subsets are packaged as a chart or graph that emphasizes some point of interest. Hence, the term "results" may refer, erroneously, to subsets of the original data, or to visual graphics intended to summarize the original data. Conclusions are the inferences drawn from the results. Results are verified; conclusions are validated. The data that is generated from the original data should not be confused with "secondary" data. See Secondary data. See Conclusions. See Verification. See Validation.

Sample size The number of samples used in a study. Methods are available for calculating the required sample size to rule out the null hypothesis, when an effect is present at a specified significance level, in a population with a known population mean, and a known standard deviation.[56] The sample size formula should not be confused with the sampling theorem. See Power. See Sampling theorem.

Sampling theorem A foundational principle of digital signal processing, also known as the Shannon sampling theorem or the Nyquist sampling theorem. The theorem states that a continuous signal can be properly sampled, only if it does not contain components with frequencies exceeding one-half of the sampling rate. For example, if you want to sample at a rate of 4000 samples per second, you would prefer a signal containing no frequencies greater than 2000 cycles per second. See DSP. See Digital Signal Processing.

Secondary data Data collected by someone else. Much of the data analyses performed today are done on secondary data.[57] Most verification and validation studies depend upon access to high-quality secondary data. Because secondary data is prepared by someone else, who cannot anticipate how you will use the data, it is important to provide secondary data that is simple and introspective. See Introspection. See Primary data.

Semantics The study of meaning (Greek root, semantikos, significant meaning). In the context of data science, semantics is the technique of creating meaningful assertions about data objects. A meaningful assertion, as used here, is a triple consisting of an identified data object, a data value, and a descriptor for the data value. In practical terms, semantics involves making assertions about data objects (ie, making triples), combining assertions about data objects (ie, merging triples), and assigning data objects to classes; hence relating triples to other triples. As a word of warning, few informaticians would define semantics in these terms, but most definitions for semantics are functionally equivalent to the definition offered here. Most language is unstructured and meaningless. Consider the assertion: Sam is tired. This is an adequately structured sentence with a subject verb and object. But what is the meaning of the sentence? There are a lot of people named Sam. Which Sam is being referred to in this sentence? What does it mean to say that Sam is tired? Is "tiredness" a constitutive property of Sam, or does it only apply to specific moments? If so, for what moment in time is the assertion, "Sam is tired" actually true? To a computer, meaning comes from assertions that have a specific, identified subject associated with some sensible piece of fully described data (metadata coupled with the data it describes). See Triple. See RDF.

Signal In a very loose sense, a signal is a way of gauging how measured quantities (eg, force, voltage, pressure) change in response to, or along with, other measured quantities (eg, time). A sound signal is caused by the changes in pressure, exerted on our eardrums, over time. A visual signal is the change in the photons impinging on our retinas, over time. An image is the change in pixel values over a two-dimensional grid. Because much of the data stored in computers consists of discrete quantities of describable objects, and because these discrete quantities change their values, with respect to one another, we can appreciate that a great deal of modern data analysis is reducible to digital signal processing. See Digital Signal Processing. See Digital signal.

Signature See Digital signature.

Simpson's paradox Occurs when a correlation that holds in two different data sets is reversed if the data sets are combined. For example, baseball player A may have a higher batting average than player B for each of two seasons, but when the data for the two seasons are combined, player B may have the higher two-season average. Simpson's paradox is just one example of unexpected changes in outcome when variables are unknowingly hidden or blended.[58]

Supercomputer Computers that can perform many times faster than a desktop personal computer. In 2015, the top supercomputers operate at about 30 petaflops. A petaflop is 10 to the 15 power floating point operations per second. By my calculations, a 1 petaflop computer performs about 250,000 operations in the time required for my laptop to finish one operation.

Timestamp Many data objects are temporal events and all temporal events must be given a timestamp indicating the time that the event occurred, using a standard measurement for time. The timestamp must be accurate, persistent, and immutable. The Unix epoch time (equivalent to the Posix epoch time) is available for most operating systems and consists of the number of seconds that have elapsed since January 1, 1970, midnight, Greenwich mean time. The Unix epoch time can easily be converted into any other standard representation of time. The duration of any event can be easily calculated by subtracting the beginning time from the ending time. Because the timing of events can be maliciously altered, scrupulous data managers may choose to employ a trusted timestamp protocol by which a timestamp can be verified.

Triple In computer semantics, a triple is an identified data object associated with a data element and the description of the data element. In the computer science literature, the syntax for the triple is commonly described as: "subject, predicate, object," wherein the subject is an identifier, the predicate is the description of the object, and the object is the data. The definition of triple, using grammatical terms, can be off-putting to the data scientist, who may think in terms of spreadsheet entries: a key that identifies the line record, a column header containing the metadata description of the data, and a cell that contains the data. In this book, the three components of a triple are described as: (1) the identifier for the data object, (2) the metadata that describes the data, and (3) the data itself. In theory, all data sets, databases, and spreadsheets can be constructed or deconstructed as collections of triples. See Introspection. See Data object. See Semantics. See RDF. See Meaning.

UUID (Universally Unique IDentifier) is a protocol for assigning unique identifiers to data objects, without using a central registry. UUIDs were originally used in the Apollo Network Computing System.[59] Most modern programming languages have modules for generating UUIDs. See Identifier.

Universally Unique IDentifier See UUID.

Validation Validation is the process that checks whether the conclusions drawn from data analysis are correct.[60] Validation usually starts with repeating the same analysis of the same data, using the methods that were originally recommended. Obviously, if a different set of conclusions is drawn from the same data and methods, the original conclusions cannot be validated. Validation may involve applying a different set of analytic methods to the same data, to determine if the conclusions are consistent. It is always reassuring to know that conclusions are repeatable, with different analytic methods. In prior eras, experiments were validated by repeating the entire experiment, thus producing a new set of observations for analysis. Many of today's scientific experiments are far too complex and costly to repeat. In such cases, validation requires access to the complete collection of the original data, and to the detailed protocols under which the data was generated. One of the most useful methods of data validation involves testing new hypotheses, based on the assumed validity of the original conclusions. For example, if you were to accept Darwin's analysis of barnacle data, leading to his theory of evolution, then you would expect to find a chronologic history of fossils in ascending layers of shale. This was the case; thus, paleontologists studying the Burgess shale provided some validation to Darwin's conclusions. Validation should not be mistaken for proof. Nonetheless, the repeatability of conclusions, over time, with the same or different sets of data, and the demonstration of consistency with related observations, is about all that we can hope for in this imperfect world. See Verification. See Reproducibility.

Verification The process by which data is checked to determine whether the data was obtained properly (ie, according to approved protocols), and that the data accurately measured what it was intended to measure, on the correct specimens, and that all steps in data processing were done using well-documented protocols. Verification often requires a level of expertise that is at least as high as the expertise of the individuals who produced the data.[60] Data verification requires a full understanding of the many steps involved in data collection and can be a time-consuming task. In one celebrated case, in which two statisticians reviewed a microarray study performed at Duke University, the number of hours devoted to verification effort was reported to be 2000 hours[61] To put this statement in perspective, the official work-year, according to the U. S. Office of Personnel Management, is 2087 hours. Verification is different from validation. Verification is performed on data; validation is done on the results of data analysis. See Validation. See Microarray. See Introspection.

XML Acronym for eXtensible Markup Language, a syntax for marking data values with descriptors (ie, metadata). The descriptors are commonly known as tags. In XML, every data value is enclosed by a start-tag, containing the descriptor and indicating that a value will follow, and an end-tag, containing the same descriptor and indicating that a value preceded the tag. For example: <name>Conrad Nervig </name >. The enclosing angle brackets, "<>", and the end-tag marker, "/", are hallmarks of HTML and XML markup. This simple but powerful relationship between metadata and data allows us to employ metadata/data pairs as though each were a miniature database. The semantic value of XML becomes apparent when we bind a metadata/data pair to a unique object, forming a so-called triple. See Triple. See Meaning. See Semantics. See HTML.

Zipf distribution George Kingsley Zipf (1902–1950) was an American linguist who demonstrated that, for most languages, a small number of words account for the majority of occurrences of all the words found in prose. Specifically, he found that the frequency of any word is inversely proportional to its placement in a list of words, ordered by their decreasing frequencies in text. The first word in the frequency list will occur about twice as often as the second word in the list, three times as often as the third word in the list, and so on. Many data collections follow a Zipf distribution (eg, income distribution in a population, energy consumption by country, and so on).[23,24] Zipf distributions cannot be sensibly described by the standard statistical measures that apply to normal distributions. Zipf distributions are instances of Pareto's principle. The Zipf distribution is discussed in depth in Section 4.4, Data Profiling. See Pareto's principle. See Power law.

REFERENCES

1. Siefgried T. *The bit and the pendulum.* New York, NY: Wiley; 2000 p. 46.
2. Cohen KB, Hunter L. Getting started in text mining. *PLoS Comput Biol* 2008;**4**:e20.
3. Tukey John W. *Exploratory data analysis.* Boston, MA: Addison-Wesley; 1977.
4. Janert PK. *Data analysis with open source tools.* Sebastopol, CA: O'Reilly Media; 2010.
5. Berman JJ. *Repurposing legacy data: innovative case studies.* Elsevier/Morgan Kaufmann imprint; 2015.
6. Boyd D. Privacy and publicity in the context of big data. In: Open Government and the World Wide Web (WWW2010). Raleigh, North Carolina, April 29, 2010; 2010. Available from: http://www.danah.org/papers/talks/2010/WWW2010.html [accessed 26.08.12].
7. Data Quality Act. 67 Fed. Reg. 8,452, February 22, 2002, addition to FY 2001 Consolidated Appropriations Act (Pub. L. No. 106-554 codified at 44 U.S.C. 3516).
8. Guidelines for ensuring and maximizing the quality, objectivity, utility, and integrity of information disseminated by federal agencies. *Fed Regist* 2002;**67**(36).
9. Sass JB, Devine Jr JP. The center for regulatory effectiveness invokes the data quality act to reject published studies on atrazine toxicity. *Environ Health Perspect* 2004;**112**:A18.
10. Tozzi JJ, Kelly Jr WG, Slaughter S. Correspondence: data quality act: response from the Center for Regulatory Effectiveness. *Environ Health Perspect* 2004;**112**:A18–9.
11. Berman JJ. *Principles of big data: preparing, sharing, and analyzing complex information.* Waltham, MA: Morgan Kaufmann; 2013.
12. Myers VC. *Practical chemical analysis of blood.* St Louis, MO: C.V. Mosby Company; 1921.
13. Goldstein JL, Brown MS. Cholesterol: a century of research. *HHMI Bull* 2012;**16**:1–4.
14. Tobert JA. Lovastatin and beyond: the history of the HMG-CoA reductase inhibitors. *Nat Rev Drug Discov* 2003;**2**:517–26.
15. Perez-Pena R. New York's Tally of Heat Deaths Draws Scrutiny. The New York Times, August 18, 2006.
16. Chiang S. *Heat waves, the "other" natural disaster: perspectives on an often ignored epidemic.* Global Pulse American Medical Student Association; 2006.

17. Berman JJ, Moore GW. The role of cell death in the growth of preneoplastic lesions: a Monte Carlo simulation model. *Cell Prolif* 1992;**25**:549–57.

18. Berman JJ. *Methods in medical informatics: fundamentals of healthcare programming in Perl, Python, and Ruby*. Boca Raton, FL: Chapman and Hall; 2010.

19. SEER. Surveillance Epidemiology End Results. National Cancer Institute. Available from: http://seer.cancer.gov/.

20. Grivell L. Mining the bibliome: searching for a needle in a haystack? *EMBO Rep* 2002;**3**:200–3.

21. Pusztai L, Mazouni C, Anderson K, Wu Y, Symmans WF. Molecular classification of breast cancer: limitations and potential. *Oncologist* 2006;**11**:868–77.

22. Tang Z, Dai Y, Zhang X. Perceptual hashing for color images using invariant moments. *Appl Math Inf Sci* 2012;**6**:643S–650S.

23. Clauset A, Shalizi CR, Newman MEJ. Power-law distributions in empirical data. *SIAM Rev* 2009;**51**:661–703. Available at: http://arxiv.org/pdf/0706.1062.pdf [accessed 23.06.15].

24. Newman MEJ. Power laws, Pareto distributions and Zipf's law. *Contemp Phys* 2005;**46**:323–51.

25. Janert PK. *Gnuplot in action: understanding data with graphs*. Greenwich, CT: Manning; 2009.

26. Gandrud C. *Reproducible research with R and R studio*. 2nd ed. New York, NY: Chapman & Hall/CRC; 2015.

27. Lewis PD. *R for medicine and biology*. Sudbury, ON: Jones and Bartlett Publishers; 2009.

28. Chang W. *R graphics cookbook*. Sebastopol, CA: O'Reilly; 2013.

29. SciPy Reference Guide, Release 0.7. Written by the SciPy community, December 07, 2008.

30. Cebrian M, Alfonseca M, Ortega A. Common pitfalls using the normalized compression distance: what to watch out for in a compressor. *Commun Inf Syst* 2005;**5**:367–84.

31. Cilibrasi R, Vitanyi PMB. Clustering by compression. *IEEE Trans Inf Theory* 2005;**51**:1523–45.

32. Deshpande R, VanderSluis B, Myers CL. Comparison of profile similarity measures for genetic interaction networks. *PLoS ONE* 2013;**8**(7):e68664.

33. A Review of the FBI's Handling of the Brandon Mayfield Case. U. S. Department of Justice, Office of the Inspector General, Oversight and Review Division, March 2006.

34. Al-Agha OM, Igbokwe AA. Malignant fibrous histiocytoma: between the past and the present. *Arch Pathol Lab Med* 2008;**132**:1030–5.

35. Nakayama R, Nemoto T, Takahashi H, Ohta T, Kawai A, Seki K, et al. Gene expression analysis of soft tissue sarcomas: characterization and reclassification of malignant fibrous histiocytoma. *Mod Pathol* 2007;**20**:749–59.

36. Katsanis SH, Wagner JK. Characterization of the standard and recommended CODIS markers. *J Forensic Sci* 2012;**58**:S169–72.

37. Brannon AR, Sawyers CL. N of 1 case reports in the era of whole-genome sequencing. *J Clin Invest* 2013;**123**:4568–70.

38. Subbiah IM, Subbiah V. Exceptional responders: in search of the science behind the miracle cancer cures. *Future Oncol* 2015;**11**:1–4.

39. Reshef DN, Reshef YA, Finucane HK, Grossman SR, McVean G, Turnbaugh PJ, et al. Detecting novel associations in large data sets. *Science* 2011;**334**:1518–24.

40. Szekely GJ, Rizzo ML. Brownian distance covariance. *Ann Appl Stat* 2009;**3**:1236–65.

41. Van den Broeck J, Cunningham SA, Eeckels R, Herbst K. Data cleaning: detecting, diagnosing, and editing data abnormalities. *PLoS Med* 2005;**2**:e267.

42. Paskin N. Identifier interoperability: a report on two recent ISO activities. *D-Lib Mag* 2006;**12**:1–23.

43. Cipra BA. The best of the 20th century: editors name top 10 algorithms. *SIAM News* 2000;**33**(4).

44. Sainani K. Error: What biomedical computing can learn from its mistakes. *Biomed Comput Rev* 2011;**7**:12–9.

45. Marsaglia G, Tsang WW. *Some difficult-to-pass tests of randomness*. J Stat Softw 2002;**7**:1–8. Available from: http://www.jstatsoft.org/v07/i03/paper [accessed 25.09.12].

46. Knuth DE. *Art of computer programming, volume 2: seminumerical algorithms*. 3rd ed. Boston, MA: Addison-Wesley; 1997.

47. McGauran N, Wieseler B, Kreis J, Schuler Y, Kolsch H, Kaiser T. Reporting bias in medical research — a narrative review. *Trials* 2010;**11**:37. Available from: http://www.trialsjournal.com/content/11/1/37 [accessed 01.01.15].
48. Dickersin K, Rennie D. Registering clinical trials. *JAMA* 2003;**290**:51.
49. Downey AB. *Think DSP: digital signal processing in python, version 0.9.8*. Needham, MA: Green Tea Press; 2014.
50. Berman JJ, Moore GW. *Implementing an RDF Schema for pathology images*; 2007. Available from: http://www.julesberman.info/spec2img.htm [accessed 01.01.15].
51. Cohen J. The earth is round (p < .05). *Am Psychol* 1994;**49**:997–1003.
52. Brin S, Page L. The anatomy of a large-scale hypertextual web search engine. *Comput Netw ISDN Syst* 1998;**33**:107–17.
53. Bloom BJ, Nicholson TL, Williams JR, Campbell SL, Bishof M, Zhang X, et al. An optical lattice clock with accuracy and stability at the 10–18 level. *Nature* 2014;**506**:71–5.
54. Department of Health and Human Services. 45 CFR (Code of Federal Regulations), parts 160 through 164. Standards for privacy of individually identifiable health information (final rule). *Fed Regist* 2000;**65** (250):82461–510.
55. Sawyer R, Berman JJ, Borkowski A, Moore GW. Elevated prostate-specific antigen levels in black men and white men. *Mod Pathol* 1996;**9**:1029–32.
56. How to determine sample size, determining sample size. Available at: http://www.isixsigma.com/tools-templates/sampling-data/how-determine-sample-size-determining-sample-size/ [accessed 08.07.15].
57. Smith AK, Ayanian JZ, Covinsky KE, Landon BE, McCarthy EP, Wee CC, et al. Conducting high-value secondary dataset analysis: an introductory guide and resources. *J Gen Intern Med* 2011;**26**:920–9.
58. Tu Y, Gunnell D, Gilthorpe MS. Simpson's Paradox, Lord's Paradox, and Suppression Effects are the same phenomenon — the reversal paradox. *Emerg Themes Epidemiol* 2008;**5**:2.
59. Leach P, Mealling M, Salz R. A Universally Unique IDentifier (UUID) URN Namespace. Network Working Group, Request for Comment 4122, Standards Track. Available from: http://www.ietf.org/rfc/rfc4122.txt [accessed 01.01.15].
60. Committee on Mathematical Foundations of Verification, Validation, and Uncertainty Quantification, Board on Mathematical Sciences and Their Applications, Division on Engineering and Physical Sciences, National Research Council. *Assessing the reliability of complex models: mathematical and statistical foundations of verification, validation, and uncertainty quantification*. Washington, DC: National Academy Press; 2012. Available from: http://www.nap.edu/catalog.php?record_id=13395 [accessed 01.01.15].
61. Misconduct in science: an array of errors. The Economist, September 10, 2011.

IDENTIFYING AND DEIDENTIFYING DATA

Intellectuals solve problems; geniuses prevent them.
-Albert Einstein

5.1 UNIQUE IDENTIFIERS

I always wanted to be somebody, but now I realize I should have been more specific.

-Lily Tomlin

An object identifier is anything associated with the object that persists throughout the life of the object and that is unique to the object (ie, does not belong to any other object). Everyone is familiar with biometric identifiers, such as fingerprints, iris patterns, and genome sequences. In the case of data objects, the identifier usually refers to a randomly chosen long sequence of numbers and letters that is permanently assigned to the object and that is never assigned to any other data object (see Glossary item, Data object).

An identifier system is a set of data-related protocols that satisfy the following conditions: (1) Completeness (ie, every unique object has an identifier); (2) Uniqueness (ie, each identifier is a unique sequence); (3) Exclusivity (ie, each identifier is assigned to only one unique object and to no other object, ever); (4) Authenticity (ie, objects that receive identification can be verified as the objects that they are intended to be); (5) Aggregation (ie, all information associated with an identifier can be collected); and (6) Permanence (ie, an identifier is never deleted).

Uniqueness is a very strange concept, especially when applied to the realm of data. For example, if I refer to the number 1, then I am referring to a unique number among other numbers (ie, there is only one number 1). Yet the number 1 may apply to many different things (eg, 1 left shoe, 1 umbrella, 1 prime number between 2 and 5). The number 1 makes very little sense to us until we know something about what it measures (eg, left shoe) and the object to which the measurement applies (eg, shoe_id_#840354751) (see Glossary item, Uniqueness).[1]

We refer to uniquely assigned computer-generated character strings as "identifiers". As such, computer-generated identifiers are abstract constructs that do not need to embody any of the natural properties of the object. A long (ie, 200 character length) character string consisting of randomly chosen numeric and alphabetic characters is an excellent identifier because the chances of two individuals being assigned the same string is essentially zero. When we need to establish the uniqueness of some object, such as a shoe or a data record, we bind the object to a contrived identifier.

Jumping ahead just a bit, if we say "part number 32027563 weighs 1 pound," then we are dealing with a meaningful assertion. The assertion tells us three things: (1) that there is a unique thing, known as part number 32027563, (2) the unique thing has a weight, and (3) the weight has a measurement of 1 pound. The phrase "weighs 1 pound" has no meaning until it is associated with a unique object (ie, part number 32027563). The assertion that "part number 32027563 weighs 1 pound" is a "triple", the embodiment of meaning in the field of computational semantics. A triple consists of a unique identified object matched to a pair of data and metadata (ie, a data element and the description of the data element). Information experts use formal syntax to express triples as data structures (see Glossary items, Meaning, RDF, RDF Schema, RDF ontology, Notation 3). We will revisit the concept of triples in Section 6.1, "Meaning and Triples".

Returning to the issue of object identification, there are various methods for generating and assigning unique identifiers to data objects,[2–5] (see Glossary items, Identification, Identifier, One-way hash, UUID, URN, URL). Some identification systems assign a group prefix to an identifier sequence that is unique for the members of the group. For example, a prefix for a research institute may be attached to every data object generated within the institute. If the prefix is registered in a public repository, data from the institute can be merged with data from other institutes, and the institutional source of the data object can always be determined. The value of prefixes and other reserved namespace designations can be undermined when implemented thoughtlessly (see Glossary item, Namespace).[1]

Identifiers are data simplifiers, when implemented properly, because they allow us to collect all of the data associated with a unique object while ensuring that we exclude that data that should be associated with some other object. As an example of the utility of personal identifier systems, please refer to the discussion of National Patient Identifiers, in the Glossary (see Glossary item, National Patient Identifier).

Universally Unique Identifier (UUID) is an example of one type of algorithm that creates collision-free identifiers that can be generated on command at the moment when new objects are created (ie, during the run-time of a software application). Linux systems have a built-in UUID utility, "uuidgen.exe", that can be called from the system prompt.

Here are a few examples of output values generated by the "uuidgen.exe" utility:

```
$ uuidgen.exe
312e60c9-3d00-4e3f-a013-0d6cb1c9a9fe

$ uuidgen.exe
822df73c-8e54-45b5-9632-e2676d178664

$ uuidgen.exe
8f8633e1-8161-4364-9e98-fdf37205df2f

$ uuidgen.exe
83951b71-1e5e-4c56-bd28-c0c45f52cb8a

$ uuidgen -t
e6325fb6-5c65-11e5-b0e1-0ceee6e0b993

$ uuidgen -r
5d74e36a-4ccb-42f7-9223-84eed03291f9
```

Notice that each of the final two examples have a parameter added to the "uuidgen" command (ie, "-t" and"-r"). There are several versions of the UUID algorithm that are available. The "-t" parameter instructs the utility to produce a UUID based on the time (measured in seconds elapsed since the first second of October 15, 1582, the start of the Gregorian calendar). The "-r" parameter instructs the utility to produce a UUID based on the generation of a pseudorandom number. In any circumstance, the UUID utility produces a fixed-length character string suitable as an object identifier. The UUID utility is trusted and widely used by computer scientists. Independent-minded readers can easily design their own unique object identifiers, using pseudorandom number generators or one-way hash generators (see Open Source Tools for this chapter, "UUID", "Pseudorandom number generators", and "One-way hash implementations").

In theory, identifier systems are incredibly easy to implement. Here is exactly how it is done:

1. Generate a unique character sequence, such as UUID, or a long random number.
2. Assign a unique character sequence (ie, identifier) to each new object at the moment that the object is created. In the case of a hospital, a patient is created at the moment he or she is registered into the hospital information system. In the case of a bank, a customer is created at the moment that he or she is provided with an account number. In the case of an object-oriented programming language, such as Ruby, this would be the moment when the "new" method is sent to a class object, instructing the class object to create a class instance.
3. Preserve the identifier number and bind it to the object. In practical terms, this means that whenever the data object accrues new data, the new data is assigned to the identifier number. In the case of a hospital system, this would mean that all of the lab tests, billable clinical transactions, pharmacy orders, and so on are linked to the patient's unique identifier number, as a service provided by the hospital information system. In the case of a banking system, this would mean that all of the customer's deposits and withdrawals and balances are attached to the customer's unique account number.

As it happens, nothing is ever as simple as it ought to be. In the case of an implementation of systems that employ long-sequence generators to produce unique identifiers, the most common problem involves indiscriminate re-assignment of additional unique identifiers to the same data object, thus nullifying the potential benefits of the unique identifier systems.

Let's look at an example wherein multiple identifiers are redundantly assigned to the same image, corrupting the identifier system. In Section 4.3, we discussed image headers and provided examples wherein the ImageMagick "identify" utility could extract the textual information included in the image header. One of the header properties created, inserted, and extracted by ImageMagick's "identify" is an image-specific unique string.

When ImageMagick is installed in our computer, we can extract any image's unique string using the "identify" utility and the "-format" attribute on the following command line:

```
c:\ftp>identify -verbose -format "%#" eqn.jpg
```

Here, the image we are examining is "eqn.jpg". The "%#" character string is ImageMagick's special syntax indicating that we would like to extract the image identifier. The output is shown.

```
219e41b4c761e4bb04fbd67f71cc84cd6ae53a26639d4bf33155a5f62ee36e33
```

We can repeat the command line whenever we like, and the same image-specific unique sequence of characters will be produced.

Using ImageMagick, we can insert text into the "comment" section of the header, using the "-set" attribute. Let's add the text, "I'm modifying myself":

```
c:\ftp>convert eqn.jpg -set comment "I'm modifying myself" eqn.jpg
```

Now, let's extract the comment that we just added to satisfy ourselves that the "-set" attribute operated as we had hoped. We do this using the "-format" attribute and the "%c" character string, which is ImageMagick's syntax for extracting the comment section of the header.

```
c:\ftp>identify -verbose -format "%c" eqn.jpg
```

The output of the command line is:

```
I'm modifying myself
```

Now, let's run one more time the command line that produces the unique character string that is unique for the eqn.jpg image file:

```
c:\ftp>identify -verbose -format "%#" eqn.jpg
```

The output is:

```
cb448260d6eeeb2e9f2dcb929fa421b474021584e266d486a6190067a278639f
```

What just happened? Why has the unique character string specific for the eqn.jpg image changed? Has our small modification of the file, which consisted of adding a text comment to the image header, resulted in the production of a new image object worthy of a new unique identifier?

Before answering these very important questions, let's pose two gedanken questions (see Glossary item, Gedanken). Imagine you have a tree. This tree, like every living organism, is unique. It has a unique history, a unique location, and a unique genome (ie, a unique sequence of nucleotides composing its genetic material). In 10 years, its leaves drop off and are replaced 10 times. Its trunk expands in size and its height increases. In the 10 years of its existence, has the identify of the tree changed?

You would probably agree that the tree has changed, but that it has maintained its identity (ie, it is still the same tree).

In informatics, a newly created object is given an identifier and this identifier is immutable (ie, cannot be changed), regardless of how the object is modified. In the case of the unique string assigned to an image by ImageMagick, the string serves as an authenticator, not as an identifier (see Glossary item, Authentication). When the image is modified, a new unique string is created. By comparing the so-called identifier string in copies of the image file, we can determine whether any modifications have been made; that is to say, we can authenticate the file.

Getting back to the image file in our example, when we modified the image by inserting a text comment, ImageMagick produced a new unique string for the image. The identity of the image had not changed, but the image was different from the original image (ie, no longer authentic). It seems that the string that we thought to be an identifier string was actually an authenticator string.

If we want an image to have a unique identifier that does not change when the image is modified, we must create our own identifier that persists when the image is modified.

Here is a short Python script, image_id.py, that uses Python's standard UUID method to create an identifier and insert it into the comment section of our image, flanking the identifier with XML tags (see Glossary item, XML).

```
#!/usr/local/bin/python
import sys, os, uuid
my_id = "<image_id>" + str(uuid.uuid4()) + "</image_id>"
in_command = "convert eqn.jpg -set comment \"" + my_id + "\" eqn.jpg"
os.system(in_command)
out_command = "identify -verbose -format \"%c\" eq2.jpg"
print ("\nHere's the unique identifier:")
os.system(out_command)
print ("\nHere's the unique authenticator:")
os.system("identify -verbose -format \"%#\" eqn.jpg")
os.system("convert eqn.jpg -resize 325x500! eqn.jpg")
print ("\nHere's the new authenticator:")
os.system("identify -verbose -format \"%#\" eqn.jpg")
print ("\nHere's the unique identifier:")
os.system(out_command)
exit
```

Here is the output of the image_id.py script:

```
Here's the unique identifier:
<image_id>c94f679f-7acd-4216-a464-eb051ab57547</image_id>
Here's the unique authenticator:
3529d28f97661b401d9ce6d9925a2dadb46c26b7350d94fff5585d7860886781
Here's the new authenticator:
7b45485ca7fca87f5b78e87b9392946b3e1895dab362d2ca5b13a0e3bc136e48
Here's the unique identifier:
<image_id>c94f679f-7acd-4216-a464-eb051ab57547</image_id>
```

What did the script do, and what does it teach us?

In three lines of code, the script produced a UUID identifier for the image, flanked by start and end tags < image_id > and </image_id>, and inserted it into the comment section of the image:

```
my_id = "<image_id>" + str(uuid.uuid4()) + "</image_id>"
in_command = "convert eqn.jpg -set comment \"" + my_id + "\" eqn.jpg"
os.system(in_command)
```

Next, the script displayed the image identifier as well as the built-in unique sequence that we now can call ImageMagick's authenticator sequence:

```
Here's the unique identifier:
<image_id>c94f679f-7acd-4216-a464-eb051ab57547</image_id>
Here's the unique authenticator:
3529d28f97661b401d9ce6d9925a2dadb46c26b7350d94fff5585d7860886781
```

Following this, the script modified the image by resizing. Then, the script once more produced the authenticator sequence and the identifier sequence:

```
Here's the new authenticator:
7b45485ca7fca87f5b78e87b9392946b3e1895dab362d2ca5b13a0e3bc136e48
Here's the unique identifier:
<image_id>c94f679f-7acd-4216-a464-eb051ab57547</image_id>
```

We see that the identifier sequence is unchanged when the image is resized (as it should be), and the authenticator sequence, following the resizing of our image, is a totally new sequence (as it should be).

If you have followed the logic of this section, you are prepared for the following exercise adapted from Zen Buddhism: Imagine you have a hammer. Over the years, you have replaced its head twice and its handle three times. In this case, with nothing remaining of the original hammer, is it still the same hammer? The informatician would answer that it is the same hammer, but it can no longer be authenticated (ie, it is what it is, though it has changed).

5.2 POOR IDENTIFIERS, HORRIFIC CONSEQUENCES

> Anticipatory plagiarism occurs when someone steals your original idea and publishes it 100 years before you were born.
>
> **-Robert Merton**

All information systems, all databases, and all good collections of data are best envisioned as identifier systems to which data (belonging to the identifier) can be added over time.

If the system is corrupted (eg, multiple identifiers for the same object; data belonging to one object incorrectly attached to other objects), then the system has no value. You can't trust any of the individual records, and you can't trust any of the analyses performed on collections of records. Furthermore, if the data from a corrupted system is merged with the data from other systems, then all analyses performed on the aggregated data becomes unreliable and useless. This holds true even when every other contributor to the system shares reliable data.

Without proper identifiers, the following may occur: Data values can be assigned to the wrong data objects; data objects can be replicated under different identifiers, with each replicant having an incomplete data record (ie, an incomplete set of data values); the total number of data objects cannot be determined; data sets cannot be verified; and the results of data set analyses will not be valid.

In the past, individuals were identified by their names. When dealing with large numbers of names, it becomes obvious, almost immediately, that personal names are woefully inadequate. Aside from the obvious fact that they are not unique (eg, surnames such as Smith, Zhang, Garcia, Lo, and given names such as John and Susan), one name can have multiple representations. The sources for these variations are many. Here is a partial listing[4]:

1. Modifiers to the surname (eg, du Bois, DuBois, Du Bois, Dubois, Laplace, La Place, van de Wilde, Van DeWilde, etc.).
2. Accents that may or may not be transcribed onto records (eg, acute accent, cedilla, diacritical comma, palatalized mark, hyphen, diphthong, umlaut, circumflex, and a host of obscure markings).
3. Special typographic characters (the combined "ae").
4. Multiple middle names for an individual that may not always be consistently transcribed onto records (eg, individuals who replace their first name with their middle name for common usage while retaining the first name for legal documents).
5. Latinized and other versions of a single name (eg, Carl Linnaeus, Carl von Linne, Carolus Linnaeus, Carolus a Linne).
6. Hyphenated names that are confused with first and middle names (eg, Jean-Jacques Rousseau or Jean Jacques Rousseau; Louis-Victor-Pierre-Raymond, Seventh duc de Broglie or Louis Victor Pierre Raymond, Seventh duc de Broglie).
7. Cultural variations in name order that are mistakenly rearranged when transcribed onto records. Many cultures do not adhere to the Western European name order (eg, given name, middle name, surname).
8. Name changes through marriage, legal action, aliasing, pseudonymous posing, or insouciant whim.

I have had numerous conversations with intelligent professionals who are tasked with the responsibility of assigning identifiers to individuals. At some point in every conversation, they will find it necessary to explain that although an individual's name cannot serve as an identifier, the combination of name plus date of birth provides accurate identification in almost every instance. They sometimes get carried away, insisting that the combination of name plus date of birth plus Social Security number provides perfect identification, as no two people will share all three identifiers: same name, same date of birth, and same Social Security number (see Glossary item, Social Security Number). This is simply wrong. Let us see what happens when we create identifiers from the name plus birthdate.

Consider this example: Mary Jessica Meagher, born June 7, 1912, decided to open a separate bank account at each of 10 different banks. Some of the banks had application forms, which she filled out accurately. Other banks registered her account through a teller, who asked her a series of questions and immediately transcribed her answers directly into a computer terminal. Ms. Meagher could not see the computer screen and therefore could not review the entries for accuracy.

Here are the entries for her name plus date of birth[4]:

1. Marie Jessica Meagher, June 7, 1912 (the teller mistook Marie for Mary).
2. Mary J. Meagher, June 7, 1912 (the form requested a middle initial, not a full name).
3. Mary Jessica Magher, June 7, 1912 (the teller misspelled the surname).
4. Mary Jessica Meagher, Jan. 7, 1912 (the birth month was constrained on the form to three letters; June was entered on the form but was transcribed as Jan.).

5. Mary Jessica Meagher, 6/7/12 (the form provided spaces for the final two digits of the birth year. Through the miracle of bank registration, Mary, born in 1912, was reborn a century later).

6. Mary Jessica Meagher, 7/6/12 (the form asked for day, month, and year, in that order, as is common in Europe).

7. Mary Jessica Meagher, June 1, 1912 (on the form, a 7 was mistaken for a 1).

8. Mary Jessie Meagher, June 7, 1912 (Marie, as a child, was called by the informal form of her middle name, which she provided to the teller).

9. Mary Jesse Meagher, June 7, 1912 (Marie, as a child, was called by the informal form of her middle name, which she provided to the teller, and which the teller entered as the male variant of the name).

10. Marie Jesse Mahrer, 1/1/12 (an underzealous clerk combined all of the mistakes on the form and the computer transcript and added a new orthographic variant of the surname).

For each of these 10 examples, a unique individual (Mary Jessica Meagher) would be assigned a different identifier at each of 10 banks. Had Mary re-registered at one bank 10 times, the results may have been the same.

If you toss the Social Security number into the mix (name + birth date + Social Security number) the problem is compounded. The Social Security number for an individual is anything but unique. Few of us carry our original Social Security cards. Our number changes due to false memory ("You mean I've been wrong all these years?"), data entry errors ("Character tranpsositoins, I mean transpositions, are very common"), intention to deceive ("I don't want to give those people my real number), desperation ("I don't have a number, so I'll invent one"), or impersonation ("I don't have health insurance, so I'll use my friend's Social Security number"). Efforts to reduce errors by requiring patients to produce their Social Security cards have not been entirely beneficial.

Beginning in the late 1930s, the E. H. Ferree Company, a manufacturer of wallets, promoted their products' card pockets by including a sample Social Security card with each wallet sold. The display card had the Social Security number of one of their employees. Many people found it convenient to use the card as their own Social Security number. Over time, the wallet display number was claimed by over 40,000 people. Today, few institutions require individuals to prove their identity by showing their original Social Security card. Doing so puts an unreasonable burden on the honest patient (who does not happen to carry his/her card) and provides an advantage to criminals (who can easily forge a card).[4]

Entities that compel individuals to provide a Social Security number have dubious legal standing. The Social Security number was originally intended as a device for validating a person's standing in the Social Security system. More recently, the purpose of the Social Security number has been expanded to track taxable transactions (ie, bank accounts, salaries). Other uses of the Social Security number are not protected by law. The Social Security Act (Section 208 of Title 42 U.S. Code 408) prohibits most entities from compelling anyone to divulge his/her Social Security number.[4]

Considering the unreliability of Social Security numbers in most transactional settings, and considering the tenuous legitimacy of requiring individuals to divulge their Social Security numbers, a prudently designed personal identifier system will limit its reliance on these numbers.

Let's examine another imperfect identifier system: Peter Kuzmak, an information specialist who works with hospital images, made an interesting observation concerning the non-uniqueness of identifiers that were thought to be unique.[6] Hospitals that use the DICOM (Digital Imaging and Communications in Medicine) image standard assign a unique object identifier to each image. Each identifier comes with a prefix consisting of a permanent registered code for the institution and the department, along with a suffix consisting of a number generated for an image at the moment the image is created.[1]

A hospital may assign consecutive numbers to its images, appending these numbers to an object identifier that is unique for the institution and for the department within the institution. For example, the first image created with a CT-scanner might be assigned an identifier consisting of the assigned code for institution and department, followed by a separator such as a hyphen, followed by "1".

In a worst-case scenario, different instruments may assign consecutive numbers to images, independently of one another. This means that the CT-scanner in room A may be creating the same identifier (ie, institution/department prefix + image number) as the CT-scanner in Room B for images on different patients. This problem could be remedied by constraining each CT-scanner to avoid using numbers assigned by any other CT-scanner.

When image counting is done properly, and the scanners are constrained to assign unique numbers (not previously assigned by other scanners in the same institution), then each image may indeed have a unique identifier (institution/department prefix + image number). Nonetheless, problems will arise when departments or institutions merge. Each of these shifts produces a change in the prefix for the institution and department. If a consecutive numbering system is used, then you can expect to create duplicate identifiers when institutional prefixes are replaced. In this case, the old records in both of the merging institutions may be assigned the same prefix and will contain replicates among the consecutively numbered suffixes (eg, image 1, image 2, etc.).

Yet another problem may occur if one unique object is provided with multiple different unique identifiers. For example, a software application may add its own unique identifier to an image that had been previously assigned a unique identifier by the radiology department. Assigning a second identifier insulates the software vendor from bad identifiers that may have been produced in the referring hospital. In so doing, the image now has two different unique identifiers. At this point, which identifier should be used to attach the various data and metadata annotations that accrue to the image over time? By redundantly layering unique identifiers onto a data object, the software vendor defeats the intended purpose of identifying the image (ie, to unambiguously connect a data object with its data).[1]

How can we avoid common design errors in identification systems? Let's look once more at the implementation steps listed in Section 5.1:

1. Generate a unique character sequence. You cannot compose an adequate identifier by concatenating a sequence of inadequate identifiers. (eg, Name + Social Security number + birthdate). A UUID or long fixed-length sequence of randomly generated alphanumeric characters will usually suffice.

2. Assign a unique character sequence (ie, identifier) to each new object at the moment that the object is created. Once the object has been created, it should already have its identifier. This means that you should never assign an identifier to a pre-existing data object. As a practical example, first-time patients seeking care at a hospital should be registered into the hospital system by a qualified registrar, who oversees the assignment of a permanent identification number to the newly created patient object (see Glossary item, Registrars and human authentication).

3. Preserve the unique identifier number and bind it to the unique object. You must never interrupt the linkage between a data object and its identifier. The enduring linkage between data object and identifier ensures that you can retrieve all of the information that accrues to a data object. As a practical example, if an individual enters a hospital and indicates that he or she is a first-time

patient, there must be some mechanism to determine that the patient is indeed a new patient (ie, to exclude the possibility that the patient had already been registered). There must also be in place a system to verify that a patient is who they claim to be. If these safeguards are not in place, then the bindings of unique identifier to unique patient are corrupted and the system fails.

Let's end this sobering section with some humor. As the story is told, a tourist, enthralled by his visit to a holy reliquary, is excited to see that one of the skulls is labeled "St. Peter". Several bones later, the tourist notices another skull, also labeled "St. Peter". The tourist asks the curator to explain why there are two skulls with the same name. Without missing a beat the curator says, "Oh, the first skull was St. Peter when he was an adult. The second skull was St. Peter when he was a child."

The moral here is: "Never give a data object more than one opportunity to be unique."

5.3 DEIDENTIFIERS AND REIDENTIFIERS

Two lawyers can make an excellent living in a town that can't support one.

-Anonymous

Imagine, for a moment, that you are a data analyst who is tasked with analyzing cancer genes. You find a large public database consisting of DNA sequences obtained from human cancer specimens. The tissues have been deidentified to protect the privacy of the individuals from whom the tissue samples were taken. All of this data is available for download. As the gigabytes stream into your computer, you think you have arrived in heaven. Before too long, you have completed your analysis on tissues from dozens of lung cancers. You draw a conclusion that most lung cancers express a particular genetic variation, and you suggest in your paper that this variation is a new diagnostic marker. You begin the process of seeking patent protection for your discovery. You believe that you are on a fast track leading to fame and fortune. At lunch, in the University cafeteria, one of your colleagues poses the following question, "If all the tissues in the public data set were deidentified, and you studied 36 samples, how would you know whether your 36 samples came from 36 different tumors in 36 patients or whether they represented 36 samples taken from one tumor in one patient?" A moment of sheer panic follows. If all the samples came from a single patient, then your research is only relevant to one person's tumor. In that case, you would expect a variation in the genome of one tumor sample to show up in every sample. Your finding would have no particular relevance to lung tumors, in general. Frantically, you contact the tissue resource from which you had obtained your data. They confess that because the tissues are deidentified, they cannot resolve your dilemma. You happen to know the director of the tissue resource, and you explain your problem to her. She indicates that she cannot answer your question, but she happens to know that all of the lung cancer specimens were contributed by a single laboratory. She puts you in touch with the principle investigator at the lab. He remembers that his lab contributed tissues, and that all their tissues were samples of a single large tumor. Your greatest fears are confirmed. Your findings have no general relevance, and no scientific value.

What is the moral of this story? Surprising as it may seem, all data, even deidentified data, must be uniquely identified if it is to be of scientific value.

To maintain confidentiality and to protect privacy, data must be disconnected from the individual, but can this be accomplished without sacrificing unique identifiers? Yes, if we have a clear understanding of our goals.

The term "identified data" is a concept central to modern data science and must be distinguished from "data that is linked to an identified individual," a concept that has legal and ethical importance. In the privacy realm, "data that is linked to an identified individual" is shortened to "identified data", and this indulgence has caused no end of confusion. All good data must be identified. If the data isn't identified, then there is no way of aggregating data that pertains to an identifier, and there is no way of distinguishing one data assertion from another (eg, one observation on 10 samples versus 10 observations on one sample).[7] It is absolutely crucial to understand and accept that the identity of data is not equivalent to the identity of the individual to whom the data applies. In particular, we can remove the links to the identity of individuals without removing data identifiers. This subtle point accounts for much of the rancor in the field of data privacy (see Glossary items, Deidentification, Deidentification versus anonymization, Reidentification).

In Section 6.1, we will be revisiting data triples and their importance in simplifying data (see Glossary item, Triple). For the moment, it suffices to say that all data can be stored as data triples that consist of a data identifier followed by a metadata tag followed by the data described by the metadata tag.

Here are a set of triples collected from other chapters in this book.

```
75898039563441      name              G. Willikers
75898039563441      gender            male
75898039563441      is_a_class_member cowboy
75898039563441      age               35
94590439540089      name              Hopalong Tagalong
94590439540089      is_a_class_member cowboy
29847575938125      calendar:date     February 4, 1986
57839109275632      social:date       Jack and Jill
83654560466294      social:date       Pyramus and Thisbe
83654560466294      calendar:date     June 16, 1904
98495efc            object_name       Andy Muzeack
98495efc            instance_of       Homo sapiens
98495efc            dob               1 January, 2001
98495efc            glucose_at_time   87, 02-12-2014 17:33:09
```

In the next chapter, we will be creating a database of triples. For now, we can see that triples are assertions about data objects that are identified by a random alphanumeric character string. The triples can be in any order we like, because we can write software that aggregates or retrieves triples by identifier, metadata, or data. For example, we could write software that aggregates all the data pertaining to a particular data object.

Notice that we can do a fair job of delinking the data that identifies individuals simply by removing triples that contain names of persons or private information (eg, age or date of birth) and occupation, as shown below:

```
75898039563441      gender            male
75898039563441      is_a_class_member cowboy
94590439540089      is_a_class_member cowboy
29847575938125      calendar:date     February 4, 1986
83654560466294      calendar:date     June 16, 1904
98495efc            instance_of       Homo sapiens
98495efc            glucose_at_time   87, 02-12-2014 17:33:09
```

This residual set of triples are disembodied and do not link to data that might identify the individual to which the data applies. Nonetheless, all of the remaining triples are fully identified in the sense that the data object identifiers are retained (eg, 75898039563441, 94590439540089, 98495efc). If we had a triplestore containing billions of triples, we could have written a short script that would have removed any triples that contained names of individuals or private information, thus yielding a set of identified triples that do not link to an identified individual (see Glossary item, Triplestore).

When you think about it, researchers almost never care about which particular individual is associated with which particular piece of data (see Glossary item, Data versus datum). The purpose of science is to draw generalizations from populations (see Glossary items, Science, Generalization). Scientists are perfectly happy using data from which the links to individuals have been removed, just so long as they can distinguish one observation from another.

Can we stop here? Have we protected the confidentiality and privacy of individuals by removing triples that can link a data object to the person from whom the data applies (see Glossary item, Privacy versus confidentiality)? Probably not. During the course of the study, new data collected on the data objects may have been generated, and this data could be damaging to individuals if it were discovered. As an example, let's add a few triples to data object 75898039563441.

```
75898039563441    gender              male
75898039563441    is_a_class_member   cowboy
75898039563441    mental_status       borderline personality disorder
75898039563441    criminal_record     multiple assaults
75898039563441    chief_complaint     kicked in head by cow
```

You can imagine that data object 75898039563441 might prefer that the data produced in the scientific study (eg, borderline personality disorder, history of assaults, cow-induced head injury) remain confidential. The problem is that a maliciously inclined individual might gain access to the original database, wherein the data object 75898039563441 is clearly linked to the name "G. Willikers". In this case, one possible solution might involve replacing the original object identifier with a new identifier that cannot be linked to data held in the original data file.

We might find it prudent to substitute a new object identifier for each object identifier in our "safe" set of triples:

```
82030201856150    gender              male
82030201856150    is_a_class_member   cowboy
44934938405062    is_a_class_member   cowboy
65840231656302    calendar:date       February 4, 1986
76206674367326    calendar:date       June 16, 1904
7392g2s1          instance_of         Homo sapiens
7392g2s1          glucose_at_time     87, 02-12-2014 17:33:09
```

By assigning new identifiers, we have essentially deidentified our original identifiers. Now, it would be impossible to link any of the experimental data in our set of triples to the set of triples that have their original identifiers. Unfortunately, in our quest to protect the names of individuals, we have created a new problem. Suppose an occasion arises when we need to establish the identity of an individual involved in a scientific study. For example, a clinical test on a deidentified blood sample might reveal that the sample contains a marker for a type of cancer that is curable when treated with an experimental drug. As another example, suppose that a virus has been isolated from a sample, indicating that the person who contributed the sample must be immediately quarantined and treated. More commonly, we can imagine that some unaccountably confusing result has prompted us to check the original dataset to determine if there was a systemic error in the collected samples. In any case, there may be legitimate reasons for reidentifying the original individuals from whom the samples were procured.

Reidentification is a term casually applied to any instance whereby information can be linked to a specific person, after the links between the information and the person associated with the information were removed. Used this way, the term reidentification connotes an insufficient deidentification process. In the U.S., privacy protection regulations define reidentification as a legally valid process whereby deidentified records can be linked back to their human subjects, under circumstances deemed compelling by a privacy board.[8]

Reidentification that is approved by a privacy board is typically accomplished via a confidential list of links between human subject names and deidentified records, held by a trusted party.[4]

In our example, a list linking the original data identifiers with the replacement data identifiers is created, as shown:

```
75898039563441 -> 82030201856150
94590439540089 -> 44934938405062
29847575938125 -> 65840231656302
83654560466294 -> 76206674367326
98495efc -> 7392g2s1
```

The list is saved by a trusted agent, and all or part of the list could be recalled by order of an institutional privacy board, if necessary.

This section covered three basic principles of deidentifiers that every data scientist must understand:

1. Every identifier can also serve as a deidentifier.
2. Data cannot be satisfactorily deidentified until it has been successfully identified.
3. Identifiers can be used to reidentify deidentified data, when necessary.

5.4 DATA SCRUBBING

> My most important piece of advice to all you would-be writers: When you write, try to leave out all the parts readers skip.
>
> **-Elmore Leonard, from "Elmore Leonard's 10 Rules of Writing"**

Data scrubbing is sometimes used as a synonym for deidentification. This is wrong. It is best to think of data scrubbing as a process that begins where deidentification ends. A data scrubber will remove unwanted information from a data record, including information of a personal nature, and any information that is not directly related to the purpose of the data record. For example, in the case of a hospital record, a data scrubber might remove: the names of physicians who treated the patient; the names of hospitals or medical insurance agencies; addresses; dates; and any textual comments that are inappropriate, incriminating, or irrelevant.[4]

There is a concept known as "minimal necessary" that applies to shared confidential data.[8] It holds that when confidential records are shared, only the minimum necessary information should be released. Any information not directly relevant to the intended purposes of the data analyst should be withheld. The process of data scrubbing gives data managers the opportunity to render a scrubbed record that is free of information that would link the record to its subject and free of extraneous information that the data analyst does not actually require.

There are many approaches to data scrubbing; most require the data manager to develop an exception list of items to be excluded from shared records (eg, names of people, cities, locations, phone numbers, email addresses, and so on). The scrubbing application moves through the records, extracting unnecessary information along the way. The end product is cleaned, but not sterilized. Though many undesired items can be successfully removed, this approach never produces a perfectly scrubbed set of data. In a large and complex data resource, it is simply impossible for the data manager to anticipate every objectionable item and to include it in an exception list.

There is, however, a method whereby data records can be cleaned without error. This method involves producing a list of "safe phrases" acceptable for inclusion in a scrubbed and deidentified data set. Any data that is not in the list of "safe phrases" is automatically deleted. What remains is the scrubbed data. This method can be described as a reverse scrubbing method. Everything is in the data set is deleted by default, unless it is an approved "exception". This method of scrubbing is very fast and can produce an error-free deidentified and scrubbed output.[4,5,9,10]

I have written a very fast scrubber that uses word doublets as its "safe phrases" list. The algorithm is simple. The text to be scrubbed is parsed word by word. All doublets that match "safe phrases" (ie, entries in the approved doublet list) are retained. The approved doublet list can be extracted from a nomenclature that comprehensively covers the knowledge domain appropriate for the research that is being conducted. For example, if I wanted to scrub medical records to search for the occurrences of diseases, then I might create a doublet list from a nomenclature of diseases. I would need to add general grammatic doublets that might not appear in a nomenclature, such as "to be, is not, for the, when the, to do", and so on. The grammatic doublets can be extracted from virtually any general text (eg, "Treasure Island," "Wuthering Heights," or "Data Simplification: Taming information with Open Source Tools"). The combined list of "safe phrases" might have a length of about 100,000 doublets.

The Ruby script, scrubit.rb, uses an external doublet list, "doubdb.txt", and scrubs out a single line of input text. Removed words from the input line are replaced by an asterisk.[11]

```ruby
#!/usr/local/bin/ruby
doub_file = File.open("c:/ftp/doubdb.txt", "r")
doub_hash = {}
doub_file.each_line{|line| line.chomp!; doub_hash[line] = " "}
doub_file.close
puts "What would you like to scrub?"
linearray = gets.chomp.downcase.split
arraysize = linearray.length - 2
lastword = "*"
for arrayindex in (0 .. arraysize)
```

```
   doublet = linearray[arrayindex] + " " + linearray[arrayindex+1]
   if doub_hash.key?(doublet)
     print " " + linearray[arrayindex]
     lastword = " " + linearray[arrayindex+1]
   else
     print lastword
     lastword = " *"
   end
   if arrayindex == arraysize
     print lastword
   end
end
exit
```

Examples of scrubbed text output are shown here[11]:

```
Basal cell carcinoma, margins involved
Scrubbed text.... basal cell carcinoma margins involved

Mr Brown has a basal cell carcinoma
Scrubbed text.... * * has a basal cell carcinoma

Mr. Brown was born on Tuesday, March 14, 1985
Scrubbed text.... * * * * * * * * *]

The doctor killed the patient
Scrubbed text.... * * * * *
```

Reviewing the output, we see that private or objectionable words, such as "Mr. Brown", "Tuesday, March 14, 1985", and "The doctor killed the patient" were all extracted.

The simple script has two main strengths:

1. The output is guaranteed to exclude all phrases other than those composed of doublets from the approved list.
2. The script is fast, executing thousands of times faster than rule-based scrubbing methods.[5,10,12]

Readers who would like to modify this script to scrub their own textual records can build their own "safe phrase" list using methods provided in Open Source Tools for Chapter 3, "Doublet lists."

Whether confidential data can be adequately deidentified and scrubbed is a highly controversial subject.[13] James Joyce is credited with saying that "there are two sides to every argument; unfortunately, I can only occupy one of them." As for myself, I have sided with the data scientists who believe that any text can be rendered deidentified and free of objectionable language, with the use of short scripts that employ simple algorithms. The method provided here removes everything from text, with the exception of pre-approved "safe" doublets. Hence, its sensitivity is only limited by the choice of safe phrases included in the doublet list. It is regrettable that scientists today refuse to share their data on the grounds of patient confidentiality. As an example, here is a quotation from a paper published in 2015 by NIH authors in the Public Library of Science (PLOS): "Data Availability Statement: All data underlying the findings are available for general research use to applicants whose data access request is approved by the National Cancer Institute dbGaP Data Access Committee (dbGaP accession number phs000720). Because of confidentiality issues associated with human subject data, they cannot be made available without restriction."[14] Tsk tsk tsk. Confidential data can, in fact, be rendered harmless through computational methods. The negative consequences caused by restricting public access to scientific data are discussed in Section 8.4. Verification, Validation, and Reanalysis.

5.5 DATA ENCRYPTION AND AUTHENTICATION

If you think technology can solve your security problems, then you don't understand the problems and you don't understand the technology.

-Bruce Schneier

On May 3, 2006, a laptop computer was stolen from the home of a U.S. Veterans Affairs data analyst. On the computer and its external drive were the names, birthdates, and Social Security numbers of 26.5 million soldiers and veterans. By the end of June, the laptop was recovered. Fortunately, there was no reason to believe that the contained data had ever been accessed. Nonetheless, the 26.5 million potential victims of identity theft suffered sufficient emotional distress to justify launching a class action suit against the Veterans Administration. Three years later, the Veterans Administration agreed to pay a lump sum of $20 million dollars to the plaintiffs.[15]

The episode opens a flood of questions:

1. Is it customary for employees to bring confidential information home? Apparently, government staff just can't help themselves. The problem extends to the top agent in the top security agency in the U.S. While he was the CIA Director, John Deutch breached his own security protocols by bringing sensitive CIA information to an unclassified computer at his home.[16]
2. Is confidential information typically bundled into a neat, no-nonsense file from which all of the information pertaining to millions of individuals can be downloaded? Apparently, all the high-tech jargon thrown around concerning encryption algorithms and security protocols just never trickles down to front-line staff.
3. Is there any way of really knowing when a confidential file has been stolen? The thing about electronic data is that it can be copied perfectly and in secret. A database with millions of records can be downloaded in a few moments, without the victim knowing that the theft has occurred.

At the U.S. National Institutes of Health (NIH), I was involved in a project in which sensitive files were to be shared with university-based investigators. The investigators were approved for viewing the data contained in the files, but we were concerned that once the data left our hands, the files could be stolen in transit or from the investigator's site. My suggestion was to devise an encryption protocol, whereby the files would leave the NIH encrypted and remain encrypted at the investigator's site. The investigator could open and view the files, using a key that we would provide. Additional data would be sent with new keys, ensuring that if a key fell into the wrong hands, the damage would be limited to one version of one file. I also suggested that the files could be easily scrubbed and deidentified, so that the data in the files contained no private information and nothing to link records to individual persons. I was satisfied that the system, when implemented, would render the data harmless beyond any reasonable concern. My assurances did not allay the fear that someone with sufficient resources might conceivably gain access to some fragment of data that they were not entitled to see. The fact that the data had been thoroughly scrubbed, and had no monetary value, was deemed irrelevant. The solution that was finally adopted was simple, but worse than useless. To my consternation, the decision was made to with-hold the data, until such time as a perfect system for safe data exchange could be implemented.

Let's be practical. Nearly everyone I know has confidential information on their computers. Often, this information resides in a few very private files. If those files fell into the hands of the wrong people, the results would be calamitous. For myself, I encrypt my sensitive files. When I need to work with those files, I decrypt them. When I'm finished working with them, I encrypt them again. These files are important to me, so I keep copies of the encrypted files on thumb drives and on an external server. I don't care if my thumb drives are lost or stolen. I don't care if a hacker gets access to the server that stores my files. The files are encrypted, and only I know how to decrypt them.

Anyone in the data sciences will tell you that it is important to encrypt your data files, particularly when you are transferring files via the Internet. Very few data scientists follow their own advice. Scientists, despite what you may believe, are not a particularly disciplined group of individuals. Few scientists get into the habit of encrypting their files. Perhaps they perceive the process as being too complex.

Here are the general desirable features for simple encryption systems that will satisfy most needs. If you have really important data, the kind that could hurt yourself or others if the data were to fall into the wrong hands, then you should totally disregard the advice that follows.

1. Save yourself a lot of grief by settling for a level of security that is appropriate and reasonable for your own needs. Don't use a bank vault when a padlock will suffice.
2. Avail yourself of no-cost solutions. Some of the finest encryption algorithms and their implementations are publicly available. For example, AES (Advanced Encryption Standard) was established by the U.S. National Institute of Standards and Technology and has been adopted by the U.S. Government and by organizations throughout the world. Methods for using AES and other encryption protocols are found in Open Source Tools for this chapter, "Encryption and decryption with OpenSSL."
3. The likelihood that you will lose your passwords is much higher than the likelihood that someone will steal your passwords. Develop a good system for passkey management that is suited to your own needs.
4. The security of the system should not be based on hiding your encrypted files or keeping the encryption algorithm secret. The greatest value of modern encryption protocols is that it makes no difference whether anyone steals or copies your encrypted files or learns your encryption algorithm.
5. File encryption and decryption should be computationally fast. Fast, open source protocols are readily available.
6. File encryption should be done automatically, as part of some computer routine (eg, a backup routine), or as a cron job (ie, a process that occurs at a predetermined time).
7. You need not be a stickler for protocol. You can use the same passkey over and over again if your level of concern for intruders is low, or if you do not value the confidentiality of your data very highly.

8. You should be able to batch-encrypt and batch-decrypt any number of files all at once (ie, from a command loop within a script), and you should be able to combine encryption with other file maintenance activities. For example, you should be able to implement a simple script that loops through every file in a directory or a directory tree (ie, all the files in all of the subdirectories under the directory) all at once, adding file header and metadata information into the file, scrubbing data as appropriate, calculating a one-way hash (ie, message digest) of the finished file, and producing an encrypted file output.

9. You should never implement an encryption system that is more complex than you can understand.[17]

Your data may be important to you and to a few of your colleagues, but the remainder of the world looks upon your output with glazed eyes. If you are the type of person who would protect your valuables with a padlock rather than a safety deposit box, then you should probably be thinking less about encryption strength and more about encryption interoperability. Ask yourself: Will the protocols that I use today be widely available platform-independent and vendor-independent protocols 5, 10, or 50 years from now? Will I always be able to decrypt my encrypted files?

For the encryptically lazy, a simple ROT13 protocol may be all you need. Rot_13 is a protocol that shifts the input text halfway around the alphabet. For example, the letter "a", ASCII value 97, is replaced by the letter "n", ASCII value 110 (see Open Source Tools for Chapter 2, ASCII).

```
#!/usr/bin/python
import codecs
print('abCdeFgHijKlM')
output = codecs.encode('abCdeFgHijKlM', 'rot_13')
print output
print(codecs.encode(output, 'rot_13'))
print('hello world')
output = codecs.encode('hello world', 'rot_13')
print output
print(codecs.encode(output, 'rot_13'))
exit
```

Here is the output of the rot_13.py script. Each input string is followed by its Rot_13 encryption:

```
c:\ftp>rot_13.py
abCdeFgHijKlM
noPqrStUvwXyZ
abCdeFgHijKlM
hello world
uryyb jbeyq
hello world
```

What happened here? The string "uryyb jbeyq" is the result of rot_13 operating on the input string "hello world". Notice that the space character is untouched by the algorithm. The Python implementation of rot_13 only operates on the 26 characters of the alphabet (ie, a-z and the uppercase equivalents, A-Z). All other ASCII characters are ignored.

The next line of output is "hello world", and this represents the rot_13 algorithm operating on the encoded string, "uryyb jbeyq". You can see that repeating the Rot_13 returns the original string.

Using Perl's transliteration operator, "tr", any string can be converted to ROT13 in one line of code.

```
#!/usr/local/bin/perl
$text = "abCdeFgHijKlM and hello world";
$text =~ tr/A-Za-z/N-ZA-Mn-za-m/;
print $text;
print "\n";
$text =~ tr/A-Za-z/N-ZA-Mn-za-m/;
print $text;
exit;
```

Here's the output of the rot_13.pl script:

```
c:\ftp>rot_13.pl
noPqrStUvwXyZ naq uryyb jbeyq
abCdeFgHijKlM and hello world
```

Of course, you will want to encrypt multiple whole files all at once. Here is a Python script, rot_13_dir.py, that will encrypt all the text files in a directory. All characters other than the 26-letter alphabet, the space character, and the underscore character are left alone (ie, uncoded).

```
#!/usr/bin/python
import sys, os, re, codecs
current_directory = os.getcwd()
filelist = os.listdir(current_directory)
pattern = re.compile(".txt$")
ascii_characters = re.compile("[a-zA-Z0-9_]")
for in_file_name in filelist:
  if pattern.search(in_file_name):
    out_file_name = pattern.sub('.rot', in_file_name)
    print(out_file_name)
    out_file_holder = open(out_file_name,'w')
    with open(in_file_name) as in_file_holder:
      while True:
        character = in_file_holder.read(1)
        if not character:
          break
        if not ascii_characters.search(character):
          out_file_holder.write(character)
        else:
          rot_13_of_character = codecs.encode(character, 'rot_13')
          out_file_holder.write(rot_13_of_character)
  else:
    continue
exit
```

For serious encryption, you will want to step up to OpenSSL. OpenSSL is an open-source collection of encryption protocols and message digest protocols (ie, protocols that yield one-way hashes). Encryption algorithms available through OpenSLL include: RSA, DES, and AES. With system calls to OpenSSL, your scripts can encrypt or decrypt thousands of files, all at once. Here is a simple Python script, aes.py , that encrypts a list of text files with the AES standard encryption algorithm (see Glossary item, AES).

```
#!/usr/local/bin/python
import sys, os, re
filelist = ['diener.txt','simplify.txt','re-ana.txt', 'phenocop.txt',
'mystery.txt','disaster.txt', 'factnote.txt', 'perlbig.txt', 'referen.txt',
'create.txt', 'exploreo.txt']
pattern = re.compile("txt")
for filename in filelist:
  out_filename = pattern.sub('enc', filename)
  out_filename = "f:\\" + out_filename
  print(out_filename)
  cmdstring = "openssl aes128 -in " + filename + " -out " + out_filename + " -pass \
pass:z4u7w28"
  os.system(cmdstring)
exit
```

In Open Source Tools for this chapter, the OpenSSL installation, documentation and protocols are described, and implementations in Perl, Python and Ruby are demonstrated.

5.6 TIMESTAMPS, SIGNATURES, AND EVENT IDENTIFIERS

Time is what keeps everything from happening at once.
-Ray Cummings in his 1922 novel, "The Girl in the Golden Atom"

Consider the following assertions:

Alexander Goodboy, 34 inches height
Alexander Goodboy, 42 inches height
Alexander Goodboy, 46 inches height
Alexander Goodboy, 52 inches height

At first glance, these assertions seem contradictory. How can Alexander Goodboy be 34, 42, 46, and 52 inches tall? The confusion is lifted when we add some timing information to the assertions:

Alexander Goodboy, age 3 years, 34 inches height
Alexander Goodboy, age 5 years, 42 inches height
Alexander Goodboy, age 7 years, 46 inches height
Alexander Goodboy, age 9 years, 52 inches height

All events, measurements, and transactions occur at a particular time, and it is essential to annotate data objects with their moment of creation and with every moment when additional data is added to the data object (ie, event times).[18] It is best to think of data objects as chronicles of a temporal sequence of immutable versions of the object (see Glossary item, Immutability). In the case of Alexander Goodboy, the boy changes in height as he grows, but each annotated version of Alexander Goodboy (ie, Alexander Goodboy, age 3 years, height 34 inches) is eternal and immutable.

Timestamps, when used consistently, achieve the impossible. They allow data managers to modify or correct data without violating data immutability (ie, without tampering with history and without hiding the truth). How might this be done?

```
Data object -> Newspaper headlines:
 "Dewey Defeats Truman"                 timestamp: November 3,1948, 6:00 AM
 "Dewey Defeats Truman" (modification) timestamp: November 3,1948, 10:00 AM
 "Truman Defeats Dewey"                 timestamp: November 3, 1948, 10:01 AM
```

The *Chicago Daily Tribune* ran an infamous banner declaring Thomas E. Dewey as victor over Harry S. Truman in the 1948 U.S. presidential election. History is immutable, and their error will live forever. Nonetheless, Dewey did not defeat Truman. To restore order to the universe, we need to do the following:

1. Timestamp the original (erroneous) headline.
2. Indicate that a modification was made and timestamp the event.
3. Produce corrected data and timestamp the corrected data.
4. Save all data assertions forever (original, modification, and new).
5. Ensure that the data assertions support introspection (discussed in Section 7.2, Introspection and Reflection).

Timestamping is nothing new. Ancient scribes were fastidious timestampers. It would be an unusual Sumerian, Egyptian, or Mayan document that lacked an inscribed date. In contrast, it is easy to find modern, web-based news reports that lack any clue to the date that the web page was created. Likewise, it is a shameful fact that most spreadsheet data lacks timestamps for individual data cells. Data sets that lack timestamps, unique identifiers, and metadata have limited value to anyone other than the individual who created the data and who happens to have personal knowledge of how the data was created and what it means.

Fortunately, all computers have an internal clock. This means that all computer events can be timestamped. Most programming languages have a method for generating the epoch time, ie, the number of seconds that have elapsed since a particular moment in time. On most systems, the epoch is the first second of January 1, 1970. Perl, Python, and Ruby have methods for producing epoch time. For trivia's sake, we must observe that the UUID timestamp is generated for an epoch time representing the number of seconds elapsed since the first second of Friday, October 15, 1582 (see Section 5.1, "Unique Identifiers"). This moment marks the beginning of the Gregorian calendar. The end of the Julian calendar occurred on October 4, 1582. The 11 days intervening, from the end of the Julian calendar to the start of the Gregorian calendar, are lost somewhere in time and space.

Here is a Perl command line generating epoch time:

```
c:\ftp>perl -e print(time())
1442353564
```

From Python's interactive environment:

```
c:\ftp>python
>>> import time
>>> print(time.time())
1442353742.456994
```

From Ruby's interactive environment:

```
c:\ftp>irb
irb(main):001:0> "%10.9f" % Time.now.to_f
=> "1442354071.895107031"
```

Perl has a built-in gmtime (Greenwich Mean Time) function that produces an array of time-related values, which can be parsed and formatted in any desired format.

Here is the Perl script, gmt.pl, that generates the date in the American style (ie, month, day, year):

```
#!/usr/bin/perl
($sec,$min,$hour,$mday,$mon,$year,$wday,$yday,$isdst) = gmtime();
$year = $year + 1900;
$mon = $mon + 1;
print "Americanized GMT date is: $mon\/$mday\/$year\n";
exit;
```

Here is the output of the gmt.pl script:

```
c:\ftp>gmt.pl
Americanized GMT date is: 9/16/2015
```

It is very important to understand that country-specific styles for representing the date are a nightmare for data scientists. As an example, consider: "2/4/97". This date signifies February 4, 1997 in America; and April 2, 1997 in Great Britain and much of the world. There basically is no way of distinguishing with certainty 2/4/97 and 4/2/97.

It is not surprising that an international standard, the ISO-8601, has been created for representing date and time.[19]

The international format for date and time is: YYYY-MM-DD hh:mm:ss

The value "hh" is the number of complete hours that have passed since midnight. The upper value of hh is 24 (midnight). If hh = 24, then the minute and second values must be zero.

An example of ISO-8601-compliant data and time is:
1995-02-04 22:45:00

An alternate form, likewise ISO-8601-compliant, is:
1995-02-04 T22:45:00Z

In the alternate form, a "T" replaces the space left between the date and the time, indicating that time follows date. A "Z" is appended to the string indicating that the time and date are computed for UTC

(Coordinated Universal Time, formerly known as Greenwich Mean Time, and popularly known as Zulu time, hence the "Z").

Here is a short Perl script, format_time.pl, that produces the date and time, in American style, and in ISO-8601-compliant forms:

```perl
#!/usr/bin/perl
($sec,$min,$hour,$mday,$mon,$year,$wday,$yday,$isdst) = gmtime();
$year = $year + 1900;
$mon = substr(("000" . ($mon+1)), -2, 2);
$mday = substr(("000" . $mday), -2, 2);
$hour = substr(("000" . $hour), -2, 2);
$min = substr(("000" . $min), -2, 2);
$sec = substr(("000" . $sec), -2, 2);
print "Americanized time is: $mday\/$wday\/$year\n";
print "ISO8601 time is:$year\-$mon\-$mday $hour\:$min\:$sec\n";
print "ISO8601 time is:$year\-$mon\-${mday}T$hour\:$min\:${sec}Z (alternate form)";
exit;
```

Here is the output of the format_time.pl script.
output

```
c:\ftp>format_time.pl
Americanized time is: 16/3/2015
ISO8601 time is:2015-09-16 12:31:41
ISO8601 time is:2015-09-16 T12:31:41Z (alternate form)
```

Here is a Python script, format_time.py, that generates the date and time, compliant with ISO-8601.

```python
#!/usr/bin/python
import time, datetime
timenow = time.time()
print(datetime.datetime.fromtimestamp(timenow).strftime('%Y-%m-%d %H:%M:%S'))
exit
```

Here is the output of the format_time.py script:

```
c:\ftp>format_time.py
2015-09-16 07:44:09
```

It is sometimes necessary to establish, beyond doubt, that a timestamp is accurate and has not been modified. Through the centuries, a great many protocols have been devised to prove that a timestamp is trustworthy. A popular method employed in the 20th century involved creating some inscrutable text extracted from a document (eg, the character sequence consisting of the first letter of each line in the document) and sending the sequence to a newspaper for publication in the classifieds section. Anyone in possession of the document could generate the same sequence from the document and find that it had been published in the newspaper on the date specified. Hence, the document must have existed on the day of publication. As more computer-savvy individuals became familiar with methods for producing one-way hashes from documents, these sequences became the digest sequences of choice for trusted time-stamp protocols (see Glossary item, Message digest). Today, newspapers are seldom used to established trusted timestamps. More commonly, a message digest of a confidential document is sent to a timestamp authority that adds a date to the digest and returns a message, encrypted with the timestamp authority's private key, containing the original one-way hash plus the trusted date. The received message can be decrypted with the timestamp authority's public key, to reveal the date/time and the message digest that is unique for the original document. It seems like the trusted timestamp process is a lot of work, but regular users of these services can routinely process hundreds of documents in seconds.

OPEN SOURCE TOOLS

It's better to wait for a productive programmer to become available than it is to wait for the first available programmer to become productive.

-Steve McConnell

PSEUDORANDOM NUMBER GENERATORS

It is not easy for computers to produce an endless collection of random numbers. Eventually, algorithms will cycle through their available variations and begin to repeat themselves, producing the same set of "random" numbers, in the same order; a phenomenon referred to as the generator's period. Because algorithms that produce seemingly random numbers are imperfect, they are known as pseudorandom number generators.

The Mersenne Twister algorithm is used as default in most current programming languages to generate pseudorandum numbers. Languages using the Mersenne Twister include R, Python, Ruby, the GNU Multiple Precision Arithmetic Library, and the GNU Scientific Library. An implementation of the Mersenne Twister is available for Perl as an external module; specifically, Math::Random::MT::Perl. The Mersenne Twister has an extremely long period, and it performs well on most of the tests that mathematicians have devised to test randomness.

Just to demonstrate how simple it is to deploy random numbers, here is a one-line Ruby command, entered on the interactive "irb(main):001:0>" prompt, that calls a pseudorandom number generator, rand(), 10 times.

```
irb(main):001:0> (1..10).each{puts rand()}
```

output:

```
0.6210719721375545
0.8275281308969118
0.5221605121682973
```

```
0.4579032986235061
0.3897775291626894
0.1859092284180266
0.9087949176336569
0.44303624386264195
0.514384506264992
0.037523700988150055
```

An equivalent Python snippet is:

```
import random
for iterations in range(10):
  print random.uniform(0,1)
```

An equivalent Perl snippet is:

```
for (0..9)
  {
  print rand() . "\n";
  }
```

Here is a short Python script, random_filenames.py, that uses a pseudorandom generator to produce a filename composed of random characters:

```
#!/usr/bin/python
import random
filename = [0]*12
filename = map(lambda x: x is "" or chr(int(random.uniform(0,25) + 97)), filename)
print ''.join(filename[0:8]) + "." + ''.join(filename[9:12])
exit
```

Here is the output of the random_filenames.py script:

```
c:\ftp\py>random_filenames.py
tjqimddr.mjb
```

Random number generators are among the more useful programming utilities available to programmers. With random number generators, we can create unique identifiers, perform resampling statistics (see Sections 8.2 and 8.3), and produce reliable non-analytic solutions to complex problems in the field of probability and combinatorics (see Glossary item, Combinatorics).

Just for fun, let's look at a short script, random_string.py, that uses Python's random number generator to test the assertion that random strings are incompressible (eg, cannot be compressed with gzip, a popular open-source compression utility).

First, let's build a file, composed of 160,000 randomly chosen ASCII characters, using a few lines of Python.

```
#!/usr/local/bin/python
from random import randint
outfile = open ("random_1.raw", "wb")
for n in range(160000):
  c = chr(randint(0,255))
  outfile.write(c)
exit
```

The output script is random_1.raw, and its size is 160,000 bytes. Now, let's try to compress this file, using the gzip utility. This produces the gzipped file, random_1.gz of size 160,077 bytes.

Not only did the gzip compression utility fail to reduce the size of random_1.raw, but the resulting file is also slightly larger than the original file. The reason for this is compression utilities reduce files by replacing repetitive sequences with shorter sequences. A random file lacks highly repetitive sequences and cannot be condensed (see Glossary item, Randomness).

UUID

The UUID, is a protocol for creating unique strings that can be used as permanent identifiers for data objects.[2] The idea here is that you create a UUID for a data object, and you take appropriate steps to permanently associate the data object with its assigned UUID. The most important benefit of the UUID is that the protocol can be implemented without the administrative overhead of a central registry. Maintaining the object-identifier association, after it is created, is the job of the data creator.

A typical UUID might look like this[5]:

```
4c108407-0570-4afb-9463-2831bcc6e4a4
```

Like most standard protocols, the UUID has been subject to modifications. Within the "standard", a UUID can be created with a pseudorandom number generator, or with timing information (eg, the moment when the UUID was generated), or with a one-way hash value produced from data contained in the data object (see Glossary items, Timestamp, One-way hash). One implementation of UUID attaches a timestamp to the random number. Implementers of UUIDs must keep in mind that uniqueness is achieved in practice but not in theory. It is possible, though remarkably unlikely, that two data objects could be assigned the same UUID. The mathematics of UUID collisions has been studied, and the chances of double assignments are incredibly remote. Nonetheless, the use of a timestamp, indicating the moment when the UUID was assigned to the data object, decreases the chance of a collision even further. The likelihood that the same 128-bit pseudorandom numbers might be assigned to different data objects at the exact same moment in time is essentially zero.

Because UUIDs have become popular, there are now many simple and convenient ways of creating UUIDs as needed. For Linux users, uuidgen.exe is a built-in command line utility. The uuidgen.exe utility is available to Windows users via its inclusion in the Cygwin distribution (Open Source Tools for Chapter 1).

```
c:\cygwin64\bin>uuidgen.exe
```

The command line generates an output that you can attach to a data object (see Glossary item, Data object)

```
9ee64643-2ff2-4 cd1-ad31-ab59f933a276
```

You can access uuidgen.exe through a system call from a Perl or Python or Ruby script to the uuidgen.exe utility residing it its Cygwin subdirectory:

```
#!/usr/bin/perl
system("c\:\\cygwin64\\bin\\uuidgen.exe");
exit;
```

A UUID module is included in the standard Python distribution and can be called directly from a script. In this case, the UUID protocol chosen is UUID-4, which generates a UUID using a random number generator.

```
#!/usr/local/bin/python
import uuid
print uuid.uuid4()
exit
```

In Ruby, UUIDs can be generated using the GUID module, available as a downloadable gem, and installed into your computer's Ruby environment using the following command (see Glossary item, Ruby gem)[5]:

```
gem install guid
```

Easier yet, if you have Ruby 1.9 or later, you can create UUIDs with the built-in SecureRandom module:

```
#!/usr/bin/ruby
require 'securerandom'
puts SecureRandom.uuid
exit
```

ENCRYPTION AND DECRYPTION WITH OPENSSL

OpenSSL is an open-source collection of encryption protocols and message digest protocols (ie, protocols that yield one-way hashes). OpenSSL comes with an Apache-style open-source license. This useful set of utilities, with implementations for various operating systems, is available at no cost from: https://www.openssl.org/related/binaries.html

Encryption algorithms and suites of cipher strategies available through OpenSLL include: RSA, DH (numerous protocols), DSS, ECDH, TLS, AES (including 128 and 256 bit keys), CAMELLIA, DES (including triple DES), RC4, IDEA, SEED, PSK, and numerous GOST protocols (see Glossary item, AES). In addition, implementations of popular one-way hash algorithms are provided (ie, MD5 and SHA, including SHA384). OpenSSL comes with an Apache-style open-source license.

For Windows users, the OpenSSL download contains three files that are necessary for file encryption: openssl.exe, ssleay32.dll, and libeay32.dll. If these three files are located in your current directory, you can encrypt any file, directly from the command prompt:

```
c:\>openssl aes128 -in public.txt -out secret.aes -pass pass:z4u7w28"
```

The command line provides a password, "z4u7w28", to the aes128 encryption algorithm, which takes the file public.txt and produces an encrypted output file, secret.aes.

The same command line could have been launched from a Perl script:

```
#!/usr/bin/perl
system("openssl aes128 -in public.txt -out secret.aes -pass pass:z4u7w28");
exit;
```

Here's a Perl script that changes the directory to the location of the OpenSSL program suite on my computer. The script encrypts the public.txt file, using the somewhat outmoded Digital Encryption Standard (DES) with password "test123".

```
#!/usr/bin/perl
chdir "c:\\ftp\\openssl\-1\.0\.11\-x64\_86\-win64";
system("openssl des -in c:\\ftp\\public.txt -out c:\\ftp\\secret.des -pass
pass:test123");
exit;
```

Of course, once you've encrypted a file, you will need a decryption method. Here's a short Perl script that decrypts secret.aes, the result of encrypting public.txt with the AES algorithm:

```
#!/usr/bin/perl
system("openssl aes128 -d -in secret.aes -out decrypted.txt -pass pass:z4u7w28");
exit;
```

We see that decryption involves inserting the "-d" option into the command line. AES is an example of a symmetric encryption algorithm, which means that the encryption password and the decryption password are identical.

Decryption works much the same way for the DES algorithm. In the following script, we change the directory to the location where the OpenSSL suite resides:

```
#!/usr/bin/perl
chdir "c\:\\ftp\\openssl\-1\.0\.11\-x64\_86\-win64";
system("openssl des -d -in c\:\\ftp\\secret.des -out c\:\\ftp\\secret.txt -pass
pass:test123");
exit;
```

Encrypting and decrypting individual strings, files, groups of files, and directory contents is extremely simple and can provide a level of security that is likely to be commensurate with your personal needs.

ONE-WAY HASH IMPLEMENTATIONS

One-way hashes are mathematical algorithms that operate on a string of any size, including large binary files, to produce a short, fixed-length, seemingly random sequence of characters that is specific for the input string. If a single byte is changed anywhere in the input string, the resulting one-way hash output string will be radically altered. Furthermore, the original string cannot be computed from the one-way hash, even when the algorithm that produced the one-way hash is known. One-way hash protocols have many practical uses in the field of information science (see Glossary items Checksum, HMAC, Digest, Message digest, Check digit, Authentication). It is very easy to implement one-way hashes, and most programming languages and operating systems come bundled with one or more implementations of one-way hash algorithms. The two most popular one-way hash algorithms are md5 (message digest version 5) and SHA (Secure Hash Algorithm).

Here we use Cygwin's own md5sum.exe utility on the command line to produce a one-way hash for an image file, named dash.png:

```
c:\ftp>c:\cygwin64\bin\md5sum.exe dash.png
```

Here is the output:

```
db50dc33800904ab5f4ac90597d7b4ea *dash.png
```

We could call the same command line from a Python script:

```
#!/usr/local/bin/python
import sys, os
os.system("c:/cygwin64/bin/md5sum.exe dash.png")
exit
```

From a Ruby script:

```
#!/usr/local/bin/ruby
system("c:/cygwin64/bin/md5sum.exe dash.png")
exit
```

From a Perl script:

```
#!/usr/local/bin/perl
system("c:/cygwin64/bin/md5sum.exe dash.png");
exit;
```

The output will always be the same, so long as the input file, dash.png, does not change:

```
db50dc33800904ab5f4ac90597d7b4ea *dash.png
```

OpenSSL contains several one-way hash implementations, including both md5 and several variants of SHA. Here is a system call to OpenSSL from Perl using a text file public.txt as input, using SHA as the algorithm, and sending the resulting hash to the file, hash.sha.

```
#!/usr/bin/perl
system("openssl dgst -sha public.txt >hash.sha");
exit;
```

The output is a file, hash.sha. Here are the contents of the hash.sha file:

```
SHA(public.txt)= af2f12663145770ac0cbd260e69675af6ac26417
```

Here is an equivalent script, in Ruby:

```
#!/usr/local/bin/ruby
system("openssl dgst -sha public.txt >hash.sha")
exit
```

Here is the output of the Ruby script:

```
SHA(public.txt)= af2f12663145770ac0cbd260e69675af6ac26417
```

Once more, notice that the output is the same whether we use Ruby or Perl, because both scripts produce a hash using the same SHA algorithm on the same file. We could have called the SHA algorithm from Python, generating the same output.

Here is a Python script, hash_dir.py, that produces an SHA hash for every file in a subdirectory, putting the collection of hash values into a file:

```
#!/usr/local/bin/python
import os
filelist = os.listdir(".")
outfile = open ("hashes_collect.txt", "w")
```

```
for filename in filelist:
    cmdstring = "openssl dgst -sha %s" % (filename)
    cmdstring = cmdstring + "> hashes.sha"
    os.system(cmdstring)
    infile = open ("hashes.sha", "r")
    getline = infile.readline()
    infile.close()
    outfile.write(getline)
outfile.close()
exit
```

The output file, hashes_collect.txt, has the following contents, listing the one-way hash value for each file that happened to reside in my current directory:

```
SHA(bunzip2.TXT)= 0547d31d7c675ae2239067611e6309dc8cb7e7db
SHA(googlez.TXT)= f96cea198ad1dd5617ac084a3d92c6107708c0ef
SHA(gunzipe.TXT)= d275bd87933f2322a97c70035aa2aa5f4c6088ac
SHA(gzip.TXT)= 0b323cb4555c8996c8100f8ad8259eec2538821b
SHA(hashes.sha)= f96cea198ad1dd5617ac084a3d92c6107708c0ef
SHA(hashes_collect.txt)= f96cea198ad1dd5617ac084a3d92c6107708c0ef
SHA(hash_dir.py)= 1db37524e54de40ff723fbc7e3ba20b18e651d48
SHA(JHSPZIP.TXT)= 32424d0d1fe75bedd5680205fbbc63bff4bb783a
SHA(libeay32.dll)= 647fae7916e8c4c45d0002fd6d2fc9c6877de085
SHA(mortzip.TXT)= 3168f52511c8289db7657b637156063c0e8c5646
SHA(Nonlinear_Science_FAQ.txt)= 6316b8531712ca2f0b192c1f662dbde446f958d9
SHA(openssl.exe)= 1cf6af2d3f720e0959d0ce49d6e4dad7a58092e8
SHA(pesonalized_blog.txt)= 25d208163e7924b8c10c7e9732d29383d61a22f1
SHA(ssleay32.dll)= 4889930b67feef5765d3aef3d1752db10ebced8f
```

Such files, containing lists of one-way hashes, can be used as authentication records (see Glossary item, Authentication)

STEGANOGRAPHY

You look at them every day; the ones that others create and the ones that you create to share with your friends or with the world. They're part of your life, and you would feel a deep sense of loss if you lost them. I'm referring to high-resolution digital images. We love them, but we give them more credit than they deserve. When you download a 16-megapixel image of your sister's lasagna, you can be certain that most of the pixel information is padded with so-called empty resolution, ie, pixel precision that is probably inaccurate and certainly exceeding the eye's ability to meaningfully resolve. Most images in the megabyte size range can safely be reduced to the kilobyte size range, without loss of visual information. Steganography is an encryption technique that takes advantage of the empty precision in pixel data by inserting secret text messages into otherwise useless data bits.

Steganography is one of several general techniques in which a message is hidden within another digital object. Steganography has been around for centuries, and was described as early as AD 1500 by Trithemious.[20] Watermarking is closely related to steganography. Digital watermarking is a way of secretly insinuating the name of the owner or creator of a digital object into the object, as a mechanism of rights management (see Glossary item, Watermarking).[21]

Steghide is an open-source GNU license utility that invisibly embeds data in image or audio files. Windows and Linux versions are available for download from SourceForge at: http://steghide. sourceforge.net/download.php.

A Steghide manual is available at: http://steghide.sourceforge.net/documentation/manpage.php.

On my computer, the Steghide executables happen to be stored on the c:\ftp\steghide\steghide sub-directory. Hence, in the following code, this subdirectory will be the launch path.

Here is an example of a command line invocation of Steghide. Your chosen password can be inserted directly into the commandline

```
c:\ftp\steghide\steghide>steghide embed -cf c:\ftp\simplify\berman_author_photo.
jpg -ef c:\ftp\berman_author_bio.txt -p hideme
```

The command line was launched from the subdirectory that holds the Steghide executable files on my computer. The command instructs Steghide to embed the text file berman_author_bio.txt into the image file berman_author_photo.jpg under the password "hideme".

That's all there is to it. The image file, containing a photo of myself, now contains an embedded text file with my short biography. I no longer need to keep track of both files. I can generate my biography file from my image file, but I've got to remember the password.

I could have called Steghide from a script. Here is an example of an equivalent Python script that invokes Steghide from a system call.

```
#!/usr/local/bin/python
import os
command_string = "steghide embed -cf c:/ftp/simplify/berman_author_photo.jpg -ef \
c:/ftp/berman_author_bio.txt -p hideme"
os.system(command_string)
exit
```

You can see how powerful this method can be. With a bit of tweaking, you can write a short script that uses the Steghide utility to embed a hidden text message in thousands of images, all at once. Anyone viewing those images would have no idea that they contained a hidden message unless you told them so.

GLOSSARY

AES The Advanced Encryption Standard (AES) is the cryptographic standard endorsed by the U.S. government as a replacement for the old government standard, Data Encryption Standard (DES). In 2001, AES was chosen from among many different encryption protocols submitted in a cryptographic contest conducted by the U.S. National Institute of Standards and Technology. AES is also known as Rijndael, after its developer. It is a symmetric encryption standard, meaning that the same password used for encryption is also used for decryption. See Symmetric key.

Authentication A process for determining if the data object that is received (eg, document, file, image) is the data object that was intended to be received. The simplest authentication protocol involves one-way hash operations on the data that needs to be authenticated. Suppose you happen to know that a certain file named z.txt will be arriving via email and that this file has an MD5 hash of "uF7pBPGgxKtabA/2zYlscQ==". You receive the z. txt, and you perform an MD5 one-way hash operation on the file, as shown here:

```
#!/usr/bin/python
import base64
import md5
md5_object = md5.new()
sample_file = open ("z.txt", "rb")
string = sample_file.read()
sample_file.close()
md5_object.update(string)
md5_string = md5_object.digest()
print(base64.encodestring(md5_string))
exit
```

Let's assume that the output of the MD5 hash operation, performed on the z.txt file, is "uF7pBPGgxKtabA/ 2zYlscQ==". This would tell us that the received z.txt file is authentic (ie, it is the file that you were intended to receive), because any file tampering would have changed the MD5 hash. Additional implementations of one-way hashes are described in Open Source Tools for this chapter. The authentication process in this example does not tell you who sent the file, the time that the file was created, or anything about the validity of the contents of the file. These would require a protocol that included signature, timestamp, and data validation, in addition to authentication. In common usage, authentication protocols often include entity authentication (ie, some method by which the entity sending the file is verified). Consequently, authentication protocols are often confused with signature verification protocols. An ancient historical example serves to distinguish the concepts of authentication protocols and signature protocols. Since earliest recorded history, fingerprints were used as a method of authentication. When a scholar or artisan produced a product, he would press his thumb into the clay tablet, or the pot, or the wax seal closing a document. Anyone doubting the authenticity of the pot could ask the artisan for a thumbprint. If the new thumbprint matched the thumbprint on the tablet, pot, or document, then all knew that the person creating the new thumbprint and the person who had put his thumbprint into the object were the same individual. Hence, ancient pots were authenticated. Of course, this was not proof that the object was the creation of the person with the matching thumbprint. For all anyone knew, there may have been a hundred different pottery artisans, with one person pressing his thumb into every pot produced. You might argue that the thumbprint served as the signature of the artisan. In practical terms, no. The thumbprint by itself does not tell you whose print was used. Thumbprints could not be read, at least not in the same way as a written signature. The ancients needed to compare the pot's thumbprint against the thumbprint of the living person who made the print. When the person died, civilization was left with a bunch of pots with the same thumbprint, but without any certain way of knowing whose thumb produced them. In essence, because there was no ancient database that permanently associated thumbprints with individuals, the process of establishing the identity of the pot maker became very difficult once the artisan died. A good signature protocol permanently binds an authentication code to a unique entity (eg, a person). Today, we can find a fingerprint at the scene of a crime; we can find a matching signature in a database and link the fingerprint to one individual. Hence, in modern times, fingerprints are true "digital" signatures, no pun intended. Modern uses of fingerprints include keying (eg, opening locked devices based on an authenticated fingerprint), tracking (eg, establishing the path and whereabouts of an individual by following a trail of fingerprints or other identifiers), and body part identification (ie, identifying the remains of individuals recovered from mass graves or from the sites of catastrophic events based on fingerprint matches). Over the past decade, flaws in the vaunted process of fingerprint identification have been documented, and the improvement of the science of identification is an active area of investigation.[22] See HMAC. See Digital signature.

Check digit A checksum that produces a single digit as output is referred to as a check digit. Some of the common identification codes in use today, such as ISBN numbers for books, come with a built-in check digit. Of course, when using a single digit as a check value, you can expect that some transmitted errors will escape the check, but the check digit is useful in systems wherein occasional mistakes are tolerated, wherein the purpose of the check digit is to find a specific type of error (eg, an error produced by a substitution in a single character or digit), and wherein the check digit itself is rarely transmitted in error. See Checksum.

Checksum An outdated term that is sometimes used synonymously with one-way hash or message digest. Checksums are performed on a string, block, or file yielding a short alphanumeric string intended to be specific for the input data. Ideally, if a single bit were to change anywhere within the input file, then the checksum for the input file would change drastically. Checksums, as the name implies, involve summing values (ie, typically weighted character values), to produce a sequence that can be calculated on a file before and after transmission. Most of the errors that were commonly introduced by poor transmission could be detected with checksums. Today, the old checksum algorithms have been largely replaced with one-way hash algorithms. A checksum that produces a single digit as output is referred to as a check digit. See Check digit. See One-way hash. See Message digest. See HMAC.

Combinatorics The analysis of complex data often involves combinatorics, ie, the evaluation, on some numeric level, of combinations of things. Often, combinatorics involves pairwise comparisons of all possible combinations of items. When the number of comparisons becomes large, as is the case with virtually all combinatoric problems involving large data sets, the computational effort becomes massive. For this reason, combinatorics research has become a subspecialty in applied mathematics and data science. There are four "hot" areas in combinatorics. The first involves building increasingly powerful computers capable of solving complex combinatoric problems. The second involves developing methods whereby combinatoric problems can be broken into smaller problems that can be distributed to many computers in order to provide relatively fast solutions to problems that could not otherwise be solved in any reasonable length of time. The third area of research involves developing new algorithms for solving combinatoric problems quickly and efficiently. The fourth area, perhaps the most promising area, involves developing innovative non-combinatoric solutions for traditionally combinatoric problems — a golden opportunity for experts in the field of data simplification.

Data object A data object is whatever is being described by the data. For example, if the data is "6 feet tall", then the data object is the person or thing to which "6 feet tall" applies. Minimally, a data object is a metadata/data pair, assigned to a unique identifier (ie, a triple). In practice, the most common data objects are simple data records, corresponding to a row in a spreadsheet or a line in a flat file. Data objects in object-oriented programming languages typically encapsulate several items of data, including an object name, an object unique identifier, multiple data/metadata pairs, and the name of the object's class. See Triple. See Identifier. See Metadata.

Data scrubbing A term that is very similar to data deidentification and is sometimes used improperly as a synonym for data deidentification. Data scrubbing refers to the removal of information from data records that is considered unwanted. This may include identifiers, private information, or any incriminating or otherwise objectionable language contained in data records, as well as any information deemed irrelevant to the purpose served by the record. See Deidentification.

Data versus datum The singular form of data is datum, but the word "datum" has virtually disappeared from the computer science literature. The word "data" has assumed both a singular and plural form. In its singular form, it is a collective noun that refers to a single aggregation of many data points. Hence, current usage would be "The data is enormous," rather than "These data are enormous."

Deidentification The process of removing all of the links in a data record that can connect the information in the record to an individual. This usually includes the record identifier, demographic information (eg, place of birth), personal information (eg, birthdate), biometrics (eg, fingerprints), and so on. The process of deidentification will vary based on the type of records examined. Deidentifying protocols exist wherein deidentificated records can be reidentified, when necessary. See Reidentification. See Data scrubbing.

Deidentification versus anonymization Anonymization is a process by which all the links between an individual and the individual's data record are irreversibly removed. The difference between anonymization and deidentification is that anonymization is irreversible. Because anonymization is irreversible, the opportunities for verifying the quality of data are limited. For example, if someone suspects that samples have been switched in a data set, thus putting the results of the study into doubt, an anonymized set of data would afford no opportunity to resolve the problem by reidentifying the original samples. See Reidentification.

Digest As used herein, "digest" is equivalent to a one-way hash algorithm. The word "digest" also refers to the output string produced by a one-way hash algorithm. See Checksum. See One-way hash. See HMAC.

Digital signature As it is used in the field of data privacy, a digital signature is an alphanumeric sequence that could only have been produced by a private key owned by one particular person. Operationally, a message digest (eg, a one-way hash value) is produced from the document that is to be signed. The person "signing" the document encrypts the message digest using his or her private key and submits the document and the encrypted message digest to the person who intends to verify that the document has been signed. This person decrypts the encrypted message digest with her public key (ie, the public key complement to the private key) to produce the original one-way hash value. Next, a one-way hash is performed on the received document. If the resulting one-way hash is the same as the decrypted one-way hash, then several statements hold true: The document received is the same document as the document that had been "signed". The signer of the document had access to the private key that complemented the public key that was used to decrypt the encrypted one-way hash. The assumption here is that the signer was the only individual with access to the private key. Digital signature protocols, in general, have a private method for encrypting a hash and a public method for verifying the signature. Such protocols operate under the assumption that only one person can encrypt the hash for the message and that the name of that person is known; hence, the protocol establishes a verified signature. It should be emphasized that a digital signature is quite different from a written signature; the latter usually indicates that the signer wrote the document or somehow attests to the veracity of the document. The digital signature merely indicates that the document was received from a particular person, contingent on the assumption that the private key was available only to that person. To understand how a digital signature protocol may be maliciously deployed, imagine the following scenario: I contact you and tell you that I am Elvis Presley and would like you to have a copy of my public key plus a file that I have encrypted using my private key. You receive the file and the public key, and you use the public key to decrypt the file. You conclude that the file was indeed sent by Elvis Presley. You read the decrypted file and learn that Elvis advises you to invest all your money in a company that manufactures concrete guitars; which, of course, you do, because Elvis knows guitars. The problem here is that the signature was valid, but the valid signature was not authentic. See Authentication.

Gedanken Gedanken, German for "thoughts" refers to conceptual exercises that clarify a scientific question. In general, gedanken problems are esoteric and not suited to experimental validation. Einstein was fond of using gedanken experiments to develop his breakthroughs in theoretical physics.

Generalization Generalization is the process of extending relationships from individual objects to classes of objects. For example, when Isaac Newton observed the physical laws that applied to apples falling to the ground, he found a way to relate the acceleration of an object to its mass and to the force of gravity. His apple-centric observations applied to all objects and could be used to predict the orbit of the moon around the earth or the orbit of the earth around the sun. Newton generalized from the specific to the universal. Similarly, Darwin's observations on barnacles could be generalized to yield the theory of evolution, thus explaining the development of all terrestrial organisms. Science would be of little value if observed relationships among objects could not be generalized to classes of objects. See Science.

HMAC Hashed Message Authentication Code. When a one-way hash is employed in an authentication protocol, it is often referred to as an HMAC. See One-way hash. See Message digest. See Checksum.

HTML HyperText Markup Language is an ASCII-based set of formatting instructions for web pages. HTML formatting instructions, known as tags, are embedded in the document and double-bracketed, indicating the start point and end points for instruction. Here is an example of an HTML tag instructing the web browser to display the word "Hello" in italics: <i>Hello</i>. All web browsers conforming to the HTML specification must contain software routines that recognize and implement the HTML instructions embedded within in web documents. In addition to formatting instructions, HTML also includes linkage instructions, in which the web browsers must retrieve and display a listed web page, or a web resource, such as an image. The protocol whereby web browsers, following HTML instructions, retrieve web pages from other Internet sites, is known as HTTP (HyperText Transfer Protocol).

Identification The process of providing a data object with an identifier, or the process of distinguishing one data object from all other data objects on the basis of its associated identifier. See Identifier.

Identifier A string that is associated with a particular thing (eg, person, document, transaction, data object), and not associated with any other thing.[23] Object identification usually involves permanently assigning a seemingly random sequence of numeric digits (0–9) and alphabet characters (a-z and A-Z) to a data object. A data object can be a specific piece of data (eg, a data record) or an abstraction, such as a class of objects or a number or a string or a variable. See Identification.

Immutability Permanent data that cannot be modified is said to be immutable. At first thought, it would seem that immutability is a ridiculous and impossible constraint. In the real world, mistakes are made, information changes, and the methods for describing information changes. This is all true, but the astute data manager knows how to accrue information into data objects without changing the pre-existing data. In practice, immutability is maintained by time-stamping all data and storing annotated data values with any and all subsequent time-stamped modifications. For a detailed explanation, see Section 5.6, "Timestamps, Signatures, and Event Identifiers."

Intellectual property Data, software, algorithms, and applications that are created by an entity capable of ownership (eg, humans, corporations, universities). The owner entity holds rights over the manner in which the intellectual property can be used and distributed. Protections for intellectual property may come in the form of copyrights, patents, and laws that apply to theft. Copyright applies to published information. Patents apply to novel processes and inventions. Certain types of intellectual property can only be protected by being secretive. For example, magic tricks cannot be copyrighted or patented; this is why magicians guard their intellectual property against theft. Intellectual property can be sold outright or used under a legal agreement (eg, license, contract, transfer agreement, royalty, usage fee, and so on). Intellectual property can also be shared freely, while retaining ownership (eg, open-source license, GNU license, FOSS license, Creative Commons license).

Introspection A method by which data objects can be interrogated to yield information about themselves (eg, properties, values, and class membership). Through introspection, the relationships among the data objects can be examined. Introspective methods are built into object-oriented languages. The data provided by introspection can be applied at run-time to modify a script's operation, a technique known as reflection. Specifically, any properties, methods, and encapsulated data of a data object can be used in the script to modify the script's run-time behavior. See Reflection.

Meaning In informatics, meaning is achieved when described data is bound to a unique identifier of a data object. "Claude Funston's height is 5 feet 11 inches," comes pretty close to being a meaningful statement. The statement contains data (5 feet 11 inches), and the data is described (height). The described data belongs to a unique object (Claude Funston). Ideally, the name "Claude Funston" should be provided with a unique identifier to distinguish one instance of Claude Funston from all the other persons who are named Claude Funston. The statement would also benefit from a formal system that ensures that the metadata makes sense (eg, What exactly is height, and does Claude Funston fall into a class of objects for which height is a property?) and that the data is appropriate (eg, Is 5 feet 11 inches an allowable measure of a person's height?). A statement with meaning does not need to be a true statement (eg, The height of Claude Funston was not 5 feet 11 inches when Claude Funston was an infant). See Semantics. See Triple. See RDF.

Message digest Within the context of this book, "message digest", "digest", "HMAC", and "one-way hash" are equivalent terms. See One-way hash. See HMAC.

Metadata The data that describes data. For example, a data element (also known as data point) may consist of the number "6". The metadata for the data may be the words "Height, in feet". A data element is useless without its metadata, and metadata is useless unless it adequately describes a data element. In XML, the metadata/data annotation comes in the form <metadata tag>data<end of metadata tag> and might look something like:

```
<weight_in_pounds>150</weight_in_pounds>
```

In spreadsheets, the data elements are the cells of the spreadsheet. The column headers are the metadata that describe the data values in the column's cells, and the row headers are the record numbers that uniquely identify each record (ie, each row of cells). See XML.

Namespace A namespace is the realm in which a metadata tag applies. The purpose of a namespace is to distinguish metadata tags that have the same name, but a different meaning. For example, within a single XML file, the metadata tag "date" may be used to signify a calendar date, or the fruit, or the social engagement. To avoid confusion, metadata terms are assigned a prefix that is associated with a web document that defines the term (ie, establishes the tag's namespace). In practical terms, a tag that can have different descriptive meanings in different contexts is provided with a prefix that links to a web document wherein the meaning of the tag, as it applies in the XML document, is specified. An example of namespace syntax is provided in Section 2.5.

National Patient Identifier Many countries employ a National Patient Identifier (NPI) system. In these cases, when a citizen receives treatment at any medical facility in the country, the transaction is recorded under the same permanent and unique identifier. Doing so enables the data collected on individuals from multiple hospitals to be merged. Hence, physicians can retrieve patient data that was collected anywhere in the nation. In countries with NPIs, data scientists have access to complete patient records and can perform health care studies that would be impossible to perform in countries that lack NPI systems. In the U.S., where a system of NPIs has not been adopted, there is a perception that such a system would constitute an invasion of privacy and would harm citizens. See Reconciliation.

Notation 3 Also called n3. A syntax for expressing assertions as triples (unique subject + metadata + data). Notation 3 expresses the same information as the more formal RDF syntax, but n3 is easier for humans to read.[24] RDF and n3 are interconvertible and either one can be parsed and equivalently tokenized (ie, broken into elements that can be re-organized in a different format, such as a database record). See RDF. See Triple.

One-way hash A one-way hash is an algorithm that transforms one string into another string (a fixed-length sequence of seemingly random characters) in such a way that the original string cannot be calculated by operations on the one-way hash value (ie, the calculation is one-way only). One-way hash values can be calculated for any string, including a person's name, a document, or an image. For any given input string, the resultant one-way hash will always be the same. If a single byte of the input string is modified, the resulting one-way hash will be changed and will have a totally different sequence than the one-way hash sequence calculated for the unmodified string. Most modern programming languages have several methods for generating one-way hash values. Here is a short Ruby script that generates a one-way hash value for a file:

```
#!/usr/local/bin/ruby
require 'digest/md5'
file_contents = File.new("simplify.txt").binmode
hash_string = Digest::MD5.base64digest(file_contents.read)
puts hash_string
exit
```

Here is the one-way hash value for the file "simplify.txt" using the md5 algorithm:

```
OCfZez7L1A6WFcT+oxMh+g==
```

If we copy our example file to another file with an alternate filename, the md5 algorithm will generate the same hash value. Likewise, if we generate a one-way hash value, using the md5 algorithm implemented in some other language, such as Python or Perl, the outputs will be identical. One-way hash values can be designed to produce long fixed-length output strings (eg, 256 bits in length). When the output of a one-way hash algorithm is very long, the chance of a hash string collision (ie, the occurrence of two different input strings generating the same one-way hash output value) is negligible. Clever variations on one-way hash algorithms have been repurposed as identifier systems.[25–28] Examples of one-way hash implementations in Perl and Python are found in Open Source Tools for this chapter, Encryption. See HMAC. See Message digest. See Checksum.

Privacy versus confidentiality The concepts of confidentiality and of privacy are often confused, and it is useful to clarify their separate meanings. Confidentiality is the process of keeping a secret with which you have been entrusted. You break confidentiality if you reveal the secret to another person. You violate privacy when you use the secret to annoy the person whose confidential information was acquired. If you give me your unlisted telephone number in confidence, then I am expected to protect this confidentiality by never revealing the number to other persons. I may also be expected to protect your privacy by never using the telephone number to call you at all hours of the day and night. In this case, the same information object (unlisted telephone number) is encumbered by separable confidentiality and privacy obligations.

RDF Resource Description Framework (RDF) is a syntax in XML notation that formally expresses assertions as triples. The RDF triple consists of a uniquely identified subject plus a metadata descriptor for the data plus a data element. Triples are necessary and sufficient to create statements that convey meaning. Triples can be aggregated with other triples from the same data set or from other data sets, so long as each triple pertains to a unique subject that is identified equivalently through the data sets. Enormous data sets of RDF triples can be merged or functionally integrated with other massive or complex data resources. For a detailed discussion see Open Source Tools for Chapter 6, "Syntax for triples." See Notation 3. See Semantics. See Triple. See XML.

RDF Schema Resource Description Framework Schema (RDFS). A document containing a list of classes, their definitions, and the names of the parent class(es) for each class. In an RDF Schema, the list of classes is typically followed by a list of properties that apply to one or more classes in the Schema. To be useful, RDF Schemas are posted on the Internet, as a web page, with a unique web address. Anyone can incorporate the classes and properties of a public RDF Schema into their own RDF documents (public or private) by linking named classes and properties, in their RDF document, to the web address of the RDF Schema where the classes and properties are defined. See Namespace. See RDFS.

RDF ontology A term that, in common usage, refers to the class definitions and relationships included in an RDF Schema document. The classes in an RDF Schema need not comprise a complete ontology. In fact, a complete ontology could be distributed over multiple RDF Schema documents. See RDF Schema.

RDFS Same as RDF Schema.

Randomness Various tests of randomness are available.[29] One of the easiest to implement takes advantage of the property that random strings are uncompressible. If you can show that if a character string, a series of numbers, or a column of data cannot be compressed by gzip, then it is pretty safe to conclude that the data is randomly distributed and without any informational value.

Reconciliation Usually refers to identifiers, and involves verifying when an object that is assigned a particular identifier in one information system has been provided the same identifier in some other system. For example, if I am assigned identifier 967bc9e7-fea0-4b09-92e7-d9327c405d78 in a legacy record system, I should like to be assigned the same identifier in the new record system. If that were the case, my records in both systems could be combined. If I am assigned an identifier in one system that is different from my assigned identifier in another system, then the two identifiers must be reconciled to determine that they both refer to the same unique data object (ie, me). This may involve creating a link between the two identifiers or a new triple that establishes the equivalence of the two identifiers. Despite claims to the contrary, there is no possible way by which information systems with poor identifier systems can be sensibly reconciled. Consider this example: A hospital has two separate registry systems, one for dermatology cases and another for psychiatry cases. The hospital would like to merge records from the two services. Because of sloppy identifier practices, a sample patient has been registered 10 times in the dermatology system and 6 times in the psychiatry system, each time with different addresses, Social Security numbers, birthdates, and spellings of the patient's name. A reconciliation algorithm is applied, and one of the identifiers from the dermatology service is matched positively against one of the records from the psychiatry service. Performance studies on the algorithm indicate that the merged records have a 99.8% chance of belonging to the same patient. So what? Though the two merged identifiers correctly point to the same patient, there are 14 (9+5) residual identifiers for the patient still unmatched. The patient's merged record will not contain his complete clinical history. Furthermore, in this hypothetical instance, analyses of patient population data will mistakenly attribute one patient's clinical findings to as many as 15 different patients, and the set of 15 records in the corrupted de-identified dataset may contain mixed-in information from an indeterminate number of additional patients! If the preceding analysis seems harsh, consider these words from the Health care Information and Management Systems Society, "A local system with a poorly maintained or 'dirty' master person index (MPI) will only proliferate and contaminate all of the other systems to which it links."[30] See Social Security Number.

Reflection A programming technique wherein a computer program will modify itself at run-time based on information it acquires through introspection. For example, a computer program may iterate over a collection of data objects, examining the self-descriptive information for each object in the collection (ie, object introspection). If the information indicates that the data object belongs to a particular class of objects, then the program may call a method appropriate for the class. The program executes in a manner determined by descriptive information obtained during run-time, metaphorically reflecting upon the purpose of its computational task. See Introspection.

Registrars and Human Authentication The experiences of registrars in U.S. hospitals serve as cautionary instruction. Hospital registrars commit a disastrous mistake when they assume that all patients wish to comply with the registration process. A patient may be highly motivated to provide false information to a registrar, acquire several different registration identifiers, seek a false registration under another person's identity (ie, commit fraud), or forego the registration process entirely. In addition, it is a mistake to believe that honest patients are able to fully comply with the registration process. Language barriers, cultural barriers, poor memory, poor spelling, and a host of errors and misunderstandings can lead to duplicative or otherwise erroneous identifiers. It is the job of the registrar to follow hospital policies that overcome these difficulties. Registration should be conducted by a trained registrar who is well-versed in the registration policies established by the institution. Registrars may require patients to provide a full legal name, any prior held names (eg maiden name), date of birth, and a government-issue photo ID card (eg, driver's license or photo ID card issued by the Department of Motor Vehicles). To be thorough, registration should require a biometric identifier (eg, fingerprints, retina scan, iris scan, voice recording, and/or photograph). If you accept the premise that hospitals have the responsibility of knowing who it is that they are treating, then obtaining a sample of DNA from every patient at the time of registration is reasonable. The DNA can be used to create a unique patient profile from a chosen set of informative loci, a procedure used by the CODIS system developed for law enforcement agencies. The registrar should document any distinguishing and permanent physical features that are plainly visible (eg, scars, eye color, colobomas, or tattoos). Neonatal and pediatric identifiers pose a special set of problems for registrars. When an individual born in a hospital and provided with an identifier returns as an adult, he or she should be assigned the same identifier that was issued in the remote past. Every patient who comes for registration should be matched against a database of biometric data that does not change from birth to death (eg, fingerprints, DNA). See Social Security Number.

Reidentification A term casually applied to any instance whereby information can be linked to a specific person after the links between the information and the person associated with the information have been removed. Used this way, the term reidentification connotes an insufficient deidentification process. In the health care industry, the term "reidentification" means something else entirely. In the U.S., regulations define "reidentification" under the "Standards for Privacy of Individually Identifiable Health Information."[8] Therein, reidentification is a legally sanctioned process whereby deidentified records can be linked back to their human subjects, under circumstances deemed legitimate and compelling, by a privacy board. Reidentification is typically accomplished via the use of a confidential list of links between human subject names and deidentified records held by a trusted party. In the health care realm, when a human subject is identified through fraud, trickery, or through the deliberate use of computational methods to break the confidentiality of insufficiently deidentified records (ie, hacking), the term "reidentification" would not apply.[4]

Ruby gem In Ruby, gems are external modules available for download from an Internet server. The Ruby gem installation module comes bundled in Ruby distribution packages. Gem installations are simple, usually consisting of commands in the form, "gem install name_of_gem" invoked at the system prompt. After a gem has been installed, scripts access the gem with a "require" statement, equivalent to an "import" statement in Python or the "use" statement in Perl.

Science Of course, there are many different definitions of science, and inquisitive students should be encouraged to find a conceptualization of science that suits their own intellectual development. For me, science is all about finding general relationships among objects. In the so-called physical sciences, the most important relationships are expressed as mathematical equations (eg, the relationship between force, mass, and acceleration; the relationship between voltage, current and resistance). In the so-called natural sciences, relationships are often expressed through classifications (eg, the classification of living organisms). Scientific advancement is the discovery of new relationships or the discovery of a generalization that applies to objects hitherto confined within disparate scientific realms (eg, evolutionary theory arising from observations of organisms and geologic strata). Engineering would be the area of science wherein scientific relationships are exploited to build new technology. See Generalization.

Semantics The study of meaning (Greek root, semantikos, significant meaning). In the context of data science, semantics is the technique of creating meaningful assertions about data objects. A meaningful assertion, as used here, is a triple consisting of an identified data object, a data value, and a descriptor for the data value. In practical terms, semantics involves making assertions about data objects (ie, making triples), combining assertions about data objects (ie, merging triples), and assigning data objects to classes, therefore relating triples to other triples. As a word of warning, few informaticians would define semantics in these terms, but most definitions for semantics are functionally equivalent to the definition offered here. Most language is unstructured and meaningless. Consider the assertion: Sam is tired. This is an adequately structured sentence, but what is its meaning? There are a lot of people named Sam. Which Sam is being referred to in this sentence? What does it mean to say that Sam is tired? Is "tiredness" a constitutive property of Sam, or does it only apply to specific moments? If so, for what moment in time is the assertion "Sam is tired" actually true? To a computer, meaning comes from assertions that have a specific, identified subject associated with some sensible piece of fully described data (metadata coupled with the data it describes). See Triple. See RDF.

Social Security Number The common strategy in the U.S. of employing Social Security numbers as identifiers is often counterproductive, owing to entry error, mistaken memory, or the intention to deceive. Efforts to reduce errors by requiring individuals to produce their original Social Security cards puts an unreasonable burden on honest individuals, who rarely carry their cards, and provides an advantage to dishonest individuals, who can easily forge Social Security cards. Institutions that compel individuals to provide a Social Security number have dubious legal standing. The Social Security number was originally intended as a device for validating a person's standing in the Social Security system. More recently, the purpose of the Social Security number has been expanded to track taxable transactions (ie, bank accounts, salaries). Other uses of the Social Security number are not protected by law. The Social Security Act (Section 208 of Title 42 U.S. Code 408) prohibits most entities from compelling anyone to divulge his/her Social Security number. Legislation or judicial action may one day stop institutions from compelling individuals to divulge their Social Security numbers as a condition for providing services. Prudent and forward-thinking institutions will limit their reliance on Social Security numbers as personal identifiers. See Registrars and human authentication.

Symmetric key A key (ie, a password) that can be used to encrypt and decrypt the same file. AES is an encryption/decryption algorithm that employs a symmetric key. See AES.

Timestamp Many data objects are temporal events and all temporal events must be given a timestamp indicating the time that the event occurred, using a standard measurement for time. The timestamp must be accurate, persistent, and immutable. The Unix epoch time (equivalent to the Posix epoch time) is available to most operating systems and consists of the number of seconds that have elapsed since January 1, 1970 at midnight, Greenwich Mean Time. The Unix epoch time can easily be converted into any other standard representation of time. The duration of any event can be calculated by subtracting the beginning time from the ending time. Because the timing of events can be maliciously altered, scrupulous data managers may choose to employ a trusted timestamp protocol by which a timestamp can be verified.

Triple In computer semantics, a triple is an identified data object associated with a data element and the description of the data element. In computer science literature, the syntax for the triple is commonly described as "subject, predicate, object," wherein the subject is an identifier, the predicate is the description of the object, and the object is the data. The definition of triple, using grammatic terms, can be off-putting to the data scientist, who may think in terms of spreadsheet entries: a key that identifies the line record, a column header containing the metadata description of the data, and a cell that contains the data. In this book, the three components of a triple are described as: (1) the identifier for the data object, (2) the metadata that describes the data, and (3) the data itself. In theory, all data sets, databases, and spreadsheets can be constructed or deconstructed as collections of triples. See Introspection. See Data object. See Semantics. See RDF. See Meaning.

Triplestore A list or database composed entirely of triples (statements consisting of an item identifier plus the metadata describing the item plus an item of data). The triples in a triple store need not be saved in any particular order, and any triplestore can be merged with any other triplestore; the basic semantic meaning of the contained triples is unaffected. See Triple.

URL Unique Resource Locator. The web is a collection of resources, each having a unique address, the URL. When you click on a link that specifies a URL, your browser fetches the page located at the unique location specified in the URL name. If the web were designed otherwise (ie, if several different web pages had the same web address, or if one web address were located at several different locations), then the web could not function with any reliability.

URN Unique Resource Name. Whereas the URL identifies objects based on the object's unique location in the web, the URN is a system of object identifiers that are location-independent. In the URN system, data objects are provided with identifiers, and the identifiers are registered with, and subsumed by, the URN. For example:

```
urn:isbn-13:9780128028827
```

Refers to the unique book *Repurposing Legacy Data: Innovative Case Studies* by Jules Berman

```
urn:uuid:e29d0078-f7f6-11e4-8ef1-e808e19e18e5
```

Refers to a data object tied to the UUID identifier e29d0078-f7f6-11e4-8ef1-e808e19e18e5. In theory, if every data object were assigned a registered URN and if the system were implemented as intended, the entire universe of information could be tracked and searched. See URL. See UUID.

UUID (Universally Unique Identifier) is a protocol for assigning unique identifiers to data objects without using a central registry. UUIDs were originally used in the Apollo Network Computing System.[2] Most modern programming languages have modules for generating UUIDs. See Identifier.

Uniqueness Uniqueness is the quality of being demonstrably different from every other thing in the universe. For data scientists, uniqueness is achieved when a data object is bound to a unique identifier (ie, a string of alphanumeric characters) that has not and will never be assigned to any other object. Interestingly, uniqueness can apply to classes of objects that happen to contain non-unique members and to two or more indistinguishable objects, if they are assigned unique identifiers (eg, unique product numbers stamped into identical auto parts).

Watermarking Watermarking, a type of steganography, is a method for insinuating the name of the owner or creator of a digital object within the object for the purpose of asserting intellectual property. See Intellectual property.

XML Acronym for Extensible Markup Language, a syntax for marking data values with descriptors (ie, metadata). The descriptors are commonly known as tags. In XML, every data value is enclosed by a start tag containing the descriptor and indicating that a value will follow and an end tag containing the same descriptor and indicating that a value preceded the tag. For example: <name>Conrad Nervig</name>. The enclosing angle brackets, "<>", and the end-tag marker, "/", are hallmarks of HTML and XML markup. This simple but powerful relationship between metadata and data allows us to employ metadata/data pairs as though each were a miniature database. The semantic value of XML becomes apparent when we bind a metadata/data pair to a unique object, forming a so-called triple. See Triple. See Meaning. See Semantics. See HTML.

REFERENCES

1. Berman JJ. *Repurposing legacy data: innovative case studies.* Burlington, MA: Elsevier, Morgan Kaufmann imprint; 2015.
2. Leach P, Mealling M, Salz R. A universally unique identifier (UUID) URN namespace. Network Working Group, Request for Comment 4122, Standards Track. Available from: http://www.ietf.org/rfc/rfc4122.txt [accessed 01.01.15].
3. Mealling M. RFC 3061. A URN namespace of object identifiers. Network Working Group, 2001. Available from: https://www.ietf.org/rfc/rfc3061.txt [accessed 01.01.15].
4. Berman JJ. *Principles of big data: preparing, sharing, and analyzing complex information.* Burlington, MA: Morgan Kaufmann; 2013.
5. Berman JJ. *Methods in medical informatics: fundamentals of healthcare programming in Perl, Python, and Ruby.* Boca Raton: Chapman and Hall; 2010.
6. Kuzmak P, Casertano A, Carozza D, Dayhoff R, Campbell K. Solving the problem of duplicate medical device unique identifiers high confidence medical device software and systems (HCMDSS). In: Workshop, Philadelphia, PA, June 2–3; 2005. Available from: http://www.cis.upenn.edu/hcmdss/Papers/submissions/ [accessed 26.08.12].
7. Committee on A Framework for Developing a New Taxonomy of Disease, Board on Life Sciences, Division on Earth and Life Studies, National Research Council of the National Academies. *Toward precision medicine: building a knowledge network for biomedical research and a new taxonomy of disease.* Washington, DC: The National Academies Press; 2011.
8. Department of Health and Human Services. 45 CFR (Code of Federal Regulations), Parts 160 through 164. Standards for privacy of individually identifiable health information (final rule). *Fed Regist* 2000;**65** (250):82461–510.

9. Berman JJ. Concept-match medical data scrubbing: how pathology datasets can be used in research. *Arch Pathol Lab Med* 2003;**127**:680–6.

10. Berman JJ. Comparing de-identification methods. Available from: http://www.biomedcentral.com/1472-6947/6/12/comments/comments.htm; 2006 [accessed 01.01.15].

11. Berman JJ. *Ruby programming for medicine and biology.* Sudbury, MA: Jones and Bartlett; 2008.

12. Berman JJ. Doublet method for very fast autocoding. *BMC Med Inform Decis Mak* 2004;**4**:16.

13. Rothstein MA. Is deidentification sufficient to protect health privacy in research? *Am J Bioeth* 2010;**10**:3–11.

14. Chen L, Shern JF, Wei JS, Yohe ME, Song YK, Hurd L, et al. Clonality and evolutionary history of rhabdomyosarcoma. *PLoS Genet* 2015;**11**.

15. Frieden T. VA will pay $20 million to settle lawsuit over stolen laptop's data. *CNN* 2009.

16. Powers T. *Computer security; the whiz kid vs. the old boys.* The New York Times; 2000.

17. Schneier B. A plea for simplicity: you can't secure what you don't understand. Information Security. Available from: http://www.schneier.com/essay-018.html; 1999 [accessed 01.07.15].

18. Reed DP. Naming and synchronization in a decentralized computer system. Doctoral Thesis, MIT; 1978.

19. Klyne G. Newman C. Date and time on the Internet: timestamps. Network Working Group Request for Comments RFC:3339. Available from: http://tools.ietf.org/html/rfc3339 [accessed 15.09.15].

20. Trithemius J. Steganographia (Secret Writing), by Johannes Trithemius. 1500.

21. Berman JJ. *Biomedical informatics.* Sudbury, MA: Jones and Bartlett; 2007.

22. A review of the FBI's handling of the Brandon Mayfield case. U.S. Department of Justice, Office of the Inspector General, Oversight and Review Division; 2006.

23. Paskin N. Identifier interoperability: a report on two recent ISO activities. *D-Lib Mag* 2006;**12**:1–23.

24. Berman JJ, Moore GW. Implementing an RDF Schema for pathology images 2007. Available from: http://www.julesberman.info/spec2img.htm [accessed 01.01.15].

25. Faldum A, Pommerening K. An optimal code for patient identifiers. *Comput Methods Programs Biomed* 2005;**79**:81–8.

26. Rivest R. Request for Comments: 1321, The MD5 Message-Digest Algorithm. Network Working Group. https://www.ietf.org/rfc/rfc1321.txt [accessed 01.01.15].

27. Bouzelat H, Quantin C, Dusserre L. Extraction and anonymity protocol of medical file. *Proc AMIA Annu Fall Symp* 1996;323–7.

28. Quantin CH, Bouzelat FA, Allaert AM, Benhamiche J, Faivre J, Dusserre L. Automatic record hash coding and linkage for epidemiological followup data confidentiality. *Methods Inf Med* 1998;**37**:271–7.

29. Marsaglia G, Tsang WW. Some difficult-to-pass tests of randomness. *J Stat Softw* 2002;**7**:1–8. Available from: http://www.jstatsoft.org/v07/i03/paper [accessed 25.09.12].

30. Patient Identity Integrity. A white paper by the HIMSS Patient Identity Integrity Work Group. Available from: http://www.himss.org/content/files/PrivacySecurity/PIIWhitePaper.pdf; 2009 [accessed 19.09.12].

GIVING MEANING TO DATA

6.1 MEANING AND TRIPLES

Increased complexity needs simplified design

-Harold Jarche[1]

Data, by itself, has no meaning. It is the job of the data scientist to assign meaning to data, and this is done with data objects, triples, and classifications (see Glossary item, Data object). Our most familiar data constructions (eg, spreadsheets, relational databases, flat-file records) convey meaning through triples and data objects; we just don't perceive them as such (see Glossary items, Spreadsheet, Database, Flat-file). The purpose of this section is to define "meaning," "data object," and "triple" and to show how all well-designed data can be reconstructed as collections of triples. Later sections will explain how triples are used to integrate and aggregate data and to express the relationships among data objects.

The three conditions for a meaningful assertion are[2]:

1. There is a specific data object about which the statement is made.
2. There is data that pertains to the specified object.
3. There is metadata that describes the data (that pertains to the specific object).

Simply put, assertions have meaning whenever a pair of metadata and data (the descriptor for the data and the data itself) is assigned to a specific object. In the informatics field, assertions come in the form of so-called triples, consisting of the object, then the metadata, and then the data.

Here are some examples of triples, as they might occur in a medical dataset:

```
"Jules Berman" "blood glucose level" "85"
"Mary Smith" "blood glucose level" "90"
"Samuel Rice" "blood glucose level" "200"
"Jules Berman" "eye color" "brown"
"Mary Smith" "eye color" "blue"
"Samuel Rice" "eye color" "green"
```

Here are a few triples, as the might occur in a haberdasher's dataset

```
"Juan Valdez" "hat size" "8"
"Jules Berman" "hat size" "9"
"Homer Simpson" "hat size" "9"
"Homer Simpson" "hat_type" "bowler"
```

We can combine the triples from a medical dataset and a habderdasher's data set that apply to a common object:

```
"Jules Berman" "blood glucose level" "85"
"Jules Berman" "eye color" "brown"
"Jules Berman" "hat size" "9"
```

Triples can port their meaning between different databases because they bind described data to an object. The portability of triples permits us to achieve data integration of heterogeneous types of data, and facilitates the design of software agents that conduct queries over multiple databases. Data integration involves merging related data objects, across diverse data sets. As it happens, if data supports introspection and data is organized as meaningful assertions (ie, as identified triples), then data integration is implicit (ie, an intrinsic property of the data) (see Glossary item, Introspection). In essence, data integration is awarded to data scientists who apply data simplification techniques.

In the previous examples, our sample identifiers were names of people; specifically the given name followed by a space followed by the surname. Names make poor identifiers because they are not unique. There is no process that ensures that no two individuals have the same name. As discussed in Section 5.1, modern informatics systems use unique alphanumeric character sequences to identify people and other data objects.

The subject, or data object's unique identifier and the subject's class (ie, the name of the class to which the subject or data object belongs) are keys to which of all the information about the subject can be collected. If you know the identifier for a data object, you can collect all of the information associated with the object, regardless of its location in the data resource. If other data resources use the same identifier for the data object, you can integrate all of the data associated with the data object, regardless of its location in external resources. Furthermore, if you know the class that holds a data object, you can infer that the data object has all of the properties of its class, along with all the properties of its ancestral classes. Consider the following example.[3]

Triples in resource #1

```
75898039563441   name     G. Willikers
75898039563441   gender   male
```

Triples in resource #2

```
75898039563441   age                35
75898039563441   is_a_class_member  cowboy
94590439540089   name               Hopalong Tagalong
94590439540089   is_a_class_member  cowboy
```

Merged triples from resource #1 and #2

```
75898039563441   name              G. Willikers
75898039563441   gender            male
75898039563441   is_a_class_member cowboy
75898039563441   age               35
94590439540089   name              Hopalong Tagalong
94590439540089   is_a_class_member cowboy
```

The merge of two triplestore resources combines data related to identifier 75898039563441 from both resources (see Glossary item, Triplestore). We now know a few things about this data object that we did not know before the merge. The merge tells us that the two data objects identified as 75898039563441 and 94590439540089 are both members of class cowboy. We now have two instance members from the same class, and this gives us information related to the types of instances contained in the class, and their properties. **The consistent application of standard methods for object identification and for class assignments enhances our ability to understand our data** (see Glossary items, Identification, Reconciliation).

The concept of namespaces was introduced in Section 2.5, "Annotation and the Simple Science of Metadata." The value of namespaces becomes very apparent when merging triplestores. Using namespaces, a single data object residing in several triplestores can be associated with assertions (ie, object-metadata-data triples) that include descriptors of the same name, without losing the intended sense of the assertions. Here is another example wherein two resources are merged:

Triples in resource #1

```
29847575938125   calendar:date   February 4, 1986
83654560466294   calendar:date   June 16, 1904
```

Triples in resource #2

```
57839109275632   social:date   Jack and Jill
83654560466294   social:date   Pyramus and Thisbe
```

Merged triples from resource #1 and #2

```
29847575938125   calendar:date   February 4, 1986
57839109275632   social:date     Jack and Jill
83654560466294   social:date     Pyramus and Thisbe
83654560466294   calendar:date   June 16, 1904
```

There you have it. The object identified as 83654560466294 is associated with a "date" metadata tag in both resources. When the resources are merged, the unambiguous meaning of the metadata tag is conveyed through the appended namespaces (ie, social: and calendar:)

Triples are the basic commodities of information science. Every triple represents a meaningful assertion, and collections of triples can be automatically integrated with other triples. As such, all the triples that share the same identifier can be collected to yield all the available information that pertains to the unique object. Furthermore, all the triples that pertain to all the members of a class of objects can be combined to provide information about the class, and to find relationships among different classes of objects. Without elaborating, the ability to find relationships among classes of objects is the chief goal of all scientific research (see Glossary items, Science, Generalization).

Triples are the basic informational unit employed by RDF (Resource Description Framework), and RDF is the syntax of the so-called semantic web.[4,5] It will come as no surprise that numerous databases have been designed to create, store, and retrieve triples. These databases are usually referred to as triplestores, or NoSQL databases, and they all operate by assigning identifiers (ie, unique record designators) to metadata/data pairs. Such databases can hold billions or trillions of key/value pairs or triples.

At the current time, software development for triplestore databases is in a state of volatility. Triplestore databases are dropping in and out of existence, changing their names, being incorporated into other systems, or being redesigned from the ground up. At the risk of showing my own personal bias, as an unapologetic Mumps fan, I would suggest that readers may want to investigate the value of using native Mumps as a triplestore database. Mumps, also known as the M programming language, is one of a small handful of ANSI-standard (American National Standard Institute) languages. It was developed in the 1960s and is still in use, primarily in hospital information systems and large production facilities. Versions of Mumps are available as open source, free distributions.[6,7] The Mumps installation process can be challenging for those who are unfamiliar with the Mumps environment. Stalwarts may find that Mumps has native features that render it suitable for storing triples and exploring their relationships.[8]

6.2 DRIVING DOWN COMPLEXITY WITH CLASSIFICATIONS

> ...individuals do not belong in the same taxon because they are similar, but they are similar because they belong to the same taxon.
> **-Simpson GG. Principles of Animal Taxonomy, Columbia University Press, New York, 1961.**

Classifications are collections of objects grouped into classes, designed to conform to a few restrictive rules, namely:

Rule 1 Each object instance belongs to one and only one class (see Glossary item, Instance).

Rule 2 Each class has one and only one parent class. Each class may be the parent class for any number (ie, zero or more) of child classes (see Glossary items, Parent class, Child class, Superclass, Subclass).

Rule 3 Instances and classes are nontransitive (ie, instances cannot change their class; classes cannot change their ancestors or descendants).

Rule 4 The properties of the parent class are inherited by the child class. By inductive inference, each class inherits all of the class properties of every class in its ancestral lineage.

The rules for constructing classifications seem obvious and simplistic. Surprisingly, the task of building a logical and self-consistent classification is extremely difficult. Most classifications are rife with logical inconsistencies and paradoxes. Let's look at a few examples.

In 1975, while touring the Bethesda, Maryland campus of the National Institutes of Health, I was informed that their Building 10 was the largest all-brick building in the world, providing a home to over 7 million bricks. Soon thereafter, an ambitious construction project was undertaken to greatly expand the size of Building 10. When the work was finished, Building 10 was no longer the largest all-brick building in the world. What happened? The builders used material other than brick, and Building 10 lost its classification as an all-brick building.

This poses something of a paradox; objects in a classification are not permitted to move about from one class to another. An object assigned to a class must stay in its class (ie, the nontransitive property of classifications). Apparent paradoxes that plague any formal conceptualization of classifications are not difficult to find. Let's look at a few more examples.

Consider the geometric class of ellipses; planar objects in which the sum of the distances to two focal points is constant. Class Circle is a child of Class Ellipse, for which the two focal points of instance members occupy the same position, in the center, producing a radius of constant size. Imagine that Class Ellipse is provided with a class method called "stretch," in which the foci are moved farther apart, thus producing flatter objects. When the parent class "stretch" method is applied to members of the Class Circle (as per Rule 4), the circle stops being a circle and becomes an ordinary ellipse. Hence the inherited "stretch" method forces members of Class Circle to transition out of their assigned class, violating Rule 3.

Let's look at the "Bag" class of objects. A "Bag" is a collection of objects, and the Class Bag is included in most object-oriented programming languages. A "Set" is also a collection of objects (ie, a subclass of Bag), with the special feature that duplicate instances are not permitted. For example, if Kansas is a member of the set of United States, then you cannot add a second state named "Kansas" to the set. If Class Bag were to have an "increment" method, that added "1" to the total count of objects in the bag, whenever an object is added to Class Bag, then the "increment" method would be inherited by all of the subclasses of Class Bag, including Class Set. But Class Set cannot increase in size when duplicate items are added. Hence, inheritance creates a paradox in the Class Set (see Glossary item, Inheritance).

SUMO is an upper-class ontology, designed to include general classes of objects that other ontologies can refer to as their superclasses (see Glossary item, SUMO, Superclass). We will learn about ontologies in Section 6.3. For now, it suffices to note that ontologies are just classifications that ignore the second restriction. That is to say, in an ontology, a class may have more than one parent class. Hence, all classifications are ontologies, but not all ontologies are classifications. SUMO permits multiple class inheritance. For example, in SUMO, the class of humans is assigned to two different parent classes: Class Hominid and Class CognitiveAgent. "HumanCorpse", another SUMO class, is defined in SUMO as "A dead thing which was formerly a Human." Human corpse is a subclass of Class OrganicObject; not of Class Human. This means that a human, once it ceases to live, transits to a class that is not directly related to the class of humans. Basically, a member of Class Human, in the SUMO ontology, will change its class and its ancestral lineage, at different timestamped moments.

One last dalliance. Consider these two classes from the SUMO ontology, both of which happen to be subclasses of Class Substance.

Subclass NaturalSubstance
Subclass SyntheticSubstance

It would seem that these two subclasses are mutually exclusive. However, diamonds occur naturally, and diamonds can be synthesized. Hence, diamond belongs to Subclass NaturalSubstance and to Subclass SyntheticSubstance. The ontology creates two mutually exclusive classes that contain some of the same objects; and this is a problem. We cannot create sensible inference rules for objects that occupy mutually exclusive classes.

How does a data scientist deal with class objects that disappear from their assigned class and reappear elsewhere? In the examples discussed here, we saw the following:

1. Building 10 at NIH was defined as the largest all-brick building in the world. Strictly speaking, Building 10 was a structure, and it had a certain weight and dimensions, and it was constructed of brick. "Brick" is an attribute or property of buildings, and properties cannot form the basis of a class of building, if they are not a constant feature shared by all members of the class (ie, some buildings have bricks; others do not). Had we not conceptualized an "all-brick" class of building, we would have avoided any confusion. We will see later in this chapter (Section 6.5, "Properties That Cross Multiple Classes") how to distinguish properties from classes.

2. Class Circle qualified as a member of Class Ellipse, because a circle can be imagined as an ellipse whose two focal points happen to occupy the same location. Had we defined Class Ellipse to specify that class members must have two separate focal points, we could have excluded circles from class Ellipse. Hence, we could have safely included the stretch method in Class Ellipse without creating a paradox.

3. Class Set was made a subset of Class Bag, but the increment method of class Bag could not apply to Class Set. We created Class Set without taking into account the basic properties of Class Bag, which must apply to all its subclasses. Perhaps it would have been better if Class Set and Class Bag were created as children of Class Collection; each with its own set of properties.

4. Class HumanCorpse was not created as a subclass of Class Human. This was a mistake, as all humans will eventually die. If we were to create two classes, one called Class Living Human and one called Class Deceased Human, we would certainly cover all possible human states of being, but we would be creating a situation where members of a class are forced to transition out of their class and into another (violating Rule 3). The solution, in this case, is simple. Life and death are properties of organisms, and all organisms can and will have both properties, but never at the same time. Assign organisms the properties of life and of death, and stop there.

5. At first glance, the concepts "NaturalSubstance" and "SyntheticSubstance" would appear to be subclasses of "Substance." Are they really? Would it not be better to think that being "natural" or being "synthetic" are just properties of substances; not types of substances. If we agree that diamonds are a member of class substance, we can say that any specific diamond may have occurred naturally or through synthesis. We can eliminate two subclasses (ie, "NaturalSubstance" and "SyntheticSubstance") and replace them with two properties of class "Substance": synthetic and natural. By assigning properties to a class of objects, we simplify the ontology (by reducing the number of subclasses), and we eliminate problems created when a class member belongs to two mutually exclusive subclasses. We will discuss the role of properties in classifications in Section 6.5.

When using classifications, it is important to distinguish a classification system from an identification system. An identification system puts a data object into its correct slot within an existing classification. In the realm of medicine, when a doctor renders a diagnosis on a patient's diseases, she is not classifying the disease; she is finding the correct slot within the preexisting classification of diseases that holds her patient's diagnosis.[3]

When creating new classes, it is important to distinguish two important concepts: object relationships and object similarities. Relationships are the fundamental properties of an object that account for the object's behavior and interactions with other objects. Mathematical equations establish relationships among the variables of the equation. For example, mass is related to force by its velocity. An object is a member of a particular class if it has a relationship to all of the other members of the class (eg, all rodents have gnawing teeth; all eukaryotic organisms have nuclei). Similarities are features or properties that two objects have in common. Related objects tend to be similar to one another, but these similarities occur as the consequence of their relationships; not vice versa. For example, you are related to your father, and you probably have many similarities to your father. The reason that you share similarities to your father is that you are related to him; you are not related to your father because you are similar to him.

Here is a specific example that demonstrates the difference between a similarity and a relationship. You look up at the clouds, and you begin to see the shape of a lion. The cloud has a tail, like a lion's tale, and a fluffy head, like a lion's mane. With a little imagination, the mouth of the lion seems to roar down from the sky. You have succeeded in finding similarities between the cloud and a lion. If you look at a cloud and you imagine a tea kettle producing a head of steam, and you recognize that the physical forces that create a cloud and the physical forces that produced steam from a heated kettle are the same, then you have found a relationship. Without science-based relationships, reality makes no sense.[9]

Currently, data scientists have at their disposal a variety of mathematical algorithms that cluster objects by similarity (see Glossary items, K-nearest neighbor algorithm, Predictive analytics, Support vector machine, SVM, Neural network, Normalized compression distance). Such algorithms are referred to as classifiers; an inaccurate and misleading name. These algorithms can take a data set consisting of data objects, and their features (ie, the data that describes the objects), and produce a hierarchical distribution of data clusters, simulating a complete classification. Such algorithms are easily fooled by data objects that share highly specific or specialized features. In the case of the classification of living organisms, two unrelated species may independently acquire identical or similar traits through adaptation; not through inheritance from a shared ancestor. Examples are: the wing of a bat and the wing of a bird; the opposable thumb of opossums and of primates; the beak of a platypus and the beak of a bird. Unrelated species frequently converge upon similar morphologic solutions to common environmental conditions or shared physiological imperatives. Algorithms that cluster organisms based on similarity will mistakenly group divergent organisms under the same species (see Glossary items, Nongeneralizable predictor, Nonphylogenetic signal).

It is sometimes assumed that classification algorithms (ie, clustering objects into classes based on finding similarities among data objects) will improve when we acquire whole-genome sequence data for many different species (see Glossary item, Phenetics). Not so.[10] Imagine an experiment wherein you take DNA samples from every organism you encounter: bacterial colonies cultured from a river, unicellular nonbacterial organisms found in a pond, small multicellular organisms found in soil, crawling creatures dwelling under rocks, and so on. You own a powerful sequencing machine, that produces the full-length sequence for each sampled organism, and you have a powerful computer that sorts and clusters every sequence. At the end, the computer prints out a huge graph, wherein groups of organisms with the greatest sequence similarities are clustered together. You may think you've created a useful classification, but you haven't really, because you don't know anything about the properties of your clusters. You don't know whether each cluster represents a species, or a class (a collection of related species), or whether a cluster may be contaminated by organisms that share some of the same gene sequences, but are phylogenetically unrelated (ie, the sequence similarities result from chance or from convergence, but not by descent from a common ancestor). The sequences do not tell you very much about the biological properties of specific organisms, and you cannot infer which biological properties characterize the classes of clustered organisms. You have no certain knowledge whether the members of any given cluster of organisms can be characterized by any particular gene sequence (ie, you do not know a characterizing gene sequence that applies to every member of a class, and to no members of other classes). You do not know the genus or species names of the organisms included in the clusters, because you began your experiment without a presumptive taxonomy (see Glossary item, Taxonomy). It is hard to begin something, if there is no beginning from which to start. Old-fashioned taxonomy is the beginning from which modern computational methods must build.

When creating a classification, it is essential to remember that the members of classes may be highly similar to one another, but their similarities result from their membership in the same class. Similarity alone can never account for class inclusion, and computational approaches to classification, based entirely on sequence similarity, have limited value.

Biologists are continually engaged in an intellectual battle over the classification of living organisms. The stakes are high. When unrelated organisms are mixed together in the same class, and when related organisms are separated into unrelated classes, the value of the classification is lost, perhaps forever (see Glossary item, Blended class). Without an accurate classification of living organisms, it would be impossible to make significant progress in the diagnosis, prevention, or treatment of infectious diseases.

6.3 DRIVING UP COMPLEXITY WITH ONTOLOGIES

> More than any other time in history, mankind faces a crossroads. One path leads to despair and utter hopelessness. The other, to total extinction. Let us pray we have the wisdom to choose correctly.
> -Woody Allen[11]

Ontologies are classifications for which the "one child class -> one parent class" restraint is lifted. Today's data scientists have largely abandoned classifications in favor of ontologies. There are several reasons why this is so, one being that a "classification" is misconstrued to be the product of a "classifier algorithm." This is not the case. Classifier algorithms organize data objects by similarity, and, as we have seen, this is a fundamentally different process than organizing data objects by relationships (see Glossary items, Classifier, Predictive analytics). More importantly, the popularity of ontologies comes from the perception that ontologies are more modern and computer-friendly than classifications. Classifications were created and implemented at a time when scientists did not have powerful computers that were capable of handling the complexities of ontologies. For example, the classification of all living organisms on earth was created over a period of two millennia. Several million species have been assigned to date to this classification. It is currently estimated that we will need to add another 10–50 million species before we come close to completing the taxonomy of living organisms. Prior generations of scientists could cope with a simple classification, wherein each class of organisms falls under a single superclass; they could not hope to cope with a complex ontology of organisms. In an ontology, the species class, "Horse," might be a child class of Equu, a zoologic term; as well as a subclass of "racing animals" and "farm animals," and "four-legged animals" (see Glossary items, Child class, Parent class). Likewise, the class "book" might be a subclass of "works of literature," as well as a subclass of "wood-pulp materials," and "inked products." Naturalists working in the precomputer age simply could not keep track of the class relationships built into ontologies.[3]

The advent of powerful and accessible computers has spawned a new generation of computer scientists who have developed powerful methods for building complex ontologies. It is the goal of these computer scientists to analyze data in a manner that allows us to find and understand relationships among data objects.

The question confronting data scientists is, "Should I model my data as a classification, wherein every class has one direct parent class; or should I model my data as an ontology, wherein classes may have multiparental inheritance?" This question lies at the heart of several related fields: database management, computational informatics, object-oriented programming, semantics, and artificial intelligence. Computer scientists are choosing sides, often without acknowledging the problem or fully understanding the stakes. For example, when a programmer builds object libraries in the Python or the Perl programming languages, he is choosing to program in a permissive environment that supports multiclass object inheritance (see Glossary items, Multiclass inheritance, Multiclass classification). In Python and Perl, any object can have as many parent classes as the programmer prefers. When a programmer chooses to program in the Ruby programming language, he shuts the door on multiclass inheritance. A Ruby object can have only one direct parent class. Most programmers are totally unaware of the liberties and restrictions imposed by their choice of programming language, until they start to construct their own object libraries, or until they begin to use class libraries prepared by another programmer.[3]

In object-oriented programming, the programming language provides a syntax whereby a named method is "sent" to data objects, and a result is calculated. The named methods are short programs contained in a library of methods created for a class. For example, a "close" method, written for file objects, typically shuts a file so that it cannot be accessed for read or write operations. In object-oriented languages, a "close" method is sent to an instance of class "File" when the programmer wants to prohibit access to the file. The programming language, upon receiving the "close" method, will look for a method named "close" somewhere in the library of methods prepared for the "File" class. If it finds the "close" method in the "File" class library, it will apply the method to the object to which the method was sent. In simplest terms, the file is closed.[3]

If the "close" method were not found among the available methods for the "File" class library, the programming language would automatically look for the "close" method in the parent class of the "File" class. In some languages, the parent class of the "File" class is the "Input/Output" class. If there were a "close" method in the "Input/Output" class, then the "close" method contained in the "Input/Output" class would be sent to the "File" Object. If not, the process of looking for a "close" method would be repeated for the parent class of the "Input/Output" class. You get the idea. **Object-oriented languages search for methods by moving up the lineage of ancestral classes for the object instance that receives the method.**

In object-oriented programming, every data object is assigned membership to a class of related objects. Once a data object has been assigned to a class, the object has access to all of the methods available to the class in which it holds membership, and to all of the methods in all the ancestral classes. This is the beauty of object-oriented programming. If the object-oriented programming language is constrained to single parental inheritance (eg, the Ruby programming language), then the methods available to the programmer are restricted to a tight lineage. When the object-oriented language permits multiparental inheritance (eg, Perl and Python programming languages), a data object can have many different ancestral classes crisscrossing the class libraries.

Freedom always has its price. Imagine what happens in a multiparental object-oriented programming language when a method is sent to a data object, and the data object's class library does not contain the method. The programming language will look for the named method in the library belonging to a parent class. Which parent class library should be searched? Suppose the object has two parent classes, and each of those two parent classes has a method of the same name in their respective class libraries? The functionality of the method will change depending on its class membership (ie, a "close" method may have a different function within Class File than it may have within Class Transactions or Class Boxes). There is no way to determine how a search for a named method will traverse its ancestral class libraries; hence, the output of a software program written in an object-oriented language that permits multiclass inheritance is unpredictable.[3]

The rules by which ontologies assign class relationships can lead to absurd outcomes. When there are no restraining inheritance rules, a class may be an ancestor of a child class that is an ancestor of its parent class (eg, a single class might be a grandfather and a grandson to the same class). An instance of a class might be an instance of two classes, at once. The combinatorics and the recursive options can become computationally difficult or impossible.

Those who use ontologies that have multiclass inheritance will readily acknowledge that they have created a system that is complex and unpredictable. The ontology expert justifies his complex and unpredictable model on the certainty that reality itself is complex and unpredictable. A faithful model of reality cannot be created with a simple-mined classification. Computational ontologists believe that with time and effort, modern approaches to complex systems will isolate and eliminate computational impedimenta, these being the kinds of problems that computer scientists are trained to solve. For example, recursion within an ontology can be avoided if the ontology is acyclic (ie, class relationships are not permitted to cycle back onto themselves). For every problem created by an ontology, an adept computer scientist will find a solution. Basically, ontologists believe that the task of organizing and understanding information no longer resides within the ancient realm of classification.[3]

For those nonprogrammers who believe in the supremacy of classifications over ontologies, their faith has nothing to do with the computational dilemmas incurred with multiclass parental inheritance. They base their faith on epistemological grounds; on the nature of objects. They hold that an object can only be one thing. You cannot pretend that one thing is really two or more things, simply because you insist that it is so. One thing can only belong to one class. One class can only have one ancestor class; otherwise, it would have a dual nature. Assigning more than one parental class to an object is a sign that you have failed to grasp the essential nature of the object. The classification expert believes that ontologies do not accurately represent reality.[3]

At the heart of classical classification is the notion that everything in the universe has an essence that makes it one particular thing, and nothing else. This belief is justified for many different kinds of systems. When an engineer builds a radio, he knows that he can assign names to components, and these components can be relied upon to behave in a manner that is characteristic of its type. A capacitor will behave like a capacitor, and a resistor will behave like a resistor. The engineer need not worry that the capacitor will behave like a semiconductor or an integrated circuit.

What is true for the radio engineer may not hold true for the data scientist. In many complex systems, the object changes its function depending on circumstances. For example, cancer researchers discovered an important protein that plays a very important role in the development of cancer. This protein, p53, was considered to be the primary cellular driver for human malignancy. When p53 mutated, cellular regulation was disrupted, and cells proceeded down a slippery path leading to cancer. In the past few decades, as more information was obtained, cancer researchers have learned that p53 is just one of many proteins that play some role in carcinogenesis, but the role changes depending on the species, tissue type, cellular microenvironment, genetic background of the cell, and many other factors. Under one set of circumstances, p53 may play a role in DNA repair; under another set of circumstances, p53 may cause cells to arrest the growth cycle.[12,13] It is difficult to classify a protein that changes its primary function based on its biological context.

Steeped as I am in the ancient art of classification, I am impressed, but not convinced, by arguments on both sides of the ontology/classification debate. Purists will argue that the complexity of the ontology must faithfully match the complexity of the data domain. As a matter of practicality, complex ontologies are difficult to implement in large and complex data projects.

Without stating a preference for single-class inheritance (classifications) or multiclass inheritance (ontologies), I would suggest that when modeling a complex system, you should always strive to design a model that is as simple as possible (see Glossary item, KISS). The practical ontologist may need to settle for a simplified approximation of the truth. Regardless of your personal preference, you should learn to recognize when an ontology has become too complex.

Here are the danger signs of an overly complex ontology[3]:

1. Nobody, even the designers, fully understands the ontology model.[14]
2. You realize that the ontology makes no sense. The solutions obtained by data analysts are impossible, or they contradict observations. Tinkering with the ontology doesn't help matters.
3. For a given problem, no two data analysts seem able to formulate the query the same way, and no two query results are ever equivalent.
4. The ontology lacks modularity. It is impossible to remove a set of classes within the ontology without collapsing its structure. When anything goes wrong, the entire ontology must be fixed or redesigned, from scratch.
5. The ontology cannot fit under a higher level ontology or over a lower-level ontology.
6. The ontology cannot be debugged when errors are detected.
7. Errors occur without anyone knowing that the error has occurred.
8. You realize, to your horror, that your ontology has violated the cardinal rule of data simplification, by increasing the complexity of your data.

6.4 THE UNREASONABLE EFFECTIVENESS OF CLASSIFICATIONS

I visited the Sage of reverend fame
And thoughtful left more burden'd than I came.
I went- - and ere I left his humble door
The busy World had quite forgot his name.

-Ecclesiastes

In 1960, Eugene Wigner wrote a fascinating essay entitled, "The Unreasonable Effectiveness of Mathematics in the Natural Sciences." The thesis of this essay is that the most fundamental and abstract concepts in mathematics seem to play important roles in almost every aspect of the sciences.[15] For myself, the most unreasonably effective equation in mathematics is Euler's identity (Fig. 6.1).

$$e^{i\pi} + 1 = 0$$

FIGURE 6.1

Euler's identity, considered one of the most beautiful equations in mathematics, demonstrates the relationships among five of the most important quantities in the mathematical universe: i, pi, 1, 0, and e (see Glossary item, Beauty).

Euler's identity is a special case of Euler's formula, from which a novice mathematician can quickly come to grasp DeMoivre's theorem, Gaussian distributions, Fourier analysis, signal analysis, and combinatorics. The fundamental quantities in mathematics seem to lead forward and backward to one another. This is true for mathematicians working in the fields or of geometry, number theory, or probability. It applies also to the worldly fields of physics, statistics, and digital signal processing. The constants in Euler's identity, i, 0, 1, pi, and e, are abstractions that have somehow come to preside over our physical reality. **It seems that the universe is organized by a few numbers that only exist in our imaginations.**

Just as everything in mathematics and physics seems to be related to a few abstract fundamentals, everything in the realm of data science seems to be related to a few classes of data objects. As an example, let me pick the least consequential subject that we can imagine: stamp collecting. Imagine that you have a great deal of time on your hands, and have chosen to while away the hours absorbed in your stamp collection. You have spent the past decade building a database of "Postage Stamps of the World," with each stamp annotated with a unique identifier and a list of attributes (eg, date of issue, ink compounds used, paper composition and manufacturer, text of stamp, font style of text, price of stamp, image of stamp). You have taken pains to assign each stamp to a class, based on the country of origin. What might you learn from such a tedious classification?

By graphing the price of stamps, country-by-country, you can determine which countries must have endured times of hyperinflation, reflected as huge rises in the cost of postage. By matching the human faces featured on stamps, by country, you can determine which cultures value scientific achievement (eg, by featuring Nobel laureates), which countries value entertainment (eg, by featuring musicians), and which countries value armed conflict (eg, by featuring generals and war heroes). You can link countries to various political and social persuasions by studying the slogans that appear on stamps (eg, calls to war, pleas for conservation, faith-based icons). Animals featured on stamps tell you something about local fauna. By examining the production levels of postage stamps within a country (ie, the number of postage stamps printed per capita), you gather that certain countries have been using postage stamps as legal tender, in lieu of minted bills. If stamps from multiple countries have the same basic design, then you can infer that these countries are too small to design and print their own stamps, and have opted to use the same manufacturer. With no additional effort on your part, it would seem that your postage stamp collection is fully integrated into other databases covering geographic regions, economies, populations, and cultures. By some miracle, your annotated stamp collection serves as a window to the world, providing an unbiased, and hyperconnected view of reality.

Ernest Rutherford (1871–1937) famously said, "All science is either physics or stamp collecting." Needless to add, Rutherford was a physicist. Rutherford's opinion echoed a sentiment, common in his heyday, that quantitative experiments advance science and engineering and broaden our understanding of the universe. Endeavors that dwell on description (eg, anatomy, zoology, and all of the so-called natural sciences), barely deserved the attention of serious scientists. It is this contempt for nonquantitative sciences, so prevalent during my own formative years, that dissuaded me, at first, from following a career in biology. It was not until after I had my undergraduate degree in mathematics that I began to think seriously about the role of classification in data analysis.

What follows here is a listing of six properties of classifications that benefit data scientists. You will notice that all of the examples for these properties are taken from the field of biology. Some readers will be put off by the emphasis on biological classes, but it cannot be helped. Almost every well-documented lesson in classification-building has come from studying the mistakes and the successes in the construction of the classification of living organisms. If you are serious about data simplification, you need to know something about taxonomy (see Glossary item, Taxonomy).[16]

1. Classifications drive down complexity

Let us take a look at the most formidable classification ever designed by humans. The classification of living organisms has been a work-in-progress for more than two millennia. This classification, sometimes called the tree-of-life, has become the grand unifying theory of all the natural sciences, including such diverse fields as genetics, geology, paleontology, microbiology, and evolution. For the past 150 years, any school child could glance at a schematic depicting the classification and gain a near instantaneous understanding of the organization of all living organisms (Fig. 6.2).

Classifications drive down the complexity of their data domain, because every instance in the domain is assigned to an exclusive class, and every class is related to the other classes through a simple hierarchy (see Glossary item, Unclassifiable objects). By creating the classification of organisms, we eliminate the burden of specifying the relationships among instances (ie, individual organisms). If oak belongs to Class Angiosperm, and birch belongs to class Angiosperm, then oak and birch are related by class. We need not specify pairwise relationships among every member of class Angiosperm. Likewise, if Class Angiosperm descends from class Plantae, then oak and birch both descend from Class Plantae. Furthermore, oak and birch both enjoy all of the class properties of Class Angiosperm and Class Plantae. Life is great!

No matter how large, a classification can be absorbed and understood by the human mind; a statement that seldom applies to ontologies. Because ontologies permit multiparental inheritance, the complexity of an ontology can easily exceed human comprehension.

2. Classifications are nonchaotic and computable

Classifications have a linear ascension through a hierarchy. The parental classes of any instance of the classification can be traced as a simple, nonbranched, and nonrecursive, ordered, and uninterrupted list of ancestral classes.

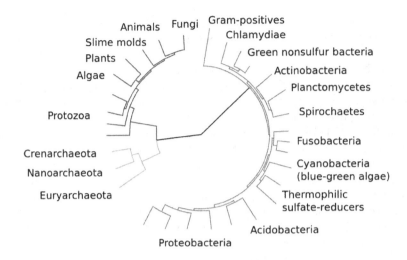

FIGURE 6.2

Modern classification of living organisms, a simple schema indicating the hierarchical relationships among the major classes of living organisms.[17]

Wikipedia, public domain.

In a prior work,[18] I described how a large, publicly available, taxonomy data file could be instantly queried to retrieve any listed organism, and to compute its complete class lineage, back to the "root" class, the primordial origin of the classification of living organisms.[18] Basically, the trick to climbing backwards up the class lineage involves building two dictionary objects, also known as associative arrays. One dictionary object (which we will be calling "namehash") is composed of key/value pairs wherein each key is the identifer code of a class (in the nomenclature of the taxonomy data file), and each value is its name or label. The second dictionary object (which we'll be calling "parenthash") is composed of key/value pairs wherein each key is the identifier code of a class, and each value is the identifier code of the parent class. The snippet that prints the lineage for any class within the classi-fication of living organisms is shown for Perl, Python, and Ruby:

In Perl:

```
while()
    {
    print OUT "$namehash{$id_name}\n";
    $id_name = $parenthash{$id_name};
    last if ($namehash{$id_name} eq "root");
    }
```

In Python:

```
for i in range(30):
    if namehash.has_key(id_name):
       print>>outtext, namehash[id_name]
    if parenthash.has_key(id_name):
       id_name = parenthash[id_name]
```

In Ruby:

```
(1..30).each do
    outtext.puts(namehash[id_name])
    id_name = parenthash[id_name]
    break if namehash[id_name].nil?
```

The parts of the script that build the dictionary objects are left as an exercise for the reader. As an example of the script's output, here is the lineage for the domestic horse (Equus caballus), calculated from the classification of living organisms:

Equus caballus
Equus subg. Equus
Equus
Equidae
Perissodactyla
Laurasiatheria
Eutheria
Theria
Mammalia
Amniota
Tetrapoda
Sarcopterygii
Euteleostomi
Teleostomi
Gnathostomata
Vertebrata
Craniata
Chordata
Deuterostomia
Coelomata
Bilateria
Eumetazoa
Metazoa
Fungi/Metazoa group
Eukaryota
Cellular organisms

The words in this zoological lineage may seem strange to laypersons, but taxonomists who view this lineage instantly grasp the place of domestic horses in the classification of all living organisms.

3. Classifications are self-correcting

New information causes us to reconsider the assumptions upon which a classification is built.[19] For example, an unfortunate error in the early classifications of living organisms involved placing fungi in the plant kingdom. On a superficial level, fungi and plants seem similar to one another. Both classes of organisms live in soil, and they both emerge from the ground, to produce stationary growths. Much like plants, fungal mushrooms can be picked, cooked, and served as a side dish.

In 1811, an interesting substance named chitin was extracted from mushrooms. In 1830, the same substance was extracted from insects. Over the following century, as we learned more about the chemistry of chitin and the cellular constituents of animals cells and plant cells, it gradually dawned on taxonomists that fungi were quite different from plants and had many similarities with animal cells. Most obviously, chitin, a constituent of fungi and insects, is absent from plant cells. Furthermore, cellulose, a constituent of plant cells, is absent from fungi and insects. These observations should have told us that fungi probably do not belong in the same class as plants.

We now know that fungi descended from a flagellated organism and belong to a large class of organisms known as the opisthokonts (organisms with one flagellum positioned at the posterior of cells). The opisthokonts include the class of metazoans (ie, animals); hence, we humans are much more closely related to fungi than to plants. To be fair, it was not easy to determine that the fungi are true opisthokonts. Most modern fungi lost their posterior flagellum somewhere along their evolutionary road. It seems that when fungi changed their habitat from water to soil, they lost their tails. The chytrids, a somewhat primitive group of fungi that never abandoned their aquatic lifestyle, have retained their posterior flagellum, using the tail to propel themselves through water. The retention of the posterior flagellum among the chytrid fungi leaves no doubt that fungi are opisthokonts, not plants.

The misconception that fungi are plants persists to this day. Academic mycologists (ie, fungal experts) are employed by botany departments, and fungal taxonomy is subsumed under the International Code of Botanical Nomenclature (ICBN).[20] It is not unusual to see modern textbooks that list the fungi among the flowers. Tsk Tsk.

The reassignment of the fungi to the Class Opisthokonta, an ancestral class of humans, raised an interesting question? If we humans are descended from Class Opisthokonta, just like the fungi, then where is our posterior flagellum? As it happens, human spermatocytes are propelled through body fluids by a posterior flagellum. Our posterior flagellum was too handy a tool for evolution to discard entirely (see Glossary item, Negative classifier).

When a class is assigned a wrong position in a classification, it can be moved, along with all its descendant classes, to its new position, under its rightful parent class. Basically, the correction involves erasing one line and constructing another. Simple! The correction of class assignments is nearly impossible in the case of complex ontologies. Because a class may have many different parent classes, a correction can disrupt the class relationships among many different classes and their subclasses. Basically, ontologies are too entangled to permit facile modifications in their structures (see Glossary item, Unstable taxonomy).

4. Classifications are self-converging

Two 20th century discoveries have greatly influenced the modern construction of the classification of living organisms: the 1909 discovery of the Burgess shale, by Walcott; and the 1961 discovery of the genetic code, by Nirenberg and Khorana. The Burgess shale provided taxonomists with an opportunity to determine the ordered epochs in which classes of organisms came into existence and out of existence. The discovery of the genetic code led to the sequencing of nucleic acids in the genes of various organisms. This data revealed the divergence of shared genes among related organisms, and added greatly to our understanding of every class of organism living on earth today.

When we look at Ernst Haeckel's classification of living organisms, as he understood it, in 1866, we learn that pre-Darwinian biologists had produced a classification that is very similar to our modern classification of organisms. If Haeckel were alive today, he would have no trouble adjusting to modern taxonomy (Fig. 6.3).

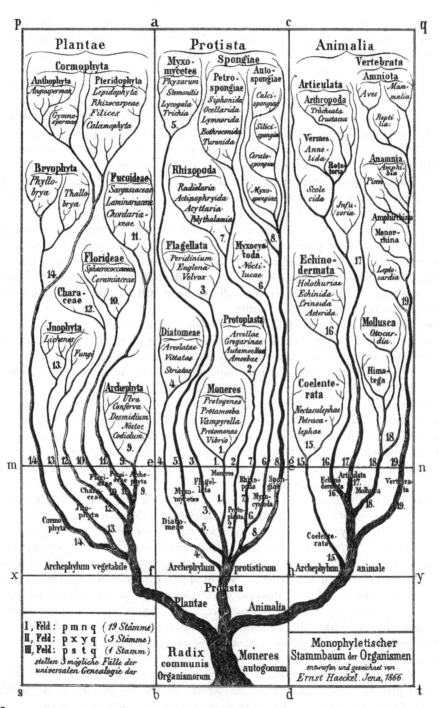

FIGURE 6.3

Ernst Haeckel's rendition of the classification of living organisms, c.1866.

Wikipedia, public domain.

How did pre-Darwinian taxonomists arrive so close to our modern taxonomy, without the benefit of the principles of evolution, modern paleontological discoveries, or molecular biology? For example, how was it possible for Aristotle to know, two thousand years ago, that a dolphin is a mammal, and not a fish? Aristotle studied the anatomy and the developmental biology of many different types of animals. One class of animals was distinguished by a gestational period in which a developing embryo is nourished by a placenta, and the offspring are delivered into the world as formed, but small versions of the adult animals (ie, not as eggs or larvae), and in which the newborn animals feed from milk excreted from nipples, overlying specialized glandular organs in the mother (mammae). Aristotle knew that these were features that specifically characterized one group of animals and distinguished this group from all the other groups of animals. He also knew that dolphins had all these features; fish did not. From these observations, he correctly reasoned that dolphins were a type of mammal, not a type of fish. Aristotle was ridiculed by his contemporaries for whom it was obvious that a dolphin is a fish. Unlike Aristotle, his contemporaries had based their classification on similarities, not on relationships.[9]

Whether a classification of living organisms is based on anatomic features that characterized classes or organisms, or on orthologic gene sequences (ie, gene sequences found in different species, inherited from a common ancestor), or on ancestral descent observed in rock strata, the resulting classification is nearly identical. **Perbhaps the greatest virtue of a classification is that regardless of the methods used to construct a classification, any two valid versions will be equivalent to one another, if the classifications represent the same reality.**

5. Classifications are multidisciplinary hypothesis-generating machines

Because a classification embodies the relationships among its members (ie, its classes and instances), we can search for relationships that may extend to members of other classifications, based on shared attributes. Such tentative relationships across classifications are equivalent to cross-disciplinary hypotheses. Let's look at a few examples.

They say that coal is a nonrenewable resource. Once we've found and consumed all of the coal that lies in the ground, no additional coal will be forthcoming. Why is this the case? Why isn't the planet producing coal today, much the same way as it produced coal hundreds of millions of years ago? The answer to this question comes, surprisingly, from the classification of living organisms. It seems that about 450 million years ago, plants began to grow on land, vertically. Erect plant growth requires the structural support provided by cellulose.

The problem that faced primeval forest organisms, early in the evolution of woody plants, was the digestion of cellulose. As it happens, cellulose, the most abundant organic compound on earth, is very difficult to digest. The early woody plants had made an evolutionary breakthrough when they first began to synthesize cellulose. The cellulose molecule, when it appeared in the earliest woody plants, was a novelty that no organism could digest; hence, early trees could not decompose. When they died, they stayed in place, like carbonized mummies. Under the weight of soil, they were slowly compressed into coal.

The age of coal lasted from the time that cellulose first appeared in plants, until the time that terrestrial organisms acquired the ability to digest cellulose. Eventually, some bacteria, fungi and other simple eukaryotes began to eat dead trees, thus heralding the end of the coal age. To this day, most organisms cannot digest cellulose. Insects, ruminants, and other animals that derive energy from cellulose outsource the job to fungal or bacterial symbiotes.

The point of this story is that the energy industry, geologists, earth scientists, ecologists, and evolutionary biologists all learned important lessons when a modern-day problem related to the sustainability of energy resources was approached as an exercise in evolutionary taxonomy.

Let's try another example.

The tip of Mount Everest is the highest point on earth, with an elevation of 29,029 feet. One might expect Mount Everest to have had a volcanic origin, wherein convulsions of earth heaped forth magma that solidified into the majestic Himalayan Mountains. If that were the case, the Himalayan Mountains, Everest included, would be composed of igneous rock such as basalt, granite, gabbro, and so on. This is definitely not the case.

The Himalayans are largely composed of limestone, a sedimentary rock that is formed at the bottom of oceans, from ocean salts and dead marine life, compressed by the weight of miles of water. The limestone at the summit of Everest contains the skeletons of long-extinct classes of marine organism (eg, trilobites), and ancient species of currently extant classes of organisms (eg, small crustaceans). The fossil-bearing limestone at the top of Mount Everest is similar to the fossil-bearing limestone found in flat ranges of sedimentary rock located in sites where oceans held sway, many millions of years ago (Fig. 6.4).

Why is Mount Everest built from ancient limestone? There can only be one answer. Everest was built by a force that pushed the ocean bottom up and up and up, until a mountain of limestone poked through the clouds, to stand dazed and naked in its own glory. What force could have caused the ocean bottom to rise up? Continental drift delivered the Indian subcontinent to Asia, about 40 or 50 million years ago. As the

FIGURE 6.4

Fossiliferous limestone, packed with the skeletons of ancient pelagic organisms.

Wikipedia, donated into the public domain by its author, Jim Stuby (Jstuby).

subcontinent closed in on Asia, a body of water, the Tethys Sea, got in its way, and the sea-bottom was squeezed backwards and upwards as the inevitable collision proceeded. Thus was born the Himalayan Mountains.

The theory of continental drift owes its existence to a set of observations and clever deductions. One of those deductions was based on understanding the timeline of evolution, which in turn was based on observations of fossils in limestone strata, which in turn was the basis for the classification of terrestrial organisms. An understanding of the classification of living organisms helped generate the continental drift hypothesis, thus providing a plausible explanation for the existence of the Indian subcontinent, and of long-dead marine life now reposing on the peak of Mt. Everest.

The classification of living organisms is directly or indirectly responsible for nearly every advance in biology, genetics, and medicine in the past half-century and for many of the advances in geology, meteorology, anthropology, and agriculture. If, as some would suggest, everything on our planet relates to every other thing, then surely the classification of living organisms is the place to learn about those relationships.

6. Classifications create our reality

In the Disney retelling of a classic fairy tale, a human-made abstraction, a puppet named Pinocchio survives a series of perils and emerges as a real live boy. It seems farfetched that an abstraction could become a living biological organism, but it happens. In point of fact, the transformation of an abstract idea into a living entity is one of the most important scientific advancements of the past half-century. For the most part, this miracle of science has gone unheralded. Nonetheless, if you think very deeply about the meaning of classifications, and if you can appreciate the role played by abstractions in the governance of our physical universe, you will appreciate the profound implications of the following story. We shall see that a human-made abstraction, that we name "species," has survived a series of perils, and has emerged as a real live biological entity.

In the classification of living terrestrial organisms, the bottom classes are known as "species." There is a species class for all the horses and another species class for all the squirrels, and so on. Speculation has it that there are 50–100 million different species of organisms on planet Earth. We humans have assigned names to a few million species, a small fraction of the total.

It has been argued that nature produces individuals, not species; the concept of species being a mere figment of the human imagination, created for the convenience of taxonomists who need to group similar organisms. Biologists can collect feature data such as gene sequences, geographic habitat, diet, size, mating rituals, hair color, shape of the skull and so on, for a variety of different animals. After some analysis, perhaps performed with the aid of a computer, we could cluster animals based on their similarities, and we could assign the clusters names, and the names of our clusters would be our species. The arbitrariness of species creation comes from the various ways we might select the features to be measured in our data sets, the choice of weights assigned to the different features (eg, should we give more weight to gene sequence than to length of gestation?), and to our choice of algorithm for assigning organisms to groups (see Glossary items, K-means algorithm, Phenetics).

For myself, and for many other scientists who use classification, there can be no human arbitrariness in the assignment of species.[21] A species is a fundamental building block of the natural world, no less substantial than the concept of a galaxy to astronomers or the number "e" to mathematicians.

The modern definition of species is "an evolving gene pool." As such, species have three properties that prove that they are biological entities.

1. Unique definition. Until recently, biologists could not agree on a definition of species. There were dozens of definitions to choose from, depending on which field of science you studied. Molecular biologists defined species by gene sequence. Zoologists defined species by mating exclusivity. Ecologists defined species by habitat constraints. The current definition equating species with an evolving gene pool serves as a great unifying theory for biologists.
2. The class "species" has a biological function that is not available to individual members of the species; namely, speciation. Species propagate, and when they do, they produce new species. Species are the only biological entities that can produce new species.
3. Species evolve. Individuals cannot evolve on their own. Evolution requires a gene pool; something that species have and individuals to not.
4. Species bear a biological relationship to individual organisms. Just as species are defined as evolving gene pools, individual organisms can be defined as set of propagating genes living within a cellular husk. Hence, the individual organism has a genome taken from the pool of genes available to his species.

The classification of living organisms has worked a true miracle, by breathing life into the concept of species, thus expanding reality.

6.5 PROPERTIES THAT CROSS MULTIPLE CLASSES

Our greatest responsibility is to be good ancestors

-Jonas Salk

Perhaps the most common mistake among builders of ontologies and classifications is to confuse a subclass with a class property. This property/class confusion is not limited to ontology builders; it is a pitfall encountered by virtually every programmer who uses object-oriented languages and every data scientist who uses RDF semantics (see Glossary items Property, Mixins, RDF Schema).

To help understand the difference between a property and a class, consider the following question: "Is a leg a subclass of the class of humans?" If you answer that a leg is most definitely a subclass of the class of humans, then you probably are basing your opinion on the following line of reasoning:

Human embryos develop to produce a leg (actually, 2);
hence every human, under normal circumstances, has a leg,
and the leg, being a component of humans, is a subclass of humans.
Furthermore, a leg, being a solid object, is not an abstraction, like a property. Hence, a leg must be a solid object, and a part of humans;
Hence, a leg is a member of a subclass of the class of humans.

No, no, no! Most students new to the subject of classification will answer, incorrectly, that a leg is a subclass of humans. First off, a subclass of a class must qualify as a member of the class. A leg is not a type of human; hence, a leg is not a subclass of class humans. If "leg" is not a subclass of class humans, then is "leg" a property of class humans? Not really. A leg is a data object that can be described by a property of class humans. For example, we can assert the following triple:

```
Batman has_component leg
```

Batman is an instance of class human. As an instance of class human, Batman is endowed with the properties and relationships of class human, one of which is the ability to have things (ie, the "has_component" property).[22] The "has_component" property may be defined to include the known body parts of humans, and this list of known body parts would include "leg." Annotating our triple, we might write:

```
Batman (a unique instance of Class Human),

has_component (a metadata property of Class Human)

leg (the data described by the "has_component" property).
```

At this point, you may be thinking that issues related to class creation and to property assignment are just too pedantic to ponder. Consider this. Abraham Lincoln was once asked, "If you call a tail a leg, then how how many legs does a horse have?" Lincoln replied, "Four, because calling a tail a leg doesn't make it one." Lincoln understood that the process of classification is neither hypothetical nor abstract. Let me try to explain the importance of understanding how classifications are organized, with the following story from my own life.

In the last decades of the 20th century, there was general agreement that the war on cancer had failed to discover drugs that were effective against advanced cases of any of the common cancers of humans (eg, lung, colon, breast, prostate). The U.S. cancer death rate was rising despite the best efforts of the U.S. National Cancer Institute. A new approach seemed warranted, and there was a growing consensus for a divide-and-conquer strategy in which treatments would be developed for biologically distinct subclasses of cancers. The idea seemed reasonable, but how would cancer researchers subclassify cancers? Several ideas were considered, but one idea gained traction. Cancers would be subclassified by their clinical stage.

Some background is needed regarding the meaning of cancer stage. When cancers are diagnosed, a determination is made regarding its size, extent of local invasion, whether tumor deposits can be found in regional or distant lymph nodes, and whether the cancer has metastasized to distant organs. As an example, a stage 3 lung cancer is one that has spread to lymph nodes. Stage 3 lung cancers are further divided into Stage 3A tumors, which have spread to lymph nodes confined to the same side of the body as the primary cancer; and Stage 3B tumors where the tumor is of any size and has spread to distant lymph nodes and invaded chest structures other than the lungs, such as the heart or esophagus. Because staging requires an accurate, well-documented assessment of the extent of spread of the tumor at the time of diagnosis, the staging process necessitates the professional services of radiologists, pathologists, oncologists, surgeons, and nurses. Furthermore, the information upon which the staging was determined would need to be reviewed by a set of experts, to verify the accuracy of the original reports.

When plans for subclassifying tumors by stage were being discussed, I indicated that the project made very little sense, from my point of view as an information scientist. The stage of a tumor is a class property; not a true class. I argued that each stage 3 cancer grew from a much smaller cancer (ie, progressed through stages over time). Given the natural course of tumor growth and metastasis, most stage 3 cancers will progress into stage 4 cancers. True classes are not transitive. The progression of cancer through stages implies that stages could not be used to classify cancers! Furthermore, a collection of patients with stage 3 cancers will include some with fast-growing cancers and others with slow-growing cancers; some cancers prone to distant metastasis and other cancers unlikely to spread to distant organs. I argued that it made no sense to lump cancers with widely different biological properties into the same class on the basis of one shared property (ie, stage) observed at one particular moment in time.

Try as I might, I failed to dissuade my colleagues from their declared course of action. The results, as you might assume, were mixed. Treatments designed for particular stages of tumor growth were effective in some individuals, ineffective in others. Molecular profiles of staged cancers showed that within any stage, some tumors shared similar profiles; other tumors did not. I would hazard to guess that every set of patients with same-stage cancer consists of a blend of undefined subclasses. Because the trials were not designed to treat a true biological class of tumors, the results were predestined to produce mixed results; an artifact of class noise.

Class noise refers to inaccuracies (eg, misleading results) introduced in the analysis of classified data due to errors in class assignments (eg, assigning a data object to class A when the object should have been assigned to class B). If you are testing the effectiveness of an antibiotic on a class of people with bacterial pneumonia, the accuracy of your results will be jeopardized if your study population includes subjects with viral pneumonia, or smoking-related lung damage (see Glossary items, Blended class, Simpson's paradox).

Some of the most promising technologies have yielded little or no scientific advancements simply because their practitioners have paid insufficient attention to the distinctions between classes and properties. The past half-century has seen incredible advances in the field of brain imaging, including the introduction of computed tomography and nuclear magnetic resonance imaging. Scientists can now determine the brain areas that are selectively activated for specific physiologic functions. These imaging techniques include: positron emission tomography, functional magnetic resonance imaging, multichannel electroencephalography, magnetoencephalography, near infrared spectroscopic imaging, and single photon emission computed tomography. With all of these available technologies, you would naturally expect that neuroscientists would be able to correlate psychiatric conditions with abnormalities in function, mapped to specific areas of the brain. Indeed, the brain research literature has seen hundreds, if not thousands, of early studies purporting to find associations that link brain anatomy to psychiatric diseases. Alas, none of these early findings has been validated. Excluding degenerative brain conditions (eg, Alzheimer's disease, Parkinson's disease), there is, at the present time, no known psychiatric condition that can be consistently associated with a specific functional brain deficit or anatomic abnormality.[23] The reasons for the complete lack of validation for what seemed to be highly promising field of research, pursued by an army of top scientists, is a deep and disturbing mystery.

In 2013, a new version of the Diagnostic and Statistical Manual of Mental Disorders (DSM) was released. The DSM is the standard classification of psychiatric disorders, and is used by psychiatrists and other healthcare professionals worldwide. The new version was long in coming, following its previous version by 20 years. Spoiling the fanfare for the much-anticipated update was a chorus of loud detractors, who included among their ranks a host of influential and respected neuroscientists. Their complaint was that the DSM classifies diagnostic entities based on collections of symptoms; not on biological principles. For every diagnostic entity in the DSM, all persons who share the same collection of symptoms will, in most cases, be assigned the same diagnosis; even when the biological cause of the symptoms are unknown or unrelated.

When individuals with unrelated diseases are studied together, simply because they have some symptoms in common, the results of the study are unlikely to have any validity.[19] Dr. Thomas Insel, a former Director of the National Institute of Mental Health, was quoted as saying, "As long as the research community takes the DSM to be a bible, we'll never make progress."[24] Apparently, the creators of the DSM do not understand the distinction between a property and a class.[9]

Returning to the definition of classification, we notice that there is nothing to say that a property for one class cannot also be a property for some unrelated class. A single property can belong to multiple unrelated classes, and to every class that descends from a class in which the property is defined (see Glossary item, Nonphylogenetic property). Knowing this, we can search classified data sets for properties shared by unrelated classes, and we can compare how values of properties vary among the different classes.

Object-oriented programming languages make good use of properties that cross unrelated classes. In object-oriented programming, methods are a type of property (see Glossary item, Method). A method can be assigned to a class (ie, a class method), or it can be placed into the repertoire of one or more classes without being assigned as a class method; sort of a freelance subroutine. Methods that apply to unrelated classes are called Mixins. Mixins enable programmers to extend the functionality of classes, without producing replicate class methods, a technique called compositional programming or layering.

Just as Mixins permit unrelated classes to have identical methods, properties permit unrelated classes to have identical features. In Section 7.4, we will see the semantic approach to assigning properties to data objects (including instances and classes), and how this simple technique, when thoughtfully applied, eliminates the hazards of confusing classes with properties.

OPEN SOURCE TOOLS

Perl: The only language that looks the same before and after RSA encryption.

-Keith Bostic

SYNTAX FOR TRIPLES

Good specifications will always improve programmer productivity far better than any programming tool or technique.

-Milt Bryce

RDF is a specialized XML syntax for creating computer-parsable files consisting of triples. The subject of an RDF triple is invoked with the rdf:about attribute. Following the subject is a metadata/data pair.

Let us create an RDF triple whose subject is the jpeg image file specified as: http://www.the_url_here.org/ldip/ldip2103.jpg. The metadata is <dc:title> and the data value is "Normal Lung".

```
<rdf:Description
    rdf:about="http://www.the_url_here.org/ldip/ldip2103.jpg">
    <dc:title>Normal Lung</dc:title>
</rdf:Description>
```

An example of three triples in RDF syntax is:

```
<rdf:Description
     rdf:about="http://www.the_url_here.org/ldip/ldip2103.jpg">
     <dc:title>Normal Lung</dc:title>
   </rdf:Description>
<rdf:Description
     rdf:about="http://www.the_url_here.org/ldip/ldip2103.jpg">
     <dc:creator>Bill Moore</dc:creator>
   </rdf:Description>
<rdf:Description
     rdf:about="http://www.the_url_here.org/ldip/ldip2103.jpg">
     <dc:date>2006-06-28</dc:date>
   </rdf:Description>
```

RDF permits you to collapse multiple triples that apply to a single subject. The following RDF:-Description statement is equivalent to the three prior triples:

```
<rdf:Description
     rdf:about="http://www.the_url_here.org/ldip/ldip2103.jpg">
     <dc:title>Normal Lung</dc:title>
     <dc:creator>Bill Moore</dc:creator>
     <dc:date>2006-06-28</dc:date>
   </rdf:Description>
```

An example of a short but well-formed RDF image specification document is:

```
<?xml version="1.0"?>
<rdf:RDF
   xmlns:rdf="http://www.w3.org/1999/02/22-rdf-syntax-ns#";
   xmlns:dc="http://purl.org/dc/elements/1.1/">
  <rdf:Description
   rdf:about="http://www.the_url_here.org/ldip/ldip2103.jpg">
   <dc:title>Normal Lung</dc:title>
   <dc:creator>Bill Moore</dc:creator>
   <dc:date>2006-06-28</dc:date>
  </rdf:Description>
</rdf:RDF>
```

The first line tells you that the document is XML. The second line tells you that the XML document is an RDF resource. The third and fourth lines are the namespace documents that are referenced within the document (see Glossary item, Namespace). Following that is the RDF statement that we have already seen.

If you think that RDF syntax creates an awful lot of text to represent a small amount of data, then your thoughts echo those of every data scientist who has tread your path. No sooner was RDF developed than a succession of simplified syntaxes, designed to convey the equivalent information, followed.

From RDF came a simplified syntax for triples, known as Notation 3 or n3.[25] From n3 came another syntactic form, thought to fit more closely to RDF, known as Turtle. From Turtle came an even more simplified form, known as N-Triples. All of these metamorphoses tell us something about the limitations and the values of syntactic rules for specifications:

1. It is impossible to write a syntax that pleases everyone.
2. Never assume that universally adopted syntaxes are permanent; data scientists are notoriously fickle.
3. Never assume that a syntax that you believe to be universally adopted is as popular as you may have been led to believe.
4. Well-designed specifications are fungible. You can always write a short script that will transform your data into any syntax you prefer.

In this book, we will use a syntax that closely resembles N-triples. N-triples are much easier to enter into a text file than RDF, and much easier to read than RDF. N-triples obey the one triple per line rule. If you know the number of lines in your triple file, you know the number of triples.

Let's look at a very short file, image.n3, containing a few triples that describe a medical image that has been archived in a hospital's electronic records system:

```
@prefix : <http://www.someplace.org/image_schema.rdf#>.
@prefix rdf: <http://www.w3.org/1999/02/22-rdf-syntax-ns#>.
:Baltimore_Hospital_Center rdf:type "Hospital".
:Baltimore_Hospital_Center_4357 rdf:type "Unique_medical_identifier".
:Baltimore_Hospital_Center_4357 :patient_name "Sam_Someone".
:Baltimore_Hospital_Center_4357 :surgical_pathology_specimen "S3456_2001".
:S_3456_2001 rdf:type "Surgical_pathology_specimen".
:S_3456_2001 :image <https://baltohosp.org/pathology/y49w3p2.jpg>.
:S_3456_2001 :log_in_date "2001-08-15".
:S_3456_2001 :clinical_history "30_years_oral_tobacco_use".
<https://baltohosp.org/pathology/y49w3p2.jpg> rdf:type "Medical_image".
<https://baltohosp.org/pathology/y49w3p2.jpg> :specimen "2".
<https://baltohosp.org/pathology/y49w3p2.jpg> :block "3".
<https://baltohosp.org/pathology/y49w3p2.jpg> :format "jpeg".
<https://baltohosp.org/pathology/y49w3p2.jpg> :width "524_pixels".
<https://baltohosp.org/pathology/y49w3p2.jpg> :height "429_pixels".
```

The file is fairly easy to read. Let's look at one triple:

```
<https://baltohosp.org/pathology/y49w3p2.jpg> rdf:type "Medical_image".
```

Here, the identified subject of the triple is the URL: <https://baltohosp.org/pathology/y49w3p2.jpg>. The data pertaining to the subject of the triple is "Medical_image". The metadata describing the data is "rdf:type". The triple tells us that the identified subject is a type of medical image. Notice that, like any complete sentence, the triple ends with a period.

You might be wondering about the "rdf:" prefix for the "type" metadata tag. The "rdf:" prefix tells us that we can look at the top of the file, where the prefix namespaces are located, to learn the prefix "rdf:" is defined in a web document, "http://www.w3.org/1999/02/22-rdf-syntax-ns#". Rather than attaching the full web document to every triple that invokes metadata described in the document, we use a prefix of our own choice, ":rdf".

You will notice that some triples use an even simpler prefix, ":". At the top of the file, we see that the ":" prefix is assigned to the namespace defined at the web site, "<http://www.someplace.org/image_schema.rdf#>". Don't try to find this web site; it is fictitious.

RDF SCHEMA

When a triple indicates that an object is a member of a certain class of objects, there must be some document that defines the class and all of its class relationships. In theory, the document that contains the triple could contain triples that define classes to which the objects in the document are assigned. Doing so would be tedious and counterproductive, because it would require a repetition of pertinent class definitions for every file in which triples are assigned the class. It makes much more sense to have accessible documents that contain class definitions that could be linked from any and all collections of triples assigned to classes. Insofar as classes will be defined, in part, by attributes (ie, features of objects) shared among class instances, it would be useful to include definitions of class properties within the same document that defines classes.

An RDF Schema is a document that lists the classes and the properties that pertain to triples residing in other documents. The properties of an RDF Schema are the metadata descriptors appearing in triples whose objects are instances of the classes listed in the RDF schema. Elements in an RDF schema may be subclasses of elements in other RDF schemas.

As the name implies, an RDF Schema can be written in formal RDF syntax. In practice, many of the so-called RDF Schema documents found on the web are prepared in alternate formats. They are nominally RDF syntax because they create a namespace for classes and properties referred by triples listed in RDF documents.

Here is a short RDF schema, written as Turtle triples, and held in a fictitious web site, "http://www.fictitious_site.org/schemas/life#"

```
@prefix rdf: <http://www.w3.org/1999/02/22-rdf-syntax-ns#>
@prefix rdfs: <http://www.w3.org/2000/01/rdf-schema#>
@base <http://www.fictitious_site.org/schemas/life#>

:Homo instance_of rdfs:Class.

:HomoSapiens instance_of rdfs:Class;
   rdfs:subClassOf :Homo.
```

Turtle triples have a somewhat different syntax than N-triples or N3 triples. As you can see, the turtle triple resembles RDF syntax in form, allowing for nested metadata/data pairs assigned to the same object. Nonetheless, turtle triples use less verbiage than RDF, but convey equivalent information. In this minimalist RDF Schema, we specify two classes that would normally be included in the much larger classification of living organisms: Homo and HomoSapiens.

A triple that refers to our "http://www.fictitious_site.org/schemas/life#" Schema might look something like this:

```
:Batman instanceOf <http://www.fictitious_site.org/schemas/life#>:HomoSapiens.
```

The triple asserts that Batman is an instance of Homo Sapiens. The data "HomoSapiens" links us to the RDF Schema, which in turn tells us that HomoSapiens is a class and is the subclass of Class Homo.

RDF PARSERS

RDF documents can be a pain to create, but they are very easy to parse. Even in instances when an RDF file is composed of an off-kilter variant of RDF, it is usually quite easy to write a short script that will parse through the file, extracting triples, and using the components of the triples to serve the programmer's goals. Such goals may include: counting occurrences of items in a class, finding properties that apply to specific subsets of items in specific classes, or merging triples extracted from various triplestore databases (see Glossary item, Triplestore).

The rdflib package is an RDF parser written for Python. Insofar as rdflib is not bundled in the standard Python distribution, Python users can download the package via the Python Package Index at: https://pypi.python.org/pypi/rdflib

Easier yet, the rdflib package can be installed from the command line, using the pip installer for Python, discussed in Open Source Tools for Chapter 1, and shown again here:

```
c:\ftp>pip install rdflib
```

To demonstrate the parsing method, let's start with an RDF file, that we will call rdf_example.xml:

```xml
<?xml version="1.0"?>
<rdf:RDF
xmlns:rdf="http://www.w3.org/1999/02/22-rdf-syntax-ns#"
xmlns:cd="http://www.recshop.fake/cd#">
<rdf:Description
rdf:about="http://www.recshop.fake/cd/Empire Burlesque">
  <cd:artist>Bob Dylan</cd:artist>
  <cd:country>USA</cd:country>
  <cd:company>Columbia</cd:company>
  <cd:price>10.90</cd:price>
  <cd:year>1985</cd:year>
</rdf:Description>
<rdf:Description
rdf:about="http://www.recshop.fake/cd/Hide your heart">
  <cd:artist>Bonnie Tyler</cd:artist>
  <cd:country>UK</cd:country>
  <cd:company>CBS Records</cd:company>
  <cd:price>9.90</cd:price>
  <cd:year>1988</cd:year>
</rdf:Description>
</rdf:RDF>
```

The Python script, rdf_parse.py, imports the rdflib package and extracts each triple, and divides the triple into three lines:

```
#!/usr/bin/python
import rdflib
g=rdflib.Graph()
g.load('rdf_example.xml')
for subject,predicate,object in g:
  print "Identified subject -", subject
  print "Metadata -", predicate
  print "Data -", object
  print
exit
```

Here are a few lines of output generated by the rdf_pars.py script:

```
c:\ftp>rdf_parse.py
No handlers could be found for logger "rdflib.term"

Identified subject - http://www.recshop.fake/cd/Hide your heart
Metadata - http://www.recshop.fake/cd#artist
Data - Bonnie Tyler

Identified subject - http://www.recshop.fake/cd/Hide your heart
Metadata - http://www.recshop.fake/cd#year
Data - 1988

Identified subject - http://www.recshop.fake/cd/Hide your heart
Metadata - http://www.recshop.fake/cd#company
Data - CBS Records

Identified subject - http://www.recshop.fake/cd/Empire Burlesque
Metadata - http://www.recshop.fake/cd#price
Data - 10.90

Identified subject - http://www.recshop.fake/cd/Empire Burlesque
Metadata - http://www.recshop.fake/cd#country
Data - USA
```

It is worth repeating that good specifications are fungible. One can be transformed into another. Just as it possible to convert RDF to n3 triples, it is possible to convert n3 triples to RDF.

Here is a Perl script, RDF_n3.pl, that converts the image.n3 file, composed as Notation 3, into long RDF syntax. You will need to pre-install Perl's RDF::Notation3 module, available from CPAN.[26]

```
#!/usr/local/bin/perl
use RDF::Notation3::Triples;
$path = "image.n3";
$rdf = RDF::Notation3::Triples->new();
$rdf->parse_file($path);
$triples = $rdf->get_triples;
use RDF::Notation3::XML;
```

```
$rdf = RDF::Notation3::XML->new();
$rdf->parse_file($path);
$string = $rdf->get_string;
print $string;
exit;
```

The RDF_n3.pl script operates on the image.n3 file, a list of N3 triples shown earlier in Open Source tools, for this chapter. Here is the truncated output, in RDF format:

```
<?xml version="1.0" encoding="utf-8"?>
<rdf:RDF
    xmlns:rdf="http://www.w3.org/1999/02/22-rdf-syntax-ns#">
<rdf:Description
    rdf:about="http://www.pathology
    informatics.org/image_schema.rdf#Baltimore_Hospital_Center">
<rdf:type
    xmlns:rdf="http://www.w3.org/1999/02/22-rdf-syntax-ns#">Hospital</rdf:type>
</rdf:Description>
<rdf:Description
    rdf:about="http://www.pathologyinfor
    matics.org/image_schema.rdf#Baltimore_Hospital_Center_4357">
<rdf:type
    xmlns:rdf="http://www.w3.org/199
    9/02/22-rdf-syntax-ns#">Unique_medical_identifier</rdf:type>
  </rdf:Description>
<rdf:Description

rdf:about="http://www.pathologyinformatics.org/image_schema.
rdf#Baltimore_Hospital_Center_4357">
  <patient_name
```

VISUALIZING CLASS RELATIONSHIPS

When working with classifications or ontologies, it is useful to have an image that represents the relationships among the classes. GraphViz is an open source software utility that produces graphic representations of object relationships (see Glossary item, Object relationships).

The GraphViz can be downloaded from: http://www.graphviz.org/

GraphViz comes with a set of applications that generate graphs of various styles. Here is an example of a Graphviz dot file, number.dot, constructed in Graphviz syntax.[27] Aside from a few lines that provide instructions for line length and graph size, the dot file is a list of classes and their child classes.

```
digraph G {
  size="7,7";
  Object -> Numeric;
  Numeric -> Integer;
  Numeric -> Float;
```

```
    Integer -> Fixnum
    Integer -> Bignum
}
```

After the Graphviz exe file (version graphviz-2.14.1.exe, on my computer) is installed, you can launch the various Graphviz methods as command lines from its working directory, or through a system call from within a script (see Glossary item, Exe file).

```
c:\ftp\dot>dot -Tpng number.dot -o number.png
```

The command line tells Graphviz to use the dot method to produce a rendering of the number.dot text file, saved as an image file, with filename number.png. The output file contains a class hierarchy, beginning with the highest class and branching until it reaches the lowest descendant class (Fig. 6.5).

With a glance, we see that the highest class is Class Object. Class Object has one child class, Class Numeric. Numeric has two child classes, Class Integer and Class Float. Class Integer has two child classes, Class Fixnum and Class Bignum. You might argue that a graphic representation of classes was unnecessary; the textual listing of class relationships was all that you needed. Maybe so, but when the class structure becomes complex, graphic visualization can greatly simplify your understanding of the relationships among classes.

Here is a visualization of a classification of human neoplasms (Fig. 6.6). It was produced by Graphviz, from a .dot file containing a list of classes and their subclasses, and rendered with the "twopi" method, shown:

```
c:\ftp>twopi -Tpng neoplasms.dot -o neoplasms_classes.png
```

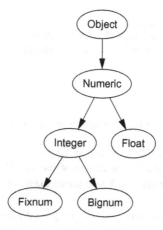

FIGURE 6.5

A class hierarchy, described by the number.dot file and converted to a visual file, using Graphviz.

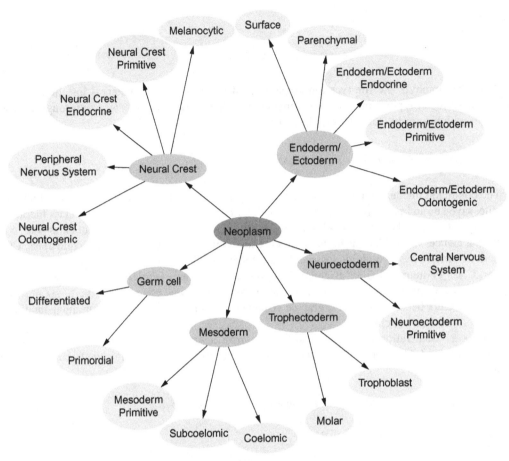

FIGURE 6.6

A visualization of relationships in a classification of tumors. The image was rendered with the Graphviz utility, using the twopi method, which produced a radial classification, with the root class in the center.

We can look at the graphic version of the classification and quickly make the following observation:

1. The root class (ie, the ancestor to every class) is Class Neoplasm. The Graphviz utility helped us find the root class, by placing it in the center of the visualization.
2. Every class is connected to other classes. There are no classes sitting out in space, unrelated to other classes.
3. Every class that has a parent class has exactly one parent class.
4. There are no recursive branches to the graph (eg, the ancestor of a class cannot also be a descendant of the class).

If we had only the textual listing of class relationships, without benefit of a graphic visualization, it would be very difficult for a human to verify, at a glance, the internal logic of the classification.

With a few tweaks to the neo.dot Graphviz file, we can create a nonsensical graphic visualization (Fig. 6.7):

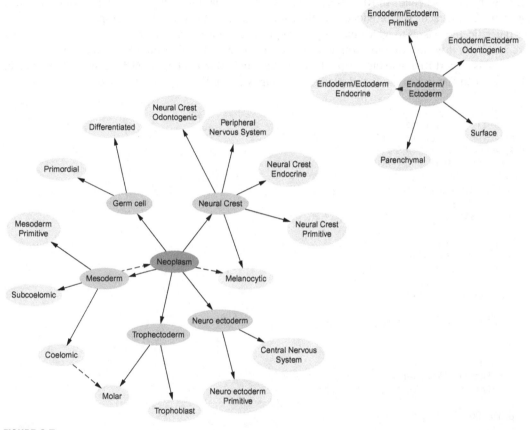

FIGURE 6.7

A corrupted classification, that might qualify as a valid ontology.

Notice that one cluster of classes is unconnected to the other, indicating that class Endoderm/Ectoderm has no parent classes. Elsewhere, Class Mesoderm is both child and parent to Class Neoplasm. Class Melanocytic and Class Molar are each the child class to two different parent classes. At a glance, we have determined that the classification is highly flawed. **The visualization simplified the relationships among classes, and allowed us to see where the classification went wrong.** Had we only looked at the textual listing of classes and subclasses, we may have missed some or all of the logical flaws in our classification.

At this point, you might be thinking that visualizations of class relationships are nice, but who has the time and energy to create the long list of classes and subclasses, in Graphviz syntax, that are the input files for the Graphviz methods?

Now comes one of the great payoffs of data specifications. **You must remember that good data specifications are fungible.** A modestly adept programmer can transform a specification into whatever format is necessary to do a particular job. In this case, the classification of neoplasms had been specified as an RDF Schema. An RDF Schema is a document that includes the definitions of classes and properties, with each class provided with the name of its parent class and each property provided with its range (ie, the classes to which the property applies). Because class relationships in an RDF Schema are specified, it is easy to transform an RDF Schema into a .dot file suitable for Graphviz.

Here is a short RDF parsing script, dot.pl, written in Perl that takes an RDF Schema (contained in the plain-text file, schema.txt) and produces a Graphviz .dot file, named schema.dot.

```perl
#!/usr/bin/perl
open (TEXT, "schema.txt");
open (OUT, ">schema.dot");
$/ = "\<\/rdfs\:Class>";
print OUT "digraph G \{\n";
print OUT "size\=\"15\,15\"\;\n";
print OUT "ranksep\=\"2\.00\"\;\n";
$line = " ";
while ($line ne "")
   {
   $line = <TEXT>;
   last if ($line !~ /\<rdfs\:/);
   if ($line =~ /\:resource\=\"[a-z0-9\:\/\_\.\-]*\#([a-z\_]+)\"/i)
      {
      $father = $1;
      }
   if ($line =~ /rdf\:ID\=\"([a-z\_]+)\"/i)
      {
      $child = $1;
      }
   print OUT "$father \-\> $child\;\n";
   print "$father \-\> $child\;\n";
   }
print OUT "\}";
exit;
```

The first 15 lines of output of the dot.pl script:

```
digraph G {
size="15,15";
ranksep="2.00";
Class -> Tumor_classification;
Tumor_classification -> Neoplasm;
Tumor_classification -> Unclassified;
Neural_tube -> Neural_tube_parenchyma;
Mesoderm -> Sub_coelomic;
Neoplasm -> Endoderm_or_ectoderm;
Unclassified -> Syndrome;
```

```
Neoplasm -> Neural_crest;
Neoplasm -> Germ_cell;
Neoplasm -> Pluripotent_non_germ_cell;
Sub_coelomic -> Sub_coelomic_gonadal;
Trophectoderm -> Molar;
```

The full schema.dot file, not shown, is suitable for use as an input file for the Graphviz utility.

GLOSSARY

Abstraction In the context of object-oriented programming, abstraction is a technique whereby a method is simplified to a generalized form that is applicable to a wide range of objects, but for which the specific characteristics of the object receiving the method may be used to return a result that is suited to the object. Abstraction, along with polymorphism, encapsulation, and inheritance, are essential features of object-oriented programming languages. See Polymorphism. See Inheritance. See Encapsulation.

Annotation Annotation involves associating data with additional data to provide description, disambiguation (eg, adding identifiers to distinguish the data from other data), links to related data, or timestamps to mark when the data was created. One of the most important functions of annotation is to provide data elements with metadata, facilitating our ability to find relationships among different data objects. Annotation is vital for effective search and retrieval of large and complex sets of data.

Autocoding When nomenclature coding is done automatically, by a computer program, the process is known as "autocoding" or "autoencoding." See Coding. See Nomenclature. See Autoencoding.

Autoencoding Synonym for autocoding. See Autocoding.

Beauty To mathematicians, beauty and simplicity are virtually synonymous, both conveying the idea that someone has managed to produce something of great meaning or value from a minimum of material. Euler's identity, relating e, i, pi, 0, and 1 in a simple equation, is held as an example of beauty in mathematics. When writing this book, I was tempted to give it the title, "The Beauty of Data," but I feared that a reductionist flourish, equating data simplification with beauty, was just too obscure.

Blended class Also known as class noise, subsumes the more familiar, but less precise term, "Labeling error." Blended class refers to inaccuracies (eg, misleading results) introduced in the analysis of data due to errors in class assignments (ie, assigning a data object to class A when the object should have been assigned to class B). If you are testing the effectiveness of an antibiotic on a class of people with bacterial pneumonia, the accuracy of your results will be forfeit when your study population includes subjects with viral pneumonia, or smoking-related lung damage. Errors induced by blending classes are often overlooked by data analysts who incorrectly assume that the experiment was designed to ensure that each data group is composed of a uniform population. A common source of class blending occurs when the classification upon which the experiment is designed is itself blended. For example, imagine that you are a cancer researcher and you want to perform a study of patients with malignant fibrous histiocytomas (MFH), comparing the clinical course of these patients with the clinical course of patients who have other types of tumors. Let's imagine that the class of tumors known as MFH does not actually exist; that it is a grab-bag term erroneously assigned to a variety of other tumors that happened to look similar to one another. This being the case, it would be impossible to produce any valid results based on a study of patients diagnosed as having MFH. The results would be a biased and irreproducible cacophony of data collected across different, and undetermined, classes of tumors. Believe it or not, this specific example, of the blended MFH class of tumors, is selected from the real-life annals of tumor biology.[28,29] The literature is rife with research of dubious quality, based on poorly designed classifications and blended classes. A detailed discussion of this topic is found in Section 6.5, Properties that Cross Multiple Classes. One caveat. Efforts to eliminate class blending can be counterproductive if undertaken with excess zeal.

For example, in an effort to reduce class blending, a researcher may choose groups of subjects who are uniform with respect to every known observable property. For example, suppose you want to actually compare apples with oranges. To avoid class blending, you might want to make very sure that your apples do not include any cumquats, or persimmons. You should be certain that your oranges do not include any limes or grapefruits. Imagine that you go even further, choosing only apples and oranges of one variety (eg, Macintosh apples and navel oranges), size (eg, 10 cm), and origin (eg, California). How will your comparisons apply to the varieties of apples and oranges that you have excluded from your study? You may actually reach conclusions that are invalid and irreproducible for more generalized populations within each class. In this case, you have succeeded in eliminating class blending, while losing representative populations of the classes. See Simpson's paradox.

Bootstrapping The act of self-creation, from nothing. The term derives from the ludicrous stunt of pulling oneself up by one's own bootstraps. Its shortened form, "booting," refers to the startup process in computers in which the operating system is somehow activated via its operating system, that has not been activated. The absurd and somewhat surrealistic quality of bootstrapping protocols serves as one of the most mysterious and fascinating areas of science. As it happens, bootstrapping processes lie at the heart of some of the most powerful techniques in data simplification (eg, classification, object-oriented programming, resampling statistics, and Monte Carlo simulations). It is worth taking the time to explore the philosophical and the pragmatic aspects of bootstrapping. Starting from the beginning, how was the universe created? For believers, the universe was created by an all-powerful deity. If this were so, then how was the all-powerful deity created? Was the deity self-created, or did the deity simply bypass the act of creation altogether? The answers to these questions are left as an exercise for the reader, but we can all agree that there had to be some kind of bootstrapping process, if something was created from nothing. Otherwise, there would be no universe, and this book would be much shorter than it is. Getting back to our computers, how is it possible for any computer to boot its operating system, when we know that the process of managing the startup process is one of the most important functions of the fully operational operating system? Basically, at startup, the operating system is nonfunctional. A few primitive instructions hardwired into the computer's processors are sufficient to call forth a somewhat more complex process from memory, and this newly activated process calls forth other processes, until the operating system is eventually up and running. The cascading rebirth of active processes takes time, and explains why booting your computer may seem to be a ridiculously slow process. What is the relationship between bootstrapping and classification? The ontologist creates a classification based on a worldview in which objects hold specific relationships with other objects. Hence, the ontologist's perception of the world is based on preexisting knowledge of the classification of things; which presupposes that the classification already exists. Essentially, you cannot build a classification without first having the classification. How does an ontologist bootstrap a classification into existence? She may begin with a small assumption that seems, to the best of her knowledge, unassailable. In the case of the classification of living organisms, she may assume that the first organisms were primitive, consisting of a few self-replicating molecules and some physiologic actions, confined to a small space, capable of hosting a self-sustaining system. Primitive viruses and prokaryotes (ie, bacteria) may have started the ball rolling. This first assumption might lead to observations and deductions, which eventually yield the classification of living organisms that we know today. Every thoughtful ontologist will admit that a classification is, at its best, a hypothesis-generating machine; not a factual representation of reality. We use the classification to create new hypotheses about the world and about the classification itself. The process of testing hypotheses may reveal that the classification is flawed; that our early assumptions were incorrect. More often, testing hypotheses will reassure us that our assumptions were consistent with new observations, adding to our understanding of the relations between the classes and instances within the classification.

Child class The direct or first generation subclass of a class. Sometimes referred to as the daughter class or, less precisely, as the subclass. See Parent class. See Classification.

Class A class is a group of objects that share a set of properties that define the class and that distinguish the members of the class from members of other classes. The word "class," lowercase, is used as a general term. The word "Class," uppercase, followed by an uppercase noun (eg, Class Animalia) represents a specific class within a formal classification. See Classification.

Classification A system in which every object in a knowledge domain is assigned to a class within a hierarchy of classes. The properties of superclasses are inherited by the subclasses. Every class has one immediate superclass (ie, parent class) although a parent class may have more than one immediate subclass (ie, child class). Objects do not change their class assignment in a classification, unless there was a mistake in the assignment. For example, a rabbit is always a rabbit, and does not change into a tiger. Classifications can be thought of as the simplest and most restrictive type of ontology, and serve to reduce the complexity of a knowledge domain.[30] Classifications can be easily modeled in an object-oriented programming language and are nonchaotic (ie, calculations performed on the members and classes of a classification should yield the same output, each time the calculation is performed). A classification should be distinguished from an ontology. In an ontology, a class may have more than one parent class and an object may be a member of more than one class. A classification can be considered a special type of ontology wherein each class is limited to a single parent class and each object has membership in one and only one class. See Nomenclature. See Thesaurus. See Vocabulary. See Classification. See Dictionary. See Terminology. See Ontology. See Parent class. See Child class. See Superclass. See Unclassifiable objects.

Classifier As used herein, refers to algorithms that assign a class (from a preexisting classification) to an object whose class is unknown.[31] It is unfortunate that the term classifier, as used by data scientists, is often misapplied to the practice of classifying, in the context of building a classification. Classifier algorithms cannot be used to build a classification, as they assign class membership by similarity to other members of the class; not by relationships. For example, a classifier algorithm might assign a terrier to the same class as a house cat because both animals have many phenotypic features in common (eg, similar size and weight, presence of a furry tail, four legs, tendency to snuggle in a lap). A terrier is dissimilar to a wolf, and a house cat is dissimilar to a lion, but the terrier and the wolf are directly related to one another; as are the housecat and the lion. **For the purposes of creating a classification, relationships are all that are important. Similarities, when they occur, arise as a consequence of relationships; not the other way around.** At best, classifier algorithms provide a clue to classification, by sorting objects into groups that may contain related individuals. Like clustering techniques, classifier algorithms are computationally intensive when the dimension is high, and can produce misleading results when the attributes are noisy (ie, contain randomly distributed attribute values) or noninformative (ie, unrelated to correct class assignment). See K-nearest neighbor algorithm. See Predictive analytics. See Support vector machine.

Coding The term "coding" has three very different meanings; depending on which branch of science influences your thinking. For programmers, coding means writing the code that constitutes a computer programmer. For cryptographers, coding is synonymous with encrypting (ie, using a cipher to encode a message). For medics, coding is calling an emergency team to handle a patient in extremis. For informaticians and library scientists, coding involves assigning an alphanumeric identifier, representing a concept listed in a nomenclature, to a term. For example, a surgical pathology report may include the diagnosis, Adenocarcinoma of prostate." A nomenclature may assign a code C4863000 that uniquely identifies the concept "Adenocarcinoma." Coding the report may involve annotating every occurrence of the work "Adenocarcinoma" with the "C4863000" identifier. For a detailed explanation of coding, and its importance for searching and retrieving data, see the full discussion in Section 3.4, "Autoencoding and Indexing with Nomenclatures." See Autocoding. See Nomenclature.

Data object A data object is whatever is being described by the data. For example, if the data is "6 feet tall," then the data object is the person or thing to which "6 feet tall" applies. Minimally, a data object is a metadata/data pair, assigned to a unique identifier (ie, a triple). In practice, the most common data objects are simple data records, corresponding to a row in a spreadsheet or a line in a flat-file. Data objects in object-oriented programming languages typically encapsulate several items of data, including an object name, an object unique identifier, multiple data/metadata pairs, and the name of the object's class. See Triple. See Identifier. See Metadata.

Database A software application designed specifically to create and retrieve large numbers of data records (eg, millions or billions). The data records of a database are persistent, meaning that the application can be turned off, then on, and all the collected data will be available to the user (see Open Source Tools for Chapter 7).

Dictionary A terminology or word list accompanied by a definition for each item. See Nomenclature. See Vocabulary. See Terminology.

Encapsulation The concept, from object-oriented programming, that a data object contains its associated data. Encapsulation is tightly linked to the concept of introspection, the process of accessing the data encapsulated within a data object. Encapsulation, Inheritance, and Polymorphism are available features of all object-oriented languages. See Inheritance. See Polymorphism.

Exe file A file with the filename suffix ".exe". In common parlance, filenames with the ".exe" suffix are executable code. See Executable file.

Executable file A file that contains compiled computer code that can be read directly from the computer's CPU, without interpretation by a programming language. A language such as C will compile C code into executables. Scripting languages, such as Perl, Python, and Ruby interpret plain-text scripts and send instructions to a run-time engine, for execution. Because executable files eliminate the interpretation step, they typically run faster than plain-text scripts. See Exe file.

Flat-file A file consisting of data records, usually with one record per file line. The individual fields of the record are typically separated by a marking character, such as "|" or "^". Flat-files are usually plain-text.

Generalization Generalization is the process of extending relationships from individual objects to classes of objects. For example, when Isaac Newton observed the physical laws that applied to apples falling to the ground, he found a way to relate the acceleration of an object to its mass and to the acceleration of gravity. His apple-centric observations applied to all objects and could be used to predict the orbit of the moon around the earth, or the orbit of the earth around the sun. Newton generalized from the specific to the universal. Similarly, Darwin's observations on barnacles could be generalized to yield the theory of evolution, thus explaining the development of all terrestrial organisms. Science would be of little value if observed relationships among objects could not be generalized to classes of objects. See Science.

HTML HyperText Markup Language is an ASCII-based set of formatting instructions for web pages. HTML formatting instructions, known as tags, are embedded in the document, and double-bracketed, indicating the start point and end points for instruction. Here is an example of an HTML tag instructing the web browser to display the word "Hello" in italics: <i>Hello</i>. All web browsers conforming to the HTML specification must contain software routines that recognize and implement the HTML instructions embedded within web documents. In addition to formatting instructions, HTML also includes linkage instructions, in which the web browsers must retrieve and display a listed web page, or a web resource, such as an image. The protocol whereby web browsers, following HTML instructions, retrieve web pages from other internet sites is known as HTTP (HyperText Transfer Protocol).

Identification The process of providing a data object with an identifier, or the process of distinguishing one data object from all other data objects on the basis of its associated identifier. See Identifier.

Identifier A string that is associated with a particular thing (eg, person, document, transaction, data object), and not associated with any other thing.[32] Object identification usually involves permanently assigning a seemingly random sequence of numeric digits (0–9) and alphabet characters (a–z and A–Z) to a data object. A data object can be a specific piece of data (eg, a data record), or an abstraction, such as a class of objects or a number or a string or a variable. See Identification.

Inheritance In object-oriented languages, data objects (ie, classes and object instances of a class) inherit the methods (eg, functions and subroutines) created for the ancestral classes in their lineage. See Abstraction. See Polymorphism. See Encapsulation.

Instance An instance is a specific example of an object that is not itself a class or group of objects. For example, Tony the Tiger is an instance of the tiger species. Tony the Tiger is a unique animal and is not itself a group of animals or a class of animals. The terms instance, instance object, and object are sometimes used interchangeably, but the special value of the "instance" concept, in a system wherein everything is an object, is that it distinguishes members of classes (ie, the instances) from the classes to which they belong.

Introspection A method by which data objects can be interrogated to yield information about themselves (eg, properties, values, and class membership). Through introspection, the relationships among the data objects can be examined. Introspective methods are built into object-oriented languages. The data provided by introspection can be applied, at run-time, to modify a script's operation; a technique known as reflection. Specifically, any properties, methods, and encapsulated data of a data object can be used in the script to modify the script's run-time behavior. See Reflection.

K-means algorithm The k-means algorithm assigns any number of data objects to one of k-clusters, where k is selected by the individual who implements the algorithm.[31] Here is how the algorithm works for sets of quantitative data: (1) The program randomly chooses k objects from the collection of objects to be clustered. We'll call each of these k objects a focus. (2) For every object in the collection, the distance between the object and all of randomly chosen k objects (chosen in step 1) is computed. (3) A round of k-clusters is computed by assigning every object to its nearest focus. (4) The centroid focus for each of the k-clusters is calculated. The centroid is the point that is closest to all of the objects within the cluster. Another way of saying this is that if you sum the distances between the centroid and all of the objects in the cluster, this summed distance will be smaller than the summed distance from any other point in space. (5) Steps 2, 3, and 4 are repeated, using the k centroid foci as the points for which all distances are computed. (6) Step 5 is repeated until the k centroid foci converge on a nonchanging set of k centroid foci (or until the program slows to an interminable crawl). There are serious drawbacks to the algorithm: The final set of clusters will sometimes depend on the initial, random choice of k data objects. This means that multiple runs of the algorithm may produce different outcomes. The algorithms are not guaranteed to succeed. Sometimes, the algorithm does not converge to a final, stable set of clusters. When the dimensionality is very high, the distances between data objects (ie, the square root of the sum of squares of the measured differences between corresponding attributes of two objects) can be ridiculously large and of no practical meaning. Computations may bog down, cease altogether, or produce meaningless results. In this case, the only recourse may require eliminating some of the attributes (ie, reducing dimensionality of the data objects). Subspace clustering is a method wherein clusters are found for computationally manageable subsets of attributes. If useful clusters are found using this method, additional attributes can be added to the mix to see if the clustering can be improved. The clustering algorithm may succeed, producing a set of clusters of similar objects, but the clusters may have no practical value, omitting essential relationships among the objects. The k-means algorithm should not be confused with the k-nearest neighbor algorithm.

K-nearest neighbor algorithm The k-nearest neighbor algorithm is a simple and popular classifier algorithm. From a collection of data objects whose class is known, the algorithm computes the distances from the object of unknown class to the objects of known class. This involves a distance measurement from the feature set of the objects of unknown class to every object of known class (the test set). After the distances are computed, the k classed objects with the smallest distance to the object of unknown class are collected. The most common class (ie, the class with the most objects) among the nearest k classed objects is assigned to the object of unknown class. If the chosen value of k is 1, then the object of unknown class is assigned the class of its closest classed object (ie, the nearest neighbor).

KISS Acronym for Keep It Simple Stupid. The motto applies to almost any area of life; nothing should be made more complex than necessary. As it happens, much of what we encounter, as data scientists, comes to us in a complex form (ie, nothing to keep simple). A more realistic acronym is MISS (Make It Simple Stupid).

Machine learning Refers to computer systems and software applications that learn or improve as new data is acquired. Examples would include language translation software that improves in accuracy as additional language data is added to the system, and predictive software that improves as more examples are obtained.

Machine learning can be applied to search engines, optical character recognition software, speech recognition software, vision software, neural networks. Machine learning systems are likely to use training data sets and test data sets.

Meaning In informatics, meaning is achieved when described data is bound to a unique identifier of a data object. "Claude Funston's height is five feet eleven inches," comes pretty close to being a meaningful statement. The statement contains data (five feet eleven inches), and the data is described (height). The described data belongs to a unique object (Claude Funston). Ideally, the name "Claude Funston" should be provided with a unique identifier, to distinguish one instance of Claude Funston from all the other persons who are named Claude Funston. The statement would also benefit from a formal system that ensures that the metadata makes sense (eg, What exactly is height, and does Claude Funston fall into a class of objects for which height is a property?) and that the data is appropriate (eg, Is 5 feet 11 inches an allowable measure of a person's height?). A statement with meaning does not need to be a true statement (eg, The height of Claude Funston was not 5 feet 11 inches when Claude Funston was an infant). See Semantics. See Triple. See RDF.

Metadata The data that describes data. For example, a data element (also known as data point) may consist of the number, "6." The metadata for the data may be the words "Height, in feet." A data element is useless without its metadata, and metadata is useless unless it adequately describes a data element. In XML, the metadata/data annotation comes in the form <metadata tag>data<end of metadata tag> and might look something like:

```
<weight_in_pounds>150</weight_in_pounds>
```

In spreadsheets, the data elements are the cells of the spreadsheet. The column headers are the metadata that describe the data values in the column's cells, and the row headers are the record numbers that uniquely identify each record (ie, each row of cells). See XML.

Method Roughly equivalent to functions, subroutines, or code blocks. In object-oriented languages, a method is a subroutine available to an object (class or instance). In Ruby and Python, instance methods are declared with a "def" declaration followed by the name of the method, in lowercase. Here is an example, in Ruby, for the "hello" method, is written for the Salutations class.

```
class Salutations
   def hello
      puts "hello there"
   end
end
```

Mixins Mixins are a technique for including modules within a class to extend the functionality of the class. The power of the mixin is that methods can be inserted into unrelated classes. In practice, mixin methods are generally useful functions that are not related to the fundamental and defining methods for a class. A good way to think about nondefining methods included in unrelated classes is that "mixins" are to object-oriented programming languages what "properties" are to classifications. A single property may apply to multiple, unrelated classes. Mixins are available in both Python and Ruby. See RDF Schema. See Property.

Multiclass classification A misnomer imported from the field of machine translation, and indicating the assignment of an instance to more than one class. Classifications, as defined in this book, impose one-class classification (ie, an instance can be assigned to one and only one class). It is tempting to think that a ball should be included in class "toy" and in class "spheroids," but mutliclass assignments create unnecessary classes of inscrutable provenance, and taxonomies of enormous size, consisting largely of replicate items. See Multiclass inheritance. See Taxonomy.

Multiclass inheritance In ontologies, multiclass inheritance occurs when a child class has more than one parent class. For example, a member of Class House may have two different parent classes: Class Shelter, and Class

Property. Multiclass inheritance is generally permitted in ontologies but is forbidden in one type of restrictive ontology, known as a classification. See Classification. See Parent class. See Multiclass classification.

Namespace A namespace is the realm in which a metadata tag applies. The purpose of a namespace is to distinguish metadata tags that have the same name, but a different meaning. For example, within a single XML file, the metadata tag "date" may be used to signify a calendar date, or the fruit, or the social engagement. To avoid confusion, metadata terms are assigned a prefix that is associated with a web document that defines the term (ie, establishes the tag's namespace). In practical terms, a tag that can have different descriptive meanings in different contexts is provided with a prefix that links to a web document wherein the meaning of the tag, as it applies in the XML document is specified.

Negative classifier One of the most common mistakes committed by ontologists involves classification by negative attribute. A negative classifier is a feature whose absence is used to define a class. An example is found in the Collembola, popularly known as springtails, a ubiquitous member of Class Hexapoda, and readily found under just about any rock. These organisms look like fleas (same size, same shape) and were formerly misclassified among the class of true fleas (Class Siphonaptera). Like fleas, springtails are wingless, and it was assumed that springtails, like fleas, lost their wings somewhere in evolution's murky past. However, true fleas lost their wings when they became parasitic. Springtails never had wings, an important taxonomic distinction separating springtails from fleas. Today, springtails (Collembola) are assigned to Class Entognatha, a separate subclass of Class Hexapoda. Alternately, taxonomists may be deceived by a feature whose absence is falsely conceived to be a fundamental property of a class of organisms. For example, all species of Class Fungi were believed to have a characteristic absence of a flagellum. Based on the absence of a flagellum, the fungi were excluded from Class Opisthokonta and were put in Class Plantae, which they superficially resembled. However, the chytrids, which have a flagellum, were recently shown to be a primitive member of Class Fungi. This finding places fungi among the true descendants of Class Opisthokonta (from which Class Animalia descended). This means that fungi are much more closely related to people than to plants, a shocking revelation!

Neural network A dynamic system in which outputs are calculated by a summation of weighted functions operating on inputs. The weights for the individual functions are determined by a learning process, simulating the learning process hypothesized for human neurons. In the computer model, individual functions that contribute to a correct output (based on the training data) have their weights increased (strengthening their influence on the calculated output). Over the past ten or fifteen years, neural networks have lost some favor in the artificial intelligence community. They can become computationally complex for very large sets of multidimensional input data. More importantly, complex neural networks cannot be understood or explained by humans, endowing these systems with a "magical" quality that some scientists find unacceptable. See Nongeneralizable predictor. See Overfitting. See Machine learning.

Nomenclature A nomenclature is a listing of terms that cover all of the concepts in a knowledge domain. A nomenclature is different from a dictionary for three reasons: (1) the nomenclature terms are not annotated with definitions, (2) nomenclature terms may be multi-word, and (3) the terms in the nomenclature are limited to the scope of the selected knowledge domain. In addition, most nomenclatures group synonyms under a group code. For example, a food nomenclature might collect submarine, hoagie, po' boy, grinder, hero, and torpedo under an alphanumeric code such as "F63958". Nomenclatures simplify textual documents by uniting synonymous terms under a common code. Documents that have been coded with the same nomenclature can be integrated with other documents that have been similarly coded, and queries conducted over such documents will yield the same results, regardless of which term is entered (ie, a search for either hoagie, or po' boy will retrieve the same information, if both terms have been annotated with the synonym code, "F63948"). Optimally, the canonical concepts listed in the nomenclature are organized into a hierarchical classification.[33,34] See Coding. See Autocoding.

Nonatomicity Nonatomicity is the assignment of a collection of objects to a single, composite object that cannot be further simplified or sensibly deconstructed. For example, the human body is composed of trillions of individual cells, each of which lives for some length of time, and then dies. Many of the cells in the body are capable of dividing to produce more cells. In many cases, the cells of the body that are capable of dividing can be cultured and grown in plastic containers, much like bacteria can be cultured and grown in Petri dishes. If the human body is composed of individual cells, why do we habitually think of each human as a single living entity? Why don't we think of humans as bags of individual cells? Perhaps the reason stems from the coordinated responses of cells. When someone steps on the cells of your toe, the cells in your brain sense pain, the cells in your mouth and vocal cords say ouch, and an army of inflammatory cells rush to the scene of the crime. The cells in your toe are not capable of registering an actionable complaint, without a great deal of assistance. The reason that organisms, composed of trillions of living cells, are generally considered to have nonatomicity, also relates to the "species" concept in biology. Every cell in an organism descended from the same zygote, and every zygote in every member of the same species descended from the same ancestral organism. Hence, there seems to be little benefit to assigning unique entity status to the individual cells that compose organisms, when the class structure for organisms is based on descent through zygotes. See Species.

Nongeneralizable predictor Sometimes data analysis can yield results that are true, but nongeneralizable (ie, irrelevant to everything outside the set of data objects under study). The most useful scientific findings are generalizable (eg, the laws of physics operate on the planet Jupiter or the star Alpha Centauri much as they do on earth). Many of the most popular analytic methods are not generalizable because they produce predictions that only apply to highly restricted sets of data; or the predictions are not explainable by any underlying theory that relates input data with the calculated predictions. Data analysis is incomplete until a comprehensible, generalizable and testable theory for the predictive method is developed.

Nonphylogenetic property Properties that do not hold true for a class; hence, cannot be used by ontologists to create a classification. For example, we do not classify animals by height or weight because animals of greatly different heights and weights may occupy the same biological class. Similarly, animals within a class may have widely ranging geographic habitats; hence, we cannot classify animals by locality. Case in point: penguins can be found virtually anywhere in the southern hemisphere, including hot and cold climates. Hence, we cannot classify penguins as animals that live in Antarctica or that prefer a cold climate. Scientists commonly encounter properties, once thought to be class-specific, that prove to be uninformative, for classification purposes. For many decades, all bacteria were assumed to be small; much smaller than animal cells. However, the bacterium Epulopiscium fishelsoni grows to about 600 microns by 80 microns, much larger than the typical animal epithelial cell (about 35 microns in diameter).[35] Thiomargarita namibiensis, an ocean-dwelling bacterium, can reach a size of 0.75 millimeter, visible to the unaided eye. What do these admittedly obscure facts teach us about the art of classification? Superficial properties, such as size, seldom inform us how to classify objects. The ontologist must think very deeply to find the essential defining features of classes.

Nonphylogenetic signal DNA sequences that cannot yield any useful conclusions related to the evolutionary pathways. Because DNA mutations arise stochastically over time (ie, at random locations in the gene, and at random times), two organisms having different ancestors may, by chance alone, achieve the same sequence in a chosen stretch of DNA. When gene sequence data is analyzed, and two organisms share the same sequence in a stretch of DNA, it can be tempting to infer that the two organisms belong to the same class (ie, that they inherited the identical sequence from a common ancestor). This inference is not necessarily correct. When mathematical phylogeneticists began modeling inferences for gene data sets, they assumed that most of the class assignment errors based on DNA sequence similarity would occur when the branches between sister taxa were long (ie, when a long time elapsed between evolutionary divergences, allowing for many random substitutions in base pairs). They called this phenomenon, wherein nonsister taxa were assigned the same ancient ancestor class, "long branch attraction." In practice, errors of this type can occur whether the branches are long, or short, or in-between. The term "nonphylogenetic signal" refers to just about any pitfall in phylogenetic grouping due to gene similarities acquired through any mechanism other than inheritance from a shared ancestor. This would include random mutational and adaptive convergence.[36]

Normalized compression distance String compression algorithms (eg, zip, gzip, bunzip) should yield better compression from a concatenation of two similar strings than from a concatenation of two highly dissimilar strings. The reason is that the same string patterns that are employed to compress a string (ie, repeated runs of a particular pattern) are likely to be found in another, similar string. If two strings are completely dissimilar, then the compression algorithm would fail to find shared repeated patterns that enhance compressibility. The normalized compression distance is a similarity measure based on the enhanced compressibility of concatenated strings of high similarity.[37] A full discussion, with examples, is found in the Open Source Tools section of Chapter 4.

Notation 3 Also called n3. A syntax for expressing assertions as triples (unique subject+metadata+data). Notation 3 expresses the same information as the more formal RDF syntax, but n3 is easier for humans to read.[38] RDF and n3 are interconvertible, and either one can be parsed and equivalently tokenized (ie, broken into elements that can be re-organized in a different format, such as a database record). See RDF. See Triple.

Object relationships We are raised to believe that science explains how the universe, and everything in it, works. Engineering and the other applied sciences use scientific explanations to create things, for the betterment of our world. This is a lovely way to think about the roles played by scientists and engineers, but it is not completely accurate. For the most part, we cannot understand very much about the universe. Nobody understands the true nature of gravity, or mass, or light, or magnetism, or atoms, or thought. We do know a great deal about the relationships between gravity and mass, mass and energy, energy and light, light and magnetism, atoms and mass, thought and neurons, and so on. Karl Pearson, a 19th century statistician and philosopher, wrote that "All science is description and not explanation." Pearson was admitting that we can describe relationships, but we cannot explain why those relationships are true. Here is an example of a mathematical relationship that we know to be true, but which defies our understanding. The constant pi is the ratio of the circumference of a circle to its diameter. Furthermore, pi figures into the Gaussian statistical distribution (ie, that describes how a normal population is spread). How is it possible that a number that determines the distribution of a population can also determine the diameter of a circle?[15] The relationships are provable and undeniable, but the full meaning of pi is beyond our grasp. **In essence, all of science can be reduced to understanding object relationships.**

Ontology An ontology is a collection of classes and their relationships to one another. Ontologies are usually rule-based systems (ie, membership in a class is determined by one or more class rules). Two important features distinguish ontologies from classifications. Ontologies permit classes to have more than one parent class and more than one child class. For example, the class of automobiles may be a direct subclass of "motorized devices" and a direct subclass of "mechanized transporters." In addition, an instance of a class can be an instance of any number of additional classes. For example, a Lamborghini may be a member of class "automobiles" and of class "luxury items." This means that the lineage of an instance in an ontology can be highly complex, with a single instance occurring in multiple classes, and with many connections between classes. Because recursive relations are permitted, it is possible to build an ontology wherein a class is both an ancestor class and a descendant class of itself. A classification is a highly restrained ontology wherein instances can belong to only one class, and each class may have only one direct parent class. Because classifications have an enforced linear hierarchy, they can be easily modeled, and the lineage of any instance can be traced unambiguously. See Classification. See Multiclass classification. See Multiclass inheritance.

Overfitting Overfitting occurs when a formula describes a set of data very closely, but does not lead to any sensible explanation for the behavior of the data, and does not predict the behavior of comparable data sets. In the case of overfitting, the formula is said to describe the noise of the system, rather than the characteristic behavior of the system. Overfitting occurs frequently with models that perform iterative approximations on training data, coming closer and closer to the training data set with each iteration. Neural networks are an example of a data modeling strategy that is prone to overfitting.[3]

Parent class The immediate ancestor, or the next-higher class (ie, the direct superclass) of a class. For example, in the classification of living organisms, Class Vertebrata is the parent class of Class Gnathostomata. Class Gnathostomata is the parent class of Class Teleostomi. In a classification, which imposes single class inheritance, each child class has exactly one parent class; whereas one parent class may have several different child classes. Furthermore, some classes, in particular the bottom class in the lineage, have no child classes (ie, a class need not always be a superclass of other classes). A class can be defined by its properties, its membership (ie, the instances that belong to the class), and by the name of its parent class. When we list all of the classes in a classification, in any order, we can always reconstruct the complete class lineage, in their correct lineage and branchings, if we know the name of each class's parent class. See Instance. See Child class. See Superclass.

Phenetics   The classification of organisms by feature similarity, rather than through relationships. Starting with a set of feature data on a collection of organisms, you can write a computer program that will cluster the organisms into classes, according to their similarities. In theory, one computer program, executing over a large dataset containing measurements for every earthly organism, could create a complete biological classification. The status of a species is thereby reduced from a fundamental biological entity, to a mathematical construction. There is a host of problems consequent to computational methods for classification. First, there are many different mathematical algorithms that cluster objects by similarity. Depending on the chosen algorithm, the assignment of organisms to one species or another would change. Secondly, mathematical algorithms do not cope well with species convergence. Convergence occurs when two species independently acquire identical or similar traits through adaptation; not through inheritance from a shared ancestor. Examples are: the wing of a bat and the wing of a bird; the opposable thumb of opossums and of primates; the beak of a platypus and the beak of a bird. Unrelated species frequently converge upon similar morphologic adaptations to common environmental conditions or shared physiological imperatives. Algorithms that cluster organisms based on similarity are likely to group divergent organisms under the same species. It is often assumed that computational classification, based on morphologic feature similarities, will improve when we acquire whole-genome sequence data for many different species. Imagine an experiment wherein you take DNA samples from every organism you encounter: bacterial colonies cultured from a river, unicellular nonbacterial organisms found in a pond, small multicellular organisms found in soil, crawling creatures dwelling under rocks, and so on. You own a powerful sequencing machine, that produces the full-length sequence for each sampled organism, and you have a powerful computer that sorts and clusters every sequence. At the end, the computer prints out a huge graph, wherein all the samples are ordered and groups with the greatest sequence similarities are clustered together. You may think you've created a useful classification, but you haven't really, because you don't know anything about the organisms that are clustered together. You don't know whether each cluster represents a species, or a class (a collection of related species), or whether a cluster may be contaminated by organisms that share some of the same gene sequences, but are phylogenetically unrelated (ie, the sequence similarities result from chance or from convergence, but not by descent from a common ancestor). The sequences do not tell you very much about the biological properties of specific organisms, and you cannot infer which biological properties characterize the classes of clustered organisms. You have no certain knowledge whether the members of any given cluster of organisms can be characterized by any particular gene sequence (ie, you do not know the characterizing gene sequences for classes of organisms). You do not know the genus or species names of the organisms included in the clusters, because you began your experiment without a presumptive taxonomy. Basically, you simply know what you knew before you started; that individual organisms have unique gene sequences that can be grouped by sequence similarity. Taxonomists, who have long held that a species is a natural unit of biological life, and that the nature of a species is revealed through the intellectual process of building a consistent taxonomy,[21] are opposed to the process of phenetics-based classification.[21] See Blended class. See Bootstrapping.

Polymorphism   Polymorphism is one of the constitutive properties of an object-oriented language (along with inheritance, encapsulation, and abstraction). Methods sent to object receivers have a response determined by the class of the receiving object. Hence, different objects, from different classes, receiving a call to a method of the same name, will respond differently. For example, suppose you have a method named "divide" and you send the method (ie, issue a command to execute the method) to an object of Class Bacteria and an object of Class Numerics. The Bacteria, receiving the divide method, will try to execute by looking for the "divide" method somewhere in its class lineage. Being bacteria, the "divide" method may involve making a copy of the bacteria (ie, reproducing) and incrementing the number of bacteria in the population. The numeric object, receiving the "divide" method, will look for the "divide" method in its class lineage and will probably find some method that provides instructions for arithmetic division. Hence, the behavior of the class object, to a received method, will be appropriate for the class of the object. See Inheritance. See Encapsulation. See Abstraction.

Predictive analytics A collection of techniques that have achieved great popularity and influence in the marketing industry. These are: recommenders, classifiers, and clustering algorithms.[39] Although these techniques can be used for purposes other than business, they are typically described using terms favored by marketers: recommenders (eg, predicting which products a person might prefer to buy), profile clustering (eg, grouping individuals into marketing clusters based on the similarity of their profiles), and product classifiers (eg, assigning a product or individual to a prediction category, based on a set of features). See Classifier. See Recommender.

Property Property, in the context of computational semantics, is a quantitative or qualitative feature of an object. In the case of spreadsheets, the column heads are all properties. In a classification, every class contains a set of properties that might apply to every member of the class (eg, male cardinals have the "red feather" property). Furthermore, instances may have their own set of properties, separate from the class. For example, the cardinal that I watch in my back yard seems to enjoy eating safflower seeds and cavorting in our bird bath, but I'm not sure that all cardinals share the same pleasures. From the standpoint of classifications, it is crucial to understand that a property may apply to multiple classes that are not directly related to one another. For example, insects, birds, and bats are not closely related classes of animals, but they all share the amazing property of flight. It is the ability to assign a single property to multiple classes that liberates classifications from the restraints imposed by the one-class/one-parent dictum. Although a class can have no more than one parent class, a class can share properties, in the form of data types and data methods, with unrelated classes. For example, Class File may be unrelated to Class Integer, but both classes may share a "print" method or the same "store" method. In object-oriented programming, assignments of shared methods to multiple classes is known as Mixins. See Mixins.

RDF Resource Description Framework (RDF) is a syntax in XML notation that formally expresses assertions as triples. The RDF triple consists of a uniquely identified subject plus a metadata descriptor for the data plus a data element. Triples are necessary and sufficient to create statements that convey meaning. Triples can be aggregated with other triples from the same data set or from other data sets, so long as each triple pertains to a unique subject that is identified equivalently through the data sets. Enormous data sets of RDF triples can be merged or functionally integrated with other massive or complex data resources. For a detailed discussion see Open Source Tools, "Syntax for Triples." See Notation 3. See Semantics. See Triple. See XML.

RDF Schema Resource Description Framework Schema (RDFS). A document containing a list of classes, their definitions, and the names of the parent class(es) for each class. In an RDF Schema, the list of classes is typically followed by a list of properties that apply to one or more classes in the Schema. To be useful, RDF Schemas are posted on the Internet, as a Web page, with a unique Web address. Anyone can incorporate the classes and properties of a public RDF Schema into their own RDF documents (public or private) by linking named classes and properties, in their RDF document, to the web address of the RDF Schema where the classes and properties are defined. See Namespace. See RDFS.

RDFS Same as RDF Schema.

Recommender A collection of methods for predicting the preferences of individuals. Recommender methods often rely on one or two simple assumptions: (1) If an individual expresses a preference for a certain type of product, and the individual encounters a new product that is similar to a previously preferred product, then he is likely to prefer the new product; (2) If an individual expresses preferences that are similar to the preferences expressed by a cluster of individuals, and if the members of the cluster prefer a product that the individual has not yet encountered, then the individual will most likely prefer the product. See Predictive analytics. See Classifier.

Reconciliation Usually refers to identifiers, and involves verifying that an object that is assigned a particular identifier in one information system has been provided the same identifier in some other system. For example, if I am assigned identifier 967bc9e7-fea0-4b09-92e7-d9327c405d78 in a legacy record system, I should like to be assigned the same identifier in the new record system. If that were the case, my records in both systems could be combined. If I am assigned an identifier in one system that is different from my assigned identifier in another system, then the two identifiers must be reconciled to determine that they both refer to the same unique data object (ie, me). This may involve creating a link between the two identifiers, or a new triple that establishes the equivalence of the two identifiers. Despite claims to the contrary, there is no possible way by which information systems with poor identifier systems can be sensibly reconciled. Consider this example. A hospital has two separate registry systems: one for dermatology cases and another for psychiatry cases. The hospital would like to merge records from the two services. Because of sloppy identifier practices, a sample patient has been registered 10 times in the dermatology system, and 6 times in the psychiatry system, each time with different addresses, social security numbers, birthdates, and spellings of the name. A reconciliation algorithm is applied, and one of the identifiers from the dermatology service is matched positively against one of the records from the psychiatry service. Performance studies on the algorithm indicate that the merged records have a 99.8% chance of belonging to the same patient. So what? Though the two merged identifiers correctly point to the same patient, there are 14 (9+5) residual identifiers for the patient still unmatched. The patient's merged record will not contain his complete clinical history. Furthermore, in this hypothetical instance, analyses of patient population data will mistakenly attribute one patient's clinical findings to as many as 15 different patients, and the set of 15 records in the corrupted de-identified dataset may contain mixed-in information from an indeterminate number of additional patients! If the preceding analysis seems harsh, consider these words, from the Healthcare Information and Management Systems Society, "A local system with a poorly maintained or "dirty" master person index (MPI) will only proliferate and contaminate all of the other systems to which it links."[40] See Social Security Number.

Reflection A programming technique wherein a computer program will modify itself, at run-time, based on information it acquires through introspection. For example, a computer program may iterate over a collection of data objects, examining the self-descriptive information for each object in the collection (ie, object introspection). If the information indicates that the data object belongs to a particular class of objects, then the program may call a method appropriate for the class. The program executes in a manner determined by descriptive information obtained during run-time; metaphorically reflecting upon the purpose of its computational task. See Introspection.

Registrars and human authentication The experiences of registrars in U.S. hospitals serve as cautionary instruction. Hospital registrars commit a disastrous mistake when they assume that all patients wish to comply with the registration process. A patient may be highly motivated to provide false information to a registrar, or to acquire several different registration identifiers, or to seek a false registration under another person's identity (ie, commit fraud), or to forego the registration process entirely. In addition, it is a mistake to believe that honest patients are able to fully comply with the registration process. Language barriers, cultural barriers, poor memory, poor spelling, and a host of errors and misunderstandings can lead to duplicative or otherwise erroneous identifiers. It is the job of the registrar to follow hospital policies that overcome these difficulties. Registration should be conducted by a trained registrar who is well-versed in the registration policies established by the institution. Registrars may require patients to provide a full legal name, any prior held names (eg, maiden name), date of birth, and a government issue photo id card (eg, driver's license or photo id card issued by the department of motor vehicles). Ideally, registration should require a biometric identifier (eg, fingerprints, retina scan, iris scan, voice recording, photograph). If you accept the premise that hospitals have the responsibility of knowing who it is that they are treating, then obtaining a sample of DNA from every patient, at the time of registration, is reasonable. The DNA can be used to create a unique patient profile from a chosen set of informative loci; a procedure used by the CODIS system developed for law enforcement agencies. The registrar should document any distinguishing and permanent physical features that are plainly visible (eg, scars, eye color, colobomas, tattoos). Neonatal and pediatric identifiers pose a special set of problems for registrars. When an individual is born in a hospital, and provided with an identifier, returns as an adult, he or she should be assigned the same identifier that was issued in the remote past. Every patient who comes for registration should be matched against a database of biometric data that does not change from birth to death (eg, fingerprints, DNA). See Social Security Number.

SUMO Knowing that ontologies reach into higher ontologies, ontologists have endeavored to create upper-level ontologies to accommodate general classes of objects, under which the lower ontologies may take their place. One such ontology is SUMO, the Suggested Upper Merged Ontology, created by a group of talented ontologists.[41] SUMO is owned by IEEE (Institute of Electrical and Electronics Engineers), and is freely available, subject to a usage license.[42]

SVM See Support vector machine.

Science Of course, there are many different definitions of science, and inquisitive students should be encouraged to find a conceptualization of science that suits their own intellectual development. For me, science is all about finding general relationships among objects. In the so-called physical sciences, the most important relationships are expressed as mathematical equations (eg, the relationship between force, mass and acceleration; the relationship between voltage, current and resistance). In the so-called natural sciences, relationships are often expressed through classifications (eg, the classification of living organisms). Scientific advancement is the discovery of new relationships or the discovery of a generalization that applies to objects hitherto confined within disparate scientific realms (eg, evolutionary theory arising from observations of organisms and geologic strata). Engineering would be the area of science wherein scientific relationships are exploited to build new technology. See Generalization.

Semantics The study of meaning (Greek root, semantikos, significant meaning). In the context of data science, semantics is the technique of creating meaningful assertions about data objects. A meaningful assertion, as used here, is a triple consisting of an identified data object, a data value, and a descriptor for the data value. In practical terms, semantics involves making assertions about data objects (ie, making triples), combining assertions about data objects (ie, merging triples), and assigning data objects to classes; hence relating triples to other triples. As a word of warning, few informaticians would define semantics in these terms, but most definitions for semantics are functionally equivalent to the definition offered here. Much of any language is unstructured and meaningless. Consider the assertion: Sam is tired. This is an adequately structured sentence with a subject verb and object. But what is the meaning of the sentence? There are a lot of people named Sam. Which Sam is being referred to in this sentence? What does it mean to say that Sam is tired? Is "tiredness" a constitutive property of Sam, or does it only apply to specific moments? If so, for what moment in time is the assertion, "Sam is tired" actually true? To a computer, meaning comes from assertions that have a specific, identified subject associated with some sensible piece of fully described data (metadata coupled with the data it describes). See Triple. See RDF.

Simpson's paradox Occurs when a correlation that holds in two different data sets is reversed if the data sets are combined. For example, baseball player A may have a higher batting average than player B for each of two seasons, but when the data for the two seasons are combined, player B may have the higher 2-season average. Simpson's paradox is just one example of unexpected changes in outcome when variables are unknowingly hidden or blended.[43]

Social Security Number The common strategy, in the U.S., of employing social security numbers as identifiers is often counterproductive, owing to entry error, mistaken memory, or the intention to deceive. Efforts to reduce errors by requiring individuals to produce their original social security cards puts an unreasonable burden on honest individuals, who rarely carry their cards, and provides an advantage to dishonest individuals, who can easily forge social security cards. Institutions that compel patients to provide a social security number have dubious legal standing. The social security number was originally intended as a device for validating a person's standing in the social security system. More recently, the purpose of the social security number has been expanded to track taxable transactions (ie, bank accounts, salaries). Other uses of the social security number are not protected by law. The Social Security Act (Section 208 of Title 42 U.S. Code 408) prohibits most entities from compelling anyone to divulge his/her social security number. Legislation or judicial action may one day stop healthcare institutions from compelling patients to divulge their social security numbers as a condition for providing medical care. Prudent and forward-thinking institutions will limit their reliance on social security numbers as personal identifiers. See Registrars and human authentication.

Species Species is the bottom-most class of any classification or ontology. Because the species class contains the individual objects of the classification, it is the only class which is not abstract. The special significance of the species class is best exemplified in the classification of living organisms. Every species of organism contains individuals that share a common ancestral relationship to one another. When we look at a group of squirrels, we know that each squirrel in the group has its own unique personality, its own unique genes (ie, genotype), and its own unique set of physical features (ie, phenotype). Moreover, although the DNA sequences of individual squirrels are unique, we assume that there is a commonality to the genome of squirrels that distinguishes it from the genome of every other species. If we use the modern definition of species as an evolving gene pool, we see that the species can be thought of as a biological life form, with substance (a population of propagating genes), and a function (evolving to produce new species).[21,44,45] Put simply, species speciate; individuals do not. As a corollary, species evolve; individuals simply propagate. Hence, the species class is a separable biological unit with form and function. We, as individuals, are focused on the lives of individual things, and we must be reminded of the role of species in biological and nonbiological classifications. The concept of species is discussed in greater detail in Section 6.4. See Blended class. See Nonatomicity.

Spreadsheet Spreadsheets are data arrays consisting of records (the rows), with each record containing data attributes (the columns). Spreadsheet applications permit the user to search records, columns, and cells (ie, the data points corresponding to a specific record and a specific column). Spreadsheets support statistical and mathematical functions operating on the elements of the spreadsheet (ie, records, columns, cells). Perhaps most importantly, spreadsheets offer a wide range of easily implemented graphing features. Quite a few data scientists perform virtually all of their work using a favorite spreadsheet application. Spreadsheets have limited utility when dealing with large data (eg, gigabytes or terabytes of data), complex data (eg, images, waveforms, text), and they do not easily support classified data (eg, data objects that belong to classes within a lineage of classes). Additionally, spreadsheets do not support the kinds of methods and data structures (eg, if statements, access to external modules, system calls, network interactions, reflection, complex data structures) that are supported in modern programming languages.

Subclass A class in which every member descends from some higher class (ie, a superclass) within the class hierarchy. Members of a subclass have properties specific to the subclass. As every member of a subclass is also a member of the superclass, the members of a subclass inherit the properties and methods of the ancestral classes. For example, all mammals have mammary glands because mammary glands are a defining property of the mammal class. In addition, all mammals have vertebrae because the class of mammals is a subclass of the class of vertebrates. A subclass is the immediate child class of its parent class. See Child class. See Parent class.

Superclass Any of the ancestral classes of a subclass. For example, in the classification of living organisms, the class of vertebrates is a superclass of the class of mammals. The immediate superclass of a class is its parent class. In common parlance, when we speak of the superclass of a class, we are usually referring to its parent class. See Parent class.

Support vector machine A machine learning classifying algorithm. The method starts with a training set consisting of two classes of objects as input. The support vector machine computes a hyperplane, in a multidimensional space, that separates objects of the two classes. The dimension of the hyperspace is determined by the number of dimensions or attributes associated with the objects. Additional objects (ie, test set objects) are assigned membership in one class or the other, depending on which side of the hyperplane they reside.

Taxonomic order In biological taxonomy, the hierarchical lineage of organisms are divided into a descending list of named orders: Kingdom, Phylum (Division), Class, Order, Family, and Genus, Species. As we have learned more and more about the classes of organisms, modern taxonomists have added additional ranks to the classification (eg, supraphylum, subphylum, suborder, infraclass, etc.). Was this really necessary? All of this taxonomic complexity could be averted by dropping named ranks and simply referring to every class as "Class." Modern specifications for class hierarchies (eg, RDF Schema) encapsulate each class with the name of its superclass. When every object yields its class and superclass, it is possible to trace any object's class lineage. For example, in the classification of living organisms, if you know the name of the parent for each class, you can write a simple script that generates the complete ancestral lineage for every class and species within the classification.[18] See Class. See Taxonomy. See RDF Schema. See Species.

Taxonomy A taxonomy is the collection of named instances (class members) in a classification or an ontology. When you see a schematic showing class relationships, with individual classes represented by geometric shapes and the relationships represented by arrows or connecting lines between the classes, then you are essentially looking at the structure of a classification, minus the taxonomy. You can think of building a taxonomy as the act of pouring all of the names of all of the instances into their proper classes. A taxonomy is similar to a nomenclature; the difference is that in a taxonomy, every named instance must have an assigned class. See Taxonomic order.

Terminology The collection of words and terms used in some particular discipline, field, or knowledge domain. It is nearly synonymous with vocabulary and with nomenclature. Vocabularies, unlike terminologies, are not to be confined to the terms used in a particular field. Nomenclatures, unlike terminologies, usually aggregate equivalent terms under a canonical synonym.

Thesaurus A vocabulary that groups together synonymous terms. A thesaurus is very similar to a nomenclature. There are two minor differences. Nomenclatures included multi-word terms; whereas a thesaurus is typically composed of one-word terms. In addition, nomenclatures are typically restricted to a well-defined topic or knowledge domain (eg, names of stars, infectious diseases, etc.). See Nomenclature. See Vocabulary. See Classification. See Dictionary. See Terminology. See Ontology.

Triple In computer semantics, a triple is an identified data object associated with a data element and the description of the data element. In the computer science literature, the syntax for the triple is commonly described as: subject, predicate, object," wherein the subject is an identifier, the predicate is the description of the object, and the object is the data. The definition of triple, using grammatical terms, can be off-putting to the data scientist, who may think in terms of spreadsheet entries: a key that identifies the line record, a column header containing the metadata description of the data, and a cell that contains the data. In this book, the three components of a triple are described as: (1) the identifier for the data object, (2) the metadata that describes the data, and (3) the data itself. In theory, all data sets, databases, and spreadsheets can be constructed or deconstructed as collections of triples. See Introspection. See Data object. See Semantics. See RDF. See Meaning.

Triplestore A list or database composed entirely of triples (ie, statements consisting of an item identifier plus the metadata describing the item plus an item of data). The triples in a triplestore need not be saved in any particular order, and any triplestore can be merged with any other triplestore; the basic semantic meaning of the contained triples is unaffected. See Triple.

Unclassifiable objects Classifications create a class for every object and taxonomies assign each and every object to its correct class. This means that a classification is not permitted to contain unclassified objects; a condition that puts fussy taxonomists in an untenable position. Suppose you have an object, and you simply do not know enough about the object to confidently assign it to a class. Or, suppose you have an object that seems to fit more than one class, and you can't decide which class is the correct class. What do you do? Historically, scientists have resorted to creating a "miscellaneous" class into which otherwise unclassifiable objects are given a temporary home, until more suitable accommodations can be provided. I have spoken with numerous data managers, and everyone seems to be of a mind that "miscellaneous" classes, created as a stopgap measure, serve a useful purpose. Not so. Historically, the promiscuous application of "miscellaneous" classes has proven to be a huge impediment to the advancement of science. In the case of the classification of living organisms, the class of protozoans stands as a case in point. Ernst Haeckel, a leading biological taxonomist in his time, created the Kingdom Protista (ie, protozoans), in 1866, to accommodate a wide variety of simple organisms with superficial commonalities. Haeckel himself understood that the protists were a blended class that included unrelated organisms, but he believed that further study would resolve the confusion. In a sense, he was right, but the process took much longer than he had anticipated; occupying generations of taxonomists over the following 150 years. Today, Kingdom Protista no longer exists. Its members have been reassigned to other classes. Nonetheless, textbooks of microbiology still describe the protozoans, just as though this name continued to occupy a legitimate place among terrestrial organisms. In the meantime, therapeutic opportunities for eradicating so-called protozoal infections, using class-targeted agents, have no doubt been missed.[16] You might think that the creation of a class of living organisms, with no established scientific relation to the real world, was a rare and ancient event in the annals of biology, having little or no chance of being repeated. Not so. A special pseudoclass of fungi, deuteromyctetes (spelled with a lowercase "d," signifying its questionable validity as a true biologic class) has been created to hold fungi of indeterminate speciation. At present, there are several thousand such fungi, sitting in a taxonomic limbo, waiting to be placed into a definitive taxonomic class.[20,16] See Blended class.

Unstable taxonomy A taxonomy that continuously changes over time. Examples abound from the classification of living organisms. You might expect that a named species would keep its name forever, and would never change its assigned class. Not so. For example, Class Fungi has recently undergone profound changes, with the exclusion of myxomycetes (slime molds) and oomycetes (water molds), and the acquisition of Class Microsporidia (formerly classed as a protozoan). The instability of fungal taxonomy impacts negatively on the practice of clinical mycology. When the name of a fungus changes, so must the name of the associated disease. Consider "Allescheria boydii," Individuals infected with this organism were said to suffer from the disease known as allescheriasis. When the organism's name was changed to Petriellidium boydii, the disease name was changed to petriellidosis. When the fungal name was changed, once more, to Pseudallescheria boydii, the disease name was changed to pseudallescheriasis.[20] All three names appear in the literature, past and present, thus hindering attempts to annotate the medical literature.[16] See Autocoding. See Annotation. See Unclassifiable objects.

Vocabulary A comprehensive collection of words and their associated meanings. In some quarters, "vocabulary" and "nomenclature" are used interchangeably, but they are different from one another. Nomenclatures typically focus on terms confined to one knowledge domain. Nomenclatures typically do not contain definitions for the contained terms. Nomenclatures typically group terms by synonymy. Lastly, nomenclatures include multiword terms. Vocabularies are collections of single words, culled from multiple knowledge domains, with their definitions, and assembled in alphabetic order. See Nomenclature. See Thesaurus. See Taxonomy. See Dictionary. See Terminology.

XML Acronym for eXtensible Markup Language, a syntax for marking data values with descriptors (ie, metadata). The descriptors are commonly known as tags. In XML, every data value is enclosed by a start-tag, containing the descriptor and indicating that a value will follow, and an end-tag, containing the same descriptor and indicating that a value preceded the tag. For example: <name>Conrad Nervig </name >. The enclosing angle brackets, "<>", and the end-tag marker, "/", are hallmarks of HTML and XML markup. This simple but powerful relationship between metadata and data allows us to employ metadata/data pairs as though each were a miniature database. The semantic value of XML becomes apparent when we bind a metadata/data pair to a unique object, forming a so-called triple. See Triple. See Meaning. See Semantics. See HTML.

REFERENCES

1. Jarche H. Increased complexity needs simplified design (blog). October 5, 2009. Available at http://jarche.com/2009/10/increased-complexity-needs-simplified-design/ [accessed 01.06.15].
2. Berman JJ. *Ruby programming for medicine and biology.* Sudbury, MA: Jones and Bartlett; 2008.

3. Berman JJ. *Principles of big data: preparing, sharing, and analyzing complex information*. Burlington, MA: Morgan Kaufmann; 2013.
4. Resource Description Framework (RDF). Available from: http://www.w3.org/RDF/ [accessed 14.1115].
5. Ahmed K, Ayers D, Birbeck M, Cousins J, Dodds D, Lubell J, et al. *Professional XML Meta Data*. Birmingham, UK: Wrox; 2001.
6. GT.M High end TP database engine: Industrial strength NoSQL application development platform. Available at: http://sourceforge.net/projects/fis-gtm/ [accessed 29.08.15].
7. MUMPS Database and Language. ANSI standard MUMPS. Available at: http://sourceforge.net/projects/mumps/files/ [accessed 29.08.15].
8. Tweed R, James G. A Universal NoSQL Engine, Using a Tried and Tested Technology; 2010. Available at: http://www.mgateway.com/docs/universalNoSQL.pdf [accessed 29.08.15].
9. Berman JJ. *Repurposing legacy data: innovative case studies*. Burlington, MA: Morgan Kaufmann; 2015.
10. Philippe H, Brinkmann H, Lavrov DV, Littlewood DT, Manuel M, Worheide G, et al. Resolving difficult phylogenetic questions: why more sequences are not enough. *PLoS Biol* 2011;**9**:e1000602.
11. Allen W. My speech to the graduates. In: *Side effects*. New York: Ballantine; 1981. p. 81.
12. Madar S, Goldstein I, Rotter V. Did experimental biology die? Lessons from 30 years of p53 research. *Cancer Res* 2009;**69**:6378–80.
13. Zilfou JT, Lowe SW. Tumor suppressive functions of p53. *Cold Spring Harb Perspect Biol* 2009;**1**(5): a001883.
14. Mitra P, Wiederhold G. An ontology-composition algebra. In: Staab S, Studer R, editors. *Handbook on ontologies*. 2nd ed. New York: Springer; 2009 [chapter 5].
15. Wigner E. The unreasonable effectiveness of mathematics in the natural sciences. *Communications in pure and applied mathematics*, vol. 13. New York: John Wiley and Sons; 1960.
16. Berman JJ. *Taxonomic guide to infectious diseases: understanding the biologic classes of pathogenic organisms*. Waltham: Academic Press; 2012.
17. Letunic I, Bork P. Interactive tree of life (iTOL): an online tool for phylogenetic tree display and annotation. *Bioinformatics* 2007;**23**:127–8.
18. Berman JJ. *Methods in medical informatics: fundamentals of healthcare programming in Perl, Python, and Ruby*. Boca Raton: Chapman and Hall; 2010.
19. Committee on A Framework for Developing a New Taxonomy of Disease, Board on Life Sciences, Division on Earth and Life Studies, National Research Council of the National Academies. *Toward precision medicine: building a knowledge network for biomedical research and a new taxonomy of disease*. Washington, DC: The National Academies Press; 2011.
20. Guarro J, Gene J, Stchigel AM. Developments in fungal taxonomy. *Clin Microbiol Rev* 1999;**12**:454–500.
21. DeQueiroz K. Ernst Mayr and the modern concept of species. *PNAS* 2005;**102**(Suppl. 1):6600–7.
22. Smith B, Ceusters W, Klagges B, Kohler J, Kumar A, Lomax J, et al. *Relations in biomedical ontologies*. *Genome Biol* 2005;**6**:R46. Available at: http://genomebiology.com/2005/6/5/R46 [accessed 09.09.15].
23. Borgwardt S, Radua J, Mechelli A, Fusar-Poli P. Why are psychiatric imaging methods clinically unreliable? Conclusions and practical guidelines for authors, editors and reviewers. *Behav Brain Funct* 2012;**8**:46.
24. Belluck P, Carey B. Psychiatry's guide is out of touch with science, Experts Say. The New York Times, May 6, 2013.
25. Primer: Getting into RDF & Semantic Web using N3. Available from: http://www.w3.org/2000/10/swap/Primer.html [accessed 17.09.15].
26. Berman JJ. *Perl programming for medicine and biology*. Sudbury, MA: Jones and Bartlett; 2007.
27. Gansner E, Koutsofios E. Drawing graphs with dot, January 26, 2006. Available at: http://www.graphviz.org/Documentation/dotguide.pdf [accessed 29.06.15].

28. Al-Agha OM, Igbokwe AA. Malignant fibrous histiocytoma: between the past and the present. *Arch Pathol Lab Med* 2008;**132**:1030–5.

29. Nakayama R, Nemoto T, Takahashi H, Ohta T, Kawai A, Seki K, et al. Gene expression analysis of soft tissue sarcomas: characterization and reclassification of malignant fibrous histiocytoma. *Mod Pathol* 2007;**20**:749–59.

30. Patil N, Berno AJ, Hinds DA, Barrett WA, Doshi JM, Hacker CR, et al. Blocks of limited haplotype diversity revealed by high-resolution scanning of human chromosome 21. *Science* 2001;**294**:1719–23.

31. Wu X, Kumar V, Quinlan JR, Ghosh J, Yang Q, Motoda H, et al. Top 10 algorithms in data mining. *Knowl Inf Syst* 2008;**14**:1–37.

32. Paskin N. Identifier interoperability: a report on two recent ISO activities. *D-Lib Mag* 2006;**12**:1–23.

33. Berman JJ. Tumor classification: molecular analysis meets Aristotle. *BMC Cancer* 2004;**4**:10. Available from: http://www.biomedcentral.com/1471-2407/4/10 [accessed 01.01.15].

34. Berman JJ. Tumor taxonomy for the developmental lineage classification of neoplasms. *BMC Cancer* 2004;**4**:88. http://www.biomedcentral.com/1471-2407/4/88 [accessed 01.01.15].

35. Angert ER, Clements KD, Pace NR. The largest bacterium. *Nature* 1993;**362**:239–41.

36. Bergsten J. A review of long-branch attraction. *Cladistics* 2005;**21**:163–93.

37. Cilibrasi R, Vitanyi PMB. Clustering by compression. *IEEE Trans Inf Theory* 2005;**51**:1523–45.

38. Berman JJ, Moore GW. Implementing an RDF Schema for pathology images; 2007. Available from: http://www.julesberman.info/spec2img.htm [accessed 01.01.15].

39. Owen S, Anil R, Dunning T, Friedman E. *Mahout in action*. Shelter Island, NY: Manning Publications Co.; 2012.

40. Patient Identity Integrity. A White Paper by the HIMSS Patient Identity Integrity Work Group, December 2009. Available from: http://www.himss.org/content/files/PrivacySecurity/PIIWhitePaper.pdf [accessed 19.09.12].

41. Niles I, Pease A. Towards a standard upper ontology. In: Welty C, Smith B, editors. Proceedings of the 2nd international conference on formal ontology in information systems (FOIS-2001), Ogunquit, Maine, October 17–19; 2001.

42. Suggested Upper Merged Ontology (SUMO). The OntologyPortal. Available from: http://www.ontologyportal.org [accessed 14.08.12].

43. Tu Y, Gunnell D, Gilthorpe MS. Simpson's Paradox, Lord's Paradox, and Suppression Effects are the same phenomenon — the reversal paradox. *Emerg Themes Epidemiol* 2008;**5**:2.

44. DeQueiroz K. Species concepts and species delimitation. *Syst Biol* 2007;**56**:879–86.

45. Mayden RL. Consilience and a hierarchy of species concepts: advances toward closure on the species puzzle. *J Nematol* 1999;**31**(2):95–116.

OBJECT-ORIENTED DATA

7

7.1 THE IMPORTANCE OF SELF-EXPLAINING DATA

> Looking at code you wrote more than two weeks ago is like looking at code you are seeing for the first time.
>
> **-Dan Hurvitz**

Data scientists use data for purposes that were unintended or unimagined by the people who prepared the data. The data that is being analyzed today may have been collected decades, centuries, or millennia in the past. If we hope to use today's data for tomorrow's purposes, we need to prepare our data in a manner that preserves meaning. Here a just a few examples.

Following the first Apollo mission to the moon (Apollo 11, July 20, 1969), the five subsequent Apollo missions left behind recording instruments on the lunar surface. The collective set of down-linked data received from these instruments is known as the Apollo Lunar Surface Experiments Package (ALSEP). More than 11,000 data tapes were recorded.[1]

While the Apollo program was active, control and use of the tapes, as well as the responsibility to safely archive the tapes, was distributed among various agencies and institutions. When the Apollo mission ended, funds were low, and a portion of the data that had been distributed to various investigators and agencies was never sent to the official archives.[2] It should come as no surprise that, at the present time, about half of the ALSEP tapes are missing; their whereabouts uncertain. Of the available tapes, much of the data is difficult to access, due to the use of abandoned data media (ie, 7- and 9-track tapes) and obsolete data formats[2] (see Glossary item, Abandonware).

Available ALSEP data, when converted into a modern data format, have proven to be a valuable asset, when reanalyzed with modern analytic tools. For example, the first analyses of ALSEP's seismic data, conducted 35 years ago, indicated that about 1300 deep moonquakes had occurred during the period when the data was being downlinked. The field of seismic analysis has advanced in the interim. A reanalysis of the same data, using modern techniques, has produced an upward revision of the first estimate; to about 7000 deep moonquakes.[2]

Today, there is a renewed push to find, collect, and archive the missing ALSEP data. Why is there a sudden urgency to finish a chore that should have been completed decades ago? Simply put, the tapes must be restored before the last of the original investigators, who alone understand the scope and organization of the data, vanish into retirement or death.

In the 1980s, the PETRA collider conducted a number of so-called atom smashing experiments designed to measure the force required to bind together quarks and gluons, the fundamental components of protons and neutrons.[1] In 1986, the PETRA collider was decommissioned and replaced with colliders that operated at higher energy levels. Several decades passed, and advances in physics raised questions that could only be answered with observations on low-energy collisions; the kind of observations collected by PETRA and omitted by present-day colliders.[3]

An archeological effort to retrieve and repurpose the 1980s data was spearheaded by Siegfried Bethke, one of the original scientists in PETRA's JADE project.[4] In the period following the decommissioning of PETRA, the original data had been dispersed to various laboratories (see Glossary item, Data archeology). Some of the JADE data was simply lost, and none of the data was collected in a format or a medium that was directly accessible.[1]

The repurposing project was divided into three tasks, involving three teams of scientists (see Glossary item, Data repurposing). One team rescued the data from archived tapes and transferred the data into a modern medium and format. The second team improved the original JADE software, fitting it to modern computer platforms. By applying new software, using updated Monte Carlo simulations, the second team generated a new set of data files (see Glossary item, Monte Carlo simulation). The third team reanalyzed the regenerated data using modern methods and improved calculations.

The project culminated in the production of numerous scientific contributions that could not have been achieved without the old JADE data. Success was credited, at least in part, to the participation of some of the same individuals who collected the original data.

On the Yucatan peninsula, concentrated within a geographic area that today encompasses the southeastern tip of Mexico, plus Belize and Guatemala, a great civilization flourished. The Mayan civilization seems to have begun about 2000 BCE, reaching its peak in the so-called classic period (AD 250–900). Abruptly, about AD 900, the great Mayan cities were abandoned, and the Mayan civilization entered a period of decline. Soon after the Spanish colonization of the peninsula, in the 16th century, the Mayans were subjected to a deliberate effort to erase any trace of their heritage. By the dawn of the 20th century, the great achievements of the Mayan civilization were forgotten, its cities and temples were thoroughly overgrown by jungle, its books had been destroyed, and no humans on the planet could decipher the enduring stone glyph tablets strewn through the Yucatan peninsula.

Over a period of several centuries, generations of archeologists, linguists, and epigraphers devoted their careers to decoding the Mayan glyphs. To succeed, they depended on the glyphs to provide some initial information to help explain their meaning. Luckily, the glyphs were created with a set of features that are essential for extracting meaning from data. The ancient Mayans provided unique, identified objects (eg, name of king and name of city), with an accurate timestamp (ie, date) on all glyph entries. The Mayans had a sophisticated calendar, highly accurate timekeeping methods, and their data was encoded in a sophisticated number system that included the concept of zero. Furthermore, their recorded data was annotated with metadata (ie, descriptions of the quantitative data). The careful recording of data as uniquely identified records, with accurate dates and helpful metadata, was the key to the first two breakthrough discoveries. In 1832, Constantine Rafinesque decoded the Mayan number system. In 1880, Forstemann, using Rafinesque's techniques to decode the numbers that appeared in a Mayan text, deduced how the Mayans recorded the passage of time, and how they used numbers to predict astronomic events. After these discoveries were made, the Mayan glyphs incrementally yielded their secrets. By 1981, the ancient Mayan scripts were essentially decoded.

What is the moral of these three examples of data repurposing (ie, The ALSEP lunar surface measurements, the PETRA collider data, and the Mayan glyphs)? The moral seems to be that if you do not want to spend decades or centuries trying to understand your data, you had better give some thought to the way you prepare your data.[5] Analysis of numerous data reconstruction efforts indicates that good historical data fulfills the following[1]:

1. Data that is immutable (see Glossary item, Immutability)
2. Data that is persistent (see Glossary item, Persistence)
3. Data that establishes the unique identify of records (ie, data objects)
4. Data that accrues over time, documenting the moments when data objects are obtained (ie, timestamped data)
5. Data that is described (ie, annotated with metadata)
6. Data that assigns data objects to classes of information
7. Data that provides a structural hierarchy for classes
8. Data that explains itself (ie, introspective data)

7.2 INTROSPECTION AND REFLECTION

> The difference between theory and practice is that in theory, there is no difference between theory and practice.
>
> **-Richard Moore**

Introspection is a term borrowed from object-oriented programming, not often found in the informatics literature. It refers to the ability of data objects to describe themselves when interrogated. With introspection, data scientists can determine the content of data objects and the hierarchical organization of data objects within complex data sets. Introspection allows users to see how different data objects are related to one another. This section describes how introspection is achieved, drawing examples from a simplified set of data, composed of triples.

To illustrate, let us see how Ruby, a popular object-oriented programming language, implements introspection (see Glossary items, Object-oriented programming, Class-oriented programming).[1]

In Ruby, we can create a new object, "x", and assign it a string, such as "hello world".

```
x = "hello world"
```

Because the data object, "x", contains a string, Ruby knows that x belongs to the String class of objects. If we send the "class" method to the object, "x", Ruby will return a message indicating that "x" belongs to class String.

```
x.class       yields String
```

In Ruby, every object is automatically given an identifier (ie, character string that is unique for the object). If we send the object the method "object_id", Ruby will tell us its assigned identifier.

```
x.object_id       yields 22502910
```

Ruby tells us that the unique object identifier assigned to the object "x" is 22502910.

In Ruby, should we need to learn the contents of "x", we can send the "inspect" method to the object. Should we need to know the methods that are available to the object, we can send the "methods" method to the object. All modern object-oriented languages support syntactic equivalents of these basic introspective tools (see Glossary item, Syntax).

An important by-product of introspection is reflection. Reflection is a programming technique wherein a computer program will modify itself, at run-time, based on information it acquires through introspection. For example, a computer program may iterate over a collection of data objects, examining the self-descriptive information for each object in the collection. If the information indicates that the data object belongs to a particular class of objects, the program might call a method appropriate for the class. The program executes in a manner determined by information obtained during run-time; metaphorically reflecting upon the purpose of its computational task. Detailed information about every piece of data in a data set (eg, the identifier associated with the data object, the class of objects to which the data object belongs, the metadata and the data values that are associated with the data object), permit data scientists to integrate, relate, and repurpose individual data objects collected from any data source or sources, even those sources that are dispersed over network servers (see Glossary items, Data fusion, Data integration, Data merging, Metadata, Software agent, Reflection).

It is worth remembering that data analysis always involves understanding the relationships among data objects. Algorithms, computers, and programming languages are simply tools that help the data analyst achieve a cognitive breakthrough. Putting tools aside, we can see that if we construct our data properly, the data will provide introspection. For successful data analysis, having object-oriented programming languages is less important than having object-oriented data.

7.3 OBJECT-ORIENTED DATA OBJECTS

The ignoramus is a leaf who doesn't know he is part of a tree.

-attributed to Michael Crichton

For programmers, the greatest benefits of preparing your data as classified triples (ie, collections of triples in which identified objects are assigned to classes) is that all of the computational benefits of object-oriented programming automatically convey to your data. To better understand why classified triples bestow the same benefits as does the object-oriented programming paradigm, let us first look at the four intrinsic features of every object-oriented programming language (see Glossary items, Inheritance, Encapsulation, Abstraction, Polymorphism):

1. Inheritance. Data objects (ie, classes and the instances that belong to classes) inherit the methods (eg, functions and subroutines) of their ancestral classes. In object-oriented programming, we can send a method request to an object, and if the method happens to be a class method belonging to any of the ancestor classes of the object, the object-oriented programming environment will find the method (by searching through the ancestral classes), and will compute a result, by feeding parameters provided by the object through its method request. Surprisingly, a list of triples provides the equivalent functionality. Suppose we have a huge database consisting of triples. We can associate a unique object with a method, and search through the triple database for the class to which the object belongs; or to any of the object's ancestral classes. Once we find the ancestral classes, we can search for triples associated with the class to see if any of the triples assert the method. If so, we can search through the triples associated with the method until we find the code associated with the method. Once we've found the code, we can execute the code, in the language for which the code is written. The process seems awkward, but it is not; computers excel at searching through hierarchical data structures.

2. Encapsulation. Encapsulation happens when a data object contains its associated data. In object-oriented programming, methods exist whereby the data that is encapsulated in a unique

object can be interrogated and examined (ie, introspected). Lists of triples are assertions about the data that are associated with a unique identifier. As such, every triple encapsulates a datum. It is easy to collect all of the triples associated with a unique identifier (ie, all the triples of a data object) and this collection will contain the totality of the unique object's data. Thus, triples encapsulate all the data associated with a data object.

3. Abstraction. In the context of object-oriented programming, abstraction is a technique whereby a method is reduced (ie, simplified) to a generalized form that is applicable to a wide range of objects, but for which the specific characteristics of the object receiving the method may be used to return a result that is suited to the particular object. When a method is sent to a triple, its output will depend on the properties of the triple, because the method receives all of the data encapsulated in the triple, and any data parameters included in the method request. The following little story may help clarify the situation. A salesman, walking along a road, passes a farmer. The salesman asks, "How long of a walk is it to town?" The farmer replies, "Keep moving." The salesman says, "Why won't you answer my question?" The farmer repeats, "Keep moving." The salesman shrugs and continues along his way. When the salesman has walked about 20 yards, the farmer shouts, "For you, 45 minutes." To the farmer, the method for computing the length of time required to reach the next town was abstracted. His answer depended on who was doing the asking and required some specific input data (collected when the salesman walked away from the farm) before an answer could be calculated.

4. Polymorphism. Methods sent to object receivers have a response determined by the class of the receiving object. Hence, different objects, from different classes, receiving a call to a method of the same name, will respond differently. For example, suppose you have a method named "divide" and you send the method (ie, issue a command to execute the method) to an object of Class Bacteria and an object of Class Numerics. The Bacteria, receiving the divide method, will try to execute by looking for the "divide" method somewhere in its class lineage. Being a bacteria, the "divide" method may involve making a copy of the bacteria object and incrementing the number of bacteria in the population. The numeric object, receiving the "divide" method, will look for the method in its class lineage and will probably find some method that provides instructions for arithmetic division. Hence, the behavior of the class object, to a received method, will be appropriate for the class of the object. The same holds true for collections of triples. A triple will only have access to the methods of its ancestral classes, and an object's ancestral classes and their methods are all described as triples. Hence, a method belonging to an unrelated class that happens to have the same method name as a method belonging to an object's ancestral class, will be inaccessible to the object.

The following example, provided in the Ruby script, lineage.rb, demonstrates how simple it is to create a new classification, and to endow the classification with inheritance, encapsulation, abstraction, and polymorphism. Readers who cannot program in Ruby will still benefit from reviewing this short example; the principles will apply to every object-oriented programming language and to every data set composed of triples.

```
#!/usr/bin/ruby

class Craniata
  def brag
    puts("I have a well-developed brain")
```

```
    end
    def myself
      puts("I am a member of Class" + self.class.to_s)
    end
end

class Gnathostomata < Craniata
  def speak
    puts("I have a jaw")
  end
end

class Teleostomi < Gnathostomata
end

class Mammalia < Teleostomi
end

class Theria < Mammalia
end

class Eutheria < Theria
end

class Canis < Eutheria
  def speak
    puts("Bow wow")
  end
end

class Primates < Eutheria
  def speak
    puts("Huf hufff")
  end
end

puts("Lassie")
Lassie = Canis.new
Lassie.speak
Lassie.brag
Lassie.myself
puts()
puts ("George_of_the_jungle")
George_of_the_jungle = Primates.new
George_of_the_jungle.speak
George_of_the_jungle.brag
George_of_the_jungle.myself
puts()
puts(Primates.method(:new).owner)
puts(Canis.method(:new).owner)

exit
```

Here is the output of the lineage.rb script:

```
c:\ftp>lineage.rb
Lassie
Bow wow
I have a well-developed brain
I am a member of Class Canis

George_of_the_jungle
Huf hufff
I have a well-developed brain
I am a member of Class Primates

Class
Class
```

In brief, the script creates two new objects: a new and unique member of Class Canis, named Lassie, and a new and unique member of Class Primates, named George_of_the_jungle. Lassie and George_of_the_jungle are both sent three methods: speak, brag, and myself. When Lassie is instructed to speak, she says "Bow wow." When George_of_the_jungle is instructed to speak, he says "Huf hufff." When Lassie and George_of_the_jungle are instructed to brag, they both say, "I have a well-developed brain." When Lassie is sent the "myself" method, she replies "I am a member of class Canis." When George_of_the_jungle is sent the "myself" method, he replies, "I am a member of Class Primates."

The special features of inheritance, abstraction, encapsulation, and polymorphism cannot be appreciated without reviewing how the methods employed by the script were implemented.

We created two unique objects, using the "new" method.

```
Lassie = Canis.new
George_of_the_jungle = Primates.new
```

These two lines of code created two new object instances: Lassie, in Class Canis, and George_of_the_jungle, in Class Primates. This was accomplished by sending the "new" method to each class and providing a name for the new instances. If you skim back the top of the script, containing the class declarations and method definitions, you will notice that there is no "new" method described for any of the classes. The reason we can call the "new" method, without defining it in our code, is that Ruby has a top-level class Class that contains an abstract "new" method that is inherited by any Ruby class that we create.

Look at the two lines of code at the bottom of the script:

```
puts(Primates.method(:new).owner)
puts(Canis.method(:new).owner)
```

This code tells Ruby to print out the class that owns the "new" method used by the Primate class and the "new" method used by the Canis class. In either case, the output indicates that the "new" method belongs to class Class.

```
Class
Class
```

All classes in Ruby are descendants of class Class, and as such, they all inherit the abstract, or general method, "new," that creates new instances of classes.

Let's look at three lines of code:

```
Lassie.speak
Lassie.brag
Lassie.myself
```

The first line sends the "speak" method to the Lassie object. Ruby finds the speak method in the objects Canis class and prints out "Bow wow." The second line sends the "brag" method to the Lassie object and hunts for the class that owns "brag." In this case, Ruby must search up the class hierarchy until it reaches Class Craniata, where it finds and executes the "brag" method. The same thing happens when we send the Lassie object the "myself" method, also found in Class Craniata, as shown:

```
def myself
   puts("I am a member of Class " + self.class.to_s)
end
```

In this case, the "myself" method calls upon the Lassie object to inspect itself and to yield its class name as a string. The "myself" method requires the Lassie object to encapsulate its own class assignment.

So far, we have seen examples of abstraction (ie, the "new" method), inheritance (ie, the "brag" method) and encapsulation (ie, the "myself" method). How does the lineage.rb script demonstrate polymorphism? Notice that a "speak" method is contained in class Gnathostomata, and class Primates and class Canis. The three "speak" methods are different from one another, as shown:

```
class Gnathostomata < Craniata
   def speak
      puts("I have a jaw")
   end
end

class Canis < Eutheria
   def speak
      puts("I tell you that I am a member of Class Canis")
   end
end

class Primates < Eutheria
   def speak
      puts("I tell you that I am a member of Class Primates")
   end
end
```

When we send the "speak" method to a member of class Primates, Ruby finds and executes the "speak" method for the Primates class. Likewise, when we send the "speak" method to a member of class Canis, Ruby finds and executes the "speak" method for the Canis class. Had there been no "speak" method in either of these classes, Ruby would have traveled up the class hierarchy until it found the "speak" method in the Gnathostomata class. In these cases, the "speak" method produces different outputs, depending on the class in which it applies, an example of polymorphism.

At this point, the reader must be wondering why she is being subjected to a lesson in Ruby object-oriented programming. As it happens, the same principles of object-oriented programming apply to every object-oriented language.[6] We will see in the next section how the benefits of object-oriented programming extend to triplestore databases, the simplest and most fundamental way of expressing meaning, with data.

7.4 WORKING WITH OBJECT-ORIENTED DATA

The unexamined life is not worth living.

-Socrates

Enormous benefits follow when data objects are expressed as triples and assigned to defined classes. All of the attributes of object-oriented programming languages (ie, inheritance, encapsulation, abstraction, and polymorphism) are available to well-organized collections of triples. Furthermore, desirable features in any set of data, including integration, interoperability, portability, and introspection are available to data scientists who analyze triplestore data. Last but not least, triples are easy to understand: a unique identifier followed by a metadata/data pair comprise the simple totality of a triple.

This section illustrates everything we've learned about classifications, triples, object-oriented data, and introspection, using a simple triplestore data set.

Here is the triplestore, as the plain-text file, triple.txt:

```
9f0ebdf2^object_name^Class
9f0ebdf2^property^subclass_of
9f0ebdf2^property^property
9f0ebdf2^property^definition
9f0ebdf2^property^object_name
9f0ebdf2^property^instance_of
9f0ebdf2^subclass_of^Class
9f0ebdf2^instance_of^Class
701cb7ed^object_name^Property
701cb7ed^subclass_of^Class
701cb7ed^definition^^the metadata class
77cb79d5^object_name^instance_of
77cb79d5^instance_of^Property
77cb79d5^definition^the name of the class to which the object is an instance
a03fbc3b^object_name^object_name
a03fbc3b^instance_of^Property
a03fbc3b^definition^word equivalent of its predicate identifying sequence
de0e5aa1^object_name^subclass_of
```

```
de0e5aa1^^instance_of^^Property
de0e5aa1^^definition^^the name of the parent class of the referred object
4b675067^^object_name^^property
4b675067^^instance_of^^Property
4b675067^^definition^^an identifier a for class property
c37529c5^^object_name^^definition
c37529c5^^instance_of^^Property
c37529c5^^definition^^the meaning of the referred object
a29c59c0^^object_name^^dob
a29c59c0^^instance_of^^Property
a29c59c0^^definition^^date of birth, as Day, Month, Year
a34a1e35^^object_name^^glucose_at_time
a34a1e35^^instance_of^^Property
a34a1e35^^definition^^glucose level in mg/Dl at time drawn (GMT)
03cc6948^^object_name^^Organism
03cc6948^^subclass_of^^Class
7d7ff42b^^object_name^^Hominidae
7d7ff42b^^subclass_of^^Organism
7d7ff42b^^property^^dob
a0ce8ec6^^object_name^^Homo
a0ce8ec6^^subclass_of^^Hominidae
a0ce8ec6^^property^^glucose_at_time
a1648579^^object_name^^Homo sapiens
a1648579^^subclass_of^^Homo
98495efc^^object_name^^Andy Muzeack
98495efc^^instance_of^^Homo sapiens
98495efc^^dob^^1 January, 2001
98495efc^^glucose_at_time^^87, 02-12-2014 17:33:09
```

Perusal of the triples provides the following observations:

1. Each triple consists of three character sequences, separated by a double-caret. The first character sequence is the object identifier. The second is the metadata and the third is the value. For example:

```
7d7ff42b^^subclass_of^^Organism
```

The individual parts of the triple are:

```
7d7ff42b is the identifier
subclass_of is the metadata
Organism is the data
```

Notice that these triples are expressed in a format different from RDF, or Notation3, or Turtle. Do we care? No. We know that with a few lines of code, we could convert our triplestore into any alternate format we might prefer. Furthermore, our triplestore could be converted into a spreadsheet, in which the identifiers are record keys, the metadata are column headings, and the data occupy cells. We could also port our triples into a database, if we so desired.

2. Using triples, we have defined various classes and properties. For example:

```
03cc6948^^object_name^^Organism
03cc6948^^subclass_of^^Class
```

With one triple, we create a new object, with name Organism, and we associate it with a unique identifier (03cc6948). With another triple, we establish that the Organism object is a class, that happens to be the child class of the root class, Class. Because Organism is a subclass of Class, it will inherit all of the properties of its parent class.

Let's skip down to the bottom of the file:

```
98495efc^^object_name^^Andy Muzeack
98495efc^^instance_of^^Homo sapiens
98495efc^^dob^^1 January, 2001
98495efc^^glucose_at_time^^87, 02-12-2014 17:33:09
```

Here we create a few triples that provide information about a person named Andy Muzeak. First, we assign a unique identifier to our new object, named Andy Museack. We learn, from the next triple that Andy Muzeack is a member of class Homo Sapiens. As such, we infer that Andy Muzeack inherits all the properties contained in class Homo (the parent class of class Homo Sapiens) and all the ancestors of class Homo, leading to the top, or root ancestor, class Class. We learn that Andy Muzeack has a "dob" of January 1, 2001. By ascending the list of triples, we learn that "dob" is a property, with a unique identifier (a29c59c0), and a definition, "date of birth, as Day, Month, Year." Finally, we learn that Andy Muzeack has a glucose_at_time of "87, 02-12-2014 17:33:09." Elsewhere in the triplestore, we find that the "glucose_at_time" metadata is defined as the glucose level in mg/Dl at time drawn, in Greenwich Mean Time.

If we wished, we could simply concatenate our triplestore with other triplestores that contain triples relevant to Andy Muzeack. It would not make any difference how the triples are ordered. If Andy Muzeack's identifier is reconcilable, and the metadata is defined, and each triple is assigned to a class, then we will be able to fully understand and analyze the data held in the triplestore (see Glossary item, Reconciliation).

Of course, when we have millions and billions of triples, we could not perform our analyses by reading through the file. We would need scripts and/or a database application.

Let's write our own scripts that tell us something about the objects in our triplestore.

Here is a short Perl script, class_prop.pl, that traverses the triple.txt file, and lists the contained properties.

```perl
#!/usr/local/bin/perl
open(TEXT, "triple.txt");
$line = " ";
$object_name = "object_name";
$class_identifier = "";
$instance = "instance_of";
$property_class = "Property";
```

```perl
$property = "property";
while ($line ne "")
  {
  $line = <TEXT>;
  $line =~ s/\n//o;
  @three = split(/\^\^/, $line) if ($line ne "");
  $triple{$three[0]}{$three[1]}{$three[2]} = "";
  }
for $identifier (keys %triple)
  {
  if (exists($triple{$identifier}{$instance}{$property_class}))
    {
    @property_names = keys (%{$triple{$identifier}{$object_name}});
    print "$property_names[0] is an instance of Class Property\n";
    }
  }
exit;
```

Here is the output of the class_prop.pl script:

```
subclass_of is an instance of Class Property
instance_of is an instance of Class Property
definition is an instance of Class Property
object_name is an instance of Class Property
glucose_at_time is an instance of Class Property
property is an instance of Class Property
dob is an instance of Class Property
```

Here is a simple Perl script, parent.pl, that will tell us the parent class of any class entered on the command line.

```perl
#/usr/local/bin/perl
open(TEXT, "triple.txt");
$line = " ";
$subclass = "subclass_of";
$object_name = "object_name";
$class_identifier = "";
$new_parent_identifier = $ARGV[0];
$class = $ARGV[0];
while ($line ne "")
  {
  $line = <TEXT>;
  $line =~ s/\n//o;
  @three = split(/\^\^/, $line) if ($line ne "");
  $triple{$three[0]}{$three[1]}{$three[2]} = "";
  }
for $identifier (keys %triple)
  {
  if (exists($triple{$identifier}{$object_name}{$class}))
```

```
    {
    $class_identifier = $identifier;
    last;
    }
  }
@parent_array = keys (%{$triple{$class_identifier}{$subclass}});
print "$class is a subclass of $parent_array[0]";
exit;
```

Here is the output of parent.pl, for three different input classes.

```
c:\ftp>parent.pl "Homo sapiens"
Homo sapiens is a subclass of Homo

c:\ftp>parent.pl "Homo"
Homo is a subclass of Hominidae

c:\ftp>parent.pl "Property"
Property is a subclass of Class
```

These simple Perl scripts demonstrate how simple it is to analyze triplestore data, using object-oriented techniques.

OPEN SOURCE TOOLS
PERSISTENT DATA

A file that big?
It might be very useful.
But now it is gone.

-Haiku by David J. Liszewski

Your scripts create data objects, and the data objects hold data. Sometimes, these data objects are transient, existing only during a block or subroutine. At other times, the data objects produced by scripts represent prodigious amounts of data, resulting from complex and time-consuming calculations. What happens to these data structures when the script finishes executing? Ordinarily, when a script stops, all the data produced by the script simply vanishes.

Persistence is the ability of data to outlive the program that produced it. The methods by which we create persistent data are sometimes referred to as marshalling or serializing. Some of the language-specific methods are called by such colorful names as data dumping, pickling, freezing/thawing, and storable/retrieve (see Glossary items, Serializing, Marshalling, Persistence).

Data persistence can be ranked by level of sophistication. At the bottom is the exportation of data to a simple flat-file, wherein records are each one line in length, and each line of the record consists of a record key, followed by a list of record attributes. The simple spreadsheet stores data as tab delimited or comma separated line records. Flat-files can contain a limitless number of line records, but spreadsheets are limited by the number of records they can import and manage. Scripts can be written that parse through flat-files line by line (ie, record by record), selecting data as they go. Software programs that write data to flat-files achieve a crude but serviceable type of data persistence.

A middle-level technique for creating persistent data is the venerable database. If nothing else, databases are made to create, store, and retrieve data records. Scripts that have access to a database can achieve persistence by creating database records that accommodate data objects. When the script ends, the database persists, and the data objects can be fetched and reconstructed for use in future scripts.

Perhaps the highest level of data persistence is achieved when complex data objects are saved in toto. Flat-files and databases may not be suited to storing complex data objects, holding encapsulated data values. Most languages provide built-in methods for storing complex objects, and a number of languages designed to describe complex forms of data have been developed. Data description languages, such as YAML (Yet Another Markup Language) and JSON (JavaScript Object Notation) can be adopted by any programming language.

Data persistence is essential to data simplification. Without data persistence, all data created by scripts is volatile, obliging data scientists to waste time recreating data that has ceased to exist. Essential tasks such as script debugging and data verification become impossible. It is worthwhile reviewing some of the techniques for data persistence that are readily accessible to Perl, Python, and Ruby programmers.

Perl will dump any data structure into a persistent, external file for later use. Here, the Perl script, data_dump.pl, creates a complex associative array, "%hash", which nests within itself a string, an integer, an array, and another associative array (see Glossary item, Associative array). This complex data structure is dumped into a persistent structure (ie, an external file named dump_struct).

```perl
#!/usr/local/bin/perl
use Data::Dump qw(dump);
%hash = (
    number => 42,
    string => 'This is a string',
    array => [ 1 .. 10 ],
    hash => { apple => 'red', banana => 'yellow'},);
open(OUT, ">dump_struct");
print OUT dump \%hash;
exit;
```

The Perl script, data_slurp.pl picks up the external file, "dump_struct", created by the data_dump.pl script, and loads it into a variable.

```perl
#!/usr/local/bin/perl
use Data::Dump qw(dump);
open(IN, "dump_struct");
undef($/);
$data = eval <IN>;
close $in;
dump $data;
exit;
```

Here is the output of the data_slurp.pl script, in which the contents in the variable "$data" are dumped onto the output screen:

```
c:\ftp>data_slurp.pl
{
    array => [1 .. 10],
    hash => { apple => "red", banana => "yellow" },
    number => 42,
    string => "This is a string",
}
```

Python pickles its data. Here, the Python script, pickle_up.py, pickles a string variable

```
#!/usr/bin/python
import pickle
pumpkin_color = "orange"
pickle.dump( pumpkin_color, open( "save.p", "wb" ) )
exit
```

The Python script, pickle_down.py, loads the pickle file, "save.p" and prints it to the screen.

```
#!/usr/bin/python
import pickle
pumpkin_color = pickle.load( open( "save.p", "rb" ) )
print(pumpkin_color)
exit
```

The output of the pickle_down.py script is shown here:

```
c:\ftp\py>pickle_down.py
orange
```

Where Python pickles, Ruby marshals. In Ruby, whole objects, with their encapsulated data, are marshalled into an external file and demarshalled at will. Here is a short Ruby script, object_marshal.rb, that creates a new class, "Shoestring", a new class object, "loafer", and marshals the new object into a persistent file, "output_file.per".

```
#!/usr/bin/ruby

class Shoestring < String
  def initialize
    @object_uuid = (`c:\\cygwin64\\bin\\uuidgen.exe`).chomp
  end
  def object_uuid
```

```
    print @object_uuid
  end
end

loafer = Shoestring.new
output = File.open("output_file.per", "wb")
output.write(Marshal::dump(loafer))
exit
```

The script produces no output other than the binary file, "output_file.per". Notice that when we created the object, loafer, we included a method that encapsulates within the object a full uuid identifier, courtesy of cygwin's bundled utility, "uuidgen.exe".

We can demarshal the persistent "output_file.per" file, using the ruby script, object_demarshal.rb:

```
#!/usr/bin/ruby

class Shoestring < String
  def initialize
    @object_uuid = `c\:\\cygwin64\\bin\\uuidgen.exe`.chomp
  end
  def object_uuid
    print @object_uuid
  end
end

array = []
$/="\n\n"
out = File.open("output_file.per", "rb").each do
  |object|
  array << Marshal::load(object)
  array.each do
    |object|
    puts object.object_uuid
    puts object.class
    puts object.class.superclass
  end
end
exit
```

The Ruby script, object_demarshal.rb, pulls the data object from the persistent file, "output_file.per" and directs Ruby to list the uuid for the object, the class of the object, and the superclass of the object.

```
c:\ftp>object_demarshal.rb
c2ace515-534f-411c-9d7c-5aef60f8c72a
Shoestring
String
```

Perl, Python, and Ruby all have access to external database modules that can build database objects that exist as external files that persist after the script has executed. These database objects can be called from any script, with the contained data accessed quickly, with a simple command syntax.[7]

Here is a Perl script, lucy.pl, that creates an associative array and ties it to an external database file, using the SDBM_file (Simple Database Management File) module.

```perl
#!/usr/local/bin/perl
use Fcntl;
use SDBM_File;
tie %lucy_hash, "SDBM_File", 'lucy', O_RDWR|O_CREAT|O_EXCL, 0644;
$lucy_hash{"Fred Mertz"} = "Neighbor";
$lucy_hash{"Ethel Mertz"} = "Neighbor";
$lucy_hash{"Lucy Ricardo"} = "Star";
$lucy_hash{"Ricky Ricardo"} = "Band leader";
untie %lucy_hash;
exit;
```

The lucy.pl script produces a persistent, external file from which any Perl script can access the associative array created in the prior script. If we look in the directory from which the lucy.pl script was launched, we will find two new files, lucy.dir and lucy.pag. These are the persistent files that will substitute for the %lucy_hash associative array when invoked within other Perl scripts.

Here is a short Perl script, lucy_untie.pl, that extracts the persistent %lucy_hash associative array from the SDBM file in which it is stored:

```perl
#!/usr/local/bin/perl
use Fcntl;
use SDBM_File;
tie %lucy_hash, "SDBM_File", 'lucy', O_RDWR, 0644;
while(($key, $value) = each (%lucy_hash))
   {
   print "$key => $value\n";
   }
untie %mesh_hash;
exit;
```

Here is the output of the lucy_untie.pl script:

```
c:\ftp>lucy_untie.pl
Fred Mertz => Neighbor
Ethel Mertz => Neighbor
Lucy Ricardo => Star
Ricky Ricardo => Band leader
```

Here is the Python script, lucy.py, that creates a tiny external database.

```
#!/usr/local/bin/python
import dumbdbm
lucy_hash = dumbdbm.open('lucy', 'c')
lucy_hash["Fred Mertz"] = "Neighbor"
lucy_hash["Ethel Mertz"] = "Neighbor"
lucy_hash["Lucy Ricardo"] = "Star"
lucy_hash["Ricky Ricardo"] = "Band leader"
lucy_hash.close()
exit
```

Here is the Python script, lucy_untie.py, that reads all of the key, value pairs held in the persistent database created for the lucy_hash dictionary object.

```
#!/usr/local/bin/python
import dumbdbm
lucy_hash = dumbdbm.open('lucy')
for character in lucy_hash.keys():
  print character, lucy_hash[character]
lucy_hash.close()
exit
```

Here is the output produced by the Python script, lucy_untie.py script.

```
c:\ftp>lucy_untie.py
Fred Mertz Neighbor
Ethel Mertz Neighbor
Lucy Ricardo Star
Ricky Ricardo Band leader
```

Ruby can also hold data in a persistent database, using the gdbm module. If you do not have the gdbm (GNU database manager) module installed in your Ruby distribution, you can install it as a Ruby GEM, using the following command line, from the system prompt:

```
c:\>gem install gdbm
```

The Ruby script, lucy.rb, creates an external database file, lucy.db:

```
#!/usr/local/bin/ruby
require 'gdbm'
lucy_hash = GDBM.new("lucy.db")
lucy_hash["Fred Mertz"] = "Neighbor"
lucy_hash["Ethel Mertz"] = "Neighbor"
lucy_hash["Lucy Ricardo"] = "Star"
lucy_hash["Ricky Ricardo"] = "Band leader"
lucy_hash.close
exit
```

The Ruby script, ruby_untie.db, reads the associate array stored as the persistent database, lucy.db:

```
#!/usr/local/bin/ruby
require 'gdbm'
gdbm = GDBM.new("lucy.db")
gdbm.each_pair do |name, role|
  print "#{name}: #{role}\n"
end
gdbm.close
exit
```

The output from the lucy_untie.rb script is:

```
c:\ftp>lucy_untie.rb
Ethel Mertz: Neighbor
Lucy Ricardo: Star
Ricky Ricardo: Band leader
Fred Mertz: Neighbor
```

Persistence is a simple and fundamental process ensuring that data created in your scripts can be recalled by yourself or by others who need to verify your results. Regardless of the programming language you use, or the data structures you prefer, you will need to familiarize yourself with at least one data persistence technique.

SQLITE DATABASES

For industrial strength persistence, providing storage for millions or billions of data objects, database applications are a good choice. SQL (Systems Query Language, pronounced like "sequel"), is a specialized language used to query relational databases. SQL allows programmers to connect with large, complex server-based network databases. A high level of expertise is needed to install and implement the software that creates server-based relational databases responding to multiuser client-based SQL queries. Fortunately, Perl, Ruby, and Python all have easy access to SQLite, a free, and widely available spin-off of SQL.[7] The source code for SQLite is public domain (see Glossary item, Public domain).

SQLite is bundled into the newer distributions of Python, and can be called from Python scripts with an "import sqlite3" command. Here is a Python script, sqlite6.py, that reads a very short dictionary into an SQL database.

```
#!/usr/local/bin/python
import sqlite3
from sqlite3 import dbapi2 as sqlite
import string, re, os
mesh_hash = {}
entry = ()
mesh_hash["Fred Mertz"] = "Neighbor"
mesh_hash["Ethel Mertz"] = "Neighbor"
mesh_hash["Lucy Ricardo"] = "Star"
```

```
mesh_hash["Ricky Ricardo"] = "Band leader"
con=sqlite.connect('test1.db')
cur=con.cursor()
cur.executescript("""
    create table mesh
    (
        name        varchar (64),
        term        varchar(64)
    );
    """)
for key, value in mesh_hash.iteritems():
    entry = (key, value)
    cur.execute("insert into mesh (name, term) values (?, ?)", entry)
con.commit()
exit
```

Once created, entries in the SQL database file, test1.db, can be retrieved, as shown in the Python script, sqlite6_read.py:

```
#!/usr/local/bin/python
import sqlite3
from sqlite3 import dbapi2 as sqlite
import string, re, os
con=sqlite.connect('test1.db')
cur=con.cursor()
cur.execute("select * from mesh")
for row in cur:
    print row[0], row[1]
exit
```

Here is the output of the sqlite6_read.py script

```
c:\ftp>sqlite6_read.py
Fred Mertz Neighbor
Ethel Mertz Neighbor
Lucy Ricardo Star
Ricky Ricardo Band leader
```

SQLite comes bundled in several of the newer Perl distributions (eg, Strawberry Perl). SQLite comes bundled in some distributions of Cygwin and is available via CPAN (see Glossary item, CPAN). A sample Perl script, perl_sqlite_in.pl, creating SQLite database records for a small associative array, is shown:

```
#!/usr/local/bin/perl
use DBI;
$mesh_hash{"Fred Mertz"} = "Neighbor";
$mesh_hash{"Ethel Mertz"} = "Neighbor";
$mesh_hash{"Lucy Ricardo"} = "Star";
$mesh_hash{"Ricky Ricardo"} = "Band leader";
```

```perl
my $dbh = DBI->connect("dbi:SQLite:dbname=dbfile","","");
my $sth = $dbh->prepare("CREATE TABLE mesh (number VARCHAR(64), term VARCHAR(64))");
$sth->execute;
$sth = $dbh->prepare("INSERT INTO mesh (number,term) VALUES(?,?)");
$dbh->do( "BEGIN TRANSACTION");
while ((my $key, my $value) = each(%mesh_hash))
    {
    $sth->execute( $key, $value );
    }
$dbh->do( "COMMIT" );
exit;
```

The Perl script, perl_sqlite_out.pl, retrieves the records created by the perl_sqlite_in.pl script:

```perl
#!/usr/local/bin/perl
use DBI;
my $dbh = DBI->connect("dbi:SQLite:dbname=dbfile","","");
$sth = $dbh->prepare("SELECT number, term FROM mesh");
$sth->execute;
while (@row = $sth->fetchrow_array())
  {
  print "@row\n";
  }
exit;
```

Here is the output of perl_sqlite_out.pl:

```
c:\ftp>perl_sqlite_out.pl
Ricky Ricardo Band leader
Lucy Ricardo Star
Fred Mertz Neighbor
Ethel Mertz Neighbor
```

Ruby users must first install SQLite on their computer, and then install the Ruby interface to SQLite, available as a Ruby gem (see Glossary item, Ruby gem), as shown:

```
c:\>gem install sqlite3
```

The Ruby script, ruby_sqlite_in.rb, calls the installed sqlite3 interface Gem, and creates an SQLite database:

```ruby
#!/usr/local/bin/ruby
require 'sqlite3'
db = SQLite3::Database.new( "test.db" )
db_hash = Hash.new()
db_hash["Fred Mertz"] = "Neighbor"
db_hash["Ethel Mertz"] = "Neighbor"
```

```
db_hash["Lucy Ricardo"] = "Star"
db_hash["Ricky Ricardo"] = "Band leader"
sql = <<SQL
    create table mesh (
      a varchar2(64),
      b varchar2(64)
    );
SQL
db.execute_batch( sql )
db.transaction
db_hash.each {|k,v| db.execute("insert into mesh values (?,?)", k,v)}
db.commit
exit
```

The resulting database is an external file, named "test.db". The data in the external file can be read out, using the ruby_sqlite_out.rb script:

```
#!/usr/local/bin/ruby
require 'sqlite3'
db = SQLite3::Database.new( "test.db" )
db.execute("select * from mesh") do
 |row|
 puts row[0] + " " + row[1]
end
exit
```

Here is the familiar output:

```
c:\ftp>ruby_sqlite_out.rb
Fred Mertz Neighbor
Ethel Mertz Neighbor
Lucy Ricardo Star
Ricky Ricardo Band leader
```

Databases, such as SQLite, are a great way to achieve data persistence, if you are adept at programming in SQL, and if you need to store millions of simple data objects. Otherwise, persistence methods that are native to your favorite programming language provide a simpler, more flexible option.

GLOSSARY

Abandonware Software that that is abandoned (eg, no longer updated, supported, distributed, or sold) after its economic value is depleted. In academic circles, the term is often applied to software that is developed under a research grant. When the grant expires, so does the software. Most of the software in existence today is abandonware.

Abstraction In the context of object-oriented programming, abstraction is a technique whereby a method is simplified to a generalized form that is applicable to a wide range of objects, but for which the specific characteristics of the object receiving the method may be used to return a result that is suited to the object. Abstraction, along with polymorphism, encapsulation, and inheritance, are essential features of object-oriented programming languages. See Polymorphism. See Inheritance. See Encapsulation. See Object-oriented programming language.

Associative array A data structure consisting of an unordered list of key/value data pairs. Also known as hash, hash table, map, symbol table, dictionary, or dictionary array. The proliferation of synonyms suggests that associative arrays, or their computational equivalents, have great utility. Associative arrays are used in Perl, Python, Ruby and most modern programming languages. Here is an example in which an associative array (ie, a member of Class Hash) is created in Ruby.

```
#!/usr/local/bin/ruby
my_hash = Hash.new
my_hash["C05"] = "Albumin"
my_hash["C39"] = "Choline"
my_hash.each {|key,value| STDOUT.print(key, " --- ", value, "\n")}
exit
```

The first line of the script creates a new associative array, named my_hash. The next two lines create two key/value elements for the associative array (C05/Albumin and C39/Choline). The next line instructs ruby to print out the elements in the my_hash associative array. Here is the output of the short ruby script.

```
Output: C05 — Albumin
C39 — Choline
```

Autocoding When nomenclature coding is done automatically, by a computer program, the process is known as "autocoding" or "autoencoding." See Coding. See Nomenclature. See Autoencoding.

Autoencoding Synonym for autocoding. See Autocoding.

Blended class Also known as class noise, subsumes the more familiar, but less precise term, "Labeling error." Blended class refers to inaccuracies (eg, misleading results) introduced in the analysis of data due to errors in class assignments (ie, assigning a data object to class A when the object should have been assigned to class B). If you are testing the effectiveness of an antibiotic on a class of people with bacterial pneumonia, the accuracy of your results will be forfeit when your study population includes subjects with viral pneumonia, or smoking-related lung damage. Errors induced by blending classes are often overlooked by data analysts who incorrectly assume that the experiment was designed to ensure that each data group is composed of a uniform and representative population. A common source of class blending occurs when the classification upon which the experiment is designed is itself blended. For example, imagine that you are a cancer researcher and you want to perform a study of patients with malignant fibrous histiocytomas (MFH), comparing the clinical course of these patients with the clinical course of patients who have other types of tumors. Let's imagine that the class of tumors known as MFH does not actually exist; that it is a grab-bag term erroneously assigned to a variety of other tumors that happened to look similar to one another. This being the case, it would be impossible to produce any valid results based on a study of patients diagnosed as having MFH. The results would be a biased and irreproducible cacophony of data collected across different, and undetermined, classes tumors. Believe it or not, this specific example, of the blended MFH class of tumors, is selected from the real-life annals of tumor biology.[8,9] The literature is rife with research of dubious quality, based on poorly designed classifications and blended classes. A detailed discussion of this topic is found in Section 6.5, Properties that Cross Multiple Classes. One caveat. Efforts to eliminate class blending can be counterproductive if undertaken with excess zeal. For example, in an effort to reduce class blending, a researcher may choose groups of subjects who are uniform with respect to every known observable property. For example, suppose you want to actually compare apples with oranges. To avoid class blending, you might want to make very sure that your apples do not included any kumquats, or persimmons. You should be certain that your oranges do not include any limes or grapefruits. Imagine that you go even further, choosing only apples and oranges of one variety (eg, Macintosh apples and navel oranges), size (eg, 10 cm), and origin (eg, California). How will your comparisons apply to the varieties of apples and oranges that you have excluded from your study? You may actually reach conclusions that are invalid and irreproducible for more generalized populations within each class. In this case, you have succeeded in elminating class blending, at the expense of losing representative populations of the classes. See Simpson's paradox.

CPAN The Comprehensive Perl Archive Network, known as CPAN, holds has nearly 154,000 Perl packages, with over 12,000 contributors. These packages greatly extend the functionality of Perl, and include virtually every type of Perl method imaginable (eg, math, statistics, communications, plotting, numerical analyses). Any CPAN Perl package can be easily downloaded and automatically installed on your computer's Perl directory when you use the CPAN installer. For instructions, see Open Source Tools for Chapter 1. You can search the multitude of Perl modules to your heart's content at: https://metacpan.org/.

Child class The direct or first generation subclass of a class. Sometimes referred to as the daughter class or, less precisely, as the subclass. See Parent class. See Classification.

Class A class is a group of objects that share a set of properties that define the class and that distinguish the members of the class from members of other classes. The word "class," lowercase, is used as a general term. The word "Class," uppercase, followed by an uppercase noun (eg, Class Animalia), represents a specific class within a formal classification. See Classification.

Class-oriented programming A type of object-oriented programming for which all object instances and all object methods must belong to a class. Hence, in a class-oriented programming language, any new methods and instances that do not sensibly fall within an existing class must be accommodated with a newly created subclass. All invocations of methods, even those sent directly to a class instance, are automatically delivered to the class containing the instance. Class-oriented programming languages embody a specified representation of the real world in which all objects reside within defined classes. Important features such as method inheritance (through class lineage), and introspection (through object and class identifiers) can be very simply implemented in class-oriented programming languages. Powerful scripts can be written with just a few short lines of code, using class-oriented programming languages, by invoking the names of methods inherited by data objects assigned to classes. More importantly, class-oriented languages provide an easy way to discover and test relationships among objects. Ruby and Python are examples of two object-oriented languages that could support a pure class-oriented approach to programming, by deliberately assigning all objects and methods to a hierarchical class system. Of the two languages, Ruby seems to be better suited to a pure class-oriented approach, as it comes with a built-in class system that is intended to accommodate additional subclassing. Nonetheless, both languages give programmers the flexibility to either permit or to circumvent a purely class-oriented approach. Perhaps Smalltalk is the language which comes closest to being a purely class-oriented language.[10] As with every technical advance, there are some pitfalls that users should understand. See Inheritance. See Introspection. See Class. See Instance. See Data object. See Object relationships.

Classification A system in which every object in a knowledge domain is assigned to a class within a hierarchy of classes. The properties of superclasses are inherited by the subclasses. Every class has one immediate superclass (ie, parent class), although a parent class may have more than one immediate subclass (ie, child class). Objects do not change their class assignment in a classification, unless there was a mistake in the assignment. For example, a rabbit is always a rabbit, and does not change into a tiger. Classifications can be thought of as the simplest and most restrictive type of ontology, and serve to reduce the complexity of a knowledge domain.[11] Classifications can be easily modeled in an object-oriented programming language and are nonchaotic (ie, calculations performed on the members and classes of a classification should yield the same output, each time the calculation is performed). A classification should be distinguished from an ontology. In an ontology, a class may have more than one parent class and an object may be a member of more than one class. A classification can be considered a special type of ontology wherein each class is limited to a single parent class and each object has membership in one and only one class. See Nomenclature. See Thesaurus.

See Vocabulary. See Classification. See Dictionary. See Terminology. See Ontology. See Parent class. See Child class. See Superclass. See Unclassifiable objects.

Coding The term "coding" has three very different meanings; depending on which branch of science influences your thinking. For programmers, coding means writing the code that constitutes a computer programmer. For cryptographers, coding is synonymous with encrypting (ie, using a cipher to encode a message). For medics, coding is calling an emergency team to handle a patient in extremis. For informaticians and library scientists, coding involves assigning an alphanumeric identifier, representing a concept listed in a nomenclature, to a term. For example, a surgical pathology report may include the diagnosis, Adenocarcinoma of prostate. A nomenclature may assign a code C4863000 that uniquely identifies the concept "Adenocarcinoma." Coding the report may involve annotating every occurrence of the work "Adenocarcinoma" with the "C4863000" identifier. For a detailed explanation of coding, and its importance for searching and retrieving data, see the full discussion in Section 3.4, Autoencoding and Indexing with Nomenclatures. See Autocoding. See Nomenclature.

Data archeology The process of recovering information held in abandoned or unpopular physical storage devices, or packaged in formats that are no longer widely recognized, and hence unsupported by most software applications. The definition encompasses truly ancient data, such as cuneiform inscriptions stored on clay tablets c.3300 BCE, and digital data stored on 5.25-in. floppy disks in Xyrite wordprocessor format, c.1994.

Data fusion Data fusion is very closely related to data integration. The subtle difference between the two concepts lies in the end result. Data fusion creates a new and accurate set of data representing the combined data sources. Data integration is an on-the-fly usage of data pulled from different domains and, as such, does not yield a residual fused set of data.

Data integration The process of drawing data from different sources and knowledge domains in a manner that uses and preserves the identities of data objects and the relationships among the different data objects. The term "integration" should not be confused with a closely related term, "interoperability." An easy way to remember the difference is to note that **integration applies to data; interoperability applies to software**.

Data merging A nonspecific term that includes data fusion, data integration, and any methods that facilitate the accrual of data derived from multiple sources. See Data fusion. See Data Integration.

Data object A data object is whatever is being described by the data. For example, if the data is "6-feet tall," then the data object is the person or thing to which "6-feet tall" applies. Minimally, a data object is a metadata/data pair, assigned to a unique identifier (ie, a triple). In practice, the most common data objects are simple data records, corresponding to a row in a spreadsheet or a line in a flat-file. Data objects in object-oriented programming languages typically encapsulate several items of data, including an object name, an object unique identifier, multiple data/metadata pairs, and the name of the object's class. See Triple. See Identifier. See Metadata.

Data repurposing Involves using old data in new ways, that were not foreseen by the people who originally collected the data. Data repurposing comes in the following categories: (1) Using the preexisting data to ask and answer questions that were not contemplated by the people who designed and collected the data; (2) Combining preexisting data with additional data, of the same kind, to produce aggregate data that suits a new set of questions that could not have been answered with any one of the component data sources; (3) Reanalyzing data to validate assertions, theories, or conclusions drawn from the original studies; (4) Reanalyzing the original data set using alternate or improved methods to attain outcomes of greater precision or reliability than the outcomes produced in the original analysis; (5) Integrating heterogeneous data sets (ie, data sets with seemingly unrelated types of information), for the purpose an answering questions or developing concepts that span diverse scientific disciplines; (6) Finding subsets in a population once thought to be homogeneous; (7) Seeking new relationships among data objects; (8) Creating, on-the-fly, novel data sets through data file linkages; (9) Creating new concepts or ways of thinking about old concepts, based on a re-examination of data; (10) Fine-tuning existing data models; and (11) Starting over and remodeling systems.[1] See Heterogeneous data.

Database A software application designed specifically to create and retrieve large numbers of data records (eg, millions or billions). The data records of a database are persistent, meaning that the application can be turned off, then on, and all the collected data will be available to the user (see Open Source Tools).

Dictionary A terminology or word list accompanied by a definition for each item. See Nomenclature. See Vocabulary. See Terminology.

Encapsulation The concept, from object-oriented programming, that a data object contains its associated data. Encapsulation is tightly linked to the concept of introspection, the process of accessing the data encapsulated within a data object. Encapsulation, Inheritance, and Polymorphism are available features of all object-oriented languages. See Inheritance. See Polymorphism.

HTML HyperText Markup Language is an ASCII-based set of formatting instructions for web pages. HTML formatting instructions, known as tags, are embedded in the document, and double-bracketed, indicating the start point and end points for instruction. Here is an example of an HTML tag instructing the web browser to display the word "Hello" in italics: <i>Hello</i>. All web browsers conforming to the HTML specification must contain software routines that recognize and implement the HTML instructions embedded within web documents. In addition to formatting instructions, HTML also includes linkage instructions, in which the web browsers must retrieve and display a listed web page, or a web resource, such as an image. The protocol whereby web browsers, following HTML instructions, retrieve web pages from other internet sites, is known as HTTP (HyperText Transfer Protocol).

Heterogeneous data Two sets of data are considered heterogeneous when they are dissimilar to one another, with regard to content, purpose, format, organization, or annotations. One of the purposes of data science is to discover relationships among heterogeneous data sources. For example, epidemiologic data sets may be of service to molecular biologists who have gene sequence data on diverse human populations. The epidemiologic data is likely to contain different types of data values, annotated and formatted in a manner different from the data and annotations in a gene sequence database. The two types of related data, epidemiologic and genetic, have dissimilar content; hence they are heterogeneous to one another.

Identification The process of providing a data object with an identifier, or the process of distinguishing one data object from all other data objects on the basis of its associated identifier. See Identifier.

Identifier A string that is associated with a particular thing (eg person, document, transaction, data object), and not associated with any other thing.[12] Object identification usually involves permanently assigning a seemingly random sequence of numeric digits (0–9) and alphabet characters (a–z and A–Z) to a data object. A data object can be a specific piece of data (eg, a data record), or an abstraction, such as a class of objects or a number or a string or a variable. See Identification.

Immutability Permanent data that cannot be modified is said to be immutable. At first thought, it would seem that immutability is a ridiculous and impossible constraint. In the real world, mistakes are made, information changes, and the methods for describing information changes. This is all true, but the astute data manager knows how to accrue information into data objects without changing the preexisting data. In practice, immutability is maintained by timestamping all data and storing annotated data values with any and all subsequent timestamped modifications. For a detailed explanation, see Section 5.6, Timestamps, Signatures, and Event Identifiers.

Inheritance In object-oriented languages, data objects (ie, classes and object instances of a class) inherit the methods (eg, functions and subroutines) created for the ancestral classes in their lineage. See Abstraction. See Polymorphism. See Encapsulation.

Instance An instance is a specific example of an object that is not itself a class or group of objects. For example, Tony the Tiger is an instance of the tiger species. Tony the Tiger is a unique animal and is not itself a group of animals or a class of animals. The terms instance, instance object, and object are sometimes used interchangeably, but the special value of the "instance" concept, in a system wherein everything is an object, is that it distinguishes members of classes (ie, the instances) from the classes to which they belong.

Introspection A method by which data objects can be interrogated to yield information about themselves (eg, properties, values, and class membership). Through introspection, the relationships among the data objects can be examined. Introspective methods are built into object-oriented languages. The data provided by introspection can be applied, at run-time, to modify a script's operation; a technique known as reflection.

Specifically, any properties, methods, and encapsulated data of a data object can be used in the script to modify the script's run-time behavior. See Reflection.

Marshalling Marshalling, like serializing, is a method for achieving data persistence (ie, saving variables and other data structures produced in a program, after the program has stopped running). Marshalling methods preserve data objects, with their encapsulated data and data structures. See Persistence. See Serializing.

Meaning In informatics, meaning is achieved when described data is bound to a unique identifier of a data object. "Claude Funston's height is 5 feet 11 inches," comes pretty close to being a meaningful statement. The statement contains data (5 feet 11 inches), and the data is described (height). The described data belongs to a unique object (Claude Funston). Ideally, the name "Claude Funston" should be provided with a unique identifier, to distinguish one instance of Claude Funston from all the other persons who are named Claude Funston. The statement would also benefit from a formal system that ensures that the metadata makes sense (eg, What exactly is height, and does Claude Funston fall into a class of objects for which height is a property?) and that the data is appropriate (eg, Is 5 feet 11 inches an allowable measure of a person's height?). A statement with meaning does not need to be a true statement (eg, The height of Claude Funston was not 5 feet 11 inches when Claude Funston was an infant). See Semantics. See Triple. See RDF.

Metadata The data that describes data. For example, a data element (also known as data point) may consist of the number, "6." The metadata for the data may be the words "Height, in feet." A data element is useless without its metadata, and metadata is useless unless it adequately describes a data element. In XML, the metadata/data annotation comes in the form <metadata tag>data<end of metadata tag > and might be look something like:

```
<weight_in_pounds>150</weight_in_pounds>
```

In spreadsheets, the data elements are the cells of the spreadsheet. The column headers are the metadata that describe the data values in the column's cells, and the row headers are the record numbers that uniquely identify each record (ie, each row of cells). See XML.

Monte Carlo simulation Monte Carlo simulations were introduced in 1946 by John von Neumann, Stan Ulam and Nick Metropolis.[13] For this technique, the computer generates random numbers and uses the resultant values to simulate repeated trials of a probabilistic event. Monte Carlo simulations can easily simulate various processes (eg, Markov models and Poisson processes) and can be used to solve a wide range of problems, discussed in detail in Section 8.2. The Achilles heel of the Monte Carlo simulation, when applied to enormous sets of data, is that so-called random number generators may introduce periodic (nonrandom) repeats over large stretches of data.[14] What you thought was a fine Monte Carlo simulation, based on small data test cases, may produce misleading results for large data sets. The wise data analyst will avail himself of the best possible random number generator, and will test his outputs for randomness (see Open Source Tools for Chapter 5, Pseudorandom number generators). Various tests of randomness are available.[15,16]

Multiclass classification A misnomer imported from the field of machine translation, and indicating the assignment of an instance to more than one class. Classifications, as defined in this book, impose one-class classification (ie, an instance can be assigned to one and only one class). It is tempting to think that a ball should be included in class "toy" and in class "spheroids," but multiclass assignments create unnecessary classes of inscrutable provenance, and taxonomies of enormous size, consisting largely of replicate items. See Multiclass inheritance. See Taxonomy.

Multiclass inheritance In ontologies, multiclass inheritance occurs when a child class has more than one parent class. For example, a member of Class House may have two different parent classes: Class Shelter and Class Property. Multiclass inheritance is generally permitted in ontologies but is forbidden in one type of restrictive ontology, known as a classification. See Classification. See Parent class. See Multiclass classification.

Nomenclature A nomenclatures is a listing of terms that cover all of the concepts in a knowledge domain. A nomenclature is different from a dictionary for three reasons: (1) the nomenclature terms are not annotated with definitions, (2) nomenclature terms may be multiword, and (3) the terms in the nomenclature are limited to the scope of the selected knowledge domain. In addition, most nomenclatures group synonyms under a group code. For example, a food nomenclature might collect submarine, hoagie, po' boy, grinder, hero, and torpedo under an alphanumeric code such as "F63958." Nomenclatures simplify textual documents by uniting synonymous terms under a common code. Documents that have been coded with the same nomenclature can be integrated with other documents that have been similarly coded, and queries conducted over such documents will yield the same results, regardless of which term is entered (ie, a search for either hoagie, or po' boy will retrieve the same information, if both terms have been annotated with the synonym code, "F63948"). Optimally, the canonical concepts listed in the nomenclature are organized into a hierarchical classification.[17,18] See Coding. See Autocoding.

Notation 3 Also called n3. A syntax for expressing assertions as triples (unique subject + metadata + data). Notation 3 expresses the same information as the more formal RDF syntax, but n3 is easier for humans to read.[19] RDF and n3 are interconvertible, and either one can be parsed and equivalently tokenized (ie, broken into elements that can be reorganized in a different format, such as a database record). See RDF. See Triple.

Object relationships We are raised to believe that science explains how the universe, and everything in it, works. Engineering and the other applied sciences use scientific explanations to create things, for the betterment of our world. This is a lovely way to think about the roles played by scientists and engineers, but it is not completely accurate. For the most part, we cannot understand very much about the universe. Nobody understands the true nature of gravity, or mass, or light, or magnetism, or atoms, or thought. We do know a great deal about the relationships between gravity and mass, mass and energy, energy and light, light and magnetism, atoms and mass, thought and neurons, and so on. Karl Pearson, a 19th-century statistician and philosopher, wrote that "All science is description and not explanation." Pearson was admitting that we can describe relationships, but we cannot explain why those relationships are true. Here is an example of a mathematical relationship that we know to be true, but which defies our understanding. The constant pi is the ratio of the circumference of a circle to its diameter. Furthermore, pi figures into the Gaussian statistical distribution (ie, that describes how a normal population is spread). How is it possible that a number that determines the distribution of a population can also determine the diameter of a circle?[20] The relationships are provable and undeniable, but the full meaning of pi is beyond our grasp. **In essence, all of science can be reduced to understanding object relationships.**

Object-oriented programming In object-oriented programming, all data objects must belong to one of the classes built into the language or to a class created by the programmer. Class methods are subroutines that belong to a class or instance. The members of a class have access to all of the class methods. There is a hierarchy of classes (with superclasses and subclasses). A data object can access any method from any superclass of its class. All object-oriented programming languages operate under this general strategy. The two most important differences among the object-oriented programming languages relate to syntax (ie, the required style in which data objects call their available methods) and content (the built-in classes and methods available to objects). Various esoteric issues, such as types of polymorphism allowed by the language, support for multiparental inheritance, and non-Boolean logic operations may influence which language is best suited for a specific project. See Data object. See Class-oriented programming.

Ontology An ontology is a collection of classes and their relationships to one another. Ontologies are usually rule-based systems (ie, membership in a class is determined by one or more class rules). Two important features distinguish ontologies from classifications. Ontologies permit classes to have more than one parent class and more than one child class. For example, the class of automobiles may be a direct subclass of "motorized devices" and a direct subclass of "mechanized transporters." In addition, an instance of a class can be an instance of any number of additional classes. For example, a Lamborghini may be a member of class "automobiles" and of class "luxury items." This means that the lineage of an instance in an ontology can be highly complex, with a single instance occurring in multiple classes, and with many connections between classes. Because recursive relations are permitted, it is possible to build an ontology wherein a class is both an ancestor class and a descendant class of itself. A classification is a highly restrained ontology wherein instances can belong to only one class, and each class may have only one direct parent class. Because classifications have an enforced linear hierarchy, they can be easily modeled, and the lineage of any instance can be traced unambiguously. See Classification. See Multiclass classification. See Multiclass inheritance.

Parent class The immediate ancestor, or the next-higher class (ie, the direct superclass) of a class. For example, in the classification of living organisms, Class Vertebrata is the parent class of Class Gnathostomata. Class Gnathostomata is the parent class of Class Teleostomi. In a classification, which imposes single class inheritance, each child class has exactly one parent class; whereas one parent class may have several different child classes. Furthermore, some classes, in particular the bottom class in the lineage, have no child classes (ie, a class need not always be a superclass of other classes). A class can be defined by its properties, its membership (ie, the instances that belong to the class), and by the name of its parent class. When we list all of the classes in a classification, in any order, we can always reconstruct the complete class lineage, in their correct lineage and branchings, if we know the name of each class's parent class. See Instance. See Child class. See Superclass.

Persistence Persistence is the ability of data to remain available in memory or storage after the program in which the data was created has stopped executing. Databases are designed to achieve persistence. When the database application is turned off, the data remains available to the database application when it is restarted at some later time. See Database. See Marshalling. See Serializing.

Polymorphism Polymorphism is one of the constitutive properties of an object-oriented language (along with inheritance, encapsulation, and abstraction). Methods sent to object receivers have a response determined by the class of the receiving object. Hence, different objects, from different classes, receiving a call to a method of the same name, will respond differently. For example, suppose you have a method named "divide" and you send the method (ie, issue a command to execute the method) to an object of Class Bacteria and an object of Class Numerics. The Bacteria, receiving the divide method, will try to execute by looking for the "divide" method somewhere in its class lineage. Being a bacteria, the "divide" method may involve making a copy of the bacteria (ie, reproducing) and incrementing the number of bacteria in the population. The numeric object, receiving the "divide" method, will look for the "divide" method in its class lineage and will probably find some method that provides instructions for arithmetic division. Hence, the behavior of the class object, to a received method, will be appropriate for the class of the object. See Inheritance. See Encapsulation. See Abstraction.

Public domain Data that is not owned by an entity. Public domain materials include documents whose copyright terms have expired, materials produced by the federal government, materials that contain no creative content (ie, materials that cannot be copyrighted), or materials donated to the public domain by the entity that holds copyright. Public domain data can be accessed, copied, and redistributed without violating piracy laws. It is important to note that plagiarism laws and rules of ethics apply to public domain data. You must properly attribute authorship to public domain documents. If you purposely fail to attribute authorship or if you purposefully and falsely attribute authorship to the wrong person (eg, yourself), then this is unethical, and an act of plagiarism.

RDF Resource Description Framework (RDF) is a syntax in XML notation that formally expresses assertions as triples. The RDF triple consists of a uniquely identified subject plus a metadata descriptor for the data plus a data element. Triples are necessary and sufficient to create statements that convey meaning. Triples can be aggregated with other triples from the same data set or from other data sets, so long as each triple pertains to a unique subject that is identified equivalently through the data sets. Enormous data sets of RDF triples can be merged or functionally integrated with other massive or complex data resources. For a detailed discussion see Open Source Tools for Chapter 6, Syntax for Triples. See Notation 3. See Semantics. See Triple. See XML.

RDF Schema Resource Description Framework Schema (RDFS). A document containing a list of classes, their definitions, and the names of the parent class(es) for each class. In an RDF Schema, the list of classes is typically followed by a list of properties that apply to one or more classes in the Schema. To be useful, RDF Schemas are posted on the Internet, as a Web page, with a unique Web address. Anyone can incorporate the classes and properties of a public RDF Schema into their own RDF documents (public or private) by linking named classes and properties, in their RDF document, to the web address of the RDF Schema where the classes and properties are defined. See RDFS.

Reconciliation Usually refers to identifiers, and involves verifying an object that is assigned a particular identifier in one information system has been provided the same identifier in some other system. For example, if I am assigned identifier 967bc9e7-fea0-4b09-92e7-d9327c405d78 in a legacy record system, I should like to be assigned the same identifier in the new record system. If that were the case, my records in both systems could be combined. If I am assigned an identifier in one system that is different from my assigned identifier in another system, then the two identifiers must be reconciled to determine that they both refer to the same unique data object (ie, me). This may involve creating a link between the two identifiers, or a new triple that establishes the equivalence of the two identifiers. Despite claims to the contrary, there is no possible way by which information systems with poor identifier systems can be sensibly reconciled. Consider this example. A hospital has two separate registry systems: one for dermatology cases and another for psychiatry cases. The hospital would like to merge records from the two services. Because of sloppy identifier practices, a sample patient has been registered 10 times in the dermatology system, and 6 times in the psychiatry system, each time with different addresses, social security numbers, birthdates and spellings of the name. A reconciliation algorithm is applied, and one of the identifiers from the dermatology service is matched positively against one of the records from the psychiatry service. Performance studies on the algorithm indicate that the merged records have a 99.8% chance of belonging to the same patient. So what? Though the two merged identifiers correctly point to the same patient, there are 14 (9+5) residual identifiers for the patient still unmatched. The patient's merged record will not contain his complete clinical history. Furthermore, in this hypothetical instance, analyses of patient population data will mistakenly attribute one patient's clinical findings to as many as 15 different patients, and the set of 15 records in the corrupted de-identified dataset may contain mixed-in information from an indeterminate number of additional patients! If the preceding analysis seems harsh, consider these words, from the Healthcare Information and Management Systems Society, "A local system with a poorly maintained or "dirty" master person index (MPI) will only proliferate and contaminate all of the other systems to which it links."[21] See Social Security Number.

Reflection A programming technique wherein a computer program will modify itself, at run-time, based on information it acquires through introspection. For example, a computer program may iterate over a collection of data objects, examining the self-descriptive information for each object in the collection (ie, object introspection). If the information indicates that the data object belongs to a particular class of objects, then the program may call a method appropriate for the class. The program executes in a manner determined by descriptive information obtained during run-time; metaphorically reflecting upon the purpose of its computational task. See Introspection.

Registrars and human authentication The experiences of registrars in U.S. hospitals serve as cautionary instruction. Hospital registrars commit a disastrous mistake when they assume that all patients wish to comply with the registration process. A patient may be highly motivated to provide false information to a registrar, or to acquire several different registration identifiers, or to seek a false registration under another person's identity (ie, commit fraud), or to forego the registration process entirely. In addition, it is a mistake to believe that honest patients are able to fully comply with the registration process. Language barriers, cultural barriers, poor memory, poor spelling, and a host of errors and misunderstandings can lead to duplicative or otherwise erroneous identifiers. It is the job of the registrar to follow hospital policies that overcome these difficulties. Registration should be conducted by a trained registrar who is well-versed in the registration policies established by the institution. Registrars may require patients to provide a full legal name, any prior held names (eg, maiden name), date of birth, and a government issue photo id card (eg, driver's license or photo id card issued by the department of motor vehicles). To be thorough, registration should require a biometric identifier (eg, fingerprints, retina scan, iris scan, voice recording, photograph). If you accept the premise that hospitals have the responsibility of knowing who it is that they are treating, then obtaining a sample of DNA from every patient, at the time of registration, is reasonable. The DNA can be used to create a unique patient profile from a chosen set of informative loci; a procedure used by the CODIS system developed for law enforcement agencies. The registrar should document any distinguishing and permanent physical features that are plainly visible (eg, scars, eye color, colobomas, tattoos). Neonatal and pediatric identifiers pose a special set of problems for registrars. When an individual born in a hospital, and provided with an identifier, returns as an adult, he or she should be assigned the same identifier that was issued in the remote past. Every patient who comes for registration should be matched against a database of biometric data that does not change from birth to death (eg, fingerprints, DNA). See Social Security Number.

Ruby gem   In Ruby, gems are external modules available for download from an internet server. The Ruby gem installation module comes bundled in Ruby distribution packages. Gem installations are simple, usually consisting of commands in the form, "gem install name_of_gem" invoked at the system prompt. After a gem has been installed, scripts access the gem with a "require" statement, equivalent to an "import" statement in Python or the "use" statement in Perl.

Semantics   The study of meaning (Greek root, semantikos, significant meaning). In the context of data science, semantics is the technique of creating meaningful assertions about data objects. A meaningful assertion, as used here, is a triple consisting of an identified data object, a data value, and a descriptor for the data value. In practical terms, semantics involves making assertions about data objects (ie, making triples), combining assertions about data objects (ie, merging triples), and assigning data objects to classes; hence relating triples to other triples. As a word of warning, few informaticians would define semantics in these terms, but most definitions for semantics are functionally equivalent to the definition offered here. Most language is unstructured and meaningless. Consider the assertion: Sam is tired. This is an adequately structured sentence with a subject verb and object. But what is the meaning of the sentence? There are a lot of people named Sam. Which Sam is being referred to in this sentence? What does it mean to say that Sam is tired? Is "tiredness" a constitutive property of Sam, or does it only apply to specific moments? If so, for what moment in time is the assertion, "Sam is tired" actually true? To a computer, meaning comes from assertions that have a specific, identified subject associated with some sensible piece of fully described data (metadata coupled with the data it describes). See Triple. See RDF.

Serializing   Serializing is a plesionym (ie, near-synonym) for marshalling and is a method for taking data produced within a script or program, and preserving it in an external file, that can be saved when the program stops, and quickly reconstituted as needed, in the same program or in different programs. The difference, in terms of common usage, between serialization and marshalling is that serialization usually involves capturing parameters (ie, particular pieces of information), while marshaling preserves all of the specifics of a data object, including its structure, content, and code content. As you might imagine, the meaning of terms might change depending on the programming language and the intent of the serializing and marshalling methods. See Persistence. See Marshalling.

Simpson's paradox   Occurs when a correlation that holds in two different data sets is reversed if the data sets are combined. For example, baseball player A may have a higher batting average than player B for each of two seasons, but when the data for the two seasons are combined, player B may have the higher 2-season average. Simpson's paradox is just one example of unexpected changes in outcome when variables are unknowingly hidden or blended.[22]

Social Security Number   The common strategy, in the U.S., of employing social security numbers as identifiers is often counterproductive, owing to entry error, mistaken memory, or the intention to deceive. Efforts to reduce errors by requiring individuals to produce their original social security cards puts an unreasonable burden on honest individuals, who rarely carry their cards, and provides an advantage to dishonest individuals, who can easily forge social security cards. Institutions that compel patients to provide a social security number have dubious legal standing. The social security number was originally intended as a device for validating a person's standing in the social security system. More recently, the purpose of the social security number has been expanded to track taxable transactions (ie, bank accounts, salaries). Other uses of the social security number are not protected by law. The Social Security Act (Section 208 of Title 42 U.S. Code 408) prohibits most entities from compelling anyone to divulge his/her social security number. Legislation or judicial action may one day stop institutions from compelling individuals to divulge their social security numbers as a condition for providing services. Prudent and forward-thinking institutions will limit their reliance on social security numbers as personal identifiers. See Registrars and human authentication.

Software agent A computer program that operates with autonomy, taking cues from the data and adjusting its behavior to perform tasks not specifically written into the program. The Internet supports software agents through the implementation of identifiers (ie, URLs) and data accessibility (ie, through TCP/IP data transport protocols). With the advent of RDF, data can be "understood," as each identified object in RDF is associated with pairs of metadata and data, and placed into defined classes. Once uniquely identified data objects are assigned into classes, it becomes relatively simple to write software agents whose activities are determined by logical inferences on retrieved data objects. See RDF. See Reflection. See URL.

Species Species is the bottom-most class of any classification or ontology. Because the species class contains the individual objects of the classification, it is the only class which is not abstract. The special significance of the species class is best exemplified in the classification of living organisms. Every species of organism contains individuals that share a common ancestral relationship to one another. When we look at a group of squirrels, we know that each squirrel in the group has its own unique personality, its own unique genes (ie, genotype), and its own unique set of physical features (ie, phenotype). Moreover, although the DNA sequences of individual squirrels are unique, we assume that there is a commonality to the genome of squirrels that distinguishes it from the genome of every other species. If we use the modern definition of species as an evolving gene pool, we see that the species can be thought of as a biological life form, with substance (a population of propagating genes), and a function (evolving to produce new species).[23–25] Put simply, species speciate; individuals do not. As a corollary, species evolve; individuals simply propagate. Hence, the species class is a separable biological unit with form and function. We, as individuals, are focused on the lives of individual things, and we must be reminded of the role of species in biological and nonbiological classifications. The concept of species is discussed in greater detail in Section 6.4. See Blended class.

Superclass Any of the ancestral classes of a subclass. For example, in the classification of living organisms, the class of vertebrates is a superclass of the class of mammals. The immediate superclass of a class is its parent class. In common parlance, when we speak of the superclass of a class, we are usually referring to its parent class. See Parent class.

Syntax Syntax is the standard form or structure of a statement. What we know as English grammar is equivalent to the syntax for the English language. Charles Mead distinctly summarized the difference between syntax and semantics: "Syntax is structure; semantics is meaning."[26] See Semantics.

Taxonomic order In biological taxonomy, the hierarchical lineage of organisms are divided into a descending list of named orders: Kingdom, Phylum (Division), Class, Order, Family, and Genus, Species. As we have learned more and more about the classes of organisms, modern taxonomists have added additional ranks to the classification (eg, supraphylum, subphylum, suborder, infraclass, etc.). Was this really necessary? All of this taxonomic complexity could be averted by dropping named ranks and simply referring to every class as "Class." Modern specifications for class hierarchies (eg, RDF Schema) encapsulate each class with the name of its superclass. When every object yields its class and superclass, it is possible to trace any object's class lineage. For example, in the classification of living organisms, if you know the name of the parent for each class, you can write a simple script that generates the complete ancestral lineage for every class and species within the classification.[7] See Class. See Taxonomy. See RDF Schema. See Species.

Taxonomy A taxonomy is the collection of named instances (class members) in a classification or an ontology. When you see a schematic showing class relationships, with individual classes represented by geometric shapes and the relationships represented by arrows or connecting lines between the classes, then you are essentially looking at the structure of a classification, minus the taxonomy. You can think of building a taxonomy as the act of pouring all of the names of all of the instances into their proper classes. A taxonomy is similar to a nomenclature; the difference is that in a taxonomy, every named instance must have an assigned class. See Taxonomic order.

Terminology The collection of words and terms used in some particular discipline, field, or knowledge domain. Nearly synonymous with vocabulary and with nomenclature. Vocabularies, unlike terminologies, are not be confined to the terms used in a particular field. Nomenclatures, unlike terminologies, usually aggregate equivalent terms under a canonical synonym.

Thesaurus A vocabulary that groups together synonymous terms. A thesaurus is very similar to a nomenclature. There are two minor differences. Nomenclatures include multiword terms; whereas a thesaurus is typically composed of one-word terms. In addition, nomenclatures are typically restricted to a well-defined topic or knowledge domain (eg, names of stars, infectious diseases, etc.). See Nomenclature. See Vocabulary. See Classification. See Dictionary. See Terminology. See Ontology.

Triple In computer semantics, a triple is an identified data object associated with a data element and the description of the data element. In the computer science literature, the syntax for the triple is commonly described as: subject, predicate, object, wherein the subject is an identifier, the predicate is the description of the object, and the object is the data. The definition of triple, using grammatical terms, can be off-putting to the data scientist, who may think in terms of spreadsheet entries: a key that identifies the line record, a column header containing the metadata description of the data, and a cell that contains the data. In this book, the three components of a triple are described as: (1) the identifier for the data object, (2) the metadata that describes the data, and (3) the data itself. In theory, all data sets, databases, and spreadsheets can be constructed or deconstructed as collections of triples. See Introspection. See Data object. See Semantics. See RDF. See Meaning.

URL Unique Resource Locator. The Web is a collection of resources, each having a unique address, the URL. When you click on a link that specifies a URL, your browser fetches the page located at the unique location specified in the URL name. If the Web were designed otherwise (ie, if several different web pages had the same web address, or if one web address were located at several different locations), then the web could not function with any reliability.

Unclassifiable objects Classifications create a class for every object and taxonomies assign each and every object to its correct class. This means that a classification is not permitted to contain unclassified objects; a condition that puts fussy taxonomists in an untenable position. Suppose you have an object, and you simply do not know enough about the object to confidently assign it to a class. Or, suppose you have an object that seems to fit more than one class, and you can't decide which class is the correct class. What do you do? Historically, scientists have resorted to creating a "miscellaneous" class into which otherwise unclassifiable objects are given a temporary home, until more suitable accommodations can be provided. I have spoken with numerous data managers, and everyone seems to be of a mind that "miscellaneous" classes, created as a stopgap measure, serve a useful purpose. Not so. Historically, the promiscuous application of "miscellaneous" classes have proven to be a huge impediment to the advancement of science. In the case of the classification of living organisms, the class of protozoans stands as a case in point. Ernst Haeckel, a leading biological taxonomist in his time, created the Kingdom Protista (ie, protozoans) in 1866 to accommodate a wide variety of simple organisms with superficial commonalities. Haeckel himself understood that the protists were a blended class that included unrelated organisms, but he believed that further study would resolve the confusion. In a sense, he was right, but the process took much longer than he had anticipated; occupying generations of taxonomists over the following 150 years. Today, Kingdom Protista no longer exists. Its members have been reassigned to other classes. Nonetheless, textbooks of microbiology still describe the protozoans, just as though this name continued to occupy a legitimate place among terrestrial organisms. In the meantime, therapeutic opportunities for eradicating so-called protozoal infections, using class-targeted agents, have no doubt been missed.[27] You might think that the creation of a class of living organisms, with no established scientific relation to the real world, was a rare and ancient event in the annals of biology, having little or no chance of being repeated. Not so. A special pseudoclass of fungi, deuteromycetes (spelled with a lowercase "d," signifying its questionable validity as a true biologic class) has been created to hold fungi of indeterminate speciation. At present, there are several thousand such fungi, sitting in a taxonomic limbo, waiting to be placed into a definitive taxonomic class.[28,27] See Blended class.

Vocabulary A comprehensive collection of the words and their associated meanings. In some quarters, "vocabulary" and "nomenclature" are used interchangeably, but they are different from one another. Nomenclatures typically focus on terms confined to one knowledge domain. Nomenclatures typically do not contain definitions for the contained terms. Nomenclatures typically group terms by synonymy. Lastly, nomenclatures include multiword terms. Vocabularies are collections of single words, culled from multiple knowledge domains, with their definitions, and assembled in alphabetic order. See Nomenclature. See Thesaurus. See Taxonomy. See Dictionary. See Terminology.

XML Acronym for eXtensible Markup Language, a syntax for marking data values with descriptors (ie, metadata). The descriptors are commonly known as tags. In XML, every data value is enclosed by a start-tag, containing the descriptor and indicating that a value will follow, and an end-tag, containing the same descriptor and indicating that a value preceded the tag. For example: <name>Conrad Nervig </name >. The enclosing angle brackets, "<>", and the end-tag marker, "/", are hallmarks of HTML and XML markup. This simple but powerful relationship between metadata and data allows us to employ metadata/data pairs as though each were a miniature database. The semantic value of XML becomes apparent when we bind a metadata/data pair to a unique object, forming a so-called triple. See Triple. See Meaning. See Semantics. See HTML.

REFERENCES

1. Berman JJ. *Repurposing legacy data: innovative case studies.* Burlington, MA: Morgan Kaufmann; 2015.
2. Solar System Exploration Research Virtual Institute. NASA. Recovering the missing ALSEP data. Available from: http://sservi.nasa.gov/articles/recovering-the-missing-alsep-data/ [accessed 13.10.14].
3. Curry A. Rescue of old data offers lesson for particle physicists. *Science* 2011;**331**:694–5.
4. Biebel O, Movilla Fernandez PA, Bethke S, The JADE Collaboration. C-parameter and jet broadening at PETRA energies. *Phys Lett* 1999;**B459**:326–34.
5. Berman JJ. *Principles of big data: preparing, sharing, and analyzing complex information.* Burlington, MA: Morgan Kaufmann; 2013.
6. Conway D. *Object oriented Perl: a comprehensive guide to concepts and programming techniques.* Sebastopol, CA: O'Reilly; 2000.
7. Berman JJ. *Methods in medical informatics: fundamentals of healthcare programming in Perl, Python, and Ruby.* Boca Raton: Chapman and Hall; 2010.
8. Al-Agha OM, Igbokwe AA. Malignant fibrous histiocytoma: between the past and the present. *Arch Pathol Lab Med* 2008;**132**:1030–5.
9. Nakayama R, Nemoto T, Takahashi H, Ohta T, Kawai A, Seki K, et al. Gene expression analysis of soft tissue sarcomas: characterization and reclassification of malignant fibrous histiocytoma. *Mod Pathol* 2007;**20**:749–59.
10. Goldberg A, Robson D, Harrison MA. *Smalltalk-80: the language and its implementation.* Boston, MA: Addison-Wesley; 1983.
11. Patil N, Berno AJ, Hinds DA, Barrett WA, Doshi JM, Hacker CR, et al. Blocks of limited haplotype diversity revealed by high-resolution scanning of human chromosome 21. *Science* 2001;**294**:1719–23.
12. Paskin N. Identifier interoperability: a report on two recent ISO activities. *D-Lib Mag* 2006;**12**:1–23.
13. Cipra BA. The best of the 20th century: editors name top 10 algorithms. *SIAM News* 2000;**33**(4).
14. Sainani K. Error: what biomedical computing can learn from its mistakes. *Biomed Comput Rev* 2011;**Fall**:12–9.
15. Marsaglia G, Tsang WW. Some difficult-to-pass tests of randomness. *J Stat Softw* 2002;**7**:1–8. Available from: http://www.jstatsoft.org/v07/i03/paper [accessed 25.09.12].
16. Knuth DE. *Art of computer programming, volume 2: seminumerical algorithms.* 3rd ed. Boston: Addison-Wesley; 1997.

17. Berman JJ. Tumor classification: molecular analysis meets Aristotle. *BMC Cancer* 2004;**4**:10. Available from: http://www.biomedcentral.com/1471-2407/4/10 [accessed 01.01.15].

18. Berman JJ. Tumor taxonomy for the developmental lineage classification of neoplasms. *BMC Cancer* 2004;**4**:88. http://www.biomedcentral.com/1471-2407/4/88 [accessed 01.01.15].

19. Berman JJ, Moore GW. Implementing an RDF Schema for pathology images. Available from: http://www.julesberman.info/spec2img.htm; 2007 [accessed 01.01.15].

20. Wigner E. The unreasonable effectiveness of mathematics in the natural sciences. *Communications in pure and applied mathematics*, vol. 13. New York: John Wiley and Sons; 1960.

21. Patient Identity Integrity. A White Paper by the HIMSS Patient Identity Integrity Work Group. Available from: http://www.himss.org/content/files/PrivacySecurity/PIIWhitePaper.pdf; 2009 [accessed 19.09.12].

22. Tu Y, Gunnell D, Gilthorpe MS. Simpson's paradox, Lord's paradox, and suppression effects are the same phenomenon: the reversal paradox. *Emerg Themes Epidemiol* 2008;**5**:2.

23. DeQueiroz K. Ernst Mayr and the modern concept of species. *PNAS* 2005;**102**(Suppl. 1):6600–7.

24. DeQueiroz K. Species concepts and species delimitation. *Syst Biol* 2007;**56**:879–86.

25. Mayden RL. Consilience and a hierarchy of species concepts: advances toward closure on the species puzzle. *J Nematol* 1999;**31**(2):95–116.

26. Mead CN. Data interchange standards in healthcare IT — computable semantic interoperability: now possible but still difficult, do we really need a better mousetrap? *J Healthc Inf Manag* 2006;**20**:71–8.

27. Berman JJ. *Taxonomic guide to infectious diseases: understanding the biologic classes of pathogenic organisms*. Waltham: Academic Press; 2012.

28. Guarro J, Gene J, Stchigel AM. Developments in fungal taxonomy. *Clin Microbiol Rev* 1999;**12**:454–500.

PROBLEM SIMPLIFICATION

8

Simplicity is the ultimate sophistication.
-Leonardo da Vinci (1452–1519)

8.1 RANDOM NUMBERS

Chaos reigns within.
Reflect, repent, and reboot.
Order shall return.

-Computer haiku by Suzie Wagner

If you are among the many students and professionals who are intimidated by statistics, then fear no more! With a little imagination, random number generators can substitute for a wide range of statistical methods.

As it happens, modern computers can perform two simple processes, easily and very quickly. These two processes are: (1) generating random numbers, and (2) repeating sets of instructions thousands or millions of times. Using these two computational steps, we can accurately predict outcomes that would be intractable to any direct mathematical analysis. You are about to be rewarded with simple methods whereby every statistical test can be replicated and every probabilistic dilemma can be resolved; usually with a few lines of code.[1–4]

To begin, let us perform a few very simple simulations that confirm what we already know, intuitively. Imagine that you have a pair of dice, and you would like to know how often you might expect each of the numbers (from 1 to 6) to appear after you have thrown one die.[5]

Let us simulate 600,000 throws of a die, using the Perl script, randtest.pl:

```
#!/usr/bin/perl
$count = 0;
while ($count < 600000)
    {
    $count++;
    $one_of_six = (int(rand(6))+1);
    $hash{$one_of_six}++;
    }
```

```
while(($key, $value) = each (%hash))
   {
print "$key => $value\n";
   }
exit;
```

The script, randtest.pl, begins by setting a loop that repeats 600,000 times, each repeat simulating the cast of a die. With each cast of the die, Perl generates a random integer, 1 through 6, simulating the outcome of a throw. The most important line of code is:

```
$one_of_six = (int(rand(6))+1);
```

The rand(6) command yields a pseudorandom number of value less than 6. We integerize the result using Perl's int() function, which truncates anything past the decimal point. This produces integer values of 0,1,2,3,4, or 5. We increment each value to produce 1,2,3,4,5, or 6. The script yields the total number of simulated die casts for each of the possible outcomes.

Here is the output of randtest.pl.

```
C:\ftp>perl randtest.pl
1 => 100002
2 => 99902
3 => 99997
4 => 100103
5 => 99926
6 => 100070
```

As one might expect, each of the six equally likely outcomes of a thrown die occurred about 100,000 times, in our simulation.

Repeating the randtest.pl script produces a different set of outcome numbers, but the general result is the same. Each die outcome had about the same number of occurrences.

```
C:\ftp>perl randtest.pl
1 => 100766
2 => 99515
3 => 100157
4 => 99570
5 => 100092
6 => 99900
```

Let us get a little more practice with random number generators, before moving onto more challenging simulations. Occasionally in scripts, we need to create a new file, automatically, during the script's run time, and we want to be fairly certain that the file we create will not have the same filename as an existing file. An easy way of choosing a filename is to grab, at random, printable characters, concatenating them into an 11 character string suitable as a filename. The chance that you will encounter two files with the same randomly chosen filename is very remote. In fact, the likelihood that any two selected filenames are identical exceeds to 2 to the 44th power.

Here is a Perl script, random_filenames.pl, that assigns a sequence of 11 randomly chosen upper-case alphabetic characters to a file name:

```
#!/usr/bin/perl
for ($count = 1; $count <= 12; $count++)
  {
  push(@listchar, chr(int(rand(26))+65));
  }
$listchar[8]= ".";
$randomfilename = join("",@listchar);
print "Your filename is $randomfilename\n";
exit;
```

Here is the output of the ranfile.pl script:

```
c:\ftp>random_filenames.pl
Your filename is OAOKSXAH.SIT
```

The key line of code in random_filenames.pl is:

```
push(@listchar, chr(int(rand(26))+65));
```

The rand(26) command yields a random value less than 26. The int() command converts the value to an integer. The number 65 is added to the value to produce a value ranging from 65 to 90, and the chr() command converts the numbers 65 through 90 to their ASCII equivalent; which just happen to be the uppercase alphabet from A to Z. The randomly chosen letter is pushed onto an array, and the process is repeated until a 12 character filename is generated.

Here is the equivalent Python script, random_filenames.py, that produces one random filename

```
#!/usr/bin/python
import random
filename = [0]*12
filename = map(lambda x: x is "" or chr(int(random.uniform(0,25) + 65)), filename)
print ".join(filename[0:8]) + "." +".join(filename[9:12])
exit
```

Here is the outcome of the random_filenames.py script:

```
c:\ftp>random_filenames.py
KYSDWKLF.RBA
```

In both these scripts, as in all of the scripts in this section, many outcomes may result from a small set of initial conditions. It is much easier to write these programs and observe their outcomes than to directly calculate all the possible outcomes of a set of governing equations.

Let us use a random number generator to calculate the value of pi, without measuring anything, and without resorting to summing an infinite series of numbers. Here is a simple python script, pi.py, that does the job.

```
#!/usr/bin/python
import random
from math import sqrt
totr = 0
totsq = 0
for iterations in range(100000):
  x = random.uniform(0,1)
  y = random.uniform(0,1)
  r = sqrt((x*x) + (y*y))
  if r < 1:
    totr = totr + 1
  totsq = totsq + 1
print float(totr)*4.0/float(totsq)
exit
```

The outcome of the pi.py script is:

```
output:
c:\ftp\py>pi.py
3.1414256
```

Here is an equivalent Ruby script.

```
#!/usr/local/bin/ruby
x = y = totr = totsq = 0.0
(1..100000).each do
  x = rand()
  y = rand()
  r = Math.sqrt((x*x) + (y*y))
  totr = totr + 1 if r < 1
  totsq = totsq + 1
end
puts (totr *4.0 / totsq)
exit
```

Here is an equivalent Perl script.

```
#!/usr/local/bin/perl
open(DATA,">pi.dat");
for (1..100000)
  {
  $x = rand();
  $y = rand();
```

```
$r = sqrt(($x*$x) + ($y*$y));
if ($r < 1)
  {
  $totr = $totr + 1;
  print DATA "$x\ $y\n";
  }
$totsq = $totsq + 1;
}
print eval(4 * ($totr / $totsq));
exit;
```

As one would hope, all three scripts produce approximately the same value of pi. The Perl script contains a few extra lines that produces an output file, named pi.dat, that will helps us visualize how these scripts work. The pi.dat script contains the *x,y* data points, generated by the random number generator, meeting the "if" statement's condition that the hypotenuse of the *x,y* coordinates must be less than 1 (ie, less than a circle of radius 1).

We can plot the output of the script with a few lines of Gnuplot code:

```
gnuplot> set size square
gnuplot> unset key
gnuplot> plot 'c:\ftp\pi.dat'
```

The resulting graph is a quarter-circle within a square (Fig. 8.1).

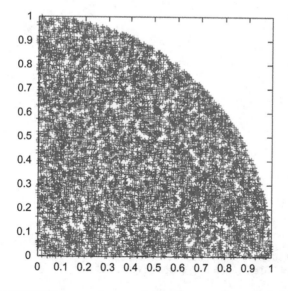

FIGURE 8.1

The data points produced by 10,000 random assignments of *x* and *y* coordinates in a range of 0-1. Randomly assigned data points whose hypotenuse exceeds "1" are excluded.

The graph shows us, at a glance, how the ratio of the number of points in the quarter-circle, as a fraction of the total number of simulations, is related to the value of pi.

Let us use our random number generators to demonstrate the cornerstone of modern statistics: the Central Limit Theorem. The Central Limit Theorem states that the distribution of the sums of independent and identically distributed variables will approximate a Gaussian distribution (ie, a Normal distribution, the so-called bell-shaped curve. Put simply, if you take a bunch of random numbers chosen from a given distribution (eg, randomly chosen numbers between 1 and 100) and add them up, and you keep repeating the process to produce sums of the same number of random numbers, then the distribution of the sums (of the random numbers) will approximate a bell-shaped curve. At first blush, the Central Limit Theorem seems nonsensical, at least to me. If you select a bunch of random numbers, would not you expect their sum to be random? If so, why would the sums of random numbers distribute as a bell curve? Regardless of my doubts, the Central Limit Theorem forms the basis for much of what we think of as probability and statistics. With a few lines of code, and a random number generator, we can simulate the Central Limit Theorem and calm our statistical angst.

Here is the Perl script, central_limit.pl, that simulates the central limit theorem, producing a data set, x_dist.dat, and plotting the contents of x_dist.dat using system calls to Gnuplot (see Open Source Tools for Chapter 4, "Gnuplot") (Fig. 8.2).

```perl
#!/usr/local/bin/perl
open (OUT, ">x_dist.dat");
for($i=0;$i<1000;$i++)
  {
  $column[$i][0]=$i;
  $column[$i][1]=0;
  }
for($i=0;$i<1000;$i++)
  {
  $n=0;
  $x=0;
  while($n < 1000)
    {
    $x = $x + rand(1);
    $n = $n + 1;
    }
  $x = int($x);
  $column[$x][1] = $column[$x][1] + 1;
  }
for($i=0;$i<1000;$i++)
  {
  print OUT "$column[$i][0] $column[$i][1]\n";
  }
close OUT;
$command = "gnuplot.exe \-e \"set term png; set output \'c\:\\ftp\\out.png\'; plot
\'c\:\\ftp\\x_dist.dat\' smooth bezier\"";
chdir "c\:\\Program Files \(x86\)\\gnuplot\\bin\\";
system($command);
exit;
```

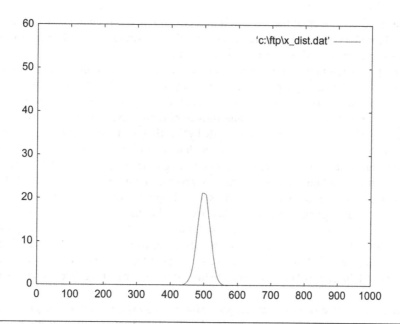

FIGURE 8.2

Output of command, showing that the sum of random numbers picked from an interval, produces a normal distribution.

8.2 MONTE CARLO SIMULATIONS

All I ever wanted to do was to paint sunlight on the side of a house

-Edward Hopper

The value of random number generators are particularly suited to Monte Carlo simulations, a technique described in 1946 by John von Neumann, Stan Ulam, and Nick Metropolis.[6] For these simulations, the computer generates random numbers and uses the resultant values to represent outcomes for repeated trials of a probabilistic event. Monte Carlo simulations can easily simulate various processes (eg, Markov models and Poisson processes) and can be used to solve a wide range of problems.[7,8]

For example, consider how biologists may want to model the growth of clonal colonies of cells. In the simplest case, wherein cell growth is continuous, a single cell divides, producing two cells. Each of the daughter cells divides, producing a total of four cells. The size of the colony increases as powers of 2. A single liver cancer cell happens to have a volume of about 30,000 cubic microns.[9] If the cell cycle time is 1 day, then the volume of a liver cell colony, grown for 45 days, and starting at day 1 with a single cell, would be 1 cubic meter. In 55 days, the volume would exceed 1000 cubic meter. If an unregulated tumor composed of malignant liver cells were to grow for the normal lifetime of a human, it would come to occupy much of the measured universe.[10] Obviously, unregulated cellular growth is unsustainable. In tumors, as in all systems that model the growth of cells and cellular organisms, the rate of cell growth is countered by the rate of cell death.

With the help of a random number generator, we can model the growth of colonies of cells by assigning each cell in the colony a probability of dying. If we say that the likelihood that a cell will die, is 50%, then we are saying that its chance of dividing (ie, producing two cells) is the same as its chance of dying (ie, producing zero cells and thus eliminating itself from the population). We can create a Monte Carlo simulation of cell growth by starting with some arbitrary number of cells (let us say 3), and assigning each cell an arbitrary chance of dying (let us say 49%). We can assign each imaginary cell to an array, and we can iterate through the array, cell by cell. As we iterate over each cell, we can use a random number generator to produce a number between 0 and 1. If the random number is less than 0.49, we say that the cell must die, dropping out of the array. If a cell is randomly assigned a number that is greater than 0.49, then we say that the cell can reproduce, to produce two cells that will take their place in the array. Every iteration over the cells in the array produces a new array, composed of the lucky winners and their offspring, from the prior array. In theory, we can repeat this process forever. More practically, we can repeat this process until the size of the colony reduces to 0, or until the colony becomes so large that additional iterations become tedious (even for a computer).

Here is the Perl script, clone.pl, that creates a Monte Carlo simulation for the growth of a colony, beginning with three cells, with a likelihood of cell death for all cells, during any generation, of 0.49:

```perl
#!/usr/local/bin/perl
$death_chance = 0.49;
@cell_array = [1];
@cell_array_incremented = [1,1,1];
while(length(@cell_array)>0)
   {
   foreach $cell (@cell_array)
       {
       $randnum = int( rand(100)) + 1;
       if ($randnum > (100 * $death_chance))
          {
          push(@cell_array_incremented, 1);
          }
       else
          {
          shift(@cell_array_incremented);
          }
       }
   die "no more cells in colony" if (scalar(@cell_array_incremented) == 0);
   $cell_array = @cell_array_incremented;
   print scalar(@cell_array_incremented) . "\,";
   }
exit;
```

The most important lines of code are:

```
if ($randnum > (100 * $death_chance))
  {
  push(@cell_array_incremented, 1);
  }
else
  {
  shift(@cell_array_incremented);
  }
```

For each cell in the array, if the random number generated for the cell exceeds the likelihood of cell death, then the colony array is incremented by 1. Otherwise, the colony array is decremented by 1. This simple step is repeated for every cell in the colony array, and is repeated for every clonal generation.

Here is a sample output when $death_chance = 0.49

```
c:\ftp>clone.pl
2,3,4,5,4,5,4,5,6,7,8,9,8,9,10,9,8,9,8,9,8,9,8,7,6,5,6,7,6,5,6,7,8,9,8,9,8,9,8,9
,8,9,10,11,10,11,12,11,10,11,10,11,10,9,10,9,8,7,8,7,8,9,10,11,10,11,12,13,12,11
,10,9,10,11,10,11,12,11,12,11,10,11,12,13,12,11,10,9,8,9,10,9,10,11,12,11,12,13,
14,15,16,15,14,13,12,11,10,9,8,7,6,7,8,9,8,7,6,5,4,3,4,5,6,7,8,9,10,9,10,9,10,11
,12,13,14,13,12,11,10,9,10,11,10,11,12,13,14,13,12,13,12,11,12,13,12,13,14,15,16
,15,16,15,14,15,14,13,12,13,14,13,14,13,14,15,14,15,14,13,14,15,16,15,14,13,14,1
3,12,13,14,13,14,13,14,15,16,15,14,13,12,11,10,11,10,11,10,9,8,9,8,7,6,7,8,9,8,9
,10,11,12,11,12,11,10,11,12,13,14,15,16,15,14,13,12,11,10,11,10,9,10,9,8,7,6,7,8
,7,8,7,6,5,6,5,6,7,6,7,8,7,6,7,8,7,8,7,6,5,4,3,2,3,2,3,2,3,4,5,4,5,4,3,4,3,4,3,2
,1,
```

Each output number represents the size of the clone at successive generations of clonal growth. Notice that, in this simulation, the clone size increases, up to a size of 20, then decreases and increases again and decreases again. Eventually, the clone dies out.

Here is a sample output when $death_chance = 0.51

```
c:\ftp>clone.pl
2,1,2,1,2,3,4,5,4,3,2,3,4,5,6,7,8,9,10,11,10,11,12,13,14,13,14,13,14,13,14,15,14
,15,16,15,14,15,14,15,14,15,16,15,14,15,16,15,14,15,14,15,14,15,16,17,18,19,18,1
7,18,17,18,19,18,19,18,17,18,19,18,19,20,19,20,21,20,19,20,21,20,19,18,19,20,19,
18,19,20,19,20,19,18,17,18,17,16,17,16,15,14,15,14,13,12,11,10,11,10,9,10,11,12,
11,12,11,12,13,14,15,14,13,14,15,16,15,14,15,16,17,18,17,16,15,14,13,14,15,16,15
,16,17,16,17,16,17,18,17,16,15,14,13,12,11,10,11,10,11,12,11,10,11,12,11,10,11,1
2,11,10,9,8,9,10,9,8,7,6,5,6,5,6,7,8,9,8,7,6,7,8,7,8,7,6,5,6,5,6,7,6,7,6,7,8,9,8
,9,10,11,12,13,12,11,10,9,10,11,10,9,8,7,8,9,10,11,12,11,12,13,12,13,12,11,12,11
,12,13,12,11,10,11,10,9,8,7,8,9,10,9,10,9,8,7,6,5,6,7,6,7,6,7,8,7,8,7,8,7,6,7,8,
9,8,7,8,9,10,9,10,11,12,11,12,13,14,13,12,13,14,13,12,13,12,13,12,11,10,11,10,11
,10,11,12,11,10,11,10,9,10,9,8,9,10,11,10,9,8,9,8,7,8,9,8,7,8,7,8,9,10,11,10,11,
12,11,10,11,12,11,10,11,12,11,10,11,12,11,12,11,10,9,8,9,8,7,6,7,6,7,8,7,6,5,4,5
,4,3,2,1,
```

Again, the clone increases and decreases and so on, until the clone dies out. These simulations indicate that clonal growth is precarious, under conditions when the cell death probability is about approximately 50%. In these two simulations, the early clones eventually die out. Had we repeated the simulation hundreds of times, we would have seen that most clonal simulations end in the extinction of the clone; while a few rare simulations culminate in a rapidly growing, large population of cells. In those rare simulations, that produce a large clone that seems to grow with no upper boundary, we notice that, from generation to generation of clonal growth, the rate of increase in clonal size is constant. At some point, when the clone size is very large, we can dispense with re-calculating the life/death outcome for each and every cell; opting instead for a model wherein the clone grows at an observed average rate per generation. The general technique, wherein an average behavior describes a population of independent members, is known as Mean Field Approximation.

In a series of papers by Dr. William Moore and myself, we developed Monte Carlo simulations of tumor cell growth. Those simulations suggested that very small changes in a tumor cell's death probability (per replication generation) profoundly affected the tumor's growth rate.[7,8,11] This suggested that chemotherapeutic agents that can incrementally increase the death rate of tumor cells may have enormous treatment benefit. Furthermore, if you simulate the growth of a cancer from a single abnormal cancer cell, most simulations result in the spontaneous extinction of the tumor, an unexpected finding that helps us to understand the high spontaneous regression rate observed in precancers (ie, very small tumors that precede the development of clinically malignant cancers).[12,13]

Here is the near-equivalent script, clone.py, in Python, that stops when the clone size exceeds 400:

```python
#!/usr/local/bin/python
import numpy.random as npr
import sys
death_chance = 0.49;
cell_array = [1, 1, 1]
cell_array_incremented = [1,1,1]
while(len(cell_array) > 0):
  for cell in cell_array:
      randnum = npr.randint(1,101)
      if randnum > 100 * death_chance:
        cell_array_incremented.append(1)
      else:
        cell_array_incremented.remove(1)
  if len(cell_array_incremented) < 1:
    sys.exit()
  if len(cell_array_incremented) > 400:
    sys.exit()
  cell_array = cell_array_incremented
  print len(cell_array_incremented),
exit
```

Here is the equivalent script, in Ruby:

```ruby
#!/usr/local/bin/ruby
death_chance = 0.49
cell_array = [1, 1, 1]
cell_array_incremented = [1,1,1]
```

```
while(cell_array.length > 0)
  cell_array.each do
    randnum = (rand(100).to_i) + 1
    if randnum > 100 * death_chance
      cell_array_incremented.push(1)
    else
      cell_array_incremented.pop(1)
    end
  end
  if cell_array_incremented.length < 1
    abort
  end
  if cell_array_incremented.length > 400
    abort
  end
  cell_array = cell_array_incremented
  print cell_array_incremented.length
  print " "
end
exit
```

With a random number generator, we can solve problems that would otherwise require Bayesian statistical analysis. Bayesian inferences involve computing conditional probabilities, based on having information about the likelihood of underlying events. For example, the probability of rain would be increased if it were known that the sky is cloudy. The fundamentals of Bayesian analysis are deceptively simple. In practice, Bayesian analysis can easily evade the grasp of intelligent data scientists. By simulating repeated trials, using a random number generator, some of the toughest Bayesian inferences can be computed in a manner that is easily understood, without resorting to any statistical methods.

Here is a problem that was previously posed by William Feller, and adapted for resampling statistics by Julian L. Simon.[1] Imagine a world wherein there are two classes of drivers. One class, the good drivers, comprise 80% of the population, and the likelihood that a member of this class will crash his car is 0.06 per year. The other class, the bad drivers, comprise 20% of the population, and the likelihood that a member of this class will crash his car is 0.6 per year. An insurance company charges clients $100 times the likelihood of having an accident, as expressed in percentage. Hence, a member of the good driver class would pay $600 per year; a member of the bad driver class would pay $6000 per year. The question is: If nothing is known about a driver other than that he had an accident in the prior year, then what should he be charged for his annual car insurance payment?

The Perl script, bayes_accident.pl, calculates the insuranace cost, based on 10,000 trial simulations:

```
#!/usr/local/bin/perl
for($trial=0;$trial<10000;$trial++)
  {
  $group_likelihood = rand();
  if ($group_likelihood < 0.2) #puts trial in poor-judgment group
    {
    $bad_likelihood = rand(); #let's roll the dice to see if an accident occurs
```

```
   if ($bad_likelihood < 0.6) #an accident occurred, simulating an initial condition
#of poor-judgment with accident
    {
    $next_bad_likelihood = rand();
    if ($next_bad_likelihood < 0.6)
        {
        $accidents_next_year = $accidents_next_year + 1;  #let's add 1 to the tally of
#trials with accidents
        }
    else
        {
        $no_accidents_next_year = $no_accidents_next_year + 1;  #let's add 1 to the
#tally of trials with no accidents
        }
    }
    }
  else  #if $group_likelihood is greater than 0.2, we bump the trial into the good-
#judgment group
    {
    $bad_likelihood = rand();  #let's roll the dice to see if an accident occurs
    if ($bad_likelihood < 0.06) #an accident occurred, simulating an initial
#condition of good-judgment with accident
        {
    $next_bad_likelihood = rand();
    if ($next_bad_likelihood < 0.06)
        {
        $accidents_next_year = $accidents_next_year + 1;  #let's add 1 to the
#tally of trials with accidents
        }
    else
        {
        $no_accidents_next_year = $no_accidents_next_year + 1;  #let's add 1 to the
#tally of trials with no accidents
        }
    }
    }
 }
$cost = int((($accidents_next_year) / ($accidents_next_year +
$no_accidents_next_year) * 100 * 100));
print "Insurance cost is $cost";
exit;
```

Here are eight consecutive executions of the bayes_accident.pl script:

```
c:\ftp>bayes_accident.pl
Insurance cost is $4527
c:\ftp>bayes_accident.pl
Insurance cost is $4301
c:\ftp>bayes_accident.pl
Insurance cost is $4514
```

```
c:\ftp>bayes_accident.pl
Insurance cost is $4669
c:\ftp>bayes_accident.pl
Insurance cost is $4360
c:\ftp>bayes_accident.pl
Insurance cost is $4550
c:\ftp>bayes_accident.pl
Insurance cost is $4340
c:\ftp>bayes_accident.pl
Insurance cost is $4480
```

In all eight executions of the script, each having 10,000 trials, we find that the insurance cost, based on initial conditions, should be about $4500.

What does our bayes_accident.pl script do? First, it creates a loop for 10,000 trial simulations. Within each simulation, it begins by choosing a random number between 0 and 1. If the random number is less than 0.2, then this simulates an encounter with a member of the bad-driver class (ie, the bottom 20% of the population). In this case, the random number generator produces another number between 0 and 1. If this number is less than 0.6 (the annual likelihood of a bad driver having an accident), then this would be simulate a member of the bad-driver class who had an accident and who is applying for car insurance. Now, we run the random number generator one more time, to simulate whether the bad driver will have an accident during the insurance year. If the generated random number is less than 0.6, we will consider this a simulation of a bad-driver, who had an accident prior to asking for applying for car insurance, having an accident in the subsequent year. We will do the same for the simulations that apply to the good drivers (ie, the trials for which our group likelihood random number was greater than 0.2). After the simulations have looped 10,000 times, all that remains is to use our tallies to calculate the likelihood of an accident, which in turn gives us the insurance cost. **In this example, as in all our other examples, we really did not need to know any statistics. We only needed to know the conditions of the problem, and how to simulate those conditions as Monte Carlo trials**.

As a final example for this section, let us use our random number generator to tackle the infamous birthday problem. It may seem unintuitive, but in a room of just 23 people, there are even odds that two or more of the group will share the same birth date. The solution of the birthday problem has become a popular lesson in introductory probability courses. The answer involves an onerous calculation, involving lots of multiplied values, divided by an enormous exponential (Fig. 8.3).

$$\frac{n(n-1)(n-2)(n-k+1)}{n^k}$$

FIGURE 8.3

Calculating the general solution of the birthday problem. "n" is the number of days in a year. "k" is the number of people.

If we wanted to know the probability of finding two or more individuals with the same birthday, in a group of 30 individuals, we could substitute 365 for n and 30 for k, and we would learn that the odds are about 70%. Or, we could design a simple little program, using a random number generator, to create an intuitively obvious simulation of the problem.

Here is the Perl script, rand_birthday.pl, that conducts conducts 10,000 random simulations of the birthday problem:

```perl
#!/usr/local/bin/perl
for($trial=0;$trial<10000;$trial++)
  {
  undef(%date_hash);
  for($i=0;$i<30;$i++)
    {
    $date = int(rand(365));
    $date_hash{$date} = $date_hash{$date} + 1;
    if ($date_hash{$date} == 2)
      {
      $success = $success + 1;
      last;
      }
    }
  }
print ($success / $trial);
exit;
```

Here is the output of the rand_birthday.pl script:

```
c:\ftp>rand_birthday.pl
0.7076
```

The Perl program indicates that the odds of two or more people, from a group of 30, sharing the same birthday, is about 70%.

Here is the equivalent Ruby script, rand_birthday.rb:

```ruby
#!/usr/local/bin/ruby
success = date = 0
date_hash = Hash.new
(1..10000).each do
  date_hash.clear
  (1..30).each do
    |date|
    date = rand(365)
    if (date_hash.has_key?(date))
      success = success + 1
      break
    else
      date_hash[date] = 1
    end
  end
end
puts success.fdiv(10000)
exit
```

The calculated probability is about the same in Perl or Ruby; about 70%.

```
c:\ftp>rand_birthday.rb
0.7004
```

What did these two scripts, in Ruby and Perl, actually do? Both scripts created variables, assigning each variable a birth date selected at random from a range of 1-365 (the number of days in the year). The program then checks among the 30 assigned variables, to see if any of them shared the same birthday (ie, the same randomly assigned number). If so, then the set of 30 assigned variables was deemed a success. The scripts repeated this exercise 10,000 times, incrementing, by 1, the number of successes whenever a match was found in the 30 assignments. At the end of it all, the total number of successes (ie, instances where there is a birthday match in the group of 30) divided by the total number of simulations (10,000 in this case) provides the likelihood that any given simulation will find a birthday match. The answer, which happens to be about 70%, is achieved without the use of any knowledge of probability theory.

Additional examples of Monte Carlo simulations are available in my previously published book, "Biomedical Informatics."[5]

8.3 RESAMPLING AND PERMUTATING

Every problem contains within itself the seeds of its own solution.

-Stanley Arnold

Up to this point, we have used a random number generator to answer a variety of questions in statistics, probability, game theory, data modeling, and even geometry. If we had a bit more stamina, we could have used our random number generator to solve problems in the areas of clustering, correlations, sample size determination, differential equations, integral equations, digital signals processing, and virtually every subdiscipline of physics.[1,3,5,14] Purists would suggest that we should have applied formal, exact, and robust mathematical techniques to all these examples. Maybe so, but there is one general set of problems for which the random number generator is the ideal tool; requiring no special assumptions about the data being explored, and producing answers that are as reliable as anything that can be produced with inscrutable mathematical techniques. This set of problems typically consists of hypothesis testing on sets of data that are small or of uncertain distribution (ie, not Gaussian), and not strictly amenable to classic statistical analysis. The methods by which these problems are solved are the closely related techniques of resampling and permutating, both of which employ random number generators (see Glossary items, Resampling statistics, Permutation test). We will devote the remainder of this section to these remarkably simple data analysis techniques.

For starters, we need to learn a new technique: shuffling. Python's numpy module, described in Open Source Tools for Chapter 4, provides a simple method for shuffling the contents of a container (such as the data objects listed in an array) to produce a random set of objects.

Here is Python's shuffle_100.py script, that produces a shuffled list of numbers ranging from 0 to 99:

```
#!/usr/local/bin/python
import numpy as np
sample = np.arange(100)
gather = []
for i in sample:
  np.random.shuffle(sample)
print sample
exit
```

Here is the output of the shuffle_100.py script:

```
c:\ftp>shuffle_100.py
[70  7 74 96 39 27  1 86 55 79 80 32 22 95 50 59 26  5 92 64 71  6 91  0 73
 56 13 99 87 20  2 81 14 36 29 67 46 12 84 15 57 24 98 62 52 35 34 61  8 77
 37 43 30 40 76 48 68 90 41 33 88 58 25 17 82 83  4 54 47 31 97 10 85 75 45
 72 19 42 65  9 28 51 16 89 44  3 53 49 69 63 38 23 93 11 94 60 78 66 21 18]
```

Shuffle is such a useful function that Perl and Ruby have an equivalent methods of the same name. The Perl script, shuffle.pl:

```
#!/usr/bin/perl
use List::Util qw(shuffle);
@data = (1..10);
print join(",", shuffle(@data));
exit;
```

Here are a few sample outputs of shuffle.pl

```
c:\ftp>shuffle.pl
5,6,2,9,4,3,8,10,1,7
c:\ftp>shuffle.pl
10,8,3,1,7,6,2,9,4,5
c:\ftp>shuffle.pl
8,10,3,1,9,4,5,6,2,7
c:\ftp>shuffle.pl
1,3,5,9,10,6,7,4,8,2
```

The Ruby script, shuffle.rb:

```
#!/usr/bin/ruby
print (1..10).to_a.shuffle!
exit
```

Here are a few sample outputs of shuffle.rb

```
c:\ftp>shuffle.rb
[1, 9, 7, 4, 5, 3, 2, 10, 6, 8]
c:\ftp>shuffle.rb
[4, 6, 9, 1, 7, 3, 8, 5, 10, 2]
c:\ftp>shuffle.rb
[3, 7, 2, 8, 1, 9, 10, 6, 5, 4]
c:\ftp>shuffle.rb
[5, 9, 7, 3, 6, 10, 8, 1, 4, 2]
c:\ftp>shuffle.rb
[1, 7, 9, 3, 8, 5, 6, 10, 2, 4]
```

Simple enough. We will be using the shuffle method to help us answer a question that arises often, whenever we examine sets of data: "Does my data represent samples from one homogeneous population of data objects, or does my data represent samples from different classes of data objects that have been blended together in one collection?" The blending of distinctive classes of data into one data set is one of the most formidable biases in experimental design, and has resulted in the failure of clinical trials, the misclassification of diseases, and the misinterpretation of the significance of outliers. How often do we fail to understand our data, simply because we cannot see the different populations lurking within? In Section 4.2, we discussed the importance of finding multimodal peaks in data distributions. Our discussion of multimodal peaks and separable subpopulations begged the question as to how we can distinguish peaks that represent subpopulations from peaks that represent random perturbations in our data.

Let us begin by using a random number generator to make two separate populations of data objects. The first population of data objects will have values that range uniformly between 1 and 80. The second population of data objects will have values that range uniformly between 20 and 100. These two populations will overlap (between 20 and 80), but they are different populations, with different population means, and different sets of properties that must account for their differences in values. We will call the population ranging from 1 to 80 our low_array and the population ranging from 20 to 100 as high_array.

Here is a Python script, low_high.py, that generates the two sets of data, representing 50 randomly selected objects from each population:

```
#!/usr/local/bin/python
import numpy as np
from random import randint
low_array = []
high_array = []
for i in range(50):
 low_array.append(randint(1,80))
print "Here's the low-skewed data set " + str(low_array)
for i in range(50):
 high_array.append(randint(21,100))
print "\nHere's the high-skewed data set " + str(high_array)
av_diff = (sum(high_array)/len(high_array)) - (sum(low_array)/len(low_array))
print "\nHere's the difference in the average value of the two arrays " + str(av_diff)
exit
```

Here is the output of the low_high.py script:

```
c:\ftp>low_high.py
Here's the low-skewed data set [75, 16, 32, 60, 59, 33, 4, 63, 50, 26, 59, 70, 6
6, 26, 31, 64, 24, 58, 15, 5, 37, 68, 10, 29, 16, 31, 21, 38, 67, 8, 15, 70, 1,
42, 75, 53, 59, 75, 13, 55, 25, 80, 53, 46, 65, 70, 30, 25, 6, 18]

Here's the high-skewed data set [76, 36, 23, 35, 44, 91, 78, 82, 22, 88, 90, 34,
78, 30, 65, 96, 77, 56, 44, 23, 48, 70, 96, 46, 30, 59, 56, 31, 40, 89, 70, 64,
44, 83, 51, 53, 32, 98, 30, 74, 33, 63, 23, 31, 24, 85, 34, 68, 53, 65]

Here's the difference in the average value of the two arrays 16
```

The low-skewed data set consists of 50 random integers selected from the interval 1 to 20. The high-skewed data set consists of 50 random numbers selected from the interval between 20 and 100. Notice that not all possible outcomes in these two intervals are represented (ie, there is no number 2 in the low-skewed data set and there is no number 25 in the high-skewed data set). If we were to repeat the low_high.py script, we would generate two different sets of numbers. Also, notice that the two populations have different average values. The difference between the average value of the low-skewed data population and the high-skewed data population is 16.

Now, we are just about ready to determine whether the two populations are statistically different. Let us combine the two sets of data into an array that we will call "total_array," containing 100 data elements. Then we will shuffle all of the values in total_array and we will create two new arrays: a left array consisting of the first 50 values in the shuffled total_array and a right array consisting of the last 50 values in the total_array. Then we will find the difference between the average of the 50 values of the left array of the right array. We will repeat this 100 times, printing out the lowest five differences in averages and the highest five differences in averages. Then we will stop and contemplate what we have done.

Here is the Python script, pop_diff.py

```python
#!/usr/local/bin/python
import numpy as np
from random import randint
low_array = []
high_array = []
gather = []
for i in range(50):
  low_array.append(randint(1,80))
for i in range(50):
  high_array.append(randint(21,100))
av_diff = (sum(high_array)/len(high_array)) - (sum(low_array)/len(low_array))
print "The difference in the average value of the high and low arrays is: " + str(av_diff)
sample = low_array + high_array
for i in sample:
  np.random.shuffle(sample)
  right = sample[50:]
  left = sample[:50]
  gather.append(abs((sum(left)/len(left)) - (sum(right)/len(right))))
```

```
sorted_gather = sorted(gather)
print "The 5 smallest and 5 largest differences of averages of left and right arrays are:"
print str(sorted_gather[:5]) + " and " + str(sorted_gather[95:])
exit
```

Here is the output of the pop_diff.py script:

```
c:\ftp>pop_diff.py
The difference in the average value of the high and low arrays is: 18
The 5 smallest and 5 largest differences of averages of left and right arrays are:
[0, 0, 0, 0, 0] and [9, 10, 11, 11, 12]
```

Believe it or not, we just demonstrated that the two arrays that we began with (ie, the array with data values 0-80; and the array with data values 20-100) represent two different populations of data (ie, to separable classes of data objects). Here is what we did, and how we reached our conclusion. We combined the two data sets and shuffled all the data values. Then we put half the shuffled data into one array and the other shuffled data into another array, and compared the average data value in the two shuffled data sets. We repeated this process 100 times, and we found that the greatest difference in average that we encountered was 12. In fact the five greatest differences between averages were [9,11,11,12, and 12]. This tells us that whenever we shuffle the combined array, we never encounter differences in the average array value that come anywhere close to the actual difference that we observed in our original arrays (18 in this example). Hence, the two arrays cannot be explained by random selection from one population. The two original arrays must represent two different populations of data objects.

Are we finished here? Not yet. We seem to have overlooked something. Let us go back to the low_high.py script, from earlier in this section. In this script, we created two arrays, one with random integers between 0 and 80 and the other with random integers between 20 and 100. In the example, we calculated that the difference between the average value of both arrays, was 16. In the preceding script, pop_diff.py, when we employed the same lines of code to create two arrays, we calculated that the difference in the average sizes of the arrays was 23. What accounts for the discrepancy. Did we do something wrong? No. The discrepancy, if you call it that, was the consequence of the randomness of our selections. In fact, when we repeat the low_high.py script several times, we encounter a somewhat wide range of results, as shown here:

```
c:\ftp>low_high.py
Here's the difference in the average value of the two arrays 20

c:\ftp>low_high.py
Here's the difference in the average value of the two arrays 23

c:\ftp>low_high.py
Here's the difference in the average value of the two arrays 19

c:\ftp>low_high.py
Here's the difference in the average value of the two arrays 12

c:\ftp>low_high.py
Here's the difference in the average value of the two arrays 22
```

```
c:\ftp>low_high.py
Here's the difference in the average value of the two arrays 21

c:\ftp>low_high.py
Here's the difference in the average value of the two arrays 20

c:\ftp>low_high.py
Here's the difference in the average value of the two arrays 15
```

In eight trials, we see outcomes that range from a low of 12 to a high of 23. Is there not something we can do to narrow the results? Our first thought is that we can just create larger arrays. Our script can generate a million random numbers just as easily as it can generate 50 numbers. In practice, data scientists do not get to create their own data. They need to work with the data that they are given, and the data that they are given is often limited in size. On such occasions, when the data set has limited size, and the statistical parameters seem unreliable, the scientist may find it advantageous to use a resampling method. In resampling, data elements from the original data are randomly selected and replaced. A copy of the data element is placed into a new array. This process is repeated as often as desired, continually appending data elements to the new array. Because the new array is composed of randomly chosen elements from the original array, it is considered to be a representation of the same population sample included in the original array. Because the selection process can be repeated indefinitely, we can create data sets of large size, from data sets of small size. When we do so, we find that our population parameters, such as the population mean, tend to fall into a tight range.

Here is a Python script, resample.py, that populates an array with 50 randomly selected integers from a range of 1-100. From this array, it creates 50 new arrays, each of length 50, composed of randomly selected integers resampled from the original array. For each of these arrays, an average is computed. From these 50 averages, an average of the 50 averages is computed.

```
#!/usr/local/bin/python
import numpy as np
import numpy.random as npr
first_array = []
total_array = []
total = 0
for i in range(50):
  first_array.append(npr.randint(1,100))
data = np.array(first_array)
for i in range(50):
   idx = npr.randint(0, len(data), (1,len(data)))
   samples_with_replacement = np.array(data[idx]).ravel()
   print (sum(samples_with_replacement)/len(samples_with_replacement)),
   total = total + (sum(samples_with_replacement)/len(samples_with_replacement))
print "\n"
print total/50
exit
```

Here are the results of three runs of the resamply.py script.

```
c:\ftp>resample.py
54 54 59 56 47 48 55 57 52 50 43 53 46 55 55 48 49 49 56 45 55 59 51 45 43 49 51
54 48 54 56 45 52 54 57 57 51 51 44 51 45 49 54 50 52 52 55 61 51 54

51

c:\ftp>resample.py
47 58 59 44 53 43 58 43 47 48 45 48 49 45 56 51 52 52 55 53 47 48 43 53 54 49 50
61 52 59 49 58 51 56 53 53 51 56 54 53 49 44 48 51 49 45 44 50 52 55

50

c:\ftp>resample.py
55 49 57 52 51 48 49 58 47 52 47 47 45 51 45 52 54 53 49 47 50 52 46 51 48 46 49
54 53 53 53 51 43 54 51 54 57 52 46 49 53 55 52 51 56 57 47 53 47 45

50
```

Notice that the average of the averages of the 50 arrays composed by resampling the original 50 element array are very close to 50. Specifically, the results are 51, 50, and 50, pretty much what you would expect when averaging an array of numbers randomly selected from a range of 1-100. Note also that the average of the averages falls into a much narrower range than the average produced by the individual resample arrays, which range from 43 to 61 in the first run; 43 to 61 in the second run, and 45 to 58 in the third run.

Have we learned everything we could possibly learn from this simple example of resampling analysis? Not quite. In our original simulation, in which we produced a low population (chosen from randomly selecting numbers between 1 and 80) and our high population (chosen from randomly selecting numbers between 1 and 80), we looked at 50 simulations for each population. We found that the difference between the average value of the two populations (about 20) always exceeded the greatest difference in the average population of a population produced by combining, shuffling, and splitting the two arrays (whose greatest value was 12). Hence, we concluded that our two original arrays were different from one another. What if we had decided to create the two sample populations by performing 25 simulations, instead of 50? How about five simulations instead of 50? We would expect that as the population sizes of the two populations shrinks, the likelihood that we could reliably distinguish one population from another will fall.

The "power" of a trial is the likelihood of detecting a difference in two populations, if the difference actually exists. The power is related to the sample size. At a sufficiently large sample size, you can be virtually certain that the difference will be found, if the difference exists. Resampling permits the experimenter to conduct repeated trials, with different sample sizes, and under conditions that simulate the population differences that are expected. For example, an experimenter might expect that a certain drug produces a 15% difference in the measured outcomes in the treated population compared with the control population. By setting the conditions of the trials, and by performing repeated trials with increasing sizes of simulated populations, the data scientist can determine the minimum sampling size that consistently (eg, in greater than 95% of the trials), demonstrates that the treated population and the control population are separable. Hence, using a random number generator and a few short scripts, the data scientist can determine the sampling size required to yield a power that is acceptable for a "real" experiment (see Glossary items, Power, Sample size, Sampling theorem).

8.4 VERIFICATION, VALIDATION, AND REANALYSIS

In God we trust, all others bring data.

-William Edwards Deming (1900–1993)

Verification and validation are two extremely important concepts that are often confused with one another. Verification involves determining that your data is, as far as anyone can reasonably determine, reliable and worthy of analysis. Validation involves showing that your conclusions are correct. Both concepts are standard components of any serious research effort, but I have never participated in a data analysis project wherein data verification and validation were performed with zeal. Nonetheless, the task is of utmost importance. **Results that cannot be verified and conclusions that cannot be validated have no scientific value.**

Two related terms that are likewise confused with one another are "results" and "conclusions." In the strictest sense, "results" include the full set of experimental data collected by measurements. In practice, "results" are provided as a small subset of data generated from the original (sometimes referred to as raw) data. Typically, selected data subsets are packaged as a chart or graph that emphasizes a point of interest. Hence, the term "results" may refer to anything from the full set of original measurements; a smaller collection of data that has been generated, by algorithms, from the original data; or a graphic prepared from subsets of the data. Conclusions are the interpretations made by studying the results of an experiment or a set of observations. The distinction between results and conclusions must be made when we try to verify and validate prior studies. **Remember, results are verified. Conclusions are validated.**[15]

Many of the data analysts with whom I have worked seem to think that data is a "given" thing, like the air we breathe, or the stars in the sky. In their opinion, they cannot criticize or improve the data they are given; that would be the job of the individuals who provided the data. Their job, as they see it, is to analyze the data that they receive. This kind of thinking certainly simplifies the job description of the data analyst, but does nothing to advance the cause of science. The absence of any serious attempt to verify data accounts for many of the irreproducible experiments that litter the field of science.[16]

Before moving into the specifics of verification and validation, it is important to understand that human nature thwarts the kind of serious self-criticism that is required to conduct an objective review of one's own work. There is an old saying that "God did not make us perfect, so he compensated by making us blind to our own faults." Hence, scientists who check their own work should use verification and validation guidelines that are developed by someone other than themselves. Fortunately, there exists a rich literature containing guidelines for validating algorithms, software, devices, statistical methods, and mathematical models.[15,17–20]

In practical terms, verification involves checking to determine whether the data was obtained properly (ie, according to approved protocols), and that the data accurately measured what it was intended to measure, on the correct specimens, and that all steps in data processing were done using well-documented and approved protocols. Verification often requires a level of expertise that is at least as high as the expertise of the individuals who produced the data.[15] Data verification requires a full understanding of the many steps involved in data collection and can be a time-consuming task.

In one celebrated case, in which two statisticians reviewed a microarray study performed at Duke University, the time devoted to verification effort was reported to be 2000 hours.[21] To put this in perspective, the official work-year, according to the U.S. Office of Personnel Management, is 2087 hours. Because data verification requires deep knowledge of the data being studied, it stands to reason that data verification is greatly facilitated by preparing well-annotated data that supports introspection.

Validation usually begins by repeating the same analysis of the same data, using the methods that were originally recommended. Obviously, if a different set of conclusions is reached, using the same data and methods, then original conclusions failed validation. Validation may involve applying a different set of analytic methods to the same data, to determine if the conclusions are consistent. **Data can be legitimately analyzed by multiple different methods. The ability to draw the same conclusion from a data set, consistently, from multiple methods of analysis, is a type of validation**.

Traditionally, validation was achieved through reproducibility; drawing the same conclusions from independently collected data. In modern times, the concept of reproducibility has lost much of its practical significance. Large and complex data sets are obtained at such great cost that they cannot be reproduced. In these cases, validation requires access to all of the original data upon which the conclusions were based.

Another type of validation involves testing new hypotheses, based on the assumed validity of the original conclusions. For example, if you were to accept Darwin's theory of evolution, then you would expect to find a chronologic archive of fossils in ascending strata of shale. This being the case, paleontologists provided independent validation to Darwin's conclusions.

Validation is serious business. In the United States the data upon which government policy is based must be available for review and reanalysis by the public. The Data Quality Act of 2002, requires the Office of Management and Budget to develop government-wide standards for data quality[22,23] (see Glossary items, Data Quality Act, Reanalysis).

As the number of data-centric studies comes under greater scrutiny, the number of studies deemed irreproducible will surely rise. When trying to understand causes of non-reproducibility, it helps to divide potential errors into three categories[24]:

1. Pre-analytic (eg, experimental design, data measurement, data collection);
2. Analytic (eg, errors in data filtering, data transformation, choice of statistical or analytic tests, execution of tests);
3. Post-analytic (eg, interpretation of results).

Examples of all three types of reproducibility errors abound in the scientific literature.[24]

As a cautionary example of pre-analytic error, consider the article, published by the journal Nature, under the droll banner, "Agony for researchers as mix-up forces retraction of ecstasy study."[25] It seems that scientists at the Johns Hopkins University School of Medicine had reported in the journal Science that the drug ecstasy, in small doses, damaged dopamine-producing brain cells in monkeys. This observation fit the authors' original hypothesis that ecstasy is a neurotoxin. As it turned out, the Johns Hopkins scientists were obliged to retract their original article when it was determined that the wrong drug had been injected, by mistake, during the experiment (ie, no ecstasy; just agony).[25]

Huntington disease is associated with a repeated trinucleotide occurring in a specific chromosome region (ie, the CAG repeat). In a review of over 1000 persons with Huntington disease, 30 were found to lack the diagnostic CAG repeat. Eighteen of these 30 "normal DNA" cases were accounted for by misdiagnosis, sample mix-up, or clerical error.[26] Likewise, anomalous and impossible results have been obtained from DNA sequence analyses of mitochondria. Laboratories were finding examples wherein a single individual was shown to have multiple ancestries; a biological impossibility. Sample mix-up and sample contamination (from other specimens) were demonstrated in these cases.[27,28]

Sample mix-ups are not rare.[29] In 2010, the UK National Health Services reported 800,000 organ donor list errors among a database of 14 million records.[30] The potential errors would include instances wherein a donor listed a particular organ intended for removal, whereas some other organ entirely might have been removed, when the time came. It happens.

An an example of an analytic error, consider this story, from the field of astronomy.[24] As a planet transits (crosses the face of the star, as seen from by an observer on earth), it focally blocks the x-rays emitted by the star. Searchers for for new exoplanets scan for dips in x-ray emissions, consistent with the transit of an exoplanet.

Early data that confirmed the discovery of new exoplanets were reanalyzed, this time taking into account effects produced by the magnetic field produced by rotating stars.[31] In the reanalysis study, the author found that certain stars could produce a periodic doppler shift that modulated the intensity of x-ray emissions. The M dwarf star Gliese 581 had been reported to host four exoplanets. When the authors corrected for Doppler shift, two of the four planets vanished.

Initial studies tend to exaggerate the importance of their findings. This is part of human nature and will never change. Reanalyses tend to take some of the air out of overinflated primary studies. In this case, two planets were evaporated. Not to be overlooked, the reanalysis verified the existence of the remaining two planets and confirmed that the original study was substantially correct. Perhaps, more importantly, the reanalysis improved our ability to identify true exoplanets, by providing a method that effectively boosts our detection of blocked x-ray signals, by compensating for a Doppler effect that would otherwise reduce signals.

At the height of the cold war, the story was told of a foot race between Russia's fastest runner and the U.S.A.'s fastest runner. In this story, the American won. A Russian newspaper reported the outcome under the following headline banner: "In International race, Russia comes in second! Struggling American comes in next to last." Strictly speaking, the headline was correct, but the post-analytic interpretation was biased and misleading.[24]

The most common source of scientific errors are post-analytic, arising from the interpretation of results.[32–37] Pre-analytic errors and analytic errors, though common, are much less frequently encountered than interpretation errors. Virtually every journal article contains, hidden in the introduction and discussion sections, some distortion of fact or misleading assertion. Scientists cannot be objective about their own work. As humans, we tend to interpret observations to reinforce our beliefs and prejudices and to advance our agendas.

One of the most common strategies whereby scientists distort their own results, is to contrive self-serving conclusions; a process called message framing.[38] In message framing, scientists omit from discussion any pertinent findings that might diminish or discredit their own conclusions. The common practice of message framing is conducted on a subconscious, or at least a sub-rational, level. A scientist is not apt to read articles whose conclusions contradict his own hypotheses and will not cite disputatious works is his manuscripts. Furthermore, if a paradigm is held in high esteem by a majority of the scientists in a field, then works that contradict the paradigm are not likely to pass peer review. Hence, it is difficult for contrary articles to be published in scientific journals. In any case, the message delivered in a journal article is almost always framed in a manner that promotes the author's interpretation.

It must be noted that throughout human history, no scientist has ever gotten into any serious trouble for misinterpreting results. Scientific misconduct comes, as a rule, from the purposeful production of bad data, either through falsification, fabrication, or through the refusal to remove and retract data that is known to be false, plagiarized, or otherwise invalid. In the United States, allegations of research misconduct are investigated by The Office of Research Integrity (ORI). Funding agencies in other countries have similar watchdog institutions. The ORI makes its findings a matter of public record.[39] Of 150 cases investigated between 1993 and 1997, all but one case had an alleged component of data falsification, fabrication, or plagiarism.[40] In 2007, of the 28 investigated cases, 100% involved allegations of falsification, fabrication, or both.[41] No cases of misconduct based on data misinterpretation were prosecuted.[24]

Post-analytic misinterpretation of data is hard-wired into the human psyche. Self-serving interpretations of data are never seriously investigated by agencies tasked with ensuring scientific integrity. Because data repurposing projects utilize primary data, and not the interpreted results based on the data, repurposing projects have the potential of uncovering and redressing misleading or erroneous results that have gained undeserved credence within the scientific community (see Glossary item, Primary data).

In 2011, amidst much fanfare, NASA scientists announced that a new form of life was found on earth, a microorganism that thrived in the high concentrations of arsenic prevalent in Mono Lake, California. The microorganism was shown to incorporate arsenic into its DNA, instead of the phosphorus used by all other known terrestrial organisms. Thus, the newfound organism synthesized a previously unknown type of genetic material.[42] NASA's associate administrator for the Science Mission Directorate, at the time, wrote, "The definition of life has just expanded."[43] The Director of the NASA Astrobiology Institute at the agency's Ames Research Center in Moffett Field, California, wrote "Until now a life form using arsenic as a building block was only theoretical, but now we know such life exists in Mono Lake."[43]

Heady stuff! Soon thereafter, other scientists tried but failed to confirm the earlier findings.[44] It seems that the new life form was just another old life form, and the arsenic was a hard-to-wash cellular contaminant, not a fundamental constituent of the organism's genetic material.[24]

As discussed in Section 1.4., "The Complexity Barrier," **The first analysis of data is usually wrong and irreproducible**. Erroneous results and misleading conclusions are regularly published by some of the finest laboratories in the most prestigious institutions in the world.[25,45–56] Every scientific study must be verified and validated, and the most effective way to ensure that verification and validation take place is to release your data for public review. Three objections typically arise whenever the issue of public release of data is discussed. Let us look at each objection, and provide a counter-argument.

Objection 1. The data that I own was collected at great expense and has great value to me. It is not reasonable to ask me to share my data with the public.

Counter-argument: If your data was collected with United States government funds (ie, under a research grant), then the data produced by the funded study is owned by the public.[57–60] In many instances, data generated with United States public funds is accessible through a formal request process described by the Freedom of Information Act 5 U.S.C. 552.[61] By law, data upon which public policy is based must be verifiable.[22] If your data was collected with private funds, then the public has no legal right to your primary data. Still, if the public has no access to the data upon which scientists have drawn their conclusions, then why would they choose to believe those conclusions? Science operates under a burdensome rule, that does not apply to religions and other belief systems: science must be validated.

Objection 2. The data that I have collected is confidential. To protect the individuals who have entrusted their data to me, I must forbid the public access to the data. That is the law.[62]

Counter-argument: There are many ways to deidentify confidential data so that the data can be shared, without violating the confidentiality or the privacy of individuals.[5,63-67] It has been argued that deidentification methods are never perfect; hence, the prudent course of action would be to always deny access to confidential data. Regulations and court rules take a dim view of the "perfection" standard applied to confidential data. Scientists are held to a "reasonable" standard for data deidentification.[64] Although strict confidentiality is a worthy goal, a balance must be struck between the public's need to verify and validate research studies, and the individual's right to privacy. When data is deidentified using any and all reasonable methods, the public's access to the data may take precedence.[68]

Objection 3. The public will misinterpret my data.

Counter-argument: The question that scientists often ask is, "Will someone misinterpret my data?" There is ample evidence that misinterpretation of large and complex data sets is commonplace. A better question to ask is, "Will someone interpret my data correctly?" It would seem that the more people there are trying to make sense of complex data, the more likely that someone will eventually hit upon a correct interpretation of the data, that can withstand the processes of verification and validation.

8.5 DATA PERMANENCE AND DATA IMMUTABILITY

How is it that you keep mutating and can still be the same virus?

-Chuck Palahniuk, in his novel, **Invisible Monsters**

Everyone is familiar with the iconic image, from Orwell's 1984, of a totalitarian government that watches its citizens from telescreens.[69] The ominous phrase, "Big Brother is watching you," evokes an important thesis of Orwell's masterpiece; that a totalitarian government can use an expansive surveillance system to crush the enemies of the state.

Orwell's book had a second thesis, that was much more insidious and much more disturbing than the threat of intrusive surveillance. Orwell was concerned that governments could change the past and the present by inserting, deleting, and otherwise distorting the information available to citizens.[37] In Orwell's 1984, old reports of military defeats, genocidal atrocities, ineffective policies, mass starvation, and any ideas that might foment unrest among the proletariat, were deleted and replaced with propaganda. In Orwell's dystopian society, retrospective data-altering activities distorted humanity's perception of reality to suit a totalitarian agenda. Today, our perception of reality can be altered by deleting or modifying, or burying electronic data.[24,70,71]

In 2009, Amazon was eagerly selling electronic editions of a popular book, much to the displeasure of the book's publisher. Amazon, to mollify the publisher, did something that seemed impossible. Amazon retracted the electronic books from the devices of readers who had already made their purchase. Where there was once a book on a personal ebook reader, there was now nothing. Amazon, to mollify the customers, credited their accounts for the price of the book. So far as Amazon and the publisher were concerned, the equilibrium of the world was restored.[72]

The public reaction to Amazon's vanishing act was a combination of bewilderment ("What just happened?"), shock ("How was it possible for Amazon to do this?"), outrage ("That book was mine!"), fear ("What else can they do to my ebook reader?"), and suspicion ("Can I ever buy another ebook?"). Amazon quickly apologized for any misunderstanding, and promised not to do it again.

To add an element of irony to the episode, the book that had been acquired, then deleted, to suit the needs of a powerful entity, was George Orwell's 1984.

In a connected, digital world it is relatively easy to experiment on individuals, without their permission or awareness.[24] In 2012, Facebook conducted an experiment on nearly 700,000 individuals, by manipulating their aggregated news feeds. One group was selectively sent sad and depressing news items. The other group was sent aggregated news feeds with content that was more upbeat. Facebook wanted to determine whether an onslaught of mind-numbing news might influence the tone of the Facebook posts that followed.[73]

News of the study evoked public outrage. Human subjects had been enrolled in an experiment without their consent and without their awareness. The information received by these unknowing human subjects had been manipulated to produce a distorted perception of reality. The experimental results, in the form of Facebook posts written by the subjects, had been monitored by data analysts.[73,74]

Following the outrage came a corporate apology. Academics, some of whom participated in the project, are now leading discussions with other academics, to develop ethical guidelines.[73]

We have all been entertained by stories of time travel wherein a protagonist is sent into the past, to stop some horrible event from happening. A series of improbable misadventures spoils the fun, proving that the past cannot be altered. We humans are enthralled with the prospect of obliterating the bad things in our lives.

The European Court of Justice, in a directive handed down in May 2014, decided that skeletons are best kept in closets. The court asked Google to remove the links, from European domains, to a 1998 article that contained material that was embarrassing, but factual, for the claimant.[75] On the first day of Google's compliance with the Court's directive, Google received 12,000 additional requests to delete links to other web pages.[24]

When a web site is delinked by Google, the content of the site is not altered. What has changed is that Google searches for the site will fail. For practical purposes, the site will be forgotten. Hence, the right to be delinked from Google, under the European Court's directive, is glibly referred to as the right to be forgotten.

If there is widespread delinking of internet sites, or if the process escalates, to involve the forced removal of materials by internet providers, then the universe of information will become mutable; changing from moment to moment. Individuals may argue that they have the right to be forgotten. **Data scientists might argue that the right to be forgotten is actually the right to alter reality**.

Much of the confusion over proper ways of updating or modifying "old" data is predicated on a somewhat overblown perception of the meaning and importance of "new" data. We think of objects as being "new," if they have no prior existence. We think of objects as being "old" if they have persisted from an earlier time. In truth, there are very few "new" objects in our universe. Most objects arise in a continuum, through a transformation or a modification of an old object. When we study Brownian motion, wherein the a particle's direction of motion, at time "t," is chosen randomly, we are aware that the location of the particle, at time "t" is predetermined by all of its prior locations, at times "t-1," "t-2," down to "t=0." The new "t+1" data is influenced by every occurrence of old data. As another example of "old" influencing "new," consider that the air temperature 1 min from now is largely determined by weather events that are occurring now. For that matter, the weather occurring now is largely determined by all of the weather events that have occurred in the history of our planet. When we speak of "new" data, alternately known as prospectively acquired data or as prospective data, we should be thinking in terms that relate the new data to the "old" data that preceded it. The dependence of new data on old data can be approached computationally. The autocorrelation function is a method for producing a type of measurement indicating the dependence of data elements on prior data elements. Long-range dependence occurs when a value is dependent on many prior values. Long-range dependence is determined when the serial correlation (ie, the autocorrelation over multiple data elements) is high when the number of sequential elements is large.[76]

Data objects should be timestamped, to ensure that we can model our data as a time series (see Section 5.6). Most importantly, we need intact (ie, immutable) old data if we have any hope of understanding the present and the future.

OPEN SOURCE TOOLS

In an information economy, the most valuable company assets drive themselves home every night. If they are not treated well, they do not return the next morning.

-Peter Chang

BURROWS WHEELER TRANSFORM (BWT)

A transform is a mathematical operation that takes a function, a signal, or a set of data and transforms it into something else, that is easier to work with than the original data. The concept of the transform is a simple but important idea that has revolutionized the fields of electrical engineering, digital signal processing (DSP), and data analysis (see Glossary items, Signal, Digital signal, DSP, Principal component analysis, Fourier transform). In the field of DSP, transforms take data from the time domain (ie, wherein the amplitude of a measurement varies over time, as in a signal), and transforms the time-domain data into the frequency domain (ie, wherein the original data can be assigned to amplitude values for an increasing set of frequencies). There are dozens, possibly hundreds, of mathematical transforms that enable data analysts to move signal data back and forth between forward transforms (eg, time domain to frequency domain), and their inverse counterparts (eg, frequency domain to time domain).

One of the most ingenious transforms in the field of data science is the BWT. Imagine an algorithm that takes a corpus of text and creates an output string consisting of a transformed text combined with its own word index, in a format that can be compressed to a smaller size than the compressed original file. The BWT does all this, and more.[77,78] A clever informatician may find many ways to use the BWT transform in search and retrieval algorithms and in data merging projects.[79] Using the BWT file, you can re-compose the original file, or you can find any portion of a file preceding or following any word from the file.

Excellent discussions of the BWT algorithm are available, along with implementations in several languages.[77,78,80] The Python script, bwt.py, is a modification of a script available on Wikipedia.[80] The script executes the BWT algorithm in just three lines of code. In this example, the input string is an excerpt from Lincoln's Gettysburg address.

```
#!/usr/bin/python
input_string = "four score and seven years ago our fathers brought forth upon"
input_string = input_string + " this continent a new nation conceived in liberty and"
input_string = input_string + "\0"
table = sorted(input_string[i:] + input_string[:i] for i in range(len(input_string)))
last_column = [row[-1:] for row in table]
print("".join(last_column))
exit
```

Here is the output of the bwt.py script, showing the transform string:

```
c:\ftp>bwt.py
dtsyesnsrtdnwaordnhn efni n snenryvcvnhbsn uatttgl tthe oioe oaai eogipccc
fr fuuuobaeoerri nhra naro ooieet
```

Let us juxtapose our input string and our BWT's transform string:

```
four score and seven years ago our fathers brought forth upon this continent a new
nation conceived in liberty and
dtsyesnsrtdnwaordnhn efni n snenryvcvnhbsn uatttgl tthe oioe oaai eogipcccfr
fuuuobaeoerri nhra naro ooieet
```

The input and output strings have the same length, so there does not seem to be any obvious advantage to the transform. If we look a bit closer, though, we see that the output string consists largely of runs of repeated individual characters, repeated substrings, and repeated spaces (eg, "ttt" "uuu"). These frequent repeats in the transform facilitate compression algorithms that hunt for repeat patterns. BWT's facility for creating runs of repeated characters accounts for its popularity in compression software (eg, Bunzip).

The Python script, bwt_inverse.py, computes the inverse BWT to re-construct the original input string. Notice that the inverse algorithm is implemented in four lines of Python code.

```
#!/usr/bin/python
input_string = "four score and seven years ago our fathers brought forth upon"
input_string = input_string + " this continent a new nation conceived in liberty and"
input_string = input_string + "\0"
table = sorted(input_string[i:] + input_string[:i] for i in range(len(input_string)))
last_column = [row[-1:] for row in table]
#The first lines re-created the forward BWT

#The next four lines compute the inverse transform
table = [""] * len(last_column)
for i in range(len(last_column)):
  table = sorted(last_column[i] + table[i] for i in range(len(input_string)))
```

```
print([row for row in table if row.endswith("\0")][0])
exit
```

The output of the bwt_inverse.py script is the original input string:

```
c:\ftp>bwt_inverse.py
four score and seven years ago our fathers brought forth upon this continent a new
nation conceived in liberty and
```

The charm of the BWT transform is demonstrated when we create an implementation that parses the input string word-by-word; not character-by-character.

Here is the Python script, bwt_trans_inv.py, that transforms an input string, word-by-word, producing its transform; then reverses the process to yield the original string, as an array of words. As an extra feature, the script produces the first column, as an array, of the transform table.

```
#!/usr/bin/python
import numpy as np
input_string = "\0 four score and seven years ago our fathers brought forth upon"
input_string = input_string + " this continent a new nation conceived in liberty and"
word_list = input_string.rsplit()
table = sorted(word_list[i:] + word_list[:i] for i in range(len(word_list)))
last_column = [row[-1:] for row in table]
first_column = [row[:1] for row in table]
print "This is the first column of the transform table:\n" + str(first_column) + "\n"
#The first lines of the script create the forward BWT
#The next four lines compute the inverse transform
table = [""] * len(last_column)
for i in range(len(last_column)):
  table = sorted(str(last_column[i]) + " " +
  str(table[i]) for i in range(len(word_list)))
original_string = [row for row in table][0]
print "Here is the inverse transform, as a word array:\n" + str(original_string)
exit
```

Notice once more that the word-by-word transform was implemented in three lines of code, and the inverse transform was implemented in four lines of code. Here is the output of the bwt_trans_inv.py script.

```
c:\ftp>bwt_trans_inv.py
This is the first column of the transform table:
[['\x00'], ['a'], ['ago'], ['and'], ['and'], ['brought'], ['conceived'],
['continent'], ['fathers'], ['forth'], ['four'], ['in'], ['liberty'], ['nation'],
['new'], ['our'], ['score'], ['seven'], ['this'], ['upon'], ['years']]

Here is the inverse transform, as a word array:
['\x00'] ['four'] ['score'] ['and'] ['seven'] ['years'] ['ago'] ['our']
['fathers'] ['brought'] ['forth'] ['upon'] ['this'] ['continent'] ['a'] ['new']
['nation'] ['conceived'] ['in'] ['liberty'] ['and']
```

The first column of the transform, created in the forward BWT, is a list of the words in the input string, in alphabetic order. Repeated words in the input appear as repeated entries in the alphabetically ordered list. Hence, the transform yields all the words from the original input, and their frequency of occurrence in the text. As expected, the inverse of the transform yields our original input string.

WINNOWING AND CHAFFING

Winnowing and chaffing is a protocol invented by Ronald Rivest for securing messages from eavesdropping, without technically employing encryption.[81] In this method, which comes in many different variations, a message is broken into small pieces (bits or bytes) and each byte is provided with a serial number (indicating its location in the message) and a message authentication string. A message authentication string is created, in one variation of the protocol, by concatenating the transmitted bit or byte and its serial number with a private unique identifier, and producing a one-way hash number for the string.

The entire message can be transmitted, with each bit or byte of the string accompanied by the heretofore described accessory items.

At this state, the message is not secure from eavesdropping, but the received message can be authenticated if the receiver is privy to the sender's private unique identifier. As you recall, the private unique identifier was not sent in the original message. The private unique identifier was included in the concatenation which was, in turn, transformed into a one-way hash and sent along with a bit or byte of data (see Glossary item, One-way hash). The receiver concatenates the received byte, the received byte serial number, inserts the shared private unique identifier, and performs a one-way hashing algorithm to reconstruct the message identification string attached to the received byte. If the message authentication strings (received from sender and computed by receiver) match, then the original byte is authenticated.

Ok, now the string, sent as bits or bytes, has been authenticated. How does any of that process secure the message from eavesdropping? It does not; not yet. Suppose the original sender got carried away and sent, along with the original message, a collection of bogus bits and bogus serial numbers and bogus message authentication codes. A receiver who has access to the sender's private identifier code could authenticate the valid bits, ignoring the bogus bits; bogus bits will fail the authentication process described in the prior paragraph.

Hence, an eavesdropper who receives a message, of the type described, corrupted with bogus bits, could never reconstruct the message, unless she had access to the sender's private identification number. Implementations of this protocol would need to provide some method for creating private identification numbers for the sender, and ensuring that only the intended recipients of the message would have access.

Ok, the protocol seems adequate, but why would anyone use winnowing and chaffing when any message can be quickly and easily encrypted, using strong encryption protocols, as previously described? To answer this question, the reader must believe a subtle argument proposed by Ronald Rivest, when he introduced the winnowing and chaffing method.[81] According to Rivest, winnowing and chaffing is not an encryption protocol, as the original message is sent as unmodified packets (ie, the bits and the bytes) along with serial numbers that can be used to reconstruct the order of the bits or bytes in the original message. Furthermore, no encryption algorithm is employed on any derivative of the message; instead, a one-way hash authentication protocol is employed. According to Rivest, because the winnowing and chaffing method is based on authentication, and not encryption, the protocol cannot be subject to regulations imposed on encryption protocols (see Glossary item, Authentication).

In a sense, Rivest has taken a simple process (ie, message encryption) and transformed it into a complex process (message obfuscation followed with bit-by-bit message authentication). This discussion reminds us that everything in informatics comes at a price, and the price is often complexification.

GLOSSARY

Authentication A process for determining if the data object that is received (eg, document, file, image) is the data object that was intended to be received. The simplest authentication protocol involves one-way has operations on the data that needs to be authenticated. Suppose you happen to know that a certain file, named z.txt will be arriving via email and that this file has an MD5 hash of "uF7pBPGgxKtabA/2zYlscQ==". You receive the z.txt, and you perform an MD5 one-way hash operation on the file, as shown here:

```
#!/usr/bin/python
import base64
import md5
md5_object = md5.new()
sample_file = open ("z.txt", "rb")
string = sample_file.read()
sample_file.close()
md5_object.update(string)
md5_string = md5_object.digest()
print(base64.encodestring(md5_string))
exit
```

Let us assume that the output of the MD5 hash operation, performed on the z.txt file, is "uF7pBPGgxKtabA/2zYlscQ==". This would tell us that the received z.txt file is authentic (ie, it is the file that you were intended to receive); because no other file has the same MD5 hash. Additional implementations of one-way hashes are described in Open Source Tools for Chapter 5. The authentication process, in this example, does not tell you who sent the file, the time that the file was created, or anything about the validity of the contents of the file. These would require a protocol that included signature, timestamp, and data validation, in addition to authentication. In common usage, authentication protocols often include entity authentication (ie, some method by which the entity sending the file is verified). Consequently, authentication protocols are often confused with signature verification protocols. An ancient historical example serves to distinguish the concepts of authentication protocols and signature protocols. Since earliest of recorded history, fingerprints were used as a method of authentication. When a scholar or artisan produced a product, he would press his thumb into the clay tablet, or the pot, or the wax seal closing a document. Anyone doubting the authenticity of the pot could ask the artisan for a thumbprint. If the new thumbprint matched the thumbprint on the tablet, pot, or document, then all knew that the person creating the new thumbprint and the person who had put his thumbprint into the object were the same individual. Of course, this was not proof that the object was the creation of the person with the matching thumbprint. For all anyone knew, there may have been a hundred different pottery artisans, with one person pressing his thumb into every pot produced. You might argue that the thumbprint served as the signature of the artisan. In practical terms, no. The thumbprint, by itself, does not tell you whose print was used. Thumbprints could not be read, at least not in the same way as a written signature. The ancients needed to compare the pot's thumbprint against the thumbprint of the living person who made the print. When the person died, civilization was left with a bunch of pots with the same thumbprint, but without any certain way of knowing whose thumb produced them. In essence, because there was no ancient database that permanently associated thumbprints with individuals, the process of establishing the identity of the pot-maker became very difficult once the artisan died. A good signature protocol permanently binds an authentication code to a unique entity (eg, a person). Today, we can find a fingerprint at the scene of a crime; we can find a matching signature in a database; and we can link the fingerprint to one individual. Hence, in modern times, fingerprints are true "digital" signatures, no pun intended. Modern uses of fingerprints include keying (eg, opening locked devices based on an authenticated fingerprint), tracking (eg, establishing the path and whereabouts of an individual by following a trail of fingerprints or other identifiers), and body part identification (ie, identifying the remains of individuals recovered from mass graves or from the sites of catastrophic events based on fingerprint matches). Over the past decade, flaws in the vaunted process of fingerprint identification have been documented, and the improvement of the science of identification is an active area of investigation.[82] See Hashed Message Authentication Code (HMAC). See Digital signature.

Check digit A checksum that produces a single digit as output is referred to as a check digit. Some of the common identification codes in use today, such as ISBN numbers for books, come with a built-in check digit. Of course, when using a single digit as a check value, you can expect that some transmitted errors will escape the check, but the check digit is useful in systems wherein occasional mistakes are tolerated; or wherein the purpose of the check digit is to find a specific type of error (eg, an error produced by a substitution in a single character or digit), and wherein the check digit itself is rarely transmitted in error. See Checksum.

Checksum An outdated term that is sometimes used synonymously with one-way hash or message digest. Checksums are performed on a string, block or file yielding a short alphanumeric string intended to be specific for the input data. Ideally, If a single bit were to change, anywhere within the input file, then the checksum for the input file would change drastically. Checksums, as the name implies, involve summing values (typically weighted character values), to produce a sequence that can be calculated on a file before and after transmission. Most of the errors that were commonly introduced by poor transmission could be detected with checksums. Today, the old checksum algorithms have been largely replaced with one-way hash algorithms. A checksum that produces a single digit as output is referred to as a check digit. See Check digit. See One-way hash. See Message digest. See HMAC.

DSP See Digital Signal Processing.

Data Quality Act In the United States the data upon which public policy is based must have quality and must be available for review by the public. Simply put, public policy must be based on verifiable data. The Data Quality Act of 2002, requires the Office of Management and Budget to develop government-wide standards for data quality.[22]

Digital Signal Processing DSP is the field that deals with creating, transforming, sending, receiving, and analyzing digital signals. DSP began as a specialized subdiscipline of signal processing. For most of the 20th century, many technologic advances came from converting non-electrical signals (temperature, pressure, sound, and other physical signals) into electric signals that could be carried via electromagnetic waves, and later transformed back into physical actions. Because electromagnetic waves sit at the center of so many transform process, even in instances when the input and outputs are non-electrical in nature, the field of electrical engineering and signal processing have paramount importance in every field of engineering. In the past several decades, intermediate signals have been moved from the analog domain (ie, waves) into the digital realm (ie, digital signals expressed as streams of 0s and 1s). Over the years, as techniques have developed by which any kind of signal can be transformed into a digital signal, the subdiscipline of DSP has subsumed virtually all of the algorithms once consigned to its parent discipline. In fact, as more and more processes have been digitized (eg, telemetry, images, audio, sensor data, communications theory), the field of DSP has come to play a central role in data science. See Digital signal.

Digital signal A signal is a description of how one parameter varies with some other parameter. The most familiar signals involve some parameter varying over time (eg, sound is air pressure varying over time). When the amplitude of a parameter is sampled at intervals, producing successive pairs of values, the signal is said to be digitized. See DSP.

Digital signature As it is used in the field of data privacy, a digital signature is an alphanumeric sequence that could only have been produced by a private key owned by one particular person. Operationally, a message digest (eg, a one-way hash value) is produced from the document that is to be signed. The person "signing" the document encrypts the message digest using her private key, and submits the document and the encrypted message digest to the person who intends to verify that the document has been signed. This person decrypts the encrypted message digest with her public key (ie, the public key complement to the private key) to produce the original one-way hash value. Next, a one-way hash is performed on the received document. If the resulting one-way hash is the same as the decrypted one-way hash, then several statements hold true: the document received is the same document as the document that had been "signed." The signer of the document had access to the private key that complemented the public key that was used to decrypt the encrypted one-way hash. The assumption here is that the signer was the only individual with access to the private key. Digital signature protocols, in general, have a private method for encrypting a hash, and a public method for verifying the signature. Such protocols operate under the assumption that only one person can encrypt the hash for the message, and that the name of that person is known; hence, the protocol establishes a verified signature. It should be emphasized that a digital signature is quite different from a written signature; the latter usually indicates that the signer wrote the document or somehow attests to the veracity of the document. The digital signature merely indicates that the document was received from a particular person, contingent on the assumption that the private key was available only to that person. To understand how a digital signature protocol may be maliciously deployed, imagine the following scenario: I contact you and tell you that I am Elvis Presley and would like you to have a copy of my public key plus a file that I have encrypted using my private key. You receive the file and the public key; and you use the public key to decrypt the file. You conclude that the file was indeed sent by Elvis Presley. You read the decrypted file and learn that Elvis advises you to invest all your money in a company that manufactures concrete guitars; which, of course, you do. Elvis knows guitars. The problem here is that the signature was valid, but the valid signature was not authentic. See Authentication.

Fourier series Periodic functions (ie, functions with repeating trends in the data, or waveforms) can be represented as the sum of oscillating functions (ie, functions involving sines, cosines, or complex exponentials). The summation function is the Fourier series.

Fourier transform A transform is a mathematical operation that takes a function or a time series (eg, values obtained at intervals of time) and transforms it into something else. An inverse transform takes the transform function and produces the original function. Transforms are useful when there are operations that can be more easily performed on the transformed function than on the original function. Possibly the most useful transform is the Fourier transform, which can be computed with great speed on modern computers, using a modified form known as the fast Fourier Transform. Periodic functions and waveforms (periodic time series) can be transformed using this method. Operations on the transformed function can sometimes eliminate periodic artifacts or frequencies that occur below a selected threshold (eg, noise). The transform can be used to find similarities between two signals. When the operations on the transform function are complete, the inverse of the transform can be calculated and substituted for the original set of data. See Fourier series.

HMAC Hashed Message Authentication Code. When a one-way hash is employed in an authentication protocol, it is often referred to as an HMAC. See One-way hash. See Message digest. See Checksum.

Introspection A method by which data objects can be interrogated to yield information about themselves (eg, properties, values, and class membership). Through introspection, the relationships among the data objects can be examined. Introspective methods are built into object-oriented languages. The data provided by introspection can be applied, at run-time, to modify a script's operation; a technique known as reflection. Specifically, any properties, methods, and encapsulated data of a data object can be used in the script to modify the script's run-time behavior. See Reflection.

Message digest Within the context of this book, "message digest," "digest," "HMAC," and "one-way hash" are equivalent terms. See One-way hash. See HMAC.

Microarray Also known as gene chip, gene expression array, DNA microarray, or DNA chips. These consist of thousands of small samples of chosen DNA sequences arrayed onto a block of support material (such as a glass slide). When the array is incubated with a mixture of DNA sequences prepared from cell samples, hybridization will occur between molecules on the array and single stranded complementary (ie, identically sequenced) molecules present in the cell sample. The greater the concentration of complementary molecules in the cell sample, the greater the number of fluorescently tagged hybridized molecules in the array. A specialized instrument prepares an image of the array, and quantifies the fluorescence in each array spot. Spots with high fluorescence indicate relatively large quantities of DNA in the cell sample that match the specific sequence of DNA in the array spot. The data comprising all the fluorescent intensity measurements for every spot in the array produces a gene profile characteristic of the cell sample.

One-way hash A one-way hash is an algorithm that transforms one string into another string (a fixed-length sequence of seemingly random characters) in such a way that the original string cannot be calculated by operations on the one-way hash value (ie, the calculation is one-way only). One-way hash values can be calculated for any string, including a person's name, a document, or an image. For any given input string, the resultant one-way hash will always be the same. If a single byte of the input string is modified, the resulting one-way hash will be changed, and will have a totally different sequence than the one-way hash sequence calculated for the unmodified string. Most modern programming languages have several methods for generating one-way hash values. Here is a short Ruby script that generates a one-way hash value for a file:

```
#!/usr/local/bin/ruby
require 'digest/md5'
file_contents = File.new("simplify.txt").binmode
hash_string = Digest::MD5.base64digest(file_contents.read)
puts hash_string
exit
```

Here is the one-way hash value for the file, simplify.txt, using the md5 algorithm:

```
OCfZez7L1A6WFcT+oxMh+g==
```

If we copy our example file to another file, with an alternate filename, the md5 algorithm will generate the same hash value. Likewise, if we generate a one-way hash value, using the md5 algorithm implemented in some other language, such as Python or Perl, the outputs will be identical. One-way hash values can be designed to produce long fixed-length output strings (eg, 256 bits in length). When the output of a one-way hash algorithm is very long, the chance of a hash string collision (ie, the occurrence of two different input strings generating the same one-way hash output value) is negligible. Clever variations on one-way hash algorithms have been repurposed as identifier systems.[83–86] Examples of one-way hash implementations in Perl and Python are found in Open Source Tools for Chapter 5, "Encryption." See HMAC. See Message digest. See Checksum.

Permutation test A method whereby the null hypothesis is accepted or rejected after testing all possible outcomes under rearrangements of the observed data elements.

Power In statistics, power describes the likelihood that a test will detect an effect, if the effect actually exists. In many cases, power reflects sample size. The larger the sample size, the more likely that an experiment will detect a true effect; thus correctly rejecting the null hypothesis. See Sample size.

Primary data The original set of data collected to serve a particular purpose or to answer a particular set of questions, and intended for use by the same individuals who collected the data. See Secondary data.

Principal component analysis A computationally intensive method for reducing the dimensionality of data sets.[87] This method takes a list of parameters and reduces it to a smaller list of variables, with each component of the smaller list constructed from combinations of variables in the longer list. Principal component analysis provides an indication of which variables in both the original and the new list are least-correlated with the other variables.

Reanalysis Subjecting a study to a new analysis, using the same data and beginning with the same questions. First analyses should always be considered tentative until such time as they undergo reanalysis and validation. One could argue that the most important purpose of analysis is to serve as the prelude to reanalysis. Although there have been instances when reanalysis has discredited published conclusions, it should be remembered that the goal of reanalysis is to confirm, strengthen, and extend prior knowledge. See Validation.

Reflection A programming technique wherein a computer program will modify itself, at run-time, based on information it acquires through introspection. For example, a computer program may iterate over a collection of data objects, examining the self-descriptive information for each object in the collection (ie, object introspection). If the information indicates that the data object belongs to a particular class of objects, then the program may call a method appropriate for the class. The program executes in a manner determined by descriptive information obtained during run-time; metaphorically reflecting upon the purpose of its computational task. See Introspection.

Reproducibility Reproducibility is achieved when repeat studies produce the same results, over and over. Reproducibility is closely related to validation, which is achieved when you draw the same conclusions, from the data, over and over again. Implicit in the concept of "reproducibility" is that the original research must somehow convey the means by which the study can be reproduced. This usually requires the careful recording of methods, algorithms, and materials. In some cases, reproducibility requires access to the data produced in the original studies. If there is no feasible way for scientists to undertake a reconstruction of the original study, or if the results obtained in the original study cannot be obtained in subsequent attempts, then the study is irreproducible. If the work is reproduced, but the results and the conclusions cannot be repeated, then the study is considered invalid. See Validation. See Verification.

Resampling statistics A technique whereby a sampling of observations is artifactually expanded by randomly selecting observations and adding them to the original data set; or by creating new sets of data by randomly selecting, without removing, data elements from the original data. For further discussion, see Section 8.3, "Resampling and Permutating."

Sample size The number of samples used in a study. Methods are available for calculating the required sample size to rule out the null hypothesis, when an effect is present at a specified significance level, in a population with a known population mean, and a known standard deviation.[88] The sample size formula should not be confused with the sampling theorem. See Power. See Sampling theorem.

Sampling theorem A foundational principle of DSP, also known as the Shannon sampling theorem or the Nyquist sampling theorem. The theorem states that a continuous signal can be properly sampled, only if it does not contain components with frequencies exceeding one-half of the sampling rate. For example, if you want to sample at a rate of 4000 samples per second, you would prefer a signal containing no frequencies greater than 2000 cycles per second. See DSP.

Secondary data Data collected by someone else. Much of the data analyses performed today are done on secondary data.[89] Most verification and validation studies depend upon access to high-quality secondary data. Because secondary data is prepared by someone else, who cannot anticipate how you will use the data, it is important to provide secondary data that is simple and introspective. See Introspection. See Primary data.

Signal In a very loose sense, a signal is a way of gauging how measured quantities (eg, force, voltage, pressure) change in response to, or along with, other measured quantities (eg, time). A sound signal is caused by the changes in pressure, exerted on our eardrums, over time. A visual signal is the change in the photons impinging on our retinas, over time. An image is the change in pixel values over a two-dimensional grid. Because much of the data stored in computers consists of discrete quantities of describable objects, and because these discrete quantities change their values, with respect to one another, we can appreciate that a great deal of modern data analysis is reducible to DSP. See DSP. See Digital signal.

Validation The process that checks whether the conclusions drawn from data analysis are correct.[15] Validation usually starts with repeating the same analysis of the same data, using the methods that were originally recommended. Obviously, if a different set of conclusions is drawn from the same data and methods, the original conclusions cannot be validated. Validation may involve applying a different set of analytic methods to the same data, to determine if the conclusions are consistent. It is always reassuring to know that conclusions are repeatable, with different analytic methods. In prior eras, experiments were validated by repeating the entire experiment, thus producing a new set of observations for analysis. Many of today's scientific experiments are far too complex and costly to repeat. In such cases, validation requires access to the complete collection of the original data, and to the detailed protocols under which the data was generated. One of the most useful methods of data validation involves testing new hypotheses, based on the assumed validity of the original conclusions. For example, if you were to accept Darwin's analysis of barnacle data, leading to his theory of evolution, then you would expect to find a chronologic history of fossils in ascending layers of shale. This was the case; thus, paleontologists studying the Burgess shale reserves provided some validation to Darwin's conclusions. Validation should not be mistaken for proof. Nonetheless, the reproducibility of conclusions, over time, with the same or different sets of data, and the demonstration of consistency with related observations, is about all that we can hope for in this imperfect world. See Verification. See Reproducibility.

Verification The process by which data is checked to determine whether the data was obtained properly (ie, according to approved protocols), and that the data accurately measured what it was intended to measure, on the correct specimens, and that all steps in data processing were done using well-documented protocols. Verification often requires a level of expertise that is at least as high as the expertise of the individuals who produced the data.[15] Data verification requires a full understanding of the many steps involved in data collection and can be a time-consuming task. In one celebrated case, in which two statisticians reviewed a microarray study performed at Duke University, the time devoted to their verification effort was reported to be 2000 hours.[21] To put this statement in perspective, the official work-year, according to the U.S. Office of Personnel Management, is 2087 hours. Verification is different from validation. Verification is performed on data; validation is done on the results of data analysis. See Validation. See Microarray. See Introspection.

REFERENCES

1. Simon J.L. *Resampling: the new statistics*. 2nd ed. The Institute for Statistics Education; 1997. Available online at: http://www.resample.com/intro-text-online/ [accessed 21.09.15].
2. Efron B, Tibshirani RJ. *An introduction to the bootstrap*. Boca Raton: CRC Press; 1998.
3. Diaconis P, Efron B. Computer-intensive methods in statistics. *Sci Am* 1983;**248**:116–30.
4. Anderson HL. Metropolis, Monte Carlo and the MANIAC. *Los Alamos Sci* 1986;**14**:96–108. Available at: http://library.lanl.gov/cgi-bin/getfile?00326886.pdf [accessed 21.09.15].
5. Berman JJ. *Biomedical informatics*. Sudbury, MA: Jones and Bartlett; 2007.
6. Cipra BA. The best of the 20th century: editors name top 10 algorithms. *SIAM News*, May 16, 2000.
7. Berman JJ, Moore GW. The role of cell death in the growth of preneoplastic lesions: a Monte Carlo simulation model. *Cell Prolif* 1992;**25**:549–57.
8. Berman JJ, Moore GW. Spontaneous regression of residual tumor burden: prediction by Monte Carlo simulation. *Anal Cell Pathol* 1992;**4**:359–68.
9. Elias H, Sherrick JC. *Morphology of the liver*. New York: Academic Press; 1969.
10. Berman JJ. *Neoplasms: principles of development and diversity*. Sudbury: Jones & Bartlett; 2009.
11. Moore GW, Berman JJ. Cell growth simulations that predict polyclonal origins for 'monoclonal' tumors. *Cancer Lett* 1991;**60**:113–9.
12. Berman JJ, Albores-Saavedra J, Bostwick D, Delellis R, Eble J, Hamilton SR, et al. Precancer: a conceptual working definition results of a consensus conference. *Cancer Detect Prev* 2006;**30**:387–94.
13. Berman JJ. *Precancer: the beginning and the end of cancer*. Sudbury: Jones and Bartlett; 2010.

14. Candes EJ, Wakin MB. An introduction to compressive sampling. *IEEE Signal Process Mag,* March, 2008.
15. Committee on Mathematical Foundations of Verification, Validation, and Uncertainty Quantification, Board on Mathematical Sciences and Their Applications, Division on Engineering and Physical Sciences, National Research Council. *Assessing the reliability of complex models: mathematical and statistical foundations of verification, validation, and uncertainty quantification.* National Academy Press; 2012. Available from: http://www.nap.edu/catalog.php?record_id=13395 [accessed 01.01.15].
16. Benowitz S. Biomarker boom slowed by validation concerns. *J Natl Cancer Inst* 2004;**96**:1356–7.
17. Oberkampf WL. Verification and validation in computational simulation. In: 2004 transport task force meeting. Salt Lake City, Utah: United States Department of Energy's National Nuclear Security Administration; 2004.
18. General Principles of Software Validation; Final Guidance for Industry and FDA Staff. U.S. Food and Drug Administration. January 11, 2002.
19. Nuzzo R. P values, the gold standard of statistical validity, are not as reliable as many scientists assume. *Nature* 2014;**506**:150–2.
20. Ransohoff DF. Rules of evidence for cancer molecular-marker discovery and validation. *Nat Rev Cancer* 2004;**4**:309–14.
21. Misconduct in science: an array of errors. The Economist. September 10, 2011.
22. Data Quality Act. 67 Fed. Reg. 8,452, February 22, 2002, addition to FY 2001 Consolidated Appropriations Act (Pub. L. No. 106–554. codified at 44 U.S.C. 3516).
23. Bornstein D. The dawn of the evidence-based budget. *New York Times,* May 30, 2012.
24. Berman JJ. *Repurposing legacy data: innovative case studies.* Burlington, MA: Morgan Kaufmann; 2015.
25. Knight J. Agony for researchers as mix-up forces retraction of ecstasy study. *Nature* 2003;**425**:109.
26. Andrew SE, Goldberg YP, Kremer B, Squitieri F, Theilmann J, Zeisler J, et al. Huntington disease without CAG expansion: phenocopies or errors in assignment? *Am J Hum Genet* 1994;**54**:852–63.
27. Bandelt H, Salas A. Contamination and sample mix-up can best explain some patterns of mtDNA instabilities in buccal cells and oral squamous cell carcinoma. *BMC Cancer* 2009;**9**:113.
28. Palanichamy MG, Zhang Y. Potential pitfalls in MitoChip detected tumor-specific somatic mutations: a call for caution when interpreting patient data. *BMC Cancer* 2010;**10**:597.
29. Sainani K. Error: what biomedical computing can learn from its mistakes. *Biomed Comput Rev* 2011;**Fall**: 12–9.
30. Satter RG. *UK investigates 800,000 organ donor list errors.* Associated Press; April 10, 2010.
31. Robertson P, Mahadevan S, Endl M, Roy A. Exoplanet detection. Stellar activity masquerading as planets in the habitable zone of the M dwarf Gliese 581. *Science* 2014;**345**:440–4.
32. Ioannidis JP. Is molecular profiling ready for use in clinical decision making? *Oncologist* 2007;**12**:301–11.
33. Ioannidis JP. Why most published research findings are false. *PLoS Med* 2005;**2**:e124.
34. Ioannidis JP. Some main problems eroding the credibility and relevance of randomized trials. *Bull NYU Hosp Jt Dis* 2008;**66**:135–9.
35. Ioannidis JP. Microarrays and molecular research: noise discovery? *Lancet* 2005;**365**:454–5.
36. Ioannidis JP, Panagiotou OA. Comparison of effect sizes associated with biomarkers reported in highly cited individual articles and in subsequent meta-analyses. *JAMA* 2011;**305**:2200–10.
37. Berman JJ. *Principles of big data: preparing, sharing, and analyzing complex information.* Burlington, MA: Morgan Kaufmann; 2013.
38. Wilson JR. Rhetorical strategies used in the reporting of implantable defibrillator primary prevention trials. *Am J Cardiol* 2011;**107**:1806–11.
39. Office of Research Integrity. Available from: http://ori.dhhs.gov.
40. Scientific Misconduct Investigations. 1993–1997. Office of Research Integrity, Office of Public Health and Science, Department of Health and Human Services, December, 1998.
41. Office of Research Integrity Annual Report 2007, June 2008. Available from: http://ori.hhs.gov/images/ddblock/ori_annual_report_2007.pdf [accessed 01.01.15].

42. Wolfe-Simon F, Switzer Blum J, Kulp TR, Gordon GW, Hoeft SE, Pett-Ridge J, et al. A bacterium that can grow by using arsenic instead of phosphorus. *Science* 2011;**332**:1163–6.

43. Discovery of "Arsenic-bug" Expands Definition of Life. NASA December 2, 2010.

44. Reaves ML, Sinha S, Rabinowitz JD, Kruglyak L, Redfield RJ. Absence of arsenate in DNA from arsenate-grown GFAJ-1 cells. *Science* 2012;**337**:470–3.

45. Hwang WS, Roh SI, Lee BC, Kang SK, Kwon DK, Kim S, et al. Patient-specific embryonic stem cells derived from human SCNT blastocysts. *Science* 2005;**308**:1777–83.

46. Hajra A, Collins FS. Structure of the leukemia-associated human CBFB gene. *Genomics* 1995;**26**:571–9.

47. Altman LK. Falsified data found in gene studies. *New York Times,* October 30, 1996.

48. Findings of scientific misconduct. NIH Guide Volume 26, Number 23, July 18, 1997. Available from: http://grants.nih.gov/grants/guide/notice-files/not97-151.html.

49. Bren L. Human Research Reinstated at Johns Hopkins, With Conditions. U.S. Food and Drug Administration, FDA Consumer magazine, September-October, 2001.

50. Kolata G. Johns Hopkins admits fault in fatal experiment. *New York Times,* July 17, 2001.

51. Brooks D. The chosen: getting in. *New York Times,* November 6, 2005.

52. Seward Z. *MIT admissions dean resigns; admits misleading school on credentials degrees from three colleges were fabricated, MIT says.* Harvard Crimson; April 26, 2007.

53. Salmon A, Hawkes N. Clone 'hero' resigns after scandal over donor eggs. *Times,* November 25, 2005.

54. Wilson D. Harvard Medical School in ethics quandary. *New York Times,* March 3, 2009.

55. Findings of Scientific Misconduct. NOT-OD-05-009. November 22, 2004. Available from: http://grants.nih.gov/grants/guide/notice-files/NOT-OD-05-009.html.

56. Hajra A, Liu PP, Wang Q, Kelley CA, Stacy T, Adelstein RS, et al. The leukemic core binding factor -smooth muscle myosin heavy chain (CBF-SMMHC) chimeric protein requires both CBF and myosin heavy chain domains for transformation of NIH 3 T3 cells. *Proc Natl Acad Sci U S A* 1995;**92**:1926–30.

57. NIH Policy on Data Sharing, 2003. Available from: http://grants.nih.gov/grants/guide/notice-files/NOT-OD-03-032.html [accessed 13.09.15].

58. NIH Public Access Working Group of the NLM Board of Regents Meeting Summary. April 10, 2006.

59. Policy on Enhancing Public Access to Archived Publications Resulting from NIH-Funded Research. Notice Number: NOT-OD-05-022, 2005.

60. Revised Policy on Enhancing Public Access to Archived Publications Resulting from NIH-Funded Research. Notice Number: NOT-OD-08-033. Release date: January 11, 2008. Effective date: April 7, 2008. Available from: http://grants.nih.gov/grants/guide/notice-files/not-od-08-033.html [accessed 28.12.09].

61. The Freedom of Information Act. 5 U.S.C. 552. Available from: http://www.nih.gov/icd/od/foia/5usc552.htm [accessed 26.08.12].

62. Data Protection Act 1998 Available from: http://www.legislation.gov.uk/ukpga/1998/29/contents [accessed 13.09.15].

63. Berman J.J. De-Identification. U.S. Office of Civil Rights (HHS), Workshop on the HIPAA Privacy Rule's De-identification Standard, March 8–9, 2010, Washington, D.C. Available from: http://hhshipaaprivacy.com/assets/4/resources/Panel1_Berman.pdf [accessed 24.08.12].

64. Department of Health and Human Services. 45 CFR (Code of Federal Regulations), Parts 160 through 164. Standards for Privacy of Individually Identifiable Health Information (Final Rule). Federal Register, Volume 65, Number 250, Pages 82461–82510, December 28, 2000.

65. Department of Health and Human Services.45 CFR (Code of Federal Regulations), 46. Protection of Human Subjects (Common Rule). Federal Register, Volume 56, p. 28003–28032, June 18, 1991.

66. Berman JJ. Threshold protocol for the exchange of confidential medical data. BMC Med Res Methodol 2002;**2**:12. Available from: http://www.biomedcentral.com/1471-2288/2/12 [accessed 27.08.15].

67. Berman JJ. Confidentiality for medical data miners. *Artif Intell Med* 2002;**26**:25–36.

68. LSU Law Center's Medical and Public Health Law Site. Cancer Registry Data May Be Available Through FOIA. Available from: http://biotech.law.lsu.edu/cases/adlaw/southern_illinoisan_brief.htm [accessed 14.11.15].

69. Orwell G. 1984. Signet, Tiptree, U.K., 1950.

70. LaFraniere S. Files vanished, young Chinese lose the future. *New York Times,* July 27, 2009.

71. Harris G. Diabetes drug maker hid test data, files indicate. *New York Times,* July 12, 2010.

72. Pogue D. Amazon.com plays big brother with famous e-books. *New York Times,* July 17, 2009.

73. Goel V. As data overflows online, researchers grapple with ethics. *New York Times,* August 12, 2014.

74. Sullivan G. *Cornell ethics board did not pre-approve Facebook mood manipulation study share on Facebook share on Twitter share on Google Plus share via email more options.* The Washington Post; July 1, 2014.

75. O'Brien KJ. European court opinion favors google in privacy battle. *New York Times,* June 25, 2013.

76. Downey AB. *Think DSP: digital signal processing in Python, version 0.9.8.* Needham, MA: Green Tea Press; 2014.

77. Burrows M., Wheeler D.J. A block-sorting lossless data compression algorithm. SRC research report 124, May 10, 1994.

78. Berman JJ. *Perl programming for medicine and biology.* Sudbury, MA: Jones and Bartlett; 2007.

79. Healy J, Thomas EE, Schwartz JT, Wigler M. Annotating large genomes with exact word matches. *Genome Res* 2003;**13**:2306–15.

80. Burrows-Wheeler transform. Wikipedia. Available at: https://en.wikipedia.org/wiki/Burrows%E2%80%93Wheeler_transform [accessed 18.08.15].

81. Rivest R.L. MIT Lab for Computer Science. March 18, 1998 (rev. April 24, 1998).

82. A Review of the FBI's Handling of the Brandon Mayfield Case. U. S. Department of Justice, Office of the Inspector General, Oversight and Review Division, March 2006.

83. Faldum A, Pommerening K. An optimal code for patient identifiers. *Comput Methods Prog Biomed* 2005;**79**:81–8.

84. Rivest R. Request for Comments: 1321, The MD5 Message-Digest Algorithm. Network Working Group. https://www.ietf.org/rfc/rfc1321.txt [accessed 01.01.15].

85. Bouzelat H, Quantin C, Dusserre L. Extraction and anonymity protocol of medical file. *Proc AMIA Annu Fall Symp* 1996;**1996**:323–7.

86. Quantin CH, Bouzelat FA, Allaert AM, Benhamiche J, Faivre J, Dusserre L. Automatic record hash coding and linkage for epidemiological followup data confidentiality. *Methods Inf Med* 1998;**37**:271–7.

87. Janert PK. *Data analysis with open source tools.* Sabastopol, CA: O'Reilly Media; 2010.

88. How to determine sample size, determining sample size. Available at: http://www.isixsigma.com/tools-templates/sampling-data/how-determine-sample-size-determining-sample-size/ [accessed 08.07.15].

89. Smith AK, Ayanian JZ, Covinsky KE, Landon BE, McCarthy EP, Wee CC, et al. Conducting high-value secondary dataset analysis: an introductory guide and resources. *J Gen Intern Med* 2011;**26**:920–9.

Index

Note: Page numbers followed by "*f*" indicate figures.

Printed in the United States
By Bookmasters